P9-CEX-119

Architect's Handbook of Formulas, Tables, and Mathematical Calculations

Other Prentice-Hall Books by the Author

The Architect's Handbook
Practical Guide to Computer Applications for Architecture and Design

Architect's Handbook of Formulas, Tables, and Mathematical Calculations

David Kent Ballast

PRENTICE HALL
Englewood Cliffs, New Jersey 07632

Prentice-Hall International (UK) Limited, *London*
Prentice-Hall of Australia Pty. Limited, *Sydney*
Prentice-Hall Canada Inc., *Toronto*
Prentice-Hall Hispanoamericana, S.A., *Mexico*
Prentice-Hall of India Private Limited, *New Delhi*
Prentice-Hall of Japan, Inc., *Tokyo*
Simon & Schuster Asia Pte. Ltd., *Singapore*
Editora Prentice-Hall do Brasil, Ltda., *Rio de Janeiro*

10 9 8 7 6 5 4

Printed in the United States of America

Library of Congress Cataloging-in-Publication Data

Ballast, David Kent.
Architect's handbook of formulas, tables, and mathematical calculations / David Ballast.
p. cm.
Includes index.
ISBN 0-13-044686-6
1. Architectural design—Tables. I. Title.
NA2750.B32 1988 88-2723
721—dc19 CIP

ISBN 0-13-044686-6

About the Author

David Ballast is a consultant and owner of Architectural Research Consulting, Denver, a firm offering applied research and information services to architects, interior designers, and others in the building industry. In addition to consulting, he teaches part time in the graduate interior design program of the College of Architecture and Planning at the University of Colorado at Denver.

As a licensed architect, Mr. Ballast has worked in all phases of practice, including interior architecture. Before starting his own firm, he worked for Gensler and Associates, Architects, as a project manager.

The author received a Bachelor of Architecture degree with special honors from the University of Colorado. He is a member of the American Institute of Architects and the Construction Specifications Institute. Mr. Ballast has written for *The Construction Specifier* magazine and is the author of *The Architect's Handbook,* published by Prentice-Hall; *Practical Guide to Computer Applications for Architecture and Design,* published by Prentice-Hall; *Guide to Quality Control for Design Professionals* and *Creative Records Management: A Guidebook for Architects, Engineers, and Interior Designers,* both published by Practice Management Associates.

What This Book Will Do for You

The *Architect's Handbook of Formulas, Tables, and Mathematical Calculations* compiles a vast range of practical, concise formulas, tables, and calculation methods useful to improve the design process. It is a problem-solving and decision-making tool for the practicing architect and interior designer. The material included in this book gives you the answers to the many types of problems you face every day—those dealing with overall site and space planning, sizes of building components, material selection, finishes, construction assemblies, and building systems. In addition, you will find useful "rules of thumb" and basic reference data.

The organization of this *Handbook* is based on how architects actually work through a project and make decisions—from establishing early programming needs, to making preliminary design and building system choices, to evaluating specific material selections. The tables and calculation methods selected are practical, proven reference information helpful for all phases of a job. To make the tables and formulas even more useful, step-by-step procedures for using them and easy-to-follow examples are included where appropriate.

Among other benefits, this *Handbook*

- provides you with space requirements of various building types to assist with preliminary planning. (See Section 1.)
- gives easy-to-use data on parking requirements, ramps, and turning radii. (See Section 1.)
- presents unique tables and diagrams for rapid planning of audio-visual facilities, including projection ratios for commonly used media. (See Section 1.)
- includes previously unpublished graphs to allow instant determination of "best estimate" sizes for structural systems—vertical supports as well as beams, floors, and roofs. (See Part 2A.)
- gives detailed tables to help you refine your preliminary structural estimates. (See Part 2A.)
- helps select the right kind of plywood for your design needs. (See Part 2A.)
- assists with the preliminary evaluation of heating and air-conditioning systems and their required spatial needs. (See Part 2B.)
- helps determine required duct space during the early stages of design. (See Part 2B.)
- speeds up the design and detailing of plumbing areas by giving number of fixtures, required sizes, pipe slopes, and other necessary dimensions. (See Part 2C.)
- makes easy work of sizing gutters and drainage piping. (See Part 2C.)
- itemizes pertinent electrical information to guide the planning of space requirements, distribution, and detailing questions. (See Part 2E.)
- shows how to determine the number and location of luminaires to help you make more informed lighting decisions. (See Part 2F.)
- presents the most current lighting design guidelines so your design solutions in this area are the best possible. (See Part 2F.)
- gives the basic information required for acoustical design decisions so they can be made early and accurately. (See Part 2G.)
- provides sound barrier criteria to help you make informed choices concerning wall and floor construction. (See Part 2G.)

- demonstrates easy-to-use methods of determining the required number of elevators, making preliminary elevator selection, and sizing shafts. (See Part 2H.)
- details how to make heat loss and heat gain calculations as the first step in designing more energy efficient buildings. (See Part 3A.)
- shows how to make the calculations necessary to comply with energy conservation standards and criteria. (See Part 3A.)
- eliminates fundamental mistakes when sizing components for passive solar energy buildings by giving tables and rules of thumb. (See Part 3C.)
- tells how to make daylighting calculations, along with the necessary tabular data on which to base your work. (See Part 3D.)
- tabulates monthly climatic data for cities across the United States, including total global radiation. (See Part 3E.)
- presents information on the selection of concrete finishes and the industry standards for concrete tolerances. (See Part 4A.)
- outlines in matrix format the essentials of selecting the correct stone for your buildings, along with tolerances and finishes. (See Part 4B.)
- demystifies the selection and specification of metal finishes with easy-to-read charts. (See Part 4C.)
- pulls together valuable information on wood species and how to factor in the effects of humidity on selection and use of wood. (See Part 4D.)
- simplifies the selection of sealants—often the focus of a troublesome type of building failure. (See Part 4E.)
- makes it easy to select the right doors and frames, along with hinges and hardware finishes. (See Part 4F.)
- gives useful data on glass properties. (See Part 4F.)
- presents guideline tables to help you in the selection and evaluation of some common finish materials. (See Part 4G.)
- compiles finger-tip reference data on conversion factors, weights of materials, live loads, geometric formulas, and more. (See Part 5.)

The tables and calculation methods have been selected from the most authoritative sources. More are based on data from trade associations and are considered industry standards, an important consideration in reducing your exposure to liability problems. Others have been derived or edited to eliminate extraneous information and give you precisely targeted data to answer your everyday questions. In addition, new material has been developed that can be found nowhere else.

A few cautions are in order. This book is intended to help you make preliminary decisions during the course of a design project under most normal situations. The material presented does not substitute for normal competent professional knowledge and judgment. Unusual circumstances will require additional study. You may also need to enlist the help of specialized consultants in the areas of structural design, mechanical and electrical engineering, and the like.

To streamline the presentation of often voluminous material, some of the tables and calculation methods have been simplified and edited. For certain projects you may need to consult the complete table available from the source listed or investigate other parameters of a problem if unusual circumstances are present. Also, remember that some of the information may be revised from time to time by the issuing organization.

In all, you will find this book a time-saving finger-tip reference for use on all types of projects and a valuable addition to your reference collection.

Contents

List of Illustrations

SECTION 1
HOW TO DETERMINE BUILDING PLANNING SPACE REQUIREMENTS

SECTION 2
CALCULATING BUILDING SYSTEMS

SECTION 3
ENERGY STANDARDS

SECTION 4
BUILDING COMPONENTS

SECTION 5
REFERENCE DATA

Architect's Handbook of Formulas, Tables, and Mathematical Calculations

SECTION 1

How to Determine Building Planning Space Requirements

In the early planning stages of a project, the architect often knows very little about the detailed functioning of a building. Typically, he or she will know only the building type and its approximate area. From this limited data, more information must be derived in order to begin making preliminary decisions concerning such things as site coverage, gross area, number of floors in the building, parking area requirements, and similar concerns.

This section includes information valuable for determining some of the more common building planning space requirements.

PARKING AND SITE WORK

Since parking, driveways, and walks use so much of the area on a typical building site, it is useful to know early in the design process how much space to allot to these functions. Initially, you can use rough rules of thumb to estimate needs. Later, as the building design is refined, more detailed layouts can be done using the information in this section.

RULES OF THUMB

- For general planning, estimate 400 sq. ft. per car to allow for parking, drives, and walks.
- For very efficient double bay aisle parking, estimate 300 sq. ft. per car for parking and drives only.
- Typical parking stall: 9 ft. wide by 19 ft. long.
- Parking structure stall: 8 1/2 ft. wide by 19 ft. long.
- Compact car stall: 7 ft. 6 in. wide by 15 ft. long.
- Handicapped parking stall: 13 ft. wide.
- Loading dock parking: 10 ft. wide by 35 ft. long by 14 ft. high.
  (**Note:** verify parking and loading dimensions with your local zoning ordinance.)
- One-way drive lane with no parking: 12 ft. wide minimum.
- Two-way drive lane with no parking: 18 ft. wide minimum.
- Recommended slope for parking: 1% minimum to 5% maximum.
- Main outdoor walks: 6 ft. to 10 ft. wide.
- Secondary outdoor walks: 3 ft. to 6 ft. wide.
- Walks adjacent to parking areas with overhanging car bumpers: 6 ft. minimum.

Planning Procedures for Parking and Site Work

When you begin detailed parking layouts, you can use Table 1–1 and Figure 1–1 to assist in the calculations. The three primary variables are the angle of parking, the stall size, and the dimension of the parking lot components. Knowing any two of these, you can easily find the other. Figure 1–1 shows the relationship of these variables.

Example

Because of a constricted site, there is only a 50 ft. wide strip of land available for parking in front of a building. What does the configuration need to be and how long of a parking area will you need to park 30 cars?

Since you know the curb-to-curb width available (50 ft.), look under column F in Table 1–1. Since the closer the parking angle is to 90° the more efficient the overall layout will be, go down the column until you find the number closest to 50 ft. Since you will probably be using a standard stall width of 9 ft. 0 in. (column B), find 50.2 as the closest figure to 50 ft. This tells you that you will need a 40° parking angle (column A).

Next, parking 30 cars on both sides of a single aisle means 15 cars per side. Reading across the same row, find the curb length required for a 40° angle and 9 ft. 0 in. stall width (column E). The answer is 14.0 ft. (14 ft. × 15 cars = 210 ft.). Add about 15 ft. more for the angled portion of the first stall not included in the curb length (Dimension E), for a total length of 225 ft. Therefore, you need a total area of 50 ft. by 225 ft., with parking angled at 40° with a one-way circulation pattern.

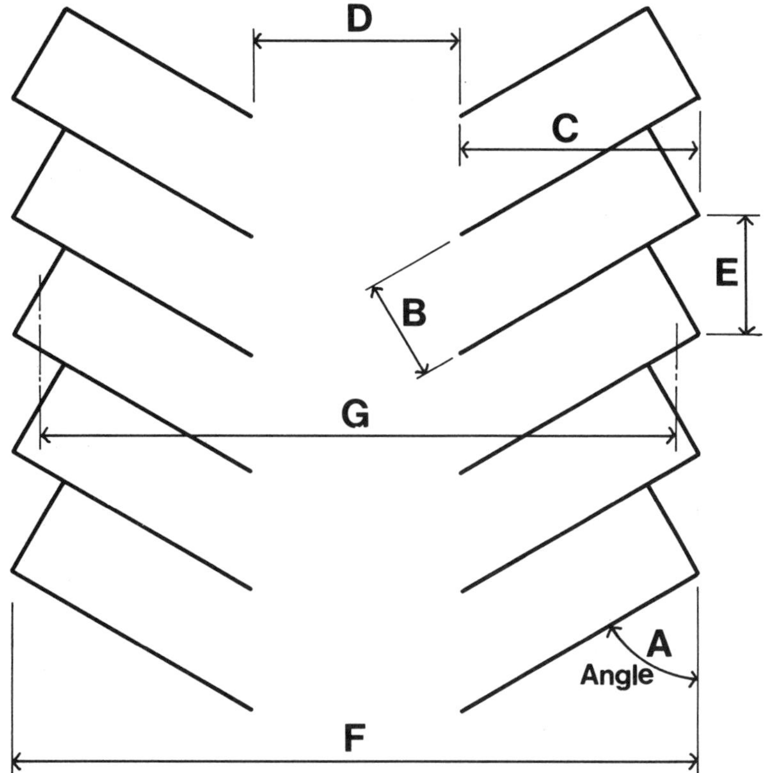

Figure 1-1: Parking Angle, Stall Size, Dimension of Parking Lot Components (See also Table 1-1.)

Table 1-1
PARKING SPACE REQUIREMENTS AT VARIOUS ANGLES

A	B	C	D	E	F	G
					Center-to-Center Width of Two Parking Rows with Access Between	
Parking Angle	*Stall Width*	*Stall to Curb*	*Aisle Width*	*Curb Length*	*Curb to Curb*	*Overlap Center Line to Center Line*
0	7 ft. 6 in.	7.5 (1)	11.0	19.0	26.0	26.0
	8 ft. 0 in.	8.0	12.0	23.0	28.0	—
	8 ft. 6 in.	8.5	12.0	23.0	29.0	—
	9 ft. 0 in.	9.0	12.0	23.0	30.0	—
	9 ft. 6 in.	9.5	12.0	23.0	31.0	—
30	7 ft. 6 in.	14.0 (1)	11.0	15.0	39.0	32.5
	8 ft. 0 in.	16.5	11.0	16.0	44.0	37.1
	8 ft. 6 in.	16.9	11.0	17.0	44.8	37.4
	9 ft. 0 in.	17.3	11.0	18.0	45.6	37.8
	9 ft. 6 in.	17.8	11.0	19.0	46.6	38.4
40	8 ft. 0 in.	18.3	13.0	12.4	49.6	43.5
	8 ft. 6 in.	18.7	12.0	13.2	49.4	42.9
	9 ft. 0 in.	19.1	12.0	14.0	50.2	43.3
	9 ft. 6 in.	19.5	12.0	14.8	51.0	43.7
45	7 ft. 6 in.	15.9 (1)	11.0	10.6	42.8	37.9
	8 ft. 0 in.	19.1	14.0	11.3	52.2	46.5
	8 ft. 6 in.	19.4	13.5	12.0	52.3	46.3
	9 ft. 0 in.	19.8	13.0	12.7	52.6	46.2
	9 ft. 6 in.	20.1	13.0	13.4	53.2	46.5
50	8 ft. 0 in.	19.7	14.0	10.5	53.4	48.3
	8 ft. 6 in.	20.0	12.5	11.1	52.5	47.0
	9 ft. 0 in.	20.4	12.0	11.7	52.8	47.0
	9 ft. 6 in.	20.7	12.0	12.4	53.4	47.3
60	7 ft. 6 in.	16.7 (1)	14.0	8.7	47.5	40.4
	8 ft. 0 in.	20.4	19.0	9.2	59.8	55.8
	8 ft. 6 in.	20.7	18.5	9.8	59.9	55.6
	9 ft. 0 in.	21.0	18.0	10.4	60.0	55.5
	9 ft. 6 in.	21.2	18.0	11.0	60.4	55.6
90	7 ft. 6 in.	15.0 (1)	18.0	7.5	48.0	48.0
	8 ft. 0 in.	19.0	26.0(2)	8.0	64.0	—
	8 ft. 6 in.	19.0	25.0(2)	8.5	63.0	—
	9 ft. 0 in.	19.0	24.0(2)	9.0	62.0	—
	9 ft. 6 in.	19.0	24.0(2)	9.5	62.0	—

(See also Figure 1-1.)

(1) Based on 15 ft. 0 in. stall length for compact cars; all others are based on 19 ft. 0 in. stall length.

(2) Two-way circulation.

When planning parking structures, the vertical dimension is also critical. Although an indoor ramp slope can be a maximum of 20%, it is better to limit yourself to 15% maximum or much less if possible. Knowing the floor-to-floor height of a parking structure (or half floors if you are designing a staggered floor garage), you can quickly determine what overall length you need from Table 1-2. If you already know what maximum length is available (from site constraints or for other reasons), you can determine what slope the ramp will be.

Table 1-2
PARKING RAMP LENGTHS—STRAIGHT RAMPS

% Ramp Grade	Angle Degrees	Floor-to-Floor Height										
		Half Floors			Full Floors							
		4	4.5	5	8	8.5	9	9.5	10	10.5	11	12
3	1.72	133	150	167	267	283	300	317	333	350	367	400
4	2.29	100	113	125	200	213	225	238	250	263	275	300
5	2.86	80	90	100	160	170	180	190	200	210	220	240
6	3.43	67	75	83	133	142	150	158	167	175	183	200
7	4.00	57	64	71	114	121	129	136	143	150	157	171
8	4.57	50	56	63	100	106	113	119	125	131	138	150
9	5.14	44	50	56	89	94	100	106	111	117	122	133
10	5.71	40	45	50	80	85	90	95	100	105	110	120
11	6.28	36	41	45	73	77	82	86	91	95	100	109
12	6.68	33	38	42	67	71	75	79	83	88	92	100
13	7.41	31	35	38	62	65	69	73	77	81	85	92
14	7.97	29	32	36	57	61	64	68	71	75	79	86
15	8.53	27	30	33	53	57	60	63	67	70	73	80

Curved portions of drives and service access can be calculated with the formulas that follow. Figure 1-2 shows the relationship of the variables involved.

Calculating Minimum Turning Radii of Vehicles

FORMULA:

$$R = R_T + C$$
$$X = R_T - \sqrt{R_T^2 - B^2}$$
$$W = A + T + X + C$$
$$r = R - W$$

where:

R_T = turning radius of vehicle
T = tread width of vehicle
B = wheel base of vehicle
R = outside radius
r = inside radius
X = difference between front and rear wheels
A = inside radius clearance (1 ft. 3 in.–1 ft. 6 in. minimum)
C = outside radius clearance (1 ft. 6 in.–2 ft. 0 in. minimum)

(See Figure 1-2.)

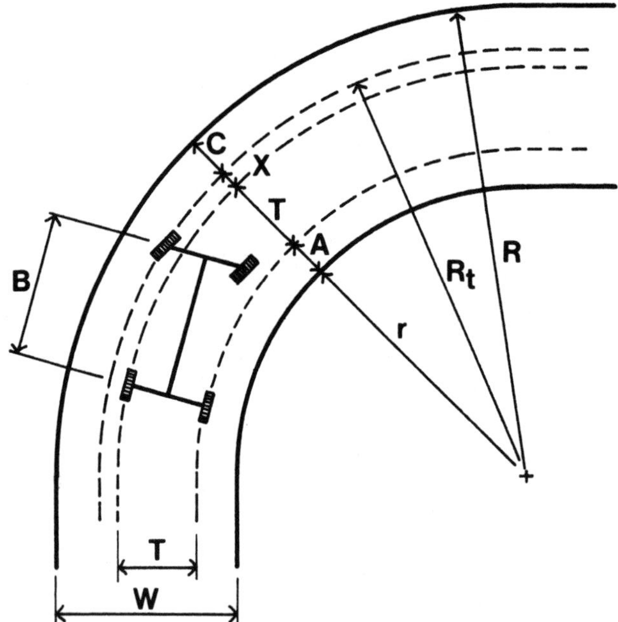

Figure 1-2: How to Calculate Minimum Turning Radii

Determining the proper slopes for various elements of site development is critical for pedestrian safety, vehicular movement, maintenance of landscaping, and proper drainage. The recommended slopes given in Table 1-3 will assist you in quickly developing spot elevations and grading plans based on site plan dimensions.

Table 1-3
RECOMMENDED SITE WORK SLOPES

	Minimum	Preferred	Maximum
Streets, with curb and gutter, asphalt	0.4	0.5	8
Streets, with curb and gutter, concrete	0.3	0.5	8
Parking, asphalt	1.5	2.5	5
Parking, concrete	1.0	2.0	5
Rough paved areas	1.5		
Smooth paved areas for runoff	0.5		
Ground areas for runoff away from building	1.0		
Ground areas for runoff near buildings	2.0	4.0	
Main collector walks	1.0		8
Approach walks to buildings	1.0		4
Building entries	1.0		2
Steps, for runoff	1.0		2
Ramps, outdoor	1.0	<6	10
Grass areas for recreation	2.0		3
Grass and mulched areas		2.0	
Landscape slopes (horizontal to vertical dimensions given)			
Grass			3:1
Soft earth			2:1
Firm earth			1.5:1
Loose gravel			1.5:1
Loose rock			.5:1

Note: Figures given are percent grades unless otherwise noted.

Example

The high point of an asphalt parking lot is elevation 105 ft. 3 in. If drainage needs to be along the length of the lot and the lot is 215 ft. long, how high can the low point of the lot be?

To determine the "highest" low point, use the minimum allowable slope, which is 1.5% for asphalt. Total slope is then 215 ft. times 0.015, or 3.23 ft., or about 3 ft. 3 in. Subtracting this from 105 ft. 3 in. gives a spot elevation of 102 ft. 0 in.

Site grading and drainage is usually given in percent, while many architectural slopes are indicated in fractions of an inch per foot. The following list compares percent slopes to inch slopes and gives the "perceived" judgment of minor slopes in relation to level construction.

COMPARISON OF PERCENT SLOPES

0.5%	About 1/16 in. per ft.; appears flat; use only for smoothest types of pavement.
1.0%	About 1/8 in. per ft.
1.5%	About 3/16 in. per ft.; good minimum for rough paving.
2.0%	About 1/4 in. per ft.; noticeable in relation to level construction.
2.5%	About 5/16 in. per ft.; quite noticeable in relation to level construction.
3.0%	About 3/8 in. per ft.; very noticeable in relation to level construction.

SPACE PLANNING GUIDELINES

Many times, all that is known about a proposed building project is a very general planning parameter, such as the number of students that must be accommodated in a school or the number of books that will be housed in a library. Square footage estimates must then be developed from these parameters to give a reasonable place to start design. The guidelines in Table 1-4 include many of the common building types and the floor area per planning unit that has been found to be reasonably accurate for initial layouts. Keep in mind, however, that occupant loads for exiting and structural loading must be determined according to local building code requirements.

Most of the figures included in Table 1-4 are based on net area; that is, area not including space for corridors, mechanical rooms, stairways, toilet rooms, and similar non-usable spaces. In order to convert estimates of *net* area to *gross* building area, the multiplying factors in Table 1-5 must be used. The lower figures represent fairly efficient plan layouts of larger buildings, while the larger number of the range should be used for smaller buildings of the particular building type or in cases where circulation is likely to be inefficient.

Example

What is the likely gross area of a restaurant designed to seat 125 people for meals, with a small 25 person bar?

From Table 1-4

Dining area: 125 × 15 sq. ft. per person =	1875
Kitchen: 125 × 6 sq. ft. per meal (under 200) =	750
Service areas: 125 × 5 sq. ft. per person =	625
Bar: 25 × 18 sq. ft. per person =	450
Allow for administration and waiting =	500
Total net area =	4200 sq. ft.

From Table 1–5 the gross to net ratio for a table service restaurant is 1.4 to 1.5. For a small restaurant, use the higher figure (4200 × 1.5 = 6300 sq. ft. total likely to be required for the restaurant).

The first portion of Table 1–4 shows some of the planning guidelines for several types of office use. Of course, usable areas per employee vary greatly depending on the type of work performed and types of support space and common areas required, such as file rooms, data processing, conference rooms, and so forth.

RULES OF THUMB

- Office use: 125 to 150 net sq. ft. area per person.
- Retail space: 30 net sq. ft. per person on ground floor.
  50 net sq. ft. per person on upper floors.
- Classrooms: 20 net sq. ft. per pupil.

Table 1–4
SPACE PLANNING BY BUILDING TYPE

Building/Use Type	Sq. Ft. per Unit		Area Basis
Office buildings, all types	100–250	net	usable
Work station, minimum clerical	40	person	usable
Work station, clerical with VDT	55	person	usable
Work station, with visitor space	65	person	usable
Work station, supervisor	100	person	usable
Manager, private office	150–225	person	usable
Law firm	450	attorney	total usable
Law firm library	25–30	attorney	usable
Law firm conference	25–30	attorney	usable
Insurance company, branch	100 average	work station	usable
Insurance company, branch Total, includes common areas and circulation	155–165	employee	total usable
Energy company	255	employee	total usable
Conference and dining rooms	15	person	net
Restaurants			
Dining areas (includes dining room but not waiting, coat room, etc.)			
Banquet	10–15	seat	net
Cafeteria, college	12–15	seat	net
Cafeteria, commercial	16–18	seat	net
Counter service	18–20	seat	net
Table service, hotel or restaurant	15–18	seat	net
Table service, minimum	11–14	seat	net

Kitchens

	Meals per Hour			
Type	< 200	200–400	400–800	800–1300
Cafeterias	7.5–5.0	5.0–4.0	4.0–3.5	3.5–3.0
Hotels	18.0–4.0	7.5–3.0	6.0–3.0	4.0–3.0
Restaurants	7.0–4.0	5.0–3.6	5.0–3.6	5.0–3.0

Serving and service areas			
Cafeterias	6	person	net
Restaurants	5	person	net

Add to totals space for food storage, administration, waiting.

Table 1-4 (Continued)

Building/Use Type	Sq. Ft. per Unit		Area Basis
Night clubs	25	person	net
Bars	18	person	net
Hotel			
1.5 persons per room without extensive conferencing facilities	550-600	room	gross
	Retail		
Large stores	30-50	person	net
	Cultural		
Public library			
Stack space	0.08	bound vols.	net
Reading rooms	20-35	user	net
Staff space	100	staff person	net
Overall	50	person	net
Museums, exhibition areas	15	person	net
Theater and assembly areas			
Seating area, fixed seats	7.5	seat	net
Seating, movable seating	15	seat	net
Theaters, fixed seating (Does not include stage, lobby, etc.)	8-12	seat	net
Stage/backstage Performing arts theater	100%	seating area	
Lobbies	3	person	net
Lobbies	30%	seating area	
	Educational		
Elementary			
The following figures are based on the number of students in the particular space listed.			
Small classrooms	20-30	student	net
Library	40	student	net
Art room	40	student	net
Secondary			
The following figures are based on the number of students in the particular space listed.			
Cafeteria	12-15	student	1/3 of total
Small classrooms	20-25	student	net
Large classrooms	15	student	net
Art classrooms	50-60	student	net
Home economics	50-60	student	net
Laboratory classrooms	55-70	student	net
Library	40	student	20% of total
Music rooms	30-35	student	net
Physical education	125	student	net
Shops/vocational rooms small	50	student	net
Shops/vocational rooms wood, metal, etc.	120-140	student	net
University			
Classrooms, small	20	student	net
Classrooms, large	12-15	student	net

Table 1-4 (Continued)

Building/Use Type	Sq. Ft. per Unit		Area Basis
Lecture halls	9–12	seat	net
Dormitory, no dining	160	student	net
Dormitory, no dining	210–240	student	gross
Dormitory, dining	235–260	student	gross
Food service, table service	18–26	seat	net, all areas
Food service, cafeteria	14–19	seat	net, all areas
Laboratories	34–45	student	net
Laboratory storage	6–10	student	net
Library			
Book stacks, less than 300,000 volumes	0.10	volume	net
Book stacks, 300,000–1,000,000 volumes	0.7–0.8	volume	net
Book stacks, over 1,000,000 volumes	0.5	volume	net
Reading, study	25–35	station	net
(provide stations equal to 25% to 40% of student population):	6.25–10	student	net
Total service space	25%	of reading	net
Residential			
Apartments	250	Occupant	net
Senior citizen housing			
Living units	300–380	1-person unit	net
Living units	350–425	2-person unit	net
Living units	400–600	unit	gross
Dining, lounge, lobby, administration, etc.	33%–45% of living unit space, gross area		
Health Care Facilities			
General hospital	1000	bed	gross
Medical center	1100	bed	gross

The above figures are based on *usable* square footage, which in the language of leasing includes the area within the boundaries of the leased space. Most building owners lease space based on the *rentable* area, which includes a tenant's prorated share of common areas such as toilet rooms, elevator lobby, public corridors, and so on. The multiplying figure can be obtained from the building owner, or a figure of 1.1 to 1.15 can be used as an estimated multiplying factor.

Table 1-5
GROSS TO NET RATIOS FOR COMMON BUILDING TYPES

Building Type	Multiplying Factor	Building Type	Multiplying Factor
Office	1.25–1.35	Library reading space	1.5
Retail	1.35	Museum	1.2
Bank	1.4	Theater	1.3–1.7
Restaurant, table service	1.4–1.5	School, classroom	1.5–1.65
Restaurant, cafeteria	1.5	School, dormitory	1.5–1.8
Bars, nightclubs	1.3–1.4	School, laboratory	1.7
Hotel	1.4–1.6	School, gymnasium	1.4–1.45
Public library	1.25–1.3	Apartment	1.25–1.5
Library stack space	1.1–1.3	Hospital	1.5–1.85

PRELIMINARY ELEVATOR PLANNING

For buildings of any size, the space required for elevators can be significant. Detailed procedures for calculating the number, size, and speed of elevators is given on page 215, but for preliminary planning the following guidelines can be used.

RULES OF THUMB

- Number of elevators, single purpose office: 1 elevator per 30,000 net sq. ft.
- Number of elevators, diversified office: 1 elevator per 40,000 net sq. ft.
- Service elevators: 1 elevator per 300,000 gross sq. ft.
- Shaft size, single elevator, 3000 lb. capacity: 8 ft. 4 in. wide by 6 ft. 3 in. deep.
- Shaft size, pair of elevators, 3000 lb. capacity: 17 ft. 0 in. wide by 7 ft. 4 in. deep.
- Add about 6 in. depth for each additional 500 lb. capacity.
- Car depth (D in Table 1-6):
  2500 lb. capacity: 4 ft. 3 in.   3500 lb. capacity: 5 ft. 3 in.
  3000 lb. capacity: 4 ft. 7 in.   4000 lb. capacity: 5 ft. 3 in.

The figure that accompanies Table 1-6 illustrates some common elevator groupings and the space required for lobbies.

Table 1-6
ELEVATOR LOBBY SPACE REQUIREMENTS

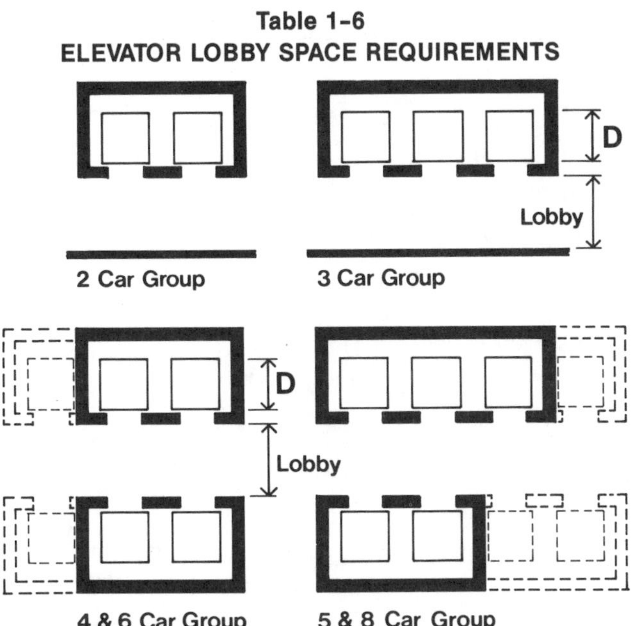

Grouping	Relative to D	But No Less Than	Other
2 car	D		
3 car	1.5 × D	6 ft.	
4 car	1.5–2 × D	10 ft.	4 cars in line 1.5 × D, min. 8 ft.
5 car	1.5–2 × D	10 ft.	
6 car	1.75–2 × D	10 ft.	
8 car	2 × D	Max. 14 ft.	Lobby open both ends

Note: Maximum of 5 ft. 0 in. from center line of lobby to wall for handicapped accessibility.

STAIRS AND RAMPS

Stairs and ramps often need to be worked out early in the design of a building, to determine total area requirements. The following stair formulas give various ways to calculate riser (R) and tread (T) dimensions.

RULES OF THUMB

- For most stairs, use the formula $2R + T = 25$.
- Maximum ramp slope: 1 : 12.

Examples

The planned floor-to-floor height in a new building is 10 ft. 9 in. and the width is 48 in. What total length should be allotted for the stair?

Try a riser height of 7 in. The total rise is 129 in. (129 in. ÷ 7 in. = 18.43 in. risers). Since 7 in. is the maximum allowable by code (Table 1–7), you will need at least 19 risers (129 in. ÷ 19 = 6.79 in., or 6 13/16 in.). Tread width is then $T = 25 - 2(6.79)$ or 11.42 in. (round off to 11 1/2 in.). Since there will be 18 treads (assuming no intermediate landings), the total run will be 18 × 11.5, or 207 in., or 17 ft. 3 in. Depending on the layout, you may need to add landing area to the top and bottom of the stairway. The landing length should be at least the same as the stair width, or 48 in. in this case.

What total length is needed for a ramp (Table 1–8) between levels 1 ft. 8 in. apart?

From the slope formulas, $L = 1.667/0.083$ or, 20.08 ft.

FORMULA: $2R + T = 25$ (use $2R + T = 26$ for exterior stairs)

This formula produces a good proportion with little computation. Other formulas:

$$R \times T = 75$$
$$R + T = 17$$
$$R = 15 - 3T/4$$
$$T = 20 - 4R/3$$
$$R = 9 - \frac{\sqrt{(T - 8)(T - 2)}}{7}$$
$$T = 5 + \sqrt{7(9 - R)^2 + 9}$$

Table 1-7
CODE REQUIREMENTS FOR STAIRS

UBC Requirements	Tread Minimum	Riser Minimum	Riser Maximum
General (includes handicapped)	11 in.	4 in.	7 in.
Private stairways	9 in.		8 in.
Winding (1) minimum required tread @ 12 in. from narrow side	6 in. at any point		
Spiral (1) measured 12 in. from column	7 1/2 in.		

(1) Private stairways in hotels and apartments and private residences.

Table 1-8
RAMP SLOPES

Type	Maximum Slope	Maximum Rise	Maximum Run
UBC, required for accessible access	1 : 12	5 ft.	
UBC, others	1 : 8	5 ft.	
Assembly with fixed seating	1 : 5		
Handicapped, new facilities	1 : 12	30 in.	30 ft.
Handicapped, existing facilities	1 : 10	6 in.	5 ft.
Handicapped, existing facilities	1 : 8	3 in.	2 ft.
Handicapped, curb ramps	1 : 10	6 in.	5 ft.

FORMULA:

Slope	*Formula*
1 : 5	$L = H/0.200$
1 : 8	$L = H/0.125$
1 : 9	$L = H/0.111$
1 : 10	$L = H/0.100$
1 : 11	$L = H/0.091$
1 : 12	$L = H/0.083$

where:

L = length in ft. or in.
H = rise in ft. or in.

Note: Allowance must be made for landings at top and bottom of ramp and at landings.

LIBRARY PLANNING

Libraries represent a unique building type in that a majority of space is devoted to housing books and not people. The number of volumes to be housed becomes the primary planning parameter, rather than numbers of people. For a detailed layout of book stacks, you can use the figures given in Table 1-9. For preliminary planning, the following general guidelines are useful.

RULES OF THUMB

- Public library: 12–18 1/2 volumes per sq. ft.
- Law library: 5–7 volumes per sq. ft.
- To stack space, add a "configuration loss" of from 6% to 20%, to account for inefficiencies in stack layout.
- Minimum aisle between open stacks: 3 ft. 0 in.
- Staff spaces: 100 net sq. ft. per person.
- Reading room seating: 15–35 sq. ft. per person plus 6% configuration loss.
- Net/Gross multiplier: 1.25.
- Maximum of 15,000–20,000 sq. ft. per floor.

Example

A 100,000 volume public library is planned. How much space should be devoted to open stacks?

Plan about 15 volumes per sq. ft. (100,000 ÷ 15 = 6667 sq. ft.). Add a configuration loss of 10%, to give a total area of 6667 + 667, or 7333 sq. ft. of stack space.

Table 1-9
LIBRARY SHELVING—VOLUMES PER LINEAR FOOT OF SHELF BASED ON SUBJECT
(standard stack section 3 ft. wide × 7 1/2 ft. high with 7 shelves)

Subject	Volumes per Ft. of Shelf	Volumes per Single Face Section
Art (excluding oversize)	7	147
Circulating, nonfiction	8	168
Economics	8	168
Fiction	8	168
General literature	7	147
History	7	147
Law	4	84
Medical	5	105
Periodicals, bound	5	105
Public documents	5	105
Technical and scientific	6	126
Average for overall estimating		125

The figures in Table 1-9 should be reduced by at least 10% to avoid overcrowding and to allow for expansion.

AUDIO-VISUAL PLANNING

Planning for audio-visual spaces requires balancing several variables, such as seating capacity, room size, projection distances, type of projection media, screen size and type, viewing angles, and seating layout. The following guidelines and tables are useful for preliminary planning of general audio-visual spaces with level floors. For large theaters, spaces with stepped flooring, and for unusual projection media, more detailed design is required.

RULES OF THUMB

- Closest viewer: minimum two times the screen height.
- Most distant viewer: maximum eight times the screen height.
- Bottom of screen: no lower than 4 ft. above floor line.
- Top of screen: no more than 30° from closest viewer's horizontal line of sight.
- Maximum viewing angle for beaded screen: 50° total—25° each side of center line of screen perpendicular to screen.
- Preferred viewing angle for matte screen: 60°.
- Maximum viewing angle for matte screen: 90°.

Formulas for Projection Media

There is a direct relationship between four variables of projection: the size of the frame of the projected image (film size), the size of the image on the screen, the focal length of the projection lens, and the projection distance. Given any three of these variables you can calculate the other.

FORMULAS:

$$T = \frac{fH}{h}$$

$$f = \frac{Th}{H}$$

$$H = \frac{hT}{f}$$

$$W = \frac{wT}{f}$$

$$\text{or} \quad T = \frac{fW}{w}$$

$$\text{or} \quad f = \frac{Tw}{W}$$

where:

T = projection distance in ft. (throw)
f = focal length of lens in in.
w = width of frame of projection media (film) in in.
h = height of frame of projection media in in.
W = width of image size on screen (or screen if you want full coverage) in ft.
H = height of image (or screen) in ft.

In most situations the projection medium is known (such as 35 mm slides, motion picture, and so on) and the projection lens focal length is known or can easily be modified by purchasing a lens that will give the desired image size for a given projection distance. Some common frame

Table 1-10
FRAME SIZES OF COMMON PROJECTION MEDIA

Projection Media	Frame Size (inches) *h*	*w*	w/h	Frame Size (metric) *h*	*w*
Standard 35 mm slide	0.902	1.346	1.49	22.9	34.2
2 × 2 super slide	1.496	1.496	1.00	38.0	38.0
126 (instamatic) slide	1.043	1.043	1.00	26.5	26.5
35 mm half-frame slide	0.626	0.902	1.44	15.9	22.9
2 1/4 × 2 1/4 slide	2.031	2.031	1.00	51.6	51.6
8 mm motion picture	0.129	0.172	1.33	3.28	4.37
Super 8	0.158	0.211	1.33	4.01	5.36
16 mm motion picture	0.284	0.380	1.33	7.21	9.65
35 mm motion picture	0.600	0.823	1.37	15.2	20.9
Overhead projector	7.5	10.0	1.33		
Overhead projector	10.0	10.0	1.00		

For rectangular formats, unless it is known that slides *always* will be shown horizontally, screen size should be square and sized for the largest dimension.

sizes are given in Table 1–10, and available focal lengths of lenses of common projectors are given in Table 1–11.

Table 1-11
TYPICAL FOCAL LENGTHS OF COMMON PROJECTION LENSES

35 mm slide projector	Lenses available from 1 in. to 12 in.; standard is 4 in. to 6 in. zoom.
16 mm movie projector	2 in. standard; 1 in. to 4 in. available.
Super 8 projector	1/2 in. standard (25 mm).
Super slide projector	5 in. standard; others available.
35 mm movie projector	50 mm (approx. 1 in.) standard; others available.

Example

You are planning a conference room in which 35 mm slides will be used. The ceiling height is 9 ft. What focal length lens is needed to give the maximum projected image size if the projection distance (length of room) is 24 ft.? If rear projection is desired, how long does the room behind the screen need to be?

Ideally, the bottom of the screen should be 4 ft. above the floor, so this gives a maximum screen height of 5 ft. (assuming nothing projects from the ceiling that would interfere with the light beam).

FORMULA:

$$f = \frac{Th}{H}$$

$$f = \frac{24(0.902)}{5} \quad \text{(0.902 frame height from Table 1–10)}$$

$$f = 4.33 \text{ in.}$$

A 4–6 in. zoom lens would work best since it could be adjusted to the exact requirement. A 4 in. fixed focal length lens would result in a larger image, while a 5 in. fixed lens would result in a smaller image than the 5 ft. screen height allows.

If H = 5 ft., then W = 5(1.49), using the aspect ratio (w/h) from Table 1–10. If all slides will only be shown horizontally, the 4.33 in. focal length is acceptable. If the same screen must accommodate vertically projected slides, then the limiting dimension will still be the 5 ft. screen height but now the short dimension of an image will be 5/1.49 = 3.36 ft. A horizontally projected image therefore will not fill the entire 5 ft. screen height available. The required focal length then becomes:

$$f = \frac{24(0.902)}{3.36} = 6.44 \text{ in.}$$

You can calculate the same figure using the screen width equal to 5 ft. (the same as the limiting vertical image), the image width of 1.346 in., and the following formula.

FORMULA: $f = \frac{Tw}{W} = \frac{24(1.346)}{5} = 6.46$ in. (slight difference is due to rounding)

For direct rear projection (no mirrors) you would probably want to select a short focal length lens to minimize space requirements, assuming a 2 1/2 in. lens with h = 0.902 and H = 5 ft.

FORMULA:

$$T = \frac{fH}{h}$$

$$T = \frac{2.5(5)}{0.902} = 13.86 \text{ ft.}$$

Adding an allowance of 1 ft. for projector space, the room would have to be about 15 ft. deep. A 1 in. lens would require about a 6 1/2 ft. room. By using mirrors, you could reduce this depth even more.

Since there is a direct relationship between the four variables, they are easily graphed. Figures 1-3 and 1-4 show graphs for determining screen height and throw distances for two common projection media: 35 mm slides and 16 mm motion picture projectors.

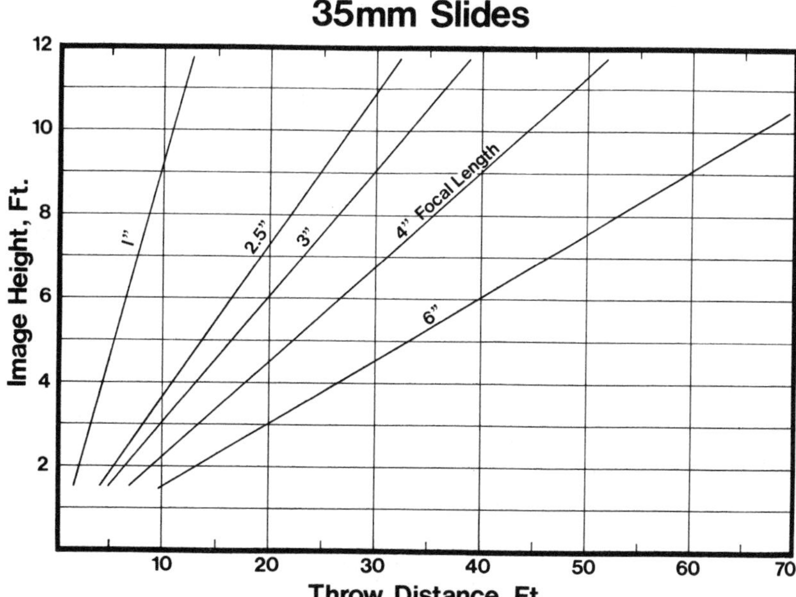

Figure 1-3: Projection Ratios—35 mm Slides

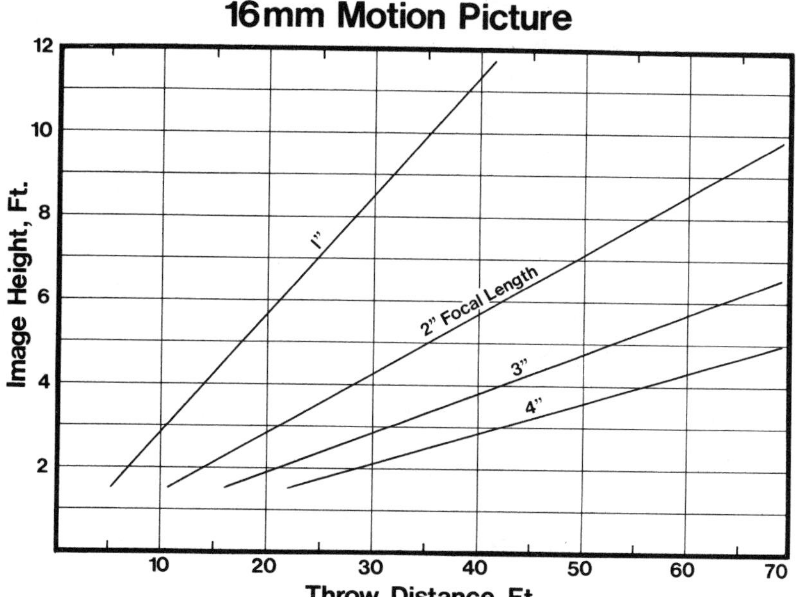

Figure 1-4: Projection Ratios—16 mm Motion Picture

Seating capacities can be estimated by determining the floor area of the desired viewing area and dividing by an allowance for square footage per person. For fixed seating, this is about 6 sq. ft. per person. For conference or seminar style seating, allow from 12 to 15 sq. ft. per person.

The maximum viewing distance should be eight times the screen height, and the minimum viewing distance two times the screen height, with the long axis of the viewing area perpendicular to the screen. The general formula for finding the area of the viewing area follows.

FORMULA:

$$A = L^2 \left(R - \frac{R^2}{4\tan a/2} - \frac{\tan a/2}{16} \right)$$

where:

A = area
L = distance to farthest viewer (last seat)
R = room ratio, length to width
a = viewing angle (In most cases this will be 50° for a beaded screen and 60° or 90° for a matte screen. See also Figure 1-5.)

This formula does not include circulation, so you must add space for side and rear aisles, as required by your layout. Seating capacities for some common room ratios at various viewing angles is given in Table 1-12.

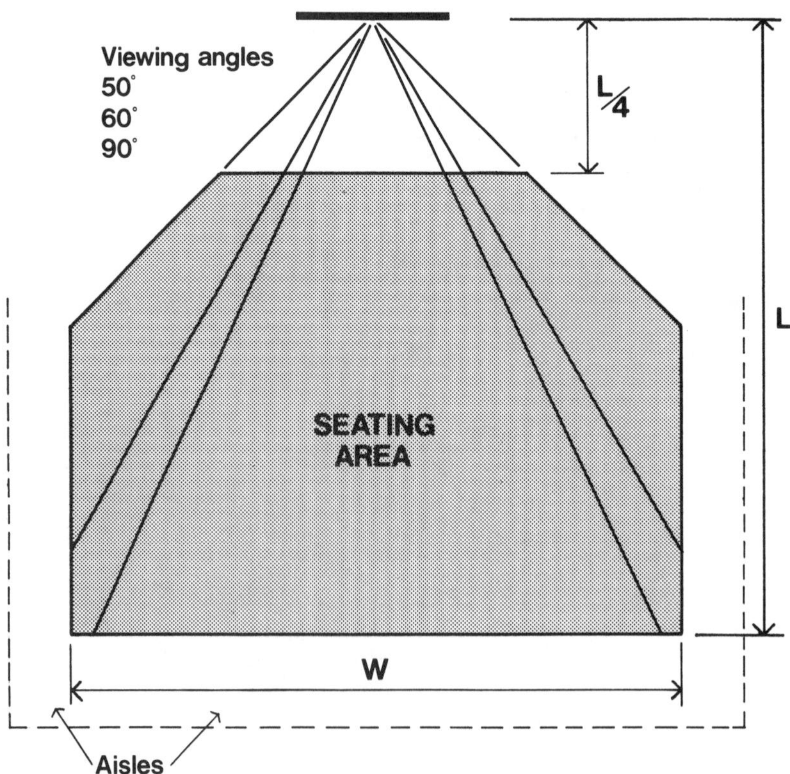

Figure 1-5: Seating Area for Projection

Table 1-12
AUDIO-VISUAL ROOM SEATING CAPACITIES

Throw L	Ratio 1 : 1 = 1.00 Viewing Angle			Ratio 4 : 3 = 0.75 Viewing Angle			Ratio 3 : 2 = 0.67 Viewing Angle			Ratio 2 : 1 = 0.50 Viewing Angle		
	50	60	90	50	60	90	50	60	90	50	60	90
20	29	35	46	28	31	36	27	29	33	22	24	25
22	35	43	55	34	38	44	32	35	40	27	29	30
24	42	51	66	40	45	53	38	42	47	32	34	36
26	49	60	77	47	53	62	45	49	56	38	40	42
28	57	69	90	55	61	71	52	57	64	44	46	49
30	65	80	103	63	71	82	60	66	74	51	53	56
32	74	91	117	72	80	93	68	75	84	57	61	64
34	84	102	132	81	91	105	77	84	95	65	69	72
36	94	115	149	91	102	118	86	95	107	73	77	81
38	105	128	165	101	113	132	96	105	119	81	86	90
40	116	142	183	112	125	146	106	117	132	90	95	100
44	140	171	222	135	152	176	129	141	159	109	115	121
48	167	204	264	161	181	210	153	168	189	129	137	144
52	196	239	310	189	212	246	180	198	222	152	160	169
56	227	277	359	219	246	286	209	229	258	176	186	196
60	261	319	413	252	282	328	240	263	296	202	213	225
64	297	362	469	286	321	373	273	299	337	230	243	256
68	335	409	530	323	362	421	308	338	380	260	274	289
72	376	459	594	362	406	473	345	379	426	291	307	324
76	418	511	662	404	453	526	384	422	475	324	342	361
80	464	566	733	447	502	583	426	467	526	359	379	400

Capacity is based on 6 sq. ft. per person. Add allowances for aisles. (See also Figure 1-5.)

SECTION 2

Calculating Building Systems

PART 2A

Structural Systems

As with many other elements of architectural design, structural calculations proceed from the general to the specific. This part contains rough rules of thumb for early "guesstimating" of structural sizes; charts for preliminary sizing and comparison of structural systems that yield a slightly more accurate answer than rules of thumb; and, finally, detailed formulas and tables for more exacting design.

Also included are tables for selection of the proper species of wood for various uses, plywood grade selection, and plywood use tables.

RULES OF THUMB

Most rules of thumb for structural estimating are based on span-to-depth ratios. The span of the beam, in inches, is divided by the ratio to get the approximate depth of the beam in inches. (You can also use the span of the beam in feet, with the resultant being in feet.) The following list includes span-to-depth ratios for common structural systems.

- Solid wood beams: 13 to 20; 10 to 30 ft. spans
- Glued laminated wood beams: 20 to 25; 20 to 60 ft. spans
- Wood joists: 20 to 25; 12 to 24 ft. spans
- Steel beams: 20; 10 to 60 ft. spans
- Open web steel joists: 20 to 24; 8 to 144 ft. spans
- Concrete beams: 12; 10 to 40 ft. spans

PRELIMINARY STRUCTURAL DESIGN CHARTS

The following charts (Figure 2A–1) can be used to compare structural systems and estimate probable sizes and spans early in the design process. These charts and the vertical support charts have been reproduced with the permission of Philip A. Corkill, University of Nebraska.

Each chart indicates the range of thickness and the depth or height to span normally required for each of the systems indicated. This normal range is a composite of analytical solutions, structural design tables, and many constructed architectural examples.

The few structures that may exceed the range of these charts are generally composed of double systems or the combination of two or more integrated systems. Sometimes one system may be an extension of another system, and in these cases the span and height should be considered for only the primary system. These charts then consider only the *normal* use of a single system and do not consider the extreme possibilities for either depth or span.

To use the charts, determine the approximate span required for the design, then choose a system appropriate to the design requirements and read vertically from the appropriate span to the center of the range, then horizontally to the left of the chart to determine the normal thickness, depth, or height. If, however, greater than normal loads are anticipated or a wider than normal spacing of members is desirable, the upper portion of the range should then be used. If light loads or closer than normal spacing of members is anticipated, the lower portion of the range should then be used.

Structures such as frames, arches, or suspension systems can be used to cover or enclose both rectangular or circular spaces. In these cases, the upper portion of the range is more appropriate for rectangular or vaulted areas, the lower portion for circular or domed areas.

Thicknesses or depths when indicated across the top of these charts reflect the averages for the spans indicated. These figures may, however, need some adjustment. For example, domed areas would require somewhat less thickness or depth of material than vaulted areas; or the thicknesses indicated for folded plates should be increased somewhat if the lower portion of the range is used, and decreased if the upper portion is used.

The use of cantilevers extended from normal spans or a continuous beam system would generally result in less thickness or depth of a system for a given span and would indicate the use of the lower portion of the range, or even below in some cases. On the other hand, pure cantilevers require a much greater thickness or depth and go beyond the range of these charts.

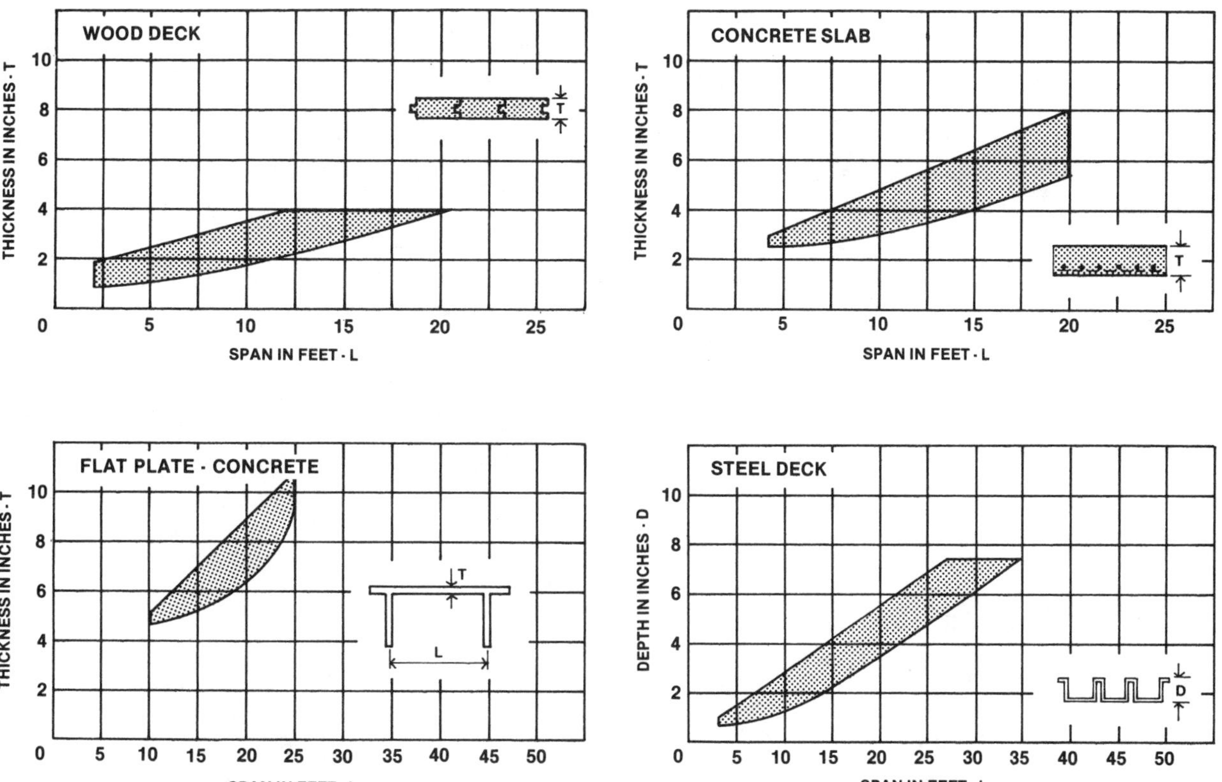

Figure 2A-1: Preliminary Structural Design Charts

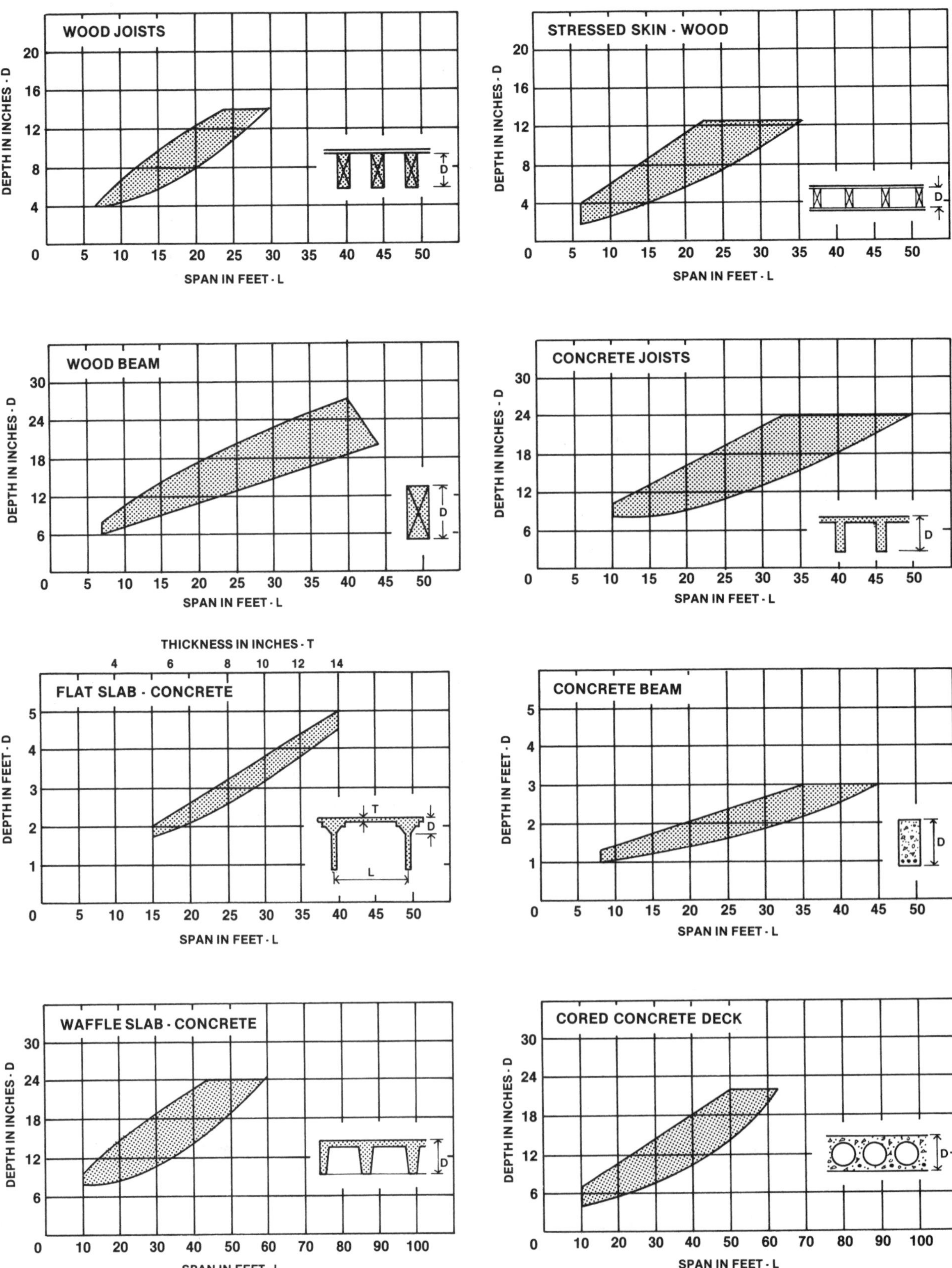

Figure 2A-1: (Continued)

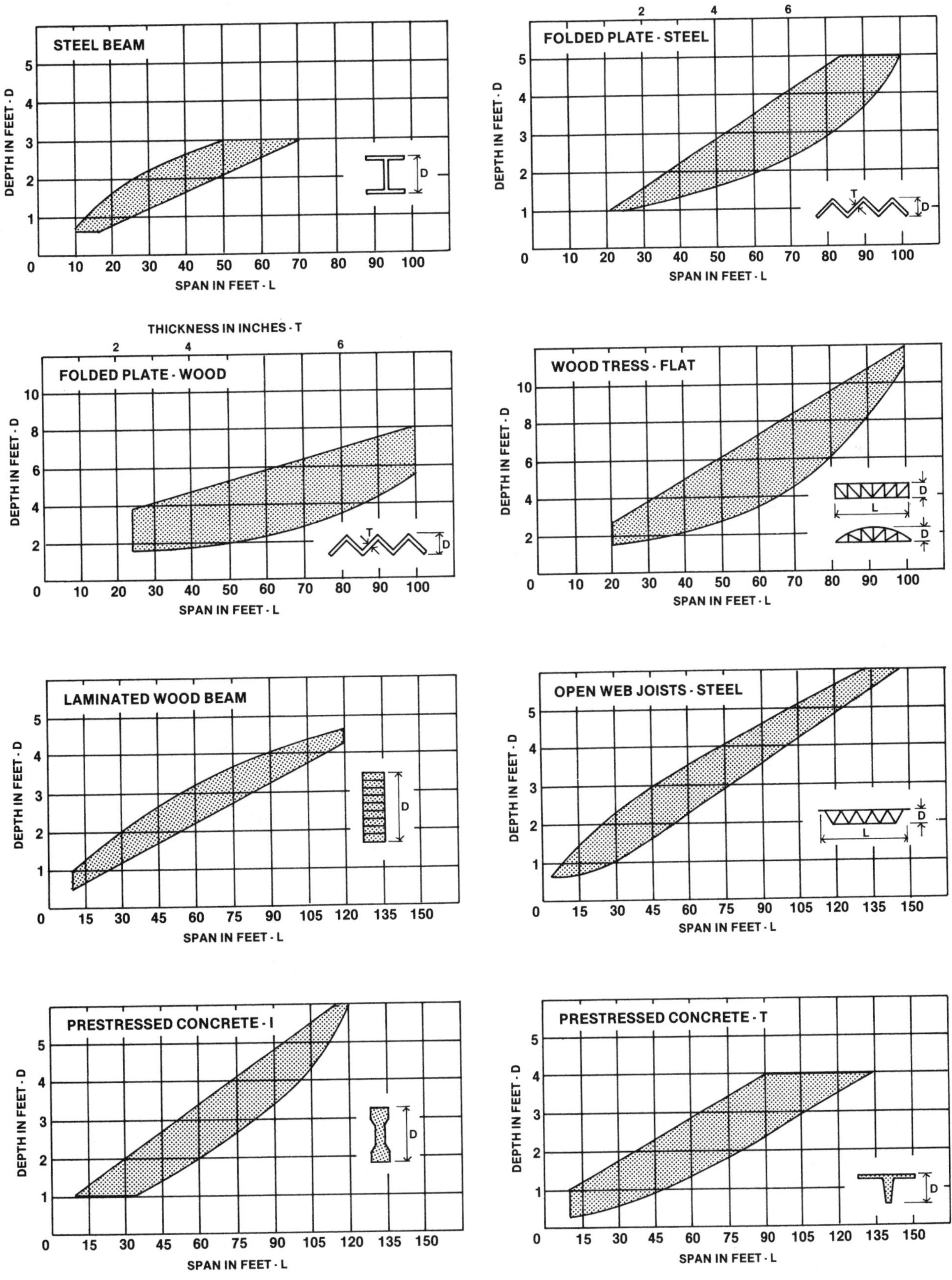
STEEL BEAM
DEPTH IN FEET - D
SPAN IN FEET - L
D
THICKNESS IN INCHES - T
FOLDED PLATE - STEEL
DEPTH IN FEET - D
SPAN IN FEET - L
T
D
THICKNESS IN INCHES - T
FOLDED PLATE - WOOD
DEPTH IN FEET - D
SPAN IN FEET - L
T
D
WOOD TRESS - FLAT
DEPTH IN FEET - D
SPAN IN FEET - L
D
L
D
LAMINATED WOOD BEAM
DEPTH IN FEET - D
SPAN IN FEET - L
D
OPEN WEB JOISTS - STEEL
DEPTH IN FEET - D
SPAN IN FEET - L
D
L
PRESTRESSED CONCRETE - I
DEPTH IN FEET - D
SPAN IN FEET - L
D
PRESTRESSED CONCRETE - T
DEPTH IN FEET - D
SPAN IN FEET - L
D

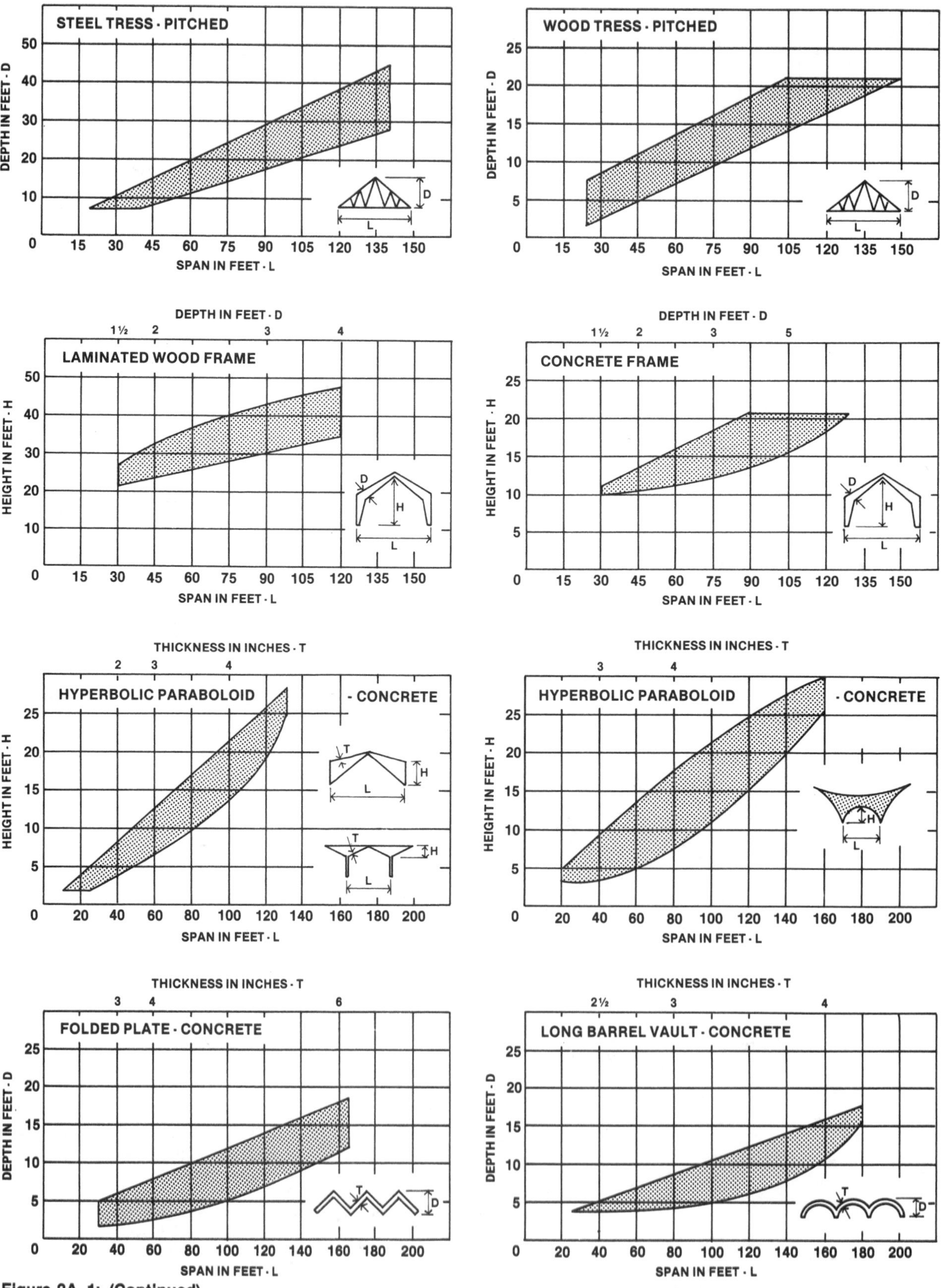

Figure 2A-1: (Continued)

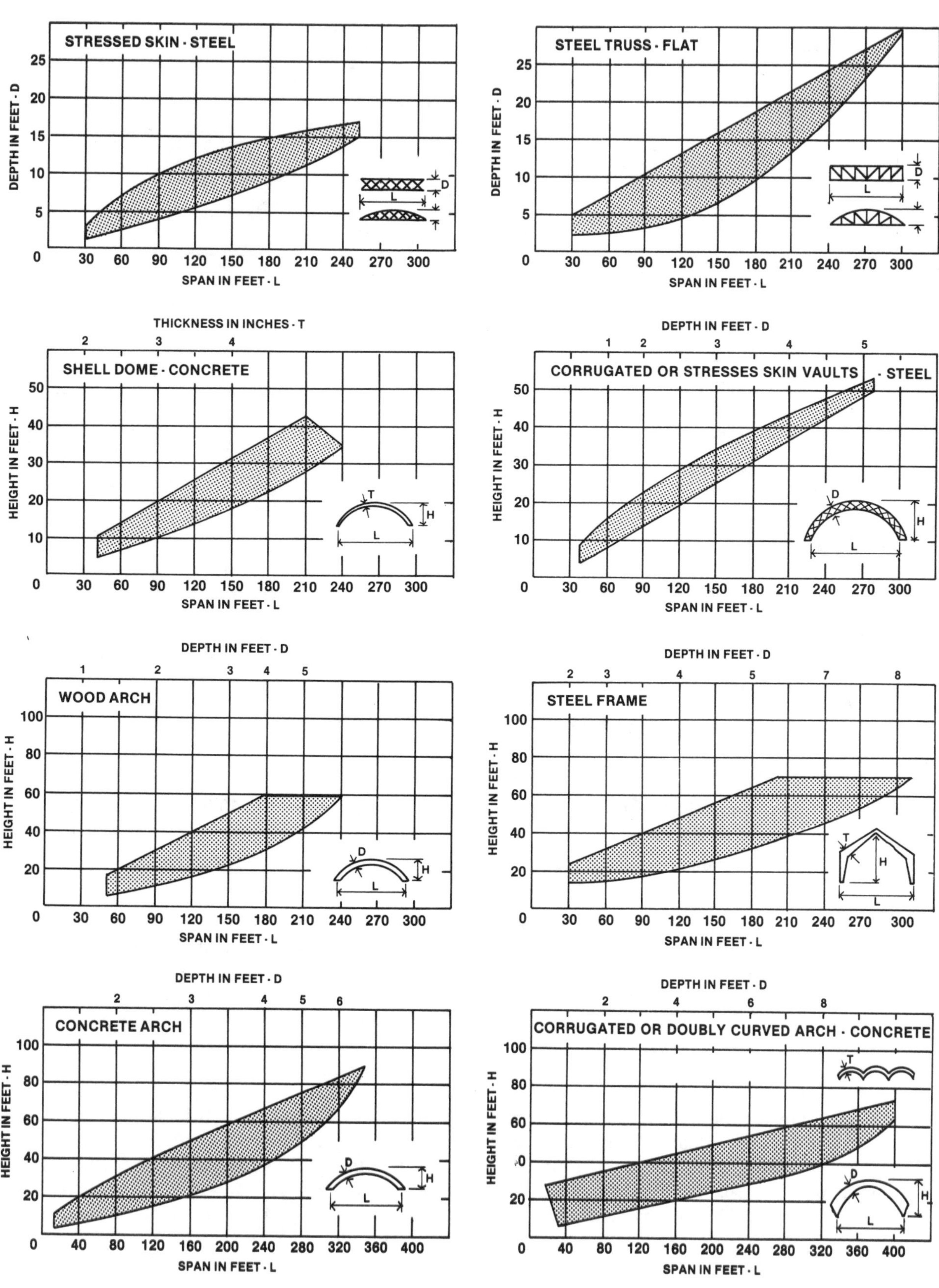
STRESSED SKIN · STEEL
DEPTH IN FEET · D
25
20
15
10
5
0
30 60 90 120 150 180 210 240 270 300
SPAN IN FEET · L
D
L
STEEL TRUSS · FLAT
DEPTH IN FEET · D
25
20
15
10
5
0
30 60 90 120 150 180 210 240 270 300
SPAN IN FEET · L
D
L
THICKNESS IN INCHES · T
2 3 4
SHELL DOME · CONCRETE
HEIGHT IN FEET · H
50
40
30
20
10
0
30 60 90 120 150 180 210 240 270 300
SPAN IN FEET · L
T
H
L
DEPTH IN FEET · D
1 2 3 4 5
CORRUGATED OR STRESSES SKIN VAULTS · STEEL
HEIGHT IN FEET · H
50
40
30
20
10
0
30 60 90 120 150 180 210 240 270 300
SPAN IN FEET · L
D
H
L
DEPTH IN FEET · D
1 2 3 4 5
WOOD ARCH
HEIGHT IN FEET · H
100
80
60
40
20
0
30 60 90 120 150 180 210 240 270 300
SPAN IN FEET · L
D
H
L
DEPTH IN FEET · D
2 3 4 5 7 8
STEEL FRAME
HEIGHT IN FEET · H
100
80
60
40
20
0
30 60 90 120 150 180 210 240 270 300
SPAN IN FEET · L
T
H
L
DEPTH IN FEET · D
2 3 4 5 6
CONCRETE ARCH
HEIGHT IN FEET · H
100
80
60
40
20
0
40 80 120 160 200 240 280 320 360 400
SPAN IN FEET · L
D
H
L
DEPTH IN FEET · D
2 4 6 8
CORRUGATED OR DOUBLY CURVED ARCH · CONCRETE
HEIGHT IN FEET · H
100
80
60
40
20
0
40 80 120 160 200 240 280 320 360 400
SPAN IN FEET · L
T
D
H
L

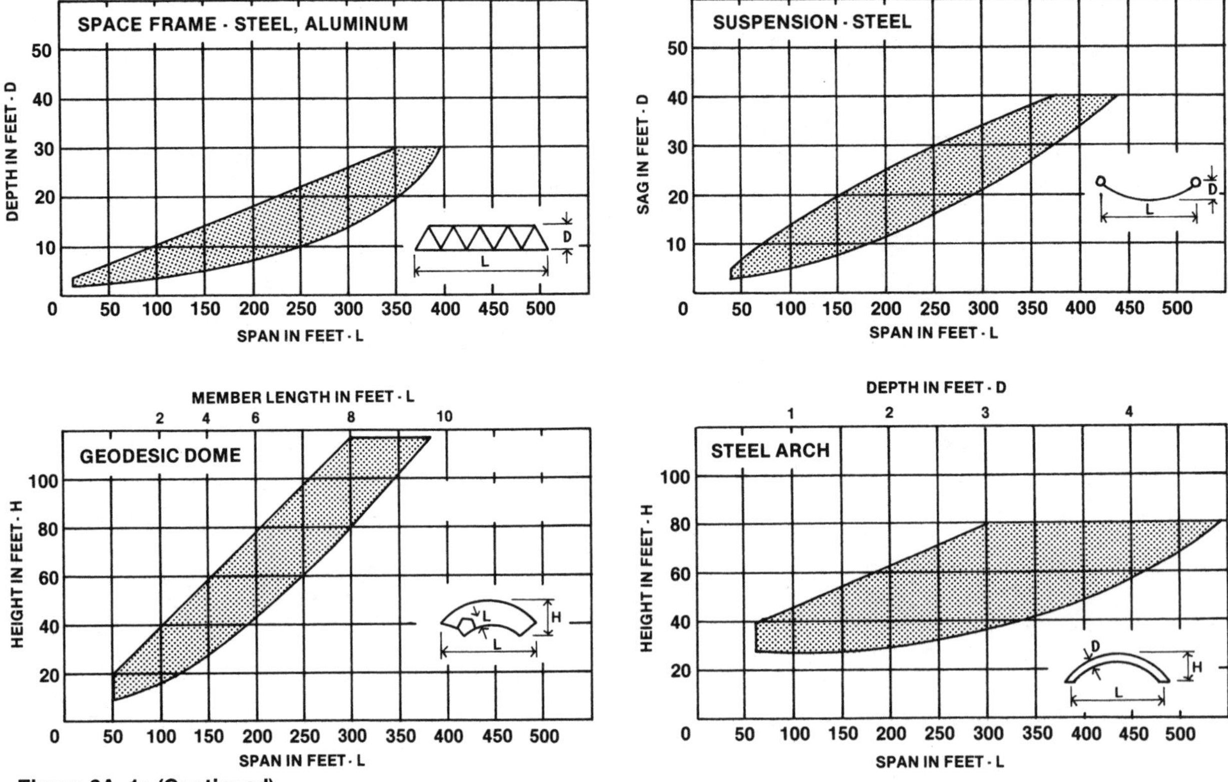

Figure 2A-1: (Continued)

VERTICAL SUPPORT CHARTS

These charts (Figure 2A–2) are presented in two parts:

1. Structural supports that have an unsupported height of from 1 to 50 feet and primarily support only a roof or a one-story load.
2. Structural supports that have a normal one-story unsupported height and must support from 1 to 50 stories.

Each chart indicates the normal range of thickness or depth of independent or continuous vertical members. This range is a composite of analytical solutions, structural design tables and codes, and many constructed architectural examples.

For single-story structures assume an unsupported height for vertical supports and choose an appropriate chart designated single-story design. From the unsupported height shown across the bottom of the chart read vertically to the center of the range, then horizontally to the left of the chart to find the required depth or thickness of the support.

For multistory design the same procedure is followed except the charts designated multistory should be used. Normal unsupported story height for these charts is from 8 to 12 feet.

Loads and spacing of supports determine whether to use the upper, middle, or lower portion of the chart range. If, for example, greater than normal loads are anticipated or column spacings are great, the upper portion of the range should be used. If, however, loads are light or the spacing of columns is closer than normal, the lower portion of the range should be used. The middle portion of the range is generally used for most designs.

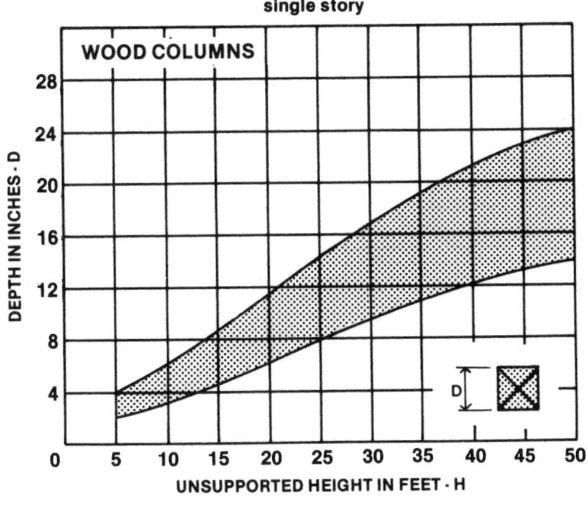

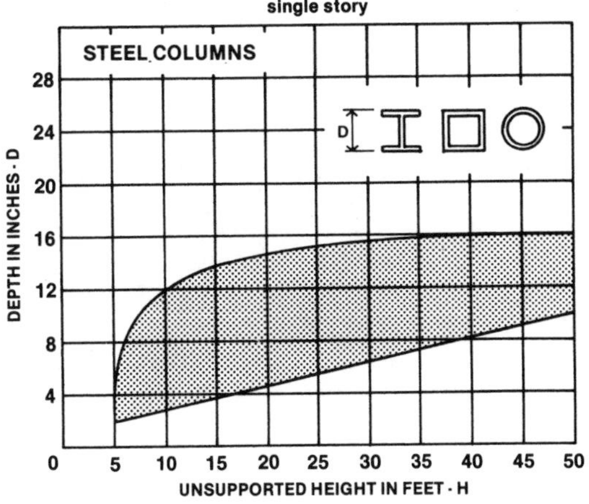

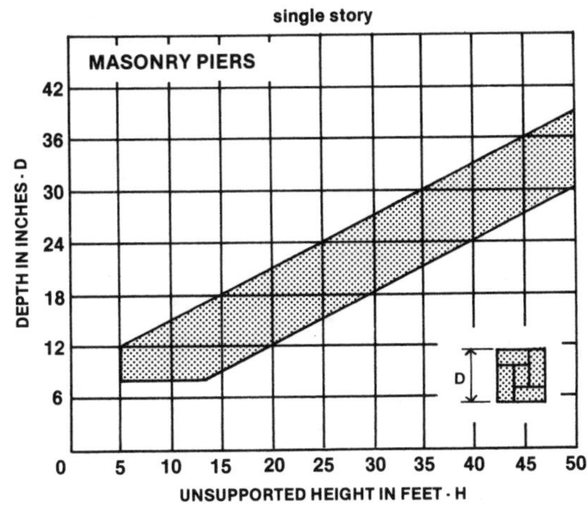

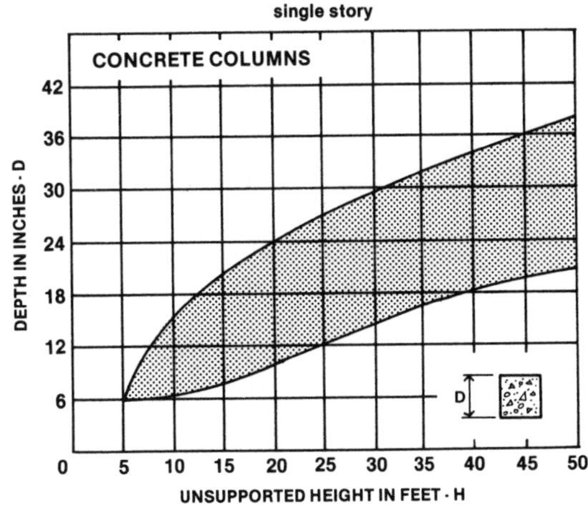

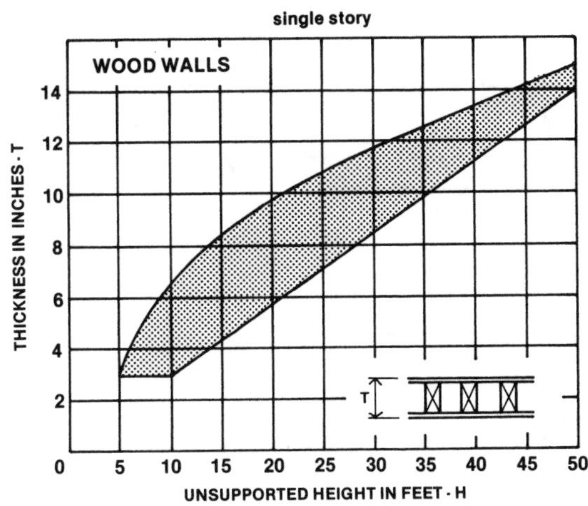

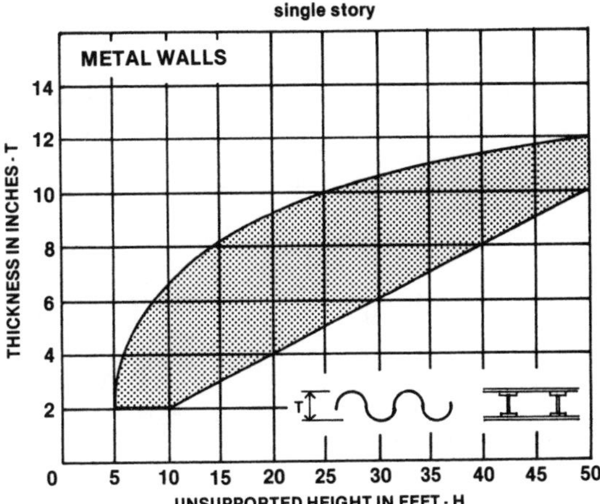

Figure 2A-2: Vertical Support Charts

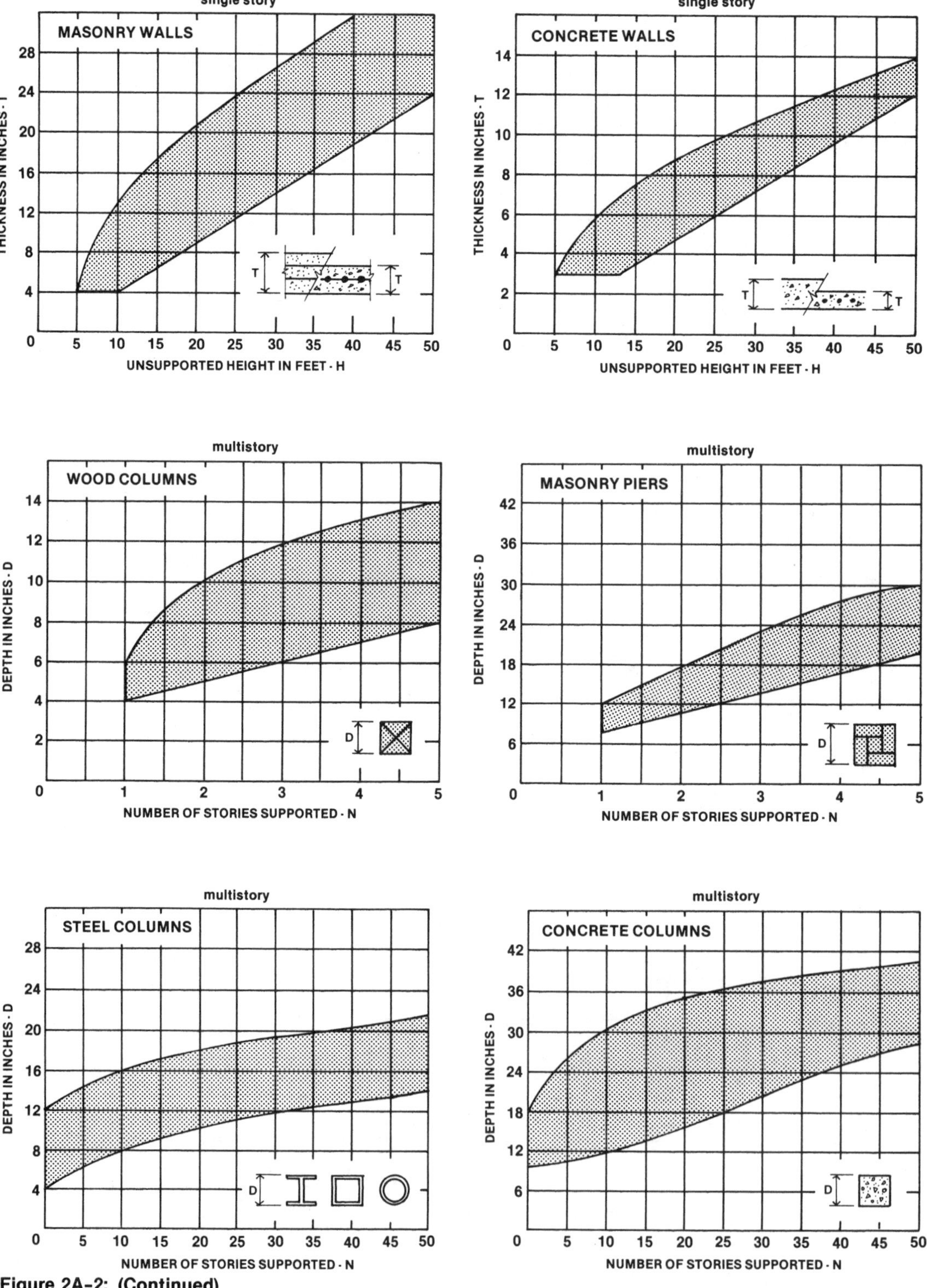

Figure 2A-2: (Continued)

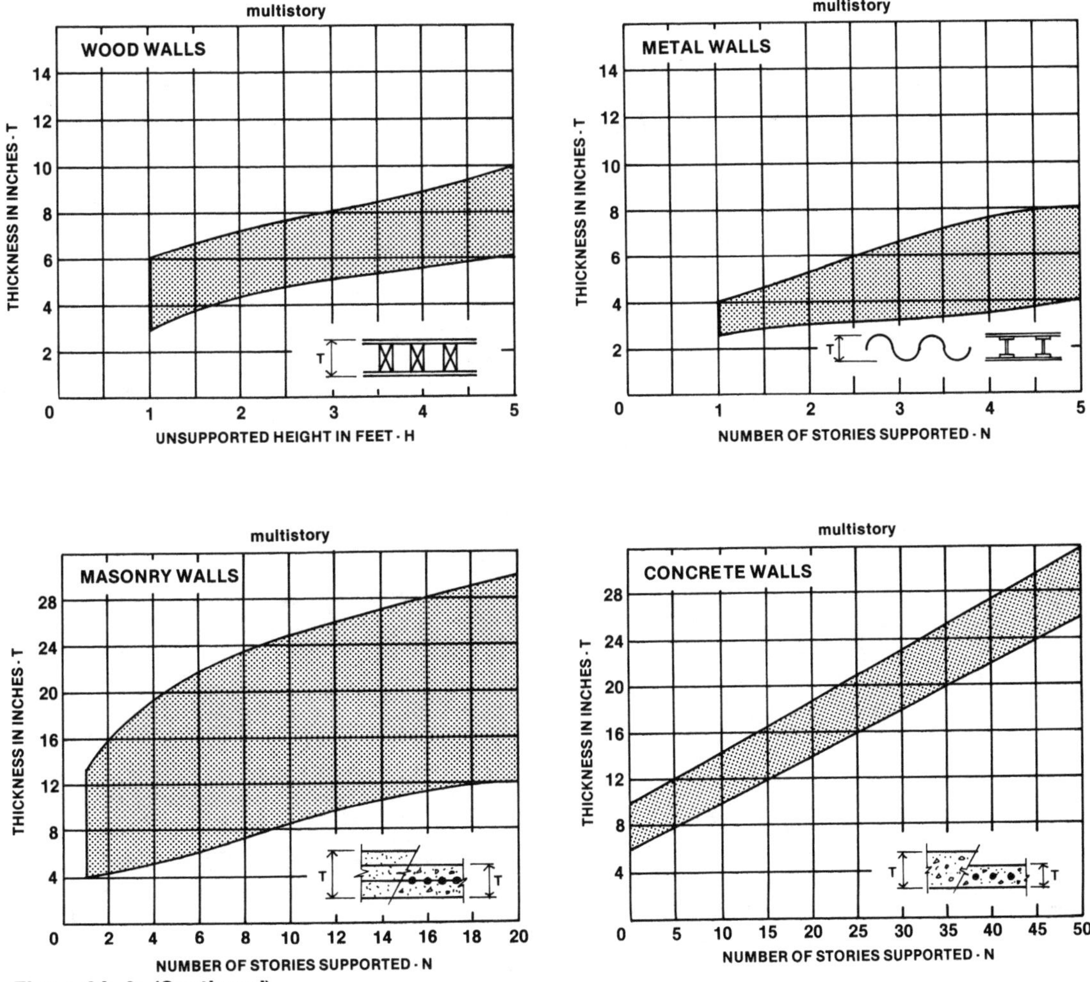

Figure 2A-2: (Continued)

HOW TO DETERMINE STATIC LOADS

Diagrams and Formulas for Static Loads

The following diagrams (Figure 2A-3) give useful formulas for analyzing and determining loads under a variety of conditions. These are applicable for beams of any material. If you know the type and amount of loading, you can quickly find reactions, shear, moment, and deflection at various points on the beam. These diagrams and formulas have been reproduced with the permission of the American Institute of Steel Construction.

BEAM DIAGRAMS AND FORMULAS

Nomenclature

- E Modulus of Elasticity of steel at 29,000 ksi.
- I Moment of Inertia of beam ($in.^4$).
- M_{max} Maximum moment (kip in.).
- M_1 Maximum moment in left section of beam (kip in.).
- M_2 Maximum moment in right section of beam (kip in.).
- M_3 Maximum positive moment in beam with combined end moment conditions (kip in.).
- M_x Moment at distance x from end of beam (kip in.).
- P Concentrated load (kips).
- P_1 Concentrated load nearest left reaction (kips).
- P_2 Concentrated load nearest right reaction, and of different magnitude than P_1 (kips).
- R End beam reaction for any condition of symmetrical loading (kips).
- R_1 Left end beam reaction (kips).
- R_2 Right end or intermediate beam reaction (kips).
- R_3 Right end beam reaction (kips).
- V Maximum vertical shear for any condition of symmetrical loading (kips).
- V_1 Maximum vertical shear in left section of beam (kips).
- V_2 Vertical shear at right reaction point, or to left of intermediate reaction point of beam (kips).
- V_3 Vertical shear at right reaction point, or to right of intermediate reaction point of beam (kips).
- V_x Vertical shear at distance x from end of beam (kips).
- W Total load on beam (kips).
- a Measured distance along beam (in.).
- b Measured distance along beam which may be greater or less than "a" (in.).
- l Total length of beam between reaction points (in.).
- w Uniformly distributed load per unit of length (kips per in.).
- w_1 Uniformly distributed load per unit of length nearest left reaction (kips per in.).
- w_2 Uniformly distributed load per unit of length nearest right reaction, and of different magnitude than w_1 (kips per in.).
- x Any distance measured along beam from left reaction (in.).
- x_1 Any distance measured along overhang section of beam from nearest reaction point (in.).
- Δ_{max} Maximum deflection (in.).
- Δ_a Deflection at point of load (in.).
- Δ_x Deflection at any point x distance from left reaction (in.).
- Δ_{x_1} Deflection of overhang section of beam at any distance from nearest reaction point (in.).

Figure 2A-3: Beam Diagrams and Formulas

1. SIMPLE BEAM—UNIFORMLY DISTRIBUTED LOAD

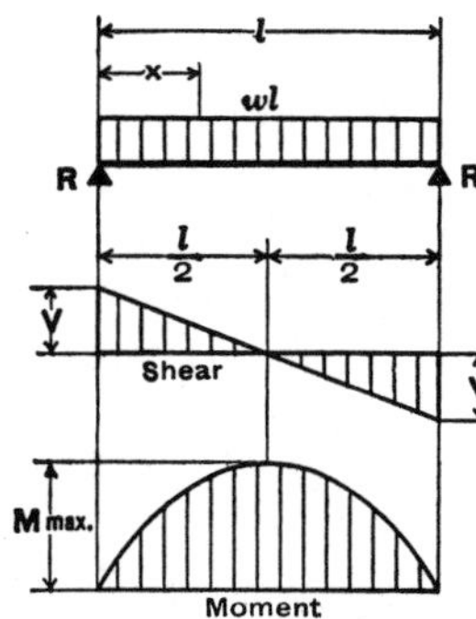

Equivalent Tabular Load . . . $= wl$

$R = V$ . . . . $= \frac{wl}{2}$

V_x . . . . $= w\left(\frac{l}{2} - x\right)$

M max. (at center) . . . . $= \frac{wl^2}{8}$

M_x . . . . $= \frac{wx}{2}(l - x)$

Δmax. (at center) . . . . $= \frac{5\,wl^4}{384\,EI}$

Δx . . . . $= \frac{wx}{24EI}(l^3 - 2lx^2 + x^3)$

2. SIMPLE BEAM—LOAD INCREASING UNIFORMLY TO ONE END

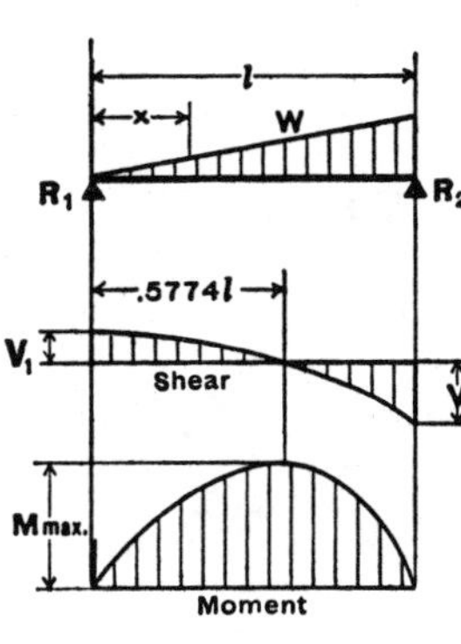

Equivalent Tabular Load . . . $= \frac{16W}{9\sqrt{3}} = 1.0264W$

$R_1 = V_1$ . . . . $= \frac{W}{3}$

$R_2 = V_2$ max. . . . . $= \frac{2W}{3}$

V_x . . . . $= \frac{W}{3} - \frac{Wx^2}{l^2}$

M max. $\left(\text{at } x = \frac{l}{\sqrt{3}} = .5774l\right)$ . . $= \frac{2Wl}{9\sqrt{3}} = .1283\,Wl$

M_x . . . . $= \frac{Wx}{3l^2}(l^2 - x^2)$

Δmax. $\left(\text{at } x = l\sqrt{1 - \sqrt{\frac{8}{15}}} = .5193l\right)$ $= .01304\,\frac{Wl^3}{EI}$

Δx . . . . $= \frac{Wx}{180EI\,l^2}(3x^4 - 10l^2x^2 + 7l^4)$

3. SIMPLE BEAM—LOAD INCREASING UNIFORMLY TO CENTER

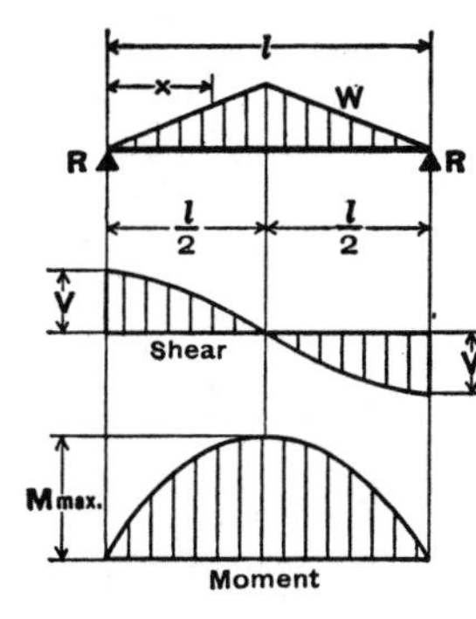

Equivalent Tabular Load . . . $= \frac{4W}{3}$

$R = V$ . . . . $= \frac{W}{2}$

V_x $\left(\text{when } x < \frac{l}{2}\right)$ . . . . $= \frac{W}{2l^2}(l^2 - 4x^2)$

M max. (at center) . . . . $= \frac{Wl}{6}$

M_x $\left(\text{when } x < \frac{l}{2}\right)$ . . . . $= Wx\left(\frac{1}{2} - \frac{2x^2}{3l^2}\right)$

Δmax. (at center) . . . . $= \frac{Wl^3}{60EI}$

Δx . . . . $= \frac{Wx}{480\,EI\,l^2}(5l^2 - 4x^2)^2$

Figure 2A-3: (Continued)

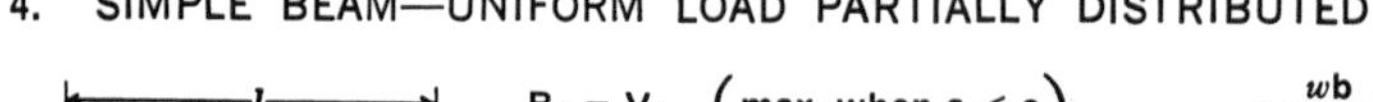

4. SIMPLE BEAM—UNIFORM LOAD PARTIALLY DISTRIBUTED

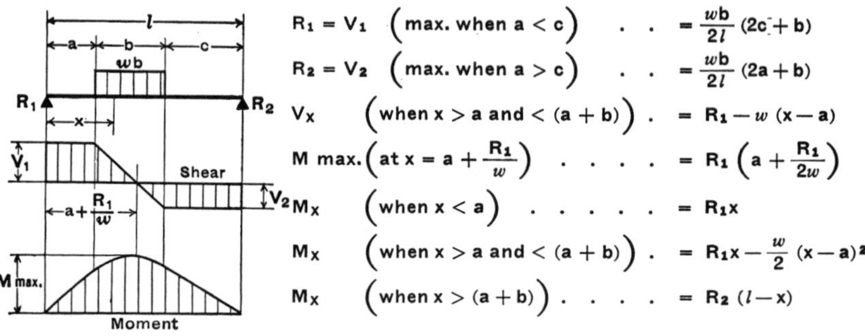

$R_1 = V_1 \left(\text{max. when } a < c\right) \quad . \quad . \quad = \frac{wb}{2l}(2c + b)$

$R_2 = V_2 \left(\text{max. when } a > c\right) \quad . \quad . \quad = \frac{wb}{2l}(2a + b)$

$V_x \left(\text{when } x > a \text{ and } < (a + b)\right) \quad . \quad = R_1 - w(x - a)$

$M \text{ max.} \left(\text{at } x = a + \frac{R_1}{w}\right) \quad . \quad . \quad . \quad . \quad = R_1\left(a + \frac{R_1}{2w}\right)$

$M_x \left(\text{when } x < a\right) \quad . \quad . \quad . \quad . \quad . \quad = R_1 x$

$M_x \left(\text{when } x > a \text{ and } < (a + b)\right) \quad . \quad = R_1 x - \frac{w}{2}(x - a)^2$

$M_x \left(\text{when } x > (a + b)\right) \quad . \quad . \quad . \quad . \quad = R_2(l - x)$

5. SIMPLE BEAM—UNIFORM LOAD PARTIALLY DISTRIBUTED AT ONE END

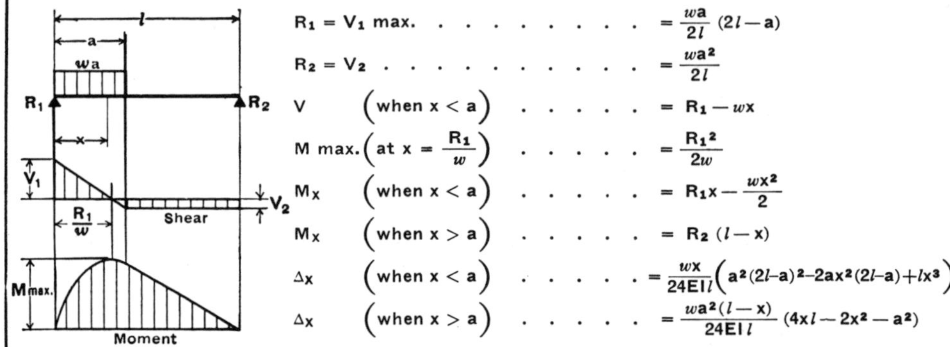

$R_1 = V_1 \text{ max.} \quad . \quad . \quad . \quad . \quad . \quad . \quad . \quad . \quad . \quad = \frac{wa}{2l}(2l - a)$

$R_2 = V_2 \quad . \quad . \quad . \quad . \quad . \quad . \quad . \quad . \quad . \quad . \quad = \frac{wa^2}{2l}$

$V \left(\text{when } x < a\right) \quad . \quad . \quad . \quad . \quad . \quad = R_1 - wx$

$M \text{ max.} \left(\text{at } x = \frac{R_1}{w}\right) \quad . \quad . \quad . \quad . \quad . \quad = \frac{R_1^2}{2w}$

$M_x \left(\text{when } x < a\right) \quad . \quad . \quad . \quad . \quad . \quad = R_1 x - \frac{wx^2}{2}$

$M_x \left(\text{when } x > a\right) \quad . \quad . \quad . \quad . \quad . \quad = R_2(l - x)$

$\Delta x \left(\text{when } x < a\right) \quad . \quad . \quad . \quad . \quad . \quad = \frac{wx}{24EIl}\left(a^2(2l - a)^2 - 2ax^2(2l - a) + lx^3\right)$

$\Delta x \left(\text{when } x > a\right) \quad . \quad . \quad . \quad . \quad . \quad = \frac{wa^2(l - x)}{24EIl}(4xl - 2x^2 - a^2)$

6. SIMPLE BEAM—UNIFORM LOAD PARTIALLY DISTRIBUTED AT EACH END

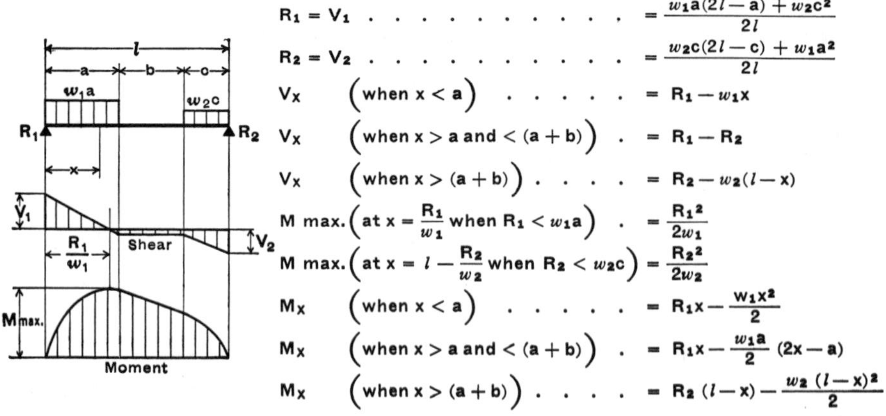

$R_1 = V_1 \quad . \quad . \quad . \quad . \quad . \quad . \quad . \quad . \quad . \quad . \quad = \frac{w_1 a(2l - a) + w_2 c^2}{2l}$

$R_2 = V_2 \quad . \quad . \quad . \quad . \quad . \quad . \quad . \quad . \quad . \quad . \quad = \frac{w_2 c(2l - c) + w_1 a^2}{2l}$

$V_x \left(\text{when } x < a\right) \quad . \quad . \quad . \quad . \quad . \quad = R_1 - w_1 x$

$V_x \left(\text{when } x > a \text{ and } < (a + b)\right) \quad . \quad = R_1 - R_2$

$V_x \left(\text{when } x > (a + b)\right) \quad . \quad . \quad . \quad . \quad = R_2 - w_2(l - x)$

$M \text{ max.} \left(\text{at } x = \frac{R_1}{w_1} \text{ when } R_1 < w_1 a\right) \quad . \quad = \frac{R_1^2}{2w_1}$

$M \text{ max.} \left(\text{at } x = l - \frac{R_2}{w_2} \text{ when } R_2 < w_2 c\right) = \frac{R_2^2}{2w_2}$

$M_x \left(\text{when } x < a\right) \quad . \quad . \quad . \quad . \quad . \quad = R_1 x - \frac{w_1 x^2}{2}$

$M_x \left(\text{when } x > a \text{ and } < (a + b)\right) \quad . \quad = R_1 x - \frac{w_1 a}{2}(2x - a)$

$M_x \left(\text{when } x > (a + b)\right) \quad . \quad . \quad . \quad . \quad = R_2(l - x) - \frac{w_2(l - x)^2}{2}$

Figure 2A-3: (Continued)

7. SIMPLE BEAM—CONCENTRATED LOAD AT CENTER

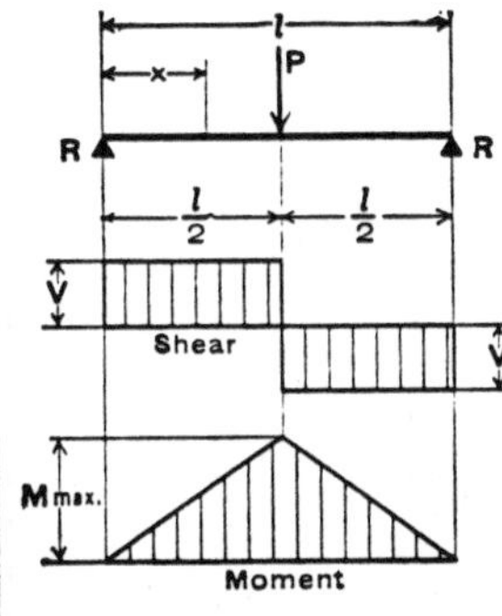

Equivalent Tabular Load . . . . . . $= 2P$

$R = V$ . . . . $= \frac{P}{2}$

M max. (at point of load) . . . . . . $= \frac{Pl}{4}$

M_x (when $x < \frac{l}{2}$) . . . . . . $= \frac{Px}{2}$

Δmax. (at point of load) . . . . . . $= \frac{Pl^3}{48EI}$

Δx (when $x < \frac{l}{2}$) . . . . . . $= \frac{Px}{48EI}(3l^2 - 4x^2)$

8. SIMPLE BEAM—CONCENTRATED LOAD AT ANY POINT

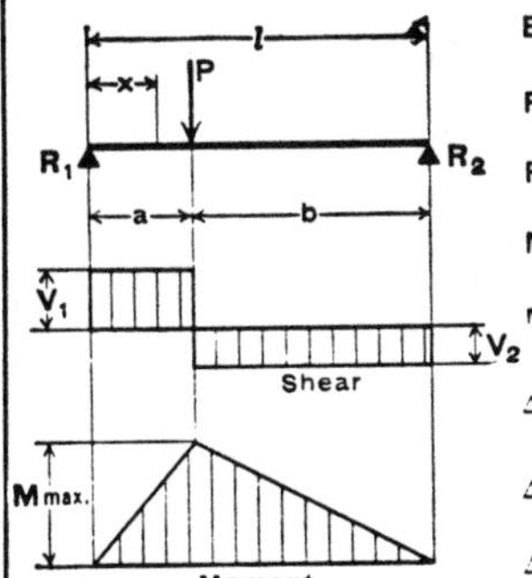

Equivalent Tabular Load . . . . . . $= \frac{8\ Pab}{l^2}$

$R_1 = V_1$ (max. when $a < b$) . . . . $= \frac{Pb}{l}$

$R_2 = V_2$ (max. when $a > b$) . . . . $= \frac{Pa}{l}$

M max. (at point of load) . . . . $= \frac{Pab}{l}$

M_x (when $x < a$) . . . . $= \frac{Pbx}{l}$

Δmax. $\left(\text{at } x = \sqrt{\frac{a(a+2b)}{3}} \text{ when } a > b\right)$ $= \frac{Pab\,(a+2b)\sqrt{3a\,(a+2b)}}{27\ EI\ l}$

Δa (at point of load) . . . . $= \frac{Pa^2b^2}{3EI\ l}$

Δx (when $x < a$) . . . . $= \frac{Pbx}{6EI\ l}(l^2 - b^2 - x^2)$

9. SIMPLE BEAM—TWO EQUAL CONCENTRATED LOADS SYMMETRICALLY PLACED

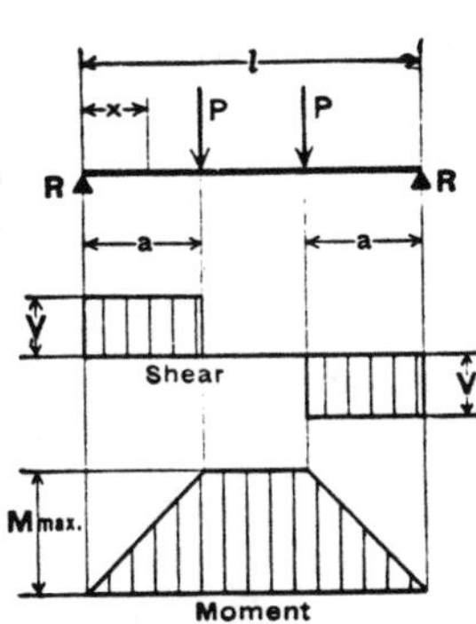

Equivalent Tabular Load . . . . . . $= \frac{8\ Pa}{l}$

$R = V$ . . . . $= P$

M max. (between loads) . . . . . . $= Pa$

M_x (when $x < a$) . . . . . . $= Px$

Δmax. (at center) . . . . $= \frac{Pa}{24EI}(3l^2 - 4a^2)$

Δx (when $x < a$) . . . . . . $= \frac{Px}{6EI}(3la - 3a^2 - x^2)$

Δx (when $x > a$ and $< (l - a)$) . . $= \frac{Pa}{6EI}(3lx - 3x^2 - a^2)$

10. SIMPLE BEAM—TWO EQUAL CONCENTRATED LOADS UNSYMMETRICALLY PLACED

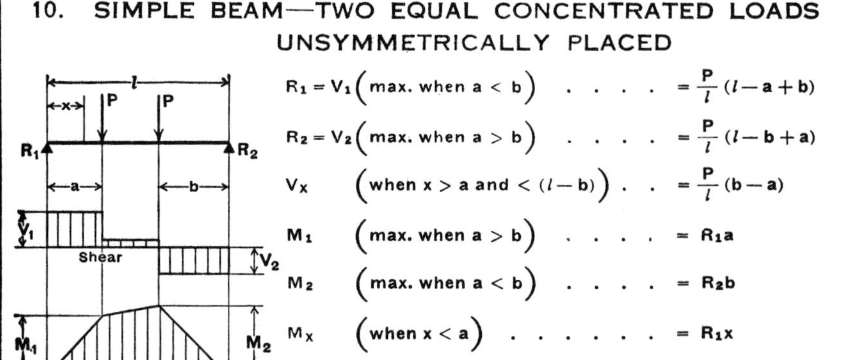

$R_1 = V_1\left(\text{max. when } a < b\right)$ . . . . $= \frac{P}{l}(l - a + b)$

$R_2 = V_2\left(\text{max. when } a > b\right)$ . . . . $= \frac{P}{l}(l - b + a)$

V_x $\left(\text{when } x > a \text{ and } < (l - b)\right)$ . . $= \frac{P}{l}(b - a)$

M_1 $\left(\text{max. when } a > b\right)$ . . . . $= R_1 a$

M_2 $\left(\text{max. when } a < b\right)$ . . . . $= R_2 b$

M_x $\left(\text{when } x < a\right)$ . . . . . . $= R_1 x$

M_x $\left(\text{when } x > a \text{ and } < (l - b)\right)$ . . $= R_1 x - P(x - a)$

11. SIMPLE BEAM—TWO UNEQUAL CONCENTRATED LOADS UNSYMMETRICALLY PLACED

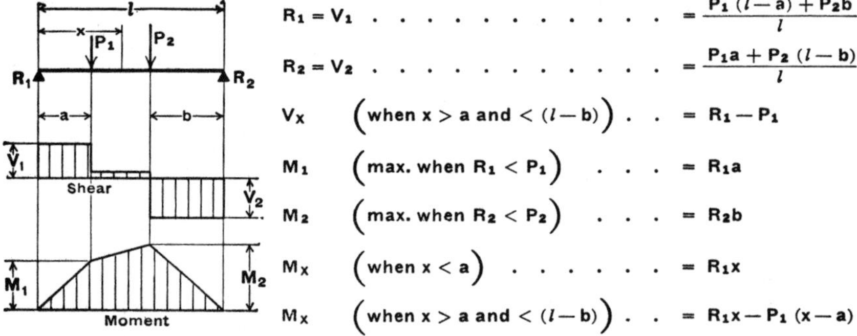

$R_1 = V_1$ . . . . $= \frac{P_1(l - a) + P_2 b}{l}$

$R_2 = V_2$ . . . . $= \frac{P_1 a + P_2(l - b)}{l}$

V_x $\left(\text{when } x > a \text{ and } < (l - b)\right)$ . . $= R_1 - P_1$

M_1 $\left(\text{max. when } R_1 < P_1\right)$ . . . $= R_1 a$

M_2 $\left(\text{max. when } R_2 < P_2\right)$ . . . $= R_2 b$

M_x $\left(\text{when } x < a\right)$ . . . . . . $= R_1 x$

M_x $\left(\text{when } x > a \text{ and } < (l - b)\right)$ . . $= R_1 x - P_1(x - a)$

12. BEAM FIXED AT ONE END, SUPPORTED AT OTHER— UNIFORMLY DISTRIBUTED LOAD

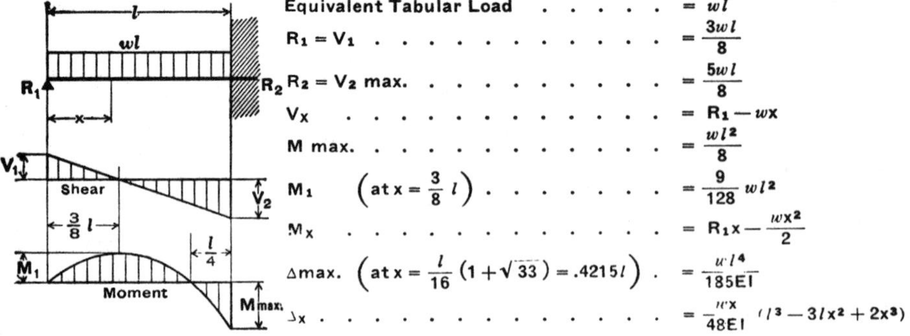

Equivalent Tabular Load . . . . . $= wl$

$R_1 = V_1$ . . . . $= \frac{3wl}{8}$

$R_2 = V_2$ max. . . . . $= \frac{5wl}{8}$

V_x . . . . $= R_1 - wx$

M max. . . . . $= \frac{wl^2}{8}$

M_1 $\left(\text{at } x = \frac{3}{8}l\right)$ . . . . $= \frac{9}{128}wl^2$

M_x . . . . $= R_1 x - \frac{wx^2}{2}$

$\Delta\text{max.}$ $\left(\text{at } x = \frac{l}{16}(1 + \sqrt{33}) = .4215l\right)$. $= \frac{wl^4}{185EI}$

Δx . . . . $= \frac{wx}{48EI}(l^3 - 3lx^2 + 2x^3)$

Figure 2A-3: (Continued)

13. BEAM FIXED AT ONE END, SUPPORTED AT OTHER— CONCENTRATED LOAD AT CENTER

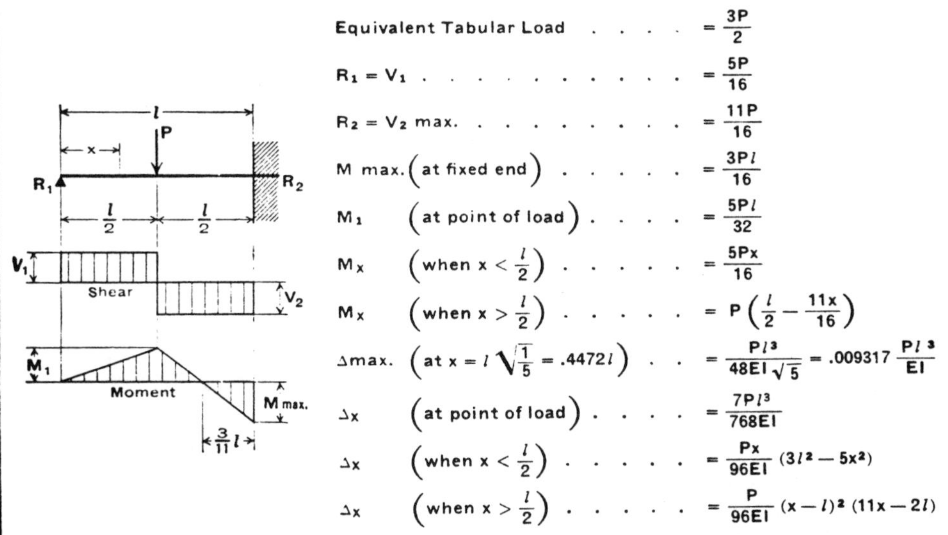

Equivalent Tabular Load		$= \frac{3P}{2}$
$R_1 = V_1$		$= \frac{5P}{16}$
$R_2 = V_2$ max.		$= \frac{11P}{16}$
M max.	(at fixed end)	$= \frac{3Pl}{16}$
M_1	(at point of load)	$= \frac{5Pl}{32}$
M_x	$\left(\text{when } x < \frac{l}{2}\right)$	$= \frac{5Px}{16}$
M_x	$\left(\text{when } x > \frac{l}{2}\right)$	$= P\left(\frac{l}{2} - \frac{11x}{16}\right)$
Δmax.	$\left(\text{at } x = l\sqrt{\frac{1}{5}} = .4472l\right)$	$= \frac{Pl^3}{48EI\sqrt{5}} = .009317\frac{Pl^3}{EI}$
Δx	(at point of load)	$= \frac{7Pl^3}{768EI}$
Δx	$\left(\text{when } x < \frac{l}{2}\right)$	$= \frac{Px}{96EI}(3l^2 - 5x^2)$
Δx	$\left(\text{when } x > \frac{l}{2}\right)$	$= \frac{P}{96EI}(x - l)^2(11x - 2l)$

14. BEAM FIXED AT ONE END, SUPPORTED AT OTHER— CONCENTRATED LOAD AT ANY POINT

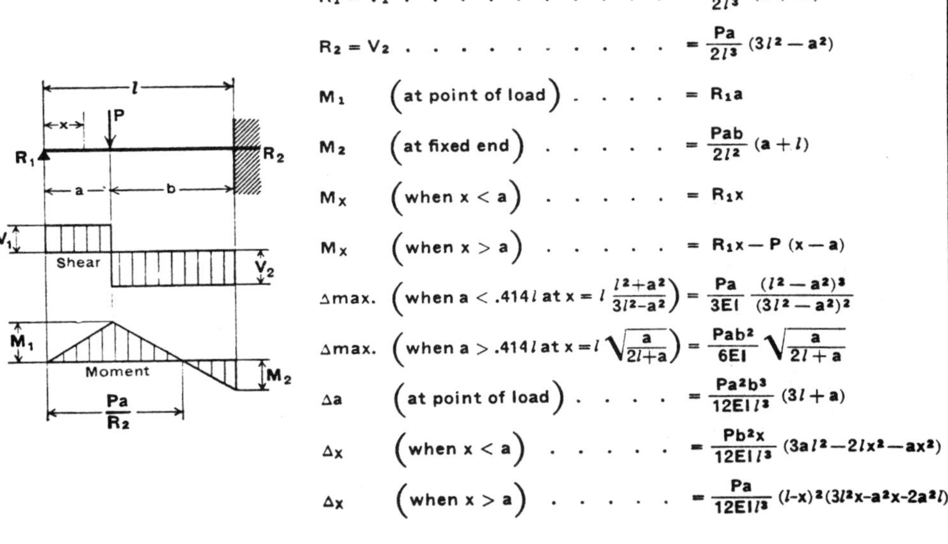

$R_1 = V_1$		$= \frac{Pb^2}{2l^3}(a + 2l)$
$R_2 = V_2$		$= \frac{Pa}{2l^3}(3l^2 - a^2)$
M_1	(at point of load)	$= R_1 a$
M_2	(at fixed end)	$= \frac{Pab}{2l^2}(a + l)$
M_x	(when $x < a$)	$= R_1 x$
M_x	(when $x > a$)	$= R_1 x - P(x - a)$
Δmax.	$\left(\text{when } a < .414l \text{ at } x = l\frac{l^2+a^2}{3l^2-a^2}\right)$	$= \frac{Pa}{3EI}\frac{(l^2 - a^2)^3}{(3l^2 - a^2)^2}$
Δmax.	$\left(\text{when } a > .414l \text{ at } x = l\sqrt{\frac{a}{2l+a}}\right)$	$= \frac{Pab^2}{6EI}\sqrt{\frac{a}{2l + a}}$
Δa	(at point of load)	$= \frac{Pa^2b^3}{12EIl^3}(3l + a)$
Δx	(when $x < a$)	$= \frac{Pb^2x}{12EIl^3}(3al^2 - 2lx^2 - ax^2)$
Δx	(when $x > a$)	$= \frac{Pa}{12EIl^3}(l-x)^2(3l^2x - a^2x - 2a^2l)$

15. BEAM FIXED AT BOTH ENDS—UNIFORMLY DISTRIBUTED LOADS

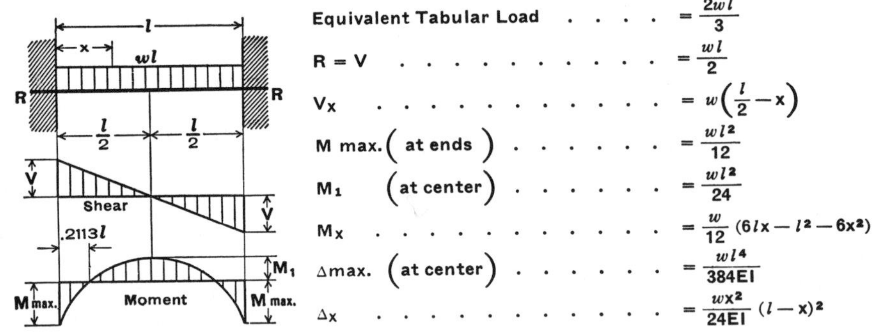

Equivalent Tabular Load	$= \frac{2wl}{3}$
R = V	$= \frac{wl}{2}$
V_x	$= w\left(\frac{l}{2} - x\right)$
M max. (at ends)	$= \frac{wl^2}{12}$
M_1 (at center)	$= \frac{wl^2}{24}$
M_x	$= \frac{w}{12}(6lx - l^2 - 6x^2)$
Δmax. (at center)	$= \frac{wl^4}{384EI}$
Δx	$= \frac{wx^2}{24EI}(l - x)^2$

16. BEAM FIXED AT BOTH ENDS—CONCENTRATED LOAD AT CENTER

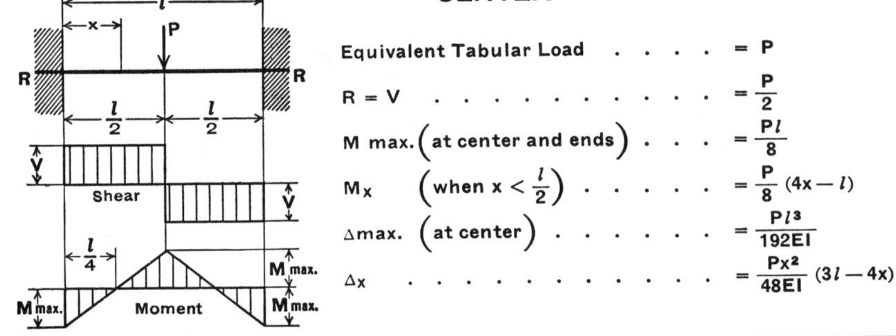

Equivalent Tabular Load	$= P$
R = V	$= \frac{P}{2}$
M max. (at center and ends)	$= \frac{Pl}{8}$
M_x (when $x < \frac{l}{2}$)	$= \frac{P}{8}(4x - l)$
Δmax. (at center)	$= \frac{Pl^3}{192EI}$
Δx	$= \frac{Px^2}{48EI}(3l - 4x)$

17. BEAM FIXED AT BOTH ENDS—CONCENTRATED LOAD AT ANY POINT

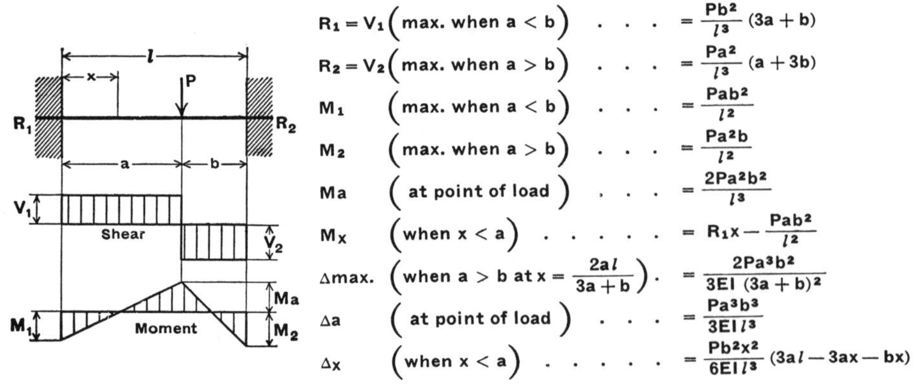

$R_1 = V_1$ (max. when $a < b$)	$= \frac{Pb^2}{l^3}(3a + b)$
$R_2 = V_2$ (max. when $a > b$)	$= \frac{Pa^2}{l^3}(a + 3b)$
M_1 (max. when $a < b$)	$= \frac{Pab^2}{l^2}$
M_2 (max. when $a > b$)	$= \frac{Pa^2b}{l^2}$
M_a (at point of load)	$= \frac{2Pa^2b^2}{l^3}$
M_x (when $x < a$)	$= R_1x - \frac{Pab^2}{l^2}$
Δmax. (when $a > b$ at $x = \frac{2al}{3a + b}$)	$= \frac{2Pa^3b^2}{3EI\,(3a + b)^2}$
Δa (at point of load)	$= \frac{Pa^3b^3}{3EIl^3}$
Δx (when $x < a$)	$= \frac{Pb^2x^2}{6EIl^3}(3al - 3ax - bx)$

Figure 2A-3: (Continued)

18. CANTILEVER BEAM—LOAD INCREASING UNIFORMLY TO FIXED END

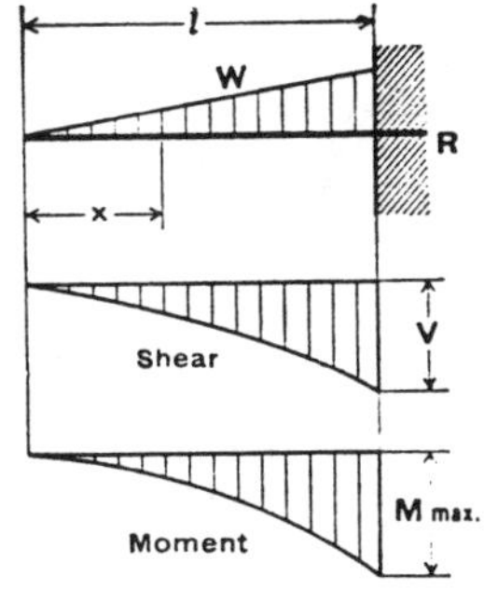

Equivalent Tabular Load . . . . $= \frac{8}{3} W$

R = V . . . . $= W$

V_x . . . . $= W \frac{x^2}{l^2}$

M max. (at fixed end) . . . . . $= \frac{Wl}{3}$

M_x . . . . $= \frac{Wx^3}{3l^2}$

Δmax. (at free end) . . . . . $= \frac{Wl^3}{15EI}$

Δx . . . . $= \frac{W}{60EIl^2}(x^5 - 5l^4x + 4l^5)$

19. CANTILEVER BEAM—UNIFORMLY DISTRIBUTED LOAD

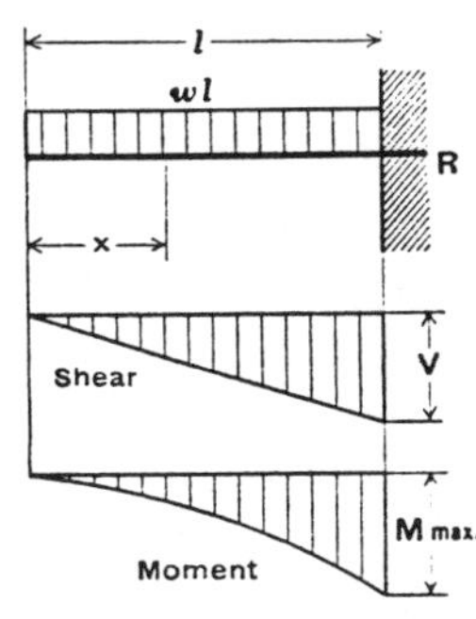

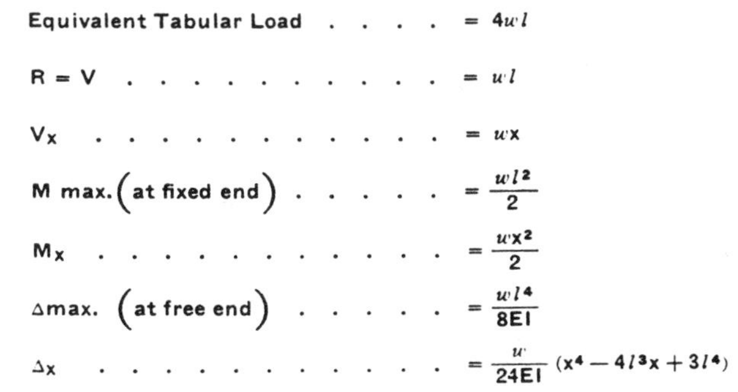

Equivalent Tabular Load . . . . $= 4wl$

R = V . . . . $= wl$

V_x . . . . $= wx$

M max. (at fixed end) . . . . . $= \frac{wl^2}{2}$

M_x . . . . $= \frac{wx^2}{2}$

Δmax. (at free end) . . . . . $= \frac{wl^4}{8EI}$

Δx . . . . $= \frac{w}{24EI}(x^4 - 4l^3x + 3l^4)$

20. BEAM FIXED AT ONE END, FREE TO DEFLECT VERTICALLY BUT NOT ROTATE AT OTHER—UNIFORMLY DISTRIBUTED LOAD

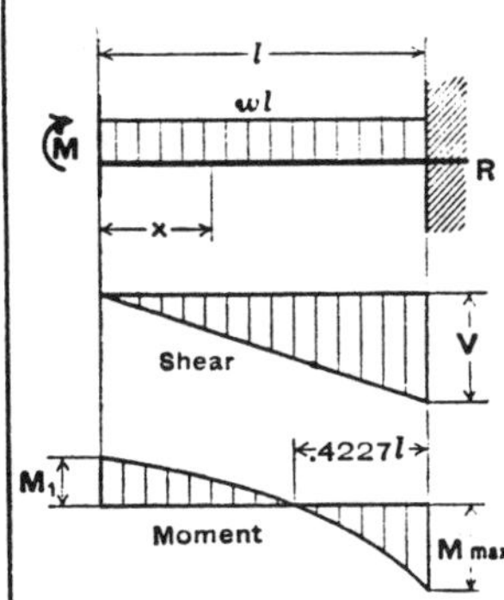

Equivalent Tabular Load . . . . $= \frac{8}{3} wl$

R = V . . . . $= wl$

V_x . . . . $= wx$

M max. (at fixed end) . . . . . $= \frac{wl^2}{3}$

M_1 (at deflected end) . . . . $= \frac{wl^2}{6}$

M_x . . . . $= \frac{w}{6}(l^2 - 3x^2)$

Δmax. (at deflected end) . . . . $= \frac{wl^4}{24EI}$

Δx . . . . $= \frac{w(l^2 - x^2)^2}{24EI}$

21. CANTILEVER BEAM—CONCENTRATED LOAD AT ANY POINT

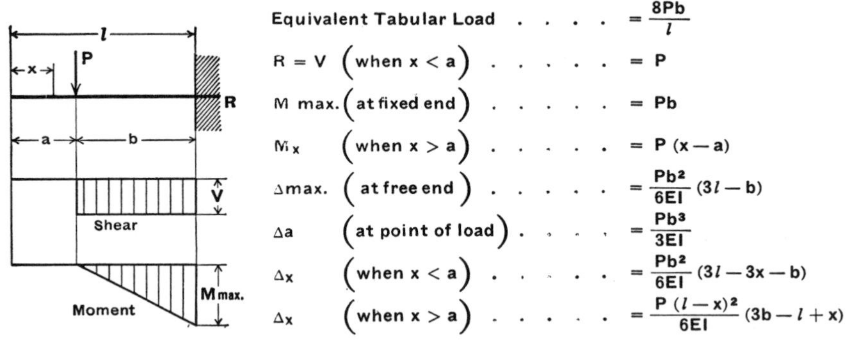

Equivalent Tabular Load . . . . $= \frac{8Pb}{l}$

$R = V$ (when $x < a$) . . . . . . $= P$

M max. (at fixed end) . . . . . . $= Pb$

M_x (when $x > a$) . . . . . . $= P(x - a)$

Δmax. (at free end) . . . . . . $= \frac{Pb^2}{6EI}(3l - b)$

Δa (at point of load) . . . . . $= \frac{Pb^3}{3EI}$

Δx (when $x < a$) . . . . . . $= \frac{Pb^2}{6EI}(3l - 3x - b)$

Δx (when $x > a$) . . . . . . $= \frac{P(l - x)^2}{6EI}(3b - l + x)$

22. CANTILEVER BEAM—CONCENTRATED LOAD AT FREE END

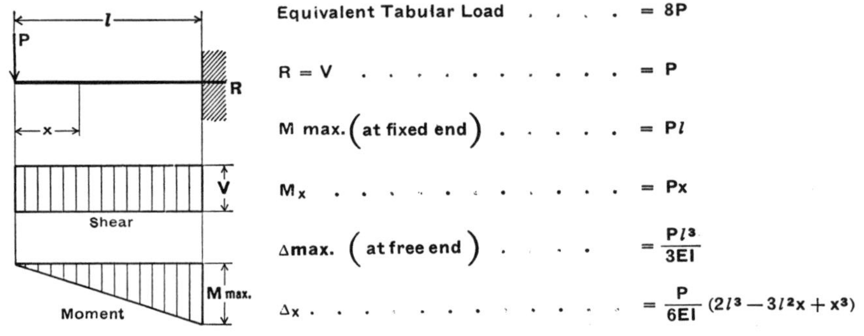

Equivalent Tabular Load . . . . $= 8P$

$R = V$ . . . . $= P$

M max. (at fixed end) . . . . . . $= Pl$

M_x . . . . $= Px$

Δmax. (at free end) . . . . $= \frac{Pl^3}{3EI}$

Δx . . . . $= \frac{P}{6EI}(2l^3 - 3l^2x + x^3)$

23. BEAM FIXED AT ONE END, FREE TO DEFLECT VERTICALLY BUT NOT ROTATE AT OTHER—CONCENTRATED LOAD AT DEFLECTED END

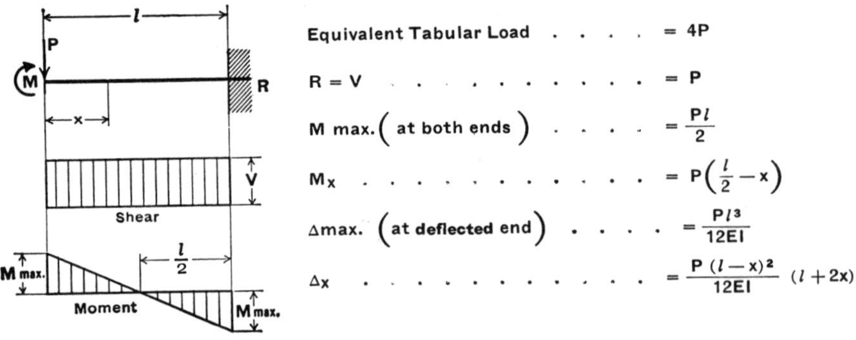

Equivalent Tabular Load . . . . $= 4P$

$R = V$ . . . . $= P$

M max. (at both ends) . . . . . $= \frac{Pl}{2}$

M_x . . . . $= P\left(\frac{l}{2} - x\right)$

Δmax. (at deflected end) . . . . $= \frac{Pl^3}{12EI}$

Δx . . . . $= \frac{P(l - x)^2}{12EI}(l + 2x)$

Figure 2A-3: (Continued)

24. BEAM OVERHANGING ONE SUPPORT—UNIFORMLY DISTRIBUTED LOAD

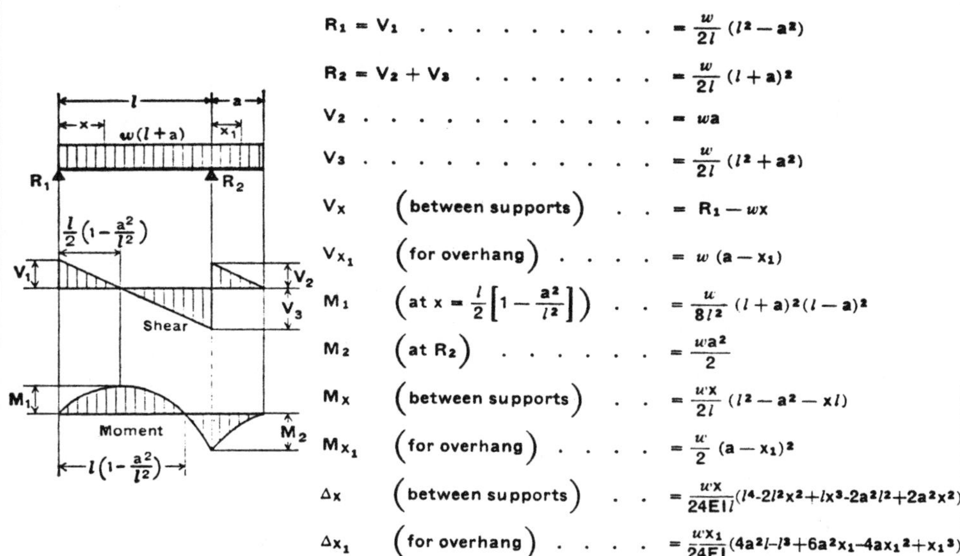

$R_1 = V_1$ . . . . $= \frac{w}{2l}(l^2 - a^2)$

$R_2 = V_2 + V_3$ . . . . $= \frac{w}{2l}(l + a)^2$

V_2 . . . . $= wa$

V_3 . . . . $= \frac{w}{2l}(l^2 + a^2)$

V_x (between supports) . . $= R_1 - wx$

V_{x_1} (for overhang) . . . . $= w(a - x_1)$

M_1 $\left(\text{at } x = \frac{l}{2}\left[1 - \frac{a^2}{l^2}\right]\right)$ . . $= \frac{w}{8l^2}(l + a)^2(l - a)^2$

M_2 (at R_2) . . . . $= \frac{wa^2}{2}$

M_x (between supports) . . $= \frac{wx}{2l}(l^2 - a^2 - xl)$

M_{x_1} (for overhang) . . . . $= \frac{w}{2}(a - x_1)^2$

Δx (between supports) . . $= \frac{wx}{24EIl}(l^4 - 2l^2x^2 + lx^3 - 2a^2l^2 + 2a^2x^2)$

Δx_1 (for overhang) . . . . $= \frac{wx_1}{24EI}(4a^2l - l^3 + 6a^2x_1 - 4ax_1^2 + x_1^3)$

25. BEAM OVERHANGING ONE SUPPORT—UNIFORMLY DISTRIBUTED LOAD ON OVERHANG

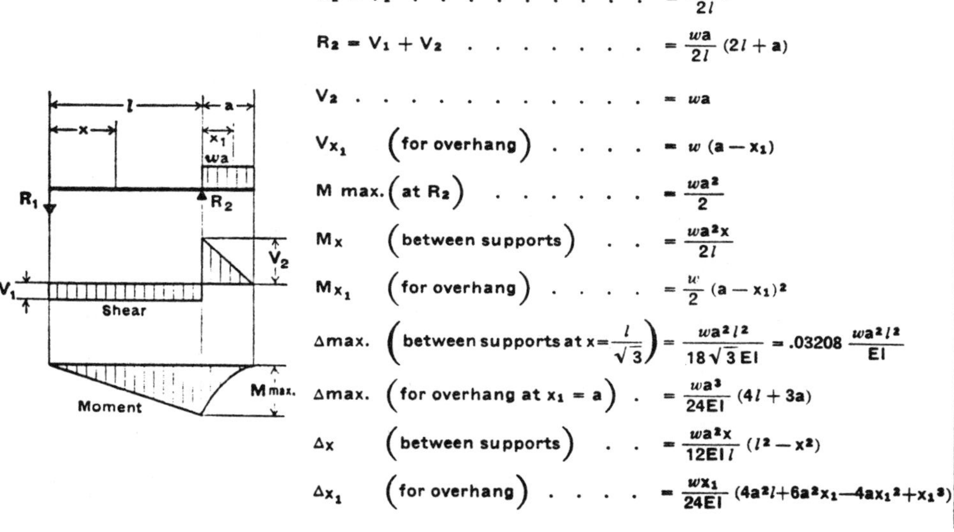

$R_1 = V_1$ . . . . $= \frac{wa^2}{2l}$

$R_2 = V_1 + V_2$ . . . . $= \frac{wa}{2l}(2l + a)$

V_2 . . . . $= wa$

V_{x_1} (for overhang) . . . . $= w(a - x_1)$

M max. (at R_2) . . . . $= \frac{wa^2}{2}$

M_x (between supports) . . $= \frac{wa^2x}{2l}$

M_{x_1} (for overhang) . . . . $= \frac{w}{2}(a - x_1)^2$

Δmax. $\left(\text{between supports at } x = \frac{l}{\sqrt{3}}\right) = \frac{wa^2l^2}{18\sqrt{3}EI} = .03208\frac{wa^2l^2}{EI}$

Δmax. (for overhang at $x_1 = a$) . $= \frac{wa^3}{24EI}(4l + 3a)$

Δx (between supports) . . $= \frac{wa^2x}{12EIl}(l^2 - x^2)$

Δx_1 (for overhang) . . . . $= \frac{wx_1}{24EI}(4a^2l + 6a^2x_1 - 4ax_1^2 + x_1^3)$

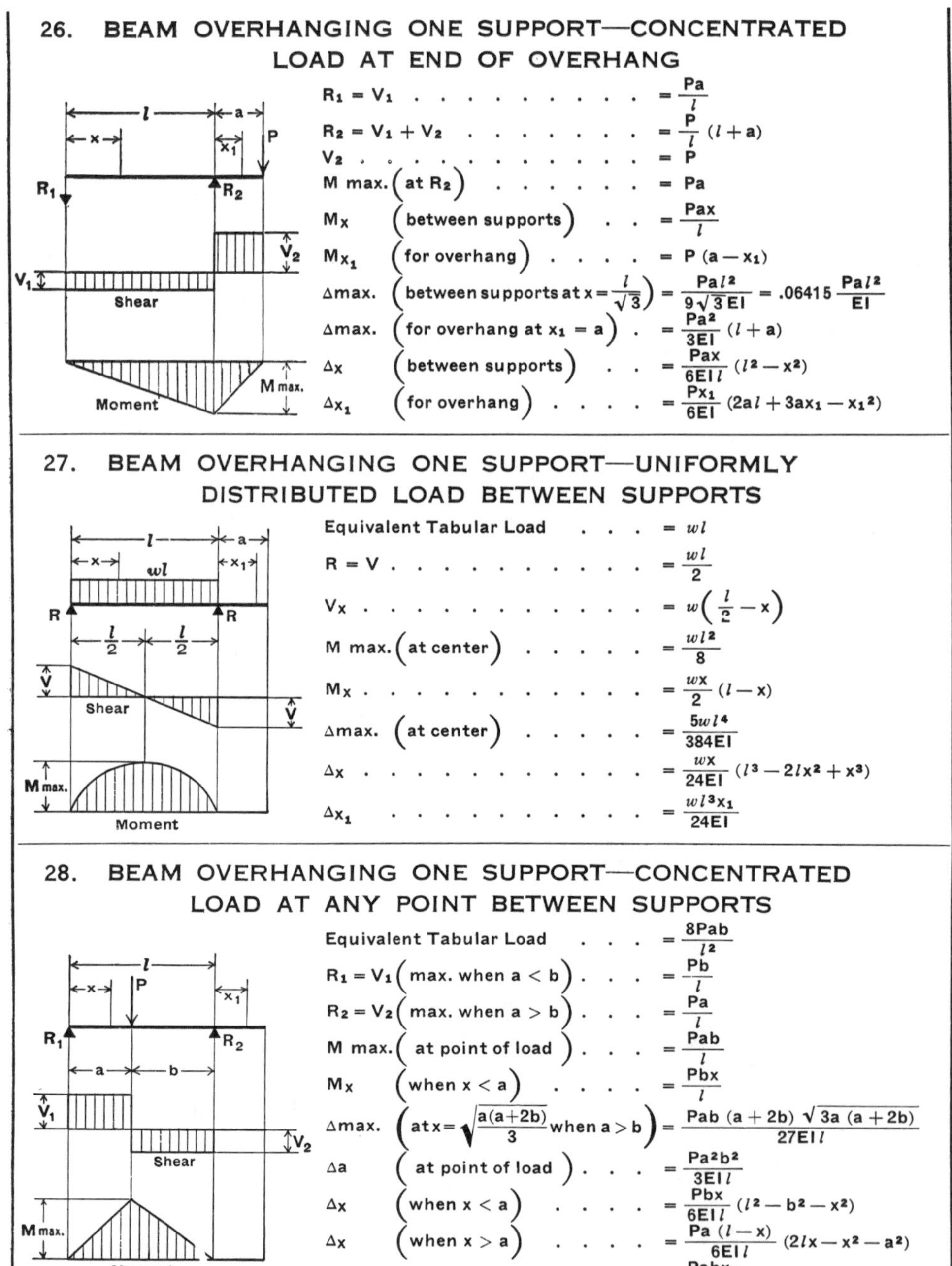

26. BEAM OVERHANGING ONE SUPPORT—CONCENTRATED LOAD AT END OF OVERHANG

$R_1 = V_1 \ldots = \frac{Pa}{l}$

$R_2 = V_1 + V_2 \ldots = \frac{P}{l}(l + a)$

$V_2 \ldots = P$

$M\ max.\left(\text{at } R_2\right) \ldots = Pa$

$M_x \left(\text{between supports}\right) \ldots = \frac{Pax}{l}$

$M_{x_1} \left(\text{for overhang}\right) \ldots = P(a - x_1)$

$\Delta max. \left(\text{between supports at } x = \frac{l}{\sqrt{3}}\right) = \frac{Pal^2}{9\sqrt{3}EI} = .06415\frac{Pal^2}{EI}$

$\Delta max. \left(\text{for overhang at } x_1 = a\right) \ldots = \frac{Pa^2}{3EI}(l + a)$

$\Delta x \left(\text{between supports}\right) \ldots = \frac{Pax}{6EIl}(l^2 - x^2)$

$\Delta x_1 \left(\text{for overhang}\right) \ldots = \frac{Px_1}{6EI}(2al + 3ax_1 - x_1^2)$

27. BEAM OVERHANGING ONE SUPPORT—UNIFORMLY DISTRIBUTED LOAD BETWEEN SUPPORTS

$\text{Equivalent Tabular Load} \ldots = wl$

$R = V \ldots = \frac{wl}{2}$

$V_x \ldots = w\left(\frac{l}{2} - x\right)$

$M\ max.\left(\text{at center}\right) \ldots = \frac{wl^2}{8}$

$M_x \ldots = \frac{wx}{2}(l - x)$

$\Delta max. \left(\text{at center}\right) \ldots = \frac{5wl^4}{384EI}$

$\Delta x \ldots = \frac{wx}{24EI}(l^3 - 2lx^2 + x^3)$

$\Delta x_1 \ldots = \frac{wl^3x_1}{24EI}$

28. BEAM OVERHANGING ONE SUPPORT—CONCENTRATED LOAD AT ANY POINT BETWEEN SUPPORTS

$\text{Equivalent Tabular Load} \ldots = \frac{8Pab}{l^2}$

$R_1 = V_1\left(\text{max. when } a < b\right) \ldots = \frac{Pb}{l}$

$R_2 = V_2\left(\text{max. when } a > b\right) \ldots = \frac{Pa}{l}$

$M\ max.\left(\text{at point of load}\right) \ldots = \frac{Pab}{l}$

$M_x \left(\text{when } x < a\right) \ldots = \frac{Pbx}{l}$

$\Delta max. \left(\text{at } x = \sqrt{\frac{a(a + 2b)}{3}} \text{ when } a > b\right) = \frac{Pab\ (a + 2b)\ \sqrt{3a\ (a + 2b)}}{27EIl}$

$\Delta a \left(\text{at point of load}\right) \ldots = \frac{Pa^2b^2}{3EIl}$

$\Delta x \left(\text{when } x < a\right) \ldots = \frac{Pbx}{6EIl}(l^2 - b^2 - x^2)$

$\Delta x \left(\text{when } x > a\right) \ldots = \frac{Pa\ (l - x)}{6EIl}(2lx - x^2 - a^2)$

$\Delta x_1 \ldots = \frac{Pabx_1}{6EIl}(l + a)$

Figure 2A-3: (Continued)

Source: American Institute of Steel Construction.

STEEL BEAMS

Table 2A–1 on the following pages of Uniform Load Constants for steel sections used as simple beams give constants for the direct calculation of the total allowable uniformly distributed load and deflection for laterally supported steel beams. The tabulated constants take into consideration the weight of the beam, which should be deducted in the calculation to determine the net load that the beam will support.

It is assumed in all cases that the loads are applied normal to the X–X axis and that the beam deflects vertically in the plane of bending. The tables are for uniformly loaded beams, but they are also applicable for concentrated loading conditions by converting concentrated loading to uniform load equivalents using Table 2A–2.

The allowable bending stress and resultant allowable load capacity of a beam is dependent upon lateral support of its compression flange in addition to its section properties. In these tables, the notation L_c is used to denote the maximum unbraced length of compression flange, in feet, for which the allowable loads for compact symmetrical shapes are calculated with an allowable stress of $0.66F_y$. The tables are not applicable for beams with an unbraced length greater than L_u.

For relatively short spans, the allowable loads for beams and channels may be limited by the shearing stress in the web, instead of by the maximum bending stress in the flanges. This limit is indicated in the tables by the notation L_v. For span lengths less than L_v the maximum total uniform load the beam can support is twice the allowable beam shear.

The Uniform Load Constant W_c is obtained from the moment and stress relationship of a simply supported, uniformly loaded beam. The relationship results in the following formula.

FORMULA: $W_c = 2SF_b/3$, kip-ft.

The following expression may be used for calculating the total allowable uniformly distributed load on a simply supported beam or girder.

FORMULA: $W = W_c/L$, kips

where:

W_c = the uniform load constant from the tables
L = span of the beam in ft.

All tables have been reproduced courtesy of the American Institute of Steel Construction. Refer to the *Manual of Steel Construction* for more information.

UNIFORM LOAD CONSTANTS
USE OF TABLES

Nomenclature

W_c = Uniform load constant, kip-ft.
$= 2S_xF_b/3$

V = Maximum web shear, kips.
$= 0.4F_ydt_w$

L_v = Span length below which shear V in beam web governs, as compared to greater span lengths where flexure constant W_c governs, ft.
$= W_c/2V$

L_c = Maximum unbraced length of the compression flange at which the allowable bending stress may be taken at $0.66F_y$ or as determined by AISC Specification Formula (1.5-5), when applicable, ft.

L_u = Maximum unbraced length of the compression flange at which the allowable bending stress may be taken at $0.6F_y$, ft.

L_b = Unbraced length of compression flange, ft.

R = Maximum end reaction for 3½ in. bearing kips. In cases where R would exceed V, the value of R is indicated by a dash.
= $0.75F_y t_w(3.5 + k)$

R_i = Increase in R for each additional inch of bearing, kips.
= $0.75F_y t_w$

N_e = Length of bearing to develop V, in.
= $(V/R_i - k)$

S = Section modulus, X-X axis, in.³

D_c = Uniform load deflection constants, in./ft.²
= $(30/29)F_b/d$

Example 1

Given:
A W 16 × 45 beam of $F_y = 36$ ksi steel spans 20 ft. Determine the uniform load capacity, end reaction, and deflection.

Solution:
Enter the Uniform Load Constants table for $F_y = 36$ ksi and note that:

W_c = 1160 kip-ft.
V = 80.7 kip
L_v = 7.2 ft.
D_c = 1.5 in./ft.²

1. Total allowable uniform load $= \dfrac{W_c}{L} = \dfrac{1160}{20} = 58$ kips

2. End reaction $= \dfrac{W_c}{2L} = \dfrac{1160}{2 \times 20} = 29$ kips

3. Deflection $= \dfrac{D_c L^2}{1000} = \dfrac{1.5 \times 20^2}{1000} = 0.6$ in.

Example 2

Given:
A W 10 × 45 beam of $F_y = 36$ ksi steel spans 6 ft. Determine the uniform load capacity, end reaction, and deflection.

Solution:
Enter the Uniform Load Constants table for $F_y = 36$ ksi and note that:
W_c = 786 kip-ft.
V = 51.3 kips
L_v = 7.7 ft.
D_c = 2.5 in./ft.²

1. The beam span is less than L_v; therefore, the total allowable uniform load, W, is limited by shear in the web.

$$W = 2V = 2 \times 51.3 = 102.6 \text{ kips}$$

2. End reaction $= V = 51.3$ kips

3. Deflection $= \dfrac{D_c L^2}{1000} \times \dfrac{2V}{(W_c/L)}$

$$= \frac{2.5 \times (6)^2}{1000} \times \frac{(2 \times 51.3)}{786/6} = 0.07 \text{ in.}$$

Example 3

Given:

Using $F_y = 36$ ksi steel, select an 18 in. deep beam to span 30 ft. and support three equal concentrated loads of 20 kips located at the quarter points of the span.

Solution:

Refer to the table of concentrated load equivalents and note that:

Equivalent uniform load $= W = 4.0P$

Deflection factor $= 0.95$

1. Required Uniform Load Constant $= WL = 4.0PL = 4.0 \times 20 \times 30 = 2400$
2. Enter the Uniform Load Constants table for $F_y = 36$ and $W_c = 2400$:

   Select W 18 × 86: $W_c = 2660$
   $D_c = 1.4$
3. Check deflection:

$$\text{Concentrated load deflection} = \frac{D_c L^2}{1000} \times \frac{\text{Req'd. } W_c}{\text{Actual } W_c} \times \text{Deflection Factor}$$

$$= \frac{1.4 \times (30)^2}{1000} \times \frac{2400}{2660} \times 0.95$$

$$= 1.1 \text{ in.}$$

If the beam depth is not restricted, a shape with less weight can usually be selected by scanning the constant tables for deeper sections. For example: Select W 21 × 73, $W_c = 2420$; W 24 × 68, $W_c = 2460$.

Example 4

Given:

Using $F_y = 36$ ksi steel and $F_y = 50$ ksi steel, select a 14 in. deep beam to span 25 ft. and support a uniform load of 1 kip/ft.

Solution:

1. Required Uniform Load Constant $= WL = wL^2 = 1 \times (25)^2 = 625$
2. Enter the Uniform Load Constants table for $F_y = 36$ ksi and $W_c = 625$:
   Select W 14 × 30: $W_c = 672$
3. Enter the Uniform Load Constants table for $F_y = 50$ ksi and $W_c = 625$:
   Select W 14 × 22: $W_c = 638$

Table 2A-1
UNIFORM LOAD CONSTANTS FOR BEAMS LATERALLY SUPPORTED

F_y = 36 ksi

BEAMS
W shapes

Uniform load constants
for beams laterally supported

Shape	W_c	V	L_v	L_c	L_u	R	R_i	N_e	S	D_c
	Kip-ft.	Kip	Ft.	Ft.	Ft.	Kip	Kip	In.	In.³	In./Ft.²
W 36 x 300	17800	503	17.6	17.6	35.3	161	25.5	16.9	1110	0.68
x 280	16500	469	17.6	17.5	33.1	148	23.9	16.9	1030	0.68
x 260	15200	442	17.3	17.5	30.5	137	22.7	16.9	953	0.68
x 245	14300	419	17.1	17.4	28.6	130	21.6	16.9	895	0.69
x 230	13400	396	16.9	17.4	26.8	121	20.5	16.9	837	0.69
W 36 x 210	11500	442	13.0	12.9	20.9	130	22.4	17.4	719	0.68
x 194	10600	405	13.1	12.8	19.4	117	20.7	17.4	664	0.68
x 182	9970	382	13.0	12.7	18.2	110	19.6	17.4	623	0.68
x 170	9280	357	13.0	12.7	17.0	101	18.4	17.4	580	0.69
x 160	8670	339	12.8	12.7	15.7	95.4	17.6	17.4	542	0.69
x 150	8060	325	12.4	12.6	14.6	90.7	16.9	17.4	504	0.69
x 135	7020	309	11.4	12.3	13.0	84.0	16.2	17.4	439	0.70
W 33 x 241	13300	411	16.1	16.7	30.1	127	22.4	16.2	829	0.73
x 221	12100	381	15.9	16.7	27.6	116	20.9	16.2	757	0.73
x 201	10900	349	15.7	16.6	24.9	105	19.3	16.1	684	0.74
W 33 x 152	7790	308	12.6	12.2	16.9	92.2	17.1	16.1	487	0.74
x 141	7170	292	12.3	12.2	15.4	85.8	16.3	16.1	448	0.75
x 130	6500	278	11.7	12.1	13.8	81.2	15.7	16.1	406	0.75
x 118	5740	262	11.0	12.0	12.6	75.2	14.9	16.1	359	0.76
W 30 x 211	10600	348	15.3	15.9	29.7	118	20.9	14.5	663	0.80
x 191	9570	316	15.1	15.9	26.9	104	19.2	14.5	598	0.81
x 173	8620	289	14.9	15.8	24.2	95.1	17.7	14.5	539	0.82
W 30 x 132	6080	270	11.2	11.1	16.1	87.2	16.6	14.5	380	0.82
x 124	5680	256	11.1	11.1	15.0	81.9	15.8	14.5	355	0.82
x 116	5260	246	10.7	11.1	13.8	78.2	15.3	14.5	329	0.83
x 108	4780	236	10.1	11.1	12.3	74.5	14.7	14.5	299	0.83
x 99	4300	224	9.6	10.9	11.4	69.3	14.0	14.5	269	0.84
W 27 x 178	8030	292	13.7	14.9	27.9	105	19.6	13.1	502	0.89
x 161	7280	264	13.8	14.8	25.4	94.7	17.8	13.0	455	0.90
x 146	6580	240	13.7	14.7	23.0	84.7	16.3	13.0	411	0.91
W 27 x 114	4780	226	10.6	10.6	15.9	78.9	15.4	13.0	299	0.91
x 102	4270	202	10.6	10.6	14.2	70.4	13.9	13.0	267	0.92
x 94	3890	191	10.2	10.5	12.8	65.3	13.2	13.0	243	0.92
x 84	3410	178	9.6	10.5	11.0	60.5	12.4	13.0	213	0.93

Notes:
Where L is the span in feet:
Total allowable uniform load in kips = W_c/L.
End reaction in kips = $W_c/2L$.
Midspan deflection in inches = $D_c \times L^2/1000$.
For unbraced lengths greater than L_c and less than L_u, multiply the constants W_c and D_c by the ratio $22/F_b$, where F_b = 24 ksi.

F_y = 36 ksi

BEAMS
W shapes

Uniform load constants
for beams laterally supported

Shape	W_c	V	L_v	L_c	L_u	R	R_i	N_e	S	D_c
	Kip-ft.	Kip	Ft.	Ft.	Ft.	Kip	Kip	In.	In.³	In./Ft.²
W 24 x 162	6620	256	13.0	13.7	29.3	105	19.0	11.4	414	0.99
x 146	5940	233	12.7	13.6	26.3	94.3	17.6	11.4	371	1.0
x 131	5260	215	12.3	13.6	23.4	85.8	16.3	11.4	329	1.0
x 117	4660	193	12.0	13.5	20.8	76.1	14.9	11.4	291	1.0
x 104	4130	174	11.8	13.5	18.4	67.5	13.5	11.4	258	1.0
W 24 x 94	3550	182	9.8	9.6	15.1	71.3	13.9	11.4	222	1.0
x 84	3140	164	9.5	9.5	13.3	64.2	12.7	11.4	196	1.0
x 76	2820	153	9.2	9.5	11.8	58.7	11.9	11.4	176	1.0
x 68	2460	143	8.6	9.5	10.2	54.6	11.2	11.4	154	1.0
W 24 x 62	2100	148	7.1	7.4	8.1	56.6	11.6	11.4	131	1.0
x 55	1820	135	6.8	7.0	7.5	51.3	10.7	11.3	114	1.1
W 21 x 147	5260	230	11.4	13.2	30.3	104.0	19.4	10.0	329	1.1
x 132	4720	206	11.5	13.1	27.2	93.2	17.6	9.9	295	1.1
x 122	4370	189	11.6	13.1	25.4	84.0	16.2	10.0	273	1.1
x 111	3980	172	11.6	13.0	23.3	76.1	14.9	9.9	249	1.2
x 101	3630	155	11.7	13.0	21.3	68.3	13.5	9.9	227	1.2
W 21 x 93	3070	182	8.4	8.9	16.8	81.2	15.7	9.9	192	1.1
x 83	2740	160	8.5	8.8	15.1	70.4	13.9	9.9	171	1.2
x 73	2420	140	8.6	8.8	13.4	61.4	12.3	9.9	151	1.2
x 68	2240	132	8.5	8.7	12.4	57.3	11.6	9.9	140	1.2
x 62	2030	122	8.3	8.7	11.2	52.7	10.8	9.9	127	1.2
W 21 x 57	1780	124	7.2	6.9	9.4	53.3	10.9	9.9	111	1.2
x 50	1510	115	6.6	6.9	7.8	49.4	10.3	9.9	94.5	1.2
x 44	1310	105	6.2	6.6	7.0	44.3	9.5	9.9	81.6	1.2
W 18 x 119	3700	180	10.3	11.9	29.1	92.8	17.7	8.4	231	1.3
x 106	3260	160	10.2	11.8	26.0	81.6	15.9	8.4	204	1.3
x 97	3010	144	10.4	11.8	24.1	73.1	14.4	8.4	188	1.3
x 86	2660	128	10.4	11.7	21.5	64.0	13.0	8.4	166	1.4
x 76	2340	112	10.4	11.6	19.1	55.9	11.5	8.4	146	1.4
W 18 x 71	2030	133	7.7	8.1	15.5	66.8	13.4	8.4	127	1.3
x 65	1870	120	7.8	8.0	14.4	60.0	12.2	8.4	117	1.4
x 60	1730	110	7.9	8.0	13.3	54.6	11.2	8.4	108	1.4
x 55	1570	102	7.7	7.9	12.1	50.7	10.5	8.4	98.3	1.4
x 50	1420	92.6	7.7	7.9	11.0	45.5	9.6	8.4	88.9	1.4

Notes:
Where L is the span in feet:
Total allowable uniform load in kips = W_c/L.
End reaction in kips = $W_c/2L$.
Midspan deflection in inches = $D_c \times L^2/1000$.
For unbraced lengths greater than L_c and less than L_u, multiply the constants W_c and D_c by the ratio $22/F_b$, where F_b = 24 ksi.

$F_y = 36$ ksi

BEAMS
W shapes
Uniform load constants for beams laterally supported

Shape	W_c	V	L_v	L_c	L_u	R	R_i	N_e	S	D_c
	Kip-ft.	Kip	Ft.	Ft.	Ft.	Kip	Kip	In.	In.³	In./Ft.²
W 18 × 46	1260	94.3	6.7	6.4	9.4	46.2	9.7	8.4	78.8	1.4
× 40	1090	81.8	6.7	6.3	8.2	39.9	8.5	8.4	68.4	1.4
× 35	922	77.0	6.0	6.3	6.7	37.5	8.1	8.4	57.6	1.4
W 16 × 100	2800	144	9.7	11.0	28.1	81.9	15.8	7.4	175	1.5
× 89	2480	128	9.7	10.9	25.0	71.8	14.2	7.4	155	1.5
× 77	2140	109	9.8	10.9	21.9	60.7	12.3	7.4	134	1.5
× 67	1870	93.5	10.0	10.8	19.3	52.0	10.7	7.4	117	1.5
W 16 × 57	1480	102	7.2	7.5	14.3	56.6	11.6	7.4	92.2	1.5
× 50	1300	89.6	7.2	7.5	12.7	49.4	10.3	7.4	81.0	1.5
× 45	1160	80.7	7.2	7.4	11.4	44.2	9.3	7.4	72.7	1.5
× 40	1040	70.8	7.3	7.4	10.2	38.6	8.2	7.4	64.7	1.6
× 36	904	67.8	6.7	7.4	8.8	36.8	8.0	7.4	56.5	1.6
W 16 × 31	755	63.3	6.0	5.8	7.1	34.3	7.4	7.4	47.2	1.6
× 26	614	56.9	5.4	5.6	6.0	30.8	6.8	7.4	38.4	1.6
W 14 × 132	3340	137	12.2	15.5	47.7	90.3	17.4	6.2	209	1.7
× 120	3040	124	12.3	15.5	44.1	81.6	15.9	6.2	190	1.7
× 109	2770	109	12.7	15.4	40.6	71.8	14.2	6.1	173	1.7
× 99	2510	99.6	12.6	15.4	37.0	64.7	13.1	6.2	157	1.8
× 90	2290	89.4	12.8	15.3	34.0	57.9	11.9	6.2	143	1.8
W 14 × 82	1970	106	9.3	10.7	28.1	70.6	13.8	6.1	123	1.7
× 74	1790	92.5	9.7	10.6	25.9	61.5	12.2	6.0	112	1.8
× 68	1650	84.5	9.8	10.6	23.9	56.0	11.2	6.0	103	1.8
× 61	1480	75.5	9.8	10.6	21.5	50.0	10.1	6.0	92.2	1.8
W 14 × 53	1240	74.7	8.3	8.5	17.7	49.3	10.0	6.0	77.8	1.8
× 48	1120	68.0	8.3	8.5	16.0	44.8	9.2	6.0	70.3	1.8
× 43	1000	60.4	8.3	8.4	14.4	39.6	8.2	6.0	62.7	1.8
W 14 × 38	874	63.4	6.9	7.1	11.5	38.2	8.4	6.5	54.6	1.8
× 34	778	57.8	6.7	7.1	10.2	34.6	7.7	6.5	48.6	1.8
× 30	672	54.2	6.2	7.1	8.7	32.3	7.3	6.5	42.0	1.8
W 14 × 26	565	51.4	5.5	5.3	7.0	30.6	6.9	6.5	35.3	1.8
× 22	464	45.8	5.1	5.3	5.6	27.2	6.2	6.5	29.0	1.8

Notes:
Where L is the span in feet:
Total allowable uniform load in kips = W_c/L.
End reaction in kips = $W_c/2L$.
Midspan deflection in inches = $D_c \times L^2/1000$.
For unbraced lengths greater than L_c and less than L_u, multiply the constants W_c and D_c by the ratio $22/F_b$, where $F_b = 24$ ksi.

$F_y = 36$ ksi

BEAMS
W shapes
Uniform load constants for beams laterally supported

Shape	W_c	V	L_v	L_c	L_u	R	R_i	N_e	S	D_c
	Kip-ft.	Kip	Ft.	Ft.	Ft.	Kip	Kip	In.	In.³	In./Ft.²
W 12 × 87	1890	93.6	10.1	12.8	36.2	69.5	13.9	5.2	118	2.0
× 79	1710	84.4	10.1	12.8	33.3	62.7	12.7	5.2	107	2.0
× 72	1560	76.4	10.2	12.7	30.5	56.6	11.6	5.2	97.4	2.0
× 65	1410	68.5	10.3	12.7	27.7	50.7	10.5	5.2	87.9	2.0
W 12 × 58	1250	63.6	9.8	10.6	24.4	47.4	9.7	5.2	78.0	2.0
× 53	1130	60.3	9.4	10.6	22.0	44.2	9.3	5.2	70.6	2.1
W 12 × 50	1040	65.4	7.9	8.5	19.6	48.7	10.0	5.2	64.7	2.0
× 45	930	58.6	7.9	8.5	17.7	43.0	9.0	5.2	58.1	2.1
× 40	830	51.1	8.1	8.4	16.0	37.8	8.0	5.2	51.9	2.1
W 12 × 35	730	54.4	6.7	6.9	12.6	36.5	8.1	5.7	45.6	2.0
× 30	618	46.5	6.6	6.9	10.8	31.2	7.0	5.7	38.6	2.0
× 26	534	40.8	6.6	6.9	9.4	27.2	6.2	5.7	33.4	2.0
W 12 × 22	406	46.4	4.4	4.3	6.4	30.7	7.0	5.7	25.4	2.0
× 19	341	41.4	4.1	4.2	5.3	27.4	6.3	5.7	21.3	2.0
× 16	274	38.2	3.6	4.1	4.3	25.2	5.9	5.7	17.1	2.1
× 14	238	34.5	3.5	3.5	4.2	22.6	5.4	5.7	14.9	2.1
W 10 × 112	2020	124	8.1	11.0	53.2	110.0	20.4	4.2	126	2.2
× 100	1790	109	8.2	10.9	48.2	96.4	18.4	4.2	112	2.2
× 88	1580	95.1	8.3	10.8	43.3	83.7	16.3	4.2	98.5	2.3
× 77	1370	81.5	8.4	10.8	38.6	71.6	14.3	4.2	85.9	2.3
× 68	1210	70.9	8.5	10.7	34.8	61.9	12.7	4.2	75.7	2.4
× 60	1070	62.2	8.6	10.6	31.1	54.6	11.3	4.2	66.7	2.4
× 54	960	54.1	8.9	10.6	28.2	47.5	10.0	4.2	60.0	2.5
× 49	874	49.2	8.9	10.6	26.0	43.0	9.2	4.2	54.6	2.5
W 10 × 45	786	51.3	7.7	8.5	22.8	44.9	9.5	4.2	49.1	2.5
× 39	674	45.3	7.4	8.4	19.8	39.3	8.5	4.2	42.1	2.5
× 33	560	40.9	6.8	8.4	16.5	35.7	7.8	4.2	35.0	2.6
W 10 × 30	518	45.5	5.7	6.1	13.1	35.9	8.1	4.7	32.4	2.4
× 26	446	38.9	5.7	6.1	11.4	30.7	7.0	4.7	27.9	2.4
× 22	371	35.4	5.2	6.1	9.4	27.5	6.5	4.7	23.2	2.4
W 10 × 19	301	37.1	4.1	4.2	7.2	29.1	6.8	4.7	18.8	2.4
× 17	259	35.2	3.7	4.2	6.1	27.5	6.5	4.7	16.2	2.5
× 15	221	33.3	3.3	4.2	5.0	26.0	6.2	4.7	13.8	2.5
× 12	174	27.2	3.2	3.9	4.3	21.2	5.1	4.7	10.9	2.5

Notes:
Where L is the span in feet:
Total allowable uniform load in kips = W_c/L.
End reaction in kips = $W_c/2L$.
Midspan deflection in inches = $D_c \times L^2/1000$.
For unbraced lengths greater than L_c and less than L_u, multiply the constants W_c and D_c by the ratio $22/F_b$, where $F_b = 24$ ksi.

Table 2A-1 (Continued)

$F_y = 36$ ksi

BEAMS
W shapes
Uniform load constants
for beams laterally supported

Shape	W_c	V	L_v	L_c	L_u	R	R_i	N_e	S	D_c
	Kip-ft.	Kip	Ft.	Ft.	Ft.	Kip	Kip	In.	In.^{3}	In./Ft.^{2}
W 8 x 67	966	74.4	6.5	8.7	39.9	—	15.4	3.4	60.4	2.8
x 58	832	64.7	6.4	8.7	35.3	—	13.8	3.4	52.0	2.8
x 48	693	49.3	7.0	8.6	30.3	—	10.8	3.4	43.3	2.9
x 40	568	43.1	6.6	8.5	25.3	—	9.7	3.4	35.5	3.0
x 35	499	36.5	6.8	8.5	22.6	—	8.4	3.4	31.2	3.1
x 31	440	33.1	6.7	8.4	20.1	—	7.7	3.4	27.5	3.1
W 8 x 28	389	33.3	5.8	6.9	17.5	—	7.7	3.4	24.3	3.1
x 24	334	28.2	5.9	6.9	15.2	—	6.6	3.4	20.9	3.1
W 8 x 21	291	30.0	4.9	5.6	11.8	29.1	6.8	3.6	18.2	3.0
x 18	243	27.1	4.5	5.5	9.9	26.4	6.2	3.6	15.2	3.1
W 8 x 15	189	28.8	3.3	4.2	7.2	28.1	6.6	3.6	11.8	3.1
x 13	159	26.6	3.0	4.2	5.9	26.0	6.2	3.6	9.91	3.1
x 10	125	19.4	3.2	4.2	4.7	18.9	4.6	3.6	7.81	3.1
W 6 x 25	267	29.6	4.5	6.4	20.0	—	8.6	2.6	16.7	3.9
x 20	214	23.4	4.6	6.4	16.4	—	7.0	2.6	13.4	4.0
x 15	*152	20.0	3.8	6.3	12.0	—	6.2	2.6	9.72	*4.1
W 6 x 16	163	23.7	3.4	4.3	12.0	—	7.0	2.6	10.2	4.0
x 12	117	20.1	2.9	4.2	8.6	—	6.2	2.6	7.31	4.1
x 9	89	14.5	3.1	4.2	6.7	—	4.6	2.6	5.56	4.2
W 5 x 19	163	20.2	4.0	5.3	19.5	—	7.3	2.0	10.2	4.8
x 16	136	17.4	3.9	5.3	16.7	—	6.5	1.9	8.51	5.0
W 4 x 13	87	16.9	2.6	4.3	15.6	—	7.6	1.5	5.46	6.0

* W_c and D_c values for this shape based upon allowable stress in accordance with AISC Specification Sect. 1.5.1.4.2.

Notes:

Dash indicates that R is greater than V.

Where L is the span in feet:

Total allowable uniform load in kips = W_c/L.
End reaction in kips = $W_c/2L$.
Midspan deflection in inches = $D_c \times L^2/1000$.

For unbraced lengths greater than L_c and less than L_u, multiply the constants W_c and D_c by the ratio $22/F_b$, where F_b = 24 ksi, except for the W6x15 shape, where F_b = 23.5 ksi.

$F_y = 36$ ksi

BEAMS
M shapes
Uniform load constants
for beams laterally supported

Shape	W_c	V	L_v	L_c	L_u	R	R_i	N_e	S	D_c
	Kip-ft.	Kip	Ft.	Ft.	Ft.	Kip	Kip	In.	In.^{3}	In./Ft.^{2}
M 14 x 18	338	43.6	3.9	3.6	4.0	23.9	5.8	6.9	21.1	1.8
M 12 x 11.8	192	30.8	3.1	2.7	3.0	19.4	4.8	5.9	12.0	2.1
M 10 x 9	124	22.8	2.7	2.6	2.7	17.2	4.2	4.8	7.76	2.5
M 8 x 6.5	74	15.7	2.4	2.4	2.5	14.6	3.6	3.8	4.62	3.1
M 6 x 20	208	21.8	4.8	6.3	17.4	—	6.8	2.3	13.0	4.1
M 6 x 4.4	38	9.9	1.9	1.9	2.4	—	3.1	2.8	2.40	4.1
M 5 x 18.9	154	22.9	3.4	5.3	19.3	—	8.5	1.8	9.63	5.0
M 4 x 13	84	14.7	2.8	4.2	16.9	—	6.9	1.3	5.24	6.2

Notes:

Dash indicates that R is greater than V.

Where L is the span in feet:

Total allowable uniform load in kips = W_c/L.
End reaction in kips = $W_c/2L$.
Midspan deflection in inches = $D_c \times L^2/1000$.

For unbraced lengths greater than L_c and less than L_u multiply the constants W_c and D_c by the ratio 22/24.

F_y = 50 ksi

BEAMS
W shapes
Uniform load constants
for beams laterally supported

Designation	W_c	V	L_v	L_c	L_u	R	R_i	N_e	S	D_c
	Kip-ft.	Kip	Ft.	Ft.	Ft.	Kip	Kip	In.	In.^{3}	In./Ft.^{2}
W 24 x 162	9110	353	12.9	11.6	21.1	145	26.4	11.3	414	1.4
x 146	8160	322	12.7	11.6	18.9	131	24.4	11.3	371	1.4
x 131	7240	296	12.2	11.5	16.8	119	22.7	11.3	329	1.4
x 117	6400	267	12.0	11.5	14.9	106	20.6	11.3	291	1.4
x 104	5680	241	11.8	11.4	13.2	93	18.8	11.3	258	1.4
W 24 x 94	4880	250	9.8	8.1	10.9	99.0	19.3	11.3	222	1.4
x 84	4310	227	9.5	8.1	9.6	89.2	17.6	11.3	196	1.4
x 76	3870	210	9.2	8.1	8.6	81.5	16.5	11.3	176	1.4
x 68	3390	197	8.6	7.4	8.5	75.9	15.6	11.3	154	1.4
W 24 x 62	2880	204	7.1	5.8	6.4	78.6	16.1	11.3	131	1.4
x 55	2510	186	6.7	5.0	6.3	71.3	14.8	11.3	114	1.4
W 21 x 147	7240	318	11.4	11.2	21.8	145	27.0	9.9	329	1.5
x 132	6490	284	11.4	11.1	19.6	129	24.4	9.8	295	1.6
x 122	6010	260	11.5	11.1	18.3	117	22.5	9.9	273	1.6
x 111	5480	237	11.6	11.1	16.8	106	20.6	9.8	249	1.6
x 101	4990	214	11.7	11.0	15.4	94.9	18.8	9.8	227	1.6
W 21 x 93	4220	251	8.4	7.5	12.1	113	21.8	9.8	192	1.6
x 83	3760	221	8.5	7.5	10.9	97.8	19.3	9.9	171	1.6
x 73	3320	193	8.6	7.4	9.6	85.3	17.1	9.8	151	1.6
x 68	3080	182	8.5	7.4	8.9	79.6	16.1	9.8	140	1.6
x 62	2790	168	8.3	7.4	8.1	73.1	15.0	9.8	127	1.6
W 21 x 57	2440	171	7.2	5.9	6.7	74.0	15.2	9.9	111	1.6
x 50	2080	158	6.6	5.6	6.0	68.6	14.3	9.8	94.5	1.6
x 44	1800	145	6.2	4.7	5.9	61.5	13.1	9.8	81.6	1.7
W 18 x 119	5080	249	10.2	10.1	21.0	129	24.6	8.4	231	1.8
x 106	4490	221	10.2	10.0	18.7	113	22.1	8.4	204	1.8
x 97	4140	199	10.4	10.0	17.4	102	20.1	8.4	188	1.8
x 86	3650	177	10.3	9.9	15.5	88.9	18.0	8.4	166	1.9
x 76	3210	155	10.4	9.9	13.7	77.7	15.9	8.3	146	1.9
W 18 x 71	2790	183	7.6	6.8	11.1	92.8	18.6	8.4	127	1.8
x 65	2570	165	7.8	6.8	10.4	83.3	16.9	8.3	117	1.9
x 60	2380	151	7.8	6.8	9.6	75.9	15.6	8.4	108	1.9
x 55	2160	141	7.7	6.7	8.7	70.4	14.6	8.3	98.3	1.9
x 50	1960	128	7.7	6.7	7.9	63.2	13.3	8.3	88.9	1.9

Notes:
Where L is the span in feet:
Total allowable uniform load in kips = W_c/L.
End reaction in kips = $W_c/2L$.
Midspan deflection in inches = $D_c \times L^2/1000$.
For unbraced lengths greater than L_c and less than L_u, multiply the constants W_c and D_c by the ratio $30/F_b$, where F_b = 33 ksi.

F_y = 50 ksi

BEAMS
W shapes
Uniform load constants
for beams laterally supported

Designation	W_c	V	L_v	L_c	L_u	R	R_i	N_e	S	D_c
	Kip-ft.	Kip	Ft.	Ft.	Ft.	Kip	Kip	In.	In.^{3}	In./Ft.^{2}
W 18 x 46	1730	130	6.7	5.4	6.8	64.1	13.5	8.4	78.8	1.9
x 40	1500	113	6.7	5.4	5.9	55.4	11.8	8.4	68.4	1.9
x 35	1270	106	6.0	4.8	5.6	52.0	11.3	8.3	57.6	1.9
W 16 x 100	3850	199	9.7	9.3	20.2	114	21.9	7.4	175	2.0
x 89	3410	176	9.7	9.3	18.0	99.7	19.7	7.4	155	2.0
x 77	2950	150	9.8	9.2	15.8	84.2	17.1	7.4	134	2.1
x 67	2570	129	10.0	9.2	13.9	72.2	14.8	7.3	117	2.1
W 16 x 57	2030	141	7.2	6.4	10.3	78.6	16.1	7.4	92.2	2.1
x 50	1780	124	7.2	6.3	9.1	68.6	14.3	7.4	81.0	2.1
x 45	1600	111	7.2	6.3	8.2	61.5	12.9	7.4	72.7	2.1
x 40	1420	97.7	7.3	6.3	7.4	53.6	11.4	7.4	64.7	2.1
x 36	1240	93.6	6.6	6.3	6.7	51.2	11.1	7.3	56.5	2.2
W 16 x 31	1040	87.3	5.9	4.9	5.2	47.7	10.3	7.3	47.2	2.1
x 26	845	78.5	5.4	4.0	5.1	42.8	9.4	7.3	38.4	2.2
W 14 x 132	4800	189	12.2	13.2	34.4	125	24.2	6.1	209	2.3
x 120	4180	171	12.2	13.1	31.7	113	22.1	6.1	190	2.4
x 109	3810	150	12.7	13.1	29.2	99.7	19.7	6.1	173	2.4
x 99	*3450	137	12.5	13.0	26.7	89.8	18.2	6.1	157	*2.4
x 90	*3080	123	12.5	13.0	24.5	80.4	16.5	6.1	143	*2.4
W 14 x 82	2710	146	9.3	9.1	20.2	98.0	19.1	6.0	123	2.4
x 74	2460	128	9.7	9.0	18.6	85.4	16.9	6.0	112	2.4
x 68	2270	117	9.7	9.0	17.2	77.8	15.6	6.0	103	2.4
x 61	2030	104	9.7	9.0	15.5	69.4	14.1	6.0	92.2	2.5
W 14 x 53	1710	103	8.3	7.2	12.7	68.5	13.9	6.0	77.8	2.5
x 48	1550	93.8	8.2	7.2	11.5	62.2	12.8	6.0	70.3	2.5
x 43	1380	83.3	8.3	7.2	10.4	55.0	11.4	6.0	62.7	2.5
W 14 x 38	1200	87.4	6.9	6.1	8.3	53.0	11.6	6.5	54.6	2.4
x 34	1070	79.7	6.7	6.0	7.3	48.1	10.7	6.5	48.6	2.4
x 30	924	74.7	6.2	6.0	6.5	44.9	10.1	6.4	42.0	2.5
W 14 x 26	777	70.9	5.5	4.5	5.1	42.4	9.6	6.5	35.3	2.5
x 22	638	63.2	5.0	4.1	4.7	37.7	8.6	6.5	29.0	2.5

* W_c and D_c values for this shape based upon allowable stress in accordance with AISC Specification Sect. 1.5.1.4.2.

Notes:
Where L is the span in feet:
Total allowable uniform load in kips = W_c/L.
End reaction in kips = $W_c/2L$.
Midspan deflection in inches = $D_c \times L^2/1000$.
For unbraced lengths greater than L_c and less than L_u, multiply the constants W_c and D_c by the ratio $30/F_b$, where F_b = 33 ksi, except as follows: For W14x99, F_b = 32.9 ksi; for W14x90, F_b = 32.3 ksi.

Table 2A-1 (Continued)

F_y = 50 ksi

BEAMS
W shapes
Uniform load constants
for beams laterally supported

Designation	W_c Kip-ft.	V Kip	L_v Ft.	L_c Ft.	L_u Ft.	R Kip	R_i Kip	N_e In.	S In.³	D_c In./Ft.²
W 12 x 87	2600	129	10.1	10.9	26.0	96.6	19.3	5.2	118	2.7
x 79	2350	116	10.1	10.8	24.0	87.0	17.6	5.2	107	2.8
x 72	2140	105	10.2	10.8	21.9	78.6	16.1	5.2	97.4	2.8
x 65	*1900	94.5	10.1	10.7	20.0	70.4	14.6	5.2	87.9	*2.8
W 12 x 58	1720	87.8	9.8	9.0	17.5	65.8	13.5	5.1	78.0	2.8
x 53	1550	83.2	9.3	9.0	15.9	61.5	12.9	5.2	70.6	2.8
W 12 x 50	1420	90.2	7.9	7.2	14.1	67.6	13.9	5.1	64.7	2.8
x 45	1280	80.8	7.9	7.2	12.8	59.7	12.6	5.2	58.1	2.8
x 40	1140	70.4	8.1	7.2	11.5	52.5	11.1	5.1	51.9	2.9
W 12 x 35	1000	75.0	6.7	5.9	9.1	50.6	11.3	5.7	45.6	2.7
x 30	849	64.2	6.6	5.8	7.8	43.3	9.8	5.6	38.6	2.8
x 26	735	56.2	6.5	5.8	6.7	37.7	8.6	5.6	33.4	2.8
W 12 x 22	559	64.0	4.4	3.6	4.6	42.7	9.8	5.7	25.4	2.8
x 19	469	57.2	4.1	3.6	3.8	38.0	8.8	5.7	21.3	2.8
x 16	376	52.8	3.6	2.9	3.6	35.1	8.3	5.6	17.1	2.8
x 14	328	47.6	3.4	2.5	3.6	31.4	7.5	5.7	14.9	2.9
W 10 x 112	2770	172	8.1	9.3	38.3	152	28.3	4.2	126	3.0
x 100	2460	151	8.2	9.3	34.7	134	25.5	4.2	112	3.1
x 88	2170	131	8.3	9.2	31.2	116	22.7	4.2	98.5	3.1
x 77	1890	112	8.4	9.1	27.8	99.4	19.9	4.2	85.9	3.2
x 68	1670	97.8	8.5	9.1	25.1	85.9	17.6	4.2	75.7	3.3
x 60	1470	85.8	8.5	9.0	22.4	75.8	15.8	4.1	66.7	3.3
x 54	1320	74.7	8.8	9.0	20.3	65.9	13.9	4.1	60.0	3.4
x 49	1200	67.9	8.9	9.0	18.7	59.8	12.8	4.1	54.6	3.4
W 10 x 45	1080	70.7	7.6	7.2	16.4	62.3	13.1	4.1	49.1	3.4
x 39	926	62.5	7.4	7.2	14.2	54.6	11.8	4.2	42.1	3.4
x 33	770	56.4	6.8	7.1	11.9	49.6	10.9	4.1	35.0	3.5
W 10 x 30	713	62.8	5.7	5.2	9.4	49.9	11.3	4.6	32.4	3.3
x 26	614	53.7	5.7	5.2	8.2	42.7	9.8	4.6	27.9	3.3
x 22	510	48.8	5.2	5.2	6.8	38.3	9.0	4.7	23.2	3.4
W 10 x 19	414	51.2	4.0	3.6	5.2	40.4	9.4	4.6	18.8	3.3
x 17	356	48.5	3.7	3.6	4.4	38.3	9.0	4.6	16.2	3.4
x 15	304	46.0	3.3	3.6	3.7	36.1	8.6	4.6	13.8	3.4
x 12	* 239	37.5	3.2	2.8	3.6	29.4	7.1	4.6	10.9	*3.4

* W_c and D_c values for this shape based upon allowable stress in accordance with AISC Specification Sect. 1.5.1.4.2.

Notes:

Where L is the span in feet:
Total allowable uniform load in kips = W_c/L.
End reaction in kips = $W_c/2L$.
Midspan deflection in inches = $D_c \times L^2/1000$.

For unbraced lengths greater than L_c and less than L_u, multiply the constants W_c and D_c by the ratio $30/F_b$, where F_b = 33 ksi, except as follows: For W12x65, F_b = 32.5 ksi; for W10x12, F_b = 32.9 ksi.

F_y = 50 ksi

BEAMS
W shapes
Uniform load constants
for beams laterally supported

Designation	W_c Kip-ft.	V Kip	L_v Ft.	L_c Ft.	L_u Ft.	R Kip	R_i Kip	N_e In.	S In.³	D_c In./Ft.²
W 8 x 67	1330	103	6.5	7.4	28.7	—	21.4	3.4	60.4	3.8
x 58	1140	89.3	6.4	7.4	25.4	—	19.1	3.4	52.0	3.9
x 48	953	68.0	7.0	7.3	21.8	—	15.0	3.3	43.3	4.0
x 40	781	59.4	6.6	7.2	18.2	—	13.5	3.3	35.5	4.1
x 35	686	50.3	6.8	7.2	16.3	—	11.6	3.3	31.2	4.2
x 31	* 605	45.6	6.6	7.2	14.5	—	10.7	3.3	27.5	*4.3
W 8 x 28	535	45.9	5.8	5.9	12.6	—	10.7	3.4	24.3	4.2
x 24	460	38.9	5.9	5.8	10.9	—	9.2	3.4	20.9	4.3
W 8 x 21	400	41.4	4.8	4.7	8.5	40.4	9.4	3.6	18.2	4.1
x 18	334	37.4	4.5	4.7	7.1	36.7	8.6	3.6	15.2	4.2
W 8 x 15	260	39.7	3.3	3.6	5.2	39.0	9.2	3.6	11.8	4.2
x 13	218	36.8	3.0	3.6	4.3	36.1	8.6	3.6	9.91	4.3
x 10	* 170	26.8	3.2	3.4	3.7	26.3	6.4	3.6	7.81	*4.3
W 6 x 25	367	40.8	4.5	5.4	14.4	—	12.0	2.6	16.7	5.4
x 20	295	32.2	4.6	5.4	11.8	—	9.8	2.6	13.4	5.5
x 15	* 203	27.6	3.7	5.4	8.7	—	8.6	2.6	9.72	*5.4
W 6 x 16	224	32.7	3.4	3.6	8.7	—	9.8	2.6	10.2	5.4
x 12	161	27.7	2.9	3.6	6.2	—	8.6	2.6	7.31	5.7
x 9	* 122	20.1	3.0	3.5	4.8	—	6.4	2.6	5.56	*5.8
W 5 x 19	224	27.8	4.0	4.5	14.0	—	10.1	1.9	10.2	6.6
x 16	187	24.0	3.9	4.5	12.0	—	9.0	1.9	8.51	6.8
W 4 x 13	120	23.3	2.6	[illegible]	11.2	—	10.5	1.5	5.46	8.2

* W_c and D_c values for this shape based upon allowable stress in accordance with AISC Specification Sect. 1.5.1.4.2.

Notes:

Dash indicates that R is greater than V.

Where L is the span in feet:
Total allowable uniform load in kips = W_c/L.
End reaction in kips = $W_c/2L$.
Midspan deflection in inches = $D_c \times L^2/1000$.

For unbraced lengths greater than L_c and less than L_u, multiply the constants W_c and D_c by the ratio $30/F_b$, where F_b = 33 ksi, except as follows: For W8x10, F_b = 32.7 ksi; for W6x15, F_b = 31.4 ksi.

Source: Manual of Steel Construction. *Courtesy of American Institute of Steel Construction.*

Table 2A-2
BEAM DIAGRAMS AND FORMULAS

BEAM DIAGRAMS AND FORMULAS
Table of Concentrated Load Equivalents

n	Loading	Coeff.	Simple Beam	Beam Fixed One End Supported at Other	Beam Fixed Both Ends
∞	Uniform load P	a	0.1250	0.0703	0.0417
		b	—	0.1250	0.0833
		c	0.5000	0.3750	—
		d	—	0.6250	0.5000
		e	0.0130	0.0054	0.0026
		f	1.0000	1.0000	0.6667
		g	1.0000	0.4151	0.3000
2	P	a	0.2500	0.1563	0.1250
		b	—	0.1875	0.1250
		c	0.5000	0.3125	—
		d	—	0.6875	0.5000
		e	0.0208	0.0093	0.0052
		f	2.0000	1.5000	1.0000
		g	0.8000	0.4770	0.4000
3	P P	a	0.3333	0.2222	0.1111
		b	—	0.3333	0.2222
		c	1.0000	0.6667	—
		d	—	1.3333	1.0000
		e	0.0355	0.0152	0.0077
		f	2.6667	2.6667	1.7778
		g	1.0222	0.4381	0.3333
4	P P P	a	0.5000	0.2656	0.1875
		b	—	0.4688	0.3125
		c	1.5000	1.0313	—
		d	—	1.9688	1.5000
		e	0.0495	0.0209	0.0104
		f	4.0000	3.7500	2.5000
		g	0.9500	0.4281	0.3200
5	P P P P	a	0.6000	0.3600	0.2000
		b	—	0.6000	0.4000
		c	2.0000	1.4000	—
		d	—	2.6000	2.0000
		e	0.0630	0.0265	0.0130
		f	4.8000	4.8000	3.2000
		g	1.0080	0.4238	0.3120

Maximum positive moment (kip-ft.): a × P × L
Maximum negative moment (kip-ft.): b × P × L
Pinned end reaction (kips): c × P
Fixed end reaction (kips): d × P
Maximum deflection (in.): e × Pl^3/EI
Equivalent simple span uniform load (kips): f × P
Deflection coeff. for equivalent simple span uniform load: g
Number of equal load spaces: n
Span of beam (ft.): L
Span of beam (in.): l

Source: Manual of Steel Construction. *Courtesy of American Institute of Steel Construction.*

STEEL COLUMNS

The following steel column tables (Tables 2A–3, 2A–4, and 2A–5) give allowable axial loads in kips for various W shapes, pipe columns, and square structural tubing. The loads are arranged according to the effective length, KL, which is the actual unbraced length, in feet, multiplied by the factor K, which depends on the rotational restraint at the ends of the unbraced length and the means available to resist lateral movement. (See Table 2A–6.) Load values are omitted when Kl/r exceeds 200. For W-shape sections, the values are calculated with respect to the minor axis.

Example 1

Given:

Design the lightest W shape of F_y = 36 ksi steel, to support a concentric load of 670 kips. The effective length with respect to its minor axis is 16 ft. The effective length with respect to its major axis is 31 ft.

Solution:

Enter the appropriate column load table for W shapes at effective length of KL = 16 ft. Since deeper columns are generally more efficient, begin with the W 14 table and work downward, weightwise.

Select W 14 × 132, good for 708 kips > 670 kips.

$r_x/r_y = 1.67$

Equivalent effective length for X–X axis:

31/1.67 = 18.6 ft.

Since 18.6 ft. > 16 ft., X–X axis controls.

Re-enter table for effective length of 18.6 ft. to satisfy axial load of 670 kips, select W 14 × 132 with $r_x/r_y = 1.67$.

By interpolation, the column is good for 679 kips.

Use: W 14 × 132 column

STEEL JOISTS

The following tables give standard load-carrying capacities of Open Web Steel Joists, K-Series; Longspan Steel Joists, LH-Series; and Deep Longspan Steel Joists, DLH-Series. They have been reproduced with the permission of the Steel Joist Institute.

Refer to *Standard Specifications, Load Tables & Weight Tables for Steel Joists & Joist Girders,* published by the Steel Joist Institute, for detailed specifications, limitations, bridging and anchoring requirements, and additional information.

K-Series, Economy Table

Table 2A–7 gives the standard load tables arranged in an "economy" format, with their weight per foot. Each joist designation for a particular span has two numbers. The top number gives the *total* safe uniformly distributed load-carrying capacity, in pounds per linear foot, of K-Series Steel Joists. The weight of *dead* loads, including the joists, must be deducted to determine the *live* load-carrying capacities of the joists. The load table may be used for parallel chord joists installed to a maximum slope of 1/2 inch per foot.

The bottom number is the *LIVE* load per linear foot of joist, which will produce an approximate deflection of 1/360 of the span. *LIVE* loads that will produce a deflection of

Table 2A-3
ALLOWABLE AXIAL LOADS FOR W SHAPE COLUMNS

COLUMNS

W shapes

$F_y = 36$ ksi

$F_y = 50$ ksi

Allowable axial loads in kips

Designation	W12									
Wt./ft.	336		305		279		252		230	
F_y	36	50	36	50	36	50	36	50	36	50
Effective length in ft. KL with respect to least radius of gyration r_y										
0	2134	**2964**	1935	**2688**	1769	**2457**	1601	**2223**	1462	**2031**
6	2031	**2788**	1840	**2526**	1681	**2306**	1519	**2085**	1387	**1903**
7	2009	**2751**	1820	**2491**	1662	**2274**	1502	**2055**	1371	**1876**
8	1986	**2711**	1799	**2454**	1642	**2240**	1484	**2023**	1355	**1847**
9	1962	**2669**	1777	**2415**	1622	**2204**	1465	**1990**	1337	**1816**
10	1937	**2625**	1753	**2375**	1600	**2166**	1445	**1955**	1319	**1784**
11	1911	**2579**	1729	**2332**	1578	**2126**	1425	**1919**	1300	**1750**
12	1884	**2531**	1704	**2288**	1554	**2085**	1403	**1881**	1280	**1715**
13	1856	**2482**	1678	**2242**	1530	**2042**	1381	**1842**	1259	**1678**
14	1827	**2430**	1651	**2194**	1505	**1998**	1358	**1801**	1238	**1641**
15	1797	**2377**	1623	**2145**	1479	**1952**	1334	**1759**	1216	**1601**
16	1766	**2322**	1594	**2094**	1452	**1905**	1309	**1715**	1193	**1561**
17	1733	**2265**	1565	**2041**	1425	**1856**	1284	**1670**	1169	**1519**
18	1701	**2206**	1534	**1987**	1396	**1805**	1258	**1623**	1145	**1476**
19	1667	**2146**	1503	**1931**	1367	**1753**	1231	**1575**	1120	**1431**
20	1632	**2084**	1471	**1873**	1337	**1699**	1203	**1526**	1095	**1386**
22	1560	**1955**	1404	**1753**	1275	**1588**	1146	**1423**	1041	**1290**
24	1484	**1819**	1333	**1627**	1209	**1470**	1085	**1314**	985	**1190**
26	1404	**1675**	1260	**1494**	1141	**1346**	1022	**1200**	927	**1084**
28	1321	**1525**	1183	**1354**	1069	**1216**	956	**1079**	866	**972**
30	1235	**1366**	1102	**1206**	994	**1078**	887	**952**	801	**855**
32	1144	**1205**	1018	**1061**	916	**948**	815	**837**	734	**751**
34	1050	**1067**	930	**940**	834	**839**	739	**742**	664	**665**
36	951	**952**	839	**839**	749	**749**	661	**661**	594	**594**
38	854	**854**	753	**753**	672	**672**	594	**594**	533	**533**
40	771	**771**	679	**679**	606	**606**	536	**536**	481	**481**
Properties										
U	2.40	**2.40**	2.41	**2.41**	2.42	**2.42**	2.45	**2.45**	2.46	**2.46**
P_{wo} (kips)	1178	**1636**	1005	**1396**	878	**1219**	738	**1024**	636	**883**
P_{wi} (kips/in.)	64	**89**	59	**81**	55	**77**	50	**70**	46	**64**
P_{wb} (kips)	14,480	**17,070**	11,110	**13,100**	9274	**10,930**	7030	**8285**	5494	**6475**
P_{fb} (kips)	1965	**2729**	1646	**2287**	1373	**1907**	1139	**1582**	964	**1339**
L_c (ft.)	14.1	**12.0**	14.0	**11.9**	13.9	**11.8**	13.7	**11.6**	13.6	**11.5**
L_u (ft.)	107.7	**77.5**	100.6	**72.5**	94.5	**68.0**	87.4	**62.9**	82.7	**59.5**
A (in.^{2})	98.8		89.6		81.9		74.1		67.7	
I_x (in.^{4})	4060		3550		3110		2720		2420	
I_y (in.^{4})	1190		1050		937		828		742	
r_y (in.)	3.47		3.42		3.38		3.34		3.31	
Ratio r_x/r_y	1.85		1.84		1.82		1.81		1.80	
B_x Bending factors	0.205		0.206		0.208		0.210		0.211	
B_y Bending factors	0.558		0.564		0.573		0.583		0.589	
a_x *	605		528		463		405		360	
a_y *	177		156		139		123		111	

* Tabulated values of a_x and a_y must be multiplied by 10^6.

$F_y = 36$ ksi

$F_y = 50$ ksi

COLUMNS

W shapes

Allowable axial loads in kips

Designation	W12											
Wt./ft.	210		190		170		152		136		120	
F_y	36	50	36	50	36	50	36	50	36	50	36	50
Effective length in ft. KL with respect to least radius of gyration r_y												
0	1335	**1854**	1205	**1674**	1080	**1500**	966	**1341**	862	**1197**	762	**1059**
6	1266	**1736**	1142	**1566**	1023	**1402**	914	**1253**	815	**1117**	721	**987**
7	1251	**1711**	1129	**1543**	1011	**1381**	903	**1233**	805	**1100**	712	**972**
8	1236	**1684**	1115	**1518**	998	**1359**	891	**1213**	795	**1082**	702	**956**
9	1219	**1655**	1100	**1492**	984	**1335**	879	**1192**	784	**1062**	692	[illegible]
10	1202	**1625**	1084	**1465**	970	**1310**	866	**1169**	772	**1042**	682	**920**
11	1185	**1594**	1068	**1437**	956	**1285**	853	**1146**	760	**1021**	671	**901**
12	1166	**1562**	1051	**1407**	940	**1258**	839	**1122**	747	**999**	660	**881**
13	1147	**1528**	1034	**1376**	924	**1230**	825	**1096**	734	**976**	648	**860**
14	1127	**1493**	1016	**1344**	908	**1200**	810	**1070**	721	**952**	636	**839**
15	1107	**1457**	997	**1311**	891	**1170**	794	**1042**	707	**927**	624	**817**
16	1086	**1419**	978	**1276**	873	**1139**	778	**1014**	693	**901**	611	**794**
17	1064	**1381**	958	**1241**	855	**1107**	762	**985**	678	**875**	597	**770**
18	1042	**1341**	937	**1204**	837	**1074**	745	**955**	662	**848**	584	**746**
19	1019	**1300**	916	**1167**	817	**1039**	728	**924**	647	**819**	569	**720**
20	995	**1257**	894	**1128**	798	**1004**	710	**892**	630	**790**	555	**694**
22	946	**1169**	849	**1047**	757	**931**	673	**825**	597	**730**	525	**640**
24	894	**1076**	802	**962**	714	**853**	633	**754**	561	**666**	493	**583**
26	840	**977**	752	**872**	668	**771**	592	**680**	524	**598**	460	**522**
28	783	**874**	700	**776**	621	**684**	549	**601**	485	**527**	425	**457**
30	723	**766**	645	**679**	571	**597**	504	**524**	444	**459**	388	**398**
32	661	**673**	588	**597**	519	**525**	457	**461**	402	**403**	349	**350**
34	596	**596**	529	**529**	465	**465**	408	**408**	357	**357**	310	**310**
36	532	**532**	472	**472**	415	**415**	364	**364**	319	**319**	277	**277**
38	477	**477**	423	**423**	372	**372**	327	**327**	286	**286**	248	**248**
40	431	**431**	382	**382**	336	**336**	295	**295**	258	**258**	224	**224**
Properties												
U	2.47	**2.47**	2.49	**2.49**	2.51	**2.51**	2.53	**2.53**	2.55	**2.55**	2.56	**2.56**
P_{wo} (kips)	558	**774**	465	**646**	389	**540**	333	**462**	276	**383**	232	**322**
P_{wi} (kips/in.)	42	**59**	38	**53**	35	**48**	31	**44**	28	**40**	26	**36**
P_{wb} (kips)	4255	**5014**	3084	**3635**	2291	**2700**	1705	**2010**	1277	**1505**	927	**1092**
P_{fb} (kips)	812	**1128**	677	**941**	548	**761**	441	**613**	352	**488**	275	**382**
L_c (ft.)	13.5	**11.5**	13.4	**11.3**	13.3	**11.3**	13.2	**11.2**	13.1	**11.1**	13.0	**11.0**
L_u (ft.)	75.9	**54.6**	71.2	**51.3**	64.3	**46.3**	58.6	**42.2**	53.2	**38.3**	48.2	**34.7**
A (in.^{2})	61.8		55.8		50.0		44.7		39.9		35.3	
I_x (in.^{4})	2140		1890		1650		1430		1240		1070	
I_y (in.^{4})	664		589		517		454		398		345	
r_y (in.)	3.28		3.25		3.22		3.19		3.16		3.13	
Ratio r_x/r_y	1.80		1.79		1.78		1.77		1.77		1.76	
B_x Bending factors	0.212		0.212		0.213		0.214		0.215		0.217	
B_y Bending factors	0.594		0.600		0.608		0.614		0.621		0.630	
a_x *	319.5		281.6		245.5		213.4		185.1		159.7	
a_y *	99.1		87.8		77.2		67.8		59.4		51.5	

* Tabulated values of a_x and a_y must be multiplied by 10^6.

Table 2A-3 (Continued)

COLUMNS
W shapes
Allowable axial loads in kips

$F_y = 36$ ksi
$F_y = 50$ ksi

Designation	W12											
Wt./ft.	106		96		87		79		72		65	
F_y	36	50	36	50	36	50	36	50	36	50	36	50†
Effective length in ft. KL with respect to least radius of gyration r_y												
0	674	**936**	609	**846**	553	**768**	501	**696**	456	**633**	413	**573**
6	637	**872**	575	**788**	522	**715**	473	**647**	430	**589**	389	**533**
7	629	**858**	568	**775**	515	**703**	467	**637**	424	**579**	384	**524**
8	620	**844**	560	**762**	508	**691**	460	**626**	418	**569**	378	**514**
9	611	**828**	552	**748**	501	**678**	453	**614**	412	**558**	373	**504**
10	602	**812**	544	**733**	493	**665**	446	**601**	406	**547**	367	**494**
11	593	**795**	535	**718**	485	**650**	439	**588**	399	**535**	361	**483**
12	583	**777**	526	**701**	477	**636**	431	**575**	392	**522**	354	**472**
13	572	**759**	516	**685**	468	**620**	423	**561**	385	**509**	348	**460**
14	561	**740**	506	**667**	459	**604**	415	**546**	377	**496**	341	**448**
15	550	**720**	496	**649**	450	**588**	407	**531**	369	**482**	334	**435**
16	539	**699**	486	**630**	440	**570**	398	**515**	361	**468**	326	**422**
17	527	**678**	475	**611**	430	**553**	389	**499**	353	**453**	319	**408**
18	514	**656**	464	**591**	420	**534**	379	**482**	344	**438**	311	**394**
19	502	**634**	452	**570**	409	**515**	370	**465**	336	**422**	303	**380**
20	489	**611**	440	**549**	398	**496**	360	**447**	326	**406**	294	**365**
22	462	**562**	416	**505**	376	**455**	339	**410**	308	**372**	277	**334**
24	433	**511**	390	**458**	352	**412**	317	**371**	288	**336**	259	**301**
26	404	**457**	362	**408**	327	**367**	294	**329**	267	**297**	240	**266**
28	372	**399**	334	**356**	301	**319**	270	**285**	245	**258**	220	**230**
30	340	**348**	304	**310**	273	**278**	245	**249**	222	**225**	199	**201**
32	305	**306**	272	**273**	244	**244**	219	**219**	197	**197**	176	**176**
34	271	**271**	242	**242**	216	**216**	194	**194**	175	**175**	156	**156**
36	241	**241**	215	**215**	193	**193**	173	**173**	156	**156**	139	**139**
38	217	**217**	193	**193**	173	**173**	155	**155**	140	**140**	125	**125**
40	196	**196**	175	**175**	156	**156**	140	**140**	126	**126**	113	**113**
Properties												
U	2.59	**2.59**	2.60	**2.60**	2.62	**2.62**	2.63	**2.63**	2.65	**2.65**	2.66	**2.42**
P_{wo} (kips)	185	**257**	161	**223**	139	**193**	122	**169**	106	**148**	92	**128**
P_{wi} (kips/in.)	22	**31**	20	**28**	19	**26**	17	**24**	15	**22**	14	**20**
P_{wb} (kips)	588	**693**	431	**508**	354	**417**	269	**317**	206	**243**	154	**181**
P_{fb} (kips)	221	**306**	182	**253**	148	**205**	122	**169**	101	**140**	82	**114**
L_c (ft.)	12.9	**10.9**	12.8	**10.9**	12.8	**10.9**	12.8	**10.8**	12.7	**10.8**	12.7	**10.7**
L_u (ft.)	43.3	**31.2**	39.9	**28.7**	36.2	**26.0**	33.3	**24.0**	30.5	**21.9**	27.7	**20.0**
A (in.²)	31.2		28.2		25.6		23.2		21.1		19.1	
I_x (in.⁴)	933		833		740		662		597		533	
I_y (in.⁴)	301		270		241		216		195		174	
r_y (in.)	3.11		3.09		3.07		3.05		3.04		3.02	
Ratio r_x/r_y	1.76		1.76		1.75		1.75		1.75		1.75	
B_x Bending factors	0.215		0.215		0.217		0.217		0.217		0.217	
B_y Bending factors	0.633		0.635		0.645		0.648		0.651		0.656	
a_x *	139.1		124.3		110.4		98.6		88.6		79.3	
a_y *	45.0		40.1		36.0		32.2		29.1		26.0	

* Tabulated values of a_x and a_y must be multiplied by 10^6.
† Flange is non-compact; see discussion preceding column load tables.

$F_y = 36$ ksi
$F_y = 50$ ksi

COLUMNS
W shapes
Allowable axial loads in kips

Designation	W12									
Wt./ft.	58		53		50		45		40	
F_y	36	50	36	50	36	50	36	50	36	50‡
Effective length in ft. KL with respect to least radius of gyration r_y										
0	367	**510**	337	**468**	318	**441**	285	**396**	255	**354**
6	341	**464**	312	**425**	286	**386**	256	**346**	229	**309**
7	335	**454**	307	**416**	279	**374**	250	**335**	222	**292**
8	329	**443**	301	**406**	271	**360**	243	**322**	217	**288**
9	322	**432**	295	**395**	263	**346**	235	**309**	210	**276**
10	315	**420**	288	**384**	254	**331**	228	**296**	203	**264**
11	308	**407**	282	**372**	246	**315**	220	**281**	196	**251**
12	301	**394**	275	**360**	236	**298**	211	**266**	188	**237**
13	293	**380**	268	**347**	226	**281**	202	**250**	180	**222**
14	285	**365**	260	**333**	216	**262**	193	**233**	172	**207**
15	276	**351**	252	**319**	206	**243**	183	**216**	163	**191**
16	268	**335**	244	**305**	195	**223**	173	**197**	154	**175**
18	249	**302**	227	**274**	171	**181**	152	**159**	135	**141**
20	230	**267**	209	**241**	146	**146**	129	**129**	114	**114**
22	209	**229**	189	**206**	121	**121**	106	**106**	94	**94**
24	187	**193**	169	**173**	102	**102**	89	**89**	79	**79**
26	164	**164**	147	**147**	87	**87**	76	**76**	67	**67**
28	142	**142**	127	**127**	75	**75**	66	**66**	58	**58**
30	123	**123**	111	**111**	65	**65**	57	**57**	51	**51**
32	108	**108**	97	**97**	57	**57**	50	**50**	45	**45**
34	96	**96**	86	**86**						
38	77	**77**	69	**69**						
41	66	**66**	59	**59**						
Properties										
U	3.21	**3.21**	3.24	**2.94**	4.10	**4.10**	4.12	**3.75**	3.77	**3.77**
P_{wo} (kips)	89	**124**	78	**108**	92	**127**	75	**105**	66	**92**
P_{wi} (kips/in.)	13	**18**	12	**17**	13	**19**	12	**17**	11	**15**
P_{wb} (kips)	121	**142**	106	**125**	131	**155**	97	**115**	66	**78**
P_{fb} (kips)	92	**128**	74	**103**	92	**128**	74	**103**	60	**83**
L_c (ft.)	10.6	**9.0**	10.6	**9.0**	8.5	**7.2**	8.5	**7.2**	8.4	**7.2**
L_u (ft.)	24.4	**17.5**	22.0	**15.9**	19.6	**14.1**	17.7	**12.8**	16.0	**11.5**
A (in.²)	17.0		15.6		14.7		13.2		11.8	
I_x (in.⁴)	475		425		394		350		310	
I_y (in.⁴)	107		95.8		56.3		50.0		44.1	
r_y (in.)	2.51		2.48		1.96		1.94		1.93	
Ratio r_x/r_y	2.10		2.11		2.64		2.65		2.66	
B_x Bending factors	0.218		0.221		0.227		0.227		0.227	
B_y Bending factors	0.794		0.813		1.058		1.065		1.073	
a_x *	70.6		63.6		58.8		52.2		46.3	
a_y *	16.0		14.3		8.4		7.4		6.5	

* Tabulated values of a_x and a_y must be multiplied by 10^6.
‡ Web may be non-compact for combined axial and bending stress; see AISC Specification Sect. 1.5.1.4.1.
Note: Heavy line indicates Kl/r of 200.

COLUMNS
W shapes

F_y = 36 ksi
F_y = 50 ksi

Allowable axial loads in kips

Designation	W10									
Wt./ft.	112		100		88		77		68	
F_y	36	50	36	50	36	50	36	50	36	50
Effective length in ft. KL with respect to least radius of gyration r_y										
0	711	**987**	635	**882**	559	**777**	488	**678**	432	**600**
6	663	**906**	592	**808**	521	**712**	454	**620**	402	**548**
7	653	**888**	583	**792**	513	**697**	447	**607**	395	**537**
8	642	**869**	573	**775**	504	**682**	439	**593**	388	**525**
9	631	**848**	562	**756**	495	**665**	431	**579**	381	**512**
10	619	**827**	551	**737**	485	**648**	422	**564**	373	**498**
11	606	**805**	540	**717**	475	**630**	413	**548**	365	**484**
12	593	**782**	528	**696**	464	**611**	404	**531**	357	**469**
13	579	**757**	516	**674**	453	**591**	394	**513**	348	**454**
14	565	**732**	503	**651**	442	**571**	384	**495**	339	**437**
15	550	**706**	489	**627**	430	**550**	373	**476**	330	**421**
16	535	**679**	476	**602**	417	**528**	362	**457**	320	**403**
17	519	**651**	461	**577**	405	**505**	351	**437**	310	**385**
18	503	**622**	446	**550**	392	**481**	339	**416**	299	**366**
19	486	**591**	431	**523**	378	**457**	327	**394**	289	**347**
20	469	**560**	416	**494**	364	**432**	315	**371**	278	**327**
22	433	**495**	383	**435**	335	**379**	289	**324**	255	**285**
24	395	**425**	348	**372**	304	**323**	261	**275**	230	**242**
26	355	**362**	312	**317**	271	**275**	232	**234**	204	**206**
28	313	**313**	273	**273**	237	**237**	202	**202**	177	**177**
30	272	**272**	238	**238**	206	**206**	176	**176**	155	**155**
32	239	**239**	209	**209**	181	**181**	155	**155**	136	**136**
34	212	**212**	185	**185**	161	**161**	137	**137**	120	**120**
36	189	**189**	165	**165**	143	**143**	122	**122**	107	**107**
38	170	**170**	148	**148**	129	**129**	110	**110**	96	**96**
40	153	**153**	134	**134**	116	**116**	99	**99**	87	**87**
Properties										
U	2.45	**2.45**	2.46	**2.46**	2.49	**2.49**	2.51	**2.51**	2.52	**2.52**
P_{wo} (kips)	255	**354**	214	**298**	177	**246**	143	**199**	116	**162**
P_{wi} (kips/in.)	27	**38**	24	**34**	22	**30**	19	**27**	17	**24**
P_{wb} (kips)	1388	**1636**	1014	**1196**	714	**842**	480	**566**	335	**395**
P_{fb} (kips)	352	**488**	282	**392**	221	**306**	170	**237**	133	**185**
L_c (ft.)	11.0	**9.3**	10.9	**9.3**	10.8	**9.2**	10.8	**9.1**	10.7	**9.1**
L_u (ft.)	53.2	**38.3**	48.2	**34.7**	43.3	**31.2**	38.6	**27.8**	34.8	**25.1**
A (in.²)	32.9		29.4		25.9		22.6		20.0	
I_x (in.⁴)	716		623		534		455		394	
I_y (in.⁴)	236		207		179		154		134	
r_y (in.)	2.68		2.65		2.63		2.60		2.59	
Ratio r_x/r_y	1.74		1.74		1.73		1.73		1.71	
B_x Bending factors	0.261		0.263		0.263		0.263		0.264	
B_y Bending factors	0.726		0.735		0.744		0.751		0.758	
a_x *	106.5		92.7		79.5		67.9		58.7	
a_y *	35.2		30.8		26.7		22.8		20.0	

* Tabulated values of a_x and a_y must be multiplied by 10^6

COLUMNS
W shapes

F_y = 36 ksi
F_y = 50 ksi

Allowable axial loads in kips

Designation	W10											
Wt./ft.	60		54		49		45		39		33	
F_y	36	50	36	50	36	50	36	50	36	50	36	50
Effective length in ft. KL with respect to least radius of gyration r_y												
0	380	**528**	341	**474**	311	**432**	287	**399**	248	**345**	210	**291**
6	353	**482**	317	**433**	289	**394**	260	**351**	224	**303**	189	**255**
7	348	**472**	312	**423**	284	**385**	253	**340**	218	**293**	184	**246**
8	341	**461**	306	**414**	279	**376**	247	**328**	213	**283**	179	**237**
9	335	**450**	300	**403**	273	**367**	240	**316**	206	**272**	173	**228**
10	328	**437**	294	**392**	268	**357**	232	**303**	200	**260**	167	**217**
11	321	**425**	288	**381**	262	**346**	224	**289**	193	**248**	161	**207**
12	313	**412**	281	**369**	256	**335**	216	**274**	186	**235**	155	**196**
13	306	**398**	274	**356**	249	**324**	208	**259**	178	**221**	149	**184**
14	297	**383**	267	**343**	242	**312**	199	**243**	170	**207**	142	**171**
15	289	**368**	259	**330**	235	**299**	190	**227**	162	**193**	135	**159**
16	280	**353**	251	**316**	228	**286**	180	**209**	154	**177**	127	**145**
17	271	**337**	243	**301**	221	**273**	170	**191**	145	**161**	120	**131**
18	262	**320**	235	**286**	213	**259**	160	**172**	136	**144**	112	**117**
19	253	**303**	226	**271**	205	**245**	149	**154**	126	**130**	103	**105**
20	243	**285**	217	**255**	197	**230**	138	**139**	116	**117**	95	**95**
22	222	**248**	199	**221**	180	**198**	115	**115**	97	**97**	78	**78**
24	201	**209**	179	**186**	161	**167**	97	**97**	81	**81**	66	**66**
26	177	**178**	158	**159**	142	**143**	82	**82**	69	**69**	56	**56**
28	154	**154**	137	**137**	123	**123**	71	**71**	60	**60**	48	**48**
30	134	**134**	119	**119**	107	**107**	62	**62**	52	**52**	42	**42**
32	118	**118**	105	**105**	94	**94**	54	**54**	46	**46**	37	**37**
33	111	**111**	99	**99**	88	**88**	51	**51**	43	**43**		
34	104	**104**	93	**93**	83	**83**						
36	93	**93**	83	**83**	74	**74**						
Properties												
U	2.55	**2.55**	2.56	**2.56**	2.57	**2.57**	3.25	**3.25**	3.28	**3.28**	3.35	**3.35**
P_{wo} (kips)	99	**138**	83	**116**	73	**101**	79	**109**	64	**89**	55	**77**
P_{wi} (kips/in.)	15	**21**	13	**19**	12	**17**	13	**18**	11	**16**	10	**15**
P_{wb} (kips)	239	**282**	163	**193**	127	**149**	138	**163**	101	**119**	79	**93**
P_{fb} (kips)	104	**145**	85	**118**	71	**98**	86	**120**	63	**88**	43	**59**
L_c (ft.)	10.6	**9.0**	10.6	**9.0**	10.6	**9.0**	8.5	**7.2**	8.4	**7.2**	8.4	**7.1**
L_u (ft.)	31.1	**22.4**	28.2	**20.3**	26.0	**18.7**	22.8	**16.4**	19.8	**14.2**	16.5	**11.9**
A (in.²)	17.6		15.8		14.4		13.3		11.5		9.71	
I_x (in.⁴)	341		303		272		248		209		170	
I_y (in.⁴)	116		103		93.4		53.4		45.0		36.6	
r_y (in.)	2.57		2.56		2.54		2.01		1.98		1.94	
Ratio r_x/r_y	1.71		1.71		1.71		2.15		2.16		2.16	
B_x Bending factors	0.264		0.263		0.264		0.271		0.273		0.277	
B_y Bending factors	0.765		0.767		0.770		1.000		1.018		1.055	
a_x *	50.5		45.0		40.6		37.2		31.2		25.4	
a_y *	17.3		15.4		13.8		8.0		6.7		5.4	

* Tabulated values of a_x and a_y must be multiplied by 10^6.
Note: Heavy line indicates Kl/r of 200.

Table 2A-3 (Continued)

COLUMNS — W shapes

$F_y = 36$ ksi
$F_y = 50$ ksi

Allowable axial loads in kips

Designation	W8											
Wt./ft.	67		58		48		40		35		31	
F_y	36	50	36	50	36	50	36	50	36	50	36	50
0	426	**591**	369	**513**	305	**423**	253	**351**	222	**309**	197	**274**
6	387	**525**	336	**455**	276	**375**	229	**310**	201	**272**	178	**241**
7	379	**510**	328	**442**	270	**363**	223	**300**	197	**264**	174	**234**
8	370	**494**	320	**428**	263	**352**	218	**290**	191	**255**	170	**226**
9	360	**477**	312	**413**	256	**339**	212	**279**	186	**246**	165	**217**
10	350	**459**	303	**397**	249	**326**	205	**268**	180	**236**	160	**208**
11	339	**440**	293	**380**	241	**312**	199	**256**	174	**225**	154	**199**
12	328	**420**	283	**363**	233	**297**	192	**244**	168	**214**	149	**189**
13	316	**399**	273	**344**	224	**282**	184	**231**	162	**202**	143	**179**
14	304	**378**	263	**325**	215	**266**	177	**217**	155	**190**	137	**168**
15	292	**355**	251	**305**	206	**249**	169	**203**	148	**177**	131	**156**
16	279	**331**	240	**284**	196	**232**	160	**188**	141	**164**	124	**145**
17	265	**307**	228	**263**	186	**214**	152	**172**	133	**150**	117	**132**
18	251	**281**	216	**240**	176	**195**	143	**156**	125	**136**	110	**119**
19	236	**254**	203	**217**	165	**175**	134	**140**	117	**122**	103	**107**
20	221	**230**	190	**196**	154	**158**	124	**126**	109	**110**	95	**97**
22	190	**190**	162	**162**	131	**131**	104	**104**	91	**91**	80	**80**
24	159	**159**	136	**136**	110	**110**	88	**88**	76	**76**	67	**67**
26	136	**136**	116	**116**	94	**94**	75	**75**	65	**65**	57	**57**
28	117	**117**	100	**100**	81	**81**	64	**64**	56	**56**	49	**49**
30	102	**102**	87	**87**	70	**70**	56	**56**	49	**49**	43	**43**
32	90	**90**	76	**76**	62	**62**	49	**49**	43	**43**	38	**38**
33	84	**84**	72	**72**	58	**58**	46	**46**	40	**40**	35	**35**
34	79	**79**	68	**68**	55	**55**	44	**44**				
35	75	**75**	64	**64**								

Effective length in ft. KL with respect to least radius of gyration r_y

Properties

	67/36	67/50	58/36	58/50	48/36	48/50	40/36	40/50	35/36	35/50	31/36	31/50
U	2.48	**2.48**	2.50	**2.50**	2.54	**2.54**	2.56	**2.56**	2.59	**2.59**	2.61	**2.61**
P_{wo} (kips)	147	**205**	120	**167**	86	**119**	69	**96**	56	**78**	48	**67**
P_{wi} (kips/in.)	21	**29**	18	**26**	14	**20**	13	**18**	11	**16**	10	**14**
P_{wb} (kips)	744	**877**	533	**628**	257	**303**	187	**221**	120	**141**	93	**110**
P_{fb} (kips)	197	**273**	148	**205**	106	**147**	71	**98**	55	**77**	43	**59**
L_c (ft.)	8.7	**7.4**	8.7	**7.4**	8.6	**7.3**	8.5	**7.2**	8.5	**7.2**	8.4	**7.2**
L_u (ft.)	39.9	**28.7**	35.3	**25.4**	30.3	**21.8**	25.3	**18.2**	22.6	**16.3**	20.1	**14.5**

	67	58	48	40	35	31
A (in.²)	19.7	17.1	14.1	11.7	10.3	9.13
I_x (in.⁴)	272	228	184	146	127	110
I_y (in.⁴)	88.6	75.1	60.9	49.1	42.6	37.1
r_y (in.)	2.12	2.10	2.08	2.04	2.03	2.02
Ratio r_x/r_y	1.75	1.74	1.74	1.73	1.73	1.72
B_x Bending factors	0.326	0.329	0.326	0.330	0.330	0.332
B_y Bending factors	0.921	0.934	0.940	0.959	0.972	0.985
a_x *	40.6	33.9	27.4	21.7	18.9	16.4
a_y *	13.2	11.2	9.1	7.3	6.3	5.6

* Tabulated values of a_x and a_y must be multiplied by 10^6.
Note: Heavy line indicates Kl/r of 200.

COLUMNS — W shapes

$F_y = 36$ ksi
$F_y = 50$ ksi

Allowable axial loads in kips

Designation	W8				W6					
Wt./ft.	28		24		25		20		15	
F_y	36	50	36	50	36	50	36	50	36†	50†
0	178	**248**	153	**212**	159	**220**	127	**176**	96	**133**
6	155	**208**	133	**178**	136	**182**	109	**145**	81	**108**
7	150	**198**	129	**170**	131	**173**	105	**137**	78	**102**
8	144	**188**	124	**161**	126	**163**	100	**129**	75	**96**
9	138	**178**	118	**152**	120	**152**	95	**121**	71	**89**
10	132	**166**	113	**142**	114	**141**	90	**112**	67	**82**
11	125	**154**	107	**132**	107	**129**	85	**102**	62	**74**
12	118	**142**	101	**121**	100	**117**	79	**92**	58	**66**
13	111	**128**	95	**109**	93	**103**	73	**81**	53	**57**
14	103	**114**	88	**97**	85	**90**	67	**70**	48	**49**
15	95	**100**	81	**85**	77	**78**	60	**61**	43	**43**
16	87	**88**	74	**74**	69	**69**	54	**54**	38	**38**
17	78	**78**	66	**66**	61	**61**	47	**47**	33	**33**
18	69	**69**	59	**59**	54	**54**	42	**42**	30	**30**
19	62	**62**	53	**53**	49	**49**	38	**38**	27	**27**
20	56	**56**	48	**48**	44	**44**	34	**34**	24	**24**
22	46	**46**	39	**39**	36	**36**	28	**28**	20	**20**
24	39	**39**	33	**33**	31	**31**	24	**24**	17	**17**
25	36	**36**	30	**30**	28	**28**	22	**22**		
26	33	**33**	28	**28**						
27	31	**31**								

Effective length in ft. KL with respect to least radius of gyration r_y

Properties

	28/36	28/50	24/36	24/50	25/36	25/50	20/36	20/50	15/36	15/50
U	3.23	**3.23**	3.27	**3.27**	2.38	**2.07**	2.43	**1.86**	1.93	**1.45**
P_{wo} (kips)	48	**67**	39	**54**	47	**65**	35	**49**	26	**36**
P_{wi} (kips/in.)	10	**14**	9	**12**	12	**16**	9	**13**	8	**12**
P_{wb} (kips)	93	**110**	59	**70**	170	**200**	91	**107**	63	**74**
P_{fb} (kips)	49	**68**	36	**50**	47	**65**	30	**42**	15	**21**
L_c (ft.)	6.9	**5.9**	6.9	**5.8**	6.4	**5.4**	6.4	**5.4**	6.3	**5.4**
L_u (ft.)	17.5	**12.6**	15.2	**10.9**	20.0	**14.4**	16.4	**11.8**	12.0	**8.7**

	28	24	25	20	15
A (in.²)	8.25	7.08	7.34	5.87	4.43
I_x (in.⁴)	98.0	82.8	53.4	41.4	29.1
I_y (in.⁴)	21.7	18.3	17.1	13.3	9.32
r_y (in.)	1.62	1.61	1.52	1.50	1.45
Ratio r_x/r_y	2.13	2.12	1.78	1.77	1.77
B_x Bending factors	0.340	0.339	0.440	0.438	0.456
B_y Bending factors	1.244	1.258	1.308	1.331	1.424
a_x *	14.63	12.34	7.97	6.19	4.33
a_y *	3.23	2.73	2.53	1.97	1.39

* Tabulated values of a_x and a_y must be multiplied by 10^6.
† Flange is non-compact; see discussion preceding column load tables.
Note: Heavy line indicates Kl/r of 200.

COLUMNS
W shapes

$F_y = 36$ ksi
$F_y = 50$ ksi

Allowable axial loads in kips

Designation	W6						W5				W4	
Wt./ft.	16		12		9		19		16		13	
F_y	36	50	36	50	36	50	36	50	36	50	36	50
Effective length in ft. KL with respect to least radius of gyration r_y												
0	102	**142**	77	**107**	58	**80**	120	**166**	101	**140**	83	**115**
2	96	**132**	72	**98**	54	**74**	115	**158**	97	**133**	78	**107**
3	92	**124**	68	**92**	51	**69**	111	**152**	94	**128**	75	**101**
4	87	**116**	64	**85**	48	**64**	107	**145**	91	**122**	71	**94**
5	82	**106**	60	**77**	45	**58**	103	**138**	87	**116**	67	**87**
6	76	**95**	55	**69**	41	**51**	99	**129**	83	**109**	62	**79**
7	69	**83**	50	**59**	37	**44**	93	**120**	79	**101**	57	**70**
8	62	**70**	44	**48**	33	**36**	88	**111**	74	**93**	52	**60**
9	54	**57**	38	**38**	28	**28**	82	**100**	69	**84**	46	**49**
10	46	**46**	31	**31**	23	**23**	76	**89**	64	**75**	39	**40**
11	38	**38**	26	**26**	19	**19**	70	**77**	58	**64**	33	**33**
12	32	**32**	22	**22**	16	**16**	63	**65**	52	**54**	28	**28**
13	27	**27**	18	**18**	13	**13**	55	**56**	46	**46**	24	**24**
14	23	**23**	16	**16**	12	**12**	48	**48**	40	**40**	20	**20**
15	20	**20**	14	**14**	10	**10**	42	**42**	35	**35**	18	**18**
16	18	**18**					37	**37**	31	**31**	16	**16**
17							33	**33**	27	**27**		
18							29	**29**	24	**24**		
19							26	**26**	22	**22**		
20							24	**24**	20	**20**		
21							21	**21**	18	**18**		
Properties												
U	3.35	**2.55**	2.89	**2.05**	2.26	**1.63**	2.25	**2.01**	2.17	**1.85**	2.30	**1.98**
P_{wo} (kips)	35	**49**	26	**36**	17	**24**	39	**55**	32	**45**	35	**48**
P_{wi} (kips/in.)	9	**13**	8	**12**	6	**9**	10	**14**	9	**12**	10	**14**
P_{wb} (kips)	91	**107**	63	**74**	25	**30**	138	**163**	97	**115**	196	**231**
P_{fb} (kips)	37	**51**	18	**25**	10	**14**	42	**58**	29	**41**	27	**37**
L_c (ft.)	4.3	**3.6**	4.2	**3.6**	4.2	**3.5**	5.3	**4.5**	5.3	**4.5**	4.3	**3.6**
L_u (ft.)	12.0	**8.7**	8.6	**6.2**	6.7	**4.8**	19.5	**14.0**	16.7	**12.0**	15.6	**11.2**
A (in.²)	4.74		3.55		2.68		5.54		4.68		3.83	
I_x (in.⁴)	32.1		22.1		16.4		26.2		21.3		11.3	
I_y (in.⁴)	4.43		2.99		2.20		9.13		7.51		3.86	
r_y (in.)	0.966		0.918		0.905		1.28		1.27		1.00	
Ratio r_x/r_y	2.69		2.71		2.73		1.70		1.68		1.72	
B_x Bending factors	0.465		0.486		0.482		0.543		0.550		0.701	
B_y Bending factors	2.155		2.367		2.414		1.526		1.560		2.016	
a_x *	4.77		3.28		2.44		3.89		3.16		1.69	
a_y *	0.66		0.45		0.33		1.35		1.12		0.57	

* Tabulated values of a_x and a_y must be multiplied by 10^6.
Note: Heavy line indicates Kl/r of 200.

COLUMNS
M shapes

$F_y = 36$ ksi
$F_y = 50$ ksi

Allowable axial loads in kips

Designation	M6		M5		M4	
Wt./ft.	20		18.9		13	
F_y	36	50	36	50	36	50
Effective length in ft. KL with respect to least radius of gyration r_y						
0	127	**177**	120	**167**	82	**114**
2	122	**168**	114	**157**	77	**105**
3	119	**163**	111	**151**	74	**99**
4	116	**157**	106	**143**	70	**92**
5	112	**150**	102	**135**	65	**84**
6	107	**142**	96	**126**	60	**75**
7	103	**134**	91	**116**	54	**65**
8	98	**125**	85	**105**	48	**54**
9	92	**115**	78	**93**	42	**43**
10	87	**105**	71	**81**	35	**35**
11	81	**94**	64	**67**	29	**29**
12	74	**83**	56	**57**	24	**24**
13	68	**71**	48	**48**	21	**21**
14	61	**61**	42	**42**	18	**18**
15	53	**53**	36	**36**	15	**15**
16	47	**47**	32	**32**		
17	41	**41**	28	**28**		
18	37	**37**	25	**25**		
19	33	**33**	23	**23**		
20	30	**30**				
21	27	**27**				
22	25	**25**				
23	23	**23**				
Properties						
U	2.53	**2.12**	2.45	**1.78**	2.45	**2.35**
P_{wo} (kips)	39	**55**	50	**69**	37	**52**
P_{wi} (kips/in.)	9	**13**	11	**16**	9	**13**
P_{wb} (kips)	90	**107**	239	**281**	170	**200**
P_{fb} (kips)	32	**45**	39	**54**	31	**43**
L_c (ft.)	6.3	**5.3**	5.3	**4.5**	4.2	**3.5**
L_u (ft.)	17.4	**12.5**	19.3	**13.9**	16.9	**12.2**
A (in.²)	5.89		5.55		3.81	
I_x (in.⁴)	39.0		24.1		10.5	
I_y (in.⁴)	11.6		7.86		3.36	
r_y (in.)	1.40		1.19		0.939	
Ratio r_x/r_y	1.84		1.75		1.77	
B_x Bending factors	0.453		0.576		0.727	
B_y Bending factors	1.510		1.768		2.228	
a_x *	5.80		3.58		1.56	
a_y *	1.72		1.17		0.50	

* Tabulated values of a_x and a_y must be multiplied by 10^6.
Note: Heavy line indicates Kl/r of 200.

Source: Manual of Steel Construction. *Courtesy of American Institute of Steel Construction.*

Table 2A-4
ALLOWABLE AXIAL LOADS FOR STEEL PIPE COLUMNS

COLUMNS — Standard steel pipe

$F_y = 36$ ksi

Allowable concentric loads in kips

Nominal Dia.	12	10	8	6	5	4	3½	3
Wall Thickness	0.375	0.365	0.322	0.280	0.258	0.237	0.226	0.216
Weight per Foot	49.56	40.48	28.55	18.97	14.62	10.79	9.11	7.58
F_y	36 ksi							
Effective length in feet KL with respect to radius of gyration								
0	315	257	181	121	93	68	58	48
6	303	246	171	110	83	59	48	38
7	301	243	168	108	81	57	46	36
8	299	241	166	106	78	54	44	34
9	296	238	163	103	76	52	41	31
10	293	235	161	101	73	49	38	28
11	291	232	158	98	71	46	35	25
12	288	229	155	95	68	43	32	22
13	285	226	152	92	65	40	29	19
14	282	223	149	89	61	36	25	16
15	278	220	145	86	58	33	22	14
16	275	216	142	82	55	29	19	12
17	272	213	138	79	51	26	17	11
18	268	209	135	75	47	23	15	10
19	265	205	131	71	43	21	14	9
20	261	201	127	67	39	19	12	
22	254	193	119	59	32	15	10	
24	246	185	111	51	27	13		
25	242	180	106	47	25	12		
26	238	176	102	43	23			
28	229	167	93	37	20			
30	220	158	83	32	17			
31	216	152	78	30	16			
32	211	148	73	29				
34	201	137	65	25				
36	192	127	58	23				
37	186	120	55	21				
38	181	115	52					
40	171	104	47					
Properties								
Area A (in.^{2})	14.6	11.9	8.40	5.58	4.30	3.17	2.68	2.23
I (in.^{4})	279	161	72.5	28.1	15.2	7.23	4.79	3.02
r (in.)	4.38	3.67	2.94	2.25	1.88	1.51	1.34	1.16
B Bending factor	0.333	0.398	0.500	0.657	0.789	0.987	1.12	1.29
* a	41.7	23.9	10.8	4.21	2.26	1.08	0.717	0.447

* Tabulated values of a must be multiplied by 10^6.
Note: Heavy line indicates Kl/r of 200.

COLUMNS — Extra strong steel pipe

$F_y = 36$ ksi

Allowable concentric loads in kips

Nominal Dia.	12	10	8	6	5	4	3½	3
Wall Thickness	0.500	0.500	0.500	0.432	0.375	0.337	0.318	0.300
Weight per Foot	65.42	54.74	43.39	28.57	20.78	14.98	12.50	10.25
F_y	36 ksi							
Effective length in feet KL with respect to radius of gyration								
0	415	348	276	181	132	95	79	65
6	400	332	259	166	118	81	66	52
7	397	328	255	162	114	78	63	48
8	394	325	251	159	111	75	59	45
9	390	321	247	155	107	71	55	41
10	387	318	243	151	103	67	51	37
11	383	314	239	146	99	63	47	33
12	379	309	234	142	95	59	43	28
13	375	305	229	137	91	54	38	24
14	371	301	224	132	86	49	33	21
15	367	296	219	127	81	44	29	18
16	363	291	214	122	76	39	25	16
18	353	281	203	111	65	31	20	12
19	349	276	197	105	59	28	18	11
20	344	271	191	99	54	25	16	
21	337	265	185	92	48	22	14	
22	334	260	179	86	44	21		
24	323	248	166	73	37	17		
26	312	236	152	62	32			
28	301	224	137	54	27			
30	289	211	122	47	24			
32	277	197	107	41				
34	264	183	95	36				
36	251	168	85	32				
38	237	152	76					
40	223	137	69					
Properties								
Area A (in.^{2})	19.2	16.1	12.8	8.40	6.11	4.41	3.68	3.02
I (in.^{4})	362	212	106	40.5	20.7	9.61	6.28	3.89
r (in.)	4.33	3.63	2.88	2.19	1.84	1.48	1.31	1.14
B Bending factor	0.339	0.408	0.521	0.688	0.822	1.03	1.17	1.36
* a	53.6	31.6	15.8	6.00	3.08	1.44	0.941	0.585

* Tabulated values of a must be multiplied by 10^6.
Note: Heavy line indicates Kl/r of 200.

Source: Manual of Steel Construction. *Courtesy of American Institute of Steel Construction.*

Table 2A-5
ALLOWABLE AXIAL LOADS FOR SQUARE STRUCTURAL TUBING

COLUMNS
Double-extra strong steel pipe

$F_y = 36$ ksi

Allowable concentric loads in kips

Nominal Dia.	8	6	5	4	3
Wall Thickness	0.875	0.864	0.750	0.674	0.600
Weight per Foot	72.42	53.16	38.55	27.54	18.58
F_y	36 ksi				
Effective length in feet KL with respect to radius of gyration					
0	461	337	244	175	118
6	431	306	216	147	91
7	424	299	209	140	84
8	417	292	202	133	77
9	410	284	195	126	69
10	403	275	187	118	60
11	395	266	178	109	51
12	387	257	170	100	43
13	378	247	160	91	37
14	369	237	151	81	32
15	360	227	141	70	28
16	351	216	130	62	24
17	341	205	119	55	22
18	331	193	108	49	
19	321	181	97	44	
20	310	168	87	40	
22	288	142	72	33	
24	264	119	61		
26	240	102	52		
28	213	88	44		
30	187	76			
32	164	67			
34	145	60			
36	130				
38	116				
40	105				
Properties					
Area A (in.²)	21.3	15.6	11.3	8.10	5.47
I (in.⁴)	162	66.3	33.6	15.3	5.99
r (in.)	2.76	2.06	1.72	1.37	1.05
B Bending factor	0.567	0.781	0.938	1.19	1.60
* a	24.2	9.86	4.98	2.27	0.899

* Tabulated values of a must be multiplied by 10^6
Note: Heavy line indicates Kl/r of 200.

COLUMNS
Square structural tubing

$F_y = 46$ ksi

Allowable concentric loads in kips

Nominal Size	8 x 8					7 x 7				
Thickness	5/8	1/2	3/8	5/16	1/4	1/2	3/8	5/16	1/4	3/16
Wt./ft.	59.32	48.85	37.60	31.84	25.82	42.05	32.59	27.59	22.42	17.08
F_y	46 ksi									
Effective length in feet KL with respect to radius of gyration										
0	480	397	306	258	209	342	264	224	182	139
6	448	370	286	242	196	314	244	207	168	128
7	441	364	281	238	193	308	239	203	165	126
8	433	358	277	234	190	301	234	199	162	123
9	425	352	272	230	187	294	229	195	158	121
10	417	345	267	226	184	287	224	190	155	118
11	408	338	262	222	180	280	218	185	151	115
12	399	330	256	217	176	272	212	180	147	113
13	389	323	251	212	173	264	206	175	143	109
14	379	315	245	207	169	255	200	170	139	106
15	369	307	238	202	165	246	193	165	135	103
16	358	298	232	197	160	237	186	159	130	100
17	347	289	225	191	156	228	179	153	125	96
18	336	280	219	186	151	218	172	147	120	92
19	324	271	212	180	147	208	165	141	115	89
20	312	261	205	174	142	197	157	134	110	85
21	300	251	197	168	137	187	149	128	105	81
22	287	241	190	162	132	176	140	121	99	77
23	274	231	182	155	127	164	132	114	94	73
24	261	220	174	148	122	152	123	106	88	68
25	247	209	165	141	116	140	114	99	82	64
26	232	198	157	134	110	130	105	91	76	59
27	218	186	148	127	105	120	98	85	70	55
28	203	174	139	120	99	112	91	79	65	51
29	189	162	130	112	93	104	85	73	61	47
30	177	151	122	105	87	98	79	69	57	44
32	155	133	107	92	76	86	70	60	50	39
34	137	118	95	82	67	76	62	53	44	35
36	123	105	84	73	60	68	55	48	40	31
38	110	94	76	65	54	61	49	43	35	28
40	99	85	68	59	49	55	45	39	32	25
Properties										
A (in.²)	17.40	14.40	11.10	9.36	7.59	12.40	9.58	8.11	6.59	5.02
I (in.⁴)	153	131	106	90.9	75.1	84.6	68.7	59.5	49.4	38.5
r (in.)	2.96	3.03	3.09	3.12	3.15	2.62	2.68	2.71	2.74	2.77
B Bending factor	0.455	0.437	0.420	0.412	0.404	0.511	0.488	0.477	0.467	0.457
* a	22.8	19.6	15.7	13.5	11.2	12.6	10.2	8.86	7.36	5.73

* Tabulated values of a must be multiplied by 10^6.
Note: Heavy line indicates Kl/r of 200.

Table 2A-5 (Continued)

F_y = 46 ksi

COLUMNS
Square structural tubing
Allowable concentric loads in kips

Effective length in feet KL with respect to radius of gyration

Nominal Size	6 x 6					5 x 5				
Thickness	1/2	3/8	5/16	1/4	3/16	1/2	3/8	5/16	1/4	3/16
Wt./ft.	35.24	27.48	23.34	19.02	14.53	28.43	22.37	19.08	15.62	11.97
F_y	46 ksi									
0	287	223	189	154	118	231	182	155	127	97
6	257	201	171	140	107	200	159	136	111	86
7	251	196	167	137	105	193	153	131	108	83
8	244	191	163	133	102	186	148	127	104	80
9	237	186	158	130	99	178	142	122	100	77
10	229	180	154	126	96	169	135	116	96	74
11	221	174	149	122	93	160	129	111	92	71
12	212	168	143	117	90	151	122	105	87	67
13	203	161	138	113	87	141	115	99	82	64
14	194	154	132	108	83	131	107	93	77	60
15	185	147	126	104	80	120	99	86	72	56
16	175	140	120	99	76	109	90	79	66	52
17	164	132	113	94	72	97	82	72	60	47
18	153	124	107	88	68	87	73	64	54	43
19	142	115	100	83	64	78	65	58	49	39
20	131	107	93	77	60	70	59	52	44	35
21	119	98	85	71	56	64	54	47	40	32
22	108	89	78	65	51	58	49	43	36	29
24	91	75	65	55	43	49	41	36	31	24
26	77	64	56	47	36	41	35	31	26	21
28	67	55	48	40	31	36	30	27	22	18
30	58	48	42	35	27	31	26	23	20	15
31	54	45	39	33	26		25	22	18	14
32	51	42	37	31	24				17	14
34	45	37	33	27	21					
36	40	33	29	24	19					
37		32	27	23	18					
38			26	22	17					
39					16					
Properties										
A (in.^{2})	10.40	8.08	6.86	5.59	4.27	8.36	6.58	5.61	4.59	3.52
I (in.^{4})	50.5	41.6	36.3	30.3	23.8	27.0	22.8	20.1	16.9	13.4
r (in.)	2.21	2.27	2.30	2.33	2.36	1.80	1.86	1.89	1.92	1.95
B Bending factor	0.615	0.583	0.567	0.553	0.539	0.773	0.722	0.699	0.677	0.656
*a	7.52	6.20	5.40	4.52	3.54	4.03	3.39	2.99	2.52	2.00

* Tabulated values of a must be multiplied by 10^6.
Note: Heavy line indicates Kl/r of 200.

F_y = 46 ksi

COLUMNS
Square structural tubing
Allowable concentric loads in kips

Effective length in feet KL with respect to radius of gyration

Nominal Size	4 x 4					3 x 3		
Thickness	1/2	3/8	5/16	1/4	3/16	5/16	1/4	3/16
Wt./ft.	21.63	17.27	14.83	12.21	9.42	10.58	8.81	6.87
F_y	46 ksi							
0	176	140	120	99	76	86	71	56
2	168	134	115	95	73	80	67	53
3	162	130	112	92	71	77	64	50
4	156	126	108	89	69	73	61	48
5	150	121	104	86	67	68	57	45
6	143	115	100	83	64	63	53	42
7	135	110	95	79	61	57	49	39
8	126	103	90	75	58	51	44	35
9	117	97	84	70	55	44	38	31
10	108	89	78	65	51	37	33	27
11	98	82	72	60	47	31	27	22
12	87	74	65	55	43	26	23	19
13	75	65	58	49	39	22	19	16
14	65	57	51	43	35	19	17	14
15	57	49	44	38	30	16	15	12
16	50	43	39	33	27	14	13	11
17	44	38	34	29	24	13	11	9
18	39	34	31	26	21		10	8
19	35	31	28	24	19			
20	32	28	25	21	17			
21	29	25	23	19	16			
22	26	23	21	18	14			
23	24	21	19	16	13			
24		19	17	15	12			
25				14	11			
Properties								
A (in.^{2})	6.36	5.08	4.36	3.59	2.77	3.11	2.59	2.02
I (in.^{4})	12.3	10.7	9.58	8.22	6.59	3.58	3.16	2.60
r (in.)	1.39	1.45	1.48	1.51	1.54	1.07	1.10	1.13
B Bending factor	1.04	0.949	0.910	0.874	0.840	1.30	1.23	1.17
*a	1.83	1.59	1.43	1.22	0.983	0.533	0.470	0.387

* Tabulated values of a must be multiplied by 10^6.
Note: Heavy line indicates Kl/r of 200.

Source: Manual of Steel Construction. *Courtesy of American Institute of Steel Construction.*

Table 2A-6
RECOMMENDED K FACTORS FOR DETERMINING EFFECTIVE LENGTH OF COLUMNS

	(a)	(b)	(c)	(d)	(e)	(f)
Buckled shape of column is shown by dashed line						
Theoretical K value	0.5	0.7	1.0	1.0	2.0	2.0
Recommended design value when ideal conditions are approximated	0.65	0.80	1.2	1.0	2.10	2.0
End condition code		Rotation fixed and translation fixed Rotation free and translation fixed Rotation fixed and translation free Rotation free and translation free				

Source: Manual of Steel Construction. *Courtesy of American Institute of Steel Construction.*

1/240 of the span may be obtained by multiplying the bottom number by 1.5. In no case shall the *total* load capacity of the joists be exceeded.

To utilize Table 2A–7, determine the span in feet and load in pounds per linear foot required; go to the required span in the left-hand column, then read across until a load equal to or greater than the required load is reached. The first joist that satisfies this loading is the most economical joist for those conditions. If this joist is too deep or too shallow or does not satisfy the deflection limitations, continue on horizontally to the right until a joist is found that satisfies the depth requirements as well as the load and deflection requirements.

Example

Floor joists @ 2 ft. 6 in. on center, supporting a structural concrete slab. Maximum deflection allowed for a span supporting a concrete slab is 1/360 of the span.

Span = 30 ft. 0 in.
Maximum joist depth allowed = 20 in.
DL = 48 psf (includes joist weight)
LL = 100 psf
TL = 148 psf
W = 148 × 2.5 = 370 lbs. per ft.
W (live load) = 100 × 2.5 = 250 lbs. per ft.

A 22K6 at a span of 30 ft. can carry 371 lbs. per ft. of total load and possesses a live load deflection figure of 266 lbs. per ft. However, it exceeds the maximum depth limitation of 20 in. A 20K7 fulfills the total load requirement but possesses a live load deflection figure of only 242 lbs. per ft. It is then found that a 20K9 is the most economical joist that satisfies all the requirements of total load, live load deflection, and maximum depth limitation.

Table 2A-7
OPEN WEB STEEL JOISTS—K-SERIES ECONOMY TABLE

Joist Designation	10K1	12K1	8K1	14K1	16K2	12K3	14K3	16K3	18K3	14K4	20K3	16K4	12K5	18K4	16K5	20K4
Depth (In.)	10	12	8	14	16	12	14	16	18	14	20	16	12	18	16	20
Approx. Wt. (lbs./ft.)	5.0	5.0	5.1	5.2	5.5	5.7	6.0	6.3	6.6	6.7	6.7	7.0	7.1	7.2	7.5	7.6
Span (ft.) ↓																
8			550 550													
9			550 550													
10	550 550		550 480													
11	550 542		532 377													
12	550 455	550 550	444 288			550 550							550 550			
13	479 363	550 510	377 225			550 510							550 510			
14	412 289	500 425	324 179	550 550		550 463	550 550			550 550			550 463			
15	358 234	434 344	281 145	511 475		543 428	550 507			550 507			550 434			
16	313 192	380 282	246 119	448 390	550 550	476 351	550 467	550 550		550 467		550 550	550 396		550 550	
17	277 159	336 234		395 324	512 488	420 291	495 404	550 526		550 443		550 526	550 366		550 526	
18	246 134	299 197		352 272	456 409	374 245	441 339	508 456	550 550	530 397		550 490	507 317	550 550	550 490	
19	221 113	268 167		315 230	408 347	335 207	395 287	455 386	514 494	475 336		547 452	454 269	550 523	550 455	
20	199 97	241 142		284 197	368 297	302 177	356 246	410 330	463 423	428 287	517 517	493 386	409 230	550 490	550 426	550 550
21		218 123		257 170	333 255	273 153	322 212	371 285	420 364	388 248	468 453	447 333	370 198	506 426	503 373	550 520
22		199 106		234 147	303 222	249 132	293 184	337 247	382 316	353 215	426 393	406 289	337 172	460 370	458 323	514 461
23		181 93		214 128	277 194	227 116	268 160	308 216	349 276	322 188	389 344	371 252	308 150	420 323	418 282	469 402
24		166 81		196 113	254 170	208 101	245 141	283 189	320 242	295 165	357 302	340 221	282 132	385 284	384 248	430 353
25				180 100	234 150		226 124	260 167	294 214	272 145	329 266	313 195		355 250	353 219	396 312
26				166 88	216 133		209 110	240 148	272 190	251 129	304 236	289 173		328 222	326 194	366 277
27				154 79	200 119		193 98	223 132	252 169	233 115	281 211	268 155		303 198	302 173	339 247
28				143 70	186 106		180 88	207 118	234 151	216 103	261 189	249 138		282 177	281 155	315 221
29					173 95			193 106	218 136		243 170	232 124		263 159	261 139	293 199
30					161 86			180 96	203 123		227 153	216 112		245 144	244 126	274 179
31					151 78			168 87	190 111		212 138	203 101		229 130	228 114	256 162
32					142 71			158 79	178 101		199 126	190 92		215 118	214 103	240 147
33									168 92		187 114			202 108		226 134
34									158 84		176 105			190 98		212 122
35									149 77		166 96			179 90		200 112
36									141 70		157 88			169 82		189 103
37											148 81					179 95
38											141 74					170 87
39											133 69					161 81
40											127 64					153 75

Joist Designation	14K6	18K5	22K4	16K6	20K5	24K4	18K6	16K7	22K5	20K6	18K7	22K6	20K7	24K5	22K7	24K6
Depth (In.)	14	18	22	16	20	24	18	16	22	20	18	22	20	24	22	24
Approx. Wt. (lbs./ft.)	7.7	7.7	8.0	8.1	8.2	8.4	8.5	8.6	8.8	8.9	9.0	9.2	9.3	9.3	9.7	9.7
Span (ft.) ↓																
14	550 550															
15	550 507															
16	550 467			550 550				550 550								
17	550 443			550 526				550 526								
18	550 408	550 550		550 490			550 550	550 490			550 550					
19	550 383	550 523		550 455			550 523	550 455			550 523					
20	525 347	550 490		550 426	550 550		550 490	550 426		550 550	550 490		550 550			
21	475 299	550 460		548 405	550 520		550 460	550 406		550 520	550 460		550 520			
22	432 259	518 414	550 548	498 351	550 490		550 438	550 385	550 548	550 490	550 438	550 548	550 490		550 548	
23	395 226	473 362	518 491	455 307	529 451		516 393	507 339	550 518	550 468	550 418	550 518	550 468		550 518	
24	362 199	434 318	475 431	418 269	485 396	520 516	473 345	465 298	536 483	528 430	526 382	550 495	550 448	550 544	550 495	550 544
25	334 175	400 281	438 381	384 238	446 350	479 456	435 305	428 263	493 427	486 380	485 337	537 464	541 421	540 511	550 474	550 520
26	308 156	369 249	404 338	355 211	412 310	442 405	402 271	395 233	455 379	449 337	448 299	496 411	500 373	499 453	550 454	543 493
27	285 139	342 222	374 301	329 188	382 277	410 361	372 241	366 208	422 337	416 301	415 267	459 367	463 333	462 404	512 406	503 439
28	265 124	318 199	348 270	306 168	355 248	381 323	346 216	340 186	392 302	386 269	385 239	427 328	430 298	429 362	475 364	467 393
29		296 179	324 242	285 151	330 223	354 290	322 194	317 167	365 272	360 242	359 215	398 295	401 268	400 325	443 327	435 354
30		276 161	302 219	266 137	308 201	331 262	301 175	296 151	341 245	336 218	335 194	371 266	374 242	373 293	413 295	406 319
31		258 146	283 198	249 124	289 182	310 237	281 158	277 137	319 222	314 198	313 175	347 241	350 219	349 266	387 267	380 289
32		242 132	265 180	233 112	271 165	290 215	264 144	259 124	299 201	295 179	294 159	326 219	328 199	327 241	363 242	357 262
33		228 121	249 164		254 150	273 196	248 131		281 183	277 163	276 145	306 199	309 181	308 220	341 221	335 239
34		214 110	235 149		239 137	257 179	233 120		265 167	261 149	260 132	288 182	290 165	290 201	321 202	315 218
35		202 101	221 137		226 126	242 164	220 110		249 153	246 137	245 121	272 167	274 151	273 184	303 185	297 200
36		191 92	209 126		213 115	229 150	208 101		236 141	232 125	232 111	257 153	259 139	258 169	286 169	281 183
37			198 116		202 106	216 138			223 130	220 115		243 141	245 128	244 155	271 156	266 169
38			187 107		191 98	205 128			211 119	208 106		230 130	232 118	231 143	256 144	252 156
39			178 98		181 90	195 118			200 110	198 98		218 120	220 109	219 132	243 133	239 144
40			169 91		172 84	185 109			190 102	188 91		207 111	209 101	208 122	231 123	227 133
41			161 85			176 101			181 95			197 103		198 114	220 114	216 124
42			153 79			168 94			173 88			188 96		189 106	209 106	206 115
43			146 73			160 88			165 82			179 89		180 98	200 99	196 107
44			139 68			153 82			157 76			171 83		172 92	191 92	187 100
45						146 76								164 86		179 93
46						139 71								157 80		171 87
47						133 67								150 75		164 82
48						128 63								144 70		157 77

Table 2A-7 (Continued)

Joist Designation	26K5	16K9	24K7	18K9	26K6	20K9	26K7	22K9	28K6	24K8	18K10	28K7	24K9	26K8	20K10	26K9
Depth (In.)	26	16	24	18	26	20	26	22	28	24	18	28	24	26	20	26
Approx. Wt. (lbs./ft.)	9.8	10.0	10.1	10.2	10.6	10.8	10.9	11.3	11.4	11.5	11.7	11.8	12.0	12.1	12.2	12.2
Span (ft.) ↓																
16		550 550														
17		550 526														
18		550 490		550 550							550 550					
19		550 455		550 523							550 523					
20		550 426		550 490		550 550					550 490				550 550	
21		550 406		550 460		550 520					550 460				550 520	
22		550 385		550 438		550 490		550 548			550 438				550 490	
23		550 363		550 418		550 468		550 518			550 418				550 468	
24		550 346	550 544	550 396		550 448		550 495		550 544	550 396		550 544		550 448	
25		514 311	550 520	550 377		550 426		550 474		550 520	550 377		550 520		550 426	
26	542 535	474 276	550 499	538 354	550 541	550 405	550 541	550 454		550 499	550 361		550 499	550 541	550 405	550 541
27	502 477	439 246	550 479	498 315	547 519	550 389	550 522	550 432		550 479	550 347		550 479	550 522	550 389	550 522
28	466 427	408 220	521 436	463 282	508 464	517 353	550 501	550 413	548 541	550 456	548 331	550 543	550 456	550 501	550 375	550 501
29	434 384	380 198	485 392	431 254	473 417	482 317	527 463	532 387	511 486	536 429	511 298	550 522	550 436	550 479	550 359	550 479
30	405 346	355 178	453 353	402 229	441 377	450 286	492 417	497 349	477 439	500 387	477 269	531 486	544 419	544 457	533 336	550 459
31	379 314	332 161	424 320	376 207	413 341	421 259	460 378	465 316	446 397	468 350	446 243	497 440	510 379	509 413	499 304	550 444
32	356 285	311 147	397 290	353 188	387 309	395 235	432 343	436 287	418 361	439 318	418 221	466 400	478 344	477 375	468 276	519 407
33	334 259		373 265	332 171	364 282	371 214	406 312	410 261	393 329	413 289	393 201	438 364	449 313	448 342	440 251	488 370
34	315 237		351 242	312 156	343 257	349 195	382 285	386 239	370 300	388 264	370 184	412 333	423 286	422 312	414 229	459 338
35	297 217		331 221	294 143	323 236	329 179	360 261	364 219	349 275	366 242	349 168	389 305	399 262	398 286	390 210	433 310
36	280 199		313 203	278 132	305 216	311 164	340 240	344 201	330 252	346 222	330 154	367 280	377 241	376 263	369 193	409 284
37	265 183		296 187		289 199	294 151	322 221	325 185	312 232	327 205		348 257	356 222	356 242	349 178	387 262
38	251 169		281 172		274 184	279 139	305 204	308 170	296 214	310 189		329 237	338 204	337 223	331 164	367 241
39	238 156		266 159		260 170	265 129	289 188	292 157	280 198	294 174		313 219	320 189	320 206	314 151	348 223
40	227 145		253 148		247 157	251 119	275 174	278 146	266 183	280 161		297 203	304 175	304 191	298 140	331 207
41	215 134		241 137		235 146		262 162	264 135	253 170	266 150		283 189	290 162	289 177		315 192
42	205 125		229 127		224 136		249 150	252 126	241 158	253 139		269 175	276 151	275 164		300 178
43	196 116		219 118		213 126		238 140	240 117	230 147	242 130		257 163	263 140	263 153		286 166
44	187 108		209 110		204 118		227 131	229 109	220 137	231 121		245 152	251 131	251 143		273 155
45	179 101		199 103		194 110		217 122		210 128	220 113		234 142	240 122	240 133		261 145
46	171 95		191 97		186 103		207 114		201 120	211 106		224 133	230 114	229 125		250 135
47	164 89		183 90		178 96		199 107		192 112	202 99		214 125	220 107	219 117		239 127
48	157 83		175 85		171 90		190 100		184 105	194 93		206 117	211 101	210 110		229 119
49	150 78				164 85		183 94		177 99			197 110		202 103		220 112
50	144 73				157 80		175 89		170 93			189 103		194 97		211 105
51	139 69				151 75		168 83		163 88			182 97		186 91		203 99
52	133 65				145 71		162 79		157 83			175 92		179 86		195 93
53									151 78			168 87				
54									145 74			162 82				
55									140 70			156 77				
56									135 66			151 73				

Joist Designation	30K7	22K10	28K8	28K9	24K10	30K8	30K9	22K11	26K10	28K10	30K10	24K12	30K11	26K12	28K12	30K12
Depth (In.)	30	22	28	28	24	30	30	22	26	28	30	24	30	26	28	30
Approx. Wt. (lbs./ft.)	12.3	12.6	12.7	13.0	13.1	13.2	13.4	13.8	13.8	14.3	15.0	16.0	16.4	16.6	17.1	17.6
Span (ft.) ↓																
22		550 548						550 548								
23		550 518						550 518								
24		550 495			550 544			550 495				550 544				
25		550 474			550 520			550 474				550 520				
26		550 454			550 499			550 454	550 541			550 499		550 541		
27		550 432			550 479			550 432	550 522			550 479		550 522		
28		550 413	550 543	550 543	550 456			550 413	550 501	550 543		550 456		550 501	550 543	
29		550 399	550 522	550 522	550 436			550 399	550 479	550 522		550 436		550 479	550 522	
30	550 543	550 385	550 500	550 500	550 422	550 543	550 543	550 385	550 459	550 500	550 543	550 422	550 543	550 459	550 500	550 543
31	534 508	550 369	550 480	550 480	550 410	550 520	550 520	550 369	550 444	550 480	550 520	550 410	550 520	550 444	550 480	550 520
32	501 461	517 337	515 438	549 463	549 393	549 500	549 500	549 355	549 431	549 463	549 500	549 393	549 500	549 431	549 463	549 500
33	471 420	486 307	484 399	527 432	532 368	520 460	532 468	532 334	532 404	532 435	532 468	532 368	532 468	532 404	532 435	532 468
34	443 384	458 280	456 364	496 395	502 337	490 420	516 441	516 314	516 378	516 410	516 441	516 344	516 441	516 378	516 410	516 441
35	418 351	432 257	430 333	468 361	473 308	462 384	501 415	494 292	501 356	501 389	501 415	501 324	501 415	501 356	501 389	501 415
36	395 323	408 236	406 306	442 332	447 283	436 353	475 383	467 269	486 334	487 366	487 392	487 306	487 392	487 334	487 366	487 392
37	373 297	386 217	384 282	418 305	423 260	413 325	449 352	442 247	460 308	474 344	474 374	474 290	474 374	474 315	474 344	474 374
38	354 274	366 200	364 260	396 282	401 240	391 300	426 325	419 228	436 284	461 325	461 353	461 275	461 353	461 299	461 325	461 353
39	336 253	347 185	346 240	376 260	380 222	371 277	404 300	397 211	413 262	447 306	449 333	449 261	449 333	449 283	449 308	449 333
40	319 234	330 171	328 222	357 241	361 206	353 256	384 278	377 195	393 243	424 284	438 315	438 247	438 315	438 269	438 291	438 315
41	303 217	314 159	312 206	340 224	344 191	335 238	365 258	359 181	374 225	404 263	427 300	427 235	427 300	427 256	427 277	427 300
42	289 202	299 148	297 192	324 208	327 177	320 221	348 240	342 168	356 210	384 245	413 282	417 224	417 284	417 244	417 264	417 284
43	276 188	285 138	284 179	309 194	312 165	305 206	332 223	326 157	339 195	367 228	394 263	406 213	407 270	407 232	407 252	407 270
44	263 176	272 128	271 167	295 181	298 154	291 192	317 208	311 146	324 182	350 212	376 245	387 199	398 258	398 222	398 240	398 258
45	251 164		259 156	282 169	285 144	278 179	303 195		310 170	334 198	359 229	370 185	389 246	389 212	389 229	389 246
46	241 153		248 146	270 158	272 135	266 168	290 182		296 159	320 186	344 214	354 174	380 236	380 203	380 219	380 236
47	230 144		237 136	258 148	261 126	255 157	277 171		284 149	306 174	329 201	339 163	372 226	369 192	372 210	372 226
48	221 135		227 128	247 139	250 118	244 148	266 160		272 140	294 163	315 188	325 153	362 215	353 180	365 201	365 216
49	212 127		218 120	237 130		234 139	255 150		261 131	282 153	303 177		347 202	339 169	357 193	357 207
50	203 119		209 113	228 123		225 130	245 141		250 124	270 144	291 166		333 190	325 159	350 185	350 199
51	195 112		201 106	219 115		216 123	235 133		241 116	260 136	279 157		320 179	313 150	338 175	343 192
52	188 106		193 100	210 109		208 116	226 126		231 110	250 128	268 148		308 169	301 142	325 165	336 184
53	181 100		186 95	203 103		200 109	218 119			240 121	258 140		296 159		313 156	330 177
54	174 94		179 89	195 97		192 103	209 112			232 114	249 132		285 150		301 147	324 170
55	168 89		173 85	188 92		185 98	202 106			223 108	240 125		275 142		290 139	312 161
56	162 84		166 80	181 87		179 92	195 100			215 102	231 118		265 135		280 132	301 153
57	156 80					173 88	188 95				223 112		256 128			290 145
58	151 76					167 83	181 90				215 106		247 121			280 137
59	146 72					161 79	175 86				208 101		239 115			271 130
60	141 69					156 75	169 81				201 96		231 109			262 124

LH-Series

Each joist designation for a particular span in Table 2A–8 has two numbers. The top number gives the *total* safe uniformly distributed load-carrying capacity, in pounds per linear foot, of LH-Series Steel Joists. The weight of *dead* loads, including the joists, must in all cases be deducted to determine the *live* load-carrying capacities of the joists. The approximate *dead* load of the joists may be determined from the weights per linear foot shown in the table.

The bottom number is the *live* load per linear foot of joist, which will produce an approximate deflection of 1/360 of the span. *Live* loads that will produce a deflection of 1/240 of the span may be obtained by multiplying the bottom number by 1.5. In no case shall the *total* load capacity of the joists be exceeded.

The LH-Series load table applies to joists with either parallel chords or standard pitched top chords. When top chords are pitched, the carrying capacities are determined by the nominal depth of the joists at the center of the span. Standard top chord pitch is 1/8 inch per foot. If pitch exceeds this standard, the load table *does not* apply. This load table may be used for parallel chord joists installed to a maximum slope of 1/2 inch per foot.

When holes are required in top or bottom chords, the carrying capacities must be reduced in proportion to reduction of chord areas.

The top chords are considered as being stayed laterally by floor slab or roof deck.

The approximate joist weights per linear foot shown in these tables *do not* include accessories.

DLH-Series

The DLH-Series table (Table 2A–9) gives the *total* safe uniformly distributed load-carrying capacities in pounds per linear foot of span. All loads shown are for roof construction only. The weight of *dead* loads, including the weight of joists, must in all cases be deducted to determine the *live* load-carrying capacity of the joists.

Each joist designation for a particular span has two numbers. The top number gives the *total* safe uniformly distributed load-carrying capacity, in pounds per linear foot, of DLH-Series Steel Joists.

The bottom number is the *live* load per linear foot of joist, which will produce an approximate deflection of 1/360 of the span. Loads that will produce a deflection of 1/240 of the span may be obtained by multiplying the bottom number by 1.5. In no case shall the *total* capacity of the joists be exceeded.

When holes are required in the top or bottom chords, the carrying capacities must be reduced in proportion to reduction of chord areas.

The top chords are considered as being stayed laterally by the roof deck.

The DLH-Series load table applies to joists with either parallel chords or standard pitched top chords. When top chords are pitched, the carrying capacities are determined by the nominal depth of the joists at the center of the span. Standard top chord pitch is 1/8 inch per foot. If pitch exceeds this standard, the load table *does not* apply. This load table may be used for parallel chord joists installed to a maximum slope of 1/2 inch per foot.

The approximate joist weights per linear foot shown in these tables do *not* include accessories.

Table 2A-8
OPEN WEB STEEL JOISTS—LH-SERIES
(Based on a Maximum Allowable Tensile Stress of 30,000 psi)

Joist Designation	Approx. Wt. in Lbs. per Linear Ft. (Joists Only)	Depth in inches	SAFE LOAD* in Lbs. BETWEEN 21—24	CLEAR SPAN IN FEET 25	26	27	28	29	30	31	32	33	34	35	36
18LH02	10	18	12000	468	442	418	391	367	345	324	306	289	273	259	245
				313	284	259	234	212	193	175	160	147	135	124	114
18LH03	11	18	13300	521	493	467	438	409	382	359	337	317	299	283	267
				348	317	289	262	236	213	194	177	161	148	136	124
18LH04	12	18	15500	604	571	535	500	469	440	413	388	365	344	325	308
				403	367	329	296	266	242	219	200	182	167	153	141
18LH05	15	18	17500	684	648	614	581	543	508	476	448	421	397	375	355
				454	414	378	345	311	282	256	233	212	195	179	164
18LH06	15	18	20700	809	749	696	648	605	566	531	499	470	443	418	396
				526	469	419	377	340	307	280	254	232	212	195	180
18LH07	17	18	21500	840	809	780	726	678	635	595	559	526	496	469	444
				553	513	476	428	386	349	317	288	264	241	222	204
18LH08	19	18	22400	876	843	812	784	758	717	680	641	604	571	540	512
				577	534	496	462	427	387	351	320	292	267	246	226
18LH09	21	18	24000	936	901	868	838	810	783	759	713	671	633	598	566
				616	571	527	491	458	418	380	346	316	289	266	245

Joist Designation	Approx. Wt. in Lbs. per Linear Ft. (Joists Only)	Depth in inches	SAFE LOAD* in Lbs. BETWEEN 22—24	25	26	27	28	29	30	31	32	33	34	35	36	37	38	39	40
20LH02	10	20	11300	442	437	431	410	388	365	344	325	307	291	275	262	249	237	225	215
				306	303	298	274	250	228	208	190	174	160	147	136	126	117	108	101
20LH03	11	20	12000	469	463	458	452	434	414	395	372	352	333	316	299	283	269	255	243
				337	333	317	302	280	258	238	218	200	184	169	156	143	133	123	114
20LH04	12	20	14700	574	566	558	528	496	467	440	416	393	372	353	335	318	303	289	275
				428	406	386	352	320	291	265	243	223	205	189	174	161	149	139	129
20LH05	14	20	15800	616	609	602	595	571	544	513	484	458	434	411	390	371	353	336	321
				459	437	416	395	366	337	308	281	258	238	219	202	187	173	161	150
20LH06	15	20	21100	822	791	763	723	679	635	596	560	527	497	469	444	421	399	379	361
				606	561	521	477	427	386	351	320	292	267	246	226	209	192	178	165
20LH07	17	20	22500	878	845	814	786	760	711	667	627	590	556	526	497	471	447	425	404
				647	599	556	518	484	438	398	362	331	303	278	256	236	218	202	187
20LH08	19	20	23200	908	873	842	813	785	760	722	687	654	621	588	558	530	503	479	457
				669	619	575	536	500	468	428	395	365	336	309	285	262	242	225	209
20LH09	21	20	25400	990	953	918	886	856	828	802	778	755	712	673	636	603	572	544	517
				729	675	626	581	542	507	475	437	399	366	336	309	285	264	244	227
20LH10	23	20	27400	1068	1028	991	956	924	894	865	839	814	791	748	707	670	636	604	575
				786	724	673	626	585	545	510	479	448	411	377	346	320	296	274	254

Joist Designation	Approx. Wt. in Lbs. per Linear Ft. (Joists Only)	Depth in inches	SAFE LOAD* in Lbs. BETWEEN 28—32	33	34	35	36	37	38	39	40	41	42	43	44	45	46	47	48
24LH03	11	24	11500	342	339	336	323	307	293	279	267	255	244	234	224	215	207	199	191
				235	226	218	204	188	175	162	152	141	132	124	116	109	102	96	90
24LH04	12	24	14100	419	398	379	360	343	327	312	298	285	273	262	251	241	231	222	214
				288	265	246	227	210	195	182	169	158	148	138	130	122	114	107	101
24LH05	13	24	15100	449	446	440	419	399	380	363	347	331	317	304	291	280	269	258	248
				308	297	285	264	244	226	210	196	182	171	160	150	141	132	124	117
24LH06	16	24	20300	604	579	555	530	504	480	457	437	417	399	381	364	348	334	320	307
				411	382	356	331	306	284	263	245	228	211	197	184	172	161	152	142
24LH07	17	24	22300	665	638	613	588	565	541	516	491	468	446	426	407	389	373	357	343
				452	421	393	367	343	320	297	276	257	239	223	208	195	182	171	161
24LH08	18	24	23800	707	677	649	622	597	572	545	520	497	475	455	435	417	400	384	369
				480	447	416	388	362	338	314	292	272	254	238	222	208	196	184	173
24LH09	21	24	28000	832	808	785	764	731	696	663	632	602	574	548	524	501	480	460	441
				562	530	501	460	424	393	363	337	313	292	272	254	238	223	209	196
24LH10	23	24	29600	882	856	832	809	788	768	737	702	668	637	608	582	556	533	511	490
				596	559	528	500	474	439	406	378	351	326	304	285	266	249	234	220
24LH11	25	24	31200	927	900	875	851	829	807	787	768	734	701	671	642	616	590	567	544
				624	588	555	525	498	472	449	418	388	361	337	315	294	276	259	243

Table 2A-8 (Continued)

Joist Designation	Approx. Wt. in Lbs. per Linear Ft. (Joists Only)	Depth in Inches	SAFE LOAD* in Lbs. BETWEEN	CLEAR SPAN IN FEET															
			33—40	**41**	**42**	**43**	**44**	**45**	**46**	**47**	**48**	**49**	**50**	**51**	**52**	**53**	**54**	**55**	**56**
28LH05	13	28	14000	337 219	323 205	310 192	297 180	286 169	275 159	265 150	255 142	245 133	237 126	228 119	220 113	213 107	206 102	199 97	193 92
28LH06	16	28	18600	448 289	429 270	412 253	395 238	379 223	364 209	350 197	337 186	324 175	313 166	301 156	291 148	281 140	271 133	262 126	253 120
28LH07	17	28	21000	505 326	484 305	464 285	445 267	427 251	410 236	394 222	379 209	365 197	352 186	339 176	327 166	316 158	305 150	295 142	285 135
28LH08	18	28	22500	540 348	517 325	496 305	475 285	456 268	438 252	420 236	403 222	387 209	371 196	357 185	344 175	331 165	319 156	308 148	297 140
28LH09	21	28	27700	667 428	639 400	612 375	586 351	563 329	540 309	519 291	499 274	481 258	463 243	446 228	430 216	415 204	401 193	387 183	374 173
28LH10	23	28	30300	729 466	704 439	679 414	651 388	625 364	600 342	576 322	554 303	533 285	513 269	495 255	477 241	460 228	444 215	429 204	415 193
28LH11	25	28	32500	780 498	762 475	736 448	711 423	682 397	655 373	629 351	605 331	582 312	561 294	540 278	521 263	502 249	485 236	468 223	453 212
28LH12	27	28	35700	857 545	837 520	818 496	800 476	782 454	766 435	737 408	709 383	682 361	656 340	632 321	609 303	587 285	566 270	546 256	527 243
28LH13	30	28	37200	895 569	874 543	854 518	835 495	816 472	799 452	782 433	766 415	751 396	722 373	694 352	668 332	643 314	620 297	598 281	577 266
			38—48	**49**	**50**	**51**	**52**	**53**	**54**	**55**	**56**	**57**	**58**	**59**	**60**	**61**	**62**	**63**	**64**
32LH06	14	32	16700	338 211	326 199	315 189	304 179	294 169	284 161	275 153	266 145	257 138	249 131	242 125	234 119	227 114	220 108	214 104	208 99
32LH07	16	32	18800	379 235	366 223	353 211	341 200	329 189	318 179	308 170	298 162	288 154	279 146	271 140	262 133	254 127	247 121	240 116	233 111
32LH08	17	32	20400	411 255	397 242	383 229	369 216	357 205	345 194	333 184	322 175	312 167	302 159	293 151	284 144	275 137	267 131	259 125	252 120
32LH09	21	32	25600	516 319	498 302	480 285	463 270	447 256	432 243	418 230	404 219	391 208	379 198	367 189	356 180	345 172	335 164	325 157	315 149
32LH10	21	32	28300	571 352	550 332	531 315	512 297	495 282	478 267	462 254	445 240	430 228	416 217	402 206	389 196	376 186	364 178	353 169	342 162
32LH11	24	32	31000	625 385	602 363	580 343	560 325	541 308	522 292	505 277	488 263	473 251	458 239	443 227	429 216	416 206	403 196	390 187	378 179
32LH12	27	32	36400	734 450	712 428	688 406	664 384	641 364	619 345	598 327	578 311	559 295	541 281	524 267	508 255	492 243	477 232	463 221	449 211
32LH13	30	32	40600	817 500	801 480	785 461	771 444	742 420	715 397	690 376	666 354	643 336	621 319	600 304	581 288	562 275	544 262	527 249	511 238
32LH14	33	32	41800	843 515	826 495	810 476	795 458	780 440	766 417	738 395	713 374	688 355	665 337	643 321	622 304	602 290	583 276	564 264	547 251
32LH15	35	32	43200	870 532	853 511	837 492	821 473	805 454	791 438	776 422	763 407	750 393	725 374	701 355	678 338	656 322	635 306	616 292	597 279
			42—56	**57**	**58**	**59**	**60**	**61**	**62**	**63**	**64**	**65**	**66**	**67**	**68**	**69**	**70**	**71**	**72**
36LH07	16	36	16800	292 177	283 168	274 160	266 153	258 146	251 140	244 134	237 128	230 122	224 117	218 112	212 107	207 103	201 99	196 95	191 91
36LH08	18	36	18500	321 194	311 185	302 176	293 168	284 160	276 153	268 146	260 140	253 134	246 128	239 123	233 118	227 113	221 109	215 104	209 100
36LH09	21	36	23700	411 247	398 235	386 224	374 214	363 204	352 195	342 186	333 179	323 171	314 163	306 157	297 150	289 144	282 138	275 133	267 127
36LH10	21	36	26100	454 273	440 260	426 248	413 236	401 225	389 215	378 206	367 197	357 188	347 180	338 173	328 165	320 159	311 152	303 146	295 140
36LH11	23	36	28500	495 297	480 283	465 269	451 257	438 246	425 234	412 224	401 214	389 205	378 196	368 188	358 180	348 173	339 166	330 159	322 153
36LH12	25	36	34100	593 354	575 338	557 322	540 307	523 292	508 279	493 267	478 255	464 243	450 232	437 222	424 213	412 204	400 195	389 187	378 179
36LH13	30	36	40100	697 415	675 395	654 376	634 359	615 342	596 327	579 312	562 298	546 285	531 273	516 262	502 251	488 240	475 231	463 222	451 213
36LH14	36	36	44200	768 456	755 434	729 412	706 392	683 373	661 356	641 339	621 323	602 309	584 295	567 283	551 270	535 259	520 247	505 237	492 228
36LH15	36	36	46600	809 480	795 464	781 448	769 434	744 413	721 394	698 375	677 358	656 342	637 327	618 312	600 299	583 286	567 274	551 263	536 252

Joist Designation	Approx. Wt. in Lbs. per Linear Ft. (Joists Only)	Depth in Inches	SAFE LOAD* in Lbs. BETWEEN	CLEAR SPAN IN FEET															
			47—64	**65**	**66**	**67**	**68**	**69**	**70**	**71**	**72**	**73**	**74**	**75**	**76**	**77**	**78**	**79**	**80**
40LH08	16	40	16600	254 150	247 144	241 138	234 132	228 127	222 122	217 117	211 112	206 108	201 104	196 100	192 97	187 93	183 90	178 86	174 83
40LH09	21	40	21800	332 196	323 188	315 180	306 173	298 166	291 160	283 153	276 147	269 141	263 136	256 131	250 126	244 122	239 118	233 113	228 109
40LH10	21	40	24000	367 216	357 207	347 198	338 190	329 183	321 176	313 169	305 162	297 156	290 150	283 144	276 139	269 134	262 129	255 124	249 119
40LH11	22	40		399 234	388 224	378 215	368 207	358 198	349 190	340 183	332 176	323 169	315 163	308 157	300 151	293 145	286 140	279 135	273 130
40LH12	25	40	31900	486 285	472 273	459 261	447 251	435 241	424 231	413 222	402 213	392 205	382 197	373 189	364 182	355 176	346 169	338 163	330 157
40LH13	30	40	37600	573 334	557 320	542 307	528 295	514 283	500 271	487 260	475 250	463 241	451 231	440 223	429 214	419 207	409 199	399 192	390 185
40LH14	35	40	43000	656 383	638 367	620 351	603 336	587 323	571 309	556 297	542 285	528 273	515 263	502 252	490 243	478 233	466 225	455 216	444 209
40LH15	36	40	48100	734 427	712 408	691 390	671 373	652 357	633 342	616 328	599 315	583 302	567 290	552 279	538 268	524 258	511 248	498 239	486 230
40LH16	42	40	53000	808 469	796 455	784 441	772 428	761 416	751 404	730 387	710 371	691 356	673 342	655 329	638 316	622 304	606 292	591 282	576 271
			52—72	**73**	**74**	**75**	**76**	**77**	**78**	**79**	**80**	**81**	**82**	**83**	**84**	**85**	**86**	**87**	**88**
44LH09	19	44	20000	272 158	265 152	259 146	253 141	247 136	242 131	236 127	231 122	226 118	221 114	216 110	211 106	207 103	202 99	198 96	194 93
44LH10	21	44	22100	300 174	293 168	286 162	279 155	272 150	266 144	260 139	254 134	249 130	243 125	238 121	233 117	228 113	223 110	218 106	214 103
44LH11	22	44	23900	325 188	317 181	310 175	302 168	295 162	289 157	282 151	276 146	269 140	264 136	258 131	252 127	247 123	242 119	236 115	232 111
44LH12	25	44	29600	402 232	393 224	383 215	374 207	365 200	356 192	347 185	339 179	331 172	323 166	315 160	308 155	300 149	293 144	287 139	280 134
44LH13	30	44	35100	477 275	466 265	454 254	444 246	433 236	423 228	413 220	404 212	395 205	386 198	377 191	369 185	361 179	353 173	346 167	338 161
44LH14	31	44	40400	549 315	534 302	520 291	506 279	493 268	481 259	469 249	457 240	446 231	436 223	425 215	415 207	406 200	396 193	387 187	379 181
44LH15	36	44	47000	639 366	623 352	608 339	593 326	579 314	565 303	551 292	537 281	524 271	512 261	500 252	488 243	476 234	466 227	455 219	445 211
44LH16	42	44	54200	737 421	719 405	701 390	684 375	668 362	652 348	637 336	622 324	608 313	594 302	580 291	568 282	555 272	543 263	531 255	520 246
44LH17	47	44	58200	790 450	780 438	769 426	759 415	750 405	732 390	715 376	699 363	683 351	667 338	652 327	638 316	624 305	610 295	597 285	584 276
			56—80	**81**	**82**	**83**	**84**	**85**	**86**	**87**	**88**	**89**	**90**	**91**	**92**	**93**	**94**	**95**	**96**
48LH10	21	48	20000	246 141	241 136	236 132	231 127	226 123	221 119	217 116	212 112	208 108	204 105	200 102	196 99	192 96	188 93	185 90	181 87
48LH11	22	48	21700	266 152	260 147	255 142	249 137	244 133	239 129	234 125	229 120	225 117	220 113	216 110	212 106	208 103	204 100	200 97	196 94
48LH12	25	48	27400	336 191	329 185	322 179	315 173	308 167	301 161	295 156	289 151	283 147	277 142	272 138	266 133	261 129	256 126	251 122	246 118
48LH13	29	48	32800	402 228	393 221	384 213	376 206	368 199	360 193	353 187	345 180	338 175	332 170	325 164	318 159	312 154	306 150	300 145	294 141
48LH14	32	48	38700	475 269	464 260	454 251	444 243	434 234	425 227	416 220	407 212	399 206	390 199	383 193	375 187	367 181	360 176	353 171	346 165
48LH15	36	48	44500	545 308	533 298	521 287	510 278	499 269	488 260	478 252	468 244	458 236	448 228	439 221	430 214	422 208	413 201	405 195	397 189
48LH16	42	48	51300	629 355	615 343	601 331	588 320	576 310	563 299	551 289	540 280	528 271	518 263	507 255	497 247	487 239	477 232	468 225	459 218
48LH17	47	48	57600	706 397	690 383	675 371	660 358	646 346	632 335	619 324	606 314	593 304	581 294	569 285	558 276	547 268	536 260	525 252	515 245

*To solve for safe uniform load between clear spans shown, divide the Safe Load in pounds by clear span in feet plus 0.67 feet. (The added 0.67 feet [eight inches] is necessary to obtain the proper length for which the load tables were developed.)

In no case shall the safe uniform load exceed the uniform load calculated for the minimum clear span listed.

To solve for live loads between clear spans shown, multiply the live load of the shortest clear span shown in the load table by the (shortest clear span plus 0.67 feet)^2, and divide by the (actual clear span plus 0.67 feet)^2. The live load shall not exceed the safe uniform load.

Reproduced by permission of the Steel Joist Institute.

Table 2A-9
OPEN WEB STEEL JOISTS—DLH-SERIES
(Based on a Maximum Allowable Tensile Stress of 30,000 psi)

Joist Designa-tion	Approx. Wt. in Lbs. per Linear Ft. (Joists Only)	Depth in Inches	SAFE LOAD* in Lbs. Between	CLEAR SPAN IN FEET															
			61—88	89	90	91	92	93	94	95	96	97	98	99	100	101	102	103	104
52DLH10	25	52	26700	298 171	291 165	285 159	279 154	273 150	267 145	261 140	256 136	251 132	246 128	241 124	236 120	231 116	227 114	223 110	218 107
52DLH11	26	52	29300	327 187	320 181	313 174	306 169	299 164	293 158	287 153	281 149	275 144	270 140	264 135	259 132	254 128	249 124	244 120	240 117
52DLH12	29	52	32700	365 204	357 197	349 191	342 185	334 179	327 173	320 168	314 163	307 158	301 153	295 149	289 144	284 140	278 135	273 132	268 128
52DLH13	34	52	39700	443 247	433 239	424 231	414 224	406 216	397 209	389 203	381 197	373 191	366 185	358 180	351 174	344 170	338 164	331 159	325 155
52DLH14	39	52	45400	507 276	497 266	486 258	476 249	466 242	457 234	447 227	438 220	430 213	421 207	413 201	405 194	397 189	390 184	382 178	375 173
52DLH15	42	52	51000	569 311	557 301	545 291	533 282	522 272	511 264	500 256	490 247	480 240	470 233	461 226	451 219	443 213	434 207	426 201	418 195
52DLH16	45	52	55000	614 346	601 335	588 324	575 314	563 304	551 294	540 285	528 276	518 267	507 260	497 252	487 245	478 237	468 230	459 224	451 217
52DLH17	52	52	63300	706 395	691 381	676 369	661 357	647 346	634 335	620 324	608 315	595 304	583 296	572 286	560 279	549 270	539 263	528 255	518 247

Joist Designa-tion	Approx. Wt. in Lbs. per Linear Ft. (Joists Only)	Depth in Inches	SAFE LOAD* in Lbs. Between	CLEAR SPAN IN FEET															
			66—96	97	98	99	100	101	102	103	104	105	106	107	108	109	110	111	112
56DLH11	26	56	28100	288 169	283 163	277 158	272 153	267 149	262 145	257 140	253 136	248 133	244 129	239 125	235 122	231 118	227 115	223 113	219 110
56DLH12	30	56	32300	331 184	324 178	318 173	312 168	306 163	300 158	295 153	289 150	284 145	278 141	273 137	268 133	263 130	259 126	254 123	249 119
56DLH13	34	56	39100	401 223	394 216	386 209	379 204	372 197	365 191	358 186	351 181	344 175	338 171	331 166	325 161	319 157	314 152	308 149	303 145
56DLH14	39	56	44200	453 249	444 242	435 234	427 228	419 221	411 214	403 209	396 202	388 196	381 190	375 186	368 181	361 175	355 171	349 167	343 162
56DLH15	42	56	50500	518 281	508 272	498 264	488 256	478 248	469 242	460 234	451 228	443 221	434 215	426 209	419 204	411 198	403 192	396 188	389 182
56DLH16	46	56	54500	559 313	548 304	537 294	526 285	516 277	506 269	496 262	487 254	478 247	469 240	460 233	452 227	444 221	436 214	428 209	420 204
56DLH17	51	56	62800	643 356	630 345	618 335	605 325	594 316	582 306	571 298	560 289	549 281	539 273	529 266	520 258	510 251	501 245	492 238	483 231

Joist Designa-tion	Approx. Wt. in Lbs. per Linear Ft. (Joists Only)	Depth in Inches	SAFE LOAD* in Lbs. Between	CLEAR SPAN IN FEET															
			70—104	105	106	107	108	109	110	111	112	113	114	115	116	117	118	119	120
60DLH12	29	60	31100	295 168	289 163	284 158	279 154	274 150	270 146	265 142	261 138	256 134	252 131	248 128	244 124	240 121	236 118	232 115	228 113
60DLH13	35	60	37800	358 203	351 197	345 191	339 187	333 181	327 176	322 171	316 167	311 163	306 158	301 154	296 151	291 147	286 143	282 139	277 135
60DLH14	40	60	42000	398 216	391 210	383 205	376 199	370 193	363 189	356 183	350 178	344 173	338 170	332 165	327 161	321 156	316 152	310 149	305 145
60DLH15	43	60	49300	467 255	458 248	450 242	442 235	434 228	427 223	419 216	412 210	405 205	398 200	392 194	385 190	379 185	373 180	367 175	361 171
60DLH16	46	60	54200	513 285	504 277	494 269	485 262	476 255	468 247	460 241	451 235	444 228	436 223	428 217	421 211	414 206	407 201	400 196	393 190
60DLH17	52	60	62300	590 324	579 315	569 306	558 298	548 290	538 283	529 275	519 267	510 261	501 254	493 247	484 241	476 235	468 228	460 223	453 217
60DLH18	59	60	71900	681 366	668 357	656 346	644 337	632 327	621 319	610 310	599 303	589 294	578 286	568 279	559 272	549 266	540 259	531 252	522 246

Joist Designation	Approx. Wt. in Lbs. per Linear Ft. (Joists Only)	Depth in Inches	SAFE LOAD* in Lbs. Between	CLEAR SPAN IN FEET															
			75—112	**113**	**114**	**115**	**116**	**117**	**118**	**119**	**120**	**121**	**122**	**123**	**124**	**125**	**126**	**127**	**128**
64DLH12	31	64	30000	264	259	255	251	247	243	239	235	231	228	224	221	218	214	211	208
				153	150	146	142	138	135	132	129	125	122	119	116	114	111	109	106
64DLH13	34	64	36400	321	315	310	305	300	295	291	286	281	277	273	269	264	260	257	253
				186	181	176	171	168	163	159	155	152	148	144	141	137	134	131	128
64DLH14	40	64	41700	367	360	354	349	343	337	332	326	321	316	311	306	301	296	292	287
				199	193	189	184	179	174	171	166	162	158	154	151	147	143	140	136
64DLH15	43	64	47800	421	414	407	400	394	387	381	375	369	363	358	352	347	341	336	331
				234	228	223	217	211	206	201	196	191	187	182	177	173	170	165	161
64DLH16	46	64	53800	474	466	458	450	443	435	428	421	414	407	401	394	388	382	376	370
				262	254	248	242	235	229	224	218	213	208	203	198	193	189	184	180
64DLH17	52	64	62000	546	536	527	518	509	501	492	484	476	468	461	454	446	439	432	426
				298	290	283	275	268	262	255	248	243	237	231	226	220	215	210	205
64DLH18	59	64	71600	630	619	608	598	587	578	568	559	549	540	532	523	515	507	499	491
				337	328	320	311	304	296	288	282	274	267	261	255	249	243	237	232
			80—120	**121**	**122**	**123**	**124**	**125**	**126**	**127**	**128**	**129**	**130**	**131**	**132**	**133**	**134**	**135**	**136**
68DLH13	37	68	35000	288	284	279	275	271	267	263	259	255	252	248	244	241	237	234	231
				171	168	164	159	155	152	149	145	142	138	135	133	130	127	124	121
68DLH14	40	68	40300	332	327	322	317	312	308	303	299	294	290	286	281	277	273	269	266
				184	179	175	171	167	163	159	155	152	148	145	141	138	135	133	130
68DLH15	40	68	45200	372	365	360	354	348	343	337	332	327	322	317	312	308	303	299	294
				206	201	196	191	187	182	178	174	170	166	162	158	155	152	148	145
68DLH16	49	68	53600	441	433	427	420	413	407	400	394	388	382	376	371	365	360	354	349
				242	236	230	225	219	214	209	204	199	195	190	186	182	178	174	171
68DLH17	55	68	60400	497	489	481	474	467	460	453	446	439	433	427	420	414	408	403	397
				275	268	262	256	249	244	238	232	228	222	217	212	208	203	198	194
68DLH18	61	68	69900	575	566	557	549	540	532	524	516	508	501	493	486	479	472	465	459
				311	304	297	289	283	276	269	263	257	251	246	240	234	230	225	219
68DLH19	67	68	80500	662	651	641	631	621	611	601	592	583	574	565	557	548	540	532	525
				353	344	336	328	320	313	305	298	291	285	278	272	266	260	254	248
			84—128	**129**	**130**	**131**	**132**	**133**	**134**	**135**	**136**	**137**	**138**	**139**	**140**	**141**	**142**	**143**	**144**
72DLH14	41	72	39200	303	298	294	290	285	281	277	274	270	266	262	259	255	252	248	245
				171	167	163	159	155	152	149	146	143	139	136	133	131	128	125	123
72DLH15	44	72	44900	347	342	336	331	326	322	317	312	308	303	299	295	291	286	282	279
				191	187	183	178	174	171	167	163	160	156	152	150	147	143	140	137
72DLH16	50	72	51900	401	395	390	384	378	373	368	363	358	353	348	343	338	334	329	325
				225	219	214	209	205	200	196	191	188	183	179	175	171	169	165	161
72DLH17	56	72	58400	451	445	438	432	426	420	414	408	402	397	391	386	381	376	371	366
				256	250	245	239	233	228	224	218	213	209	205	200	196	191	188	184
72DLH18	59	72	68400	528	520	512	505	497	490	483	479	470	463	457	450	444	438	432	426
				289	283	276	270	265	258	252	247	242	236	231	227	222	217	212	209
72DLH19	70	72	80200	619	609	600	591	582	573	565	557	549	541	533	526	518	511	504	497
				328	321	313	306	300	293	286	280	274	268	263	257	251	247	241	236

*To solve for safe uniform load between clear spans shown, divide the Safe Load in pounds by clear span in feet plus 0.67 feet. (The added 0.67 feet [eight inches] is necessary to obtain the proper length for which the load tables were developed.)

In no case shall the safe uniform load exceed the uniform load calculated for the minimum clear span listed.

To solve for live loads between clear spans shown, multiply the live load of the shortest clear span shown in the load table by the (shortest clear span plus 0.67 feet)^2, and divide by the (actual clear span plus 0.67 feet)^2. The live load shall not exceed the safe uniform load.

FORMULAS FOR STRUCTURAL LUMBER BEAMS

Bending Formula:

FORMULA: $M = F_bS$

where:

M = maximum bending moment, inch-pounds
F_b = extreme fiber stress in bending, psi
S = section modulus of beam, in^3

Bending moments for various loading conditions can be found in Figure 2A-3. Values for the section modulus of wood sections are given in Table 2A-10. Extreme fiber stress values for many wood species are given in Tables 2A-14 and 2A-18.

For uniformly loaded beams that are simply supported at each end, the maximum moment follows.

FORMULA:

$$M = \frac{3wL^2}{2}$$

where:

M = moment, inch-pounds
w = load per foot, pounds
L = length of beam, feet

The two formulas can be equated.

FORMULAS:

$$F_bS = \frac{3wL^2}{2}$$

or

$$S = \frac{3wL^2}{2F_b}$$

This formula can be used to determine the beam size for a given span, load condition, and lumber species. For other loading conditions use the formulas given in Figure 2A-3.

Beams must be laterally supported if their ratio of depth to width exceeds 2 to 1. If the ratio is 3 to 1 to 4 to 1, the ends should be held in position. If the ratio is 5 to 1, one edge should be continuously supported. If the ratio is 6 to 1 or more, the beam should be supported at intervals of 8 feet. In addition, lateral bracing should be provided at locations of major point loads and at bearing points of cantilevers.

As the depth of a beam increases, there is a slight decrease in bending strength. For rectangular sawn beams over 12 inches deep the previous formula becomes:

$$M = F_bSC_f$$

where:

C_f (size factor) is computed by the formula:

$$C_f = \left(\frac{12}{d}\right)^{1/9}$$

In this formula, d is the actual depth of the beam in inches.

Deflection Formula

Formulas for deflection of beams under various loading conditions are given in Figure 2A-3. Criteria for maximum allowable deflections are often a matter of judgment, but usually are 1/360 of the span (in inches) for floor and ceiling joists with plaster or drywall ceilings and 1/240 for roof framing where 1 is the length of the beam in inches. To allow for long-term deflection under permanent loading, multiply the calculated deflection by 1.5 for seasoned sawn beams and laminated timber or by 2.0 for unseasoned lumber.

HORIZONTAL SHEAR (RECTANGULAR BEAMS) FORMULA:

$$f_v = \frac{3V}{2bd}$$

where:

f_v = horizontal shear stress, psi
V = total vertical shear, pounds
(**Note:** V = 1/2 total load on a beam simply supported at both ends)
b = actual width of beam, inches
d = actual depth of beam, inches

The calculated shear must not exceed the design value of F_v for the wood species used. F_v values are given in Tables 2A-14 and 2A-18.

Beams notched at their ends increase the horizontal shear stresses. Notches should not exceed one fourth of the beam's depth when located at the ends and should not be located in the middle third of the span. To calculate horizontal shear of an end-notched beam the value of d should be the depth of the beam minus the depth of the notch.

TABLES FOR DESIGN VALUES, JOIST SIZING, AND GRADE SELECTION

Table 2A-10
PROPERTIES OF WOOD SECTIONS

Nominal Size Inches b d	Actual Size Inches b d	Area In.^{2}	AXIS XX S In.^{3}	AXIS XX I In.^{4}	AXIS YY S In.^{3}	AXIS YY I In.^{4}	Board Measure per Lineal Foot	Weight per Lineal Foot Lbs.
2 x 2	1-1/2 x 1-1/2	2.25	.56	.42	.56	.42	.33	.63
3	2-1/2	3.75	1.56	1.95	.94	.70	.50	1.05
4	3-1/2	5.25	3.06	5.36	1.31	.99	.67	1.46
2 x 5	1-1/2 x 4-1/2	6.75	5.06	11.39	1.69	1.27	.83	1.87
6	5-1/2	8.25	7.56	20.80	2.06	1.55	1.00	2.29
8	7-1/4	10.88	13.14	47.63	2.72	2.06	1.33	2.98
10	9-1/4	13.88	21.39	98.93	3.57	2.62	1.67	3.87
12	11-1/4	16.88	31.64	177.98	4.23	3.18	2.00	4.68
14	13-1/4	19.88	43.89	290.77	4.97	3.75	2.33	5.50
3 x 3	2-1/2 x 2-1/2	6.25	2.61	3.25	2.6	3.24	.75	1.73
4	3-1/2	8.75	5.10	8.93	3.64	4.56	1.00	2.43
6	5-1/2	13.75	12.60	34.66	5.73	7.16	1.50	3.82
8	7-1/4	18.13	21.90	79.39	7.56	9.53	2.00	5.03
10	9-1/4	23.13	35.65	164.88	9.63	12.16	2.50	6.44
12	11-1/4	28.13	52.73	296.63	11.75	14.79	3.00	7.83
14	13-1/4	33.13	73.15	484.63	14.91	17.34	3.50	9.18
4 x 4	3-1/2 x 3-1/2	12.25	7.15	12.50	7.14	12.52	1.33	3.39
6	5-1/2	19.25	17.65	48.53	11.23	19.64	2.00	5.34
8	7-1/4	25.38	30.66	111.15	14.82	26.15	2.67	7.05
10	9-1/4	32.38	49.91	230.84	18.97	33.23	3.33	8.98
12	11-1/4	39.38	73.82	415.28	23.03	40.30	4.00	10.91
14	13-1/4	46.38	102.41	678.48	27.07	47.59	4.67	12.90
★ 6 x 6	5-1/2 x 5-1/2	30.25	27.73	76.25	27.73	76.25	3	8.40
8	7-1/2	41.25	51.56	193.35	37.81	103.98	4	11.46
10	9-1/2	52.25	82.73	392.96	47.89	131.71	5	14.51
12	11-1/2	63.25	121.23	697.07	57.98	159.44	6	17.57
14	13-1/2	74.25	167.06	1127.67	68.06	187.17	7	20.62
★ 8 x 8	7-1/2 x 7-1/2	56.25	70.31	263.67	70.31	263.67	5.33	15.62
10	9-1/2	71.25	112.81	535.86	89.06	333.98	6.67	19.79
12	11-1/2	86.25	165.31	950.55	107.81	404.30	8	23.96
14	13-1/2	101.25	227.81	1537.73	126.56	474.61	9.33	28.12
★ 10 x 10	9-1/2 x 9-1/2	90.25	142.89	678.75	142.89	678.75	8.33	25.07
12	11-1/2	109.25	209.39	1204.03	172.98	821.65	10	30.35
14	13-1/2	128.25	288.56	1947.80	203.06	964.25	11.67	35.62
★ 12 x 12	11-1/2 x 11-1/2	132.25	253.48	1457.51	253.48	1457.51	12	36.74
14	13-1/2	155.25	349.31	2357.86	297.56	1710.98	14	43.12
★ 14 x 14	13-1/2 x 13-1/2	182.25	410.06	2767.92	410.06	2767.92	16.33	50.62

★ *Note: Properties are based on minimum dressed green size which is ½ inch off nominal in both b and d dimensions.*

Courtesy: Western Wood Products Association.

Table 2A-11
WESTERN WOOD PRODUCTS: GRADE SELECTOR CHARTS
(Numbers in Parentheses refer to WWPA Grading Rules Section Numbers.)

APPEARANCE GRADES	**SELECTS**	B & BETTER C SELECT D SELECT	(IWP—SUPREME)[1] (IWP—CHOICE)[1] (IWP—QUALITY)[1]	(10.11) (10.12) (10.13)
	FINISH	SUPERIOR PRIME E	(10.51) (10.52) (10.53)	
	PANELING	ANY SELECT OR FINISH GRADE OR SELECTED 2 COMMON FOR KNOTTY PANELING SELECTED 3 COMMON FOR KNOTTY PANELING		 (30.22) (30.23)
	BEVEL OR BUNGALOW SIDING	SUPERIOR PRIME (Refer to WWPA "Wood Siding" Catalog for other siding grades)	(16.11) (16.12)	
GENERAL PURPOSE BOARDS	**COMMON[2] BOARDS (WWPA)**	1 COMMON 2 COMMON 3 COMMON 4 COMMON 5 COMMON	(IWP—COLONIAL)[1] (IWP—STERLING)[1] (IWP—STANDARD)[1] (IWP—UTILITY)[1] (IWP—INDUSTRIAL)[1]	(30.11) (30.12) (30.13) (30.14) (30.15)
	ALTERNATE[2] BOARDS (WCLIB)	SELECT MERCHANTABLE CONSTRUCTION STANDARD UTILITY ECONOMY		(118-a) (118-b) (118-c) (118-d) (118-e)

1. Idaho White Pine carries its own comparable grade designations.
2. Structural applications (sheathing) are regulated by model codes.

Courtesy: Western Wood Products Association.

Table 2A-12
WESTERN WOOD PRODUCTS: DIMENSION/STRESS-RATED FRAMING LUMBER

LIGHT FRAMING 2 x 2 Through 4 x 4	CONSTRUCTION STANDARD UTILITY	(40.11) (40.12) (40.13)	This category for use where high strength values are not required; such as studs, plates, sills, cripples, blocking, etc. (Tables 1, 1a, and 1b).
STUDS 2 x 2 Through 4 x 6 10' and Shorter	STUD	(41.13)	An optional all-purpose grade limited to 10' and shorter. Characteristics affecting strength and stiffness values are limited so that the "Stud" grade is suitable for all stud uses, including load bearing walls. (Table 1 — 2 x 2 through 4 x 4, Table 3 — 2 x 6 through 4 x 6.)
STRUCTURAL LIGHT FRAMING 2 x 2 Through 4 x 4	SELECT STRUCTUAL NO. 1 NO. 2 NO. 3	(42.10) (42.11) (42.12) (42.13)	These grades are designed to fit those engineering applications where higher bending strength ratios are needed in light framing sizes. Typical uses would be for trusses, concrete pier wall forms, etc. (Table 2.)
STRUCTURAL JOISTS & PLANKS 2 x 5 Through 4 x 16	SELECT STRUCTURAL NO. 1 NO. 2 NO. 3	(62.10) (62.11) (62.12) (62.13)	These grades are designed especially to fit in engineering applications for lumber 5" and wider, such as joists, rafters and general framing uses. (Table 3.)

Courtesy: Western Wood Products Association.

Table 2A-13
WESTERN WOOD PRODUCTS: STANDARD LUMBER SIZES/NOMINAL AND DRESSED, BASED ON WWPA RULES

Product	Description	Nominal Size: Thickness In.	Nominal Size: Width In.	Dressed Dimensions: Thicknesses and Widths In. Surfaced Dry	Dressed Dimensions: Thicknesses and Widths In. Surfaced Unseasoned	Dressed Dimensions: Lengths Ft.
DIMENSION	S4S .... Other surface combinations are available. See "Abbreviations" below.	2 3 4	2 3 4 5 6 8 10 12 Over 12	$1\frac{1}{2}$ $2\frac{1}{2}$ $3\frac{1}{2}$ $4\frac{1}{2}$ $5\frac{1}{2}$ $7\frac{1}{4}$ $9\frac{1}{4}$ $11\frac{1}{4}$ Off $\frac{3}{4}$	$1\frac{9}{16}$ $2\frac{9}{16}$ $3\frac{9}{16}$ $4\frac{5}{8}$ $5\frac{5}{8}$ $7\frac{1}{2}$ $9\frac{1}{2}$ $11\frac{1}{2}$ Off $\frac{1}{2}$	6' and longer in multiples of 1'
SCAFFOLD PLANK	Rough Full Sawn or S4S....... (Usually shipped unseasoned)	$1\frac{1}{4}$ & Thicker	8 and Wider	If Dressed refer to "DIMENSION" sizes.		6' and longer in multiples of 1'
TIMBERS	Rough or S4S................ (Shipped unseasoned)	5 and Larger		Thickness In. Width In. $\frac{1}{2}$ Off Nominal (S4S) See 3.20 of WWPA Grading Rules for Rough.		6' and longer in multiples of 1'

Product	Description	Nominal Size: Thickness In.	Nominal Size: Width In.	Dressed Dimensions (Dry): Thickness In.	Dressed Dimensions (Dry): Face Width In.	Dressed Dimensions (Dry): Lengths Ft.
DECKING	2" (Single T&G)	2	5 6 8 10 12	$1\frac{1}{2}$	4 5 $6\frac{3}{4}$ $8\frac{3}{4}$ $10\frac{3}{4}$	6' and longer in multiples of 1'
	3" and 4" (Double T&G)	3 4	6	$2\frac{1}{2}$ $3\frac{1}{2}$	$5\frac{1}{4}$	
FLOORING	(D&M), (S2S & CM)	$\frac{3}{8}$ $\frac{1}{2}$ $\frac{5}{8}$ 1 $1\frac{1}{4}$ $1\frac{1}{2}$	2 3 4 5 6	$\frac{5}{16}$ $\frac{7}{16}$ $\frac{9}{16}$ $\frac{3}{4}$ 1 $1\frac{1}{4}$	$1\frac{1}{8}$ $2\frac{1}{8}$ $3\frac{1}{8}$ $4\frac{1}{8}$ $5\frac{1}{8}$	4' and longer in multiples of 1'
CEILING AND PARTITION	(S2S & CM)	$\frac{3}{8}$ $\frac{1}{2}$ $\frac{5}{8}$ $\frac{3}{4}$	3 4 5 6	$\frac{5}{16}$ $\frac{7}{16}$ $\frac{9}{16}$ $\frac{11}{16}$	$2\frac{1}{8}$ $3\frac{1}{8}$ $4\frac{1}{8}$ $5\frac{1}{8}$	4' and longer in multiples of 1'
FACTORY AND SHOP LUMBER	S2S	1 (4/4) $1\frac{1}{4}$ (5/4) $1\frac{1}{2}$ (6/4) $1\frac{3}{4}$ (7/4) 2 (8/4) $2\frac{1}{2}$ (10/4) 3 (12/4) 4 (16/4)	5 and wider except (4" and wider in 4/4 No. 1 Shop and 4/4 No. 2 Shop)	$\frac{3}{4}$ (4/4) $1\frac{5}{32}$ (5/4) $1\frac{13}{32}$ (6/4) $1\frac{19}{32}$ (7/4) $1\frac{13}{16}$ (8/4) $2\frac{3}{8}$ (10/4) $2\frac{3}{4}$ (12/4) $3\frac{3}{4}$ (16/4)	Usually sold random width	4' and longer in multiples of 1'

ABBREVIATIONS
Abbreviated descriptions appearing in the size table are explained below.
S1S—Surfaced one side.
S2S—Surfaced two sides.
S4S—Surfaced four sides.
S1S1E—Surfaced one side, one edge.
S1S2E—Surfaced one side, two edges.
CM—Center matched.
D&M—Dressed and matched.
T&G—Tongue and grooved.
Rough Full Sawn—Unsurfaced lumber cut to full specified size.

Product	Description	Nominal Size: Thickness In.	Nominal Size: Width In.	Dry Dressed Dimensions: Thickness In.	Dry Dressed Dimensions: Width In.	Dry Dressed Dimensions: Lengths Ft.
SELECTS AND COMMONS	S1S, S2S, S4S, S1S1E, S1S2E .	4/4 5/4 6/4 7/4 8/4 9/4 10/4 11/4 12/4 16/4	2 3 4 5 6 7 8 and wider	3/4 1 5/32 1 13/32 1 19/32 1 13/16 2 3/32 2 3/8 2 9/16 2 3/4 3 3/4	1 1/2 2 1/2 3 1/2 4 1/2 5 1/2 6 1/2 3/4 Off nominal	6' and longer in multiples of 1' except Douglas Fir and Larch Selects shall be 4' and longer with 3% of 4' and 5' permitted.
FINISH AND BOARDS	S1S, S2S, S4S, S1S1E, S1S2E Only these sizes apply to Alternate Board Grades.	3/8 1/2 5/8 3/4 1 1 1/4 1 1/2 1 3/4 2 2 1/2 3 3 1/2 4	2 3 4 5 6 7 8 and wider	5/16 7/16 9/16 5/8 3/4 1 1 1/4 1 3/8 1 1/2 2 2 1/2 3 3 1/2	1 1/2 2 1/2 3 1/2 4 1/2 5 1/2 6 1/2 3/4 Off nominal	3' and longer. In Superior grade, 3% of 3' and 4' and 7% of 5' and 6' are permitted. In Prime Grade, 20% of 3' to 6' is permitted.
RUSTIC AND DROP SIDING	(D&M) . . . . If 3/8" or 1/2" T&G specified, same over-all widths apply. (Shiplapped, 3/8" or 1/2" lap).	1	6 8 10 12	23/32	5 3/8 7 1/8 9 1/8 11 1/8	4' and longer in multiples of 1'
PANELING AND SIDING	T&G or Shiplap	1	6 8 10 12	23/32	5 7/16 7 1/8 9 1/8 11 1/8	4' and longer in multiples of 1'
CEILING AND PARTITION	T&G.	5/8 1	4 6	9/16 23/32	3 3/8 5 3/8	4' and longer in multiples of 1'
BEVEL SIDING	Bevel or Bungalow Siding . . . . . . Western Red Cedar Bevel Siding available in 1/2",5/8",3/4" nominal thickness. Corresponding thick edge is 15/32",9/16" and 3/4". Widths for 8" and wider, 1/2" off nominal.	1/2	4 5 6	15/32 butt,3/16 tip	3 1/2 4 1/2 5 1/2	3' and longer in multiples of 1'
		3/4	8 10 12	3/4 butt,3/16 tip	7 1/4 9 1/4 11 1/4	3' and longer in multiples of 1'
				Surfaced **Dry** / **Green**	**Surfaced** **Dry** / **Green**	
STRESS- RATED BOARDS	S1S, S2S, S4S, S1S1E, S1S2E .	1 1 1/4 1 1/2	2 3 4 5 6 7 8 and Wider	3/4 / 25/32 1 / 1 1/32 1 1/4 / 1 9/32	1 1/2 / 1 9/16 2 1/2 / 2 9/16 3 1/2 / 3 9/16 4 1/2 / 4 5/8 5 1/2 / 5 5/8 6 1/2 / 6 5/8 Off 3/4 / Off 1/2	6' and longer in multiples of 1'

MINIMUM ROUGH SIZES. Thickness and Widths, Dry or Unseasoned, All Lumber
80% of the pieces in a shipment shall be at least 1/8" thicker than the standard surfaced size, the remaining 20% at least 3/32" thicker than the surfaced size. Widths shall be at least 1/8" wider than standard surfaced widths.

When specified to be full sawn, lumber may not be manufactured to a size less than the size specified.

Courtesy: Western Wood Products Association.

Table 2A-14
WESTERN WOOD PRODUCTS DESIGN VALUES

LIGHT FRAMING and STUDS—2 x 2 through 4 x 4

Design Values in Pounds Per Square Inch

Fb, Ft and Fc design values apply only to 4" width of Construction, Standard and Utility grades. See also Tables 1a and 1b.

Species or Group	Grade	Extreme Fiber Stress in Bending "Fb"		Tension Parallel to Grain "Ft"	Hori-zontal Shear "Fv"	Compression		Modulus of Elasticity "E"
		Single	Repetitive			Perpen-dicular "Fc⊥"	Parallel to Grain "Fc"	
DOUGLAS FIR-LARCH	Construction	1050	1200	625	95	625	1150	1,500,000
	Standard	600	675	350	95	625	925	1,500,000
	Utility	275	325	175	95	625	600	1,500,000
	Stud	800	925	475	95	625	600	1,500,000
DOUGLAS FIR SOUTH	Construction	1000	1150	600	90	520	1000	1,100,000
	Standard	550	650	325	90	520	850	1,100,000
	Utility	275	300	150	90	520	550	1,100,000
	Stud	775	875	450	90	520	550	1,100,000
HEM-FIR	Construction	825	975	500	75	405	925	1,200,000
	Standard	475	550	275	75	405	775	1,200,000
	Utility	225	250	125	75	405	500	1,200,000
	Stud	650	725	375	75	405	500	1,200,000
MOUNTAIN HEMLOCK-HEM-FIR	Construction	825	975	500	75	405	900	1,000,000
	Standard	475	550	275	75	405	725	1,000,000
	Utility	225	250	125	75	405	475	1,000,000
	Stud	650	725	375	75	405	475	1,000,000
WESTERN HEMLOCK	Construction	925	1050	550	90	410	1050	1,300,000
	Standard	525	600	300	90	410	850	1,300,000
	Utility	250	275	150	90	410	550	1,300,000
	Stud	700	800	425	90	410	550	1,300,000
ENGELMANN SPRUCE-LODGEPOLE PINE (Engelmann Spruce-Alpine Fir)	Construction	700	800	400	70	320	675	1,000,000
	Standard	375	450	225	70	320	550	1,000,000
	Utility	175	200	100	70	320	375	1,000,000
	Stud	525	600	300	70	320	375	1,000,000
LODGEPOLE PINE	Construction	775	875	450	70	400	800	1,000,000
	Standard	425	500	250	70	400	675	1,000,000
	Utility	200	225	125	70	400	425	1,000,000
	Stud	600	675	350	70	400	425	1,000,000
PONDEROSA PINE-LODGEPOLE PINE	Construction	725	825	425	70	375	775	1,000,000
	Standard	400	450	225	70	375	625	1,000,000
	Utility	200	225	100	70	375	400	1,000,000
	Stud	550	625	325	70	375	400	1,000,000
WESTERN CEDARS	Construction	775	875	450	75	425	850	900,000
	Standard	425	500	250	75	425	700	900,000
	Utility	200	225	125	75	425	450	900,000
	Stud	600	675	350	75	425	450	900,000
WHITE WOODS (Western Woods)	Construction	675	775	400	70	315	675	900,000
	Standard	375	425	225	70	315	550	900,000
	Utility	175	200	100	70	315	375	900,000
	Stud	525	600	300	70	315	375	900,000

STRUCTURAL LIGHT FRAMING — 2 x 2 through 4 x 4
Design Values in Pounds Per Square Inch

Species or Group	Grade	Extreme Fiber Stress in Bending "Fb"		Tension Parallel to Grain "Ft"	Hori-zontal Shear "Fv"	Compression		Modulus of Elasticity "E"
		Single	Repetitive			Perpen-dicular "Fc⊥"	Parallel to Grain "Fc"	
DOUGLAS FIR-LARCH	Select Structural	2100	2400	1200	95	625	1600	1,800,000
	No. 1/Appearance	1750	2050	1050	95	625	1250/1500	1,800,000
	No. 2	1450	1650	850	95	625	1000	1,700,000
	No. 3	800	925	475	95	625	600	1,500,000
DOUGLAS FIR SOUTH	Select Structural	2000	2300	1150	90	520	1400	1,400,000
	No. 1/Appearance	1700	1950	975	90	520	1150/1350	1,400,000
	No. 2	1400	1600	825	90	520	900	1,300,000
	No. 3	775	875	450	90	520	550	1,100,000
HEM-FIR	Select Structural	1650	1900	975	75	405	1300	1,500,000
	No. 1/Appearance	1400	1600	825	75	405	1050/1250	1,500,000
	No. 2	1150	1350	675	75	405	825	1,400,000
	No. 3	650	725	375	75	405	500	1,200,000
MOUNTAIN HEMLOCK-HEM-FIR	Select Structural	1650	1900	975	75	405	1250	1,300,000
	No. 1/Appearance	1400	1600	825	75	405	1000/1200	1,300,000
	No. 2	1150	1350	675	75	405	775	1,100,000
	No. 3	650	725	375	75	405	475	1,000,000
WESTERN HEMLOCK	Select Structural	1800	2100	1050	90	410	1450	1,600,000
	No. 1/Appearance	1550	1800	900	90	410	1150/1350	1,600,000
	No. 2	1300	1450	750	90	410	900	1,400,000
	No. 3	700	800	425	90	410	550	1,300,000
ENGELMANN SPRUCE LODGEPOLE PINE (Engelmann Spruce-Alpine Fir)	Select Structural	1350	1550	800	70	320	950	1,300,000
	No. 1/Appearance	1150	1350	675	70	320	750/900	1,300,000
	No. 2	950	1100	550	70	320	600	1,100,000
	No. 3	525	600	300	70	320	375	1,000,000
LODGEPOLE PINE	Select Structural	1500	1750	875	70	400	1150	1,300,000
	No. 1/Appearance	1300	1500	750	70	400	900/1050	1,300,000
	No. 2	1050	1200	625	70	400	700	1,200,000
	No. 3	600	675	350	70	400	425	1,000,000
PONDEROSA PINE-LODGEPOLE PINE	Select Structural	1400	1650	825	70	375	1050	1,200,000
	No. 1/Appearance	1200	1400	700	70	375	850/1000	1,200,000
	No. 2	1000	1150	575	70	375	675	1,100,000
	No. 3	550	625	325	70	375	400	1,000,000
WESTERN CEDARS	Select Structural	1500	1750	875	75	425	1200	1,100,000
	No. 1/Appearance	1300	1500	750	75	425	950/1100	1,100,000
	No. 2	1050	1200	625	75	425	750	1,000,000
	No. 3	600	675	350	75	425	450	900,000
WHITE WOODS (Western Woods)	Select Structural	1350	1550	775	70	315	950	1,100,000
	No. 1/Appearance	1150	1300	650	70	315	750/900	1,100,000
	No. 2	925	1050	550	70	315	600	1,000,000
	No. 3	525	600	300	70	315	375	900,000

Table 2A-14 (Continued)

STRUCTURAL JOISTS and PLANKS — 2 x 5 through 4 x 16
Design Values in Pounds Per Square Inch

Species or Group	Grade	Extreme Fiber Stress in Bending "Fb"		Tension Parallel to Grain "Ft"[1]	Horizontal Shear "Fv"	Compression		Modulus of Elasticity "E"
		Single	Repetitive			Perpendicular "Fc⊥"	Parallel to Grain "Fc"	
DOUGLAS FIR-LARCH	Select Structural	1800	2050	1200	95	625	1400	1,800,000
	No. 1/Appearance	1500	1750	1000	95	625	1250/1500	1,800,000
	No. 2	1250	1450	650	95	625	1050	1,700,000
	No. 3/STUD	725	850	375	95	625	675	1,500,000
DOUGLAS FIR SOUTH	Select Structural	1700	1950	1150	90	520	1250	1,400,000
	No. 1/Appearance	1450	1650	975	90	520	1150/1350	1,400,000
	No. 2	1200	1350	625	90	520	950	1,300,000
	No. 3/STUD	700	800	350	90	520	600	1,100,000
HEM-FIR	Select Structural	1400	1650	950	75	405	1150	1,500,000
	No. 1/Appearance	1200	1400	800	75	405	1050/1250	1,500,000
	No. 2	1000	1150	525	75	405	875	1,400,000
	No. 3/STUD	575	675	300	75	405	550	1,200,000
MOUNTAIN HEMLOCK-HEM-FIR	Select Structural	1400	1650	950	75	405	1100	1,300,000
	No. 1/Appearance	1200	1400	800	75	405	1000/1200	1,300,000
	No. 2	1000	1150	525	75	405	825	1,100,000
	No. 3/STUD	575	675	300	75	405	525	1,000,000
WESTERN HEMLOCK	Select Structural	1550	1800	1050	90	410	1300	1,600,000
	No. 1/Appearance	1350	1550	900	90	410	1150/1350	1,600,000
	No. 2	1100	1250	575	90	410	975	1,400,000
	No. 3/STUD	650	750	325	90	410	625	1,300,000
ENGELMANN SPRUCE LODGEPOLE PINE (Engelmann Spruce-Alpine Fir)	Select Structural	1200	1350	775	70	320	850	1,300,000
	No. 1/Appearance	1000	1150	675	70	320	750/900	1,300,000
	No. 2	825	950	425	70	320	625	1,100,000
	No. 3/STUD	475	550	250	70	320	400	1,000,000
LODGEPOLE PINE	Select Structural	1300	1500	875	70	400	1000	1,300,000
	No. 1/Appearance	1100	1300	750	70	400	900/1050	1,300,000
	No. 2	925	1050	475	70	400	750	1,200,000
	No. 3/STUD	525	625	275	70	400	475	1,000,000
PONDEROSA PINE-LODGEPOLE PINE	Select Structural	1200	1400	825	70	375	950	1,200,000
	No. 1/Appearance	1050	1200	700	70	375	850/1000	1,200,000
	No. 2	850	975	450	70	375	700	1,100,000
	No. 3/STUD	500	575	250	70	375	450	1,000,000
WESTERN CEDARS	Select Structural	1300	1500	875	75	425	1050	1,100,000
	No. 1/Appearance	1100	1300	750	75	425	950/1100	1,100,000
	No. 2	925	1050	475	75	425	800	1,000,000
	No. 3/STUD	525	625	275	75	425	500	900,000
WHITE WOODS (Western Woods)	Select Structural	1150	1300	775	70	315	850	1,100,000
	No. 1/Appearance	975	1100	650	70	315	750/900	1,100,000
	No. 2	800	925	425	70	315	625	1,000,000
	No. 3/STUD	475	550	250	70	315	400	900,000

1. Tabulated values apply to 5" and 6" widths. For 8" width, use 90% of tabulated tension parallel to grain value for Select Structural and 80% for all other grades. For 10" and wider widths, use 80% of tabulated tension parallel to grain value for Select Structural and 60% for all other grades.

BEAMS and STRINGERS — 5" and Thicker — Width More Than 2" Greater Than Thickness (i.e. 6 x 10)

Design Values in Pounds Per Square Inch

Species or Group	Grade	Extreme Fiber Stress in Bending "Fb"	Tension Parallel to Grain	Horizontal Shear	Compression		Modulus of Elasticity
		Single Members[1]	"Ft"	"Fv"	Perpendicular "Fc⊥"	Parallel to Grain "Fc"	"E"
DOUGLAS FIR-LARCH	Select Structural	1600	950	85	625	1100	1,600,000
	No. 1	1350	675	85	625	925	1,600,000
	No. 2	875	425	85	625	600	1,300,000
DOUGLAS FIR SOUTH	Select Structural	1550	900	85	520	1000	1,200,000
	No. 1	1300	625	85	520	850	1,200,000
	No. 2	825	425	85	520	525	1,000,000
HEM-FIR	Select Structural	1250	725	70	405	925	1,300,000
	No. 1	1050	525	70	405	775	1,300,000
	No. 2	675	325	70	405	475	1,100,000
WESTERN HEMLOCK	Select Structural	1400	825	85	410	1000	1,400,000
	No. 1	1150	575	85	410	850	1,400,000
	No. 2	750	375	85	410	550	1,100,000
ENGELMANN SPRUCE—LODGEPOLE PINE (Engelmann Spruce-Alpine Fir)	Select Structural	1050	625	65	320	675	1,100,000
	No. 1	875	450	65	320	550	1,100,000
	No. 2	575	275	65	320	350	900,000
LODGEPOLE PINE	Select Structural	1150	700	65	400	800	1,100,000
	No. 1	975	500	65	400	675	1,100,000
	No. 2	625	325	65	400	425	900,000
PONDEROSA PINE-LODGEPOLE PINE	Select Structural	1100	650	65	375	750	1,100,000
	No. 1	925	450	65	375	625	1,100,000
	No. 2	600	300	65	375	400	900,000
WESTERN CEDARS	Select Structural	1150	700	70	425	875	1,000,000
	No. 1	975	475	70	425	725	1,000,000
	No. 2	625	325	70	425	475	800,000

1. When the depth of a rectangular sawn lumber bending member exceeds 12 inches, the design value for extreme fiber in bending, Fb, shall be multiplied by the size factor, C_F, as determined by the following formula: $C_F = \left(\frac{12}{d}\right)^{1/9}$

Table 2A-14 (Continued)

POSTS and TIMBERS — 5"x 5" and Larger — Width Not More Than 2" Greater Than Thickness (i.e. 6 x 6, 6 x 8)

Design Values in Pounds Per Square Inch

Species or Group	Grade	Extreme Fiber Stress in Bending "Fb"	Tension Parallel to Grain	Hori-zontal Shear	Compression		Modulus of Elasticity
		Single Members[1]	"Ft"	"Fv"	Perpen-dicular "Fc⊥"	Parallel to Grain "Fc"	"E"
DOUGLAS FIR-LARCH	Select Structural	1500	1000	85	625	1150	1,600,000
	No. 1	1200	825	85	625	1000	1,600,000
	No. 2	700	475	85	625	475	1,300,000
DOUGLAS FIR SOUTH	Select Structural	1400	950	85	520	1050	1,200,000
	No. 1	1150	775	85	520	925	1,200,000
	No. 2	650	400	85	520	425	1,100,000
HEM-FIR	Select Structural	1200	800	70	405	975	1,300,000
	No. 1	950	650	70	405	850	1,300,000
	No. 2	525	350	70	405	375	1,100,000
WESTERN HEMLOCK	Select Structural	1300	875	85	410	1100	1,400,000
	No. 1	1050	700	85	410	950	1,400,000
	No. 2	600	400	85	410	425	1,100,000
ENGELMANN SPRUCE— LODGEPOLE PINE (Engelmann Spruce-Alpine Fir)	Select Structural	975	650	65	320	700	1,100,000
	No. 1	800	525	65	320	625	1,100,000
	No. 2	450	300	65	320	275	900,000
LODGEPOLE PINE	Select Structural	1100	725	65	400	850	1,100,000
	No. 1	875	600	65	400	725	1,100,000
	No. 2	500	350	65	400	350	900,000
PONDEROSA PINE- LODGEPOLE PINE	Select Structural	1000	675	65	375	800	1,100,000
	No. 1	825	550	65	375	700	1,100,000
	No. 2	475	325	65	375	325	900,000
WESTERN CEDARS	Select Structural	1100	725	70	425	925	1,000,000
	No. 1	875	600	70	425	800	1,000,000
	No. 2	500	350	70	425	375	800,000

1. When the depth of a rectangular sawn lumber bending member exceeds 12 inches, the design value for extreme fiber in bending, Fb, shall be multiplied by the size factor, C_F, as determined by the following formula: $C_F = \left(\frac{12}{d}\right)^{1/9}$

Courtesy: Western Wood Products Association.

Table 2A-15
WESTERN WOOD PRODUCTS FLOOR AND CEILING JOIST SPAN TABLES

Floor Joist Span Tables (Feet and Inches)

40# Live Load
10# Dead Load

Design Criteria:
Strength—10 lbs. per sq. ft. dead load plus 40 lbs. per sq. ft. live load.
Deflection—Limited to span in inches divided by 360 for live load only.

L/360

Species or Group	Grade*	Span (feet and inches)											
		2 x 6			2 x 8			2 x 10			2 x 12		
		12" oc	16" oc	24" oc	12" oc	16" oc	24" oc	12" oc	16" oc	24" oc	12" oc	16" oc	24" oc
DOUGLAS FIR-LARCH	2	10-11	9-11	8-6	14-4	13-1	11-3	18-4	16-9	14-5	22-4	20-4	17-6
	3	9-3	8-0	6-6	12-2	10-7	8-8	15-7	13-6	11-0	18-11	16-5	13-5
DOUGLAS FIR SOUTH	2	10-0	9-1	7-11	13-2	12-0	10-6	16-9	15-3	13-4	20-5	18-7	16-3
	3	9-0	7-9	6-4	11-9	10-3	8-4	15-1	13-1	10-8	18-4	15-11	13-0
HEM-FIR	2	10-3	9-4	7-7	13-6	12-3	10-0	17-3	15-8	12-10	20-11	19-1	15-7
	3	8-3	7-2	5-10	10-10	9-5	7-8	13-10	12-0	9-10	16-10	14-7	11-11
MOUNTAIN HEMLOCK-HEM-FIR	2	9-5	8-7	7-6	12-5	11-4	9-11	15-11	14-6	12-8	19-4	17-7	15-4
	3	8-3	7-2	5-10	10-10	9-5	7-8	13-10	12-0	9-10	16-10	14-7	11-11
WESTERN HEMLOCK	2	10-3	9-4	7-11	13-6	12-3	10-6	17-3	15-8	13-4	20-11	19-1	16-3
	3	8-8	7-6	6-1	11-5	9-11	8-1	14-7	12-8	10-4	17-9	15-5	12-7
ENGELMANN SPRUCE LODGEPOLE PINE (Engelmann Spruce-Alpine Fir)	2	9-5	8-7	6-11	12-5	11-2	9-1	15-11	14-3	11-7	19-4	17-3	14-2
	3	7-5	6-5	5-3	9-9	8-6	6-11	12-6	10-10	8-10	15-3	13-2	10-9
LODGEPOLE PINE	2	9-8	8-10	7-3	12-10	11-8	9-7	16-4	14-11	12-3	19-10	18-1	14-11
	3	7-10	6-10	5-7	10-5	9-1	7-5	13-4	11-7	9-5	16-3	14-1	11-6
PONDEROSA PINE-LODGEPOLE PINE	2	9-5	8-7	7-0	12-5	11-4	9-3	15-11	14-5	11-9	19-4	17-7	14-4
	3	7-7	6-6	5-4	10-0	8-8	7-1	12-9	11-1	9-1	15-7	13-6	11-0
WESTERN CEDARS	2	9-2	8-4	7-3	12-0	11-0	9-7	15-4	14-0	12-3	18-9	17-0	14-11
	3	7-10	6-10	5-6	10-5	9-1	7-5	13-4	11-6	9-5	16-3	14-0	11-6
WHITE WOODS (Western Woods)	2	9-2	8-4	6-10	12-0	11-0	9-0	15-5	14-0	11-6	18-9	17-0	14-0
	3	7-5	6-5	5-3	9-9	8-6	6-11	12-6	10-10	8-10	15-3	13-2	10-9

*Spans were computed for commonly marketed grades. Spans for other grades can be computed utilizing the WWPA Span Computer.

Ceiling Joist Span Tables (Feet and Inches)

10# Live Load (No Storage)
5# Dead Load

Design Criteria:
Strength—5 lbs. per sq. ft. dead load plus 10 lbs. per sq. ft. live load. No storage above.
Deflection—Limited to span in inches divided by 240 for live load only.

L/240

Species or Group	Grade*	Span (feet and inches)						
		2 x 4			2 x 6		2 x 8	
		16" oc	24" oc	Grade*	16" oc	24" oc	16" oc	24" oc
DOUGLAS FIR-LARCH	STD	8-3	6-9	2	18-1	15-7	23-10	20-7
				3	14-8	11-11	19-4	15-9
DOUGLAS FIR SOUTH	STD	8-1	6-8	2	16-6	14-5	21-9	19-0
				3	14-2	11-7	18-9	15-3
HEM-FIR	STD	7-6	6-1	2	16-11	13-11	22-4	18-4
				3	13-1	10-8	17-2	14-0
MOUNTAIN HEMLOCK-HEM-FIR	STD	7-8	6-2	2	15-7	13-8	20-7	18-0
				3	13-1	10-8	17-2	14-0
WESTERN HEMLOCK	STD	7-10	6-4	2	16-11	14-6	22-4	19-1
				3	13-9	11-3	18-1	14-10
ENGELMANN SPRUCE-LODGEPOLE PINE (Engelmann Spruce-Alpine Fir)	STD	6-9	5-6	2	15-6	12-8	20-7	16-8
				3	11-9	9-7	15-6	12-8
LODGEPOLE PINE	STD	7-1	5-10	2	16-1	13-3	21-2	17-6
				3	12-7	10-3	16-7	13-6
PONDEROSA PINE-LODGEPOLE PINE	STD	6-9	5-6	2	15-7	12-10	20-7	16-10
				3	12-0	9-10	15-10	12-11
WESTERN CEDARS	STD	7-1	5-10	2	15-1	13-2	20-0	17-6
				3	12-7	10-3	16-7	13-7
WHITE WOODS (Western Woods)	STD	6-7	5-4	2	15-1	12-6	20-2	16-5
				3	11-9	9-8	15-6	12-8

*Spans were computed for commonly marketed grades. Spans for other grades can be computed utilizing the WWPA Span Computer.

Courtesy: Western Wood Products Association.

Table 2A-16
WESTERN WOOD PRODUCTS RAFTER SPAN TABLES

Rafter Span Tables No Finished Ceiling/Light Roof Covering/Roof Pitch 3/12 Or More

Design Criteria: Spans were computed for commonly marketed grades and species. Spans for other grades and species can be computed utilizing the WWPA Span Computer.

Strength: 7 lbs. per sq. ft. dead load plus live load indicated in each heading determines required fiber stress.

Deflection: Based on live load only as indicated in each heading and limited to span in inches divided by 180.

20# Live Load (7 Day) 7# Dead Load — L/180

Species or Group	Grade	2 x 4 16" oc	2 x 4 24" oc	Grade	2 x 6 16" oc	2 x 6 24" oc	2 x 8 16" oc	2 x 8 24" oc
DOUGLAS FIR-LARCH	STD	6-10	5-7	2 3	15-9 12-2	13-0 9-11	20-9 16-1	17-1 13-1
DOUGLAS FIR SOUTH	STD	6-9	5-6	2 3	14-5 11-10	12-7 9-8	19-0 15-7	16-6 12-9
HEM-FIR	STD	6-2	5-1	2 3	14-2 10-10	11-7 8-10	18-8 14-3	15-3 11-8
WHITE WOODS (Western Woods)	STD	5-5	4-5	2 3	12-9 9-9	10-4 7-11	16-9 12-11	13-8 10-6

30# Live Load (Snow) 7# Dead Load — L/180

Species or Group	Grade	2 x 4 16" oc	2 x 4 24" oc	Grade	2 x 6 16" oc	2 x 6 24" oc	2 x 8 16" oc	2 x 8 24" oc
DOUGLAS FIR-LARCH	STD	5-8	4-7	2 3	13-0 10-0	10-7 8-2	17-2 13-2	14-0 10-9
DOUGLAS FIR SOUTH	STD	5-6	4-6	2 3	12-7 9-8	10-3 7-10	16-7 12-9	13-6 10-5
HEM-FIR	STD	5-1	4-2	2 3	11-7 8-11	9-6 7-3	15-3 11-9	12-6 9-7
WHITE WOODS (Western Woods)	STD	4-6	3-8	2 3	10-4 8-0	8-6 6-6	13-9 10-6	11-2 8-6

40# Live Load (7 Day) 7# Dead Load — L/180

Species or Group	Grade	2 x 6 16" oc	2 x 6 24" oc	2 x 8 16" oc	2 x 8 24" oc	2 x 10 16" oc	2 x 10 24" oc
DOUGLAS FIR-LARCH	2 3	11-7 8-10	9-5 7-3	15-3 11-8	12-6 9-6	19-6 14-10	15-11 12-1
DOUGLAS FIR SOUTH	2 3	11-2 8-7	9-1 7-0	14-8 11-4	12-0 9-3	18-9 14-6	15-4 11-9
HEM-FIR	2 3	10-4 7-11	8-5 6-5	13-7 10-4	11-1 8-6	17-3 13-3	14-2 10-10
WHITE WOODS (Western Woods)	2 3	9-3 7-1	7-6 5-9	12-2 11-4	9-11 7-8	15-6 12-0	12-8 9-9

Rafter Span Tables Supporting Drywall Ceiling/Flat Or Sloped With No Attic Space

Design Criteria: Spans were computed for commonly marketed grades and species. Spans for other grades and species can be computed utilizing the WWPA Span Computer.

Strength: 15 pounds per sq. ft. dead load plus live load indicated in each heading determines required fiber stress.

Deflection: Based on live load only as indicated in each heading and limited to span in inches divided by 240.

20# Live Load (7 Day) 15# Dead Load — L/240

Species or Group	Grade	2 x 6		2 x 8		2 x 10	
		16" oc	24" oc	16" oc	24" oc	16" oc	24" oc
DOUGLAS FIR-LARCH	2 3	13-11 10-8	11-5 8-9	18-5 14-1	15-0 11-6	23-6 17-11	19-2 14-8
DOUGLAS FIR SOUTH	2 3	12-11 10-4	11-0 8-6	17-3 13-8	14-6 11-2	22-8 17-6	18-6 14-3
HEM-FIR	2 3	12-5 9-6	10-2 7-9	16-5 12-6	13-4 10-3	20-11 16-0	17-2 13-0
WHITE WOODS (Western Woods)	2 3	11-2 8-7	9-2 7-0	14-9 11-4	12-0 9-3	18-10 14-6	15-4 11-10

30# Live Load (Snow) 15# Dead Load — L/240

Species or Group	Grade	2 x 6		2 x 8		2 x 10	
		16" oc	24" oc	16" oc	24" oc	16" oc	24" oc
DOUGLAS FIR-LARCH	2 3	11-10 9-1	9-7 7-4	15-7 11-11	12-9 9-9	19-11 15-3	16-3 12-5
DOUGLAS FIR SOUTH	2 3	11-4 8-9	9-4 7-2	15-0 11-7	12-3 9-5	19-2 14-9	15-8 12-1
HEM-FIR	2 3	10-6 8-1	8-7 6-7	13-10 10-8	11-4 8-8	17-8 13-7	14-5 11-1
WHITE WOODS (Western Woods)	2 3	9-5 7-3	7-8 5-11	12-6 9-7	10-1 7-10	15-10 12-2	12-11 10-0

40# Live Load (Snow) 15# Dead Load — L/240

Species or Group	Grade	2 x 6		2 x 8		2 x 10	
		16" oc	24" oc	16" oc	24" oc	16" oc	24" oc
DOUGLAS FIR-LARCH	2 3	10-8 8-2	8-8 6-8	14-1 10-9	11-6 8-10	18-0 13-9	14-8 11-3
DOUGLAS FIR SOUTH	2 3	10-4 7-11	8-5 6-6	13-7 10-5	11-1 8-6	17-4 13-4	14-2 10-11
HEM-FIR	2 3	9-6 7-3	7-9 5-11	12-7 9-7	10-3 7-10	16-0 12-3	13-1 10-0
WHITE WOODS (Western Woods)	2 3	8-6 6-7	6-11 5-4	11-3 8-8	9-2 7-1	14-4 11-1	11-8 9-0

Courtesy: Western Wood Products Association.

Table 2A-17
RECOMMENDED GRADES OF SOUTHERN PINE

Use-Item	MINIMUM GRADES RECOMMENDED
FRAMING	
Sills on Foundation Walls or Slab on Ground*	Utility
Sills on Piers* — Built-up	No. 2
Joists, Rafters, Headers	No. 3
Plates, Caps, Bucks	Utility
Studs	Stud Grade
Ribbon Boards, Bracing, Ridge Boards (1'' nominal thickness)	No. 2
Collar Beams	No. 2
Furring Grounds	
1'' nominal thickness	No. 3
Subflooring	No. 3
Wall Sheathing	No. 3
Roof Sheathing, Pitched	No. 3
Roof Decking, Flat	
1'' thick	No. 2 KD
2'' thick	No. 2 KD
Exposed Decking — where appearance is of prime concern	
3'' & 4'' thick	Dense Standard DT&G Deck
Industrial — appearance not prime concern	
3'' & 4'' thick	Commercial DT&G
Stair Stringers or Carriages	No. 1
Cellar and Attic Stair Treads and Risers	No. 1 Dense
Roof Truss Members	
2'' to 4'' thick	
Upper and Lower Chords	No. 2
Other	No. 3
5'' & thicker	No. 2 SR
Heavy Timber Construction	
Beams	
Built-up — 2'' to 4'' thick	No. 2
Solid — over 5'' thick	No. 2 SR
Posts and Columns	
2'' to 4'' thick	No. 2
over 5'' thick	No. 2 SR
SIDING, PANELING, FINISH AND MILLWORK	
Siding	
Bevel, Drop, Rough Sawn	
For rustic applications	No. 2
For appearance applications	C&Btr
Exterior Trim	
Cornice	C Finish or C Ceiling
Mouldings, Drip Cap, Water Table	C Mouldings
Trim, Facia, Corner Boards, Soffits	No. 1
Window and Door	
Frames, Sash, Shutters, Screens	C
Doors, Garage and Warehouse	No. 1
SIDING, PANELING, FINISH AND MILLWORK (cont'd)	
Porch	
Ceiling	No. 2 Ceiling
Flooring**††	No. 2
Stair Treads	No. 1 Dense
Stair Stringers or Carriages & Risers††	No. 1
Columns, Built-up††	No. 2
Newel Posts, Railings, Balustrades††	No. 1
Finished or Top Flooring**††	
Uncovered Floors, Natural, Stained	C Flooring
Covered Floors	No. 2 Flooring
Industrial or Workroom Floors	No. 2 Flooring or End Grain Block Flooring
Interior Finish and Trim	
Stair Treads or Stepping	C
Trim	C
Mouldings	C
Ceiling	C
Partition	C
Closet Lining	No. 2 Ceiling
Shelving	No. 1
Paneling	
For rustic application	No. 2 KD
For appearance application	C
FENCING AND ACCESSORIES††	
Fencing	
Framing, Posts, Boards	No. 3
Pickets	No. 2
Gates, 1-inch thick	No. 2
Gates, 2-inch thick	No. 3
BALCONY, DECKS, PATIOS AND BOARDWALKS††	
Posts and Caps	
2'' to 4'' thick	No. 1 Dense
5'' & thicker	No. 1 SR
Sills	
2'' to 4'' thick	No. 1
5'' & thicker	No. 1 SR
Beams, Stringers	
2'' to 4'' thick	No. 1
5'' & thicker	No. 1 SR
Railings, Rail Posts	No. 1
Steps and Ramps	No. 2
Decking	No. 2 (Specify ''Bark side up'')
Decking, Laminated, on Edge	No. 2
Decking, Radius Edge	Premium Standard (Specify ''Bark side up'')

*For slab on ground where sill on foundation wall or piers is within 18" of ground on inside or 12" on outside, use pressure preservative treated sills. See SFPA publication "Pressure Treated Southern Pine" regarding preservative treatment.

**Flooring may be specified "end-matched" the grade being the same as if plain-end.

††See SFPA brochure "Pressure Treated Southern Pine" regarding preservative treatments and applications.

Source: SOUTHERN FOREST PRODUCTS ASSOCIATION.

Table 2A-18
DESIGN VALUES OF SOUTHERN PINE

GRADE	EXTREME FIBER IN BENDING "F_b"	TENSION PARALLEL TO THE GRAIN "F_t"**	COMPRESSION PARALLEL TO THE GRAIN "F_c"	HORIZONTAL SHEAR "F_v"	COMPRESSION PERPENDICULAR TO THE GRAIN "F_c"	MODULUS OF ELASTICITY "E"
STRUCTURAL LUMBER						
2" to 4" thick KD 15 or MC 15						
Dense Str. 86	2800	1900	2300	165	660	1,900,000
Dense Str. 72	2400	1600	1950	135	660	1,900,000
Dense Str. 65	2150	1450	1750	125	660	1,900,000
2" to 4" thick S. DRY or KD 19						
Dense Str. 86	2600	1750	2000	155	660	1,800,000
Dense Str. 72	2200	1450	1650	130	660	1,800,000
Dense Str. 65	2000	1300	1500	115	660	1,800,000
2½" & thicker over 19% MC						
Dense Str. 86	2100	1400	1300	145	440	1,600,000
Dense Str. 72	1750	1200	1100	120	440	1,600,000
Dense Str. 65	1600	1050	1000	110	440	1,600,000
STRUCTURAL LIGHT FRAMING AND STUDS						
2" to 4" thick 2" to 4" wide KD 15 or MC 15						
Dense Select Structural	2500	1500	2100	105	660	1,900,000
Select Structural	2150	1250	1800	105	565	1,800,000
No. 1 Dense	2150	1250	1700	105	660	1,900,000
No. 1	1850	1050	1450	105	565	1,800,000
No. 2 Dense	1800	1050	1350	95	660	1,700,000
No. 2	1550	900	1150	95	565	1,600,000
No. 3 Dense	1000	575	800	95	660	1,500,000
No. 3	850	500	675	95	565	1,500,000
Stud	850	500	675	95	565	1,500,000
2" to 4" thick 2" to 4" wide S. DRY or KD 19						
Dense Select Structural	2350	1350	1800	100	660	1,800,000
Select Structural	2000	1150	1550	100	565	1,700,000
No. 1 Dense	2000	1150	1450	100	660	1,800,000
No. 1	1700	1000	1250	100	565	1,700,000
No. 2 Dense	1650	975	1150	90	660	1,600,000
No. 2	1400	825	975	90	565	1,600,000
No. 3 Dense	925	525	675	90	660	1,500,000
No. 3	775	450	575	90	565	1,400,000
Stud	775	450	575	90	565	1,400,000
2½" to 4" thick 2½" to 4" wide over 19% MC						
Dense Select Structural	1850	1100	1200	95	440	1,600,000
Select Structural	1600	925	1050	95	375	1,500,000
No. 1 Dense	1600	925	950	95	440	1,600,000
No. 1	1350	800	825	95	375	1,500,000
No. 2 Dense	1350	775	750	85	440	1,400,000
No. 2	1150	675	650	85	375	1,400,000
No. 3 Dense	725	425	450	85	440	1,300,000
No. 3	625	375	400	85	375	1,200,000
Stud	625	375	400	85	375	1,200,000
STRUCTURAL JOISTS & PLANKS						
2" to 4" thick 5" and wider KD 15 or MC 15						
Dense Selected Structural	2200	1450	1850	95	660	1,900,000
Select Structural	1850	1200	1600	95	565	1,800,000
No. 1 Dense	1850	1250	1700	95	660	1,900,000
No. 1	1600	1050	1480	95	565	1,800,000
No. 2 Dense	1550	800	1400	95	660	1,700,000
No. 2	1300	675	1200	95	565	1,600,000
No. 3 Dense	875	450	850	95	660	1,500,000
No. 3	750	400	725	95	565	1,500,000
* Stud	800	400	725	95	565	1,500,000
S. DRY or KD 19						
Dense Select Structural	2050	1300	1600	90	660	1,800,000
Select Structural	1750	1150	1350	90	565	1,700,000

Table 2A-18 (Continued)

GRADE	EXTREME FIBER IN BENDING "F_b"	TENSION PARALLEL TO THE GRAIN "F_t"**	COMPRESSION PARALLEL TO THE GRAIN "F_c"	HORIZONTAL SHEAR "F_v"	COMPRESSION PERPENDICULAR TO THE GRAIN "F_c"	MODULUS OF ELASTICITY "E"
STRUCTURAL JOISTS & PLANKS (cont'd)						
No. 1 Dense	1700	1150	1450	90	660	1,800,000
No. 1	1450	975	1250	90	565	1,700,000
No. 2 Dense	1400	725	1200	90	660	1,600,000
No. 2	1200	625	1000	90	565	1,600,000
No. 3 Dense	825	425	725	90	660	1,500,000
No. 3	700	350	625	90	565	1,400,000
* Stud	725	350	625	90	565	1,400,000
2½" to 4" thick 5" and wider over 19% MC						
Dense Select Structural	1600	1050	1050	85	440	1,600,000
Select Structural	1400	900	900	85	375	1,500,000
No. 1 Dense	1400	925	950	85	440	1,600,000
No. 1	1200	775	825	85	375	1,500,000
No. 2 Dense	1150	600	800	85	440	1,400,000
No. 2	975	500	675	85	375	1,400,000
No. 3 Dense	650	350	475	85	440	1,300,000
No. 3	550	300	425	85	375	1,200,000
* Stud	575	300	425	85	375	1,200,000
LIGHT FRAMING[1] 2" to 4" thick 2" to 4" wide KD 15 or MC 15						
Construction	1100	650	1300	105	565	1,500,000
Standard	625	375	1050	95	565	1,500,000
Utility	275	175	675	95	565	1,500,000
S. DRY or KD 19						
Construction	1000	600	1100	100	565	1,400,000
Standard	575	350	900	90	565	1,400,000
Utility	275	150	575	90	565	1,400,000
3" to 4" thick 3" to 4" wide over 19% MC						
Construction	825	475	725	95	375	1,200,000
Standard	475	275	600	85	375	1,200,000
Utility	200	125	400	85	375	1,200,000
TIMBER 5" and thicker						
No. 1 Dense SR	1550	1050	925	110	440	1,600,000
No. 1 SR	1350	875	775	110	375	1,500,000
No. 2 Dense SR	1250	850	725	95	440	1,400,000
No. 2 SR	1100	725	625	95	375	1,400,000
INDUSTRIAL LUMBER 1" to 4" thick (KD 15 or MC 15)						
Dense Ind. 86 KD	2800	1900	2300	160	660	1,900,000
Industrial 86 KD	2400	1600	1950	160	565	1,800,000
Dense Ind. 72 KD	2400	1600	1950	135	660	1,900,000
Industrial 72 KD	2050	1350	1650	135	565	1,800,000
Dense Ind. 65 KD	2150	1400	1750	125	660	1,900,000
Industrial 65 KD	1850	1200	1500	125	565	1,800,000
1" to 4" thick (S. DRY or KD 19)						
Dense Ind. 86	2600	1750	2000	150	660	1,800,000
Industrial 86	2250	1500	1700	150	565	1,700,000
Dense Ind. 72	2200	1450	1650	130	660	1,800,000
Industrial 72	1900	1250	1400	130	565	1,700,000
Dense Ind. 65	2000	1300	1500	115	660	1,800,000
Industrial 65	1700	1150	1250	115	565	1,700,000
2½" & thicker over 19% MC						
Dense Ind. 86	2100	1400	1300	145	440	1,600,000
Industrial 86	1800	1200	1150	145	375	1,500,000
Dense Ind. 72	1750	1200	1100	120	440	1,600,000
Industrial 72	1500	1000	950	120	375	1,500,000
Dense Ind. 65	1600	1050	1000	110	440	1,600,000
Industrial 65	1350	900	850	110	375	1,500,000

* Applies to 5" and 6" widths only.

** For Select Structural joist & plank grades, use 90% of the tabulated "F_t" values for 8" width and 80% for 10" and wider. For No. 1, No. 2, No. 3 joist & plank grades, use 80% of the tabulated "F_t" values for 8" widths and 60% for 10" and wider.

(1) Recommended in 4" width — stress information on 2" and 3" widths available upon request from Southern Pine Inspection Bureau.

Source: *SOUTHERN FOREST PRODUCTS ASSOCIATION.*

Table 2A-19
SOUTHERN PINE GRADE DESCRIPTIONS

PRODUCT	GRADE	CHARACTER OF GRADE AND TYPICAL USES
FINISH	*B&B	Highest recognized grade of finish. Generally clear although a limited number of pin knots permitted. Finest quality for natural or stain finish.
	C	Excellent for painted or natural finish where requirements are less exacting. Reasonably clear but permits limited number of surface checks, and small tight knots.
	C&Btr	Combination of ''B&B'' and ''C'' grades, satisfies requirements for high quality finish.
	D	Economical, serviceable grade for natural or painted finish.
* PANELING INCLUDING FILLETS	B&B C C&Btr	Similar to above grades with additional restrictions on stain and wane.
	D	Top quality knotty pine paneling for natural or stained finish. Knots are smooth and even with surrounding surface.
	No. 1	Not contained in current SPIB Grading Rules; however, if specified, will be designated and graded as ''D'' grade.
	No. 2	Knotty pine grade somewhat less exacting than ''D'' but suitable for natural or stained finish. Tight-knotted, with knots generally smooth across surface. Minor surface pits and cavities permitted. Wane not permitted on face.
	No. 3	More manufacturing imperfections allowed than in No. 2 but suitable for economical use.
* FLOORING CEILING PARTITION DROP SIDING BEVEL SIDING	B&B C C&Btr D	See Finish grades.
	No. 1	No. 1 Flooring not provided under SPIB Grading Rules as separate grade, but if specified, will be designated and graded as ''D''. No. 1 drop siding is graded as No. 1 boards.
	No. 2	Slightly better than No. 2 boards. High utility value where appearance is not factor.
	No. 3	More manufacturing imperfections allowed than in No. 2 but suitable for economical use.
BOARDS S4S SHIPLAP S2S&CM	No. 1	High quality with good appearance characteristics. Generally sound and tight-knotted. Largest hole permitted is 1/16''. A superior product suitable for wide range of uses including shelving, form and crating lumber.
	No. 2	High quality sheathing material, characterized by tight knots. Generally free of holes.
	No. 3	Good, serviceable sheathing, usable for many applications without waste.
	No. 4	Admit pieces below No. 3 which can be used without waste or contain usable portion at least 24'' in length.
STRUCTURAL LUMBER	*Dense Str. 86 *Dense Str. 72 *Dense Str. 65	Number at end of grade names indicates the percentage stress of clear wood value. (All grades identified as ''Structural'' contain only sound wood free from any form of decay.)

***Caution!** Most mills do not manufacture all products and make all grade separations. Those products and grades manufactured by a relatively few mills are noted with an asterisk.

Table 2A-19 (Continued)

PRODUCT	GRADE	CHARACTER OF GRADE AND TYPICAL USES
DIMENSION **Structural Light Framing** **2" to 4" thick** **2" to 4" wide**	***Select Structural** ***Dense Select Structural**	High quality, relatively free of characteristics with impair strength or stiffness. Recommended for uses where high strength, stiffness and good appearance are required.
	No. 1 **No. 1 Dense**	Provide high strength, recommended for general utility and construction purposes. Good appearance, especially suitable where exposed because of the knot limitations.
	No. 2 **No. 2 Dense**	Although less restricted than No. 1, suitable for all types of construction. Tight knots.
	No. 3 **No. 3 Dense**	Assigned design values meet wide range of design requirements. Recommended for general construction purposes where appearance is not a controlling factor. Many pieces included in this grade would qualify as No. 2 except for single limiting characteristic. Provides high quality and low cost construction.
STUDS **2" to 4" thick** **2" to 6" wide** **10' and Shorter**	**Stud**	Stringent requirements as to straightness, strength and stiffness adapt this grade to all stud uses, including load-bearing walls. Crook restricted in 2" x 4" — 8' to 1/4", with wane restricted to 1/3 of thickness.
Structural Joists & Planks **2" to 4" thick** **5" and wider**	***Select Structural** **Dense Select** ***Structural**	High quality, relatively free of characteristics which impair strength or stiffness. Recommended for uses where high strength, stiffness and good appearance are required.
	No. 1 **No. 1 Dense**	Provide high strength, recommended for general utility and construction purposes. Good appearance, especially suitable where exposed because of the knot limitations.
	No. 2 **No. 2 Dense**	Although less restricted than No. 1, suitable for all types of construction. Tight knots.
	No. 3 **No. 3 Dense**	Assigned stress values meet wide range of design requirements. Recommended for general construction purposes where appearance is not a controlling factor. Many pieces included in this grade would qualify as No. 2 except for single limiting characteristic. Provides high quality and low cost construction.
* **Light Framing** **2" to 4" thick** **2" to 4" wide**	***Construction**	Recommended for general framing purposes. Good appearance, strong and serviceable.
	***Standard**	Recommended for same uses as Construction grade, but allows larger defects.
	***Utility**	Recommended where combination of strength and economy is desired. Excellent for blocking, plates and bracing.
	***Economy**	Usable lengths suitable for bracing, blocking, bulkheading and other utility purposes where strength and appearance not controlling factors.
Appearance Framing **2" to 4" thick** **2" and wider**	***Appearance**	Designed for uses such as exposed-beam roof systems. Combines strength characteristics of No. 1 with appearance of "C&Btr."

***Caution!** Most mills do not manufacture all products and make all grade separations. Those products and grades manufactured by a relatively few mills are noted with an asterisk.

PRODUCT	GRADE	CHARACTER OF GRADE AND TYPICAL USES
TIMBERS 5" x 5" & larger	**No. 1 SR No. 1 Dense SR No. 2 SR No. 2 Dense SR**	No. 1 and No. 2 are similar in appearance to corresponding grades of 2" dimension. Recommended for general construction uses. SR in grade name STRESS RATED.
	Square Edge and Sound No. 1, No. 2, No. 3	Not stress-rated but economical for general construction purposes.
INDUSTRIAL LUMBER	***Dense Industrial 86 *Industrial 86 *Dense Industrial 72 *Industrial 72 *Dense Industrial 65 *Industrial 65**	These classifications cover a variety of industrial grades where resistance to abrasive action, mechanical wear, or ability to absorb shock is desirable on specific use conditions.
* **FACTORY FLOORING AND DECKING**	**Dense Standard**	High quality product, suitable for plank floor where face serves as finish floor. Has a better appearance than No. 1 Dense because of additional restrictions on pitch, knots, pith and wane.
	Select Dense Select	Slightly less restrictive than Dense Standard but more restrictive than No. 1 dimension. Sound, solid appearance.
	Commercial Dense Commercial	Same requirements as corresponding grades of No. 2 dimension.
SCAFFOLD PLANK	***Dense Industrial 72 Scaffold Plank**	Extra high quality. Available in dimensions 2" and thicker and all widths. (For design values see Table 2.)
	Dense Industrial 65 Scaffold Plank	High quality. Available in dimensions 2" and thicker and all widths. (For design values see Table 2.)
STADIUM SEATS	***No. 1 Dense Stadium Grade**	Superior material with one face of pitch and otherwise complying with No. 1 Dense dimension.
	***No. 1 Stadium Grade**	Similar to No. 1 Dense Stadium Grade, except density not required.
RADIUS EDGE DECKING	**Premium**	High quality product, recommended where smallest knots are desired and appearance is of utmost importance, excellent for painting or staining.
	Standard	Slightly less restrictive than premium grade. A very good product to use where appearance is not the major factor. Excellent for painting or staining.

***Caution!** Most mills do not manufacture all products and make all grade separations. Those products and grades manufactured by a relatively few mills are noted with an asterisk.

Source: *SOUTHERN FOREST PRODUCTS ASSOCIATION.*

Table 2A-20

SPAN TABLES FOR SOUTHERN PINE JOISTS AND RAFTERS

FLOOR JOISTS—30 psf live load. Sleeping rooms and attic floors. (Spans shown in light face type are based on a deflection limitation of $l/360$. Spans shown in bold face type are limited by the recommended extreme fiber stress in bending value of the grade and includes a 10 psf dead load.)

Size and Spacing in.	Grade in. o.c.	Dense Sel Str KD and No. 1 Dense KD	Dense Sel Str, Sel Str KD, No. 1 Dense and No. 1 KD	Sel Str, No. 1 and No. 2 Dense KD	No. 2 Dense, No. 2 KD and No. 2	No. 3 Dense KD	No. 3 Dense	No. 3 KD	No. 3
2 x 6	12.0	12-6	12-3	12-0	11-10	**11-3**	**10-11**	**10-5**	**10-1**
	13.7	11-11	11-9	11-6	11-3	**10-6**	**10-3**	**9-9**	**9-5**
	16.0	11-4	11-2	10-11	10-9	**9-9**	**9-6**	**9-0**	**8-9**
	19.2	10-8	10-6	10-4	10-1	**8-11**	**8-8**	**8-3**	**8-0**
	24.0	9-11	9-9	9-7	9-4	**8-0**	**7-9**	**7-4**	**7-1**
2 x 8	12.0	16-6	16-2	15-10	15-7	**14-10**	**14-5**	**13-9**	**13-3**
	13.7	15-9	15-6	15-2	14-11	**13-11**	**13-6**	**12-10**	**12-5**
	16.0	15-0	14-8	14-5	14-2	**12-10**	**12-6**	**11-11**	**11-6**
	19.2	14-1	13-10	13-7	13-4	**11-9**	**11-5**	**10-10**	**10-6**
	24.0	13-1	12-10	12-7	12-4	**10-6**	**10-2**	**9-9**	**9-5**
2 x 10	12.0	21-0	20-8	20-3	19-10	**18-11**	**18-5**	**17-6**	**16-11**
	13.7	20-1	19-9	19-4	19-0	**17-9**	**17-2**	**16-5**	**15-10**
	16.0	19-1	18-9	18-5	18-0	**16-5**	**15-11**	**15-2**	**14-8**
	19.2	18-0	17-8	17-4	17-0	**15-0**	**14-6**	**13-10**	**13-5**
	24.0	16-8	16-5	16-1	15-9[1]	**13-5**	**13-0**	**12-5**	**12-0**
2 x 12	12.0	25-7	25-1	24-8	24-2	**23-0**	**22-4**	**21-4**	**20-7**
	13.7	24-5	24-0	23-7	23-1	**21-7**	**20-11**	**19-11**	**19-3**
	16.0	23-3	22-10	22-5	21-11	**19-11**	**19-4**	**18-6**	**17-10**
	19.2	21-10	21-6	21-1	20-8	**18-3**	**17-8**	**16-10**	**16-3**
	24.0	20-3	19-11	19-7	19-2[1]	**16-3**	**15-10**	**15-1**	**14-7**

1. The span for No. 2 grade, 24 inches o.c. spacing is: 2x10, **15-8**; 2x12, **19-1**.

FLOOR JOISTS—40 psf live load. All rooms except sleeping rooms and attic floors. (Spans shown in light face type are based on a deflection limitation of $l/360$. Spans shown in bold face type are limited by the recommended extreme fiber stress in bending value of the grade and includes a 10 psf dead load.)

Size and Spacing in	Grade / in. o.c.	Dense Sel Str KD and No. 1 Dense KD	Dense Sel Str, Sel Str KD, No. 1 Dense and No. 1 KD	Sel Str, No. 1 and No. 2 Dense KD	No. 2 Dense, No. 2 KD and No. 2	No. 3 Dense KD	No. 3 Dense	No. 3 KD	No. 3
2 x 6	12.0	11-4	11-2	10-11	10-9	**10-1**	**9-9**	**9-4**	**9-0**
	13.7	10-10	10-8	10-6	10-3	**9-5**	**9-2**	**8-9**	**8-5**
	16.0	10-4	10-2	9-11	9-9	**8-9**	**8-6**	**8-1**	**7-10**
	19.2	9-8	9-6	9-4	9-2	**8-0**	**7-9**	**7-4**	**7-1**
	24.0	9-0	8-10	8-8	8-6[1]	**7-1**	**6-11**	**6-7**	**6-4**
2 x 8	12.0	15-0	14-8	14-5	14-2	**13-3**	**12-11**	**12-4**	**11-11**
	13.7	14-4	14-1	13-10	13-6	**12-5**	**12-1**	**11-6**	**11-1**
	16.0	13-7	13-4	13-1	12-10	**11-6**	**11-2**	**10-8**	**10-3**
	19.2	12-10	12-7	12-4	12-1	**10-6**	**10-2**	**9-9**	**9-5**
	24.0	11-11	11-8	11-5	11-3[1]	**9-5**	**9-1**	**8-8**	**8-5**
2 x 10	12.0	19-1	18-9	18-5	18-0	**16-11**	**16-5**	**15-8**	**15-2**
	13.7	18-3	17-11	17-7	17-3	**15-10**	**15-5**	**14-8**	**14-2**
	16.0	17-4	17-0	16-9	16-5	**14-8**	**14-3**	**13-7**	**13-1**
	19.2	16-4	16-0	15-9	15-5	**13-5**	**13-0**	**12-5**	**12-0**
	24.0	15-2	14-11	14-7	14-4[1]	**12-0**	**11-8**	**11-1**	**10-9**
2 x 12	12.0	23-3	22-10	22-5	21-11	**20-7**	**20-0**	**19-1**	**18-5**
	13.7	22-3	21-10	21-5	21-0	**19-3**	**18-9**	**17-10**	**17-3**
	16.0	21-1	20-9	20-4	19-11	**17-10**	**17-4**	**16-6**	**16-0**
	19.2	19-10	19-6	19-2	18-9	**16-3**	**15-10**	**15-1**	**14-7**
	24.0	18-5	18-1	17-9	17-5[1]	**14-7**	**14-2**	**13-6**	**13-0**

1. The span for No. 2 grade, 24 inches o.c. spacing is: 2x5, **6-10**; 2x6, **8-4**; 2x8, **11-0**; 2x10, **14-0**; 2x12, **17-1**.

Table 2A-20 (Continued)

CEILING JOISTS—Drywall Ceiling—10 psf live load. No future sleeping rooms and no attic storage, roof slopes 3 in 12 or less. (Spans shown in light face type are based on a deflection limitation of $l/240$. Spans shown in bold face type are limited by the recommended extreme fiber stress in bending value of the grade and includes a 5 psf dead load.)

Size in.	Grade / Spacing in. o.c.	Dense Sel Str KD and No. 1 Dense KD	Dense Sel Str, Sel Str KD, No. 1 Dense and No. 1 KD	Sel Str, No. 1 and No. 2 Dense KD	No. 2 Dense, No. 2 KD and No. 2	No. 3 Dense KD	No. 3 Dense	No. 3 KD	No. 3	Construction KD	Construction	Standard KD	Standard
2 x 4	12.0	13-2	12-11	12-8	12-5	12-2	**12-0**	**11-6**	**11-0**	12-2	11-10	**9-11**	**9-6**
	13.7	12-7	12-4	12-1	11-10	11-7	**11-3**	**10-9**	**10-4**	11-7	11-4	**9-3**	**8-11**
	16.0	11-11	11-9	11-6	11-3	**10-10**	**10-5**	**10-0**	**9-6**	11-0	10-9	**8-7**	**8-3**
	19.2	11-3	11-0	10-10	10-7	**9-11**	**9-6**	**9-1**	**8-8**	**10-4**	**9-11**	**7-10**	**7-6**
	24.0	10-5	10-3	10-0	9-10	**8-10**	**8-6**	**8-2**	**7-9**	**9-3**	**8-10**	**7-0**	**6-9**
2 x 6	12.0	20-8	20-3	19-11	19-6	**18-5**	**17-10**	**17-0**	**16-5**				
	13.7	19-9	19-5	19-0	18-8	**17-2**	**16-8**	**15-11**	**15-5**				
	16.0	18-9	18-5	18-1	17-8	**15-11**	**15-6**	**14-9**	**14-3**				
	19.2	17-8	17-4	17-0	16-8	**14-6**	**14-1**	**13-6**	**13-0**				
	24.0	16-4	16-1	15-9	15-6[1]	**13-0**	**12-8**	**12-0**	**11-8**				
2 x 8	12.0	27-2	26-9	26-2	25-8	**24-3**	**23-6**	**22-5**	**21-8**				
	13.7	26-0	25-7	25-1	24-7	**22-8**	**22-0**	**21-0**	**20-3**				
	16.0	24-8	24-3	23-10	23-4	**21-0**	**20-5**	**19-5**	**18-9**				
	19.2	23-3	22-10	22-5	21-11	**19-2**	**18-7**	**17-9**	**17-2**				
	24.0	21-7	21-2	20-10	20-5[1]	**17-2**	**16-8**	**15-10**	**15-4**				
2 x 10	12.0	34-8	34-1	33-5	32-9	**30-11**	**30-0**	**28-8**	**27-8**				
	13.7	33-2	32-7	32-0	31-4	**28-11**	**28-1**	**26-9**	**25-11**				
	16.0	31-6	31-0	30-5	29-9	**26-9**	**26-0**	**24-10**	**23-11**				
	19.2	29-8	29-2	28-7	28-0	**24-5**	**23-9**	**22-8**	**21-10**				
	24.0	27-6	27-1	26-6	26-0[1]	**21-10**	**21-3**	**20-3**	**19-7**				

1. The span for No. 2 grade, 24 inches o.c. spacing is: 2x5, **12-6**; 2x6, **15-3**; 2x8, **20-1**; 2x10, **25-7**.

CEILING JOISTS—Drywall Ceiling—20 psf live load. No future sleeping rooms but limited storage available. (Spans shown in light face type are based on a deflection limitation of $l/240$. Spans shown in bold face type are limited by the recommended extreme fiber stress in bending value of the grade and includes a 10 psf dead load.)

Size and Spacing in.	Grade / in. o.c.	Dense Sel Str KD and No. 1 Dense KD	Dense Sel Str, Sel Str KD, No. 1 Dense and No. 1 KD	Sel Str, No. 1 and No. 2 Dense KD	No. 2 Dense	No. 2 KD	No. 2	No. 3 Dense KD	No. 3 Dense	No. 3 KD	No. 3	Con-struc-tion KD	Con-struc-tion	Stand-ard KD	Stand-ard
2 x 4	12.0	10-5	10-3	10-0	9-10	9-10	9-10	**8-10**	**8-6**	**8-2**	**7-9**	**9-3**	**8-10**	**7-0**	**6-9**
	13.7	10-0	9-9	9-7	9-5	9-5	9-5	**8-3**	**8-0**	**7-8**	**7-3**	**8-8**	**8-3**	**6-7**	**6-3**
	16.0	9-6	9-4	9-1	8-11	8-11	8-11	**7-8**	**7-4**	**7-1**	**6-9**	**8-0**	**7-8**	**6-1**	**5-10**
	19.2	8-11	8-9	8-7	8-5	8-5	**8-3**	**7-0**	**6-9**	**6-5**	**6-2**	**7-4**	**7-0**	**5-6**	**5-4**
	24.0	8-3	8-1	8-0	7-10	**7-9**	**7-5**	**6-3**	**6-0**	**5-9**	**5-6**	**6-7**	**6-3**	**4-11**	**4-9**
2 x 6	12.0	16-4	16-1	15-9	15-6	15-6	**15-3**	**13-0**	**12-8**	**12-0**	**11-8**				
	13.7	15-8	15-5	15-1	14-9	14-9	**14-3**	**12-2**	**11-10**	**11-3**	**10-11**				
	16.0	14-11	14-7	14-4	14-1	**13-9**	**13-2**	**11-3**	**10-11**	**10-5**	**10-1**				
	19.2	14-0	13-9	13-6[2]	**13-0**	**12-6**	**12-0**	**10-3**	**10-0**	**9-6**	**9-2**				
	24.0	13-0	12-9[1]	12-6[2,3]	**11-8**	**11-2**	**10-9**	**9-2**	**8-11**	**8-6**	**8-3**				
2 x 8	12.0	21-7	21-2	20-10	20-5	20-5	**20-1**	**17-2**	**16-8**	**15-10**	**15-4**				
	13.7	20-8	20-3	19-11	19-6	19-6	**18-9**	**16-0**	**15-7**	**14-10**	**14-4**				
	16.0	19-7	19-3	18-11	18-6	**18-1**	**17-5**	**14-10**	**14-5**	**13-9**	**13-3**				
	19.2	18-5	18-2	17-9[2]	**17-2**	**16-6**	**15-10**	**13-7**	**13-2**	**12-7**	**12-1**				
	24.0	17-2	16-10[1]	16-6[2,3]	**15-4**	**14-9**	**14-2**	**12-1**	**11-9**	**11-3**	**10-10**				
2 x 10	12.0	27-6	27-1	26-6	26-0	26-0	**25-7**	**21-10**	**21-3**	**20-3**	**19-7**				
	13.7	26-4	25-10	25-5	24-11	24-11	**24-0**	**20-6**	**19-10**	**18-11**	**18-4**				
	16.0	25-0	24-7	24-1	23-8	**23-1**	**22-2**	**18-11**	**18-5**	**17-6**	**16-11**				
	19.2	23-7	23-2	22-8[2]	**21-10**	**21-1**	**20-3**	**17-3**	**16-9**	**16-0**	**15-6**				
	24.0	21-10	21-6[1]	21-1[2,3]	**19-7**	**18-10**	**18-1**	**15-6**	**15-0**	**14-4**	**13-10**				

1. The span for No. 1 KD grade, 24 inches o.c. is: 2x5, **10-2**; 2x6, **12-5**; 2x8, **16-5**; 2x10, **20-11**.

2. The span for No. 1 grade is: 2x5, 19.2 o.c., **10-10**; 24 o.c., **9-8**; 2x6, 19.2 o.c., **13-3**; 24 o.c., **11-10**; 2x8, 19.2 o.c., **17-5**; 24 o.c., **15-7**; 2x10, 19.2 o.c., **22-3**; 24 o.c., **19-11**.

3. The span for No. 2 Dense KD grade, 24 inches o.c. is: 2x5, **10-0**; 2x6, **12-3**; 2x8, **16-2**; 2x10, **20-7**.

Table 2A-20 (Continued)

RAFTERS—Low Slope (3 in 12 or less)—With No Finished Ceiling—20 psf live load. (Spans shown in light face type are based on a deflection limitation of $l/240$. Spans shown in bold face type are limited by the recommended extreme fiber stress in bending value of the grade and includes a 10 psf dead load.)

Size and Spacing (in.)	Grade / in. o.c.	Dense Sel Str KD and No. 1 Dense KD	Dense Sel Str, Sel Str KD, No. 1 Dense and No. 1 KD	Sel Str, No. 2 Dense KD	No. 1	No. 2 Dense	No. 2 KD	No. 2	No. 3 Dense KD	No. 3 Dense	No. 3 KD	No. 3
2 x 6	12.0	16-4	16-1	15-9	15-9	15-6	15-6	**15-3**	**13-0**	**12-8**	**12-0**	**11-8**
	13.7	15-8	15-5	15-1	15-1	14-9	14-9	**14-3**	**12-2**	**11-10**	**11-3**	**10-11**
	16.0	14-11	14-7	14-4	14-4	14-1	**13-9**	**13-2**	**11-3**	**10-11**	**10-5**	**10-1**
	19.2	14-0	13-9	13-6	**13-3**	**13-0**	**12-6**	**12-0**	**10-3**	**10-0**	**9-6**	**9-2**
	24.0	13-0	12-9[1]	12-6[2]	**11-10**	**11-8**	**11-2**	**10-9**	**9-2**	**8-11**	**8-6**	**8-3**
2 x 8	12.0	21-7	21-2	20-10	20-10	20-5	20-5	**20-1**	**17-2**	**16-8**	**15-10**	**15-4**
	13.7	20-8	20-3	19-11	19-11	19-6	19-6	**18-9**	**16-0**	**15-7**	**14-10**	**14-4**
	16.0	19-7	19-3	18-11	18-11	18-6	**18-1**	**17-5**	**14-10**	**14-5**	**13-9**	**13-3**
	19.2	18-5	18-2	17-9	**17-5**	**17-2**	**16-6**	**15-10**	**13-7**	**13-2**	**12-7**	**12-1**
	24.0	17-2	16-10[1]	16-6[2]	**15-7**	**15-4**	**14-9**	**14-2**	**12-1**	**11-9**	**11-3**	**10-10**
2 x 10	12.0	27-6	27-1	26-6	26-6	26-0	26-0	**25-7**	**21-10**	**21-3**	**20-3**	**19-7**
	13.7	26-4	25-10	25-5	25-5	24-11	24-11	**24-0**	**20-6**	**19-10**	**18-11**	**18-4**
	16.0	25-0	24-7	24-1	24-1	23-8	**23-1**	**22-2**	**18-11**	**18-5**	**17-6**	**16-11**
	19.2	23-7	23-2	22-8	**22-3**	**21-10**	**21-1**	**20-3**	**17-3**	**16-9**	**16-0**	**15-6**
	24.0	21-10	21-6[1]	21-1[2]	**19-11**	**19-7**	**18-10**	**18-1**	**15-6**	**15-0**	**14-4**	**13-10**
2 x 12	12.0	33-6	32-11	32-3	32-3	31-8	31-8	**31-2**	**26-7**	**25-10**	**24-8**	**23-9**
	13.7	32-0	31-6	30-10	30-10	30-3	30-3	**29-2**	**24-11**	**24-2**	**23-0**	**22-3**
	16.0	30-5	29-11	29-4	29-4	28-9	**28-1**	**27-0**	**23-0**	**22-4**	**21-4**	**20-7**
	19.2	28-8	28-2	27-7	**27-1**	**26-7**	**25-8**	**24-8**	**21-0**	**20-5**	**19-6**	**18-10**
	24.0	26-7	26-1[1]	25-7[2]	**24-3**	**23-9**	**22-11**	**22-0**	**18-10**	**18-3**	**17-5**	**16-10**

1. The span for No. 1 KD, 24 inches o.c. is: 2x5, **10-2**; 2x6, **12-5**; 2x8, **16-5**; 2x10, **20-11**; 2x12, **25-5**.

2. The span for No. 2 Dense KD, 24 inches o.c. is: 2x5, **10-0**; 2x6, **12-3**; 2x8, **16-2**; 2x10, **20-7**; 2x12, **25-0**.

RAFTERS—Low Slope (3 in 12 or less)—With No Finished Ceiling—30 psf live load. (Spans shown in light face type are based on a deflection limitation of $l/240$. Spans shown in bold face type are limited by the recommended extreme fiber stress in bending value of the grade and includes a 10 psf dead load.)

Size and Spacing in.	Grade / in. o.c.	Dense Sel Str KD and No. 1 Dense KD	Dense Sel Str and Sel Str KD	No. 1 Dense and No. 1 KD	Sel Str	No. 2 Dense KD	No. 1	No. 2 Dense	No. 2 KD	No. 2	No. 3 Dense KD	No. 3 Dense	No. 3 KD	No. 3
2 x 6	12.0	14-4	14-1	14-1	13-9	13-9	13-9	13-6	13-6	**13-2**	**11-3**	**10-11**	**10-5**	**10-1**
	13.7	13-8	13-5	13-5	13-2	13-2	13-2	12-11	**12-10**	**12-4**	**10-6**	**10-3**	**9-9**	**9-5**
	16.0	13-0	12-9	12-9	12-6	12-6	12-6	12-3	**11-11**	**11-5**	**9-9**	**9-6**	**9-0**	**8-9**
	19.2	12-3	12-0	12-0	11-9	11-9	**11-6**	**11-3**	**10-10**	**10-5**	**8-11**	**8-8**	**8-3**	**8-0**
	24.0	11-4	11-2	**11-1**[1]	10-11	**10-7**	**10-3**	**10-1**	**9-8**	**9-4**	**8-0**	**7-9**	**7-4**	**7-1**
2 x 8	12.0	18-10	18-6	18-6	18-2	18-2	18-2	17-10	17-10	**17-5**	**14-10**	**14-5**	**13-9**	**13-3**
	13.7	18-0	17-9	17-9	17-5	17-5	17-5	17-0	**16-11**	**16-3**	**13-11**	**13-6**	**12-10**	**12-5**
	16.0	17-2	16-10	16-10	16-6	16-6	16-6	16-2	**15-8**	**15-1**	**12-10**	**12-6**	**11-11**	**11-6**
	19.2	16-1	15-10	15-10	15-6	15-6	**15-1**	**14-10**	**14-4**	**13-9**	**11-9**	**11-5**	**10-10**	**10-6**
	24.0	15-0	14-8	**14-8**[1]	14-5	**14-0**	**13-6**	**13-3**	**12-10**	**12-4**	**10-6**	**10-2**	**9-9**	**9-5**
2 x 10	12.0	24-1	23-8	23-8	23-2	23-2	23-2	22-9	22-9	**22-2**	**18-11**	**18-5**	**17-6**	**16-11**
	13.7	23-0	22-7	22-7	22-2	22-2	22-2	21-9	**21-7**	**20-9**	**17-9**	**17-2**	**16-5**	**15-10**
	16.0	21-10	21-6	21-6	21-1	21-1	21-1	20-8	**20-0**	**19-3**	**16-5**	**15-11**	**15-2**	**14-8**
	19.2	20-7	20-2	20-2	19-10	19-10	**19-3**	**18-11**	**18-3**	**17-6**	**15-0**	**14-6**	**13-10**	**13-5**
	24.0	19-1	18-9	**18-8**[1]	18-5	**17-10**	**17-3**	**16-11**	**16-4**	**15-8**	**13-5**	**13-0**	**12-5**	**12-0**
2 x 12	12.0	29-3	28-9	28-9	28-2	28-2	28-2	27-8	27-8	**27-0**	**23-0**	**22-4**	**21-4**	**20-7**
	13.7	28-0	27-6	27-6	27-0	27-0	27-0	26-5	**26-3**	**25-3**	**21-7**	**20-11**	**19-11**	**19-3**
	16.0	26-7	26-1	26-1	25-7	25-7	25-7	25-1	**24-4**	**23-4**	**19-11**	**19-4**	**18-6**	**17-10**
	19.2	25-0	24-7	24-7	24-1	24-1	**23-5**	**23-0**	**22-2**	**21-4**	**18-3**	**17-8**	**16-10**	**16-3**
	24.0	23-3	22-10	**22-8**[1]	22-5	**21-8**	**21-0**	**20-7**	**19-10**	**19-1**	**16-3**	**15-10**	**15-1**	**14-7**

1. The span for No. 1 KD, 24 inches o.c. is:
2x5, **8-10**; 2x6, **10-9**; 2x8, **14-2**; 2x10, **18-1**; 2x12, **22-0**.

Table 2A-20 (Continued)

RAFTERS—Low Slope (3 in 12 or less)—With No Finished Ceiling—40 psf live load. (Spans shown in light face type are based on a deflection limitation of $l/240$. Spans shown in bold face type are limited by the recommended extreme fiber stress in bending value of the grade and includes a 10 psf dead load.)

Size and Spacing in.	Grade in. o.c.	Dense Sel Str KD and No. 1 Dense KD	Dense Sel Str and Sel Str KD	No. 1 Dense	No. 1 KD	Sel Str	No. 2 Dense KD	No. 1	No. 2 Dense	No. 2 KD	No. 2	No. 3 Dense KD	No. 3 Dense	No. 3 KD	No. 3
2 x 6	12.0	13-0	12-9	12-9	12-9	12-6	12-6	12-6	12-3	12-3	**11-10**	**10-1**	**9-9**	**9-4**	**9-0**
	13.7	12-5	12-3	12-3	12-3	12-0	12-0	12-0	11-9	**11-6**	**11-0**	**9-5**	**9-2**	**8-9**	**8-5**
	16.0	11-10	11-7	11-7	11-7	11-5	11-5	**11-3**	**11-0**	**10-8**	**10-3**	**8-9**	**8-6**	**8-1**	**7-10**
	19.2	11-1	10-11	10-11	**10-9**	10-8	**10-7**	**10-3**	**10-1**	**9-8**	**9-4**	**8-0**	**7-9**	**7-4**	**7-1**
	24.0	10-4	10-2	**9-11**	**9-8**	9-11	**9-6**	**9-6**	**9-0**	**8-8**	**8-4**	**7-1**	**6-11**	**6-7**	**6-4**
2 x 8	12.0	17-2	16-10	16-10	16-10	16-6	16-6	16-6	16-2	16-2	**15-7**	**13-3**	**12-11**	**12-4**	**11-11**
	13.7	16-5	16-1	16-1	16-1	15-9	15-9	15-9	15-6	**15-2**	**14-7**	**12-5**	**12-1**	**11-6**	**11-1**
	16.0	15-7	15-3	15-3	15-3	15-0	15-0	**14-10**	**14-7**	**14-0**	**13-6**	**11-6**	**11-2**	**10-8**	**10-3**
	19.2	14-8	14-5	14-5	**14-2**	14-1	**14-0**	**13-6**	**13-3**	**12-10**	**12-4**	**10-6**	**10-2**	**9-9**	**9-5**
	24.0	13-7	13-4	**13-1**	**12-8**	13-1	**12-6**	**12-1**	**11-11**	**11-5**	**11-0**	**9-5**	**9-1**	**8-8**	**8-5**
2 x 10	12.0	21-10	21-6	21-6	21-6	21-1	21-1	21-1	20-8	20-8	**19-10**	**16-11**	**16-5**	**15-8**	**15-2**
	13.7	20-11	20-6	20-6	20-6	20-2	20-2	20-2	19-9	**19-4**	**18-7**	**15-10**	**15-5**	**14-8**	**14-2**
	16.0	19-10	19-6	19-6	19-6	19-2	19-2	**18-11**	**18-7**	**17-11**	**17-2**	**14-8**	**14-3**	**13-7**	**13-1**
	19.2	18-8	18-4	18-4	**18-1**	18-0	**17-10**	**17-3**	**16-11**	**16-4**	**15-8**	**13-5**	**13-0**	**12-5**	**12-0**
	24.0	17-4	17-0	**16-8**	**16-2**	16-9	**15-11**	**15-5**	**15-2**	**14-7**	**14-0**	**12-0**	**11-8**	**11-1**	**10-9**
2 x 12	12.0	26-7	26-1	26-1	26-1	25-7	25-7	25-7	25-1	25-1	**24-2**	**20-7**	**20-0**	**19-1**	**18-5**
	13.7	25-5	25-0	25-0	25-0	24-6	24-6	24-6	24-0	**23-6**	**22-7**	**19-3**	**18-9**	**17-10**	**17-3**
	16.0	24-2	23-9	23-9	23-9	23-3	23-3	**23-0**	**22-7**	**21-9**	**20-11**	**17-10**	**17-4**	**16-6**	**16-0**
	19.2	22-9	22-4	22-4	**22-0**	21-11	**21-8**	**21-0**	**20-7**	**19-10**	**19-1**	**16-3**	**15-10**	**15-1**	**14-7**
	24.0	21-1	20-9	**20-4**	**19-8**	20-4	**19-5**	**18-9**	**18-5**	**17-9**	**17-1**	**14-7**	**14-2**	**13-6**	**13-0**

RAFTERS—High Slope (over 3 in 12)—With No Finished Ceiling. 20 psf live load + 15 psf dead load—heavy roofing.
(Spans shown in light face type are based on a deflection limitation of $l/180$. Spans shown in bold face type are limited by the recommended extreme fiber stress in bending value of the grade and includes a 15 psf dead load.)

Size and Spacing in.	Grade / in. o.c.	Dense Sel Str KD	Dense Sel Str	No. 1 Dense KD and Sel Str KD	Sel Str	No. 1 Dense	No. 1 KD	No. 2 Dense KD	No. 1	No. 2 Dense	No. 2 KD	No. 2	No. 3 Dense KD	No. 3 Dense	No. 3 KD	No. 3	Con-struc-tion KD	Con-struc-tion	Stand-ard KD	Stand-ard
2 x 4	12.0	11-6	11-3	11-6[1]	11-1	11-3	11-2	11-0	10-8	10-6	10-2	9-8	8-2	7-11	7-7	7-3	8-7	8-2	6-6	6-3
	13.7	11-0	10-9	11-0[1]	10-7	10-9	10-5	10-3	10-0	9-10	9-6	9-1	7-8	7-4	7-1	6-9	8-0	7-8	6-1	5-10
	16.0	10-5	10-3	10-5[1]	10-0	10-0	9-8	9-6	9-3	9-1	8-10	8-5	7-1	6-10	6-6	6-3	7-5	7-1	5-7	5-5
	19.2	9-10	9-8	9-6	9-2	9-2	8-10	8-8	8-5	8-4	8-1	7-8	6-6	6-3	6-0	5-8	6-9	6-6	5-1	4-11
	24.0	9-1	8-11	8-6	8-2	8-2	7-11	7-9	7-7	7-5	7-3	6-10	5-9	5-7	5-4	5-1	6-1	5-9	4-7	4-5
2 x 6	12.0	18-0	17-8	17-6	17-0	16-9	16-3	16-0	15-6	15-3	14-8	14-1	12-0	11-8	11-2	10-9				
	13.7	17-3	16-11	16-5	15-11	15-8	15-3	15-0	14-6	14-3	13-9	13-2	11-3	10-11	10-5	10-1				
	16.0	16-4	16-0	15-2	14-9	14-6	14-1	13-11	13-5	13-2	12-9	12-3	10-5	10-1	9-8	9-4				
	19.2	15-1	14-7	13-10	13-6	13-3	12-10	12-8	12-3	12-0	11-7	11-2	9-6	9-3	8-10	8-6				
	24.0	13-6	13-0	12-5	12-0	11-10	11-6	11-4	11-0	10-9	10-5	10-0	8-6	8-3	7-11	7-7				
2 x 8	12.0	23-9	23-4	23-1	22-5	22-1	21-6	21-1	20-5	20-1	19-4	18-7	15-10	15-5	14-8	14-2				
	13.7	22-9	22-4	21-7	21-0	20-8	20-1	19-9	19-1	18-9	18-1	17-5	14-10	14-5	13-9	13-3				
	16.0	21-7	21-0	20-0	19-5	19-2	18-7	18-4	17-8	17-5	16-9	16-1	13-9	13-4	12-9	12-4				
	19.2	19-11	19-2	18-3	17-9	17-6	17-0	16-8	16-2	15-10	15-4	14-8	12-7	12-2	11-7	11-3				
	24.0	17-10	17-2	16-4	15-10	15-8	15-2	14-11	14-5	14-2	13-8	13-2	11-3	10-11	10-5	10-0				
2 x 10	12.0	30-4	29-9	29-5	28-8	28-3	27-5	26-11	26-1	25-7	24-8	23-9	20-3	19-8	18-9	18-1				
	13.7	29-0	28-6	27-7	26-9	26-5	25-7	25-3	24-5	24-0	23-1	22-2	18-11	18-5	17-6	16-11				
	16.0	27-6	26-10	25-6	24-10	24-5	23-9	23-4	22-7	22-2	21-4	20-6	17-6	17-0	16-3	15-8				
	19.2	25-5	24-6	23-3	22-8	22-4	21-8	21-4	20-7	20-3	19-6	18-9	16-0	15-7	14-10	14-4				
	24.0	22-8	21-11	20-10	20-3	19-11	19-4	19-1	18-5	18-1	17-5	16-9	14-4	13-11	13-3	12-10				

1. The span for Select Structural KD, 2x4, 12 inches o.c. is 11-3; 13.7 inches o.c., 10-9, and 16 inches o.c., 10-3.

Table 2A-20 (Continued)

RAFTERS—High Slope (over 3 in 12)—With No Finished Ceiling. 30 psf live load + 15 psf dead load—heavy roofing.
(Spans shown in light face type are based on a deflection limitation of $l/180$. Spans shown in bold face type are limited by the recommended extreme fiber stress in bending value of the grade and includes a 15 psf dead load.)

Size and Spacing in.	Grade in. o.c.	Dense Sel Str KD	Dense Sel Str	No. 1 Dense KD and Sel Str KD	Sel Str	No. 1 Dense	No. 1 KD	No. 2 Dense KD	No. 1	No. 2 Dense	No. 2 KD	No. 2	No. 3 Dense KD	No. 3 Dense	No. 3 KD	No. 3	Construction KD	Construction	Standard KD	Standard
2 x 4	12.0	10-0	9-10	10-0[1]	9-8	9-10	9-10	9-8	9-5	9-3	9-0	8-7	7-3	6-11	6-8	6-4	7-7	7-3	5-9	5-6
	13.7	9-7	9-5	9-7[1]	9-3	9-5	9-2	9-1	8-10	8-8	8-5	8-0	6-9	6-6	6-3	5-11	7-1	6-9	5-4	5-1
	16.0	9-1	8-11	9-1[1]	8-9	8-10	8-6	8-5	8-2	8-0	7-9	7-5	6-3	6-0	5-9	5-6	6-7	6-3	4-11	4-9
	19.2	8-7	8-5	8-4	8-1	8-1	7-9	7-8	7-5	7-4	7-1	6-9	5-9	5-6	5-3	5-0	6-0	5-9	4-6	4-4
	24.0	7-11	7-10	7-6	7-3	7-3	6-11	6-10	6-8	6-7	6-4	6-1	5-1	4-11	4-9	4-6	5-4	5-1	4-0	3-10
2 x 6	12.0	15-9	15-6	15-5	15-0	14-10	14-4	14-2	13-8	13-5	12-11	12-5	10-7	10-4	9-10	9-6				
	13.7	15-1	14-9	14-5	14-1	13-10	13-5	13-3	12-9	12-7	12-1	11-8	9-11	9-8	9-2	8-11				
	16.0	14-4	14-1	13-4	13-0	12-10	12-5	12-3	11-10	11-8	11-2	10-9	9-2	8-11	8-6	8-3				
	19.2	13-4	12-10	12-2	11-10	11-8	11-4	11-2	10-10	10-7	10-3	9-10	8-5	8-2	7-9	7-6				
	24.0	11-11	11-6	10-11	10-7	10-6	10-2	10-0	9-8	9-6	9-2	8-10	7-6	7-3	6-11	6-9				
2 x 8	12.0	20-9	20-5	20-4	19-10	19-6	18-11	18-8	18-0	17-8	17-1	16-5	14-0	13-7	12-11	12-6				
	13.7	19-10	19-6	19-0	18-6	18-3	17-8	17-5	16-10	16-7	16-0	15-4	13-1	12-9	12-1	11-9				
	16.0	18-10	18-6	17-7	17-2	16-11	16-5	16-2	15-7	15-4	14-9	14-2	12-1	11-9	11-3	10-10				
	19.2	17-7	16-11	16-1	15-8	15-5	15-0	14-9	14-3	14-0	13-6	12-11	11-1	10-9	10-3	9-11				
	24.0	15-8	15-2	14-5	14-0	13-10	13-5	13-2	12-9	12-6	12-1	11-7	9-11	9-7	9-2	8-10				
2 x 10	12.0	26-6	26-0	26-0	25-3	24-11	24-2	23-9	23-0	22-7	21-9	20-11	17-10	17-4	16-6	16-0				
	13.7	25-4	24-11	24-4	23-8	23-3	22-7	22-3	21-6	21-2	20-4	19-7	16-8	16-3	15-6	14-11				
	16.0	24-1	23-8	22-6	21-10	21-7	20-11	20-7	19-11	19-7	18-10	18-1	15-6	15-0	14-4	13-10				
	19.2	22-5	21-7	20-6	20-0	19-8	19-1	18-9	18-2	17-10	17-2	16-6	14-1	13-8	13-1	12-8				
	24.0	20-0	19-4	18-4	17-10	17-7	17-1	16-10	16-3	16-0	15-5	14-9	12-8	12-3	11-8	11-4				

1. The span for Select Structural KD, 2x4, 12 inches o.c. is 9-10; 13.7 inches o.c., 9-5, and 16 inches o.c., 8-11.

RAFTERS—High Slope (over 3 in 12)—With No Finished Ceiling—40 psf live load + 7 psf dead load—light roofing. (Spans shown in light face type are based on a deflection limitation of $l/180$. Spans shown in bold face type are limited by the recommended extreme fiber stress in bending value of the grade and includes a 7 psf dead load.)

Size (in.)	Spacing (in. o.c.)	Dense Sel Str KD	Sel Str KD and Dense Sel Str	No. 1 Dense KD	Sel Str	No. 1 Dense	No. 1 KD	No. 2 Dense KD	No. 1	No. 2 Dense	No. 2 KD	No. 2	No. 3 Dense KD	No. 3 Dense	No. 3 KD	No. 3	Construction KD	Construction	Standard KD	Standard
2 x 4	12.0	9-1	8-11	9-1	8-9	8-11	8-11	8-9	8-9	8-7	8-7	8-4	7-1	6-10	6-6	6-3	7-5	7-1	5-7	5-4
	13.7	8-8	8-7	8-8	8-5	8-7	8-7	8-5	8-5	8-3	8-3	7-10	6-7	6-4	6-1	5-10	6-11	6-7	5-3	5-0
	16.0	8-3	8-1	8-3	8-0	8-1	8-1	8-0	8-0	7-10	7-7	7-3	6-1	5-11	5-8	5-5	6-5	6-1	4-10	4-8
	19.2	7-9	7-8	7-9	7-6	7-8	7-7	7-6	7-3	7-2	6-11	6-7	5-7	5-4	5-2	4-11	5-10	5-7	4-5	4-3
	24.0	7-3	7-1	7-3	7-0	7-1	6-10	6-8	6-6	6-5	6-3	5-11	5-0	4-10	4-7	4-5	5-3	5-0	3-11	3-9
2 x 6	12.0	14-4	14-1	14-4	13-9	14-1	14-1	13-9	13-4	13-2	12-8	12-2	10-5	10-1	9-7	9-4				
	13.7	13-8	13-5	13-8	13-2	13-5	13-2	12-11	12-6	12-4	11-10	11-5	9-9	9-5	9-0	8-8				
	16.0	13-0	12-9	13-0	12-6	12-6	12-2	12-0	11-7	11-5	11-0	10-6	9-0	8-9	8-4	8-1				
	19.2	12-3	12-0[1]	11-11	11-7	11-5	11-1	10-11	10-7	10-5	10-10	9-7	8-3	8-0	7-7	7-4				
	24.0	11-4	11-2[1]	10-8	10-5	10-3	9-11	9-9	9-5	9-4	8-11	8-7	7-4	7-2	6-10	6-7				
2 x 8	12.0	18-10	18-6	18-10	18-2	18-6	18-6	18-2	17-8	17-4	16-8	16-0	13-8	13-4	12-8	12-3				
	13.7	18-0	17-9	18-0	17-5	17-9	17-4	17-1	16-6	16-2	15-7	15-0	12-10	12-5	11-10	11-6				
	16.0	17-2	16-10	17-2	16-6	16-6	16-0	15-9	15-3	15-0	14-5	13-11	11-10	11-6	11-0	10-7				
	19.2	16-1	15-10[1]	15-9	15-4	15-1	14-8	14-5	13-11	13-8	13-2	12-8	10-10	10-6	10-0	9-8				
	24.0	15-0	14-8[1]	14-1	13-8	13-6	13-1	12-11	12-6	12-3	11-10	11-4	9-8	9-5	9-0	8-8				
2 x 10	12.0	24-1	23-8	24-1	23-2	23-8	23-8	23-2	22-6	22-1	21-4	20-6	17-6	17-0	16-2	15-8				
	13.7	23-0	22-7	23-0	22-2	22-7	22-1	21-9	21-1	20-8	19-11	19-2	16-4	15-10	15-2	14-7				
	16.0	21-10	21-6	21-10	21-1	21-1	20-6	20-2	19-6	19-2	18-5	17-9	15-2	14-8	14-0	13-6				
	19.2	20-7	20-2[1]	20-1	19-6	19-3	18-8	18-5	17-9	17-6	16-10	16-2	13-10	13-5	12-9	12-4				
	24.0	19-1	18-9[1]	18-0	17-6	17-3	16-8	16-5	15-11	15-8	15-1	14-6	12-4	12-0	11-5	11-1				

1. The span for Select Structural KD is: 2x5, 19.2 inches o.c., 9-9; 24 inches o.c., 8-9; 2x6, 19.2 inches o.c., 11-11; 24 inches o.c., 10-8;

Table 2A-20 (Continued)

RAFTERS—High Slope (over 3 in 12)—With No Finished Ceiling—20 psf live load + 7 psf dead load—light roofing. (Spans shown in light face type are based on a deflection limitation of $l/180$. Spans shown in bold face type are limited by the recommended extreme fiber stress in bending value of the grade and includes a 7 psf dead load.)

Size and Spacing (Grade) in.	in. o.c.	Dense Sel Str KD	Sel Str KD and Dense Sel Str	No. 1 Dense KD	Sel Str	No. 1 Dense	No. 1 KD	No. 2 Dense KD	No. 1	No. 2 Dense	No. 2 KD	No. 2	No. 3 Dense KD	No. 3 Dense	No. 3 KD	No. 3	Con-struc-tion KD	Con-struc-tion	Stand-ard KD	Stand-ard
	12.0	11-6	11-3	11-6	11-1	11-3	11-3	11-1	11-1	10-10	10-10	10-10	**9-4**	**9-0**	**8-7**	**8-3**	**9-9**	**9-4**	**7-4**	**7-1**
	13.7	11-0	10-9	11-0	10-7	10-9	10-9	10-7	10-7	10-4	10-4	**10-4**	**8-9**	**8-5**	**8-1**	**7-8**	**9-2**	**8-9**	**6-11**	**6-7**
2 x 4	16.0	10-5	10-3	10-5	10-0	10-3	10-3	10-0	10-0	9-10	9-10	**9-7**	**8-1**	**7-9**	**7-5**	**7-1**	**8-6**	**8-1**	**6-5**	**6-1**
	19.2	9-10	9-8	9-10	9-5	9-8	9-8	9-5	9-5	9-3	**9-2**	**8-9**	**7-4**	**7-1**	**6-10**	**6-6**	**7-9**	**7-4**	**5-10**	**5-7**
	24.0	9-1	8-11	9-1	8-9	8-11	8-11	8-9	**8-7**	**8-6**	**8-3**	**7-10**	**6-7**	**6-4**	**6-1**	**5-10**	**6-11**	**6-7**	**5-3**	**5-0**
	12.0	18-0	17-8	18-0	17-4	17-8	17-8	17-4	17-4	17-0	**16-8**	**16-1**	**13-8**	**13-4**	**12-8**	**12-3**				
	13.7	17-3	16-11	17-3	16-7	16-11	16-11	16-7	**16-6**	**16-3**	**15-8**	**15-0**	**12-10**	**12-5**	**11-10**	**11-6**				
2 x 6	16.0	16-4	16-1	16-4	15-9	16-1	**16-1**	15-9	**15-3**	**15-0**	**14-6**	**13-11**	**11-10**	**11-6**	**11-0**	**10-7**				
	19.2	15-5	15-2	15-5	14-10	**15-1**	**14-8**	**14-5**	**13-11**	**13-8**	**13-3**	**12-8**	**10-10**	**10-6**	**10-0**	**9-8**				
	24.0	14-4	14-1	**14-1**	**13-8**	**13-6**	**13-1**	**12-11**	**12-6**	**12-3**	**11-10**	**11-4**	**9-8**	**9-5**	**9-0**	**8-8**				
	12.0	23-9	23-4	23-9	22-11	23-4	23-4	22-11	22-11	22-5	**22-0**	**21-2**	**18-1**	**17-7**	**16-9**	**16-2**				
	13.7	22-9	22-4	22-9	21-11	22-4	22-4	21-11	**21-9**	**21-5**	**20-7**	**19-10**	**16-11**	**16-5**	**15-8**	**15-1**				
2 x 8	16.0	21-7	21-2	21-7	20-10	21-2	**21-2**	20-10	**20-2**	**19-10**	**19-1**	**18-4**	**15-8**	**15-2**	**14-6**	**14-0**				
	19.2	20-4	19-11	20-4	19-7	**19-11**	**19-4**	**19-0**	**18-5**	**18-1**	**17-5**	**16-9**	**14-3**	**13-10**	**13-3**	**12-9**				
	24.0	18-10	18-6	**18-7**	**18-1**	**17-10**	**17-3**	**17-0**	**16-5**	**16-2**	**15-7**	**15-0**	**12-9**	**12-5**	**11-10**	**11-5**				
	12.0	30-4	29-9	30-4	29-2	29-9	29-9	29-2	29-2	28-7	**28-1**	**27-0**	**23-1**	**22-5**	**21-4**	**20-7**				
	13.7	29-0	28-6	29-0	27-11	28-6	28-6	27-11	**27-9**	**27-3**	**26-3**	**25-3**	**21-7**	**20-11**	**20-0**	**19-3**				
2 x 10	16.0	27-6	27-1	27-6	26-6	27-1	**27-0**	26-6	**25-8**	**25-3**	**24-4**	**23-5**	**20-0**	**19-5**	**18-6**	**17-10**				
	19.2	25-11	25-5	25-11	25-0	**25-5**	**24-8**	**24-3**	**23-6**	**23-1**	**22-3**	**21-4**	**18-3**	**17-8**	**16-10**	**16-4**				
	24.0	24-1	23-8	**23-8**	**23-1**	**22-9**	**22-1**	**21-8**	**21-0**	**20-7**	**19-10**	**19-1**	**16-4**	**15-10**	**15-1**	**14-7**				

RAFTERS—High Slope (over 3 in 12)—With No Finished Ceiling—30 psf live load + 7 psf dead load—light roofing. (Spans shown in light face type are based on a deflection limitation of $l/180$. Spans shown in bold face type are limited by the recommended extreme fiber stress in bending value of the grade and includes a 7 psf dead load.)

Size (in.)	Spacing (in. o.c.)	Dense Sel Str KD	Sel Str KD and Dense Sel Str	No. 1 Dense KD	Sel Str	No. 1 Dense	No. 1 KD	No. 2 Dense KD	No. 1	No. 2 Dense	No. 2 KD	No. 2	No. 3 Dense KD	No. 3 Dense	No. 3 KD	No. 3	Construction KD	Construction	Standard KD	Standard
	12.0	10-0	9-10	10-0	9-8	9-10	9-10	9-8	9-8	9-6	9-6	**9-5**	**8-0**	**7-8**	**7-4**	**7-0**	**8-4**	**8-0**	**6-4**	**6-0**
	13.7	9-7	9-5	9-7	9-3	9-5	9-5	9-3	9-3	9-1	9-1	**8-10**	**7-5**	**7-2**	**6-10**	**6-7**	**7-10**	**7-5**	**5-11**	**5-8**
2 x 4	16.0	9-1	8-11	9-1	8-9	8-11	8-11	8-9	8-9	8-7	**8-7**	**8-2**	**6-11**	**6-8**	**6-4**	**6-1**	**7-3**	**6-11**	**5-5**	**5-3**
	19.2	8-7	8-5	8-7	8-3	8-5	8-5	8-3	**8-3**	8-1	**7-10**	**7-5**	**6-4**	**6-1**	**5-10**	**5-7**	**6-7**	**6-4**	**5-0**	**4-9**
	24.0	7-11	7-10	7-11	7-8	7-10	**7-8**	**7-7**	**7-4**	**7-3**	**7-0**	**6-8**	**5-8**	**5-5**	**5-2**	**5-0**	**5-11**	**5-8**	**4-5**	**4-3**
	12.0	15-9	15-6	15-9	15-2	15-6	15-6	15-2	**15-1**	**14-10**	**14-3**	**13-9**	**11-9**	**11-4**	**10-10**	**10-6**				
	13.7	15-1	14-9	15-1	14-6	14-9	14-9	14-6	**14-1**	**13-10**	**13-4**	**12-10**	**10-11**	**10-8**	**10-2**	**9-10**				
2 x 6	16.0	14-4	14-1	14-4	13-9	14-1	**13-9**	**13-6**	**13-1**	**12-10**	**12-4**	**11-11**	**10-2**	**9-10**	**9-5**	**9-1**				
	19.2	13-6	13-3	**13-6**	13-0	**12-11**	**12-6**	**12-4**	**11-11**	**11-9**	**11-3**	**10-10**	**9-3**	**9-0**	**8-7**	**8-3**				
	24.0	12-6	12-3[1]	**12-0**	**11-9**	**11-6**	**11-2**	**11-0**	**10-8**	**10-6**	**10-1**	**9-8**	**8-3**	**8-0**	**7-8**	**7-5**				
	12.0	20-9	20-5	20-9	20-0	20-5	20-5	20-0	**19-10**	**19-6**	**18-10**	**18-1**	**15-5**	**15-0**	**14-3**	**13-10**				
	13.7	19-10	19-6	19-10	19-2	19-6	19-6	19-2	**18-7**	**18-3**	**17-7**	**16-11**	**14-5**	**14-0**	**13-4**	**12-11**				
2 x 8	16.0	18-10	18-6	18-10	18-2	18-6	**18-1**	**17-9**	**17-2**	**16-11**	**16-4**	**15-8**	**13-4**	**13-0**	**12-5**	**11-11**				
	19.2	17-9	17-5	**17-9**	17-1	**17-0**	**16-6**	**16-3**	**15-9**	**15-5**	**14-10**	**14-3**	**12-2**	**11-10**	**11-4**	**10-11**				
	24.0	16-6	16-2[1]	**15-10**	**15-5**	**15-3**	**14-9**	**14-6**	**14-1**	**13-10**	**13-4**	**12-9**	**10-11**	**10-7**	**10-1**	**9-9**				
	12.0	26-6	26-0	26-6	25-6	26-0	26-0	25-6	**25-4**	**24-11**	**24-0**	**23-1**	**19-8**	**19-1**	**18-3**	**17-7**				
	13.7	25-4	24-11	25-4	24-5	24-11	24-11	24-5	**23-9**	**23-4**	**22-5**	**21-7**	**18-5**	**17-11**	**17-1**	**16-6**				
2 x 10	16.0	24-1	23-8	24-1	23-2	23-8	**23-1**	**22-8**	**21-11**	**21-7**	**20-9**	**20-0**	**17-1**	**16-7**	**15-9**	**15-3**				
	19.2	22-8	22-3	**22-8**	21-10	**21-8**	**21-1**	**20-9**	**20-1**	**19-8**	**19-0**	**18-3**	**15-7**	**15-1**	**14-5**	**13-11**				
	24.0	21-0	20-8[1]	**20-3**	**19-8**	**19-5**	**18-10**	**18-6**	**17-11**	**17-7**	**17-0**	**16-4**	**13-11**	**13-6**	**12-11**	**12-5**				

1. The span for Select Structural KD, 24 inches o.c. is:
2x5, **9-10**; 2x6, **12-0**; 2x8, **15-10**; 2x10, **20-3**.

Table 2A-20 (Continued)

RAFTERS—High Slope (over 3 in 12)—With No Finished Ceiling. 40 psf live load + 15 psf dead load—heavy roofing.
(Spans shown in light face type are based on a deflection limitation of $l/180$. Spans shown in bold face type are limited by the recommended extreme fiber stress in bending value of the grade and includes a 15 psf dead load.)

Size and Spacing in.	Grade / in. o.c.	Dense Sel Str KD	Sel Str Dense	No. 1 Dense KD and Sel Str KD	Sel Str	No. 1 Dense	No. 1 KD	No. 2 Dense KD	No. 1	No. 2 Dense	No. 2 KD	No. 2	No. 3 Dense KD	No. 3 Dense	No. 3 KD	No. 3	Con-struc-tion KD	Con-struc-tion	Stand-ard KD	Stand-ard
	12.0	9-1	8-11	9-1[1]	8-9	8-11	8-11	8-9	8-6	8-5	8-2	7-9	6-6	6-3	6-0	5-9	6-10	6-6	5-2	4-11
	13.7	8-8	8-7	8-8[1]	8-5	8-7	8-4	8-2	8-0	7-10	7-7	7-3	6-1	5-11	5-8	5-5	6-5	6-1	4-10	4-8
2 x 4	16.0	8-3	8-1	8-3[1]	8-0	8-0	7-8	7-7	7-5	7-3	7-1	6-8	5-8	5-5	5-3	5-0	5-11	5-8	4-6	4-3
	19.2	7-9	7-8	7-7	7-4	7-4	7-0	6-11	6-9	6-8	6-5	6-1	5-2	5-0	4-9	4-7	5-5	5-2	4-1	3-11
	24.0	7-3	7-1	6-9	6-6	6-6	6-3	6-2	6-0	5-11	5-9	5-6	4-7	4-5	4-3	4-1	4-10	4-7	3-8	3-6
	12.0	14-4	14-1	14-0	13-7	13-5	13-0	12-9	12-4	12-2	11-8	11-3	9-7	9-4	8-11	8-7				
	13.7	13-8	13-5	13-1	12-8	12-6	12-2	12-0	11-7	11-4	10-11	10-6	9-0	8-9	8-4	8-0				
2 x 6	16.0	13-0	12-9	12-1	11-9	11-7	11-3	11-1	10-8	10-6	10-2	9-9	8-4	8-1	7-8	7-5				
	19.2	12-0	11-7	11-0	10-9	10-7	10-3	10-1	9-9	9-7	9-3	8-11	7-7	7-4	7-0	6-9				
	24.0	10-9	10-5	9-10	9-7	9-6	9-2	9-0	8-9	8-7	8-3	7-11	6-9	6-7	6-3	6-1				
	12.0	18-10	18-6	18-5	17-11	17-8	17-1	16-10	16-4	16-0	15-5	14-10	12-8	12-4	11-9	11-4				
	13.7	18-0	17-9	17-3	16-9	16-6	16-0	15-9	15-3	15-0	14-5	13-10	11-10	11-6	11-0	10-7				
2 x 8	16.0	17-2	16-9	15-11	15-6	15-3	14-10	14-7	14-1	13-10	13-4	12-10	11-0	10-8	10-2	9-10				
	19.2	15-10	15-4	14-7	14-2	13-11	13-6	13-4	12-11	12-8	12-2	11-9	10-0	9-9	9-3	8-11				
	24.0	14-2	13-8	13-0	12-8	12-6	12-1	11-11	11-6	11-4	10-11	10-6	8-11	8-8	8-3	8-0				
	12.0	24-1	23-8	23-6	22-10	22-6	21-10	21-6	20-10	20-5	19-8	18-11	16-2	15-8	14-11	14-5				
	13.7	23-0	22-7	22-0	21-4	21-1	20-5	20-1	19-5	19-1	18-5	17-8	15-1	14-8	14-0	13-6				
2 x 10	16.0	21-10	21-5	20-4	19-9	19-6	18-11	18-7	18-0	17-8	17-1	16-5	14-0	13-7	12-11	12-6				
	19.2	20-3	19-7	18-7	18-1	17-10	17-3	17-0	16-5	16-2	15-7	14-11	12-9	12-5	11-10	11-5				
	24.0	18-1	17-6	16-7	16-2	15-11	15-5	15-2	14-8	14-5	13-11	13-5	11-5	11-1	10-7	10-3				

1. The span for Select Structural KD, 2x4, 12 inches o.c. is 8-11; 13.7 inches o.c., 8-7, and 16 inches o.c., 8-1.

Source: SOUTHERN FOREST PRODUCTS ASSOCIATION.

PLYWOOD

Tables 2A–21 through 2A–29 provide convenient assistance in selection of plywood for various uses and structural loading conditions. Table 2A–22 summarizes the common grades of plywood, their uses, and the common thicknesses in which they are available. Also included in this table is the typical trademark stamp that is placed on each panel if rated by the American Plywood Association and the exposure durability classification; that is, where the particular grade should be used.

Panels with an "exterior" classification are designed for applications exposed permanently to the weather or moisture. Exposure 1 panels are intended for protected construction applications where the ability to resist moisture during long construction delays or where exposure to conditions of similar severity is required. Exposure 2 panels are intended for protected construction applications where moderate delays in providing protection from moisture are expected.

Table 2A–21 itemizes what species of wood belong to the five groups of plywood, while Table 2A–23 describes the appearance of the various face grades of plywood. For practical purposes, most plywood is of Douglas fir, birch, or pine.

Tables 2A–24 through 2A–28 allow a quick determination of the proper grade and thickness of plywood for various use conditions. Note that when span ratings are used, such as "32/16," they indicate the maximum recommended center-to-center spacing of supports in inches when the panels are installed with the long dimension across three or more supports. The number on the left of the slash indicates the maximum recommended spacing of supports when the plywood is used for roof sheathing. The number on the right indicates the spacing of supports when the plywood is used for subflooring.

Example

The snow load in a mountain area is 70 lbs. per sq. ft. What grade and thickness of plywood should be used for sheathing if asphalt shingles are to be used?

Look in Table 2A–24. Assume the rafters are to be placed 16 in. on center. Look down the column indicated "16" in the "Spacing of Supports" group until you find a figure meeting or exceeding 70. In this case, the allowable load is 100 psf. Looking across the row to the left, the panel span rating should be 24/16 and the minimum thickness 7/16 or 1/2 in. The *maximum* span is 24 in. so this is well within the assumed spacing of 16 in. Since 1/2 in. is more common and available than 7/16 in., the final choice should be 1/2 in., 24/16 sheathing.

Table 2A-21
CLASSIFICATION OF PLYWOOD SPECIES

Group 1	Group 2	
Apitong (a)(b)	Cedar, Port Orford	Maple, Black
Beech, American	Cypress	Mengkulang (a)
Birch	Douglas Fir 2 (c)	Meranti, Red (a)(d)
Sweet	Fir	Mersawa (a)
Yellow	Balsam	Pine
Douglas Fir 1 (c)	California Red	Pond
Kapur (a)	Grand	Red
Keruing (a)(b)	Noble	Virginia
Larch, Western	Pacific Silver	Western White
Maple, Sugar	White	Spruce
Pine	Hemlock, Western	Black
Caribbean	Lauan	Red
Ocote	Almon	Sitka
Pine, Southern	Bagtikan	Sweetgum
Loblolly	Mayapis	Tamarack
Longleaf	Red Lauan	Yellow Poplar
Shortleaf	Tangile	
Slash	White Lauan	
Tanoak		
Group 3	**Group 4**	**Group 5**
Alder, Red	Aspen	Basswood
Birch, Paper	Bigtooth	Poplar, Balsam
Cedar, Alaska	Quaking	
Fir, Subalpine	Cativo	
Hemlock, Eastern	Cedar	
Maple, Bigleaf	Incense	
Pine	Western Red	
Jack	Cottonwood	
Lodgepole	Eastern	
Ponderosa	Black (Western Poplar)	
Spruce	Pine	
Redwood	Eastern White	
Spruce	Sugar	
Englemann		
White		

(a) Each of these names represents a trade group of woods consisting of a number of closely related species.

(b) Species from the genus *Dipterocarpus* are marketed collectively: Apitong if originating in the Philippines; Keruing if originating in Malaysia or Indonesia.

(c) Douglas fir from trees grown in the states of Washington, Oregon, California, Idaho, Montana, Wyoming, and the Canadian Provinces of Alberta and British Columbia shall be classed as Douglas fir No. 1. Douglas fir from trees grown in the states of Nevada, Utah, Colorado, Arizona and New Mexico shall be classed as Douglas fir No. 2.

(d) Red Meranti shall be limited to species having a specific gravity of 0.41 or more based on green volume and oven dry weight.

Courtesy American Plywood Association.

Table 2A-22
PLYWOOD GRADES AND USES

	GRADE		Trademarks Shown Are Typical Facsimiles	EXPOSURE DURABILITY CLASSIFICATIONS				COMMON THICKNESSES											
				Exterior	Exposure 1	Exposure 2	Interior	1/4	5/16	11/32	3/8	7/16	15/32	1/2	19/32	5/8	23/32	3/4	1-1/8
PERFORMANCE-RATED PANELS	**APA RATED SHEATHING**	Specially designed for subflooring, wall sheathing and roof sheathing, but also used for broad range of other construction, industrial and do-it-yourself applications. Can be manufactured as conventional plywood, as a composite, or as a reconstituted wood panel (waferboard, oriented strand board, structural particle-board). For special engineered applications, veneered panels conforming to PS 1 may be required. SPAN RATINGS: 16/0, 20/0, 24/0, 24/16, 32/16, 40/20, 48/24.	APA RATED SHEATHING 32/16 15/32 INCH SIZED FOR SPACING EXPOSURE 1 000 NER-108	●	●	●			●		●	●	●	●	●	●	●	●	
	APA STRUCTURAL I RATED SHEATHING	Unsanded all-veneer PS 1 plywood grades for use where cross-panel strength and stiffness or shear properties are of maximum importance, such as box beams, gusset plates, stressed-skin panels, containers, pallet bins. All plies in Structural I panels are special improved grades and limited to Group 1 species. (Structural II panels, limited to Group 1, 2, or 3 species, are also sometimes available. However, application recommendations for Structural II plywood are identical to those for RATED SHEATHING plywood marked PS 1.) SPAN RATINGS: 20/0, 24/0, 32/16, 40/20, 48/24.	APA RATED SHEATHING STRUCTURAL I 48/24 23/32 INCH SIZED FOR SPACING EXTERIOR 000 PS 1-83 C-C NER-108	●	●				●		●		●	●	●	●	●	●	
	APA RATED STURD-I-FLOOR	Specially designed as combination subfloor-underlayment. Provides smooth surface for application of carpet and pad and possesses high concentrated and impact load resistance. Can be manufactured as conventional plywood, as a composite, or as a reconstituted wood panel (waferboard, oriented strand board, structural particle-board). Available square edge or tongue-and-groove. SPAN RATINGS: 16, 20, 24.	APA RATED STURD-I-FLOOR 20 oc 19/32 INCH SIZED FOR SPACING EXPOSURE 1 000 NER-108	●	●	●									●	●	●	●	
	APA RATED STURD-I-FLOOR 48 oc (2-4-1)	For combination subfloor-underlayment on 32- and 48-inch spans and for heavy timber roof construction. Manufactured only as conventional plywood. Available square edge or tongue-and-groove. SPAN RATING: 48.	APA RATED STURD-I-FLOOR 48 oc 1-1/8 INCH 2-4-1 SIZED FOR SPACING EXPOSURE 1 T&G 000 UNDERLAYMENT PS 1-83 NER-108		●														●
APA 303 SIDING	**APA 303 SIDING**	APA proprietary plywood products for exterior and interior applications: siding, paneling, fencing, accent panels, mansard roofs, balcony screens, signs, chimney enclosures, etc. Available in numerous face grades and with a variety of surface textures and patterns. SPAN RATINGS: 16 and 24.	APA 303 SIDING 6-S/W 24 oc GROUP 2 EXTERIOR 000 PS 1-83 FHA-UM-64	●						●	●		●	●	●	●			
	APA TEXTURE 1-11	Special 303 Siding panel with grooves 1/4" deep, 3/8" wide, typically spaced 4" or 8" oc. Other spacings (2", 6", 12") may be available on special order. Shiplapped edges. Available in various surface textures. SPAN RATING: 16 only.	APA 303 SIDING 6-W 16 oc 19/32 INCH GROUP 1 EXTERIOR T1-11 000 PS 1-83 FHA-UM-64	●											●	●			
SANDED	**APA A-A**	Use where appearance of both sides is important for interior applications such as built-ins, cabinets, furniture, partitions; and exterior applications such as fences, signs, boats, shipping containers, tanks, ducts, etc. Smooth surfaces suitable for painting.	A-A · G-1 · EXPOSURE1 · APA · 000 · PS1-83	●	●		●	●		●	●		●	●	●	●	●	●	
	APA A-B	For use where appearance of one side is less important but where two solid surfaces are necessary.	A-B · G-1 · EXPOSURE1 · APA · 000 · PS1-83	●	●		●	●		●	●		●	●	●	●	●	●	

Table 2A-22 (Continued)

	GRADE		Trademarks Shown Are Typical Facsimiles	Exterior	Exposure 1	Exposure 2	Interior	1/4		11/32	3/8		15/32	1/2	19/32	5/8	23/32	3/4	
				EXPOSURE DURABILITY CLASSIFICATIONS				COMMON THICKNESSES											
SANDED & TOUCH-SANDED PLYWOOD	**APA B-C**	Utility panel for farm service and work buildings, boxcar and truck linings, containers, tanks, agricultural equipment, as a base for exterior coatings and other exterior uses.	APA B-C GROUP 1 EXTERIOR 000 PS 1-83	●				●		●	●		●	●	●	●	●	●	
	APA B-D	Utility panel for backing, sides of built-ins, industry shelving, slip sheets, separator boards, bins and other interior or protected applications.	APA B-D GROUP 2 INTERIOR 000 PS 1-83		●		●	●		●	●		●	●	●	●	●	●	
	APA A-C	For use where appearance of one side is important in exterior applications such as soffits, fences, structural uses, boxcar and truck linings, farm buildings, tanks, trays, commercial refrigerators, etc.	APA A-C GROUP 1 EXTERIOR 000 PS 1-83	●				●		●	●		●	●	●	●	●	●	
	APA A-D	For use where appearance of only one side is important in interior applications, such as paneling, built-ins, shelving, partitions, flow racks, etc.	APA A-D GROUP 1 EXPOSURE 1 000 PS 1-83		●		●	●		●	●		●	●	●	●	●	●	
	APA B-B	Utility panels with two solid sides.	B-B · G-2 · EXPOSURE 1- APA · 000 · PS1-83	●	●		●	●		●	●		●	●	●	●	●	●	
	APA C-C PLUGGED	For use as an underlayment over structural subfloor, refrigerated or controlled atmosphere storage rooms, pallet fruit bins, tanks, boxcar and truck floors and linings, open soffits, and other exterior applications. Provides smooth surface for application of carpet and possesses high concentrated and impact load resistance. Touch-sanded.	APA C-C PLUGGED GROUP 2 EXTERIOR 000 PS 1-83	●							●			●	●	●	●	●	
	APA C-D PLUGGED	For built-ins, cable reels, walkways, separator boards and other interior or protected applications. Not a substitute for Underlayment or APA Rated Sturd-I-Floor as it lacks their puncture resistance. Touch-sanded.	APA C-D PLUGGED GROUP 2 EXPOSURE 1 000 PS 1-83		●		●				●			●	●	●	●	●	
	APA UNDERLAYMENT	For application over structural subfloor. Provides smooth surface for application of carpet and pad and possesses high concentrated and impact load resistance. Touch-sanded. For areas to be covered with resilient non-textile flooring, specify panels with "sanded face."	APA UNDERLAYMENT GROUP 1 EXPOSURE 1 000 PS 1-83		●		●			●	●			●	●	●	●	●	

			Trademarks Shown Are Typical Facsimiles	EXPOSURE DURABILITY CLASSIFICATION				COMMON THICKNESSES										
				Exterior	Exposure 1	Exposure 2	Interior	1/4	5/16	11/32	3/8	15/32	1/2	19/32	5/8	23/32	3/4
SPECIALTY PANELS	**APA HIGH DENSITY OVERLAY (HDO)**	Plywood panel manufactured with a hard, semi-opaque resin-fiber overlay on both sides. Extremely abrasion resistant and ideally suited to scores of punishing construction and industrial applications, such as concrete forms, industrial tanks, work surfaces, signs, agricultural bins, exhaust ducts, etc. Also available with skid-resistant screen-grid surface and in Structural I.	HDO · A-A · G-1 · EXT· APA · 000 · PS1-83	●							●		●		●		●
SPECIALTY PANELS	**APA MEDIUM DENSITY OVERLAY (MDO)**	Plywood panel manufactured with smooth, opaque, resin-treated fiber overlay providing ideal base for paint on one or both sides. Excellent material choice for shelving, factory work surfaces, paneling, built-ins, signs and numerous other construction and industrial applications. Also available as a 303 Siding with texture-embossed or smooth surface on one side only and in Structural I.	APA M. D. OVERLAY GROUP 1 EXTERIOR 000 PS 1-83	●						●	●	●	●	●	●	●	●
SPECIALTY PANELS	**APA DECORATIVE**	Rough sawn, brushed, grooved, or striated faces. For paneling, interior accent walls, built-ins, counter facing, exhibit displays, etc. Made by some manufacturers in Exterior for exterior siding, gable ends, fences and other exterior applications. Use recommendations for Exterior panels vary; check with the manufacturer.	APA DECORATIVE GROUP 2 INTERIOR 000 PS 1-83	●	●		●		●		●		●		●		
SPECIALTY PANELS	**APA MARINE**	Specially designed plywood panel made only with Douglas fir or western larch, solid jointed cores, and highly restrictive limitations on core gaps and face repairs. Ideal for boat hulls and other marine applications. Also available with HDO or MDO faces.	MARINE · A-A · EXT· APA · 000 · PS1-83	●				●			●		●		●		●
SPECIALTY PANELS	**APA B-B PLYFORM CLASS I AND CLASS II**	APA proprietary concrete form panels designed for high reuse. Sanded both sides and mill-oiled unless otherwise specified. Class I, the strongest, stiffest and more commonly available, is limited to Group 1 faces, Group 1 or 2 crossbands, and Group 1, 2, 3, or 4 inner plies. Class II is limited to Group 1 or 2 faces (Group 3 under certain conditions) and Group 1, 2, 3, or 4 inner plies. Also available in HDO for very smooth concrete finish, in Structural I, and with special overlays.	APA PLYFORM B-B CLASS I EXTERIOR 000 PS 1-83	●										●	●	●	●
SPECIALTY PANELS	**APA PLYRON**	Non-PS 1 plywood panel with hardboard face on both sides. Faces tempered, untempered, smooth or screened. For countertops, shelving, cabinet doors, concentrated load flooring, etc.	PLYRON· EXPOSURE1-APA	●	●		●						●		●		●

Courtesy American Plywood Association

Table 2A-23
PLYWOOD VENEER GRADES

N	Smooth surface "natural finish" veneer; select, all heartwood or all sapwood; free of open defects; allows not more than 6 repairs, wood only, per 4 × 8 panel, made parallel to grain and well matched for grain and color; available only on special order from some manufacturers.
A	Smooth, paintable; not more than 18 neatly made repairs, boat, sled, or router type, and parallel to grain permitted; may be used for natural finish in less demanding applications.
B	Solid surface; shims, circular repair plugs, and tight knots to 1 in. across grain permitted; some minor splits permitted.
C	Tight knots to 1 1/2 in.; knotholes to 1 in. across grain and some to 1 1/2 in. if total width of knots and knotholes is within specified limits; synthetic or wood repairs; discoloration and sanding defects that do not impair strength permitted; limited splits allowed.
C plg.	Plugged; improved C veneer with splits limited to 1/8 in. width and knotholes and borer holes limited to 1/4 × 1/2 in.; admits some broken grain; synthetic repairs permitted.
D	Knots and knotholes to 2 1/2 in. width across grain and 1/2 in. larger within specified limits; limited splits are permitted.

Courtesy American Plywood Association.

Table 2A-24
RECOMMENDED UNIFORM ROOF LIVE LOADS FOR APA PANEL SHEATHING WITH LONG DIMENSION PERPENDICULAR TO SUPPORTS (c)
(APA Rated Sheathing and APA Structural I and II Rated Sheathing)

Panel Span Rating	Panel Thickness (in in.)	Max. Span (in in.) Edge Supports		Allowable Live Loads, psf (d) Spacing of Supports Center to Center							
		with (a)	without	12	16	20	24	32	40	48	60
12/0	5/16	12	12	30							
16/0	5/16, 3/8	16	16	55	30						
20/0	5/16, 3/8	20	20	70	50	30					
24/0	3/8, 7/16, 1/2	24	20(b)	90	65	55	30				
24/16	7/16, 1/2	24	24	135	100	75	40				
32/16	15/32, 1/2, 5/8	32	28	135	100	75	55	30			
40/20	9/16, 19/32, 5/8, 3/4, 7/8	40	32	165	120	100	75	55	30		
48/24	23/32, 3/4, 7/8	48	36	210	155	130	100	65	50	35	
48 oc(e)	1-1/8	60	48				375	205	100	65	40

(a) Tongue-and-groove edges, panel edge clips (one between each support, except two between supports 48 in. on center), lumber blocking, or other.

(b) 24 in. for 1/2 in. panels.

(c) When roofing is to be guaranteed by a performance bond, check with roofing manufacturer for minimum thickness, span, and edge support requirements.

(d) 10 psf dead load assumed.

(e) Span Rating applies to APA Rated Sturd-I-Floor "2-4-1".

Note: The recommendations in this table apply to APA Rated Sheathing Exterior, Exposure 1 or Exposure 2, and APA Structural I and II Rated Sheathing Exterior or Exposure 1. Uniform load deflection limits are 1/180 of span under live load plus dead load, and 1/240 under live load only. Panels are assumed installed with the long dimension across three or more supports.

Courtesy American Plywood Association.

Table 2A-25
PANEL RECOMMENDATIONS FOR APA GLUED FLOOR SYSTEM (a)

Joist Spacing	Flooring Type	APA Panel Grade and Span Rating	Possible Thickness (in in.)
16	Carpet and pad Separate underlayment or structural finish flooring	Sturd-I-Floor 16 oc Rated Sheathing 24/16, 32,16, 40/20, 48/24	19/32, 5/8, 21,32 7/16, 15, 32, 1/2, 19/32, 5/8, 23/32, 3/4
19.2	Carpet and pad Separate underlayment or structural finish flooring	Sturd-I-Floor 20 oc Rated Sheathing 40/20, 48/24	19/32, 5/8, 23/32, 3/4 9/16, 19/32, 5/8, 23/32, 3/4
24	Carpet and pad Separate underlayment or structural finish flooring	Sturd-I-Floor 24 oc Rated Sheathing 48/24	11/16, 23/32, 3/4, 7/8, 1 23/32, 3/4
32 or 48	Carpet and pad	Sturd-I-Floor 48 oc (2-4-1)	1 1/8

(a) For panel recommendations under ceramic tile, see Table 2A-28.

Courtesy American Plywood Association.

Table 2A-26
APA PANEL SUBFLOORING (a)
(APA Rated Sheathing)

Panel Span Rating (or group number)	**Panel Thickness** (in in.)	**Maximum Span** (in in.)
24/16	7/16	16
32/16	15/32, 1/2, 5/8	16 (b)
40/20	9/16, 19/32, 5/8, 3/4, 7/8	20 (c)
48/24	23/32, 3/4, 7/8	24
1 1/8 Groups 1 & 2 (d)	1 1/8	48
1 1/4 Groups 3 & 4 (d)	1 1/4	48

(a) For subfloor recommendations under ceramic tile, refer to Table 2A-28. For subfloor recommendations under gypsum concrete, contact manufacturer of floor topping.

(b) Span may be 24 in. if 25/32 in. wood strip flooring is installed at right angles to joists.

(c) Span may be 24 in. if 25/32 in. wood strip flooring is installed at right angles to joists, or if a minimum 1 1/2 in. of lightweight concrete (or 1 in. of some gypsum concrete products) is applied over panels.

(d) Check dealer for availability.

Courtesy American Plywood Association.

Table 2A-27
APA PLYWOOD UNDERLAYMENT (a)

Plywood Grades (b) and Species Group	Application	Minimum Plywood Thickness
Groups 1, 2, 3, 4, 5 APA UNDERLAYMENT INT (with int. or ext. glue)	Over smooth subfloor	1/4
APA UNDERLAYMENT EXT APA C-C Plugged Ext	Over lumber subfloor or other uneven surfaces	11/32
Same grades as above, but Group 1 only	Over lumber floor up to 4 in. wide. Face grain must be perpendicular to boards.	1/4

(a) For underlayment recommendations under ceramic tile, refer to Table 2A-28.
(b) When 19/32 in. or thicker underlayment is desired, APA RATED STURD-I-FLOOR may be specified. In areas to be finished with thin floor coverings such as tile, linoleum, or vinyl, specify Underlayment, C-C Plugged, or STURD-I-FLOOR with fully sanded face.

Courtesy American Plywood Association.

Table 2A-28
APA PLYWOOD SYSTEMS FOR CERAMIC TILE FLOORING
(Based on ANSI Standard A108 and recommendations of the Tile Council of America)

Joist Spacing (in in.)	Minimum Panel Thickness (in in.)		
	Subfloor (a)	Underlayment (b)	Tile installation
Residential			
16	15/32	(d)	"Dry-Set" mortar or latex-Portland Cement mortar
16	19/32	—	Cement mortar (3/4 in.–1 1/4 in.)
16	19/32	11/32	Organic adhesive
16	19/32	15/32 (e)	Epoxy mortar
16	19/32 T & G (c,e)	—	Epoxy mortar
Commercial			
16	15/32	(d)	"Dry-Set" mortar or latex-Portland Cement mortar
16	19/32	—	Cement mortar (3/4 in.–1 1/4 in.)
16	19/32	19/32 (c,e)	Epoxy mortar

(a) APA Rated Sheathing with subfloor Span Rating of 16 in. oc (15/32 in. panel) or 20 in. oc (19/32 in. panel), except as noted.

(b) APA Underlayment or sanded Exterior grade, except as noted.
(c) APA Rated Sturd-I-Floor with 20 in. oc Span Rating.
(d) Bond glass mesh mortar units to subfloor with latex-Portland Cement mortar prior to spreading mortar for setting ceramic tile.
(e) Leave 1/4 in. space at panel ends and edges; trim panels as necessary to maintain end spacing and panel support on framing. Fill joints with epoxy mortar when it is spread for setting tile. With single-layer residential floors, use solid lumber blocking or framing under all panel end and edge joints (including T&G joints).

Courtesy American Plywood Association.

Table 2A-29
MINIMUM BENDING RADII FOR PLYWOOD PANELS

Panel Thickness (in in.)	Bending Radii for Panel Bent in Direction (in ft.)	
	Across Grain	Parallel to Grain
1/4	2	5
5/16	2	6
11/32 & 3/8	3	8
15/32 & 1/2	6	12
19/32 & 5/8	8	16
23/32 & 3/4	12	20

Courtesy American Plywood Association.

GLUED, LAMINATED CONSTRUCTION

Glued, laminated construction is a popular method of wood construction when spans and loading conditions make the use of solid wood timbers impractical or impossible. Table 2A-30 can be used to size simple beams.

Example

What size glue-laminated beam should be used to support a floor of wood decking if the design live load is 40 psf, the beams are 8 ft. apart, and the beam span is 22 ft.?

First, calculate the total load on the beam. Since the allowable loads in the table are in pounds per lineal foot, the loads must be calculated in this manner. For an interior beam, the load area is 8 ft. × 1 ft. × 50 psf (assume a 10 psf dead load) or 400 lbs. per lineal ft. of beam. Look in the table for 5 in. wide floor beams and find the row for a 22 ft. span. Read across the row until you find a figure meeting or exceeding 400 lbs. In this case it is 443. Read up the column and find that a 16 1/2 in. deep beam can carry this load. If a shallower beam is required, look in the 6 3/4 in. wide floor beam table. Following the same procedure, you find that a 15 1/8 in. deep beam will carry 460 lbs. per lineal ft.

Table 2A-30
CAPACITIES FOR GLUED, LAMINATED ROOF AND FLOOR BEAMS

Table Specifications

The beam tables are applicable only for straight, simply-supported beams which are laterally supported by decking, joists or purlins, etc. Also, the ends of beams must be restrained against rotation.

Roofs should have a minimum slope of ¼ inch per foot for drainage to help avoid ponding of water.

The allowable loads shown are in pounds per lineal foot, PLF, and include the beam weights.

Design values
(dry conditions of use):

a. Bending stress, F_b = 2400 psi* (reduced by size effect factor)

b. Shear stress, F_v = 200 psi** (loads within the depth of the member from the supports were neglected in shear calculations)

c. Modulus of elasticity, E = 1,700,000 psi

d. Design values F_b and F_v have been increased 15% for two months duration of load for *roof beams.* No increases have been included for the *floor beams.*

e. Deflections have been limited to 1/180 span for total load for *roof beams* and 1/360 span for *floor beams.* Floor beams may be designed using deflection limits of 1/360 for live load only. If stiffer beams are desired, 1/360 for total load should be used.

*This rating only applies with the beams oriented properly. Install beams with "top" marks up. If beams are used for conditions other than simple spans, special lumber combinations may be required. If the lower grade compression zone is stressed in tension (such as on cantilevered or continuous span beams), the allowable bending design value is only 1200 psi.

**Tabulated values are for Southern Pine. Maximum F_v values for Douglas Fir-Larch and Hem-Fir are 165 psi and 155 psi, respectively.

Alternate widths

To determine *approximate* load-carrying capacities for alternate beam and header widths, multiply the tabulated applied load capacities by the factors shown below:

Tabulated Width, in.	Factors for Alternate Widths			
	3⅛"	5⅛"	8¾"	10¾"
3"	1.042	—	—	—
5"	—	1.025	—	—
8½"	—	—	1.029	—
10½"	—	—	—	1.024

The use of these factors will result in *approximate* load values. Actual load values should be calculated when greater accuracy is required.

ROOF BEAMS 3"x

Span'	5½"	6⅞"	8¼"	9⅝"	11"	12⅜"	13¾"	15⅛"	16½"	17⅞"
8	409	679	978	1332	1641	1917	2216	2540	2891	3275
10	210	409	626	852	1113	1404	1641	1861	2094	2342
12	121	237	409	592	773	975	1190	1424	1641	1823
14		149	258	409	568	716	874	1047	1233	1435
16		100	173	274	409	548	669	801	944	1099
18			121	193	287	409	529	633	746	868
20				140	210	298	409	513	604	703
22				105	157	224	307	409	500	581
24					121	173	237	315	409	488
26						136	186	248	322	409
28						109	149	198	258	328
30							121	161	210	266

FLOOR BEAMS 3"x

Span'	5½"	6⅞"	8¼"	9⅝"	11"	12⅜"	13¾"	15⅛"	16½"	17⅞"
8	205	400	691	1097	1427	1667	1927	2208	2514	2848
10	105	205	354	561	838	1193	1427	1618	1821	2037
12		118	205	325	485	691	947	1239	1427	1585
14			129	205	305	435	596	794	1031	1248
16				137	205	291	400	532	691	878
18					144	205	281	374	485	617
20					105	149	205	272	354	449
22						112	154	205	266	338
24							118	158	205	260
26								124	161	205
28									129	164
30									105	133

ROOF BEAMS 5"x

Span'	12⅜"	13¾"	15⅛"	16½"	17⅞"	19¼"	20⅝"	22"	23⅜"	24¾"	26⅛"	27½"	28⅞"
8	3196	3693	4233	4819	5459	6160	6932	7785	8733	9794	10987	12341	13890
10	2340	2735	3101	3490	3904	4346	4819	5326	5872	6460	7095	7785	8535
12	1625	1983	2374	2735	3038	3357	3693	4048	4423	4819	5239	5685	6160
14	1194	1457	1744	2056	2391	2735	2994	3265	3547	3843	4153	4478	4819
16	914	1115	1335	1574	1831	2106	2399	2710	2961	3196	3440	3693	3958
18	682	881	1055	1244	1447	1664	1896	2141	2401	2675	2936	3143	3357
20	497	682	855	1007	1172	1348	1535	1734	1945	2167	2400	2644	2899
22	374	512	682	833	968	1114	1269	1433	1607	1791	1983	2185	2396
24	288	395	525	682	814	936	1066	1205	1351	1505	1666	1836	2013
26	226	310	413	536	682	798	909	1026	1151	1282	1420	1564	1715
28	181	249	331	429	546	682	783	885	992	1105	1224	1349	1479
30	147	202	269	349	444	554	682	771	864	963	1067	1175	1288
32	121	167	222	288	366	457	562	678	760	846	937	1033	1132
34	101	139	185	240	305	381	468	569	673	750	830	915	1003
36		117	156	202	257	321	395	479	575	669	741	816	895
38			132	172	218	273	336	407	488	580	665	732	803
40			113	147	187	234	288	349	419	497	585	661	725
42				127	162	202	249	302	362	429	505	589	657
44				111	141	176	216	262	315	374	439	512	593
46					123	154	189	230	275	327	384	448	519
48					108	135	167	202	242	288	338	395	457
50						120	147	179	214	255	299	349	404

FLOOR BEAMS 5"x

Span'	12⅜"	13¾"	15⅛"	16½"	17⅞"	19¼"	20⅝"	22"	23⅜"	24¾"	26⅛"	27½"	28⅞"
8	2779	3212	3681	4190	4747	5357	6027	6769	7594	8516	9554	10732	12078
10	1989	2378	2696	3034	3395	3779	4190	4632	5106	5617	6170	6769	7422
12	1151	1579	2064	2378	2642	2919	3212	3520	3846	4190	4556	4944	5357
14	725	994	1323	1718	2079	2378	2604	2839	3085	3342	3611	3894	4190
16	486	666	886	1151	1463	1828	2086	2357	2575	2779	2991	3212	3441
18	341	468	623	808	1028	1284	1579	1862	2088	2326	2553	2733	2919
20	249	341	454	589	749	936	1151	1397	1675	1884	2087	2299	2521
22	187	256	341	443	563	703	865	1049	1259	1494	1725	1900	2083
24	144	197	263	341	434	541	666	808	970	1151	1354	1579	1751
26	113	155	207	268	341	426	524	636	763	905	1065	1242	1437
28		124	165	215	273	341	419	509	611	725	852	994	1151
30		101	134	175	222	277	341	414	496	589	693	808	936
32			111	144	183	228	281	341	409	486	571	666	771
34				120	152	190	234	284	341	405	476	555	643
36				101	128	160	197	239	287	341	401	468	541
38					109	136	168	204	244	290	341	398	460
40						117	144	175	209	249	292	341	395

Span′	ROOF BEAMS 6¾″ x 12⅜″	13¾″	15⅛″	16½″	17⅞″	19¼″	20⅝″	22″	23⅜″	24¾″	26⅛″	27½″	28⅞″	30¼″	31⅝″	33″	34⅜″	35¾″	37⅛″	38½″
20	671	921	1154	1360	1582	1820	2073	2342	2626	2925	3240	3569	3914	4186	4444	4711	4986	5270	5564	5867
22	504	692	921	1124	1307	1504	1713	1935	2170	2417	2677	2950	3234	3532	3841	4140	4373	4613	4860	5114
24	388	533	709	921	1099	1264	1439	1626	1823	2031	2250	2479	2718	2967	3227	3498	3778	4068	4314	4532
26	305	419	558	724	921	1077	1227	1386	1554	1731	1917	2112	2316	2528	2750	2980	3219	3467	3723	3987
28	245	336	447	580	737	921	1058	1195	1340	1492	1653	1821	1997	2180	2371	2570	2776	2989	3210	3438
30	199	273	363	471	599	749	921	1041	1167	1300	1440	1586	1739	1899	2066	2238	2418	2604	2796	2995
32	164	225	299	388	494	617	759	915	1026	1143	1265	1394	1529	1669	1815	1967	2125	2288	2458	2632
34	137	187	249	324	412	514	632	768	909	1012	1121	1235	1354	1479	1608	1743	1882	2027	2177	2332
36	115	158	210	273	347	433	533	647	776	903	1000	1102	1208	1319	1434	1554	1679	1808	1942	2080
38		134	179	232	295	368	453	550	659	783	897	989	1084	1184	1287	1395	1507	1623	1743	1867
40		115	153	199	253	316	388	471	565	671	789	892	978	1068	1162	1259	1360	1465	1573	1685
42			132	172	218	273	336	407	488	580	682	795	887	969	1054	1142	1234	1328	1427	1528
44			115	149	190	237	292	354	425	504	593	692	801	883	960	1041	1124	1210	1300	1392
46			101	131	166	208	255	310	372	441	519	605	701	806	879	952	1028	1107	1189	1274
48				115	146	183	225	273	327	388	457	533	617	709	807	874	944	1017	1092	1170
50				102	129	162	199	241	289	344	404	471	546	627	717	806	870	937	1007	1078
52					115	144	177	215	257	305	359	419	485	558	637	724	805	867	931	997
54					103	128	158	192	230	273	321	374	433	498	569	647	731	804	863	924
56						115	142	172	206	245	288	336	388	447	510	580	655	737	802	860
58						104	127	155	185	220	259	302	350	402	459	522	590	663	743	801
60							115	140	168	199	234	273	316	363	415	471	533	599	671	749

Span′	FLOOR BEAMS 6¾″ x 12⅜″	13¾″	15⅛″	16½″	17⅞″	19¼″	20⅝″	22″	23⅜″	24¾″	26⅛″	27½″	28⅞″	30¼″	31⅝″	33″	34⅜″	35¾″	37⅛″	38½″
20	336	460	613	795	1011	1263	1554	1886	2262	2543	2817	3104	3403	3640	3865	4097	4336	4583	4838	5102
22	252	346	460	598	760	949	1167	1417	1699	2017	2328	2565	2813	3071	3340	3600	3803	4011	4226	4447
24	194	266	355	460	585	731	899	1091	1309	1554	1827	2131	2363	2580	2806	3041	3285	3538	3752	3941
26	153	210	279	362	460	575	707	858	1029	1222	1437	1676	1940	2199	2391	2591	2799	3014	3237	3467
28	122	168	223	290	369	460	566	687	824	978	1151	1342	1554	1786	2041	2234	2414	2599	2791	2990
30		136	182	236	300	374	460	559	670	795	936	1091	1263	1452	1660	1886	2102	2264	2431	2604
32		112	150	194	247	308	379	460	552	655	771	899	1041	1197	1367	1554	1756	1975	2137	2289
34			125	162	206	257	316	384	460	546	643	750	868	998	1140	1295	1464	1647	1844	2028
36			105	136	173	217	266	323	388	460	541	631	731	840	960	1091	1233	1387	1554	1733
38				116	147	184	227	275	330	391	460	537	622	715	817	928	1049	1180	1321	1473
40					126	158	194	236	283	336	395	460	533	613	700	795	899	1011	1133	1263

Span′	ROOF BEAMS 8½″ x 19¼″	20⅝″	22″	23⅜″	24¾″	26⅛″	27½″	28⅞″	30¼″	31⅝″	33″	34⅜″	35¾″	37⅛″	38½″	39⅞″	41¼″	42⅝″	44″	45⅜″	46¾″
24	1591	1813	2048	2296	2558	2833	3121	3422	3737	4064	4404	4757	5123	5433	5707	5989	6279	6576	6882	7196	7518
26	1356	1545	1745	1956	2179	2414	2659	2916	3184	3463	3753	4054	4365	4688	5021	5365	5622	5880	6144	6415	6693
28	1159	1332	1504	1687	1879	2081	2293	2514	2745	2986	3236	3495	3764	4042	4329	4626	4932	5247	5550	5787	6030
30	943	1159	1311	1470	1637	1813	1998	2190	2392	2601	2819	3045	3279	3521	3771	4030	4296	4571	4853	5144	5442
32	777	955	1152	1292	1439	1594	1756	1925	2102	2286	2477	2676	2882	3095	3315	3542	3776	4017	4266	4521	4783
34	648	796	967	1144	1275	1412	1555	1705	1862	2025	2195	2370	2553	2741	2936	3137	3345	3559	3779	4005	4237
36	545	671	814	977	1137	1259	1387	1521	1661	1806	1957	2114	2277	2445	2619	2799	2984	3174	3370	3572	3779
38	464	570	692	830	986	1130	1245	1365	1491	1621	1757	1898	2044	2195	2351	2512	2678	2849	3025	3206	3392
40	398	489	594	712	845	994	1124	1232	1345	1463	1586	1713	1844	1981	2121	2267	2417	2571	2730	2893	3061
42	344	423	513	615	730	859	1002	1118	1220	1327	1438	1553	1673	1796	1924	2056	2192	2332	2476	2624	2777
44	299	367	446	535	635	747	871	1008	1112	1209	1310	1415	1524	1637	1753	1873	1997	2125	2256	2391	2530
46	261	322	390	468	556	654	762	882	1015	1106	1199	1295	1395	1498	1604	1714	1827	1944	2064	2188	2315
48	230	283	344	412	489	575	671	777	893	1016	1101	1189	1281	1375	1473	1574	1678	1786	1896	2009	2126
50	204	250	304	365	433	509	594	687	790	903	1015	1096	1180	1268	1358	1451	1547	1646	1747	1852	1959
52	181	223	270	324	385	452	528	611	702	803	912	1013	1091	1172	1255	1341	1430	1521	1615	1712	1811
54	162	199	241	289	344	404	471	545	627	717	814	920	1012	1087	1164	1244	1326	1411	1498	1588	1680
56	145	178	216	259	308	362	423	489	562	643	730	825	928	1011	1082	1157	1233	1312	1393	1476	1562
58	130	160	195	234	277	326	380	440	506	578	657	743	836	936	1009	1078	1149	1223	1298	1376	1456
60	118	145	176	211	250	295	344	398	457	522	594	671	755	845	943	1007	1074	1143	1213	1286	1361

Span′	FLOOR BEAMS 8½″ x 19¼″	20⅝″	22″	23⅜″	24¾″	26⅛″	27½″	28⅞″	30¼″	31⅝″	33″	34⅜″	35¾″	37⅛″	38½″	39⅞″	41¼″	42⅝″	44″	45⅜″	46¾″
24	921	1132	1374	1648	1956	2301	2684	2976	3249	3534	3830	4137	4455	4724	4963	5208	5460	5718	5984	6257	6538
26	724	891	1081	1296	1539	1810	2111	2444	2769	3011	3263	3525	3796	4076	4366	4665	4889	5113	5343	5578	5820
28	580	713	865	1038	1232	1449	1690	1956	2249	2570	2814	3039	3273	3515	3765	4023	4289	4563	4826	5032	5244
30	471	580	704	844	1002	1178	1374	1591	1829	2090	2374	2648	2851	3062	3280	3504	3736	3975	4220	4473	4732
32	388	478	580	695	825	971	1132	1311	1507	1722	1956	2211	2487	2691	2882	3080	3284	3493	3709	3931	4159
34	324	398	483	580	688	809	944	1093	1256	1436	1631	1844	2074	2322	2553	2728	2909	3095	3286	3482	3684
36	273	335	407	488	580	682	795	921	1058	1209	1374	1553	1747	1956	2182	2424	2594	2760	2931	3106	3286
38	232	285	346	415	493	580	676	783	900	1028	1168	1321	1485	1664	1855	2061	2282	2477	2630	2788	2950
40	199	245	297	356	423	497	580	671	772	882	1002	1132	1274	1426	1591	1767	1956	2159	2374	2516	2662

Table 2A-30 (Continued)

Span'	ROOF BEAMS 10½" x																				
	20⅝"	22"	23⅜"	24¾"	26⅛"	27½"	28⅞"	30¼"	31⅝"	33"	34⅜"	35¾"	37⅛"	38½"	39⅞"	41¼"	42⅝"	44"	45⅜"	46¾"	48⅛"
24	2239	2529	2836	3160	3499	3856	4228	4616	5020	5441	5877	6329	6711	7050	7399	7756	8123	8501	8889	9288	9698
26	1908	2155	2417	2692	2982	3285	3602	3933	4278	4636	5007	5392	5791	6203	6628	6945	7264	7590	7924	8267	8619
28	1645	1858	2084	2321	2571	2833	3106	3391	3688	3997	4318	4650	4993	5348	5715	6093	6482'	6855	7149	7449	7756
30	1432	1619	1815	2022	2240	2468	2706	2954	3213	3482	3761	4050	4350	4659	4978	5307	5646	5995	6354	6723	7050
32	1180	1423	1595	1777	1968	2169	2378	2597	2824	3060	3306	3560	3823	4095	4375	4665	4963	5269	5585	5909	6241
34	984	1194	1413	1574	1744	1921	2107	2300	2501	2711	2928	3153	3386	3627	3876	4132	4396	4668	4947	5234	5529
36	829	1006	1206	1404	1555	1714	1879	2052	2231	2418	2612	2813	3021	3235	3457	3686	3921	4164	4413	4669	4931
38	705	855	1026	1218	1396	1538	1686	1841	2003	2170	2344	2524	2711	2904	3103	3308	3519	3737	3960	4190	4426
40	604	733	880	1044	1228	1388	1522	1662	1807	1959	2116	2278	2447	2621	2800	2985	3176	3372	3574	3782	3994
42	522	633	760	902	1061	1237	1380	1507	1639	1777	1919	2066	2219	2377	2540	2708	2881	3059	3242	3430	3623
44	454	551	661	784	923	1076	1246	1373	1494	1619	1748	1883	2022	2166	2314	2467	2625	2787	2954	3125	3301
46	397	482	578	686	807	942	1090	1253	1367	1481	1600	1723	1850	1982	2117	2257	2402	2550	2703	2859	3020
48	350	424	509	604	711	829	959	1103	1255	1360	1469	1582	1699	1820	1945	2073	2206	2342	2482	2626	2774
50	309	375	450	535	629	733	849	976	1115	1254	1354	1458	1566	1677	1792	1911	2033	2158	2288	2420	2556
52	275	334	400	475	559	652	755	868	991	1126	1252	1348	1448	1551	1657	1767	1879	1996	2115	2238	2364
54	246	298	357	424	499	582	674	775	885	1006	1137	1250	1342	1438	1536	1638	1743	1850	1961	2075	2192
56	220	267	321	380	447	522	604	695	794	902	1019	1147	1248	1337	1429	1523	1620	1721	1824	1929	2038
58	198	241	289	342	403	470	544	625	714	812	918	1032	1156	1246	1332	1420	1511	1604	1700	1799	1900
60	179	217	261	309	364	424	491	565	645	733	829	932	1044	1164	1245	1327	1412	1499	1589	1681	1775

Source: Courtesy of American Institute of Timber Construction. While these data have been prepared in accordance with recognized engineering principles and based on the most accurate and reliable technical data available, they should not be used or relied upon for any general or specific application without competent professional examination and verification of its accuracy, suitability, and applicability by a licensed professional engineer, designer, or architect. By publication of this material, AITC intends no representation or warrant, expressed or implied, that the information contained herein is suitable for any general or specific use, or is free from infringement of any patent or copyright. Any user of this information assumes all risk and liability arising from such use.

PART 2B

Heating, Ventilating, and Air-Conditioning Space Allowances

HOW TO DO PRELIMINARY SIZING OF MECHANICAL EQUIPMENT SPACE

During preliminary design, one of the architect's first needs related to the HVAC system is to determine approximately how much space will be required by the various components: air-conditioning equipment, fan rooms, boilers, major duct space, and the like. Space requirements are dependent on the type of system selected and the capacity of the system, which in turn is dependent on the building type, climate, total area (or volume), building construction, heat loss and heat gain, and other variables.

While detailed calculations and sizing are usually the province of the mechanical engineer, many space requirements for commercial buildings can be estimated early in the design process.

Knowledge of several variables is usually required: the type of mechanical system to be used, the total gross floor area of the building being designed, the air quantities to be supplied, and an approximate estimate of the refrigeration loads. Table 2B–1 summarizes many of the HVAC systems used in various occupancy types. Tables 2B–2 and 2B–3 give some guidelines for refrigeration loads and air quantities for various occupancies. Table 2B–3 is especially useful where solar loading is a significant factor in the building design.

To find approximate refrigeration requirements in tons, divide the refrigeration load from Table 2B–2 or 2B–3 into the total area of the building under design.

To estimate the total air volume in cfm, one of two methods can be used:

1. Select an average air quantity per square foot from Table 2B–2 or Table 2B–3 and multiply by the total area.
2. Use the following formula:

FORMULA: $\text{cfm} = [A - (Pd)]C_1 + (Pd)C_2$

where:

cfm = air required for air conditioning
A = total area of building or floor in sq. ft.
P = length of perimeter zone of building or floor in ft. (measure at mid-depth)
d = depth of perimeter zone in ft. (usually 15 ft.)
C_1 = cfm/sq. ft. for internal zone from Table 2B–2
C_2 = cfm/sq. ft. for exterior zone from Table 2B–2

The figure for exterior zone cfm can be the total of amounts of the four building exposures.

Table 2B-1
GUIDE TO SYSTEMS AND APPLICATIONS

Applications		Individual Room or Zone Unit Systems				Central Station Apparatus Systems						
		D-X Self-Contained		All-Water		All-Air				Air-Water		
				Room Fan-Coil		Single Air Stream				Primary Air Systems		
								Reheat				
		Room ⅓ to 2 Tons	Area 2 Tons and Over	Recir. Air	With Outdoor Air	Variable Volume[3]	Bypass	At Terminal	Zone In Duct	Multi-zone Single Duct	Secondary Water H-V H-P Induction	Room Fan-Coil With O.A.
Single-purpose Occupancies												
Residential	Medium	x										
	Large		x	x						x		
Variety and Specialty Shops			x			x						
Restaurants	Medium		x			x			x			
	Large		x			x	x	x	x	x		
Bowling Alleys			x			x	x					
Radio and TV Studios	Small		x			x	x		x	x		
	Large		x			x	x		x	x		
Country Clubs			x			x	x		x	x		
Funeral Homes			x			x				x		
Beauty Salons		x	x			x						
Barber Shops		x	x			x						
Churches			x			x	x			x		
Theaters						x	x					
Auditoriums						x	x					
Dance and Roller Skating Pavilions			x			x	x					
Factories (comfort)			x				x		x			
Multi-purpose Occupancies												
Office Buildings						x				x	x	
Hotels, Dormitories				x	x	x					x	x
Motels				x								
Apartment Buildings					x						x	x
Hospitals					x	x			x		x	
Schools and Colleges					x	x	x	x	x			
Museums						x			x	x		
Libraries	Standard		x			x	x		x	x		
	Rare Books		x			x			x			
Department Stores						x	x					
Shopping Centers			x			x	x			x		
Laboratories	Small		x			x			x	x		
	Large					x		x			x	
Marine								x			x	

Reproduced courtesy of Carrier Corporation.

Table 2B-2
COOLING LOAD CHECK FIGURES

Classifications	Cooling Load Check Figures																	
	Occupancy Sq Ft/Person			Lights Watts/Sq Ft			Refrigeration Sq Ft/Ton‡			Air Quantities CFM/Sq Ft								
										East-South-West			North			Internal		
	Lo	Av	Hi	Lo	Av	Hi	Lo	Av	Hi	Lo	Av	Hi	Lo	Av	Hi	Lo	Av	Hi
Apartment, High Rise	325	175	100	1.0	2.0	4.0	450	400	350	0.8	1.2	1.7	0.5	0.8	1.3	–	–	–
Auditoriums, Churches, Theaters	15	11	6	1.0	2.0	3.0	400	250	90	–	–	–	–	–	–	1.0	2.0	3.0
Educational Facilities Schools, Colleges, Universities	30	25	20	2.0	4.0	6.0	240	185	150	1.0	1.6	2.2	0.9	1.3	2.0	0.8	1.2	1.9
Factories Assembly Areas	50	35	25	3.0†	4.5†	6.0†	240	150	90	–	–	–	–	–	–	2.0	3.6	5.5
Light Manufacturing	200	150	100	9.0†	10.0†	12.0†	200	150	100	–	–	–	–	–	–	1.6	2.5	3.8
Heavy Manufacturing△	300	250	200	15.0†	45.0†	60.0†	100	80	60	–	–	–	–	–	–	2.5	4.0	6.5
Hospitals Patient Rooms°	75	50	25	1.0	1.5	2.0	275	220	165	0.33	0.55	0.67	0.33	0.50	0.67	–	–	–
Public Areas	100	80	50	1.0	1.5	2.0	175	140	110	1.0	1.25	1.45	1.0	1.1	1.2	0.95	1.0	1.1
Hotels, Motels, Dormitories	200	150	100	1.0	2.0	3.0	350	300	220	1.0	1.40	1.5	0.9	1.2	1.4	–	–	–
Libraries and Museums	80	60	40	1.0	1.5	3.0	340	280	200	1.0	1.6	2.1	0.9	1.1	1.3	0.9	1.0	1.1
Office Buildings°	130	110	80	4.0	6.0†	9.0†	360	280	190	0.25	0.5	0.9	0.25	0.5	0.8	0.8	1.1	1.8
Private Offices°	150	125	100	2.0	5.8	8.0	–	–	–	0.25	0.5	0.9	0.25	0.5	0.8	–	–	–
Stenographic Department	100	85	70	5.0†	7.5†	10.0†	–	–	–	–	–	–	–	–	–	0.9	1.3	2.0
Residential Large	600	400	200	1.0	2.0	4.0	600	500	380	0.8	1.2	1.6	0.5	0.8	1.3	–	–	–
Medium	600	360	200	0.7	1.5	3.0	700	550	400	0.7	1.1	1.4	0.5	0.7	1.2	–	–	–
Restaurants Large	17	15	13	1.5	1.7	2.0	135	100	80	1.8	2.4	3.7	1.2	1.6	2.1	0.9	1.1	1.4
Medium							150	120	100	1.5	2.0	3.0	1.1	1.4	1.8	0.9	1.0	1.3
Shopping Centers, Department Stores and Specialty Shops																		
Beauty and Barber Shops	45	40	25	3.0†	5.0†	9.0†	240	160	105	1.5	2.6	4.2	1.1	1.7	2.6	0.9	1.3	2.0
Department stores Basement	30	25	20	2.0	3.0	4.0	340	285	225	–	–	–	–	–	–	0.7	1.0	1.2
Main Floor	45	25	16	3.5	6.0†	9.0†	350	245	150	–	–	–	–	–	–	0.9	1.4	2.0
Upper Floors	75	55	40	2.0	2.5	3.5†	400	340	280	–	–	–	–	–	–	0.8	1.0	1.2
Dress Shops	50	40	30	1.0	2.0	4.0	345	280	185	0.9	1.2	1.6	0.7	1.0	1.4	0.6	0.8	1.1
Drug Stores	35	23	17	1.0	2.0	3.0	180	135	110	1.8	2.3	3.0	1.0	1.4	1.8	0.7	1.0	1.3
5¢ and 10¢ Stores	35	25	15	1.5	3.0	5.0	345	220	120	0.7	1.4	2.0	0.6	1.2	1.6	0.5	0.9	1.1
Hat Shops	50	43	30	1.0	2.0	3.0	315	270	185	1.0	1.3	1.9	0.7	1.0	1.5	0.6	0.8	1.2
Shoe Stores	50	30	20	1.0	2.0	3.0	300	220	150	1.2	1.6	2.1	1.0	1.4	1.8	0.8	1.0	1.2
Malls	100	75	50	1.0	1.5	2.0	365	230	160	–	–	–	–	–	–	1.1	1.8	2.5
Refrigeration for Central Heating and Cooling Plant																		
Urban Districts							475	380	285									
College Campuses							400	320	240									
Commercial Centers							330	265	200									
Residential Centers							625	500	375									

Notes:

‡ Refrigeration loads are for entire application.

† Includes other loads expressed in Watts/sq ft.

△ Air quantities for heavy manufacturing areas are based on supplementary means to remove excessive heat.

° Air Quantities for hospital patient rooms and office buildings (except internal areas) are based on Induction (air-water) system.

Refrigeration and air quantities for applications listed in this table of cooling load check figures are based on all-air system and normal outdoor air quantities for ventilation except as noted.

Reproduced courtesy of Carrier Corporation.

Table 2B-3
REFRIGERATION LOAD AND AIR QUANTITY BASED ON GLASS EXPOSURE

Load and Air Quantity

Item	Bldg. Shape	Glass Area—% Wall Area										
		0%	20%		40%		60%		80%		100%	
		Shading (venetian blinds)										
			With	Without	With	Without	With	Without	With	Without	With	Without
Refrigeration	1	320	292	286	264	252	236	218	208	184	180	150
Load*	2	330	304	298	278	266	252	234	226	202	200	170
(sq ft/ton)	3	322	296	290	270	258	244	226	217	193	190	160
Air†	1	1.20	1.46	1.52	1.72	1.84	1.98	2.16	2.24	2.48	2.50	2.80
Quantity	2	1.05	1.25	1.30	1.45	1.55	1.65	1.80	1.85	2.05	2.05	2.30
(cfm/sq ft)	3	1.15	1.35	1.41	1.55	1.67	1.75	1.93	1.95	2.29	2.15	2.45

*Refrigeration load based on 100 sq ft/person, 6 watts/sq ft, .15 cfm outdoor air/sq ft, wall U=.32; roof U=.10, single glazing, 10-story building, 40° N latitude, 12-hour operation.

†Air Quantity is average for entire building and is based on use of an all-air system.

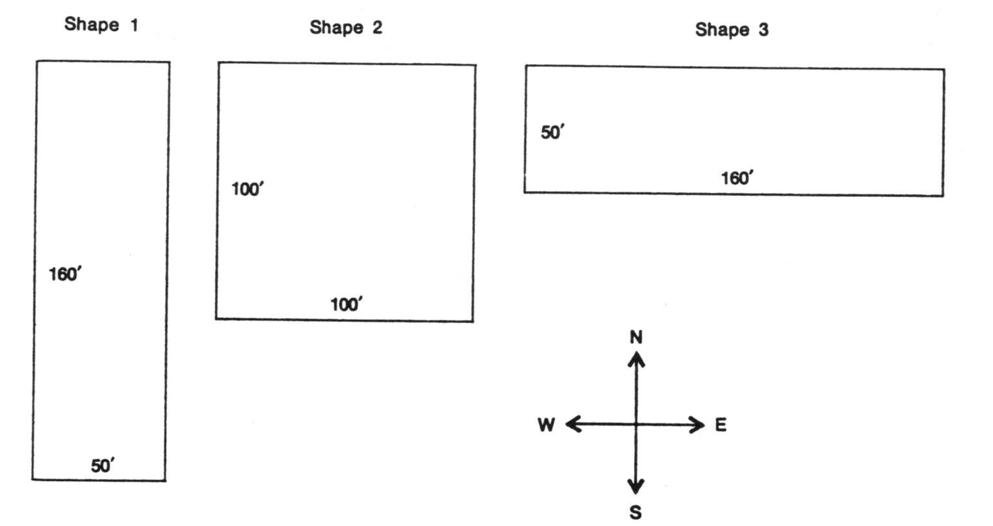

Examples of Using Tables

Case	Area Sq. Ft.	% Glass	Shading	Bldg. Shape	Tonnage	Cfm
1	30,000	20	Yes	1	100	44,000
2	30,000	60	Yes	1	127	59,500
3	30,000	60	Yes	3	123	52,500
4	30,000	60	No	1	137	65,000

Reproduced courtesy of Carrier Corporation.

RULES OF THUMB

The following are some of the frequently used guides to preliminary planning of mechanical equipment space based on the variables just described.

- Mechanical equipment space will typically occupy about 6% to 9% of the total area of the building. This includes fan rooms, boilers, and refrigeration equipment.
- If the tonnage and system type are known, multiply the figures in Table 2B-4 by tonnage.
- If the gross floor area and general system type are known, use the percentages listed in Table 2B-5.
- If you will be using one of the system types listed in Table 2B-6, multiply the gross floor by the percentages in the table.

Table 2B-4
PRELIMINARY SIZING OF MECHANICAL EQUIPMENT ROOMS BASED ON TONNAGE

System Type	Equipment (sq. ft./ton)	Air Handlers (sq. ft./ton)
Gas-fired multizone direct-expansion cycle	2.8	5.0
Gas-fired multizone chilled-water cycle	4.0	5.0
Hot water–chilled water cycle	4.4	6.7
Hot water direct-expansion cycle	3.7	6.2

Note: Figures are generous and include allowance for domestic hot water heaters and electrical panels to operate equipment.

Table 2B-5
PRELIMINARY SIZING OF MECHANICAL EQUIPMENT ROOMS BASED ON GROSS FLOOR AREA

	Percent of Gross Floor Area	
	Larger Buildings	Smaller Buildings, Less Than 10,000 sq. ft. or with Heavy Cooling Loads
All-Air Systems (1)	3%	8%
Air and Water Systems (1)	3%	6%
All-Water Systems	1.5%	5%
Small Package Units Throughout or on Roof	1%	3%

(1) Separate rooms for air-handling equipment may require an additional 2% to 4% of the building's total occupied area.

Table 2B-6
TYPICAL SPACE REQUIREMENTS FOR VARIOUS MECHANICAL SYSTEMS
Percent of Gross Floor Area (1)

		Percent of Gross Area or Cubage				
		Equipment Room		Ductwork Distribution		
		Air Handling %	Refrig.	Riser	Horizontal	Piping
Low Velocity Conventional		2.2–3.5	0.2–1.0	(2)	0.7–0.9 (3)	—
High Velocity Conventional		2.0–3.3	"	(2)	0.4–0.5 (3)	—
Terminal Reheat (hot water)		2.0–3.3	"	(2)	"	0.03–0.04 (3)
Terminal Reheat (electric)		2.0–3.3	"	(2)	"	—
Variable Volume		—	"	(2)	0.1–0.2 (3)	—
Multizone Unit		—	"	(2)	0.7–0.9 (3)	—
Double Duct		2.2–3.5	"	(2)	0.6–0.8 (3)	—
Dual Conduit		2.4–3.4	"	(2)	0.3–0.4 (3)	—
All-Air Induction		2.0–3.3	0.2–1.0	(2)	0.4–0.5 (3)	0.1–0.2
Air-Water	2-pipe	0.5–1.5	"	0.25–0.35 (4)		—
Induction	4 pipe	0.5–1.5	"	0.3–0.4 (4)		—
Fan-Coil Unit	2-pipe	—	"	—	—	0.1–0.2
	4-pipe	—	"	—	—	0.25–0.3

(1) To determine equipment room size, use gross area of entire building. For others, use gross area of space served.
(2) Included in equipment room area.
(3) Percent of gross cubical content.
(4) Includes space for pipe risers.

Reproduced courtesy of Carrier Corporation.

Formulas for Mechanical Equipment Space

Mechanical space

Low occupancy buildings: 3.5% to 7% of total gross area
Office buildings: 5% to 10%
Labs and hospitals: 6.25% to 15%

Air-conditioning plant size

0.3 cu. ft. per each cfm of air exchanged
100 cu. ft. per ton of refrigeration, assuming 350 cfm/ton

Volume of fan room

0.4 cu. ft. per each cfm of air exchanged

FORMULA:

$$V = \frac{cfm}{2.5}$$

where:

V = volume of fan room

Fan rooms

Fan rooms occupy 3% to 7% of the total gross building area, with ceiling heights from 15 ft. to 18 ft.

Volume of mechanical equipment room

FORMULA: $V = \text{tons}\,(60)$

where:

V = volume in cu. ft.

Vertical duct shaft space in sq. ft.

FORMULA:

$$A = \frac{\text{air quantity in cfm}}{1000} \times 1.3$$

Vertical duct space

3 to 4 sq. ft. for every 1000 sq. ft. of floor space served.

Vertical duct shaft space

Occupies from 2% to 5% of total floor area of building

HOW TO ESTIMATE DUCT SIZES

Since duct work sizes can affect floor to floor heights and vertical shaft space during preliminary design of buildings, it is helpful to have a quick way to estimate their size. Duct sizes are primarily dependent on the quantity of air to be moved, the velocity of the air, and friction losses of the duct and fittings.

Recommended and maximum air velocities in ducts are given in Table 2B–7. The quantity of air to be moved depends both on air-condition loads and ventilation requirements. Air quantities in cubic feet per minute per square foot are given in Tables 2B–2 and 2B–3. These are useful where cooling loads are dominant. Table 2B–12 gives recommended outdoor air requirements for ventilation. These are useful where air-conditioning is not used or where ventilation requirements are dominant over cooling loads. Local building codes also give minimum required ventilation requirements.

Tables 2B–8, 2B–9, 2B–10, and 2B–11 give values for duct area per square foot of floor area served for three different duct shapes: round ducts, nearly square ducts, and thin rectangular ducts. These four tables include a friction allowance based on the duct shape. To use the tables, first calculate the volume of air to be moved in cubic feet *per hour* per square foot. Values from Tables 2B–2 and 2B–3 are simply multiplied by 60 minutes per hour to arrive at cubic feet per hour.

If a value for air changes per hour is given, multiply this by the height of the ceiling to get cubic feet per hour per square foot. For other values such as cubic feet per person, you will need to calculate the occupancy load, multiply by the recommended cfm per person, and then divide by the room or building area to get cfm/sq. ft. Then multiply by 60 to get cfh/sq. ft.

After you determine the volume of air, determine the velocity to use from Table 2B–7 and look in the appropriate table for the duct area per square foot of floor area. Multiply this by the floor area served to get approximate duct area in *square inches*. Divide by 144 to get a square footage area or divide by either a required width or height to determine the corresponding dimension for a rectangular duct in inches. Allow additional area for insulation and duct support.

Remember that this calculation procedure is only for preliminary estimates of sizing for space-planning purposes. Unusual heating or cooling design conditions, duct layout, unusual friction losses, and the like will affect final sizing.

Example

Find the approximate size of the main duct serving one floor of a small air-conditioned office building that is 95 ft. wide and 150 ft. long. Ceiling space is limited.

Total area is $150 \times 95 = 14{,}250$ sq. ft.

Assume a perimeter zone of 15 ft. and select the "average" air quantities for office buildings from Table 2B–2 of 1.1 cfm/sq. ft. for internal loading and 0.5 cfm/sq. ft. for the perimeter zone. (Table 2B–2 assumes office buildings are based on an air–water system.)

Use the following formula.

FORMULA: $\text{cfm} = [A - (Pd)]C_1 + (Pd)C_2$

(To find area of perimeter zone, use the midpoint of the zone, 7.5 ft. in from the actual perimeter. The perimeter then becomes that of a 135 ft. by 80 ft. building.)

FORMULA:

$$P = 2 \times 135 + 2 \times 80 = 430 \text{ ft.}$$
$$\text{cfm} = [14{,}250 - (430 \times 15)]\ 0.5 + (430 \times 15)\ 1.1$$
$$\text{cfm} = 3900 + 7095$$
$$\text{cfm} = 10{,}995 \text{ for the entire floor}$$

To find the cu. ft. per hr. per sq. ft. required by the tables:

$$\text{cfh/sq. ft.} = 10{,}995/14{,}250 \times 60 = 46.3 \text{ cfh/sq. ft.}$$

From Table 2B–7, select the low recommended velocity of main ducts of 1000 fpm. Using Table 2B–11 for thin rectangular ducts (since presumably you want a duct with minimum depth) look under the 1000 fpm column and the 45 cfh/sq. ft. row to get 0.135 sq. in. per sq. ft.

FORMULA: $0.135 \times 14{,}250 = 1923$ sq. in., or 13.35 sq. ft.

If the depth of the duct was 20 in., then the width should be $1923/20 = 96$ in. This is approximately a 1 : 5 ratio.

The main return air duct should be at least 80% of supply air for a centralized system, so this area would also have to be allowed. Of course, as the main duct branched out to serve individual zones or spaces, its size would decrease from the maximum just calculated. Also note that the cfm figure is conservative since the total area of 14,250 sq. ft. includes areas taken up by stairways, elevator shafts, partitions, structure, storage closets, and other non-air-conditioned spaces.

Example

Find the approximate size of a round duct used to ventilate a 1400 sq. ft. bar/cocktail lounge where smoking is allowed.

From Table 2B–12 the recommended ventilation requirement is 50 cfm per person and the assumed occupancy is 100 persons per 1000 sq. ft., or 1 person per 10 sq. ft.

FORMULA: 50 cfm/person × 140 people = 7000 cfm for the total area
7000/1400 = 5.0 cfm/sq. ft., or 300 cfh/sq. ft. (5.0 × 60)

Using the high range of recommended velocities for branch ducts from Table 2B–7 of 900 fpm and Table 2B–8 for round ducts, interpolate to find the duct area per sq. ft. of 0.810.

0.810 × 1400 = 1134 sq. in.

Since the area of a round duct is $A = \pi r^2$, r = 19 in. and the diameter should be about 38 in.

Table 2B-7
RECOMMENDED AND MAXIMUM AIR VELOCITIES FOR DUCTS

Designation	Recommended Velocities (fpm)		
	Residences	Schools, Theaters, Public Buildings	Industrial Buildings
Outdoor air intakes (a)	500	500	500
Filters (a)	250	300	350
Heating coils (a),(b)	450	500	600
Cooling coils (a)	450	500	600
Air washers (a)	500	500	500
Fan outlets	1000–1600	1300–2000	1600–2400
Main ducts (b)	700–900	1000–1300	1200–1800
Branch ducts (b)	600	600–900	800–1000
Branch risers (b)	500	600–700	800
	Maximum Velocities (fpm)		
Outdoor air intakes (a)	800	900	1200
Filters (a)	300	350	350
Heating coils (a),(b)	500	600	700
Cooling coils (a)	450	500	600
Air washers (a)	500	500	500
Fan outlets	1700	1500–2200	1700–2800
Main ducts (b)	800–1200	1100–1600	1300–2200
Branch ducts (b)	700–1000	800–1300	1000–1800
Branch risers (b)	650–800	800–1200	1000–1600

(a) These velocities are for total face area, not the net free area; other velocities in table are for net free area.

(b) For low velocity systems only.

Source: Copyright by the American Society of Heating, Refrigerating, and Air Conditioning Engineers, Inc., Atlanta, GA. Reprinted by permission from ASHRAE Handbook Systems and Equipment, 1967.

Table 2B-8
DUCT AREA PER SQUARE FOOT OF FLOOR AREA (in sq. in.)
Round Ducts
Friction Allowance = 1.00

Velocity (fpm)

CFH/sq. ft.	400	600	800	1000	1200	1400	1600	1800	2000	2200
30	0.180	0.120	0.090	0.072	0.060	0.051	0.045	0.040	0.036	0.033
35	0.210	0.140	0.105	0.084	0.070	0.060	0.053	0.047	0.042	0.038
40	0.240	0.160	0.120	0.096	0.080	0.069	0.060	0.053	0.048	0.044
45	0.270	0.180	0.135	0.108	0.090	0.077	0.068	0.060	0.054	0.049
50	0.300	0.200	0.150	0.120	0.100	0.086	0.075	0.067	0.060	0.055
55	0.330	0.220	0.165	0.132	0.110	0.094	0.083	0.073	0.066	0.060
60	0.360	0.240	0.180	0.144	0.120	0.103	0.090	0.080	0.072	0.065
65	0.390	0.260	0.195	0.156	0.130	0.111	0.098	0.087	0.078	0.071
70	0.420	0.280	0.210	0.168	0.140	0.120	0.105	0.093	0.084	0.076
75	0.450	0.300	0.225	0.180	0.150	0.129	0.113	0.100	0.090	0.082
80	0.480	0.320	0.240	0.192	0.160	0.137	0.120	0.107	0.096	0.087
85	0.510	0.340	0.255	0.204	0.170	0.146	0.128	0.113	0.102	0.093
90	0.540	0.360	0.270	0.216	0.180	0.154	0.135	0.120	0.108	0.098
95	0.570	0.380	0.285	0.228	0.190	0.163	0.143	0.127	0.114	0.104
100	0.600	0.400	0.300	0.240	0.200	0.171	0.150	0.133	0.120	0.109
105	0.630	0.420	0.315	0.252	0.210	0.180	0.158	0.140	0.126	0.115
110	0.660	0.440	0.330	0.264	0.220	0.189	0.165	0.147	0.132	0.120
115	0.690	0.460	0.345	0.276	0.230	0.197	0.173	0.153	0.138	0.125
120	0.720	0.480	0.360	0.288	0.240	0.206	0.180	0.160	0.144	0.131
130	0.780	0.520	0.390	0.312	0.260	0.223	0.195	0.173	0.156	0.142
140	0.840	0.560	0.420	0.336	0.280	0.240	0.210	0.187	0.168	0.153
150	0.900	0.600	0.450	0.360	0.300	0.257	0.225	0.200	0.180	0.164
160	0.960	0.640	0.480	0.384	0.320	0.274	0.240	0.213	0.192	0.175
170	1.020	0.680	0.510	0.408	0.340	0.291	0.255	0.227	0.204	0.185
180	1.080	0.720	0.540	0.432	0.360	0.309	0.270	0.240	0.216	0.196
190	1.140	0.760	0.570	0.456	0.380	0.326	0.285	0.253	0.228	0.207
200	1.200	0.800	0.600	0.480	0.400	0.343	0.300	0.267	0.240	0.218
220	1.320	0.880	0.660	0.528	0.440	0.377	0.330	0.293	0.264	0.240
240	1.440	0.960	0.720	0.576	0.480	0.411	0.360	0.320	0.288	0.262
260	1.560	1.040	0.780	0.624	0.520	0.446	0.390	0.347	0.312	0.284
280	1.680	1.120	0.840	0.672	0.560	0.480	0.420	0.373	0.336	0.305
300	1.800	1.200	0.900	0.720	0.600	0.514	0.450	0.400	0.360	0.327
320	1.920	1.280	0.960	0.768	0.640	0.549	0.480	0.427	0.384	0.349
340	2.040	1.360	1.020	0.816	0.680	0.583	0.510	0.453	0.408	0.371
360	2.160	1.440	1.080	0.864	0.720	0.617	0.540	0.480	0.432	0.393
380	2.280	1.520	1.140	0.912	0.760	0.651	0.570	0.507	0.456	0.415
400	2.400	1.600	1.200	0.960	0.800	0.686	0.600	0.533	0.480	0.436

Table 2B-9
DUCT AREA PER SQUARE FOOT OF FLOOR AREA (in sq. in.)
Nearly Square Ducts Less Than 1000 cfm
Friction Allowance = 1.10
Velocity (fpm)

CFH/sq. ft.	400	600	800	1000	1200	1400	1600	1800	2000	2200
30	0.198	0.132	0.099	0.079	0.066	0.057	0.050	0.044	0.040	0.036
35	0.231	0.154	0.116	0.092	0.077	0.066	0.058	0.051	0.046	0.042
40	0.264	0.176	0.132	0.106	0.088	0.075	0.066	0.059	0.053	0.048
45	0.297	0.198	0.149	0.119	0.099	0.085	0.074	0.066	0.059	0.054
50	0.330	0.220	0.165	0.132	0.110	0.094	0.083	0.073	0.066	0.060
55	0.363	0.242	0.182	0.145	0.121	0.104	0.091	0.081	0.073	0.066
60	0.396	0.264	0.198	0.158	0.132	0.113	0.099	0.088	0.079	0.072
65	0.429	0.286	0.215	0.172	0.143	0.123	0.107	0.095	0.086	0.078
70	0.462	0.308	0.231	0.185	0.154	0.132	0.116	0.103	0.092	0.084
75	0.495	0.330	0.248	0.198	0.165	0.141	0.124	0.110	0.099	0.090
80	0.528	0.352	0.264	0.211	0.176	0.151	0.132	0.117	0.106	0.096
85	0.561	0.374	0.281	0.224	0.187	0.160	0.140	0.125	0.112	0.102
90	0.594	0.396	0.297	0.238	0.198	0.170	0.149	0.132	0.119	0.108
95	0.627	0.418	0.314	0.251	0.209	0.179	0.157	0.139	0.125	0.114
100	0.660	0.440	0.330	0.264	0.220	0.189	0.165	0.147	0.132	0.120
105	0.693	0.462	0.347	0.277	0.231	0.198	0.173	0.154	0.139	0.126
110	0.726	0.484	0.363	0.290	0.242	0.207	0.182	0.161	0.145	0.132
115	0.759	0.506	0.380	0.304	0.253	0.217	0.190	0.169	0.152	0.138
120	0.792	0.528	0.396	0.317	0.264	0.226	0.198	0.176	0.158	0.144
130	0.858	0.572	0.429	0.343	0.286	0.245	0.215	0.191	0.172	0.156
140	0.924	0.616	0.462	0.370	0.308	0.264	0.231	0.205	0.185	0.168
150	0.990	0.660	0.495	0.396	0.330	0.283	0.248	0.220	0.198	0.180

Table 2B-10
DUCT AREA PER SQUARE FOOT OF FLOOR AREA (in sq. in.)
Nearly Square Ducts More Than 1000 cfm
Friction Allowance = 1.05
Velocity (fpm)

CFH/sq. ft.	400	600	800	1000	1200	1400	1600	1800	2000	2200
150	0.945	0.630	0.473	0.378	0.315	0.270	0.236	0.210	0.189	0.172
160	1.008	0.672	0.504	0.403	0.336	0.288	0.252	0.224	0.202	0.183
170	1.071	0.714	0.536	0.428	0.357	0.306	0.268	0.238	0.214	0.195
180	1.134	0.756	0.567	0.454	0.378	0.324	0.284	0.252	0.227	0.206
200	1.260	0.840	0.630	0.504	0.420	0.360	0.315	0.280	0.252	0.229
220	1.386	0.924	0.693	0.554	0.462	0.396	0.347	0.308	0.277	0.252
240	1.512	1.008	0.756	0.605	0.504	0.432	0.378	0.336	0.302	0.275
260	1.638	1.092	0.819	0.655	0.546	0.468	0.410	0.364	0.328	0.298
280	1.764	1.176	0.882	0.706	0.588	0.504	0.441	0.392	0.353	0.321
300	1.890	1.260	0.945	0.756	0.630	0.540	0.473	0.420	0.378	0.344
320	2.016	1.344	1.008	0.806	0.672	0.576	0.504	0.448	0.403	0.367
340	2.142	1.428	1.071	0.857	0.714	0.612	0.536	0.476	0.428	0.389
360	2.268	1.512	1.134	0.907	0.756	0.648	0.567	0.504	0.454	0.412
380	2.394	1.596	1.197	0.958	0.798	0.684	0.599	0.532	0.479	0.435
400	2.520	1.680	1.260	1.008	0.840	0.720	0.630	0.560	0.504	0.458

Table 2B-11
DUCT AREA PER SQUARE FOOT OF FLOOR AREA (in sq. in.)
Thin Rectangular Ducts (width to depth 1 : 5)
Friction Allowance 1.25
Velocity (fpm)

CFH/sq. ft.	400	600	800	1000	1200	1400	1600	1800	2000	2200
30	0.225	0.150	0.113	0.090	0.075	0.064	0.056	0.050	0.045	0.041
35	0.263	0.175	0.131	0.105	0.088	0.075	0.066	0.058	0.053	0.048
40	0.300	0.200	0.150	0.120	0.100	0.086	0.075	0.067	0.060	0.055
45	0.338	0.225	0.169	0.135	0.113	0.096	0.084	0.075	0.068	0.061
50	0.375	0.250	0.188	0.150	0.125	0.107	0.094	0.083	0.075	0.068
55	0.413	0.275	0.206	0.165	0.138	0.118	0.103	0.092	0.083	0.075
60	0.450	0.300	0.225	0.180	0.150	0.129	0.113	0.100	0.090	0.082
65	0.488	0.325	0.244	0.195	0.163	0.139	0.122	0.108	0.098	0.089
70	0.525	0.350	0.263	0.210	0.175	0.150	0.131	0.117	0.105	0.095
75	0.563	0.375	0.281	0.225	0.188	0.161	0.141	0.125	0.113	0.102
80	0.600	0.400	0.300	0.240	0.200	0.171	0.150	0.133	0.120	0.109
85	0.638	0.425	0.319	0.255	0.213	0.182	0.159	0.142	0.128	0.116
90	0.675	0.450	0.338	0.270	0.225	0.193	0.169	0.150	0.135	0.123
95	0.713	0.475	0.356	0.285	0.238	0.204	0.178	0.158	0.143	0.130
100	0.750	0.500	0.375	0.300	0.250	0.214	0.188	0.167	0.150	0.136
105	0.788	0.525	0.394	0.315	0.263	0.225	0.197	0.175	0.158	0.143
110	0.825	0.550	0.413	0.330	0.275	0.236	0.206	0.183	0.165	0.150
115	0.863	0.575	0.431	0.345	0.288	0.246	0.216	0.192	0.173	0.157
120	0.900	0.600	0.450	0.360	0.300	0.257	0.225	0.200	0.180	0.164
130	0.975	0.650	0.488	0.390	0.325	0.279	0.244	0.217	0.195	0.177
140	1.050	0.700	0.525	0.420	0.350	0.300	0.263	0.233	0.210	0.191
150	1.125	0.750	0.563	0.450	0.375	0.321	0.281	0.250	0.225	0.205
160	1.200	0.800	0.600	0.480	0.400	0.343	0.300	0.267	0.240	0.218
170	1.275	0.850	0.638	0.510	0.425	0.364	0.319	0.283	0.255	0.232
180	1.350	0.900	0.675	0.540	0.450	0.386	0.338	0.300	0.270	0.245
190	1.425	0.950	0.713	0.570	0.475	0.407	0.356	0.317	0.285	0.259
200	1.500	1.000	0.750	0.600	0.500	0.429	0.375	0.333	0.300	0.273
220	1.650	1.100	0.825	0.660	0.550	0.471	0.413	0.367	0.330	0.300
240	1.800	1.200	0.900	0.720	0.600	0.514	0.450	0.400	0.360	0.327
260	1.950	1.300	0.975	0.780	0.650	0.557	0.488	0.433	0.390	0.355
280	2.100	1.400	1.050	0.840	0.700	0.600	0.525	0.467	0.420	0.382
300	2.250	1.500	1.125	0.900	0.750	0.643	0.563	0.500	0.450	0.409
320	2.400	1.600	1.200	0.960	0.800	0.686	0.600	0.533	0.480	0.436
340	2.550	1.700	1.275	1.020	0.850	0.729	0.638	0.567	0.510	0.464
360	2.700	1.800	1.350	1.080	0.900	0.771	0.675	0.600	0.540	0.491
380	2.850	1.900	1.425	1.140	0.950	0.814	0.713	0.633	0.570	0.518
400	3.000	2.000	1.500	1.200	1.000	0.857	0.750	0.667	0.600	0.545

VENTILATION REQUIREMENTS

Table 2B-12
OUTDOOR AIR REQUIREMENTS FOR VENTILATION

OUTDOOR AIR REQUIREMENTS FOR VENTILATION Commercial Facilities (offices, stores, shops, hotels, sports facilities, etc.)						
	Estimated Occupancy (persons per 1000 ft^2 or 100 m^2 floor area) (use only when design occupancy is not known)	Outdoor Air Requirements				Comments
		Smoking	Non-smoking	Smoking	Non-smoking	
Dry Cleaners and Laundries		cfm/person		L/s · person		
Commercial	10	—	15	—	7.75	A blank (—) indicates that smoking (or non-smoking) in a space should not occur.
Storage/pickup areas	30	35	10	17.5	5	
Coin-operated laundries	20	35	15	17.5	7.5	Dry cleaning processes may require more air.
Coin-operated dry cleaning	20	—	15	—	7.5	
Food and Beverage Services						
Dining rooms	70	35	7	17.5	3.5	
Kitchens	20	—	10	—	5	
Cafeterias, fast food facilities	100	35	7	17.5	3.5	
Bars and cocktail lounges	100	50	10	25	5	

Table 2B-12 (Continued)

OUTDOOR AIR REQUIREMENTS FOR VENTILATION
Commercial Facilities

	Estimated Occupancy (persons per 1000 ft^2 or 100 m^2 floor area) (use only when design occupancy is not known)	Outdoor Air Requirements				Comments
		Smoking	Non-smoking	Smoking	Non-smoking	
Garages, Auto Repair Shops, Service Stations		**cfm/ft² floor**		**L/s · m² floor**		
Parking garages (enclosed)	—	1.5	1.5	7.5	7.5	Distribution must consider worker location and concentration of running engines; stands where engines are run must incorporate systems for positive engine exhaust withdrawal.
Auto repair workrooms (general)	—	1.5	1.5	7.5	7.5	
Hotels, Motels, Resorts, Dormitories, and Correctional Facilities		**cfm/room**		**L/s · room**		See also food and beverage services, merchandising, barber and beauty shops, garages.
Bedrooms (single, double)	5	30	15	15	7.5	Independent of room size
Living rooms (suites)	20	50	25	25	12.5	
Baths, toilets (attached to bedrooms)		50	50	25	25	Independent of room size: installed capacity for intermittent use

		cfm/person		L/s · person	
Lobbies	30	15	5	7.5	2.5
Conference rooms (small)	50	35	7	17.5	3.5
Assembly rooms (large)	120	35	7	17.5	3.5
Gambling casinos	120	35	7	17.5	3.5
Offices					
Office space	7	20	5	10	2.5
Meeting and waiting spaces	60	35	7	17.5	3.5
Public Spaces		**cfm/ft² floor**		**L/s · m² Floor**	
Corridors and utility rooms		0.02	0.02	0.10	0.10
		cfm/stall or urinal		**L/s · stall or urinal**	
Public restrooms	100	75	—	37.5	—
		cfm/locker		**L/s · locker**	
Locker and dressing rooms	50	35	15	17.5	7.5
Retail Stores		**cfm/person**		**L/s · person**	
Sales floors and showrooms					
Basement and street floors	30	25	5	12.5	2.5
Upper floors	20	25	5	12.5	2.5
Storage areas (serving sales and storerooms)	15	25	5	12.5	2.5
Dressing rooms	—	25	5	12.5	3.5
Malls and arcades	20	10	5	5	2.5
Shipping and receiving areas	10	10	5	5	2.5
Warehouses	5	10	5	5	2.5
Elevators	—	—	15	—	7.5
Smoking rooms	70	50	—	25	—

Table 2B-12 (Continued)

OUTDOOR AIR REQUIREMENTS FOR VENTILATION
Commercial Facilities

	Estimated Occupancy (persons per 1000 ft² or 100 m² floor area) (use only when design occupancy is not known)	Outdoor Air Requirements				Comments
		Smoking	Non-smoking	Smoking	Non-smoking	
Specialty Shops		cfm/person		L/s · person		
Barber and beauty shops	25	35	20	17.5	10	
Reducing salons, health spas (exercise rooms)	20	—	15	—	7.5	
Florists	10	25	5	12.5	2.5	Ventilation to optimize plant growth may dictate requirements.
Greenhouses	1	—	5	—	2.5	
Show repair shops (combined workrooms/ trade areas)	10	15	10	7.5	5	
		cfm/ft² floor		L/s · m² floor		
Pet shops	—	1	1	5	5	
Sports and Amusement Facilities		cfm/person		L/s · person		
Ballrooms and discos	100	35	7	17.5	3.5	
Bowling alleys (seating area)	70	35	7	17.5	3.5	
Playing floors (e.g., gymnasiums, ice arenas)	30	—	20	—	10	When internal combustion engines are operated for maintenance of playing surfaces, increased ventilation rates will be required.
Spectator areas	150	35	7	17.5	3.5	

Game rooms (e.g., cards and billiards rooms)	70	35	7	17.5	3.5	
Swimming pools		**cfm/ft² area**		**L/s · m² area**		
Pool and deck areas	—	—	0.5	—	2.5	Higher values may be required for humidity control.
		cfm/person		**L/s · person**		
Spectators' area	70	35	7	17.5	3.5	
Theaters		**cfm/person**		**L/s · person**		
Ticket booths	—	20	5	10	2.5	
Lobbies, foyers, and lounges, and auditoriums in motion picture theaters, lecture, concert, and opera halls	150	35	7	17.5	3.5	
Stages, TV and movie studios	70	—	10	—	5	Special ventilation will be needed to eliminate special stage effects (e.g., dry ice vapors, mists, etc.).
Transportation		**cfm/person**		**L/s · person**		
Waiting rooms, ticket and baggage areas, corridors and gate areas, platforms, concourses	150	35	7	17.5	3.5	Ventilation within vehicles will require special consideration.

Table 2B-12 (Continued)

OUTDOOR AIR REQUIREMENTS FOR VENTILATION Commercial Facilities						
	Estimated Occupancy (persons per 1000 ft^2 or 100 m^2 floor area) (use only when design occupancy is not known)	Outdoor Air Requirements				Comments
		Smoking	Non-smoking	Smoking	Non-smoking	
Workrooms		**cfm/person**		**L/s · person**		
Meat processing rooms	10	—	5	—	2.5	Spaces maintained at low temperatures (−10 F to +50 F or −23°C to +10°C) are not covered by these requirements unless the occupancy is continuous. Ventilation from adjoining spaces is permissible. When the occupancy is intermittent, infiltration will normally exceed the ventilation requirement.
Pharmacists' workroom	20	—	7	—	3.5	
Bank vaults	10	—	5	—	2.5	
Photo studios						
Camera room, stages	10	—	5	—	2.5	
Darkrooms	10	—	20	—	10	

		cfm/ft² floor		L/s · m² floor		
Duplicating and printing rooms		—	0.5	—	2.5	Installed equipment must incorporate positive exhaust and control (as required) of undesirable contaminants (toxic or otherwise).
Educational Facilities		cfm/person		L/s · person		
Classrooms	50	25	5	12.5	2.5	
Laboratories	30	—	10	—	5	Special contaminant control systems may be required for processes or functions including laboratory animal occupancy.
Training shops	30	35	7	17.5	3.5	
Music rooms	50	35	7	17.5	3.5	
Libraries	20	—	5	—	2.5	
Hospital, Nursing and Convalescent Homes						Special requirements or codes and pressure relationships may determine minimum ventilation rates and filter efficiency.
		cfm/bed		L/s · bed		
Patient rooms	10	35	7	17.5	3.5	

Table 2B-12 (Continued)

OUTDOOR AIR REQUIREMENTS FOR VENTILATION
Commercial Facilities

	Estimated Occupancy (persons per 1000 ft^2 or 100 m^2 floor area) (use only when design occupancy is not known)	Outdoor Air Requirements				Comments
		Smoking	Non-smoking	Smoking	Non-smoking	
		cfm/person		L/s · person		
Medical procedure areas	10	35	7	17.5	3.5	
Operating rooms, delivery rooms	20	—	40	—	20	Procedures generating contaminants may require higher rates.
Recovery and intensive care rooms	20	—	15	—	7.5	Air shall not be recirculated into other spaces.
Autopsy rooms	20	—	100	—	50	Air shall not be recirculated into other spaces.
Physical therapy areas	20	—	15	—	7.5	

OUTDOOR AIR REQUIREMENTS FOR VENTILATION
Commercial Facilities

Outdoor Air Requirements	Comments
	Operable windows or mechanical ventilation systems shall be provided for use when occupancy is greater than usual conditions or when unusual contaminant levels are generated within the space.

	cfm/room	L/s · room	
General living areas	10	5	Ventilation rate is independent of room size.
Bedrooms	10	5	
All other rooms	10	5	
Kitchens	100	50	Installed capacity for intermittent use
Baths, toilets	50	25	
	cfm/car space	**L/s · car space**	
Garages (separate for each dwelling unit)	100	50	
	cfm/ft² floor	**L/s · m² floor**	
Garages (common for several units)	1.5	7.5	

OUTDOOR AIR REQUIREMENTS FOR VENTILATION
Commercial Facilities

Occupational safety laws in various states usually regulate process ventilation requirements. The following list gives the requirements for the occupants only, assuming that the ventilated airs is of a quality equal to or exceeding limits listed in Section 6.1 in Standard 62-1981. Air of this quality may be included as part of the process ventilation.

	Outdoor Air Requirements				
	Smoking	**Non-smoking**	**Smoking**	**Non-smoking**	**Comments**
	cfm/person		**L/s · person**		
High activity level (2.5 met)*	35	20	17.5	10	Mining, foundry, etc.
Medium activity level (2.0 met)	35	10	17.5	5	Automotive repair, assembly line, etc.
Low activity level (1.5 met)	35	7	17.5	3.5	Laboratory work, light assembly, etc.

*1.0 met = sedentary activity level = 18.4 Btu/hr · ft² body surface (58.2 W/m²)

Source: ASHRAE Standard 62-1981.

Attic Ventilation for Moisture Control

FORMULA:

$$V = \frac{A}{300}$$

where:

V = total net area of vents in sq. ft.
A = building area below attic in sq. ft.

Notes:

1. Vent each joist space where ceiling is on the underside of joists; allow 1 1/2 in. free space above insulation.
2. Provide at least two vents on opposite sides of a gable roof.
3. Provide A/600 additional vent area at ridge of a hip roof.
4. Increase the net area by 1.25 for # 8 screen and by 2.00 for # 16 screen and by 3.00 for # 16 screen with louver.

Crawl Space Ventilation

FORMULAS: For covered soil:

$$V = \frac{A}{1600}$$

For uncovered soil:

$$V = \frac{A}{160} \text{ or } V = \frac{2L}{100} + \frac{A}{300}$$

where:

V = net area of vents in sq. ft.
A = crawl space area in sq. ft.
L = perimeter of crawl space in ft.

Notes

1. Provide at least four vents, one near each corner.
2. Increase net area by factors just listed for screens and louvers.

PART 2C

Plumbing

MINIMUM PLUMBING FIXTURES

Table 2C–1 gives requirements for the minimum number of plumbing fixtures for various occupancies based on the *Uniform Plumbing Code* requirements. You should also verify requirements for disabled persons with ANSI A117.1, *Specifications for Making Buildings and Facilities Accessible to and Usable by Physically Handicapped People.*

WATER PIPE SIZING USING TABLES

Where the maximum length of supply piping is 200 feet or less and the system serves less than 50 fixture units, the *Uniform Plumbing Code* requires piping to be sized according to tables. Larger systems may also be sized using the tables or by more detailed methods.

When sizing piping according to this method, a few requirements apply:

1. No building supply pipe can be less than 3/4 inch.
2. Pressure losses from water filters, water softeners, backflow prevention valves, and similar devices must be included in the pressure loss calculations.
3. Where fluctuations of pressure occur in the supply main during the day, the design must be based on the minimum pressure available.
4. The tables included here are for a maximum water velocity of 8 feet per second. Above this velocity noise becomes a problem in many situations.

PROCEDURES FOR SIZING

1. Determine the available pressure from the supply main.
2. Calculate the difference in elevation between the supply point and the highest water supply outlet in the system. Multiply this difference by 1/2 psi and subtract from the water main pressure. This gives the pressure range to use.
3. Calculate the maximum length in piping to the most remote fixture.
4. Determine the total number of fixture units based on plans of the facility and the number of fixture units per fixture, as given in Table 2C–2.
5. Using the pressure calculated in step 2, use the appropriate pressure range in Table 2C–3. Select the "length" column that is equal to or greater than the length you calculated in step 3 and read down until you find the number of fixture units equal to or greater than what you determined in step 4. Read across to find the required meter and street service size and the building supply pipe size.
6. Individual branch lines can be sized according to the same procedures.

Table 2C-1
MINIMUM PLUMBING FIXTURES

Each building shall be provided with sanitary facilities, including provisions for the physically handicapped as prescribed by the Department having jurisdiction. In the absence of such requirements, this table—which provides a guideline for the minimum facilities for the various types of occupancies (See Section 910, Plumbing Fixtures Required, of the Uniform Plumbing Code)—may be used. For handicapped requirements, ANSI A117.1-1961 (R1971). Specifications for Making Buildings and Facilities Accessible to and Usable by the Physically Handicapped, may be used.

Type of Building or Occupancy[2]	**Water Closets** (fixtures per person)		**Urinals**[10] (fixtures per person)	**Lavatories** (fixtures per person)		**Bathtubs or Showers** (fixtures per person)	**Drinking Fountains**[3,13] (fixtures per person)
	Male	*Female*		*Male*	*Female*		
Assembly places—theaters auditoriums, convention halls, etc.—for permanent employee use	1 : 1–15 2 : 16–35 3 : 36–55 Over 50, add 1 fixture for each additional 40 persons	1 : 1–15 2 : 16–35 3 : 36–55	1 per 50	1 per 40	1 per 40	—	—
	Male	*Females*		*Male*	*Female*		
Assembly places—theaters, auditoriums, convention halls, etc.—for public use	1 : 1–100 2 : 101–200 3 : 201–400 Over 400, add 1 fixture for each additional 500 males and 2 for each 300 females	3 : 1–100 6 : 101–200 8 : 201–400	1 : 1–100 2 : 101–200 3 : 201–400 4 : 401–600 Over 600 add 1 fixture for each additional 300 males	1 : 1–200 2 : 201–400 3 : 401–750 Over 750, add 1 fixture for each additional 500 persons	1 : 1–200 2 : 201–400 3 : 401–750	—	1 per 75[12]
	Male	*Female*		*Male*	*Female*		
Dormitories[9]-school or labor	1 per 10 Add 1 fixture for each additional 25 males (over 10) and 1 for each additional 20 females (over 8)	1 per 8	1 per 25 Over 150, add 1 fixture for each additional 50 males	1 per 12 Over 12, add 1 fixture for each additional 20 males and 1 for each 15 females	1 per 12	1 per 8 For female, add 1 bathtub per 30; over 150, add 1 per 20	1 per 75[12]

Type of Building or Occupancy[2]	Water Closets (fixtures per person)		Urinals[10] (fixtures per person)	Lavatories (fixtures per person)		Bathtubs or Showers (fixtures per person)	Drinking Fountains[3,13] (fixtures per person)
	Male	*Female*		*Male*	*Female*		
Dormitories—for staff use	1 : 1–15 2 : 16–35 3 : 36–55	1 : 1–15 2 : 16–35 3 : 36–55	1 per 50	1 per 40	1 per 40	—	—
	Over 55, add 1 fixture for each additional 40 persons						
Dwellings[4]							
Single dwelling	1 per dwelling		—	1 per dwelling		1 per dwelling	—
Multiple dwelling or apartment house	1 per dwelling or apartment unit			1 per dwelling or apartment unit		1 per dwelling or apartment unit	
Hospitals							
Waiting room	1 per room		—	1 per room		—	1 per 75[12]
For employee use	*Male*	*Female*	1 per 50	*Male*	*Female*	—	
	1 : 1–15 2 : 16–35 3 : 36–55	1 : 1–15 2 : 16–35 3 : 36–55		1 per 40	1 per 40		
	Over 55, add 1 fixture for each additional 40 persons						
Hospitals							
Individual room	1 per room		—	1 per room		1 per room	—
Ward room	1 per 8 patients		—	1 per 10 patients		1 per 20 patients	1 per 75[12]

Table 2C-1 (Continued)

Type of Building or Occupancy[2]	Water Closets (fixtures per person)		Urinals[10] (fixtures per person)	Lavatories (fixtures per person)		Bathtubs or Showers (fixtures per person)	Drinking Fountains[3,13] (fixtures per person)
Industrial[6] warehouses Workshops, foundries, and similar establishments (for employee use)	*Male* 1 : 1–10 2 : 11–25 3 : 26–50 4 : 51–75 5 : 76–100 Over 100, add 1 fixture for each additional 30 persons	*Female* 1 : 1–10 2 : 11–25 3 : 26–50 4 : 51–75 5 : 76–100		Up to 100, 1 per 10 persons Over 100, 1 per 15 persons[7,8]		1 shower for each 15 persons exposed to excessive heat or to skin contamination with poisonous, infectious, or irritating material	1 per 75[12]
Institutional—other than hospitals or penal institutions (on each occupied floor)	*Male* 1 per 25	*Female* 1 per 20	1 per 50	*Male* 1 per 10	*Female* 1 per 10	1 per 8	1 per 75[12]
Institutional—other than hospitals or penal institutions (on each occupied floor)—for employee use	*Male* 1 : 1–15 2 : 16–35 3 : 36–55 Over 55, add 1 fixture for each additional 40 persons	*Female* 1 : 1–15 2 : 16–35 3 : 36–55	1 per 50	*Male* 1 per 40	*Female* 1 per 40	—	—

Type of Building or Occupancy[2]	Water Closets (fixtures per person)		Urinals[10] (fixtures per person)	Lavatories (fixtures per person)		Bathtubs or Showers (fixtures per person)	Drinking Fountains[3,13] (fixtures per person)
	Male	*Female*		*Male*	*Female*		
Office or public buildings	1 : 1–15 2 : 16–35 3 : 36–55 4 : 56–80 5 : 81–110 6 : 111–150	1 : 1–15 2 : 16–35 3 : 36–55 4 : 56–80 5 : 81–110 6 : 111–150		1 : 1–15 2 : 16–35 3 : 36–60 4 : 61–90 5 : 91–125	1 : 1–15 2 : 16–35 3 : 36–60 4 : 61–90 5 : 91–125	—	1 per 75[12]
	Over 150, add 1 fixture for each additional 40 persons			Over 125, add 1 fixture for each additional 45 persons			
Office or public buildings—for employee use	*Male* 1 : 1–15 2 : 16–35 3 : 36–55	*Female* 1 : 1–15 2 : 16–35 3 : 36–55	1 per 50	*Male* 1 per 40	*Female* 1 per 40	—	—
	Over 55, add 1 fixture for each additional 40 persons						
Penal institutions—for employee use	*Male* 1 : 1–15 2 : 16–35 3 : 36–55	*Female* 1 : 1–15 2 : 16–35 3 : 36–55	1 per 50	*Male* 1 per 40	*Female* 1 per 40	— —	1 per 75[12]
Penal institutions—for prisoner use							
Cell	1 per cell		—	1 per cell		—	1 per cell block floor
Exercise room	1 per exercise room		1 per exercise room	1 per exercise room		—	1 per exercise room

Table 2C-1 (Continued)

Type of Building or Occupancy[2]	Water Closets (fixtures per person)	Urinals[10] (fixtures per person)	Lavatories (fixtures per person)	Bathtubs or Showers (fixtures per person)	Drinking Fountains[3,13] (fixtures per person)
Restaurants, pubs, and lounges[11]	*Male* 1:1–50, 2:51–150, 3:151–300 *Female* 1:1–50, 2:51–150, 3:151–300 Over 300, add 1 fixture for each additional 200 persons	1:1–150 Over 150, add 1 fixture for each additional 150 males	*Male* 1:1–150, 2:151–200, 3:201–400 *Female* 1:1–150, 2:151–200, 3:201–400 Over 400, add 1 fixture for each additional 400 persons	—	—
Schools—for staff use All schools	*Male* 1:1–15, 2:16–35, 3:36–55 *Female* 1:1–15, 2:16–35, 3:36–55 Over 55, add 1 fixture for each additional 40 persons	1 per 50	*Male* 1 per 40 *Female* 1 per 40	—	—
Schools[5]—for student use Nursery	*Male* 1:1–20, 2:21–50 *Female* 1:1–20, 2:21–50 Over 50, add 1 fixture for each additional 50 persons	—	*Male* 1:1–25, 2:26–50 *Female* 1:1–25, 2:26–50 Over 50, add 1 fixture for each additional 50 persons	—	1 per 75[12]
Elementary	*Male* 1 per 30 *Female* 1 per 25	1 per 75	*Male* 1 per 35 *Female* 1 per 35	—	1 per 75[12]
Secondary	*Male* 1 per 40 *Female* 1 per 30	1 per 35	*Male* 1 per 40 *Female* 1 per 40	—	1 per 75[12]
Others (colleges, universities, adult centers, etc.)	*Male* 1 per 40 *Female* 1 per 30	1 per 35	*Male* 1 per 40 *Female* 1 per 40	—	1 per 75[12]
Worship places Educational and activities unit	*Male* 1 per 250 *Female* 1 per 125	1 per 250	1 per toilet room	—	1 per 75[12]
Worship places Principal assembly place	*Male* 1 per 300 *Female* 1 per 150	1 per 300	1 per toilet room	—	1 per 75[12]

Whenever urinals are provided, one (1) water closet less than the number specified may be provided for each urinal installed, except the number of water closets in such cases shall not be reduced to less than two-thirds (⅔) of the minimum specified.

1. The figures shown are based upon one (1) fixture being the minimum required for the number of persons indicated or any fraction thereof.
2. Building categories not shown on this table shall be considered separately by the Administrative Authority.
3. Drinking fountains shall not be installed in toilet rooms.
4. Laundry trays. One (1) laundry tray or one (1) automatic washer standpipe for each dwelling unit or two (2) laundry trays or two (2) automatic washer standpipes, or combination thereof, for each ten (10) apartments. Kitchen sinks. One (1) for each dwelling or apartment unit.
5. This schedule has been adopted by the National Council on Schoolhouse Construction.
6. As required by ANSI Z4.1-1968, Sanitation in Places of Employment.
7. Where there is exposure to skin contamination with poisonous, infectious, or irritating materials, provide one (1) lavatory for each five (5) persons.
8. Twenty-four (24) lineal inches (609.6 mm) of wash sink or eighteen (18) inches (457.2 mm) of a circular basin, when provided with water outlets for such space, shall be considered equivalent to one (1) lavatory.
9. Laundry trays. One (1) for each fifty (50) persons. Slop sinks, one (1) for each hundred (100) persons.
10. General. In applying this schedule of facilities, consideration must be given to the accessibility of the fixtures. Conformity purely on a numerical basis may not result in an installation suited to the need of the individual establishment. For example, schools should be provided with toilet facilities on each floor having classrooms. Temporary workingmen facilities. One (1) water closet and one (1) urinal for each thirty (30) workmen.
    a. Surrounding materials. Wall and floor space to a point two (2) feet (0.6 m) in front of urinal lip and four (4) feet (1.2 m) above the floor, and at least two (2) feet (0.6 m) to each side of the urinal shall be lined with non-absorbent material.
    b. Trough urinals are prohibited.
11. A restaurant is defined as a business which sells food to be consumed on the premises.
    a. The number of occupants for a drive-in restaurant shall be considered as equal to the number of parking stalls.
    b. Employee toilet facilities are not to be included in the above restaurant requirements. Hand washing facilities must be available in the kitchen for employees.
12. Where food is consumed indoors, water stations may be substituted for drinking fountains. Theaters, auditoriums, dormitories, offices, or public buildings for use by more than six (6) persons shall have one (1) drinking fountain for the first seventy-five (75) persons and one (1) additional fountain for each one hundred and fifty (150) persons thereafter.
13. There shall be a minimum of one (1) drinking fountain per occupied floor in schools, theaters, auditoriums, dormitories, offices or public buildings.

Table 2C-2
EQUIVALENT FIXTURE UNITS

Fixture	Number of Fixture Units	
	Private Use	Public Use
Bar sink	1	2
Bathtub (with or without shower over)	2	4
Bidet	2	4
Dental unit or cuspidor	—	1
Drinking fountain (each head)	1	2
Hose bibb or sill cock (standard type)	3	5
Mobile home (each)	6	6
Laundry tub or clotheswasher (each pair of faucets)	2	4
Lavatory	1	2
Lavatory (dental)	1	1
Lawn sprinklers (standard type, each head)	1	1
Shower (each head)	2	4
Sink (bar)	1	2
Sink or dishwasher	2	4
Sink (flushing rim, clinic)	—	10
Sink (washup, each set of faucets)	—	2
Sink (washup, circular spray)	—	4
Urinal (pedestal or similar type)	—	10
Urinal (stall)	—	5
Urinal (wall)	—	5
Urinal (flush tank)	—	3
Water closet (flush tank)	3	5
*Water closet (flushometer valve)	*	*
Water supply outlets for items not listed above shall be computed at their maximum demand but in no case less than:		
3/8 inch (9.5 mm)	1	2
1/2 inch (12.7 mm)	2	4
3/4 inch (19.1 mm)	3	6
1 inch (25.4 mm)	6	10

Sizing for Flushometer Valves

In order to size branches and mains serving flushometer valves using Table 2C-3, assign the following values to each flushometer valve beginning with the most remote valve on each branch.

For the first flushometer valve	40 fixture units
For the second valve	30 fixture units
For the third valve	20 fixture units
For the fourth valve	15 fixture units
For the fifth valve	10 fixture units

Five fixture unit flushometer valves may be computed at half the above values assigned but in no case less than five fixture units. After the fifth valve on any branch or main, subsequent fixture unit loading may be computed using the value of the fifth flushometer.

Sizing Systems with Hot Water Piping

For systems with a total demand of 50 fixture units or less, the length of the hot water piping may be ignored when hot water pipe friction loss is compensated for by the following method:

1. Compute the total hot water fixture demand using the values given in Table 2C-2.
2. Assign the total demand computed, as required in step 1, as the fixture unit demand at the hot water heater inlet.
3. Starting at the most remote outlet on the cold water piping and working back toward the water meter, compute the pipe sizing for the system from the column originally selected in Table 2C-3, using the fixture unit values given in Table 2C-2 and adding in the fixture unit demand of the hot water heater supply inlet, as computed in step 1, at the point where it occurs. The final size of the cold water branch or main need not exceed the originally established size of the building supply.

Alternate Method of Sizing Systems with Hot Water Piping

Take the total length of the supply piping from the source of cold water supply through the water heater to the most remote hot water outlet and assess flow values of 75% of the combined hot and cold water demand, as given in Table 2C-2, to the piping supplying either hot or cold water to those fixtures served by both. Size piping serving water heaters to deliver the above required hot water demand, plus all required cold water demands, but in no case does the piping need to be larger in size than that required by Table 2C-3 for the total building supply.

HOW TO CALCULATE THE REQUIRED SIZE OF DRAINAGE PIPING

The minimum size of traps and trap arms for individual fixtures is given in Table 2C-4. Table 2C-4 also gives drainage fixture units for each type of fixture. To calculate the required sizes of drainage piping in a system or part of a system, determine the total number of drainage fixture units served and the horizontal and vertical lengths of pipe required and refer to Table 2C-5. This gives the maximum fixture unit loading allowed, along with permissible length of horizontal and vertical piping, as well as requirements for sizing vent piping.

For fixtures not shown in Table 2C-4, refer to Table 2C-6 for determining unit load based on discharge capacity.

Maximum lengths of trap arms from the trap weir to the inner edge of the vent are given in Table 2C-7. This information is useful in situations where a sink must be located some distance from a wall where the vent may be located.

Table 2C-3
FIXTURE UNIT TABLE FOR DETERMINING WATER PIPE AND METER SIZES FOR FLUSH TANK SYSTEMS 8 FEET PER SECOND MAXIMUM WATER VELOCITY

PRESSURE RANGE—30 to 45 psi

Meter and Street Service (in in.)	**Building Supply and Branches** (in in.)	**Maximum Allowable Length** (in ft.)														
		40	60	80	100	150	200	250	300	400	500	600	700	800	900	1000
¾	½**	6	5	4	3*	2*	1*	1*	1*	0*	0*	0*	0*	0*	0*	0*
¾	¾	18	16	14*	12*	9*	6*	5*	5*	4*	4*	3*	2	2	2	1
¾	1	29	25	23	21	17	15	13	12	10	9	7	6	6	6	6
1	1	33	31	27	25	20	17	15	13	12	10	8	6	6	6	6
1	1¼	54	47	42	38	32	28	25	23	19	17	14	12	12	11	11
1½	1¼	75	68	57	48	38	32	28	25	21	18	15	12	12	11	11
1½	1½	129	124	105	91	70	57	49	45	36	31	26	23	21	20	20
2	1½	129	129	129	110	80	64	53	46	38	32	27	23	21	20	20
1½	2	220	205	190	176	155	138	127	120	104	85	70	61	57	54	51
2	2	293	293	292	265	217	185	164	147	124	96	70	61	57	54	51
2	2½	445	418	390	370	330	300	280	265	240	220	198	175	158	143	133

PRESSURE RANGE—46 to 60 psi

Meter and Street Service (in in.)	**Building Supply and Branches** (in in.)	**Maximum Allowable Length** (in ft.)														
		40	60	80	100	150	200	250	300	400	500	600	700	800	900	1000
¾	½**	9	7*	6*	5*	4*	3*	2*	2*	1*	1*	1*	0*	0*	0*	0*
¾	¾	19	19	19	17	14*	11*	9*	8*	6*	5*	4*	4*	3*	3*	3*
¾	1	33	33	33	33	28	23	21	19	17	14	12	10	9	8	8
1	1	33	33	33	33	30	25	23	20	18	15	12	10	9	8	8
1	1¼	75	75	75	67	52	44	39	36	30	27	22	20	19	17	16
1½	1¼	75	75	75	75	66	52	44	39	33	29	24	20	19	17	16
1½	1½	129	129	129	129	128	105	90	78	62	52	42	38	35	32	30
2	1½	129	129	129	129	129	117	98	84	67	55	42	38	35	32	30
1½	2	293	293	293	293	272	240	220	198	170	150	135	123	110	102	94
2	2	293	293	293	293	293	293	280	250	205	165	142	123	110	102	94
2	2½	474	474	474	474	474	474	470	440	400	365	335	315	285	267	250

PRESSURE RANGE—Over 60 psi

Meter and Street Service (in in.)	**Building Supply and Branches** (in in.)	**Maximum Allowable Length** (in ft.)														
		40	60	80	100	150	200	250	300	400	500	600	700	800	900	1000
¾	½**	11	9	7*	6*	5*	4*	3*	3*	2*	1*	1*	1*	1*	1*	0*
¾	¾	19	19	19	19	17	13*	11*	10*	8*	7*	6*	6*	5*	4*	4*
¾	1	33	33	33	33	33	30	27	24	21	17	14	13	12	12	11
1	1	33	33	33	33	33	32	29	26	22	18	14	13	12	12	11
1	1¼	75	75	75	75	74	62	53	47	39	31	26	25	23	22	21
1½	1¼	75	75	75	75	75	74	62	54	43	34	26	25	23	22	21
1½	1½	129	129	129	129	129	129	129	113	88	73	51	51	46	43	40
2	1½	129	129	129	129	129	129	129	122	98	82	64	51	46	43	40
1½	2	293	293	293	293	293	293	293	282	244	212	187	172	153	141	129
2	2	293	293	293	293	293	293	293	293	288	245	204	172	153	141	129
2	2½	474	474	474	474	474	474	474	474	474	460	430	404	380	356	329

*Branch pipes up to 20 ft. developed length (from main to outlet or fixture) may supply maximum of four fixture units for ½ in. size and maximum 16 fixture units for ¾ in. nominal size.

**Building supply, ¾ in. nominal size minimum

FIXTURE UNIT TABLE FOR DETERMINING WATER PIPE AND METER SIZES FOR FLUSH TANK SYSTEMS 15 FEET PER SECOND MAXIMUM WATER VELOCITY

PRESSURE RANGE—30 to 45 psi

Meter and Street Service (in in.)	**Building Supply and Branches** (in in.)	**Maximum Allowable Length** (in ft.)														
		40	60	80	100	150	200	250	300	400	500	600	700	800	900	1000
¾	½**	6	5	4	3*	2*	1*	1*	1*	0*	0*	0*	0*	0*	0*	0*
¾	¾	18	16	14*	12*	9*	6*	5*	5*	4*	4*	3*	2	2	2	1
¾	1	29	25	23	21	17	15	13	12	10	9	7	6	6	6	6
1	1	36	31	27	25	20	17	15	13	12	10	8	6	6	6	6
1	1¼	54	47	42	38	32	28	25	23	19	17	14	12	12	11	11
1½	1¼	90	68	57	48	38	32	28	25	21	18	15	12	12	11	11
1½	1½	151	124	105	91	70	57	49	45	36	31	26	23	21	20	20
2	1½	210	162	132	110	80	64	53	46	38	32	27	23	21	20	20
1½	2	220	205	190	176	155	138	127	120	104	85	70	61	57	54	51
2	2	372	329	292	265	217	185	164	147	124	96	70	61	57	54	51
2	2½	445	418	390	370	330	300	280	265	240	220	198	175	158	143	133

PRESSURE RANGE—46 to 60 psi

Meter and Street Service (in in.)	**Building Supply and Branches** (in in.)	**Maximum Allowable Length** (in ft.)														
		40	60	80	100	150	200	250	300	400	500	600	700	800	900	1000
¾	½**	9	7*	6*	5*	4*	3*	2*	2*	1*	1*	1*	0*	0*	0*	0*
¾	¾	27	23	19	17	14*	11*	9*	8*	6*	5*	4*	4*	3*	3*	3*
¾	1	44	40	36	33	28	23	21	19	17	14	12	10	9	8	8
1	1	60	47	41	36	30	25	23	20	18	15	12	10	9	8	8
1	1¼	102	87	76	67	52	44	39	36	30	27	22	20	19	17	16
1½	1¼	156	130	106	89	66	52	44	39	33	29	24	20	19	17	16
1½	1½	270	225	193	167	128	105	90	78	62	52	42	38	35	32	30
2	1½	286	286	242	204	150	117	98	84	67	55	42	38	35	32	30
1½	2	360	360	340	318	272	240	220	198	170	150	135	123	110	102	94
2	2	570	510	470	430	368	318	280	250	205	165	142	123	110	102	94
2	2½	680	640	610	580	535	500	470	440	400	365	335	315	285	267	250

PRESSURE RANGE—Over 60 psi

Meter and Street Service (in in.)	**Building Supply and Branches** (in in.)	**Maximum Allowable Length** (in ft.)														
		40	60	80	100	150	200	250	300	400	500	600	700	800	900	1000
¾	½**	11	9	7*	6*	5*	4*	3*	3*	2*	1*	1*	1*	1*	1*	0*
¾	¾	31	28	24	22	17	13*	11*	10*	8*	7*	6*	6*	5*	4*	4*
¾	1	63	53	47	42	35	30	27	24	21	17	14	13	12	12	11
1	1	72	66	55	48	38	32	29	26	22	18	14	13	12	12	11
1	1¼	140	126	108	96	74	62	53	47	39	31	26	25	23	22	21
1½	1¼	156	156	150	127	93	74	62	54	43	34	26	25	23	22	21
1½	1½	286	286	273	240	186	154	130	113	88	73	51	51	46	43	40
2	1½	286	286	286	275	220	170	142	122	98	82	64	51	46	43	40
1½	2	360	360	360	360	360	335	305	282	244	212	187	172	153	141	129
2	2	611	611	610	560	478	420	375	340	288	245	204	172	153	141	129
2	2½	690	690	690	690	690	650	610	570	510	460	430	404	380	356	329

*Branch pipes up to 20 ft. developed length (from main to outlet or fixture) may supply maximum of four fixture units for ½ in. size and maximum 16 fixture units for ¾ in. nominal size.

**Building supply, ¾ in. nominal size minimum

Table 2C-4
MINIMUM TRAP AND TRAP ARM SIZES

Kind of Fixture	Minimum Trap and Trap Arm Size		
	(in in.)	(in mm)	Units
Bathtubs	1½	(38.1)	2
Bidets	1½	(38.1)	2
Dental units or cuspidors	1¼	(31.8)	1
Drinking fountains	1¼	(31.8)	1
Floor drains	2	(50.8)	2
*Interceptors for grease, oil, solids, etc.	2	(50.8)	3
*Interceptors for sand, auto wash, etc.	3	(76.2)	6
Laundry tubs	1½	(38.1)	2
Clotheswashers	2	(50.8)	2
*Receptors (floor sinks), indirect waste receptors for refrigerators, coffee urns, water stations, etc.	1½	(38.1)	1
*Receptors, indirect waste receptors for commercial sinks, dishwashers, airwashers, etc.	2	(50.8)	3
Showers, single stalls	2	(50.8)	2
*Showers, gangs, (one unit per head)	2	(50.8)	
Sinks, bar, private (1½ in. (38.1 mm) min. waste)	1½	(38.1)	1
Sinks, bar, commercial (2 in. (50.8 mm) min. waste)	1½	(38.1)	2
Sinks, commercial or industrial, schools, etc. including dishwashers, wash-up sinks, and wash fountains (2 in. (50.8 mm) min. waste)	1½	(38.1)	3
Sinks, flushing rim, clinic	3	(76.2)	6
Sinks, and/or dishwashers (residential) (2 in. (50.8 mm) min. waste)	1½	(38.1)	2
Sinks, service	2	(50.8)	3
Mobile home park traps (one (1) for each trailer)	3	(76.2)	6
Urinals, pedestal, trap arm only	3	(76.2)	6
Urinals, stall	2	(50.8)	2
Urinals, wall (2 in. (50.8 mm) min. waste)	1½	(38.1)	2
Wash basins (lavatories) single	1¼	(31.8)	1
Wash basins, in sets	1½	(38.1)	2
*Water closet, private installation, trap arm only	3	(76.2)	4
Water closet, public installation, trap arm only	3	(76.2)	6

***Note:** The size and discharge rating of each indirect waste receptor and each interceptor shall be based on the total rated discharge.

Reproduced from the Uniform Plumbing Code, 1985 Edition, by permission of the copyright holder, International Association of Plumbing and Mechanical Officials. Copyright, 1985.

Table 2C–5

MAXIMUM UNIT LOADING AND MAXIMUM LENGTH OF DRAINAGE AND VENT PIPING

Size of Pipe											
(in in.)	1-1/4	1-1/2	2	2-1/2	3	4	5	6	8	10	12
(in mm)	31.8	38.1	50.8	63.5	76.2	101.6	127	152.4	203.2	254	304.8
Maximum Units											
Drainage Piping[1]											
Vertical	1	2[2]	16[3]	32[3]	48[4]	256	600	1380	3600	5600	8400
Horizontal[5]	1	1	8[3]	14[3]	35[4]	216	428	720	2640	4680	8200
Maximum Length											
Drainage Piping											
Vertical (ft.)	45	65	85	148	212	300	390	510	750		
(m)	13.7	19.8	25.8	45	64.5	91.2	118.6	155	228		
Horizontal (unlimited)											
Vent Piping											
Horizontal and Vertical											
Max. Units	1	8[3]	24	48	84	256	600	1380	3600		
Max. Lengths (ft.)	45	60	120	180	212	300	390	510	750		
(m)	13.7	18.2	36.5	54.7	64.5	91.2	118.6	155	228		
(See Note.)											

[1]Excluding trap arm

[2]Except sinks and urinals

[3]Except six-unit traps or water closets

[4]Only four (4) water closets or six-unit traps allowed on any vertical pipe or stack; and not to exceed three (3) water closets or six-unit traps on any horizontal branch or drain.

[5]Based upon one-fourth (¼) in./ft. (20.9 mm/m) slope. For one-eighth (⅛) in./ft. (10.4 mm/m) slope, multiply horizontal fixture units by a factor of 0.8.

Note: The diameter of an individual vent shall not be less than one and one-fourth (1¼) in. (31.8 mm) nor less than one-half (½) the diameter of the drain to which it is connected. Fixture unit load values for drainage and vent piping shall be computed from Tables 2C-2 and 2C-4. Not to exceed one-third (⅓) of the total permitted length of any vent may be installed in a horizontal position. When vents are increased one (1) pipe size for their entire length, the maximum length limitations specified in this table do not apply.

Table 2C-6
DISCHARGE CAPACITY
(in gals. per min.) (liters per sec.)
For Intermittent Flow Only

GPM	L/s		
Up to 7½	Up to .47	Equals	1 Unit
8 to 15	.50 to .95	Equals	2 Units
16 to 30	1 to 1.89	Equals	4 Units
31 to 50	1.95 to 3.15	Equals	6 Units

Over 50 gals. per min. (3.15 L/s) shall be determined by the Administrative Authority.

For a continuous flow into a drainage system, such as from a pump, sump ejector, air-conditioning equipment, or similar device, two (2) fixture units shall be allowed for each gal. per min. (0.06 L/s) of flow.

Table 2C-7
HORIZONTAL DISTANCE OF TRAP ARMS
(except for water closets and similar fixtures)

Trap Arm (*in in.*)	Distance Trap to Vent *ft.*	*in.*	(Metric) Trap Arm *mm*	Distance Trap to Vent *m*
1¼	2	6	31.8	0.76
1½	3	6	38.1	1.07
2	5	0	50.8	1.52
3	6	0	76.2	1.83
4 and larger	10	0	101.6 and larger	3.05

Slope one-fourth (¼) in./ft. (20.9 mm/m).

HOW TO CALCULATE THE REQUIRED SIZING OF RAINWATER PIPING

Sizing of Gutters

Determine the maximum rainfall per hour from local sources or from Figure 2C–1 and calculate the roof area served by the gutter. Refer to Table 2C–8 and read down the appropriate rainfall column in the section for the gutter slope you are using until you find the roof area that is equal to or greater than the design roof area. Read across to find the diameter of a semicircular gutter.

Sizing of Vertical Rainwater Piping

Calculate the horizontal projected roof area under consideration and determine the maximum rainfall per hour. Using the appropriate row of inches of rainfall per hour in Table 2C–9, read across until you find a number equal to or greater than the horizontal projected roof area. Read the top of the column to find the required drain or leader size.

Sizing of Horizontal Rainwater Piping

Calculate the roof area to be served and determine the maximum rainfall per hour from local sources. Using the appropriate section of Table 2C–10 based on pipe slope, read down the appropriate column of inches of rainfall per hour until you find a number equal to or greater than the roof area under consideration. Read across to find the required pipe size.

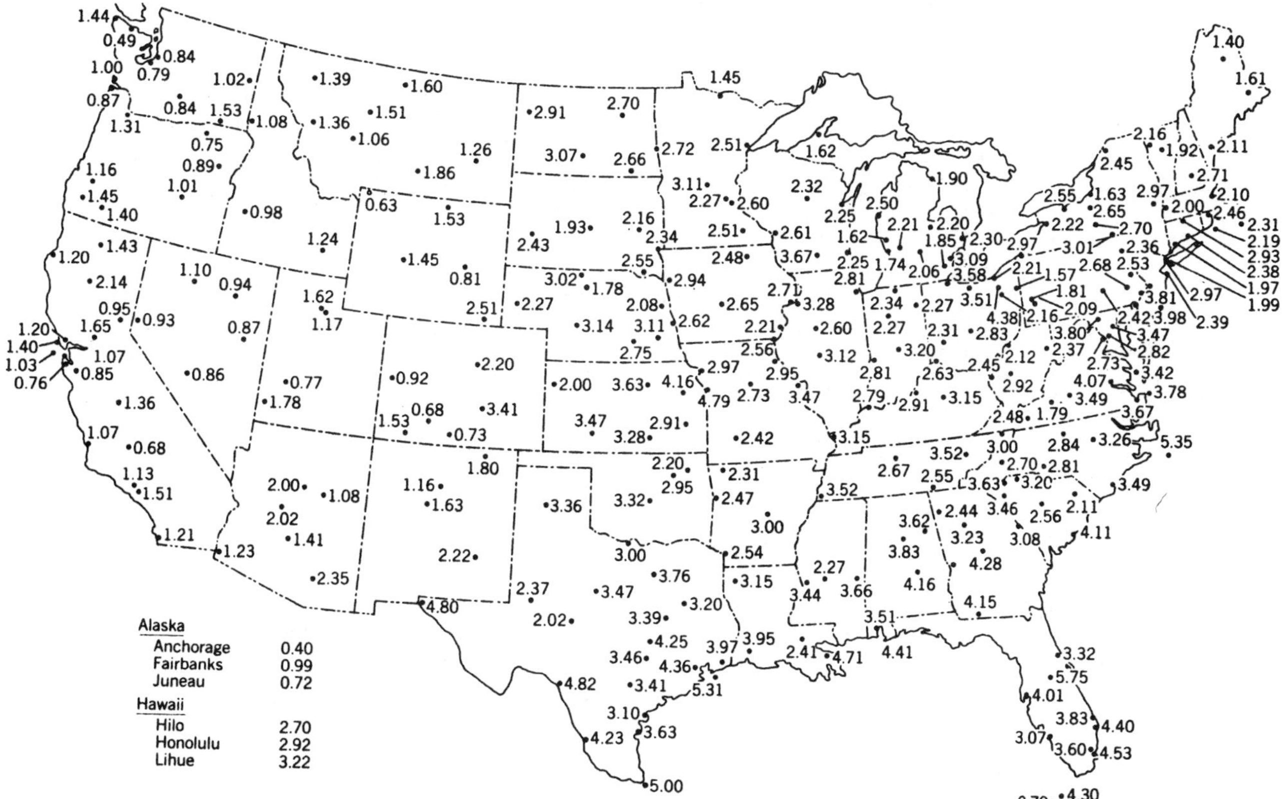

Source: U.S. Weather Bureau Technical Paper #2.

Figure 2C–1: Maximum Recorded Hourly Rainfall (in inches)

Table 2C-8
GUTTER SIZING

Diameter of Gutter 1/16 in. Slope	Maximum Rainfall (in inches per hour)				
	2	3	4	5	6
3	340	226	170	136	113
4	720	480	360	288	240
5	1250	834	625	500	416
6	1920	—	960	768	640
7	2760	1840	1380	1100	918
8	3980	2655	1990	1590	1325
10	7200	4800	3600	2880	2400

Diameter of Gutter 1/8 in. Slope	Maximum Rainfall (in inches per hour)				
	2	3	4	5	6
3	480	320	240	192	160
4	1020	681	510	408	340
5	1760	1172	880	704	587
6	2720	1815	1360	1085	905
7	3900	2600	1950	1560	1300
8	5600	3740	2800	2240	1870
10	10200	6800	5100	4080	3400

Diameter of Gutter 1/4 in. Slope	Maximum Rainfall (in inches per hour)				
	2	3	4	5	6
3	680	454	340	272	226
4	1440	960	720	576	480
5	2500	1668	1250	1000	834
6	3840	2560	1920	1536	1280
7	5520	3680	2760	2205	1840
8	7960	5310	3980	3180	2655
10	14400	9600	7200	5750	4800

Diameter of Gutter 1/2 in. Slope	Maximum Rainfall (in inches per hour)				
	2	3	4	5	6
3	960	640	480	384	320
4	2040	1360	1020	816	680
5	3540	2360	1770	1415	1180
6	5540	3695	2770	2220	1850
7	7800	5200	3900	3120	2600
8	11200	7460	5600	4480	3730
10	20000	13330	10000	8000	6660

Table 2C-9
SIZING OF ROOF DRAINS AND RAINWATER PIPING

Rainfall (in inches)	**Size of Drain or Leader** (in inches) 2	3	4	5	6	8
1	2880	8800	18400	34600	54000	116000
2	1440	4400	9200	17300	27000	58000
3	960	2930	6130	11530	17995	38660
4	720	2200	4600	8650	13500	29000
5	575	1760	3680	6920	10800	23200
6	480	1470	3070	5765	9000	19315
7	410	1260	2630	4945	7715	16570
8	360	1100	2300	4325	6750	14500
9	320	980	2045	3845	6000	12890
10	290	880	1840	3460	5400	11600
11	260	800	1675	3145	4910	10545
12	240	730	1530	2880	4500	9660

Reproduced from the Uniform Plumbing Code, 1985 Edition, by permission of the copyright holder, International Association of Plumbing and Mechanical Officials. Copyright, 1985.

Table 2C-10
SIZING HORIZONTAL RAINWATER PIPING

Size of Pipe (in inches)	**Maximum Rainfall** (in inches per hour)				
⅛ in. Slope	2	3	4	5	6
3	1644	1096	822	657	548
4	3760	2506	1880	1504	1253
5	6680	4453	3340	2672	2227
6	10700	7133	5350	4280	3566
8	23000	15330	11500	9200	7600
10	41400	27600	20700	16580	13800
12	66600	44400	33300	26650	22200
15	109000	72800	59500	47600	39650
Size of Pipe (in inches)	**Maximum Rainfall** (in inches per hour)				
¼ in. Slope	2	3	4	5	6
3	2320	1546	1160	928	773
4	5300	3533	2650	2120	1766
5	9440	6293	4720	3776	3146
6	15100	10066	7550	6040	5033
8	32600	21733	16300	13040	10866
10	58400	38950	29200	23350	19450
12	94000	62600	47000	37600	31350
15	168000	112000	84000	67250	56000
Size of Pipe (in inches)	**Maximum Rainfall** (in inches per hour)				
½ in. Slope	2	3	4	5	6
3	3288	2295	1644	1310	1096
4	7520	5010	3760	3010	2500
5	13360	8900	6680	5320	4450
6	21400	13700	10700	8580	7140
8	46000	30650	23000	18400	15320
10	82800	55200	41400	33150	27600
12	133200	88800	66600	53200	44400
15	238000	158800	119000	95300	79250

Reproduced from the Uniform Plumbing Code, 1985 Edition, by permission of the copyright holder, International Association of Plumbing and Mechanical Officials. Copyright, 1985.

Table 2C-11
MINIMUM RESIDENTIAL WATER HEATER CAPACITIES

Number of Baths	1 to 1.5			2 to 2.5				3 to 3.5		
Number of Bedrooms	1	2	3	2	3	4	5	3	4	5
Gas[a]										
Storage, gal.	20	30	30	30	40	40	50	40	50	50
1000 Btu/h input	27	36	36	36	36	38	47	38	38	47
1-hr draw, gal.	43	60	60	60	70	72	90	72	82	90
Recovery, gph	23	30	30	30	30	32	40	32	32	40
Electric[a]										
Storage, gal.	20	30	40	40	50	50	66	50	66	66
kW input	2.5	3.5	4.5	4.5	5.5	5.5	5.5	5.5	5.5	5.5
1-hr draw, gal.	30	44	58	58	72	72	88	72	88	88
Recovery, gph	10	14	18	18	22	22	22	22	22	22
Oil[a]										
Storage, gal.	30	30	30	30	30	30	30	30	30	30
1000 Btu/h input	70	70	70	70	70	70	70	70	70	70
1-hr draw gal.	89	89	89	89	89	89	89	89	89	89
Recovery, gph	59	59	59	59	59	59	59	59	59	59
Tank-type, indirect[b,c]										
1-W-H rated draw, gal. in 3-hr, 100°F rise		40	40		66	66[d]	66	66	66	66
Mfg.-rated draw, gal. in 3-hr, 100°F rise		49	49		75	75[d]	75	75	75	75
Tank capacity, gal.		66	66		66	66[d]	82	66	82	82
Tankless-type, indirect[c,e]										
1-W-H rated, gpm 100°F rise		2.75	2.75		3.25	3.25[d]	3.75	3.25	3.75	3.75
Mfg.-rated draw, gal. in 5 min., 100°F rise		15	15		25	25[d]	35	25	35	35

[a]Storage capacity, input, and recovery requirements indicated in the table are typical and may vary with each individual manufacturer. Any combination of these requirements to produce the stated 1-h draw will be satisfactory.

[b]Boiler-connected water heater capacities (180°F boiler water, internal or external connection).

[c]Heater capacities and inputs are minimum allowable. Variations in tank size are permitted when recovery is based on 4 gph/kW @ 100°F rise for electrical. A.G.A. recovery ratings for gas heaters and IBR ratings for steam and hot water heaters.

[d]Also for 1 to 1.5 baths and 4 bedrooms for indirect water heaters.

[e]Boiler-connected heater capacities (200°F boiler water, internal or external connection).

Source: *U.S. HUD-FHA for one- and two-family living units. Copyright by the American Society of Heating, Refrigerating and Air Conditioning Engineers, Inc., Atlanta, GA. Reprinted by permission from the ASHRAE Systems Handbook, 1984.*

Table 2C-12
COMBUSTION AIR REQUIREMENTS FOR GAS-BURNING WATER HEATERS*

Input Rating**	Condition 1 Minimum total area of ducts or openings where floor area of compartment is less than twice the floor area of the appliances therein	Condition 2 Minimum total area of ducts or openings where floor area of compartment is more than twice the floor area of all appliances therein
0-500,000 BTUs (0-146500 W)	2 sq. in. (1290.3 mm^2) per 1000 BTUs (293 W)	1 sq. in. (645.2 mm^2) per 1000 BTUs (293 W)
500,000-1,000,000 BTUs (146500.3-293000 W)	1000 sq. in. (0.7 m^2) plus 2 sq. in. (1290.3 mm^2) per 1500 BTUs (439.5 W) over 500,000 BTUs (146500 W)	500 sq. in. (0.3 m^2) plus 1 sq. in. (645.2 mm^2) per 1500 BTUs (439.5 W) over 500,000 BTUs (146500 W)
In excess of 1,000,000 BTUs (293000 W)	1666 sq. in. (1.1 m^2) plus 2 sq. in. (1290.3 mm^2) per 2000 BTUs (586 W) over 1,000,000 BTUs (293000 W)	833 sq. in. (0.5 m^2) plus 1 sq. in. (645.2 mm^2) per 2000 BTUs (586 W) over 1,000,000 BTUs (293000 W)

*For water heaters burning solid or liquid fuels, the required areas shall be one and one-half (1½) times that required for gas burning water heaters.
**Minimum one hundred (100) sq. in. (0.07 m^2) required equally divided top and bottom.

Reproduced from the Uniform Plumbing Code, 1985 Edition, by permission of the copyright holder, International Association of Plumbing and Mechanical Officials. Copyright, 1985.

PLUMBING PIPE SIZES

Table 2C-13
PIPE SIZES—OUTSIDE DIAMETERS

					Cast Iron Hub and Spigot	
Nominal Size	Copper Tubing	Copper and Steel Pipe	CPVC Plastic	PVC DWV Pipe	Maximum Hub Diameter	Pipe Outside Diameter
1/4	3/8	0.540	0.540			
3/8	1/2	0.675	0.675			
1/2	5/8	0.840	0.840			
3/4	7/8	1.050	1.050			
1	1 1/8	1.315	1.315			
1 1/4	1 3/8	1.660	1.660	1.660		
1 1/2	1 5/8	1.900	1.900	1.900		
2	2 1/8	2.375	2.375	2.375	3 15/16	2 1/4
2 1/2	2 5/8	2.875	2.875			
3	3 1/8	3.500	3.500	3.500	5	3 1/4
3 1/2	3 5/8	4.000	4.000			
4	4 1/8	4.500	4.500	4.500	6	4 1/4
5	5 1/8	5.562	5.563		7	5 1/4
6	6 1/8	6.625	6.625	6.625	8	6 1/4
8		8.625	8.625	8.625	10 1/2	8 3/8
10		10.750	10.750		12 13/16	10 1/2
12		12.750	12.750		14 15/16	12 1/2
15					18 5/16	15 5/8

PART 2D

Fire Protection

Fire protection has become an important part of building planning. One of the primary concerns of architects is the location of sprinklers relative to room layout and ceiling design. To determine required numbers and location of sprinklers, use the procedure here.

HOW TO DETERMINE REQUIRED NUMBER OF SPRINKLERS AND THEIR LOCATION

1. Determine the hazard classification of the building under design. Refer to Table 2D–1. Most of the building types architects deal with are of the "Light-Hazard" type.
2. Refer to Table 2D–2 to determine the maximum coverage per sprinkler. Dividing the appropriate figure into the floor area will give the number of sprinklers required. This

Table 2D–1
RELATIVE FIRE HAZARD FOR VARIOUS OCCUPANCIES, AS RELATED TO SPRINKLER INSTALLATIONS

Classification of Occupancies

A-1-7.1 Occupancy examples in the listings as shown in the various hazard classifications are intended to represent the norm for those occupancy types. Unusual or abnormal fuel loadings or combustible characteristics and susceptibility for changes in these characteristics for a particular occupancy are considerations that should be weighed in the selection and classification.

The Light-Hazard Classification is intended to encompass residential occupancies; however, this is not intended to preclude the use for listed residential sprinklers in residential occupancies or residential portions of other occupancies.

Light-Hazard Occupancies include occupancies having conditions similar to:

- Churches
- Clubs
- Eaves and overhangs, if combustible construction with no combustibles beneath
- Educational
- Hospitals
- Institutional
- Libraries, except large stack rooms
- Museums
- Nursing or convalescent homes
- Office, including data processing
- Residential
- Restaurant seating areas
- Theaters and auditoriums, excluding stages and prosceniums
- Unused attics

Reprinted with permission from NFPA 13-1985, Standard for the Installation of Sprinkler Systems, Copyright © 1985, National Fire Protection Association, Quincy, MA 02269. This reprinted material is not the complete and official position of the NFPA on the referenced subject which is represented only by the standard in its entirety.

Ordinary-Hazard Occupancies (Group 1) include occupancies having conditions similar to:

Automobile parking garages
Bakeries
Beverage manufacturing
Canneries
Dairy products manufacturing and processing
Electronic plants
Glass and glass products manufacturing
Laundries
Restaurant service areas

Ordinary-Hazard Occupancies (Group 2) include occupancies having conditions similar to:

Cereal mills
Chemical plants—ordinary
Cold storage warehouses
Confectionery products
Distilleries
Leather goods manufacturing
Libraries—large stack room areas
Machine shops
Metal working
Mercantiles
Printing and publishing
Textile manufacturing
Tobacco products manufacturing
Wood product assembly

Ordinary-Hazard Occupancies (Group 3) include occupancies having conditions similar to:

Feed mills
Paper and pulp mills
Paper process plants
Piers and wharves
Repair garages
Tire manufacturing
Warehouses (having moderate to higher combustibility of content, such as paper, household furniture, paint, general storage, whiskey, etc.)
Wood machining

When hazards in those buildings or portions of buildings of this occupancy group are severe, the authority having jurisdiction should be consulted for special rulings regarding water supplies, types of equipment, pipe sizes, types of sprinklers, and sprinkler spacing.

New installations protecting extra-hazard occupancies should be hydraulically designed, where standards giving design criteria are available.

Extra-Hazard Occupancies (Group 1) include occupancies having conditions similar to:

Combustible hydraulic fluid use areas
Die casting
Metal extruding
Plywood and particle board manufacturing
Printing (using inks with below 100°F (37.8°C) flash points)
Rubber reclaiming, compounding, drying, milling, vulcanizing
Saw mills
Textile picking, opening, blending, garnetting, carding, combining of cotton synthetics, wood shoddy or burlap
Upholstering with plastic foams

Extra-Hazard Occupancies (Group 2) include occupancies having conditions similar to:

Asphalt saturating
Flammable liquids spraying
Flow coating
Mobile home or modular building assemblies (where finished enclosure is present and has combustible interiors)
Open oil quenching
Solvent cleaning
Varnish and paint dipping

number should be checked against the maximum spacing requirements given at the bottom of the table.

Note: Most sprinkler systems for commercial buildings are hydraulically calculated either by the fire protection engineer or the fire protection contractor, so the maximum coverage of 225 square feet is typically used in light-hazard occupancies.

3. If the area under design has any dropped beams, coffered ceilings, or similar projections, check the required distance of the sprinkler head from the projection based on the information in Table 2D–3.

Table 2D–2
SPRINKLER SPACING

Maximum Coverage per Sprinkler	
Light Hazard	200 sq. ft. smooth ceiling and beam and girder construction 225 sq. ft. if hydraulically calculated for smooth ceiling and beam and girder construction 130 sq. ft. open wood joists 168 sq. ft. all other types of construction
Ordinary Hazard	130 sq. ft. all types of construction except, 100 sq. ft. high pile storage (solid piled storage or palletized or rack storage in excess of 12 ft. in height.)
Extra Hazard	90 sq. ft. for all types of construction 100 sq. ft. if hydraulically calculated

MAXIMUM SPACING BETWEEN LINES AND SPRINKLERS

Light and Ordinary Hazard: 15 ft., except 12 ft. for high-piled storage

Extra hazard: 12 ft.

Maximum distance from walls to last sprinkler: one half the allowable distance between sprinklers except for small room rule.

Minimum distance from walls to last sprinkler: 4 in.

Small room rule: A small room is a room with a smooth ceiling area not exceeding 800 sq. ft. of Light-Hazard Occupancy classification. Within small rooms, sprinklers may be located not more than 9 ft. from any single wall as long as sprinkler spacing limitations and area limitations are not exceeded.

NFPA specifies requirements for the location of sprinkler deflectors near open web joists, trusses, and similar conditions that occur at the ceiling line. One condition that often concerns the architect or interior designer is the allowable locations of sprinklers near exposed beams or dropped ceilings. The following sketch and table give maximum permissible dimensions.

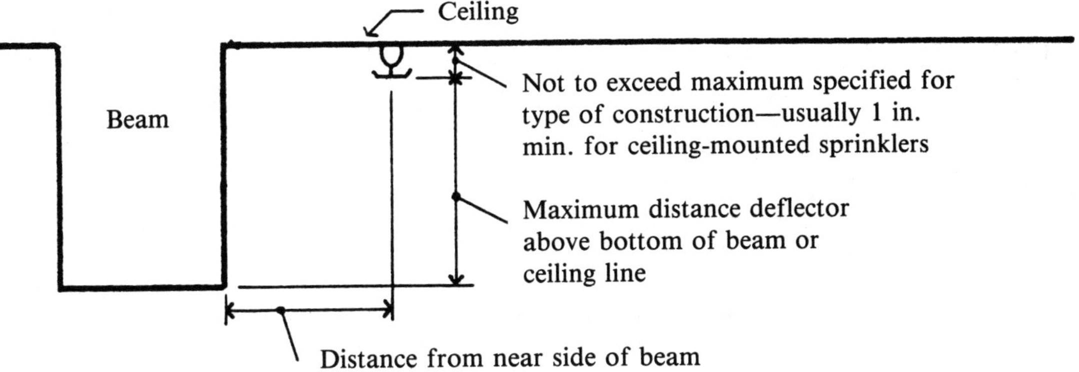

Table 2D-3
POSITION OF DEFLECTOR NEAR BEAMS OR DROPPED CEILINGS

Distance from Sprinkler to Side of Beam	Maximum Allowable Distance Deflector Above Bottom of Beam (in in.)
Less than 1 ft.	0
1 ft. to less than 2 ft.	1
2 ft. to less than 2 ft.–6 in.	2
2 ft.–6 in. to less than 3 ft.	3
3 ft. to less than 3 ft.–6 in.	4
3 ft.–6 in. to less than 4 ft.	6
4 ft. to less than 4 ft.–6 in.	7
4 ft.–6 in. to less than 5 ft.	9
5 ft. to less than 5 ft.–6 in.	11
5 ft.–6 in. to less than 6 ft.	14

PART 2E

Electrical Data

FORMULA FOR OHM'S LAW FOR AC CIRCUITS:

$$I = \frac{V}{Z}$$

where:

I = current in amperes
V = voltage in volts
Z = impedance in ohms

FORMULA FOR POWER IN AC CIRCUITS:

$$W = VI(pf)$$

where:

W = power in watts
pf = power factor

The power factor is the ratio of actual power in a circuit measured in watts to the apparent power in volt-amperes. In a circuit with only resistive loads, such as incandescent lights or electric heating elements, impedance equals resistance, and the power factor is 1.0. Therefore, W = VI.

Example

Find the current in a 120 volt circuit serving nine 150 watt downlights. From the formula just given,

$$I = \frac{W}{V(pf)}$$

Since the power factor is 1, then

$$I = \frac{9 \times 150}{120} = 11.25 \text{ amps}$$

Energy Formula

Energy is a measure of use of power over time, so energy measured in kilowatt-hours is equal to kilowatts times hours. For example, an 1150 watt appliance used for 30 minutes would consume 1150/1000 × 0.5 = 0.58 kWh of energy.

SIZES OF METALLIC CONDUIT

In detailing situations where electrical service is required and space is limited, it is often necessary to know the outside diameter of conduit and what the minimum bend can be for conduit. Table 2E–1 gives outside diameters of conduit. Table 2E–2 gives the radius of the curve of the inner edge of any field bend and the exception to the basic rule, which is for field bends for conductors without lead sheaths and made with a single operation bending machine designed for the purpose. Note that the exception dimension is measured to the *center* of the conduit. The maximum number of bends between fittings or outlets shall not exceed the equivalent of four quarter bends, or a total of 360 degrees.

The following table gives the bend radius, in inches, for flexible metallic tubing:

Size of Conduit	For Fixed Bends	For Flexing Use
3/8	3 1/2	10
1/2	4	12 1/2
3/4	5	17 1/2

Table 2E–1
OUTSIDE DIAMETERS OF CONDUIT

Nominal Size	Outside Diameter		
	EMT	IMC	RS
1/2	0.71	0.82	0.84
3/4	0.92	1.03	1.05
1	1.16	1.29	1.32
1 1/4	1.51	1.64	1.66
1 1/2	1.74	1.88	1.90
2	2.20	2.36	2.38
2 1/2	2.88	2.86	2.88
3	3.50	3.48	3.50
3 1/2	4.00	3.97	4.00
4	4.50	4.47	4.50
5			5.56
6			6.63

RS Rigid Steel Conduit
IMC Intermediate Weight Conduit
EMT Electric Metallic Tubing

Table 2E-2
MINIMUM CONDUIT BENDS
Radius of Conduit Bends (in inches)

Size of Conduit (in in.)	**Conductors Without Lead Sheath** (in in.)	**Conductors With Lead Sheath** (in in.)
1/2	4	6
3/4	5	8
1	6	11
1 1/4	8	14
1 1/2	10	16
2	12	21
2 1/2	15	25
3	18	31
3 1/2	21	36
4	24	40
5	30	50
6	36	61

For SI units: (Radius) one inch = 25.4 millimeters.

Exception
Radius of Conduit Bends (in inches)

Size of Conduit (in. in.)	**Radius to Center of Conduit** (in in.)
1/2	4
3/4	4 1/2
1	5 3/4
1 1/4	7 1/4
1 1/2	8 1/4
2	9 1/2
2 1/2	10 1/2
3	13
3 1/2	15
4	16
5	24
6	30

For SI units: (Radius) one inch = 25.4 millimeters.

MAXIMUM NUMBER OF CONDUCTORS ALLOWED IN CONDUIT

Table 2E–3 gives the *maximum* number of conductors that can be placed in a conduit based on the National Electrical Code's* requirements for maximum percentage of cross-sectional fill allowed. From a practical standpoint, however, these maximums are seldom employed because of the difficulty of pulling the conductors through the conduit. Additional space should also be allowed for future conductors. In most cases, 3/4 inch conduit is the smallest used in commercial applications.

Table 2E–3
MAXIMUM NUMBER OF CONDUCTORS IN TRADE SIZES OF CONDUIT OR TUBING

Conduit Trade Size (Inches)		½	¾	1	1¼	1½	2	2½	3	3½	4	5	6
Type Letters	**Conductor Size AWG, MCM**												
TW, T, RUH,	14	9	15	25	44	60	99	142					
RUW,	12	7	12	19	35	47	78	111	171				
XHHW (14 thru 8)	10	5	9	15	26	36	60	85	131	176			
	8	2	4	7	12	17	28	40	62	84	108		
RHW and RHH	14	6	10	16	29	40	65	93	143	192			
(without outer	12	4	8	13	24	32	53	76	117	157			
covering),	10	4	6	11	19	26	43	61	95	127	163		
THW	8	1	3	5	10	13	22	32	49	66	85	133	
TW,	6	1	2	4	7	10	16	23	36	48	62	97	141
T,	4	1	1	3	5	7	12	17	27	36	47	73	106
THW,	3	1	1	2	4	6	10	15	23	31	40	63	91
RUH (6 thru 2),	2	1	1	2	4	5	9	13	20	27	34	54	78
RUW (6 thru 2),	1		1	1	3	4	6	9	14	19	25	39	57
FEPB (6 thru 2),	0		1	1	2	3	5	8	12	16	21	33	49
RHW and	00		1	1	1	3	5	7	10	14	18	29	41
RHH (with-	000		1	1	1	2	4	6	9	12	15	24	35
out outer	0000			1	1	1	3	5	7	10	13	20	29
covering)													

Conduit Trade Size (Inches)		½	¾	1	1¼	1½	2	2½	3	3½	4	5	6
Type Letters	**Conductor Size AWG, MCM**												
	14	13	24	39	69	94	154						
	12	10	18	29	51	70	114	164					
THWN,	10	6	11	18	32	44	73	104	160				
	8	3	5	9	16	22	36	51	79	106	136		
THHN,	6	1	4	6	11	15	26	37	57	76	98	154	
FEP (14 thru 2),	4	1	2	4	7	9	16	22	35	47	60	94	137
FEPB (14 thru 8),	3	1	1	3	6	8	13	19	29	39	51	80	116
PFA (14 thru 4/0)	2	1	1	3	5	7	11	16	25	33	43	67	97
PFAH (14 thru 4/0)	1		1	1	3	5	8	12	18	25	32	50	72
Z (14 thru 4/0)													
XHHW (4 thru	0		1	1	3	4	7	10	15	21	27	42	61
500MCM)	00		1	1	2	3	6	8	13	17	22	35	51
	000		1	1	1	3	5	7	11	14	18	29	42
	0000		1	1	1	2	4	6	9	12	15	24	35
	250			1	1	1	3	4	7	10	12	20	28
	300			1	1	1	3	4	6	8	11	17	24
	350			1	1	1	2	3	5	7	9	15	21
	400				1	1	1	3	5	6	8	13	19
	500				1	1	1	2	4	5	7	11	16
	600				1	1	1	1	3	4	5	9	13
	700					1	1	1	3	4	5	8	11
	750					1	1	1	2	3	4	7	11
XHHW	6	1	3	5	9	13	21	30	47	63	81	128	185
	600				1	1	1	1	3	4	5	9	13
	700					1	1	1	3	4	5	7	11
	750					1	1	1	2	3	4	7	10

*National Electrical Code ® and NEC® are registered trademarks of the National Fire Protection Association, Inc., Quincy, MA 02269.

Table 2E-3 (Continued)

Conduit Trade Size (Inches)		½	¾	1	1¼	1½	2	2½	3	3½	4	5	6
Type Letters	**Conductor Size AWG, MCM**												
	14	3	6	10	18	25	41	58	90	121	155		
	12	3	5	9	15	21	35	50	77	103	132		
RHW,	10	2	4	7	13	18	29	41	64	86	110		
	8	1	2	4	7	9	16	22	35	47	60	94	137
RHH	6	1	1	2	5	6	11	15	24	32	41	64	93
	4	1	1	1	3	5	8	12	18	24	31	50	72
(with	3	1	1	1	3	4	7	10	16	22	28	44	63
outer	2		1	1	3	4	6	9	14	19	24	38	56
covering)	1		1	1	1	3	5	7	11	14	18	29	42
	0		1	1	1	2	4	6	9	12	16	25	37
	00			1	1	1	3	5	8	11	14	22	32
	000			1	1	1	3	4	7	9	12	19	28
	0000			1	1	1	2	4	6	8	10	16	24

Table 2E-3 is helpful in estimating probable conduit sizes when space in partitions, ceilings, and other critical areas is limited. If space is very limited, also make an allowance for connectors and other fittings.

Table 2E-4 is helpful when planning for electrical closets and other types of electrical service rooms.

Table 2E-4
WORKING SPACE REQUIRED AROUND ELECTRICAL EQUIPMENT

Voltage to Ground Nominal	**Minimum Clear Distance** (feet)		
	Condition		
	1	2	3
0-150	3	3	3
151-600	3	3 1/2	4
	Minimum depth of clear working space in front of electrical equipment		
601-2500	3	4	5
2501-9000	4	5	6
9001-25,000	5	6	9
25,001-75 kV	6	8	10
Above 75 kV	8	10	12

CONDITIONS

1. Exposed live parts on one side and no live or grounded parts on the other side of the working space, or exposed live parts on both sides effectively guarded by suitable wood or other insulating materials. Insulated wire or insulated busbars operating at not over 300 volts shall not be considered live parts.
2. Exposed live parts on one side and grounded parts on the other side.
3. Exposed live parts on both sides of the work space (not guarded as provided in Condition 1, with the operator between).

Exception No. 1: Working space shall not be required in back of assemblies such as dead-front switchboards or motor control centers where there are no renewable or adjustable parts such as fuses or switches on the back and where all connections are accessible from locations other than the back.

Exception No. 2: By special permission, smaller spaces may be permitted (1) where it is judged that the particular arrangement of the installation will provide adequate accessibility or (2) where all uninsulated parts are at a voltage no greater than 30 volts RMS or 42V dc.

PART 2F

Illumination

MEASURING LIGHT AND ILLUMINATION TERMS

(See Figure 2F–1.)

Luminous Intensity, I, is the solid angular flux density in a given direction measured in candlepower in American Standard (AS) units and candela in SI units. The candela and candlepower have the same magnitude.

Lumen, lm, is the unit of luminous flux equal to the flux in a unit solid angle of one steradian from a uniform point source of one candela. On a unit sphere, an area of one square foot (or square meter) will subtend an angle of one steradian. Since the area of a unit sphere is 4 × pi, a source of one candlepower (candela) produces 12.57 lumens.

Illuminance E, is the density of luminous flux *incident* on a surface in lumens per unit area. One lumen uniformly incident on one square foot of area produces an illuminance of one footcandle. The unit of measurement, therefore, is the footcandle (fc) in AS units. In SI units, the measurement is lux (lx), or lumens square meter.

FORMULAS: one footcandle = 10.764 lux

$$fc = \frac{lm}{ft^2}$$

$$fc = \frac{lm}{m^2}$$

In many cases, 10 lux is taken as being approximately equal to one footcandle.

Luminance, L, is the luminous flux per unit of projected (apparent) area and unit solid angle *leaving* a surface, either reflected or transmitted. The unit is the footlambert (fL) where one footlambert = 1/pi candelas per square foot. In SI units, it is candela per square meter. Luminance takes into account the reflectance and transmittance properties of materials and the direction in which they are viewed (the apparent area). Thus, 100 footcandles striking a surface with 50% reflectance would result in a luminance of 50 footlamberts.

Another way to view luminance is to say that a surface emitting, transmitting, or reflecting one lumen per square foot in the direction being viewed has a luminance of one footlambert.

CONVERSION FACTORS OF UNITS OF ILLUMINATION

Given	Multiply by	to obtain
Illuminance (E) in lux	0.0929	footcandles
Illuminance (E) in footcandles	10.764	lux
Luminance (L) in cd/sq. m	0.2919	footlamberts
Luminance (L) in footlamberts	3.4263	cd/sq. m
Intensity (I) candelas	1.0	candlepower

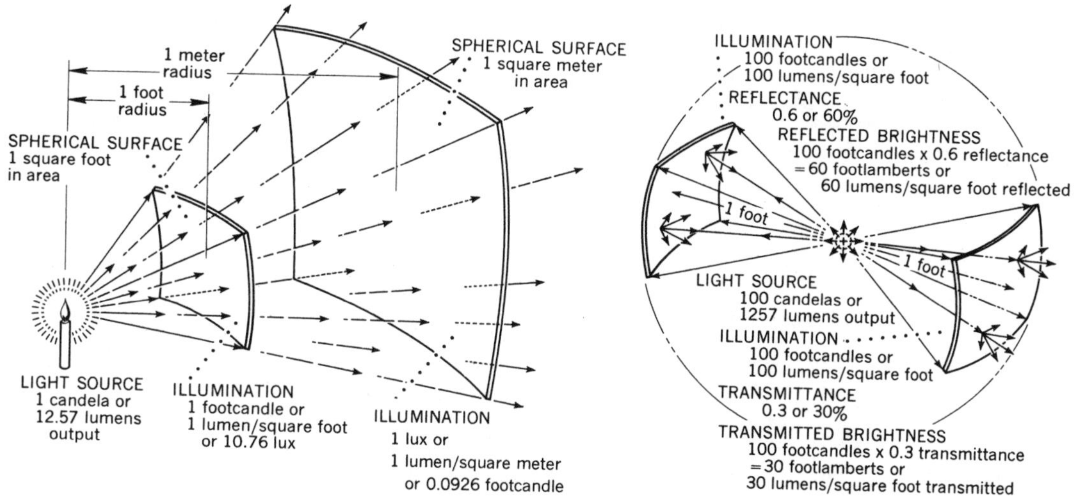

Source: GE Lighting Business Group

Figure 2F-1: Relationship of Light Source, Illumination, Transmittance, and Reflectance

FORMULAS:

Inverse Square Law

The illumination at a point on a surface when the surface is perpendicular to the direction of the source varies directly with the luminous intensity of the source and inversely with the square of the distance between the source and the point:

$$E = \frac{I}{d^2}$$

where:

E = illumination in footcandles (or lux)
I = luminous intensity in candlepower (or candelas)
d = distance in ft. (or m)

This equation assumes the source is a *point source.* Since a point source is only theoretical, the formula is applicable when the maximum dimension of the source is less than five times the distance to the point where the illumination is being calculated.

The value for I at various angles can be obtained from the candlepower distribution curves or tables supplied by the manufacturer of the luminaire under consideration.

Cosine Law

The illumination of any surface varies as the cosine of the angle of incidence, θ, where the angle of incidence is the angle between the normal to the surface and the direction of the incident light. (See Figure F2-2.) Combined with the equation just given, the formula becomes:

FORMULA:

$$E = \frac{I}{d^2} \cos \theta$$

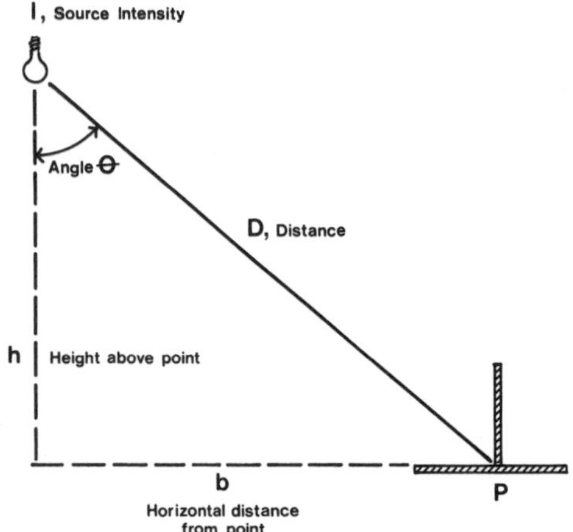

Figure 2F-2: Cosine Law of Illumination

This is the illumination on a horizontal surface at point P. For illumination on a vertical surface at point P, the equation becomes:

$$E(v) = \frac{I}{d^2} \sin \theta$$

since:

$$\cos \theta = \frac{h}{d}$$

and

$$\sin \theta = \frac{b}{d}$$

the equations for horizontal and vertical illumination can be rewritten as follows.

$$E(h) = \frac{I}{h^2} \cos^3 \theta$$

$$E(v) = \frac{I}{b^2} \sin^3 \theta$$

Example

What is the vertical surface illumination on a wall 6 ft. down from the ceiling that is illuminated by a downlight placed 3 ft. from the wall? The candlepower distribution curve for the fixture indicates an intensity of 2550 fc at 25 degrees from vertical.

The angle, θ, is arctan 3/6, or 26.6°. Since this is very close to the reading at 25 degrees, use I = 2550 fc.

FORMULA:

$$E(v) = \frac{2550}{3^2} \sin^3 26.6$$

$$E(v) = 25 \text{ footcandles}$$

If the reflectance of the wall is 55%, the luminance, L, is 25 × 0.55, or about 14 footlamberts.

HOW TO SELECT THE RECOMMENDED ILLUMINANCE LEVEL

Different tasks under different conditions require different levels of illumination. The variables include the task itself, the age of the person performing the task, the reflectances of the room, and the demand for speed and/or accuracy in performing the task. The Illuminating Engineering Society (IES) has established a range of illumination levels for various tasks, areas, and activities to take into account these variables.

To determine the required illumination level in footcandles (or lux), first determine the illuminance category for the task under consideration from Table 2F-1. This table lists representative activities for common occupancies. For a detailed listing, refer to the complete table in the *IES Lighting Handbook.* Illuminance categories are given a letter from *A* to *I, A* representing the lowest values for general lighting in noncritical areas and *I* representing requirements for specialized and difficult visual tasks.

Table 2F-2 gives the corresponding range of illuminances for each category.

With the illuminance category and a knowledge of the age of the occupant, the approximate (or assumed) surface reflectances, and the importance of the task, find which of the three values should be used by referring to Table 2F-3. Note that the values in this table are in lux. For recommended footcandle levels, divide the values by 10.

The following caveats apply to selecting illumination levels and using them in lighting calculations:

1. All aspects of a quality design must be considered—control of glare, contrast ratios, color rendering properties, and so on—not just raw illumination levels.
2. The values determined in the illumination categories are *maintained* values in the space, not initial values.
3. The values in categories *A* to *C* are average maintained illuminances and are most appropriate for lighting calculations using the zonal cavity method, as described in the next section on "Calculating Number of Luminaires Required" and for daylighting calculations. The values in categories *D* to *I* are illumination levels on the task. Point calculation methods, as described in the previous section "Basic Formulas," are more appropriate for these categories, although achieving the recommended illumination level may be accomplished with a combination of general and task lighting.
4. Special analysis and design is required for lighting for visual tasks in categories *G* through *I.*

Table 2F-1
ILLUMINANCE CATEGORIES FOR SELECTED ACTIVITIES

Area/Activity	Illuminance Category
Auditoriums	
Assembly	C
Social activity	B
Banks	
General lobby area	C
Lobby writing area	D
Tellers' stations	E
Barber shops and beauty parlors	E
Conference rooms—conferring	D
For critical seeing, refer to individual task	
Drafting	
High contrast	E
Low contrast	F

Table 2F-1 (Continued)

Area/Activity	Illuminance Category
Educational facilities	
General classrooms (see Reading)	
Science laboratories	E
Lecture rooms—audience (see Reading)	
Lecture rooms—demonstrations	F
Cafeterias (see Food Service)	
Food service facilities	
Cashier	D
Cleaning	C
Dining	B
Kitchen	E
Hotels	
Bathrooms, for grooming	D
Bedrooms, for reading	D
Corridors, elevators, and stairs	C
Front desk	E
Lobby, general lighting	C
Libraries	
Reading areas (see Reading)	
Active stacks	D
Inactive stacks	B
Card files	E
Circulation desks	D
Merchandising spaces	
Dressing areas	D
Fitting areas	F
Wrapping and packaging	D
Sales transaction area	E
Offices	
Conference (see Conference rooms)	
General and private offices (see Reading)	
Lobbies, lounges, and reception areas	C
Mail sorting	E
Reading	
Copied tasks	
Microfiche reader	B
Photographs, moderate detail	E
Xerograph	D
Electronic data-processing tasks	
CRT screens	B
Impact printer, good ribbon	D
Keyboard reading	D
Machine rooms, active operations	D
Handwritten tasks	
# 3 pencil and softer leads	E
# 4 pencil and harder leads	F
Felt-tip pen	D
Chalkboards	E

Area/Activity	Illuminance Category
Printed tasks	
6 point type	E
8 and 10 point type	D
Maps	E
Typed originals	D
Telephone books	E
Residences	
General lighting	B
Dining	C
Grooming	D
Kitchen duties, critical seeing	E
Kitchen duties, non-critical	D
Reading, normal	D
Reading, prolonged	E
Service spaces	
Stairways, corridors	C
Elevators	C
Toilets and washrooms	C

Note: Refer to the *IES Lighting Handbook* for a detailed list of requirements for individual spaces and for industrial, transportation, and outdoor activities.

Source: Data extracted from IES Lighting Handbook, *1981 Reference Volume.*

Table 2F-2
ILLUMINANCE CATEGORIES AND ILLUMINANCE VALUES FOR GENERIC TYPES OF ACTIVITES IN INTERIORS

Type of Activity	Illuminance Category	Range of Illuminances (in footcandles)
General lighting throughout space:		
Public spaces with dark surroundings	A	2-3-5
Simple orientation for short temporary visits	B	5-7.5-10
Working spaces where visual tasks are only occasionally performed	C	10-15-20
Illuminance on task:		
Performance of visual tasks of high contrast or large size	D	20-30-50
Performance of visual tasks of medium contrast of small size	E	50-75-100
Performance of visual tasks of low contrast or very small size	F	100-150-200
Illuminance on task, obtained by a combination of general and local (supplementary) lighting:		
Performance of visual tasks of low contrast and very small size over a prolonged period	G	200-300-500
Performance of very prolonged and exacting visual tasks	H	500-750-1000
Performance of very special visual tasks of extremely low contrast and small size	I	1000-1500-2000

Source: IES Lighting Handbook.

Table 2F-3
ILLUMINANCE VALUES, MAINTAINED, IN LUX, FOR A COMBINATION OF ILLUMINANCE CATEGORIES AND USER, ROOM, AND TASK CHARACTERISTICS (FOR ILLUMINANCE IN FOOTCANDLES, DIVIDE BY 10)

a. General Lighting Throughout Room

Weighting Factors		Illuminance Categories		
Average of Occupants Ages	Average Room Surface Reflectance (per cent)	A	B	C
Under 40	Over 70	20	50	100
	30–70	20	50	100
	Under 30	20	50	100
40–55	Over 70	20	50	100
	30–70	30	75	150
	Under 30	50	100	200
Over 55	Over 70	30	75	150
	30–70	50	100	200
	Under 30	50	100	200

b. Illuminance on Task

Weighting Factors			Illuminance Categories					
Average of Workers Ages	Demand for Speed and/or Accuracy*	Task Background Reflectance (per cent)	D	E	F	G**	H**	I**
Under 40	NI	Over 70	200	500	1000	2000	5000	10000
		30–70	200	500	1000	2000	5000	10000
		Under 30	300	750	1500	3000	7500	15000
	I	Over 70	200	500	1000	2000	5000	10000
		30–70	300	750	1500	3000	7500	15000
		Under 30	300	750	1500	3000	7500	15000
	C	Over 70	300	750	1500	3000	7500	15000
		30–70	300	750	1500	3000	7500	15000
		Under 30	300	750	1500	3000	7500	15000
40–55	NI	Over 70	200	500	1000	2000	5000	10000
		30–70	300	750	1500	3000	7500	15000
		Under 30	300	750	1500	3000	7500	15000
	I	Over 70	300	750	1500	3000	7500	15000
		30–70	300	750	1500	3000	7500	15000
		Under 30	300	750	1500	3000	7500	15000
	C	Over 70	300	750	1500	3000	7500	15000
		30–70	300	750	1500	3000	7500	15000
		Under 30	500	1000	2000	5000	10000	20000
Over 55	NI	Over 70	300	750	1500	3000	7500	15000
		30–70	300	750	1500	3000	7500	15000
		Under 30	300	750	1500	3000	7500	15000
	I	Over 70	300	750	1500	3000	7500	15000
		30–70	300	750	1500	3000	7500	15000
		Under 30	500	1000	2000	5000	10000	20000
	C	Over 70	300	750	1500	3000	7500	15000
		30–70	500	1000	2000	5000	10000	20000
		Under 30	500	1000	2000	5000	10000	20000

* NI = not important, I – important, and C = critical
** Obtained by a combination of general and supplementary lighting.

Source: IES Lighting Handbook.

HOW TO CALCULATE NUMBER OF LUMINAIRES REQUIRED

The number of luminaires required to light a space to a desired illumination level (footcandles) can be calculated knowing certain characteristics of the room and the light source. The following method is the zonal cavity method of calculating illumination.

FORMULA:

$$\text{Area/luminaire} = \frac{\text{N} \times \text{Lumens per lamp} \times \text{CU} \times \text{LLF}}{\text{footcandles required (E)}}$$

where:

N = number of lamps
CU = coefficient of utilization
LLF = light loss factor
E = recommended illumination (maintained)

The formula can be rewritten to find the number of luminaires or to determine the maintained footcandle level.

FORMULA:

$$\text{Number of luminaires} = \frac{\text{footcandles required} \times \text{area of room}}{\text{N} \times \text{lumens per lamp} \times \text{CU} \times \text{LLF}}$$

$$\text{Footcandles} = \frac{\text{N} \times \text{lumens per lamp} \times \text{CU} \times \text{LLF}}{\text{area per luminaire}}$$

The coefficient of utilization (CU) is a factor that reflects the fact that not all of the lumens produced by a luminaire reach the work surface. It depends on the particular light fixture used as well as the characteristics of the room in which it is placed, including the room size and the surface reflectances of the room. If you know what specific luminaire you want to use, obtain coefficient of utilization factors from the manufacturer and use those. They are usually included in product catalogs.

If you do not know specifically what fixture you will be selecting, you can use general CU tables based on luminaire types. (See Table 2F–4.)

Light Loss Factor (LLF)

The light loss factor is a fraction that represents the amount of light that will be lost due to things such as dirt on lamps, reduction of light output of a lamp over time, and similar factors. The following items are the individual components of the LLF. The total LLF is calculated by multiplying all of the individual factors together.

Ambient Temperature: For normal indoor temperatures, use 1. For air-handling luminaires, use 1.10.

Voltage: Use 1 for luminaire operation at rated temperature.

Luminaire Surface Depreciation: Over time, the various surfaces of a light fixture will change (some plastic lens yellow, for example). In the absence of data, use a value of 1.

Non-Standard Components: Use of different components such as ballasts, louvers, and so on can affect light output. Use a value of 1 if no other information is available.

In the absence of other data, use a factor of 0.9 for the combination of the four factors just mentioned. This is usually adequate for most situations.

Table 2F-4
COEFFICIENTS OF UTILIZATION

Typical Luminaire	Typical Intensity Distribution and Per Cent Lamp Lumens		ρ_{CC} →	80			70			50			30			10			0
			ρ_W →	50	30	10	50	30	10	50	30	10	50	30	10	50	30	10	0
	Maint. Cat.	SC	RCR ↓	Coefficients of Utilization for 20 Per Cent Effective Floor Cavity Reflectance (ρ_{FC} = 20)															
1	V	1.5	0	.87	.87	.87	.81	.81	.81	.70	.70	.70	.59	.59	.59	.49	.49	.49	.45
			1	.71	.67	.63	.66	.62	.59	.56	.53	.50	.47	.45	.42	.38	.37	.35	.31
			2	.60	.54	.49	.56	.50	.45	.47	.43	.39	.39	.36	.33	.32	.29	.27	.23
			3	.52	.45	.39	.48	.42	.37	.41	.36	.31	.34	.30	.26	.27	.24	.22	.18
	35½% ↑		4	.46	.38	.33	.42	.36	.30	.36	.30	.26	.30	.26	.22	.24	.21	.18	.15
			5	.40	.33	.27	.37	.30	.25	.31	.26	.22	.26	.22	.18	.21	.18	.15	.12
	45% ↓		6	.36	.28	.23	.33	.26	.21	.28	.23	.19	.23	.19	.16	.19	.15	.13	.10
			7	.32	.25	.20	.29	.23	.18	.25	.20	.16	.21	.16	.13	.17	.13	.11	.09
			8	.29	.22	.17	.26	.20	.16	.23	.17	.14	.19	.15	.12	.15	.12	.09	.07
Pendant diffusing sphere with incandescent lamp			9	.26	.19	.15	.24	.18	.14	.20	.15	.12	.17	.13	.10	.14	.11	.08	.06
			10	.23	.17	.13	.22	.16	.12	.19	.14	.10	.16	.12	.09	.13	.09	.07	.05
2	II	N.A.	0	.83	.83	.83	.72	.72	.72	.50	.50	.50	.30	.30	.30	.12	.12	.12	.03
			1	.72	.69	.66	.62	.60	.57	.43	.42	.40	.26	.25	.25	.10	.10	.10	.03
			2	.63	.58	.54	.54	.50	.47	.38	.36	.33	.23	.22	.21	.09	.09	.08	.02
			3	.55	.49	.45	.48	.43	.39	.33	.30	.28	.20	.19	.17	.08	.08	.07	.02
			4	.48	.42	.37	.42	.37	.33	.29	.26	.24	.18	.16	.15	.07	.07	.06	.02
	83% ↑		5	.43	.36	.32	.37	.32	.28	.26	.23	.20	.16	.14	.13	.06	.06	.05	.01
			6	.38	.32	.27	.33	.28	.24	.23	.20	.17	.14	.12	.11	.06	.05	.04	.01
	3½% ↓		7	.34	.28	.23	.30	.24	.21	.21	.17	.15	.13	.11	.09	.05	.04	.04	.01
			8	.31	.25	.20	.27	.21	.18	.19	.15	.13	.12	.10	.08	.05	.04	.03	.01
Concentric ring unit with incandescent silvered-bowl lamp			9	.28	.22	.18	.24	.19	.16	.17	.14	.11	.10	.09	.07	.04	.03	.03	.01
			10	.25	.20	.16	.22	.17	.14	.16	.12	.10	.10	.08	.06	.04	.03	.03	.01
3	IV	1.3	0	.99	.99	.99	.97	.97	.97	.93	.93	.93	.89	.89	.89	.85	.85	.85	.83
			1	.88	.85	.82	.86	.83	.81	.83	.80	.78	.79	.78	.76	.77	.75	.73	.72
	0% ↑		2	.78	.73	.68	.76	.72	.67	.73	.69	.66	.71	.67	.64	.68	.65	.63	.61
			3	.69	.62	.57	.67	.61	.57	.65	.60	.56	.63	.58	.55	.61	.57	.54	.52
			4	.61	.54	.49	.60	.53	.48	.58	.52	.48	.56	.51	.47	.54	.50	.46	.45
	83½% ↓		5	.54	.47	.41	.53	.46	.41	.51	.45	.41	.50	.44	.40	.48	.43	.40	.38
			6	.48	.41	.35	.47	.40	.35	.46	.39	.35	.44	.39	.34	.43	.38	.34	.32
			7	.43	.35	.30	.42	.35	.30	.41	.34	.30	.39	.34	.30	.38	.33	.29	.28
			8	.38	.31	.26	.38	.31	.26	.37	.30	.26	.36	.30	.26	.35	.30	.26	.24
Porcelain-enameled ventilated standard dome with incandescent lamp			9	.35	.28	.23	.34	.27	.23	.33	.27	.23	.32	.27	.23	.31	.26	.22	.21
			10	.31	.25	.20	.31	.24	.20	.30	.24	.20	.29	.24	.20	.29	.23	.20	.18
4	V	1.3	0	.89	.89	.89	.85	.85	.85	.77	.77	.77	.70	.70	.70	.63	.63	.63	.60
			1	.78	.75	.72	.74	.72	.69	.68	.66	.64	.62	.60	.58	.56	.55	.54	.51
	18½% ↑		2	.69	.65	.61	.66	.62	.58	.61	.57	.54	.56	.53	.50	.51	.49	.47	.44
			3	.62	.57	.52	.60	.55	.50	.55	.51	.47	.50	.47	.44	.46	.43	.41	.39
			4	.56	.50	.46	.54	.49	.44	.50	.45	.42	.46	.42	.39	.42	.39	.37	.35
	60½% ↓		5	.51	.45	.40	.49	.43	.39	.45	.41	.37	.42	.38	.35	.39	.36	.33	.31
			6	.46	.40	.36	.45	.39	.35	.42	.37	.33	.39	.35	.31	.36	.32	.30	.28
			7	.42	.36	.32	.41	.35	.31	.38	.33	.29	.35	.31	.28	.33	.29	.27	.25
			8	.38	.32	.28	.37	.32	.28	.35	.30	.26	.32	.28	.25	.30	.27	.24	.22
			9	.35	.29	.25	.34	.29	.25	.32	.27	.24	.30	.26	.23	.28	.24	.22	.20
Prismatic square surface drum			10	.32	.27	.23	.31	.26	.22	.29	.25	.21	.27	.23	.20	.26	.22	.20	.18
5	IV	0.8	0	1.19	1.19	1.19	1.16	1.16	1.16	1.11	1.11	1.11	1.06	1.06	1.06	1.02	1.02	1.02	1.00
			1	1.09	1.07	1.04	1.07	1.05	1.02	1.03	1.01	.99	.99	.98	.96	.96	.95	.93	.92
	0% ↑		2	1.01	.97	.93	.99	.95	.92	.96	.93	.90	.93	.90	.88	.90	.88	.86	.84
			3	.93	.88	.84	.92	.87	.83	.89	.85	.81	.87	.83	.80	.84	.81	.79	.77
			4	.87	.81	.76	.85	.80	.75	.83	.78	.75	.81	.77	.74	.79	.76	.73	.71
	100% ↓		5	.80	.74	.69	.79	.73	.69	.77	.72	.68	.76	.71	.67	.74	.70	.67	.65
			6	.74	.68	.63	.73	.67	.63	.72	.66	.62	.70	.66	.62	.69	.65	.61	.60
			7	.69	.62	.57	.68	.62	.57	.67	.61	.57	.65	.60	.56	.64	.60	.56	.55
			8	.64	.57	.53	.63	.57	.52	.62	.56	.52	.61	.56	.52	.60	.55	.52	.50
			9	.59	.52	.48	.59	.52	.48	.58	.52	.48	.57	.51	.48	.56	.51	.47	.46
R-40 flood without shielding			10	.55	.49	.44	.55	.48	.44	.54	.48	.44	.53	.48	.44	.52	.47	.44	.42
6	IV	0.7	0	1.01	[illegible]	1.01	.99	.99	.99	.94	.94	.94	.90	.90	.90	.87	.87	.87	.85
			1	.96	.94	.92	.94	.92	.91	.90	.89	.88	.87	.86	.85	.84	.84	.83	.82
	0% ↑		2	.91	.88	.86	.90	.87	.85	.87	.85	.83	.84	.83	.82	.82	.81	.80	.79
			3	.87	.84	.81	.86	.83	.81	.84	.81	.79	.82	.80	.78	.80	.78	.77	.76
			4	.83	.80	.77	.82	.79	.77	.81	.78	.76	.79	.77	.75	.78	.76	.74	.73
	85% ↓		5	.79	.76	.73	.79	.75	.73	.77	.74	.72	.76	.73	.71	.75	.73	.71	.70
			6	.76	.73	.70	.76	.72	.70	.75	.72	.69	.74	.71	.69	.73	.70	.68	.67
			7	.73	.69	.66	.73	.69	.66	.72	.68	.66	.71	.68	.66	.70	.67	.65	.64
			8	.70	.66	.63	.70	.66	.63	.69	.65	.63	.68	.65	.63	.67	.65	.63	.62
R-40 flood with specular anodized reflector skirt; 45° cutoff			9	.67	.63	.60	.67	.63	.60	.66	.62	.60	.65	.62	.60	.65	.62	.60	.59
			10	.64	.60	.58	.64	.60	.58	.63	.60	.58	.63	.60	.57	.62	.59	.57	.56

Typical Luminaire	Typical Intensity Distribution and Per Cent Lamp Lumens			ρ_{CC} →	80			70			50			30			10			0
				ρ_W →	50	30	10	50	30	10	50	30	10	50	30	10	50	30	10	0
		Maint. Cat.	SC	RCR ↓	Coefficients of Utilization for 20 Per Cent Effective Floor Cavity Reflectance (ρ_{FC} = 20)															
7	0% ↑	IV	0.7	0	.52	.52	.52	.51	.51	.51	.48	.48	.48	.46	.46	.46	.45	.45	.45	.44
	43½% ↓			1	.49	.48	.48	.48	.48	.47	.47	.46	.46	.45	.45	.44	.44	.43	.43	.42
				2	.47	.46	.45	.46	.45	.44	.45	.44	.43	.44	.43	.42	.43	.42	.42	.41
				3	.45	.44	.43	.45	.43	.42	.44	.42	.42	.43	.42	.41	.42	.41	.40	.40
				4	.43	.42	.41	.43	.41	.40	.42	.41	.40	.41	.40	.39	.41	.40	.39	.38
				5	.42	.40	.39	.41	.40	.38	.41	.39	.38	.40	.39	.38	.39	.38	.38	.37
EAR-38 lamp above 51 mm (2″) diameter aperture (increase efficiency to 54 ½% for 76 mm (3″) diameter aperture)*				6	.40	.39	.37	.40	.38	.37	.39	.38	.37	.39	.38	.37	.38	.37	.36	.36
				7	.39	.37	.36	.39	.37	.36	.38	.37	.35	.38	.36	.35	.37	.36	.35	.35
				8	.37	.36	.34	37	.35	.34	.37	.35	.34	.36	.35	.34	.36	.35	.34	.33
				9	.36	.34	.33	.36	.34	.33	.35	.34	.33	.35	.34	.33	.35	.33	.33	.32
				10	.35	.33	.32	.35	.33	.32	.34	.33	.32	.34	.33	.32	.34	.32	.31	.31
8	0% ↑	V	1.0	0	.65	.65	.65	.63	.63	.63	.60	.60	.60	.58	.58	.58	.55	.55	.55	.54
	54½% ↓			1	.60	.58	.57	.58	.57	.56	.56	.55	.54	.54	.53	.52	.52	.52	.51	.50
				2	.55	.53	.51	.54	.52	.50	.52	.50	.49	.51	.49	.48	.49	.48	.47	.46
				3	.51	.48	.46	.50	.47	.45	.49	.46	.44	.47	.45	.44	.46	.44	.43	.42
				4	.47	.44	.41	.47	.44	.41	.45	.43	.41	.44	.42	.40	.43	.41	.40	.39
				5	.44	.40	.38	.43	.40	.38	.42	.39	.37	.41	.39	.37	.40	.38	.37	.36
				6	.41	.37	.35	.40	.37	.35	.39	.36	.34	.39	.36	.34	.38	.36	.34	.33
				7	.38	.34	.32	.37	.34	.32	.37	.34	.31	.36	.33	.31	.35	.33	.31	.30
				8	.35	.32	.29	.35	.31	.29	.34	.31	.29	.34	.31	.29	.33	.30	.29	.28
Medium distribution unit with lens plate and inside frost lamp				9	.33	.29	.27	.32	.29	.27	.32	.29	.26	.31	.28	.26	.31	.28	.26	.25
				10	.30	.27	.25	.30	.27	.24	.30	.27	.24	.29	.26	.24	.29	.26	.24	.23
9	0% ↑	IV	0.5	0	.82	.82	.82	.80	.80	.80	.76	.76	.76	.73	.73	.73	.70	.70	.70	.69
	68½% ↓			1	.78	.77	.76	.77	.76	.75	.74	.74	.73	.72	.71	.71	.69	.69	.69	.68
				2	.76	.74	.73	.75	.73	.72	.73	.71	.70	.71	.70	.69	.69	.68	.67	.67
				3	.74	.72	.70	.73	.71	.70	.71	.70	.69	.70	.69	.68	.68	.67	.67	.66
				4	.72	.70	.68	.71	.69	.68	.70	.68	.67	.69	.67	.66	.67	.66	.66	.65
				5	.70	.68	.66	.69	.67	.66	.68	.67	.65	.67	.66	.65	.67	.65	.64	.64
				6	.69	.66	.65	.68	.66	.65	.67	.66	.64	.67	.65	.64	.66	.65	.64	.63
Recessed baffled downlight, 140 mm (5 ½″) diameter aperture—150-PAR/FL lamp				7	.67	.65	.63	.67	.65	.63	.66	.64	.63	.65	.64	.63	.65	.64	.62	.62
				8	.66	.64	.62	.65	.63	.62	.65	.63	.62	.64	.63	.62	.64	.62	.61	.61
				9	.65	.63	.61	.64	.62	.61	.64	.62	.61	.63	.62	.61	.63	.62	.61	.60
				10	.63	.61	.60	.63	.61	.60	.63	.61	.60	.62	.61	.60	.62	.61	.60	.59
10	0% ↑	IV	0.5	0	1.01	1.01	1.01	.99	.99	.99	.95	.95	.95	.91	.91	.91	.87	.87	.87	.85
	85% ↓			1	.97	.95	.94	.95	.94	.92	.92	.91	.90	.88	.88	.87	.86	.85	.84	.83
				2	.93	.91	.89	.91	.89	.88	.89	.87	.86	.86	.85	.84	.84	.83	.82	.81
				3	.90	.87	.85	.89	.86	.84	.87	.85	.83	.85	.83	.82	.83	.82	.81	.79
				4	.87	.84	.82	.86	.83	.81	.84	.82	.80	.83	.81	.79	.81	.80	.79	.78
				5	.84	.81	.79	.83	.80	.78	.82	.79	.78	.81	.79	.77	.80	.78	.76	.75
				6	.82	.79	.76	.81	.78	.76	.80	.78	.76	.79	.77	.75	.78	.76	.75	.74
Recessed baffled downlight, 140 mm (5 ½″) diameter aperture—75ER30 lamp				7	.79	.76	.74	.79	.76	.74	.78	.75	.73	.77	.75	.73	.76	.74	.73	.72
				8	.77	.74	.72	.77	.74	.72	.76	.73	.71	.75	.73	.71	.75	.72	.71	.70
				9	.75	.72	.70	.75	.72	.70	.74	.71	.69	.73	.71	.69	.73	.71	.69	.68
				10	.73	.70	.68	.73	.70	.68	.72	.69	.68	.72	.69	.67	.71	.69	.67	.67
11	0% ↑	V	1.4	0	.63	.63	.63	.62	.62	.62	.59	.59	.59	.57	.57	.57	.54	.54	.54	.53
	53½% ↓			1	.58	.56	.54	.57	.55	.54	.54	.53	.52	.52	.51	.50	.50	.50	.49	.48
				2	.53	.50	.48	.52	.49	.47	.50	.48	.46	.48	.47	.45	.47	.45	.44	.43
				3	.48	.45	.42	.47	.44	.42	.46	.43	.41	.44	.42	.40	.43	.41	.40	.39
				4	.44	.40	.37	.43	.40	.37	.42	.39	.37	.41	.38	.36	.40	.37	.36	.35
				5	.40	.36	.33	.39	.36	.33	.38	.35	.33	.37	.35	.32	.36	.34	.32	.31
				6	.36	.32	.30	.36	.32	.29	.35	.32	.29	.34	.31	.29	.33	.31	.29	.28
				7	.33	.29	.26	.33	.29	.26	.32	.28	.26	.31	.28	.26	.30	.28	.26	.25
Wide distribution unit with lens plate and inside frost lamp				8	.30	.26	.23	.30	.26	.23	.29	.26	.23	.28	.25	.23	.28	.25	.23	.22
				9	.27	.23	.21	.27	.23	.21	.26	.23	.21	.26	.23	.20	.25	.22	.20	.19
				10	.25	.21	.18	.25	.21	.18	.24	.21	.18	.24	.20	.18	.23	.20	.18	.17
12	1½% ↑	V	1.3	0	.62	.62	.62	.60	.60	.60	.57	.57	.57	.54	.54	.54	.52	.52	.52	.51
	50½% ↓			1	.53	.51	.48	.52	.49	.47	.49	.47	.46	.47	.45	.44	.45	.43	.42	.41
				2	.46	.42	.39	.45	.42	.39	.43	.40	.38	.41	.39	.36	.39	.37	.35	.34
				3	.40	.36	.33	.40	.35	.32	.38	.34	.31	.36	.33	.31	.35	.32	.30	.29
				4	.36	.31	.28	.35	.31	.28	.34	.30	.27	.32	.29	.26	.31	.28	.26	.25
				5	.32	.27	.24	.31	.27	.24	.30	.26	.23	.29	.25	.23	.28	.25	.22	.21
				6	.29	.24	.20	.28	.24	.20	.27	.23	.20	.26	.22	.20	.25	.22	.19	.18
				7	.26	.21	.18	.25	.21	.18	.24	.20	.17	.23	.20	.17	.22	.19	.17	.16
				8	.23	.19	.16	.23	.18	.15	.22	.18	.15	.21	.18	.15	.20	.17	.15	.14
Recessed unit with dropped diffusing glass				9	.21	.17	.14	.21	.16	.14	.20	.16	.13	.19	.16	.13	.19	.15	.13	.12
				10	.19	.15	.12	.19	.15	.12	.18	.14	.12	.18	.14	.12	.17	.14	.12	.11

* Also, reflector downlight with baffles and inside frosted lamp.

Table 2F-4 (Continued)

Typical Luminaire	Typical Intensity Distribution and Per Cent Lamp Lumens		ρ_{CC} →	80			70			50			30			10			0
			ρ_W →	50	30	10	50	30	10	50	30	10	50	30	10	50	30	10	0
	Maint. Cat.	SC	RCR ↓	Coefficients of Utilization for 20 Per Cent Effective Floor Cavity Reflectance (ρ_{FC} = 20)															
31 150 mm × 150 mm (6" × 6") cell parabolic wedge louver (multiply by 1.1 for 250 × 250 mm (10 × 10") cells)	IV	1.5/1.2	0	.69	.69	.69	.67	.67	.67	.64	.64	.64	.62	.62	.62	.59	.59	.59	.58
			1	.63	.61	.59	.62	.60	.58	.59	.58	.57	.57	.56	.55	.55	.54	.53	.52
	0% ↑		2	.57	.54	.52	.56	.53	.51	.54	.52	.50	.52	.50	.49	.51	.49	.48	.47
			3	.52	.48	.45	.51	.47	.45	.49	.46	.44	.48	.45	.43	.46	.44	.42	.41
			4	.47	.42	.39	.46	.42	.39	.44	.41	.38	.43	.40	.38	.42	.40	.38	.36
			5	.42	.37	.34	.41	.37	.34	.40	.36	.34	.39	.36	.33	.38	.35	.33	.32
	58% ↓		6	.38	.33	.30	.37	.33	.30	.36	.32	.29	.35	.32	.29	.34	.31	.29	.28
			7	.34	.29	.26	.33	.29	.26	.32	.29	.26	.32	.28	.26	.31	.28	.25	.24
			8	.30	.26	.22	.30	.25	.22	.29	.25	.22	.28	.25	.22	.28	.24	.22	.21
			9	.27	.22	.19	.27	.22	.19	.26	.22	.19	.25	.22	.19	.25	.21	.19	.18
			10	.24	.20	.17	.24	.20	.17	.23	.19	.17	.23	.19	.17	.22	.19	.17	.16
32 2 lamp, surface mounted, bare lamp unit—Photometry with 460 mm (18") wide panel above luminaire (lamps on 150 mm (6") centers)	I	1.3	0	1.02	1.02	1.02	.99	.99	.99	.92	.92	.92	.86	.86	.86	.81	.81	.81	.78
			1	.86	.82	.78	.83	.79	.75	.78	.74	.71	.73	.70	.67	.68	.66	.64	.61
	9½% ↑		2	.74	.67	.61	.71	.65	.60	.66	.61	.57	.62	.58	.54	.58	.55	.52	.49
			3	.64	.56	.50	.62	.55	.49	.58	.52	.47	.54	.49	.45	.51	.47	.43	.41
			4	.56	.48	.42	.55	.47	.41	.51	.45	.39	.48	.42	.38	.45	.40	.36	.34
			5	.49	.41	.35	.48	.40	.34	.45	.38	.33	.42	.36	.32	.39	.34	.30	.28
	78% ↓		6	.44	.36	.30	.43	.35	.29	.40	.33	.28	.38	.32	.27	.35	.30	.26	.24
			7	.39	.31	.25	.38	.30	.25	.36	.29	.24	.34	.28	.23	.32	.27	.23	.21
			8	.35	.27	.22	.34	.27	.22	.32	.26	.21	.30	.24	.20	.29	.23	.19	.18
			9	.32	.24	.19	.31	.23	.18	.29	.22	.18	.27	.21	.17	.26	.20	.17	.15
			10	.29	.21	.17	.28	.21	.16	.26	.20	.16	.25	.19	.15	.23	.18	.15	.13
33 Luminous bottom suspended unit with extra-high output lamp	VI	N.A.	0	.77	.77	.77	.68	.68	.68	.50	.50	.50	.34	.34	.34	.19	.19	.19	.12
			1	.67	.64	.62	.59	.57	.54	.44	.42	.41	.30	.29	.28	.17	.16	.16	.10
			2	.59	.54	.50	.52	.48	.45	.38	.36	.34	.26	.25	.23	.15	.14	.13	.09
			3	.51	.46	.42	.45	.41	.37	.34	.31	.28	.23	.21	.20	.13	.12	.12	.07
			4	.45	.40	.35	.40	.35	.31	.30	.27	.24	.20	.18	.17	.12	.11	.10	.06
	66% ↑		5	.40	.34	.30	.35	.30	.27	.26	.23	.20	.18	.16	.14	.10	.09	.08	.05
			6	.36	.30	.26	.32	.27	.23	.24	.20	.18	.16	.14	.12	.09	.08	.07	.05
			7	.32	.26	.22	.28	.23	.20	.21	.18	.15	.15	.12	.11	.08	.07	.06	.04
	12% ↓		8	.29	.23	.19	.25	.21	.17	.19	.16	.13	.13	.11	.09	.08	.06	.06	.03
			9	.26	.20	.17	.23	.18	.15	.17	.14	.12	.12	.10	.08	.07	.06	.05	.03
			10	.24	.18	.15	.21	.16	.13	.16	.12	.10	.11	.09	.07	.06	.05	.04	.03
34 Prismatic bottom and sides, open top, 4 lamp suspended unit—see note 7	VI	1.4/1.2	0	.91	.91	.91	.85	.85	.85	.74	.74	.74	.64	.64	.64	.54	.54	.54	.50
			1	.80	.77	.74	.75	.73	.70	.66	.64	.62	.57	.56	.54	.49	.48	.47	.43
			2	.71	.66	.62	.67	.63	.59	.59	.56	.53	.51	.49	.47	.44	.43	.41	.38
	33% ↑		3	.63	.58	.53	.60	.55	.50	.53	.49	.45	.46	.43	.41	.40	.38	.36	.33
			4	.57	.50	.45	.53	.48	.43	.47	.43	.39	.41	.38	.35	.36	.34	.32	.29
			5	.50	.44	.39	.48	.42	.37	.42	.38	.34	.37	.34	.31	.33	.30	.28	.25
	50% ↓		6	.45	.39	.34	.43	.37	.33	.38	.33	.30	.34	.30	.27	.30	.27	.24	.22
			7	.41	.34	.30	.39	.33	.28	.34	.30	.26	.30	.27	.24	.27	.24	.21	.19
			8	.37	.30	.26	.35	.29	.25	.31	.26	.23	.27	.24	.21	.24	.21	.19	.17
			9	.33	.27	.22	.31	.26	.22	.28	.23	.20	.25	.21	.18	.22	.19	.16	.15
			10	.30	.24	.20	.28	.23	.19	.25	.21	.18	.23	.19	.16	.20	.17	.14	.13
35 2 lamp prismatic wraparound—see note 7	V	1.5/1.2	0	.81	.81	.81	.78	.78	.78	.72	.72	.72	.66	.66	.66	.61	.61	.61	.59
	11½% ↑		1	.71	.69	.66	.69	.66	.64	.64	.62	.60	.59	.58	.56	.55	.54	.53	.50
			2	.64	.59	.56	.61	.58	.54	.57	.54	.51	.53	.51	.49	.49	.48	.46	.44
			3	.57	.52	.48	.55	.50	.47	.51	.48	.45	.48	.45	.42	.45	.42	.40	.38
			4	.51	.46	.41	.49	.44	.41	.46	.42	.39	.43	.40	.37	.41	.38	.35	.34
	58½% ↓		5	.46	.40	.36	.44	.39	.35	.41	.37	.34	.39	.35	.32	.37	.33	.31	.29
			6	.41	.35	.31	.40	.35	.31	.38	.33	.30	.35	.31	.28	.33	.30	.27	.26
			7	.37	.31	.27	.36	.31	.27	.34	.29	.26	.32	.28	.25	.30	.27	.24	.23
			8	.33	.28	.24	.32	.27	.23	.30	.26	.22	.29	.25	.22	.27	.24	.21	.19
			9	.30	.24	.20	.29	.24	.20	.27	.23	.19	.26	.22	.19	.24	.21	.18	.17
			10	.27	.22	.18	.26	.21	.18	.25	.20	.17	.23	.19	.16	.22	.18	.16	.15
36 2 lamp prismatic wraparound—see note 7	V	1.2	0	.82	.82	.82	.77	.77	.77	.69	.69	.69	.61	.61	.61	.53	.53	.53	.50
			1	.71	.68	.65	.67	.65	.62	.60	.58	.56	.53	.51	.50	.47	.45	.44	.41
			2	.63	.58	.54	.59	.55	.52	.53	.50	.47	.47	.45	.42	.42	.40	.38	.35
	24% ↑		3	.56	.50	.46	.53	.48	.44	.47	.44	.40	.42	.39	.37	.38	.35	.33	.31
			4	.50	.44	.40	.48	.42	.38	.43	.39	.35	.38	.35	.32	.34	.32	.29	.27
			5	.45	.39	.34	.43	.37	.33	.38	.34	.31	.35	.31	.28	.31	.28	.26	.24
	50% ↓		6	.41	.35	.30	.39	.33	.29	.35	.30	.27	.32	.28	.25	.28	.25	.23	.21
			7	.37	.31	.27	.35	.30	.26	.32	.27	.24	.29	.25	.22	.26	.23	.20	.19
			8	.33	.27	.23	.32	.26	.23	.29	.24	.21	.26	.22	.20	.23	.20	.18	.16
			9	.30	.24	.20	.29	.23	.20	.26	.22	.19	.24	.20	.17	.21	.18	.16	.14
			10	.27	.22	.18	.26	.21	.18	.24	.19	.16	.22	.18	.15	.19	.16	.14	.13

Typical Luminaire	Typical Intensity Distribution and Per Cent Lamp Lumens		ρ_{CC} →	80			70			50			30			10			0
			ρ_W →	50	30	10	50	30	10	50	30	10	50	30	10	50	30	10	0
	Maint. Cat.	SC	RCR ↓	Coefficients of Utilization for 20 Per Cent Effective Floor Cavity Reflectance (ρ_{FC} = 20)															
37	V	1.3	0	.52	.52	.52	.50	.50	.50	.46	.46	.46	.43	.43	.43	.39	.39	.39	.38
			1	.45	.43	.41	.43	.41	.39	.40	.38	.37	.36	.35	.34	.34	.33	.32	.30
	8% ↑		2	.39	.35	.33	.37	.34	.32	.34	.32	.30	.32	.30	.28	.29	.28	.26	.25
			3	.34	.30	.27	.33	.29	.26	.30	.27	.25	.28	.26	.24	.26	.24	.22	.21
			4	.30	.26	.23	.29	.25	.22	.27	.24	.21	.25	.22	.20	.23	.21	.19	.18
	37½% ↓		5	.26	.22	.19	.25	.21	.19	.23	.20	.18	.22	.19	.17	.20	.18	.16	.15
			6	.23	.19	.16	.23	.19	.16	.21	.18	.15	.19	.17	.14	.18	.16	.14	.13
			7	.21	.17	.14	.20	.16	.14	.19	.16	.13	.18	.15	.13	.16	.14	.12	.11
			8	.19	.15	.12	.18	.14	.12	.17	.14	.11	.16	.13	.11	.15	.12	.10	.09
2 lamp diffuse wraparound—see note 7			9	.17	.13	.10	.16	.13	.10	.15	.12	.10	.14	.11	.09	.13	.11	.09	.08
			10	.15	.12	.09	.15	.11	.09	.14	.11	.09	.13	.10	.08	.12	.10	.08	.07
38	IV	1.0	0	.60	.60	.60	.58	.58	.58	.56	.56	.56	.53	.53	.53	.51	.51	.51	.50
	0% ↑		1	.54	.52	.50	.52	.51	.49	.50	.49	.48	.48	.47	.46	.47	.46	.45	.44
			2	.48	.45	.43	.47	.44	.42	.45	.43	.41	.44	.42	.40	.42	.41	.39	.39
			3	.43	.40	.37	.42	.39	.37	.41	.38	.36	.40	.37	.36	.39	.37	.35	.34
			4	.39	.35	.32	.38	.35	.32	.37	.34	.32	.36	.33	.31	.35	.33	.31	.30
	50% ↓		5	.35	.31	.28	.35	.31	.28	.34	.30	.28	.33	.30	.28	.32	.29	.27	.26
			6	.32	.28	.25	.32	.28	.25	.31	.27	.25	.30	.27	.25	.29	.26	.24	.23
			7	.29	.25	.22	.29	.25	.22	.28	.25	.22	.27	.24	.22	.27	.24	.22	.21
			8	.26	.22	.20	.26	.22	.20	.25	.22	.20	.25	.22	.19	.24	.21	.19	.18
4 lamp, 610 mm (2') wide troffer with 45° plastic louver—see note 7			9	.24	.20	.17	.24	.20	.17	.23	.20	.17	.23	.19	.17	.22	.19	.17	.16
			10	.22	.18	.16	.22	.18	.16	.21	.18	.16	.21	.18	.15	.20	.17	.15	.15
39	IV	0.9	0	.55	.55	.55	.54	.54	.54	.51	.51	.51	.49	.49	.49	.47	.47	.47	.46
	0% ↑		1	.50	.48	.47	.49	.47	.46	.47	.46	.45	.45	.44	.43	.43	.43	.42	.41
			2	.45	.43	.41	.44	.42	.40	.43	.41	.39	.41	.40	.38	.40	.39	.37	.37
			3	.41	.38	.36	.40	.38	.35	.39	.37	.35	.38	.36	.34	.37	.35	.34	.33
			4	.37	.34	.32	.37	.34	.31	.36	.33	.31	.35	.32	.31	.34	.32	.30	.29
			5	.34	.30	.28	.33	.30	.28	.32	.30	.27	.32	.29	.27	.31	.29	.27	.26
	46% ↓		6	.31	.28	.25	.31	.27	.25	.30	.27	.25	.29	.27	.25	.29	.26	.24	.24
			7	.29	.25	.23	.28	.25	.23	.28	.25	.22	.27	.24	.22	.26	.24	.22	.21
			8	.26	.23	.20	.26	.23	.20	.25	.22	.20	.25	.22	.20	.24	.22	.20	.19
4 lamp, 610 mm (2') wide troffer with 45° white metal louver—see note 7			9	.24	.20	.18	.24	.20	.18	.23	.20	.18	.23	.20	.18	.22	.20	.18	.17
			10	.22	.19	.16	.22	.19	.16	.21	.18	.16	.21	.18	.16	.20	.18	.16	.15
40	V	1.2	0	.73	.73	.73	.71	.71	.71	.68	.68	.68	.65	.65	.65	.62	.62	.62	.60
			1	.64	.61	.59	.62	.60	.58	.60	.58	.56	.57	.56	.54	.55	.54	.52	.51
	1% ↑		2	.56	.52	.49	.55	.51	.48	.52	.49	.47	.50	.48	.46	.48	.46	.44	.43
			3	.50	.45	.41	.49	.44	.41	.47	.43	.40	.45	.42	.39	.43	.41	.38	.37
			4	.44	.39	.35	.43	.38	.35	.42	.37	.34	.40	.36	.33	.39	.36	.33	.32
	60½% ↓		5	.39	.34	.30	.38	.33	.29	.37	.32	.29	.36	.32	.29	.34	.31	.28	.27
			6	.35	.30	.26	.34	.29	.25	.33	.29	.25	.32	.28	.25	.31	.27	.25	.23
			7	.31	.26	.22	.31	.26	.22	.30	.25	.22	.29	.25	.22	.28	.24	.22	.20
			8	.28	.23	.19	.28	.23	.19	.27	.22	.19	.26	.22	.19	.25	.22	.19	.18
Fluorescent unit dropped diffuser, 4 lamp 610 mm (2') wide—see note 7			9	.25	.20	.17	.25	.20	.17	.24	.20	.17	.23	.19	.16	.23	.13	.16	.15
			10	.23	.18	.15	.23	.18	.15	.22	.18	.15	.21	.17	.15	.21	.17	.14	.13
41	V	1.2	0	.69	.69	.69	.67	.67	.67	.64	.64	.64	.61	.61	.61	.59	.59	.59	.58
			1	.61	.58	.56	.59	.57	.56	.57	.55	.54	.55	.53	.52	.53	.52	.51	.49
	0% ↑		2	.53	.50	.47	.52	.49	.46	.50	.48	.45	.49	.46	.44	.47	.45	.43	.42
			3	.47	.43	.40	.47	.42	.39	.45	.41	.38	.43	.40	.38	.42	.39	.37	.36
			4	.42	.37	.34	.41	.37	.33	.40	.36	.33	.39	.35	.33	.37	.35	.32	.31
	57½% ↓		5	.37	.32	.29	.37	.32	.28	.35	.31	.28	.34	.31	.28	.33	.30	.27	.26
			6	.33	.28	.25	.33	.28	.25	.32	.28	.24	.31	.27	.24	.30	.27	.24	.23
			7	.30	.25	.22	.30	.25	.21	.29	.24	.21	.28	.24	.21	.27	.24	.21	.20
Fluorescent unit with flat bottom diffuser, 4 lamp 610 mm (2') wide—see note 7			8	.27	.22	.19	.27	.22	.19	.26	.22	.18	.25	.21	.18	.24	.21	.18	.17
			9	.24	.19	.16	.24	.19	.16	.23	.19	.16	.23	.19	.16	.22	.18	.16	.15
			10	.22	.17	.14	.22	.17	.14	.21	.17	.14	.21	.17	.14	.20	.17	.14	.13
42	V	1.4/1.2	0	.75	.75	.75	.73	.73	.73	.70	.70	.70	.67	.67	.67	.64	.64	.64	.63
			1	.67	.65	.63	.66	.64	.62	.63	.62	.60	.61	.60	.58	.59	.58	.57	.55
	0 ↑		2	.60	.57	.54	.59	.56	.53	.57	.54	.52	.55	.53	.51	.53	.51	.50	.49
			3	.54	.50	.47	.53	.49	.46	.52	.48	.45	.50	.47	.45	.48	.46	.44	.43
		60°	4	.49	.44	.40	.48	.44	.40	.47	.43	.40	.45	.42	.39	.44	.41	.39	.37
	63% ↓		5	.44	.39	.35	.43	.38	.35	.42	.38	.34	.41	.37	.34	.40	.36	.34	.33
			6	.40	.34	.31	.39	.34	.31	.38	.34	.30	.37	.33	.30	.36	.32	.30	.29
			7	.36	.30	.27	.35	.30	.27	.34	.30	.27	.33	.29	.26	.32	.29	.26	.25
Fluorescent unit with flat prismatic lens, 4 lamp 610 mm (2') wide—see note 7			8	.32	.27	.23	.32	.27	.23	.31	.26	.23	.30	.26	.23	.29	.26	.23	.22
			9	.29	.24	.20	.28	.23	.20	.28	.23	.20	.27	.23	.20	.26	.23	.20	.19
			10	.26	.21	.18	.26	.21	.18	.25	.21	.18	.24	.20	.18	.24	.20	.18	.16

Table 2F-4 (Continued)

Typical Luminaire	Typical Intensity Distribution and Per Cent Lamp Lumens: Maint. Cat.	SC	ρ_{CC} → / ρ_W → / RCR ↓	80			70			50			30			10			0
			ρ_W →	50	30	10	50	30	10	50	30	10	50	30	10	50	30	10	0
			RCR ↓	Coefficients of Utilization for 20 Per Cent Effective Floor Cavity Reflectance (ρ_{FC} = 20)															
43	V	1.4/1.3	0	.78	.78	.78	.76	.76	.76	.73	.73	.73	.70	.70	.70	.67	.67	.67	.66
	0 ▲		1	.71	.69	.67	.70	.68	.66	.67	.65	.64	.64	.63	.62	.62	.61	.60	.59
	65½ ▼		2	.64	.61	.58	.63	.60	.58	.61	.59	.56	.59	.57	.55	.57	.55	.54	.53
			3	.58	.54	.51	.58	.54	.51	.56	.52	.50	.54	.51	.49	.52	.50	.48	.47
			4	.53	.48	.45	.52	.48	.44	.51	.47	.44	.49	.46	.43	.48	.45	.43	.42
			5	.48	.43	.39	.47	.42	.39	.46	.42	.39	.45	.41	.38	.43	.40	.38	.37
			6	.43	.38	.35	.43	.38	.34	.42	.37	.34	.40	.37	.34	.40	.36	.34	.32
4 lamp, 610 mm (2′) wide unit with sharp cutoff (high angle—low luminance) flat prismatic lens—see note 7			7	.39	.34	.30	.38	.34	.30	.38	.33	.30	.37	.33	.30	.36	.32	.30	.28
			8	.35	.30	.26	.35	.30	.26	.34	.29	.26	.33	.29	.26	.32	.29	.26	.25
			9	.31	.26	.23	.31	.26	.23	.30	.26	.23	.30	.26	.23	.29	.25	.23	.21
			10	.28	.24	.20	.28	.23	.20	.28	.23	.20	.27	.23	.20	.26	.23	.20	.19
44	IV	N.A.	0	.71	.71	.71	.70	.70	.70	.66	.66	.66	.64	.64	.64	.61	.61	.61	.60
	0 ▲		1	.65	.63	.61	.63	.62	.60	.61	.59	.58	.59	.57	.56	.57	.56	.55	.54
	60 ▼		2	.59	.55	.53	.58	.55	.52	.55	.53	.51	.54	.52	.50	.52	.50	.49	.48
			3	.53	.49	.46	.52	.48	.45	.50	.47	.45	.49	.46	.44	.47	.45	.43	.42
			4	.47	.43	.40	.47	.43	.40	.45	.42	.39	.44	.41	.39	.43	.40	.38	.37
			5	.42	.38	.34	.42	.37	.34	.41	.37	.34	.40	.36	.34	.39	.36	.33	.32
			6	.38	.33	.30	.38	.33	.30	.37	.33	.30	.36	.32	.29	.35	.32	.29	.28
			7	.34	.29	.26	.33	.29	.26	.33	.28	.25	.32	.28	.25	.31	.28	.25	.24
			8	.30	.25	.22	.30	.25	.22	.29	.25	.22	.28	.24	.22	.27	.24	.21	.20
Bilateral batwing distribution—louvered fluorescent unit			9	.27	.22	.18	.26	.22	.18	.26	.21	.18	.25	.21	.18	.24	.21	.18	.17
			10	.24	.19	.16	.24	.19	.16	.23	.19	.16	.22	.19	.16	.22	.18	.16	.15
45	V	N.A.	0	.57	.57	.57	.56	.56	.56	.53	.53	.53	.51	.51	.51	.49	.49	.49	.48
	0 ▲		1	.50	.48	.47	.49	.47	.46	.47	.46	.44	.45	.44	.43	.44	.43	.42	.41
	48 ▼		2	.44	.41	.38	.43	.40	.38	.41	.39	.37	.40	.38	.36	.38	.37	.35	.34
			3	.39	.35	.32	.38	.34	.31	.37	.33	.31	.35	.33	.30	.34	.32	.30	.29
			4	.34	.30	.27	.33	.29	.26	.32	.29	.26	.31	.28	.26	.30	.27	.25	.24
			5	.30	.25	.22	.29	.25	.22	.28	.24	.22	.27	.24	.21	.26	.23	.21	.20
			6	.26	.22	.19	.26	.22	.18	.25	.21	.18	.24	.21	.18	.23	.20	.18	.17
Bilateral batwing distribution—4 lamp, 610 mm (2′) wide fluorescent unit with flat prismatic lens and overlay—see note 7			7	.23	.19	.16	.23	.19	.16	.22	.18	.16	.21	.18	.15	.21	.18	.15	.14
			8	.21	.16	.13	.20	.16	.13	.19	.16	.13	.19	.15	.13	.18	.15	.13	.12
			9	.18	.14	.11	.18	.14	.11	.17	.14	.11	.17	.13	.11	.16	.13	.11	.10
			10	.16	.12	.09	.16	.12	.09	.16	.12	.09	.15	.12	.09	.15	.12	.09	.08
46	V	N.A.	0	.87	.87	.87	.84	.84	.84	.77	.77	.77	.72	.72	.72	.66	.66	.66	.64
	12½ ▲		1	.76	.73	.70	.73	.70	.67	.67	.65	.63	.63	.61	.59	.58	.57	.55	.53
	63½ ▼		2	.66	.61	.57	.64	.59	.56	.59	.56	.52	.55	.52	.49	.51	.49	.47	.44
			3	.59	.53	.48	.56	.51	.47	.53	.48	.44	.49	.45	.42	.46	.43	.40	.38
			4	.52	.45	.40	.50	.44	.40	.47	.42	.38	.44	.39	.36	.41	.37	.34	.32
			5	.46	.39	.34	.44	.38	.33	.41	.36	.32	.38	.34	.31	.36	.32	.29	.27
			6	.41	.34	.29	.39	.33	.29	.37	.31	.27	.34	.30	.26	.32	.28	.25	.23
			7	.36	.30	.25	.35	.29	.24	.33	.27	.23	.31	.26	.23	.29	.25	.22	.20
Bilateral batwing distribution—one lamp, surface mounted fluorescent with prismatic wraparound lens			8	.32	.26	.21	.31	.25	.21	.29	.24	.20	.27	.23	.19	.26	.21	.18	.17
			9	.29	.22	.18	.28	.22	.18	.26	.21	.17	.24	.20	.16	.23	.19	.15	.14
			10	.26	.20	.16	.25	.19	.15	.23	.18	.15	.22	.17	.14	.20	.16	.13	.12
47	V	1.7	0	.71	.71	.71	.69	.69	.69	.66	.66	.66	.63	.63	.63	.61	.61	.61	.60
	0 ▲		1	.62	.60	.58	.61	.59	.57	.59	.57	.55	.56	.55	.53	.54	.53	.52	.51
	59½ ▼		2	.55	.51	.47	.53	.50	.47	.51	.48	.46	.49	.47	.45	.48	.45	.44	.42
			3	.48	.43	.39	.47	.43	.39	.45	.41	.38	.44	.40	.38	.42	.39	.37	.36
			4	.42	.37	.33	.41	.37	.33	.40	.36	.32	.39	.35	.32	.37	.34	.31	.30
			5	.37	.32	.27	.36	.31	.27	.35	.30	.27	.34	.30	.27	.33	.29	.26	.25
			6	.33	.27	.23	.32	.27	.23	.31	.26	.23	.30	.26	.23	.29	.25	.23	.21
			7	.29	.24	.20	.29	.24	.20	.28	.23	.20	.27	.23	.20	.26	.22	.19	.18
Radial batwing distribution—4 lamp, 610 mm (2′) wide fluorescent unit with flat prismatic lens—see note 7			8	.26	.21	.17	.25	.20	.17	.25	.20	.17	.24	.20	.17	.23	.19	.16	.15
			9	.23	.18	.14	.23	.18	.14	.22	.17	.14	.21	.17	.14	.21	.17	.14	.13
			10	.21	.16	.12	.20	.16	.12	.20	.15	.12	.19	.15	.12	.19	.15	.12	.11
48	I	1.6/1.2	0	1.01	1.01	1.01	.96	.96	.96	.87	.87	.87	.79	.79	.79	.72	.72	.72	.68
	20½ ▲		1	.85	.81	.77	.81	.77	.73	.73	.70	.67	.66	.64	.62	.60	.58	.56	.53
	68 ▼		2	.73	.66	.61	.69	.63	.58	.63	.58	.54	.57	.53	.50	.51	.48	.45	.42
			3	.63	.56	.50	.60	.53	.48	.55	.49	.44	.50	.45	.41	.45	.41	.38	.35
			4	.56	.47	.41	.53	.46	.40	.48	.42	.37	.44	.39	.34	.40	.35	.32	.29
			5	.49	.40	.34	.46	.39	.33	.42	.36	.31	.38	.33	.29	.35	.30	.26	.24
			6	.43	.35	.29	.41	.34	.28	.38	.31	.26	.34	.29	.24	.31	.26	.23	.20
			7	.39	.31	.25	.37	.29	.24	.34	.27	.23	.31	.25	.21	.28	.23	.19	.17
			8	.34	.27	.21	.33	.26	.21	.30	.24	.19	.27	.22	.18	.25	.20	.17	.15
			9	.31	.23	.18	.30	.23	.18	.27	.21	.17	.25	.19	.15	.22	.18	.14	.12
2 lamp fluorescent strip unit			10	.28	.21	.16	.27	.20	.16	.25	.19	.15	.22	.17	.14	.20	.16	.13	.11

Lamp Burnouts: If lamps are replaced as they burn out, use a factor of 0.95. If a group replacement maintenance program is employed, use a factor of 1.

Lamp Lumen Depreciation: All lamps put out less light as they age. Specific information is available from each manufacturer, or you can use the figures in Table 2F–12. For preliminary calculations the following factors can also be used:

Lamp Type	Group Replacement	Burnout Replacement
Fluorescent	0.90	0.85
Incandescent	0.94	0.88
Metal-halide	0.87	0.80
Mercury	0.82	0.74
Tungsten-halogen	0.94	0.88
High-pressure sodium	0.94	0.88

Luminaire Dirt Depreciation (LDD)

This factor depends on the type of luminaire, its design, the maintenance schedule of cleaning, and the cleanliness of the room in which the luminaire is used. The manufacturer's literature should give the maintenance category to which an individual fixture belongs. If not, follow the procedure given in Table 2F–5 to find the maintenance category to which a fixture belongs. Next, determine the degree of dirt conditions from the following examples:

Very clean: High-grade offices, not near production; laboratories; clean rooms.

Clean: Offices in older buildings or near production; light assembly; inspection.

Medium: Mill offices; paper processing; light machining.

Dirty: Heat treating; high-speed printing; rubber processing.

Very dirty: Similar to dirty but luminaires within immediate area of contamination.

Finally, estimate the expected cleaning cycle. With these three factors, use Table 2F–6 to determine the LDD factor.

Room Surface Dirt

This factor depends on the type of luminaire (how much it depends on surface reflectances), the type of use conditions, and the maintenance schedule. There are detailed ways of calculating this factor, but for preliminary design purposes, use the factors given in Table 2F–7.

In lieu of combining all of the factors just given, the LLF can be estimated by using the following combination of task and area types:

Clean	0.70
Light dirt	0.65
Medium dirt	0.60
Dirty	0.55
Very dirty	0.50

To calculate the number of luminaires required for a particular room complete the following steps.

Table 2F-5
PROCEDURE FOR DETERMINING LUMINAIRE MAINTENANCE CATEGORIES

To assist in determining Luminaire Dirt Depreciation (LDD) factors, luminaires are separated into six maintenance categories (I through VI). To arrive at categories, luminaires are arbitrarily divided into sections, a Top Enclosure and a Bottom Enclosure, by drawing a horizontal line through the light center of the lamp or lamps. The characteristics listed for the enclosures are then selected as best describing the luminaire. Only one characteristic for the top enclosure and one for the bottom enclosure should be used in determining the category of a luminaire. Percentage of uplight is based on 100% for the luminaire.

The maintenance category is determined when there are characteristics in both enclosure columns. If a luminaire falls into more than one category, the lower numbered category is used.

Maintenance Category	Top Enclosure	Bottom Enclosure
I	1. None	1. None
II	1. None 2. Transparent with 15% or more uplight through apertures. 3. Translucent with 15% or more uplight through apertures. 4. Opaque with 15% or more uplight through apertures.	1. None 2. Louvers or baffles
III	1. Transparent with less than 15% upward light through apertures. 2. Translucent with less than 15% upward light through apertures. 3. Opaque with less than 15% upward light through apertures.	1. None 2. Louvers or baffles
IV	1. Transparent unapertured. 2. Translucent unapertured. 3. Opaque unapertured.	1. None 2. Louvers
V	1. Transparent unapertured. 2. Translucent unapertured. 3. Opaque unapertured.	1. Transparent unapertured 2. Translucent unapertured
VI	1. None 2. Transparent unapertured. 3. Translucent unapertured. 4. Opaque unapertured.	1. Transparent unapertured 2. Translucent unapertured 3. Opaque unapertured

Source: IES Lighting Handbook *1981 Reference Volume.*

1. Compile the following information:

- Length and width of room.
- Height of floor cavity; the distance from the floor to the work surface (usually taken as 2 1/2 ft.).
- Height of the ceiling cavity; the distance from the ceiling to the light fixture. If the fixture is recessed or ceiling mounted, the value is zero.

Table 2F-6
LUMINAIRE DIRT DEPRECIATION FACTORS

Dirt Conditions	Cleaning Cycle in Years	Luminaire Maintenance Categories I	II	III	IV	V	VI
Very clean	1.0	0.96	0.97	0.92	0.93	0.92	0.93
	1.5	0.95	0.96	0.90	0.91	0.91	0.90
	2.0	0.94	0.95	0.88	0.89	0.89	0.87
	3.0	0.92	0.94	0.84	0.86	0.87	0.82
Clean	1.0	0.93	0.93	0.90	0.88	0.88	0.87
	1.5	0.91	0.92	0.87	0.84	0.85	0.81
	2.0	0.89	0.90	0.84	0.81	0.83	0.77
	3.0	0.86	0.87	0.80	0.75	0.80	0.68
Medium	1.0	0.89	0.90	0.87	0.81	0.83	0.80
	1.5	0.86	0.88	0.83	0.75	0.79	0.73
	2.0	0.84	0.85	0.79	0.70	0.76	0.67
	3.0	0.79	0.82	0.73	0.62	0.71	0.56
Dirty	1.0	0.85	0.86	0.83	0.73	0.78	0.75
	1.5	0.81	0.83	0.78	0.66	0.73	0.67
	2.0	0.77	0.80	0.74	0.60	0.70	0.59
	3.0	0.71	0.75	0.67	0.50	0.64	0.47
Very dirty	1.0	0.74	0.83	0.79	0.64	0.73	0.67
	1.5	0.67	0.79	0.73	0.55	0.67	0.57
	2.0	0.62	0.75	0.68	0.47	0.63	0.48
	3.0	0.53	0.69	0.60	0.37	0.56	0.35

Source: IES Lighting Handbook *1981 Reference Volume.*

Table 2F-7
APPROXIMATE ROOM SURFACE DIRT DEPRECIATION FACTORS

Room Cleanliness	Luminaire Distribution Types: Direct	Semidirect	Direct-Indirect	Semi-indirect	Indirect
Very clean	0.97	0.95	0.94	0.94	0.89
Clean	0.95	0.91	0.87	0.85	0.80
Medium	0.94	0.88	0.83	0.81	0.73
Dirty	0.92	0.85	0.79	0.78	0.67
Very dirty	0.91	0.83	0.76	0.74	0.61

Source: IES Lighting Handbook *1981 Reference Volume.*

- Height of the room cavity; the distance from the work surface to the light fixture.
- Surface reflectances of the ceiling, the walls, and the floor. If the wall surface of the floor cavity is different from the room cavity wall surface (as with a wainscot, for example) obtain both figures. Surface reflectances are usually available from paint companies, ceiling tile manufacturers, and manufacturers of other finishes. If these are not readily available, use the values in Table 2F-8.

2. Determine cavity ratios.

FORMULA:

$$CR = 2.5 \times \frac{\text{area of cavity wall}}{\text{area of base of cavity}}$$

Table 2F-8
REFLECTANCE VALUES OF VARIOUS MATERIALS AND COLORS

Material	Approximate Reflectance (in %)
Acoustical ceiling tile	75–85
Aluminum, brushed	55–58
Aluminum, polished	60–70
Clear glass	8–10
Granite	20–25
Marble	30–70
Stainless steel	55–65
Wood	
Light oak	25–35
Dark oak	10–15
Mahogany	6–12
Walnut	5–10
Color	
White	80–85
Light gray	45–70
Dark gray	20–25
Ivory white	70–80
Ivory	60–70
Pearl gray	70–75
Buff	40–70
Tan	30–50
Brown	20–40
Green	25–50
Azure blue	50–60
Sky blue	35–40
Pink	50–70
Cardinal red	20–25
Red	20–40

For rectangular spaces the formula becomes

$$CR = 5h \times \frac{1 + w}{1 \times w}$$

where:

h = height of the cavity
l = length of the room
w = width of the room

Note that if the work surface is the floor or if the luminaires are surface mounted, the floor cavity ratio or ceiling cavity ratio, respectively, are zero. Also, since the three cavity ratios are related, after finding one you can find the other two by ratios:

$$CCR = RCR \frac{h(cc)}{h(rc)}$$

$$FCR = RCR \frac{h(fc)}{h(rc)}$$

where:

CCR = ceiling cavity ratio
FCR = floor cavity ratio
RCR = room cavity ratio
h(cc) = height of ceiling cavity
h(fc) = height of floor cavity
h(rc) = height of room cavity

You can find the cavity ratios by calculation or use the values given in Table 2F–9. First find the RCR and then use the ratios to find the values of the CCR and FCR.

3. Determine the effective ceiling cavity reflectance and the effective floor cavity reflectance. These are values of the imaginary planes at the height of the luminaire and the work surface that will be used in finding the coefficient of utilization of a particular light fixture. If the luminaires are recessed or surface mounted, the effective ceiling cavity reflectance is the same as the reflectance of the ceiling itself. Use Table 2F–10 to find the effective reflectances, knowing the cavity ratios you determined in step 2.

4. Determine the coefficient of utilization of the fixture under consideration by using the CU tables from the manufacturer's literature or from Table 2F–4. Straight line interpolation will probably be necessary. Most tables are set up for a floor reflectance of 20%. If the effective floor reflectance varies significantly from this, use the correction factors given in Table 2F–11 and multiply by the CU for the fixture.

5. Determine the recommended illumination for the space being designed. Follow the procedures outlined in the section "Selection of Recommended Illumination Levels."

6. Determine the lumen output of the lamps that will be used in the luminaire you have selected. Values for lumen output for some representative lamps are given in Table 2F–12. More accurate data can be obtained from the fixture manufacturer or a lamp manufacturer. Determine the number of lamps that will be used in each luminaire.

7. With the information compiled in the previous steps and with the light loss factor (LLF), use the following formula.

FORMULA:

$$\text{Number of luminaires} = \frac{\text{footcandles required} \times \text{area of room}}{\text{N} \times \text{lumens per lamp} \times \text{CU} \times \text{LLF}}$$

You can also determine the area per luminaire using the formula given at the beginning of this section.

Table 2F-9
ROOM CAVITY RATIOS

Room W	Room L	Cavity Depth 2.5	5.5	6.0	6.5	7.0	7.5	8.0	8.5	9.0	10.0	12.0	14.0	16.0	18.0
10	10	2.5	5.5	6.0	6.5	7.0	7.5	8.0	8.5	9.0					
	12	2.3	5.0	5.5	6.0	6.4	6.9	7.3	7.8	8.3					
	14	2.1	4.7	5.1	5.6	6.0	6.4	6.9	7.3	7.7	8.6				
	15	2.1	4.6	5.0	5.4	5.8	6.3	6.7	7.1	7.5	8.3				
	16	2.0	4.5	4.9	5.3	5.7	6.1	6.5	6.9	7.3	8.1				
12	12	2.1	4.6	5.0	5.4	5.8	6.3	6.7	7.1	7.5	8.3				
	14	1.9	4.3	4.6	5.0	5.4	5.8	6.2	6.6	7.0	7.7				
	16	1.8	4.0	4.4	4.7	5.1	5.5	5.8	6.2	6.6	7.3				
	18	1.7	3.8	4.2	4.5	4.9	5.2	5.6	5.9	6.3	6.9				
	20	1.7	3.7	4.0	4.3	4.7	5.0	5.3	5.7	6.0	6.7				
14	14	1.8	3.9	4.3	4.6	5.0	5.4	5.7	6.1	6.4	7.1	8.6			
	16	1.7	3.7	4.0	4.4	4.7	5.0	5.4	5.7	6.0	6.7	8.0			
	18	1.6	3.5	3.8	4.1	4.4	4.8	5.1	5.4	5.7	6.3	7.6			
	20	1.5	3.3	3.6	3.9	4.3	4.6	4.9	5.2	5.5	6.1	7.3			
	22	1.5	3.2	3.5	3.8	4.1	4.4	4.7	5.0	5.3	5.8	7.0			
16	16	1.6	3.4	3.8	4.1	4.4	4.7	5.0	5.3	5.6	6.3	7.5	8.8		
	18	1.5	3.2	3.5	3.8	4.1	4.4	4.7	5.0	5.3	5.9	7.1	8.3		
	20	1.4	3.1	3.4	3.7	3.9	4.2	4.5	4.8	5.1	5.6	6.8	7.9		
	22	1.3	3.0	3.2	3.5	3.8	4.0	4.3	4.6	4.9	5.4	6.5	7.6		
	24	1.3	2.9	3.1	3.4	3.6	3.9	4.2	4.4	4.7	5.2	6.3	7.3		
18	18	1.4	3.1	3.3	3.6	3.9	4.2	4.4	4.7	5.0	5.6	6.7	7.8	8.9	
	22	1.3	2.8	3.0	3.3	3.5	3.8	4.0	4.3	4.5	5.1	6.1	7.1	8.1	
	26	1.2	2.6	2.8	3.1	3.3	3.5	3.8	4.0	4.2	4.7	5.6	6.6	7.5	
	30	1.1	2.4	2.7	2.9	3.1	3.3	3.6	3.8	4.0	4.4	5.3	6.2	7.1	
	34	1.1	2.3	2.5	2.8	3.0	3.2	3.4	3.6	3.8	4.2	5.1	5.9	6.8	

20	20	1.3	2.8	3.0	3.3	3.5	3.8	4.0	4.3	4.5	5.0	6.0	7.0	8.0	9.0
	24	1.1	2.5	2.8	3.0	3.2	3.4	3.7	3.9	4.1	4.6	5.5	6.4	7.3	8.3
	28	1.1	2.4	2.6	2.8	3.0	3.2	3.4	3.6	3.9	4.3	5.1	6.0	6.9	7.7
	32	1.0	2.2	2.4	2.6	2.8	3.0	3.3	3.5	3.7	4.1	4.9	5.7	6.5	7.3
	36	1.0	2.1	2.3	2.5	2.7	2.9	3.1	3.3	3.5	3.9	4.7	5.4	6.2	7.0
24	24	1.0	2.3	2.5	2.7	2.9	3.1	3.3	3.5	3.8	4.2	5.0	5.8	6.7	7.5
	28	1.0	2.1	2.3	2.5	2.7	2.9	3.1	3.3	3.5	3.9	4.6	5.4	6.2	7.0
	32	0.9	2.0	2.2	2.4	2.6	2.7	2.9	3.1	3.3	3.6	4.4	5.1	5.8	6.6
	36	0.9	1.9	2.1	2.3	2.4	2.6	2.8	3.0	3.1	3.5	4.2	4.9	5.6	6.3
	40	0.8	1.8	2.0	2.2	2.3	2.5	2.7	2.8	3.0	3.3	4.0	4.7	5.3	6.0
28	34	0.8			2.1	2.3	2.4	2.6	2.8	2.9	3.3	3.9	4.6	5.2	5.9
	40	0.8			2.0	2.1	2.3	2.4	2.6	2.7	3.0	3.6	4.3	4.9	5.5
	46	0.7			1.9	2.0	2.2	2.3	2.4	2.6	2.9	3.4	4.0	4.6	5.2
	52	0.7			1.8	1.9	2.1	2.2	2.3	2.5	2.7	3.3	3.8	4.4	4.9
32	38	0.7					2.2	2.3	2.4	2.6	2.9	3.5	4.0	4.6	5.2
	44	0.7					2.0	2.2	2.3	2.4	2.7	3.2	3.8	4.3	4.9
	50	0.6					1.9	2.1	2.2	2.3	2.6	3.1	3.6	4.1	4.6
	56	0.6					1.8	2.0	2.1	2.2	2.5	2.9	3.4	3.9	4.4
38	46	0.6					1.8	1.9	2.0	2.2	2.4	2.9	3.4	3.8	4.3
	54	0.6					1.7	1.8	1.9	2.0	2.2	2.7	3.1	3.6	4.0
	62	0.5					1.6	1.7	1.8	1.9	2.1	2.5	3.0	3.4	3.8
	70	0.5							1.7	1.8	2.0	2.4	2.8	3.2	3.7
44	50	0.5							1.8	1.9	2.1	2.6	3.0	3.4	3.8
	60	0.5							1.7	1.8	2.0	2.4	2.8	3.2	3.5
	70	0.5							1.6	1.7	1.9	2.2	2.6	3.0	3.3
	80	0.4							1.5	1.6	1.8	2.1	2.5	2.8	3.2

Table 2F-10

PERCENT EFFECTIVE CEILING OR FLOOR CAVITY REFLECTANCES FOR VARIOUS REFLECTANCE COMBINATIONS

Per Cent Base* Reflectance	90									
Per Cent Wall Reflectance	90	80	70	60	50	40	30	20	10	0
Cavity Ratio										
0.2	89	88	88	87	86	85	85	84	84	82
0.4	88	87	86	85	84	83	81	80	79	76
0.6	87	86	84	82	80	79	77	76	74	73
0.8	87	85	82	80	77	75	73	71	69	67
1.0	86	83	80	77	75	72	69	66	64	62
1.2	85	82	78	75	72	69	66	63	60	57
1.4	85	80	77	73	69	65	62	59	57	52
1.6	84	79	75	71	67	63	59	56	53	50
1.8	83	78	73	69	64	60	56	53	50	48
2.0	83	77	72	67	62	56	53	50	47	43
2.2	82	76	70	65	59	54	50	47	44	40
2.4	82	75	69	64	58	53	48	45	41	37
2.6	81	74	67	62	56	51	46	42	38	35
2.8	81	73	66	60	54	49	44	40	36	34
3.0	80	72	64	58	52	47	42	38	34	30
3.2	79	71	63	56	50	45	40	36	32	28
3.4	79	70	62	54	48	43	38	34	30	27
3.6	78	69	61	53	47	42	36	32	28	25
3.8	78	69	60	51	45	40	35	31	27	23
4.0	77	69	58	51	44	39	33	29	25	22
4.2	77	62	57	50	43	37	32	28	24	21
4.4	76	61	56	49	42	36	31	27	23	20
4.6	76	60	55	47	40	35	30	26	22	19
4.8	75	59	54	46	39	34	28	25	21	18
5.0	75	59	53	45	38	33	28	24	20	16
6.0	73	61	49	41	34	29	24	20	16	11
7.0	70	58	45	38	30	27	21	18	14	08
8.0	68	55	42	35	27	23	18	15	12	06
9.0	66	52	38	31	25	21	16	14	11	05
10.0	65	51	36	29	22	19	15	11	09	04

Per Cent Base* Reflectance	80									
Per Cent Wall Reflectance	90	80	70	60	50	40	30	20	10	0
Cavity Ratio										
0.2	79	78	78	77	77	76	76	75	74	72
0.4	79	77	76	75	74	73	72	71	70	68
0.6	78	76	75	73	71	70	68	66	65	63
0.8	78	75	73	71	69	67	65	63	61	57
1.0	77	74	72	69	67	65	62	60	57	55
1.2	76	73	70	67	64	61	58	55	53	51
1.4	76	72	68	65	62	59	55	53	50	48
1.6	75	71	67	63	60	57	53	50	47	44
1.8	75	70	66	62	58	54	50	47	44	41
2.0	74	69	64	60	56	52	48	45	41	38
2.2	74	68	63	58	54	49	45	42	38	35
2.4	73	67	61	56	52	47	43	40	36	33
2.6	73	66	60	55	50	45	41	38	34	31
2.8	73	65	59	53	48	43	39	36	32	29
3.0	72	65	58	52	47	42	37	34	30	27
3.2	72	65	57	51	45	40	35	33	28	25
3.4	71	64	56	49	44	39	34	32	27	24
3.6	71	63	54	48	43	38	32	30	25	23
3.8	70	62	53	47	41	36	31	28	24	22
4.0	70	61	53	46	40	35	30	26	22	20
4.2	69	60	52	45	39	34	29	25	21	18
4.4	69	60	51	44	38	33	28	24	20	17
4.6	69	59	50	43	37	32	27	23	19	15
4.8	68	58	49	42	36	31	26	22	18	14
5.0	68	58	48	41	35	30	25	21	18	14
6.0	66	55	44	38	31	27	22	19	15	10
7.0	64	53	41	35	28	24	19	16	12	07
8.0	62	50	38	32	25	21	17	14	11	05
9.0	61	49	36	30	23	19	15	13	10	04
10.0	59	46	33	27	21	18	14	11	08	03

Per Cent Base* Reflectance	70									
Per Cent Wall Reflectance	90	80	70	60	50	40	30	20	10	0
Cavity Ratio										
0.2	70	69	68	68	67	67	66	66	65	64
0.4	69	68	67	66	65	64	63	62	61	58
0.6	69	67	65	64	63	61	59	58	57	54
0.8	68	66	64	62	60	58	56	55	53	50
1.0	68	65	62	60	58	55	53	52	50	47
1.2	67	64	61	59	57	54	50	48	46	44
1.4	67	63	60	58	55	51	47	45	44	41
1.6	67	62	59	56	53	47	45	43	41	38
1.8	66	61	58	54	51	46	42	40	38	35
2.0	66	60	56	52	49	45	40	38	36	33
2.2	66	60	55	51	48	43	38	36	34	32
2.4	65	60	54	50	46	41	37	35	32	30
2.6	65	59	54	49	45	40	35	33	30	28
2.8	65	59	53	48	43	38	33	30	28	26
3.0	64	58	52	47	42	37	32	29	27	24
3.2	64	58	51	46	40	36	31	28	25	23
3.4	64	57	50	45	39	35	29	27	24	22
3.6	63	56	49	44	38	33	28	25	22	20
3.8	63	56	49	43	37	32	27	24	21	19
4.0	63	55	48	42	36	31	26	23	20	17
4.2	62	55	47	41	35	30	25	22	19	16
4.4	62	54	46	40	34	29	24	21	18	15
4.6	62	53	45	39	33	28	24	21	17	14
4.8	62	53	45	38	32	27	23	20	16	13
5.0	61	52	44	36	31	26	22	19	16	12
6.0	60	51	41	35	28	24	19	16	13	09
7.0	58	48	38	32	26	22	17	14	11	06
8.0	57	46	35	29	23	19	15	13	10	05
9.0	56	45	33	27	21	18	14	12	09	04
10.0	55	43	31	25	19	16	12	10	08	03

Per Cent Base* Reflectance	60									
Per Cent Wall Reflectance	90	80	70	60	50	40	30	20	10	0
Cavity Ratio										
0.2	60	59	59	59	58	57	56	56	55	53
0.4	60	59	59	58	57	55	54	53	52	50
0.6	60	58	57	56	55	53	51	51	50	46
0.8	59	57	56	55	54	51	48	47	46	43
1.0	59	57	55	53	51	48	45	44	43	41
1.2	59	56	54	51	49	46	44	42	40	38
1.4	59	56	53	49	47	44	41	39	38	36
1.6	59	55	52	48	45	42	39	37	35	33
1.8	58	55	51	47	44	40	37	35	33	31
2.0	58	54	50	46	43	39	35	33	31	29
2.2	58	53	49	45	42	37	34	31	29	28
2.4	58	53	48	44	41	36	32	30	27	26
2.6	58	53	48	43	39	35	31	28	26	24
2.8	58	53	47	43	38	34	29	27	24	22
3.0	57	52	46	42	37	32	28	25	23	20
3.2	57	51	45	41	36	31	27	23	22	18
3.4	57	51	45	40	35	30	26	23	20	17
3.6	57	50	44	39	34	29	25	22	19	16
3.8	57	50	43	38	33	29	24	21	19	15
4.0	57	49	42	37	32	28	23	20	18	14
4.2	56	49	42	37	32	27	22	19	17	14
4.4	56	49	42	36	31	27	22	19	16	13
4.6	56	49	41	35	30	26	21	18	16	13
4.8	56	48	41	34	29	25	21	18	15	12
5.0	56	48	40	34	28	24	20	17	14	11
6.0	55	45	37	31	25	21	17	14	11	07
7.0	54	43	35	30	24	20	15	12	09	05
8.0	53	42	33	28	22	18	14	11	08	04
9.0	52	40	31	26	20	16	12	10	07	03
10.0	51	39	29	24	18	15	11	09	07	02

Per Cent Base* Reflectance	50									
Per Cent Wall Reflectance	90	80	70	60	50	40	30	20	10	0
Cavity Ratio										
0.2	50	50	49	49	48	48	47	46	46	44
0.4	50	49	48	48	47	46	45	45	44	42
0.6	50	48	47	46	45	44	43	42	41	38
0.8	50	48	47	45	44	42	40	39	38	36
1.0	50	48	46	44	43	41	38	37	36	34
1.2	50	47	45	43	41	39	36	35	34	29
1.4	50	47	45	42	40	38	35	34	32	27
1.6	50	47	44	41	39	36	33	32	30	26
1.8	50	46	43	40	38	35	31	30	28	25
2.0	50	46	43	40	37	34	30	28	26	24
2.2	50	46	42	38	36	33	29	27	24	22
2.4	50	46	42	37	35	31	27	25	23	21
2.6	50	46	41	37	34	30	26	23	21	20
2.8	50	46	41	36	33	29	25	22	20	19
3.0	50	45	40	36	32	28	24	21	19	17
3.2	50	44	39	35	31	27	23	20	18	16
3.4	50	44	39	35	30	26	22	19	17	15
3.6	50	44	39	34	29	25	21	18	16	14
3.8	50	44	38	34	29	25	21	17	15	13
4.0	50	44	38	33	28	24	20	17	15	12
4.2	50	43	37	32	28	24	20	17	14	12
4.4	50	43	37	32	27	23	19	16	13	11
4.6	50	43	36	31	26	22	18	15	13	10
4.8	50	43	36	31	26	22	18	15	12	09
5.0	50	42	35	30	25	21	17	14	12	09
6.0	50	42	34	29	23	19	15	13	10	06
7.0	49	41	32	27	21	18	14	11	08	05
8.0	49	40	30	25	19	16	12	10	07	03
9.0	48	39	29	24	18	15	11	09	07	03
10.0	47	37	27	22	17	14	10	08	06	02

* Ceiling, floor or floor of cavity.

Per Cent Base* Reflectance	40									
Per Cent Wall Reflectance	90	80	70	60	50	40	30	20	10	0
Cavity Ratio										
0.2	40	40	39	39	39	38	38	37	36	36
0.4	41	40	39	39	38	37	36	35	34	34
0.6	41	40	39	38	37	36	34	33	32	31
0.8	41	40	38	37	36	35	33	32	31	29
1.0	42	40	38	37	35	33	32	31	29	27
1.2	42	40	38	36	34	32	30	29	27	25
1.4	42	39	37	35	33	31	29	27	25	23
1.6	42	39	37	35	32	30	27	25	23	22
1.8	42	39	36	34	31	29	26	24	22	21
2.0	42	39	36	34	31	28	25	23	21	19
2.2	42	39	36	33	30	27	24	22	19	18
2.4	43	39	35	33	29	27	24	21	18	17
2.6	43	39	35	32	29	26	23	20	17	15
2.8	43	39	35	32	28	25	22	19	16	14
3.0	43	39	35	31	27	24	21	18	16	13
3.2	43	39	35	31	27	23	20	71	15	13
3.4	43	39	34	30	26	23	20	17	14	12
3.6	44	39	34	30	26	22	19	16	14	11
3.8	44	38	33	29	25	22	18	16	13	10
4.0	44	38	33	29	25	21	18	15	12	10
4.2	44	38	33	29	24	21	17	15	12	10
4.4	44	38	33	28	24	20	17	14	11	09
4.6	44	38	32	28	23	19	16	14	11	08
4.8	44	38	32	27	22	19	16	13	10	08
5.0	45	38	31	27	22	19	15	13	10	07
6.0	44	37	30	25	20	17	13	11	08	05
7.0	44	36	29	24	19	16	12	10	07	04
8.0	44	35	28	23	18	15	11	09	06	03
9.0	44	35	26	21	16	13	10	08	05	02
10.0	43	34	25	20	15	12	08	07	05	02

Per Cent Base* Reflectance	30									
Per Cent Wall Reflectance	90	80	70	60	50	40	30	20	10	0
Cavity Ratio										
0.2	31	31	30	30	29	29	29	28	28	27
0.4	31	31	30	30	29	28	28	27	26	25
0.6	32	31	30	29	28	27	26	26	25	23
0.8	32	31	30	29	28	26	25	25	23	22
1.0	33	32	30	29	27	25	24	23	22	20
1.2	33	32	30	28	27	25	23	22	21	19
1.4	34	32	30	28	26	24	22	21	19	18
1.6	34	33	29	27	25	23	22	20	18	17
1.8	35	33	29	27	25	23	21	19	17	16
2.0	35	33	29	26	24	22	20	18	16	14
2.2	36	32	29	26	24	22	19	17	15	13
2.4	36	32	29	26	24	22	19	16	14	12
2.6	36	32	29	25	23	21	18	16	14	12
2.8	37	33	29	25	23	21	17	15	13	11
3.0	37	33	29	25	22	20	17	15	12	10
3.2	37	33	29	25	22	19	16	14	12	10
3.4	37	33	29	25	22	19	16	14	11	09
3.6	38	33	29	24	21	18	15	13	10	09
3.8	38	33	28	24	21	18	15	13	10	08
4.0	38	33	28	24	21	18	14	12	09	07
4.2	38	33	28	24	20	17	14	12	09	07
4.4	39	33	28	24	20	17	14	11	09	06
4.6	39	33	28	24	20	17	13	10	08	06
4.8	39	33	28	24	20	17	13	10	08	05
5.0	39	33	28	24	19	16	13	10	08	05
6.0	39	33	27	23	18	15	11	09	06	04
7.0	40	33	26	22	17	14	10	08	05	03
8.0	40	33	26	21	16	13	09	07	04	02
9.0	40	33	25	20	15	12	09	07	04	02
10.0	40	32	24	19	14	11	08	06	03	01

Per Cent Base* Reflectance	20									
Per Cent Wall Reflectance	90	80	70	60	50	40	30	20	10	0
Cavity Ratio										
0.2	21	20	20	20	20	20	19	19	19	17
0.4	22	21	20	20	20	19	19	18	18	16
0.6	23	21	21	20	19	19	18	18	17	15
0.8	24	22	21	20	19	19	18	17	16	14
1.0	25	23	22	20	19	18	17	16	15	13
1.2	25	23	22	20	19	17	17	16	14	12
1.4	26	24	22	20	18	17	16	15	13	12
1.6	26	24	22	20	18	17	16	15	13	11
1.8	27	25	23	20	18	17	15	14	12	10
2.0	28	25	23	20	18	16	15	13	11	09
2.2	28	25	23	20	18	16	14	12	10	09
2.4	29	26	23	20	18	16	14	12	10	08
2.6	29	26	23	20	18	16	14	11	09	08
2.8	30	27	23	20	18	15	13	11	09	07
3.0	30	27	23	20	17	15	13	11	09	07
3.2	31	27	23	20	17	15	12	11	09	06
3.4	31	27	23	20	17	15	12	10	08	06
3.6	32	27	23	20	17	15	12	10	08	05
3.8	32	28	23	20	17	15	12	10	07	05
4.0	33	28	23	20	17	14	11	09	07	05
4.2	33	28	23	20	17	14	11	09	07	04
4.4	34	28	24	20	17	14	11	09	07	04
4.6	34	29	24	20	17	14	11	09	07	04
4.8	35	29	24	20	17	13	10	08	06	04
5.0	35	29	24	20	16	13	10	08	06	04
6.0	36	30	24	20	16	13	10	08	05	02
7.0	36	30	24	20	15	12	09	07	04	02
8.0	37	30	23	19	15	12	08	06	03	01
9.0	37	29	23	19	14	11	08	06	03	01
10.0	37	29	22	18	13	10	07	05	03	01

Per Cent Base* Reflectance	10									
Per Cent Wall Reflectance	90	80	70	60	50	40	30	20	10	0
Cavity Ratio										
0.2	11	11	11	10	10	10	10	09	09	09
0.4	12	11	11	11	11	10	10	09	09	08
0.6	13	13	12	11	11	10	10	09	08	08
0.8	15	14	13	12	11	10	10	09	08	07
1.0	16	14	13	12	12	11	10	09	08	07
1.2	17	15	14	13	12	11	10	09	07	06
1.4	18	16	14	13	12	11	10	09	07	06
1.6	19	17	15	14	12	11	09	08	07	06
1.8	19	17	15	14	13	11	09	08	06	05
2.0	20	18	16	14	13	11	09	08	06	05
2.2	21	19	16	14	13	11	09	07	06	05
2.4	22	19	17	15	13	11	09	07	06	05
2.6	23	20	17	15	13	11	09	07	06	04
2.8	23	20	18	16	13	11	09	07	05	03
3.0	24	21	18	16	13	11	09	07	05	03
3.2	25	21	18	16	13	11	09	07	05	03
3.4	26	22	18	16	13	11	09	07	05	03
3.6	26	22	19	16	13	11	09	06	04	03
3.8	27	23	19	17	14	11	09	06	04	02
4.0	27	23	20	17	14	11	09	06	04	02
4.2	28	24	20	17	14	11	09	06	04	02
4.4	28	24	20	17	14	11	08	06	04	02
4.6	29	25	20	17	14	11	08	06	04	02
4.8	29	25	20	17	14	11	08	06	04	02
5.0	30	25	20	17	14	11	08	06	04	02
6.0	31	26	21	18	14	11	08	06	03	01
7.0	32	27	21	17	13	11	08	06	03	01
8.0	33	27	21	17	13	10	07	05	03	01
9.0	34	28	21	17	13	10	07	05	02	01
10.0	34	28	21	17	12	10	07	05	02	01

Per Cent Base* Reflectance	0									
Per Cent Wall Reflectance	90	80	70	60	50	40	30	20	10	0
Cavity Ratio										
0.2	02	02	02	01	01	01	01	00	00	0
0.4	04	03	03	02	02	02	01	01	00	0
0.6	05	05	04	03	03	02	02	01	01	0
0.8	07	06	05	04	04	03	02	02	01	0
1.0	08	07	06	05	04	03	02	02	01	0
1.2	10	08	07	06	05	04	03	02	01	0
1.4	11	09	08	07	06	04	03	02	01	0
1.6	12	10	09	07	06	05	03	02	01	0
1.8	13	11	09	08	07	05	04	03	01	0
2.0	14	12	10	09	07	05	04	03	01	0
2.2	15	13	11	09	07	06	04	03	01	0
2.4	16	13	11	09	08	06	04	03	01	0
2.6	17	14	12	10	08	06	05	03	02	0
2.8	17	15	13	10	08	07	05	03	02	0
3.0	18	16	13	11	09	07	05	03	02	0
3.2	19	16	14	11	09	07	05	03	02	0
3.4	20	17	14	12	09	07	05	03	02	0
3.6	20	17	15	12	10	08	05	04	02	0
3.8	21	18	15	12	10	08	05	04	02	0
4.0	22	18	15	13	10	08	05	04	02	0
4.2	22	19	16	13	10	08	06	04	02	0
4.4	23	19	16	13	10	08	06	04	02	0
4.6	23	20	17	13	11	08	06	04	02	0
4.8	24	20	17	14	11	08	06	04	02	0
5.0	25	21	17	14	11	08	06	04	02	0
6.0	27	23	18	15	12	09	06	04	02	0
7.0	28	24	19	15	12	09	06	04	02	0
8.0	30	25	20	15	12	09	06	04	02	0
9.0	31	25	20	15	12	09	06	04	02	0
10.0	31	25	20	15	12	09	06	04	02	0

* Ceiling, floor or floor of cavity.

Table 2F-11
MULTIPLYING FACTORS FOR OTHER THAN 20 PERCENT EFFECTIVE FLOOR CAVITY REFLECTANCE

% Effective Ceiling Cavity Reflectance, ρ_{cc}	80				70				50			30			10		
% Wall Reflectance, ρ_w	70	50	30	10	70	50	30	10	50	30	10	50	30	10	50	30	10
For 30 Per Cent Effective Floor Cavity Reflectance (20 Per Cent = 1.00)																	
Room Cavity Ratio																	
1	1.092	1.082	1.075	1.068	1.077	1.070	1.064	1.059	1.049	1.044	1.040	1.028	1.026	1.023	1.012	1.010	1.008
2	1.079	1.066	1.055	1.047	1.068	1.057	1.048	1.039	1.041	1.033	1.027	1.026	1.021	1.017	1.013	1.010	1.006
3	1.070	1.054	1.042	1.033	1.061	1.048	1.037	1.028	1.034	1.027	1.020	1.024	1.017	1.012	1.014	1.009	1.005
4	1.062	1.045	1.033	1.024	1.055	1.040	1.029	1.021	1.030	1.022	1.015	1.022	1.015	1.010	1.014	1.009	1.004
5	1.056	1.038	1.026	1.018	1.050	1.034	1.024	1.015	1.027	1.018	1.012	1.020	1.013	1.008	1.014	1.009	1.004
6	1.052	1.033	1.021	1.014	1.047	1.030	1.020	1.012	1.024	1.015	1.009	1.019	1.012	1.006	1.014	1.008	1.003
7	1.047	1.029	1.018	1.011	1.043	1.026	1.017	1.009	1.022	1.013	1.007	1.018	1.010	1.005	1.014	1.008	1.003
8	1.044	1.026	1.015	1.009	1.040	1.024	1.015	1.007	1.020	1.012	1.006	1.017	1.009	1.004	1.013	1.007	1.003
9	1.040	1.024	1.014	1.007	1.037	1.022	1.014	1.006	1.019	1.011	1.005	1.016	1.009	1.004	1.013	1.007	1.002
10	1.037	1.022	1.012	1.006	1.034	1.020	1.012	1.005	1.017	1.010	1.004	1.015	1.009	1.003	1.013	1.007	1.002
For 10 Per Cent Effective Floor Cavity Reflectance (20 Per Cent = 1.00)																	
Room Cavity Ratio																	
1	.923	.929	.935	.940	.933	.939	.943	.948	.956	.960	.963	.973	.976	.979	.989	.991	.993
2	.931	.942	.950	.958	.940	.949	.957	.963	.962	.968	.974	.976	.980	.985	.988	.991	.995
3	.939	.951	.961	.969	.945	.957	.966	.973	.967	.975	.981	.978	.983	.988	.988	.992	.996
4	.944	.958	.969	.978	.950	.963	.973	.980	.972	.980	.986	.980	.986	.991	.987	.992	.996
5	.949	.964	.976	.983	.954	.968	.978	.985	.975	.983	.989	.981	.988	.993	.987	.992	.997
6	.953	.969	.980	.986	.958	.972	.982	.989	.977	.985	.992	.982	.989	.995	.987	.993	.997
7	.957	.973	.983	.991	.961	.975	.985	.991	.979	.987	.994	.983	.990	.996	.987	.993	.998
8	.960	.976	.986	.993	.963	.977	.987	.993	.981	.988	.995	.984	.991	.997	.987	.994	.998
9	.963	.978	.987	.994	.965	.979	.989	.994	.983	.990	.996	.985	.992	.998	.988	.994	.999
10	.965	.980	.989	.995	.967	.981	.990	.995	.984	.991	.997	.986	.993	.998	.988	.994	.999
For 0 Per Cent Effective Floor Cavity Reflectance (20 Per Cent = 1.00)																	
Room Cavity Ratio																	
1	.859	.870	.879	.886	.873	.884	.893	.901	.916	.923	.929	.948	.954	.960	.979	.983	.987
2	.871	.887	.903	.919	.886	.902	.916	.928	.926	.938	.949	.954	.963	.971	.978	.983	.991
3	.882	.904	.915	.942	.898	.918	.934	.947	.936	.950	.964	.958	.969	.979	.976	.984	.993
4	.893	.919	.941	.958	.908	.930	.948	.961	.945	.961	.974	.961	.974	.984	.975	.985	.994
5	.903	.931	.953	.969	.914	.939	.958	.970	.951	.967	.980	.964	.977	.988	.975	.985	.995
6	.911	.940	.961	.976	.920	.945	.965	.977	.955	.972	.985	.966	.979	.991	.975	.986	.996
7	.917	.947	.967	.981	.924	.950	.970	.982	.959	.975	.988	.968	.981	.993	.975	.987	.997
8	.922	.953	.971	.985	.929	.955	.975	.986	.963	.978	.991	.970	.983	.995	.976	.988	.998
9	.928	.958	.975	.988	.933	.959	.980	.989	.966	.980	.993	.971	.985	.996	.976	.988	.998
10	.933	.962	.979	.991	.937	.963	.983	.992	.969	.982	.995	.973	.987	.997	.977	.989	.999

LAMP SELECTION AND SURFACE REFLECTION RECOMMENDATIONS

Table 2F-12
CHARACTERISTICS OF TYPICAL LAMPS

Standard Incandescent

Bulb Description	Watts	Length/ Size (in in.)	Lamp Life (in hours) (1)	Color Temp. °K (1)	Initial Lumens (1)	Lamp Lumen Depreciation (1)
A-19	60		1000	2790	860	0.93
A-19	75		750	2840	1180	0.92
A-19	100		750	2900	1740	0.91
A-19	100		2500		1490	0.93
A-21	100		750	2880	1690	0.90
A-21	150		750	2960	2880	0.89
A-23	150		2500		2350	0.89
PS-25	150		750	2900	2660	0.88
A-23	200		750	2980	4000	0.90
A-23	200		2500		3400	0.88
PS-25	300		750	3010	6360	0.88
PS-30	300		2500		5200	0.79
PS-35	500		1000	3050	10600	0.89

R, PAR, and ER Lamps

Bulb Description	Watts	Length/ Size (in in.)	Lamp Life (in hours) (1)	Color Temp. (1)	Initial Lumens (1,2)	Lamp Lumen Depreciation (1)
R-30 Spot/Flood	75		2000		850	
R-40 Spot/Flood	150		2000		1825	
R-40 Spot/Flood	300		2000		3600	
PAR-38 Spot/Flood	100		2000		1250	
PAR-38 Spot/Flood	150		2000		1730	
ER-30	50		2000		525	
ER-30	75		2000		850	
ER-30	90		5000		950	
ER-40	120		2000		1475	

Fluorescent

Bulb Description	Watts	Length/ Size (in in.)	Lamp Life (in hours) (1,3)	Color Temp. (1,4)	Initial Lumens (1,5)	Lamp Lumen Depreciation (1)
F40T12CW/RS	40	48	20000	4300	3150	0.84
F40T12WW/RS	40	48	20000	3100	3170	0.84
F40T12CWX/RS	40	48	20000	4100	2200	0.84
F40T12WWX/RS	40	48	20000	3000	2170	0.84
F40T12D/RS	40	48	20000	6500	2600	0.84
F40T12W/RS	40	48	20000	3600	3180	0.84
F96T12CW	75	96	12000	4300	6300	0.89
F96T12WW	75	96	12000	3100	6335	0.89
F96T12CWX	75	96	12000	4100	4465	0.89
F96T12WWX	75	96	12000	3000	4365	

Table 2F-12 (Continued)

Tungsten-Halogen (Quartz-Iodine)

Bulb Description	Watts	Length/ Size (in in.)	Lamp Life (in hours) (1)	Color Temp. (1)	Initial Lumens (1)	Lamp Lumen Depreciation (1)
T-4	100		1000		1800	0.93
T-4	150		1500	3000	2900	0.93
T-4	250		2000	2950	5000	0.97
PAR-38	250		6000		3500	0.95

Mercury

Bulb Description	Watts	Length/ Size (in in.)	Lamp Life (in hours) (1)	Color Temp. (1)	Initial Lumens (1)	Lamp Lumen Depreciation (1)
H45AY-40/50 DX	50		16000		1680	
H43AY-75/DX	75		24000		3000	
H38BP-100/DX	100		24000+		2865	
H38JA-100/WDX	100		24000+		4000	
H38MP-100/DX	100		24000		4275	
H39BN-175/DX	175		24000		5800	
H39KC-175/DX	175		24000+		8600	
H37KC-250/DX	250		24000+		12775	

Metal-Halide

Bulb Description	Watts	Length/ Size (in in.)	Lamp Life (in hours) (1)	Color Temp. (1)	Initial Lumens (1)	Lamp Lumen Depreciation (1)
M57PF-175	175		7500	3600	14000	
M58PH-250	250		10000		20500	
M59PK-400	400		1500	3800	34000	

High-Pressure Sodium

Bulb Description	Watts	Length/ Size (in in.)	Lamp Life (in hours) (1)	Color Temp. (1)	Initial Lumens (1)	Lamp Lumen Depreciation (1)
S68MT-50	50		24000		3800	
S54MC-100	100		24000		8800	
S55MD-150	150		24000		15000	

(1) Figures listed are approximate. Exact values vary with manufacturer.

(2) Initial lumens for R, PAR, and ER lamps is for total lumens.

(3) Lamp life for fluorescent depends on number of hours per start; figures given are for approximately 10 hours per start.

(4) Technically, "color temperature" applies only to incandescent sources, but it is often used to describe the degree of whiteness of other light sources.

(5) Lumens at 40% of rated life.

Table 2F-13
GUIDE TO LAMP SELECTION

Lamp Type and Efficacy (1)	Lamp Appearance Effect on Neutral Surfaces	Effect on "Atmosphere"	Colors Strengthened	Colors Grayed	Effect on Complexions	Remarks
Fluorescent						
Cool white (#4) (2)	White	Neutral to moderately cool	Orange, blue, yellow	Red	Pale pink	Blends with natural daylight—good color acceptance
Deluxe cool white (#2) (2)	White	Neutral to moderately cool	All nearly equal	None appreciably	Most natural	Best overall color rendition, simulates natural daylight
Warm white (#4) (3)	Yellowish white	Warm	Orange, yellow	Red, green, blue	Sallow	Blends with incandescent light—poor color acceptance
Deluxe warm white (#2) (3)	Yellowish white	Warm	Red, orange, yellow, green	Blue	Ruddy	Good color rendition; simulates incandescent light
Daylight (#3)	Bluish white	Very cool	Green, blue	Red, orange	Grayed	Usually replaceable with cool white
White (#4)	Pale yellowish white	Moderately warm	Orange, yellow	Red, green, blue	Pale	Usually replaceable with cool white or warm white

(1) Efficacy (lumens/watt): #1 = low; #2 = medium; #3 = medium high; #4 = high.
(2) Greater preference at higher levels.
(3) Greater preference at lower levels.

Source: *GE Lighting Business Group.*

Table 2F-13 (Continued)

Lamp Type and Efficacy (1)	Lamp Appearance Effect on Neutral Surfaces	Effect on "Atmosphere"	Colors Strengthened	Colors Grayed	Effect on Complexions	Remarks
Incandescent, Tungsten-Halogen						
Filament (#1) (3)	Yellowish white	Warm	Red, orange, yellow	Blue	Ruddiest	Good color rendering
High-Intensity Discharge						
Clear mercury (#2)	Greenish blue-white	Very cool, greenish	Yellow, green, blue	Red, orange	Greenish	Very poor color rendering
White mercury (#2)	Greenish white	Moderately cool, greenish	Yellow, green, blue	Red, orange	Very pale	Moderate color rendering
Deluxe white mercury (#2)	Purplish white	Warm, purplish	Red, yellow, blue	Green	Ruddy	Color acceptance similar to cool white fluorescent
Metal-Halide (#4) (2)	Greenish white	Moderately cool greenish	Yellow, blue, green	Red	Grayed	Color acceptance similar to cool white
High-pressure sodium (#4)	Yellowish	Warm, yellowish	Yellow, green, orange	Red, blue	Yellowish	Color acceptance approaches warm white fluorescent

(1) Efficacy (lumens/watt): #1 = low; #2 = medium; #3 = medium high; #4 = high.
(2) Greater preference at higher levels.
(3) Greater preference at lower levels.

Source: GE Lighting Business Group.

Table 2F-14
RECOMMENDED REFLECTANCES OF INTERIOR SURFACES

	Recommended Reflectances in Percent					
	Ceilings	**Walls**	**Floors**	**Furniture**	**Other**	
Offices	80+	50-70	20-40	25-45	40-70	Partitions
Schools	70-90	40-60	30-50	35-50	up to 20	Chalkboards
Industrial	80-90	40-60	20+		25-45	Benchtops, machines, etc.
Residential	60-90	35-60 (1)	15-35 (1)		45-85	Large drapery areas

(1) Where specific visual tasks are more important than lighting for environment, minimum reflectances should be 40% for walls and 25% for floors.

Source: Data extracted from IES Lighting Handbook, *1981 Applications Volume.*

Table 2F-15
RECOMMENDED LUMINANCE RATIOS

		Recommended Ratios (1)				
		Between task and immediate darker surroundings		Between task and immediate lighter surroundings	Between task and general surroundings	
Use	**Task**	**Minimum**	**Desired**	**Maximum**	**Minimum**	**Desired**
Residential	1	1/5	1/3		0.1-10	0.2-5
Office	1		1/3			0.1-10
Classroom	1	1/3		5 (2)	1/3	
Merchandising	1	1/3	1/5			
Industrial	1		1/3	3	0.5-20	0.1-10

(1) These are recommended guidelines for most applications. Ratios higher or lower are acceptable if they do not exceed a significant portion of the visual field.

(2) Any significant surface normally viewed directly should be no greater than five times the luminance of the task.

Source: IES Lighting Handbook, *1981 Applications Volume.*

PART 2G

Acoustics

HOW TO USE BASIC ACOUSTIC FORMULAS

Sound has three basic qualities: velocity, frequency, and power.

Velocity of sound depends on the medium in which it is traveling—in air at sea level it is approximately 1130 feet per second (344 m/sec).

Frequency is the number of cycles completed per second and is measured in Hertz (Hz). (1 Hz = 1 cycle per second.) Since most common sound sources contain energy over a wide range of frequencies, measurement and analysis is often divided into eight octave frequency bands identified by the center frequency. These are 63, 125, 250, 500, 1000, 2000, 4000 and 8000 Hz. For detailed purposes, smaller bands are often used.

Frequency and velocity are related by the following formula.

FORMULA:

$$f = \frac{c}{w}$$

where:

f = frequency of the sound in Hertz (cycles per sec.)
c = velocity of the sound (ft. per sec.)
w = wavelength (ft.)

Power is the quality of acoustical energy as measured in watts. Since a point source emits waves in a spherical shape in free space, the sound intensity (watts per unit area) is given by the following formula.

FORMULA:

$$I = \frac{P}{4 \pi r^2}$$

where:

I = sound intensity (watts/cm^2)
P = acoustic power (watts)
r = distance from the source (cm)

Since 1 square foot equals 930 square centimeters, the formula can be rewritten for English units as:

$$I = \frac{P}{(930)\, 4\, \pi\, r^2}$$

The basic inverse square law is derived from this formula where sound intensity is inversely proportional to the square of the distance from the source:

$$\frac{I_1}{I_2} = \frac{{r_2}^2}{{r_1}^2}$$

where:

I = intensity in watts/cm^2 at distances r_1 and r_2 from source
r = distance in centimeters from sound source at distances r_1 and r_2

Since the sensation of hearing is proportional to the logarithm of the source intensity and since the range of human hearing covers a vast range (from 10^{-16} w/cm^2 to 10^{-3} w/cm^2), the decibel is used to relate the intensity level perceived by the human ear to the intensity of sound based on a logarithmic scale.

FORMULA:

$$IL = 10\log \frac{I}{I_0}$$

where:

IL = sound intensity level in decibels (dB)
I = sound intensity in watts/cm^2
I_0 = 10^{-16} watts/cm^2 (the minimum sound intensity audible to the average human ear)

Some common sound intensity levels are given in Table 2G–1.

In performing acoustical calculations, logarithms must be manipulated. The following formulas are useful.

FORMULAS:

$$\log xy = \log x + \log y$$

$$\log \frac{x}{y} = \log x - \log y$$

$$\log x^n = n \log x$$

$$\log 1 = 0$$

Table 2G-1
COMMON SOUND INTENSITY LEVELS

dB	Example	Subjective Evaluation	Intensity watts/cm²
140	Jet plane takeoff		
130	Gunfire	Threshold of pain	10^{-3}
120	Hard-rock band; siren at 100 ft.	Deafening	10^{-4}
110	Accelerating motorcycle	Sound can be felt	10^{-5}
100	Auto horn at 10 ft.	Conversation difficult to hear	10^{-6}
90	Loud street noise, kitchen blender	Very loud	10^{-7}
80	Noisy office; average factory	Difficult to use phone	10^{-8}
70	Average street noise; quiet typewriter; average radio	Loud	10^{-9}
60	Average office; noisy home	Usual background	10^{-10}
50	Average conversation; quiet radio	Moderate	10^{-11}
40	Quiet home; private office	Noticeably quiet	10^{-12}
30	Quiet conversation	Faint	10^{-13}
20	Whisper		10^{-14}
10	Rustling leaves; soundproof room	Very faint	10^{-15}
0	Threshold of hearing		10^{-16}

ADDITION OF DECIBELS OF UNCORRELATED SOUNDS

Because decibels are logarithmic, they cannot be added directly. A detailed calculation can be performed by using the following formula.

FORMULA: $IL\ (total) = 10 \log (10^{IL[1]/10} + 10^{IL[2]/10} + 10^{IL[3]/10} + \ldots)$

where:

IL[1] = Intensity level of source 1, IL[2] = source 2, etc.

However, for most calculations, a rule of thumb that rounds off to whole numbers gives results accurate to within 1%.

Given two decible values, see Table 2G–2.

Table 2G-2
ADDITION OF DECIBELS

When difference between the two values is	Add this value to the higher value
0 or 1 dB	3 dB
2 or 3 dB	2 dB
4 to 8 dB	1 dB
9 or more	0 dB

For a more detailed calculation, use Table 2G–3.

Table 2G-3
DETAILED ADDITION OF DECIBELS

Difference between two values, dB	Add this value to the higher value
0	3.0
1	2.5
2	2.1
3	1.8
4	1.4
5	1.2
6	0.9
7	0.8
8	0.6
9	0.5
10	0.4
11	0.3

For three or more sources, first add two, then the result to the third number, and so on.

Example

Find the combined intensity level of two office machines, one generating 70 dB and the other generating 76 dB.

FORMULA:

$$\begin{aligned} \text{IL (total)} &= 10 \log (10^{7.0} + 10^{7.6}) \\ &= 10 \log (4.98 \times 10^{7}) \\ &= 10 \times 7.7 \\ \text{IL (total)} &= 77 \text{ dB} \end{aligned}$$

The difference between 76 and 70 is 6; therefore, add 1 dB to 76, which gives 77 dB.
Using the more detailed table, the difference of 7 gives 0.78 to be added to the higher value of 76, which gives 76.78. Since fractions of a decibel are imperceptible, round off to the next higher number to yield 77 dB.
The formula for the addition of several sources of identical value follows.

FORMULA: $\text{IL (total)} = \text{IL (source)} + 10 \log (\text{number of sources})$

Example

What would be the sound level in a room of eight typewriters, each producing 73 dB?

$$\begin{aligned} \text{IL (total)} &= 73 + 10 \log 8 \\ \text{IL (total)} &= 82 \text{ dB} \end{aligned}$$

Loudness is very subjective, but Table 2G-4 gives general guidelines for evaluating various architectural acoustic situations.

Table 2G-4
SUBJECTIVE CHANGE IN LOUDNESS BASED ON DECIBEL LEVEL CHANGE

Change in Intensity Level in dB	Change in Apparent Loudness
1	Almost imperceptible
3	Just perceptible
5	Clearly noticeable
6	Change when distance to source in a free field is doubled or halved
10	Twice or half as loud
18	Very much louder or quieter
20	Four times or one fourth as loud

HOW TO CALCULATE NOISE REDUCTION BETWEEN SPACES

One important aspect of acoustical design is reducing the transmission of unwanted air-borne sound from one space to another through a barrier. For example, you may want to minimize the passage of sounds generated in a noisy kitchen from passing into a quiet dining room, or you may want to avoid conversation in one office from being heard in another. Sound isolation calculations can either help you predict noise reduction between two spaces to see if it meets design criteria or, if given the noise reduction desired, can help you select the appropriate type of construction assembly to separate the two spaces.

There are two important concepts in noise reduction: transmission loss and actual noise reduction.

Transmission loss (TL): the difference (in decibels) between the sound power incident on a barrier in a source room and the sound power radiated into a receiving room on the opposite side of the barrier. This is the measurement typically derived in a testing laboratory.

Remember that although the primary variable in transmission loss of a barrier is its mass (the greater the mass, the greater the transmission loss), the stiffness of the barrier is also important. Given two barriers of the same weight per square foot, the one with less stiffness will perform better than the other.

Noise reduction (NR): the arithmetical difference (in decibels) between the intensity levels in two rooms separated by a barrier of a given transmission loss. Noise reduction is dependent on the transmission loss of the barrier, the *area* of the barrier, and the *absorption* of the surfaces in the receiving room.

Noise reduction is calculated by the following formula.

FORMULA:

$$NR = TL + 10 \log \frac{A}{S}$$

where:

TL = transmission loss in decibles of the barrier

A = absorption in the receiving room in sabins (A sabin is a unit of absorption of a surface—refer to the section "Noise Reduction Within a Space" for a complete discussion.)

S = area of the barrier in sq. ft.

The actual transmission loss of a barrier varies with the frequencies of the sounds being tested. Tests reports are often published with manufacturer's literature, including the transmission loss over six or more octave bands. A single number average that is often used is the

Sound Transmission Class (STC). The higher the STC rating, the better the barrier is (theoretically) in stopping sound.

Example

What is the total noise reduction from a conference room to an office connected by a common wall 13 ft. long and 9 ft. high if the wall has an STC rating of 54? The total absorption of the office has been calculated to be 220 sabins.

FORMULA:

$$\begin{aligned} NR &= 54 + 10 \log \frac{220}{9 \times 13} \\ &= 54 + 10 \log 1.88 \\ &= 54 + 2.7 \\ NR &= 57 \text{ dB} \end{aligned}$$

There are many times when a partition will be comprised of two or more types of construction; for example, a door in a wall or a glass panel in a wall. The combined transmission loss can be found by the following formula.

FORMULA:

$$\text{TL (composite)} = 10 \log \frac{A}{\Sigma tS}$$

where:

A = total area of wall in sq. ft.
S = area of the individual component in the wall
t = coefficient of transmission of a material

NOTE:

$$\text{TL (transmission loss of a material)} = 10 \log \frac{1}{t}$$

or

$t = 10^{-(TL/10)}$
Σ = summation of transmission coefficients times their areas

Example

What is the combined transmission loss of a wall 9 ft. high and 15 ft. long with a 3 ft. by 7 ft. door in it? Assume TL of the wall is 54 and the door with full perimeter seals is 29 (refer to Table 2G–5).

Total wall area: $9 \times 15 = 135$ sq. ft.
Area of door: 21 sq. ft.
Area of partition: $135 - 21 = 114$ sq. ft.
t of partition $= 10^{-5.4}$
t of door $= 10^{-2.9}$

$$\begin{aligned} \text{TL (composite)} &= 10 \log \frac{135}{(10^{-5.4} \times 114) + 10^{-2.9} \times 21)} \\ &= 10 \log 5020 \\ \text{TL (composite)} &= 37 \text{ dB} \end{aligned}$$

Tables 2G–5 to 2G–9 give transmission loss data for some common building constructions and the recommended criteria for sound isolation between various occupancies. For more accurate transmission loss data, refer to the manufacturer's or trade association's literature. Also remember that STC ratings represent the *ideal* loss under laboratory conditions. Walls, partitions, and floors built in the field are seldom constructed as well as those in the laboratory. Also, breaks in the barrier, such as cracks, electrical outlets, doors, and the like will significantly reduce the overall noise reduction.

In critical situations, transmission loss and selection of barriers should be calculated using the values for the various frequencies rather than the single STC average value. However, for preliminary design purposes in typical situations, the STC value is adequate.

Note: These recommended STC ratings are guidelines only, for preliminary design. Whether or not a sound transmitted through a partition or floor will be heard depends on the level of background noise in the receiving space. For example, a steady hum of an air-conditioning system or background music will mask sounds that might otherwise be heard in a quiet office environment.

Recognizing that these requirements are minimums and that actual construction seldom reaches the laboratory values given in the tables, a conservative approach is to add 5 to 10 STC points to the above values and then select or design a barrier to match that number.

You should also give consideration to whether you want complete masking of all sounds or whether *speech privacy* is required, such as in many office situations. In this case, the goal may be simply to prevent conversations from being understood rather than stopping *all* the sound. (See Table 2G–12.)

The Uniform Building Code requires an STC of 50 between living units and living units and public spaces if design is based on published values for a particular type of construction. It allows an STC of 45 if the barrier is field-tested.

Additional variables that affect transmitted sound include:

1. Quality of the constructed partition or floor.
2. Gaps or "leaks" in the barrier, such as uncaulked edges, electrical outlets, and so on.
3. Flanking paths for sound, such as partitions that stop at the ceiling instead of continuing to the floor above, air ducts, adjacent doorways, and so on.
4. "Weaker" construction within the barrier, such as doors, glazing, and so on.
5. Paths for impact sound transmission, such as pipes through walls rigidly attached, work counters attached to walls, and so on.
6. Unusual sound conditions or frequencies—amplified sound, low-frequency rumbling, exterior walls in unusually loud environments, and the like, which require special design study by an acoustical consultant.

The following tables give criteria developed by the Department of Housing and Urban Development in conjunction with the Federal Housing Administration for Sound Transmission Classes (STC) and Impact Isolation Class (IIC) in multifamily dwellings. Three "grades" of acoustic environments are recognized, each requiring a different STC and IIC.

Grade I is applicable to suburban and peripheral suburban residential areas generally regarded as "quiet," where nighttime exterior noise levels are around 35 to 40 dB(A) or lower. Recommended interior noise criteria is NC 20 to 25.

Grade II is the most important category and is applicable to "average" noise environments, where the nighttime exterior noise levels are about 40 to 45 dB(A); interior noise criteria is NC 25 to 30.

Grade III is applicable to "noisy" environments such as urban areas, where nighttime exterior noise levels are about 55 dB(A) or higher; interior noise criteria should not exceed NC 35.

Table 2G-5
TRANSMISSION LOSS DATA FOR TYPICAL BUILDING CONSTRUCTIONS

Construction Description	STC	IIC
Walls		
Typical interior partitions:		
5/8 in. gypsum board, each side 3 5/8 in. metal studs	42	
Same as above with 3 in. sound attenuation blankets in cavity	48	
2 layers 1/2 in. gypsum board, each side 2 1/2 in. metal studs with 1 1/2 in. sound attenuation blankets in cavity	54	
Same as above except only one layer drywall on one side of partition	50	
5/8 in. gypsum board, each side 2 × 4 studs	34	
Same as above using resilient channels on wood studs	45	
5/8 in. gypsum board on 2 × 4 staggered wood studs on common 2 × 6 plate with 2 in. sound attenuation blanket in cavity	45	
2 layers 1/2 in. gypsum board each side 2 × 4 studs, gypsum board mounted on one side on resilient clips, 3 in. sound attenuation blanket in cavity	59	
Brick		
4 in. brick	45	
Same as above with 1/2 in. plaster one side	50	
8 in. solid brick (2 wythes)	52	
Same as above with 1/2 in. gypsum board on furring strips one side	53	
10 in. reinforced brick	59	
2 wythes 4 in. brick with 2 in. air space	50	
Concrete Masonry		
4 in. lightweight concrete block (18 psf)	40	
4 in. standard concrete block (33 psf)	45	
4 in. standard concrete block painted each side	44	
4 in. standard concrete block, 5/8 in. plaster each side	51	
4 in. standard concrete block, 1/2 in. gypsum board each side	48	
8 in. lightweight concrete block (39 psf)	49	
Same as above with cells filled with insulation	51	
8 in. standard concrete block with 1/2 in. gypsum board each side	49	
8 in. reinforced and grouted with 1/2 in. gypsum board each side	60	
4 in. concrete brick, 2 in. air space, 4 in. lightweight concrete block with 1/2 in. gypsum board on block face	59	
Add for one side resilient furred gypsum board	10	
Add for two sides resilient furred gypsum board	15	
Concrete		
6 in. solid concrete	47	
8 in. solid concrete	50	
10 in. solid concrete	53	

Note: Partition STC ratings include fully caulked perimeter and no flanking loss due to ceiling construction.

Table 2G-5 (Continued)

Construction Description	STC	IIC
Floors/Ceilings		
Construction Description	STC	IIC (See note below.)
2 in. wood floor joists 16 in. o.c. with 5/8 in. plywood subfloor. 1/8 in. vinyl tile on 1/2 in. plywood underlayment with 1/2 in. gypsum board nailed to underside of joists.	37	34
Same as above but with vinyl on 3/8 in. underlayment and 5/8 in. gypsum board screwed to resilient channels. 3 in. fiberglass insulation in joist space.	46	44
Same as above but with 44 oz. carpet on 3/8 in. underlayment and 5/8 in. gypsum board nailed directly to joists. 3 in. insulation	40	58
2 in. wood floor joists 16 in. o.c. with 1/2 in. plywood subfloor. 44 oz. carpet on 3/4 in. nominal oak strip flooring and 1/2 in. gypsum board screwed to resilient channels. 3 in. mineral wood insulation in joist space.	50	71
2 in. wood floor joists 16 in. o.c. with 1/2 in. subfloor. Sleepers glued to 1/2 in. soundboard over subfloor with 3/4 in. nominal wood strip flooring over. Ceiling 5/8 in. gypsum board screwed to resilient channels. Insulation in joist space and between sleepers.	55	51
2 in. wood floor joists 16 in. o.c. with 1 1/2 in. lightweight concrete over 5/8 in. plywood subfloor. Carpet and pad over concrete and 5/8 in. gypsum board ceiling screwed to resilient channels.	55	67
Long span truss-joists with 1 5/8 in. lightweight concrete over 5/8 in. plywood subfloor. Carpet on pad finish. 5/8 in. gypsum board ceiling nailed to bottom chord of joist.	46	62
Bar joists with 2 1/2 in. concrete slab over metal decking with suspended acoustical ceiling below. Carpet.	40–45	60–70
Glass		
Single-Strength Float Glass	26	
1/4 in. float glass	29	
1/2 in. float glass	33	
3/4 in. float glass	33	
1/4 in. laminated glass (0.030 interlayer)	35	
1/2 in. laminated glass (0.060 interlayer)	38	
3/4 in. laminated glass (2–0.060 interlayers)	41	
2 1/4 in. layers glass with 1 in. air space	35	
1/4 in. and 1/2 in. layers with 2 in. air space	39	
1/4 in. and 1/2 in. layers glass with 4 in. air space	40	
Generally, laminated glass performs better as a sound barrier because of the damping effect of the interlayer. In critical situations and to achieve the above ratings, glass panels must be sealed at all edges. When using two layers of glass separated by an air space, the thicknesses of glass should not be the same.		

Note: Floor construction is especially susceptible to impact noise. Even with a high STC rating, a floor can transmit undesirable sound from footfalls, dropped objects, and the like. Therefore, the IIC (Impact Insulation Class) is just as important as STC in evaluating floor construction. Usually, adding a material such as carpeting is sufficient to bring a floor assembly up to recommended levels.

Table 2G-5 (Continued)

Construction Description	STC	IIC
Doors		
1 3/4 in. hollow core with 1/4 in. gap at sill	17	
1 3/4 in. solid-core wood with no seal	20	
1 3/4 in. solid-core wood with perimeter seal and automatic door bottom (2.5 psf)	29	
2-1 3/4 in. solid-core doors with full seals separated by 3 ft. (5.0 psf)	47	

Note: These figures were compiled from various industry sources and represent typical ratings useful for preliminary design decisions. Refer to manufacturer's test data for more detailed data.

Table 2G-6
SOUND ISOLATION CRITERIA

Type of Occupancy	Area Considered (source)	Adjacent Area (receiver)	Minimum STC
Single-family residential	Bedrooms and living rooms	Bedrooms	40–48
		Living rooms	42–50
		Bathrooms	45–52
		Kitchens	45–52
		Building exterior	45–52
Multifamily residential	See Tables 2G-7, 2G-8, and 2G-9		
Offices—normal privacy requirements	Offices	Adjacent offices	45
		General office areas	45
		Conference rooms	45
		Toilets	47
		Corridors	45
		Kitchen/dining areas	47
		Mechanical equipment	52+
	Conference rooms	Conference rooms	45
		General office areas	45
		Toilets	47
Offices—confidential, privacy required	Offices	Adjacent offices	52
		Conference rooms	
		Other areas	
Offices—large general areas	General office areas	Corridors, lobby	37
		Data processing	42
		Kitchen/dining areas	42
Hotels/motels	Bedrooms	Adjacent bedrooms	48+
		Bathrooms	52+
		Corridor, public area	48+
		Mechanical room	52+
Apartments	Bedrooms	Adjacent bedrooms	48–55
		Bathrooms, same unit	45–52
		Bathrooms, adjacent unit	52–58
		Corridor, public area	48–55
		Kitchen, adjacent unit	50–57

Table 2G-6 (Continued)

Type of Occupancy	Area Considered (source)	Adjacent Area (receiver)	Minimum STC
Apartments (continued)		Kitchen, same unit	45–52
		Mechanical room	58–65
	Living rooms	Adjacent living room	48–55
		Bathrooms, same unit	45–52
		Bathrooms, adjacent unit	50–57
		Kitchen, adjacent unit	48–55
Schools	Classrooms	Adjacent classrooms	42–48
		Corridors/public area	42
		Shops	52+
		Music rooms	52+
		Toilets	47
		Kitchen/lunchroom	47
	Music rooms	Corridors	52

Table 2G-7
CRITERIA FOR AIRBORNE SOUND INSULATION OF WALL PARTITIONS BETWEEN DWELLING UNITS

Partition Function Between Dwellings Apt. A		Apt. B	Grade I STC	Grade II STC	Grade III STC
Bedroom	to	Bedroom	55	52	48
Living room	to	Bedroom (1),(2)	57	54	50
Kitchen (3)	to	Bedroom (1),(2)	58	55	52
Bathroom	to	Bedroom (1),(2)	59	56	52
Corridor	to	Bedroom (2),(4)	55	52	48
Living room	to	Living room	55	52	48
Kitchen (3)	to	Living room (1),(2)	55	52	48
Bathroom	to	Living room (1)	57	54	50
Corridor	to	Living room (2),(4),(5)	55	52	48
Kitchen	to	Kitchen (6),(7)	52	50	46
Bathroom	to	Kitchen (1),(7)	55	52	48
Corridor	to	Kitchen (2),(4),(5)	55	52	48
Bathroom	to	Bathroom (7)	52	50	46
Corridor	to	Bathroom (2),(4)	50	48	46

(1) The most desirable plan would have the dwelling unit partition separating spaces with equivalent functions—for example, living room opposite living room, and so on—however, when this arrangement is not feasible, the partition must have greater sound-insulating properties.

(2) Whenever a partition wall might serve to separate several functional spaces, the highest criterion must prevail.

(3) Or dining, or family, or recreation room.

(4) It is assumed that there is no entrance door leading from corridor to living unit.

(5) If a door is part of the corridor partition, it must have the same rating as the corridor. The most desirable arrangement has the entrance door leading from the corridor to a partially enclosed vestibule or foyer in the living unit.

(6) Double-wall construction is recommended to provide, in addition to airborne sound insulation, isolation from impact noises generated by the placement of articles on pantry shelves and the slamming of cabinet doors.

(7) Special detailing is required for vibration isolation of plumbing in kitchens and bathrooms.

Source: "A Guide to Airborne, Impact, and Structureborne Noise Control in Multifamily Dwellings," U.S. Dept. of Housing and Urban Development, HUD-TS-24 (1974).

Table 2G-8
CRITERIA FOR AIRBORNE AND IMPACT SOUND INSULATON OF FLOOR-CEILING ASSEMBLIES BETWEEN DWELLING UNITS

Partition Function Between Dwellings			Grade I		Grade II		Grade III	
Apt. A		Apt. B	STC	IIC	STC	IIC	STC	IIC
Bedroom	above	Bedroom	55	55	52	52	48	48
Living room	above	Bedroom (1),(2)	57	60	54	57	50	53
Kitchen (3)	above	Bedroom (1),(2),(4)	58	65	55	62	52	58
Family room	above	Bedroom (1),(2),(5)	60	65	56	62	52	58
Corridor	above	Bedroom (1),(2)	55	65	52	62	48	58
Bedroom	above	Living room (6)	57	55	54	52	50	48
Living room	above	Living room	55	55	52	52	48	48
Kitchen	above	Living room (1),(2),(4)	55	60	52	57	48	53
Family room	above	Living room (1),(2),(5)	58	62	54	60	52	56
Corridor	above	Living room (1),(2)	55	60	52	57	48	53
Bedroom	above	Kitchen (1),(4),(6)	58	55	55	50	52	46
Living room	above	Kitchen (1),(4),(6)	55	55	52	52	48	48
Kitchen	above	Kitchen (4)	52	55	50	52	46	48
Bathroom	above	Kitchen (1),(2),(4)	55	55	52	52	48	48
Family room	above	Kitchen (1),(2),(4),(5)	55	60	52	58	48	54
Corridor	above	Kitchen (1),(2),(4)	50	55	48	52	46	48
Bedroom	above	Family room (1),(6)	60	50	56	48	52	46
Living room	above	Family room (1),(6)	58	52	54	50	52	48
Kitchen	above	Family room (1),(6)	55	55	52	52	48	50
Bathroom	above	Bathroom (4)	52	52	50	50	48	48
Corridor	above	Corridor (7)	50	50	48	48	46	46

(1) The most desirable plan would have the floor-ceiling assembly separating spaces with equivalent function—for example, living room above living room, and so on—however, when this is not feasible, the assembly must have greater acoustical-insulating properties.
(2) This arrangement requires greater impact sound insulation than the converse, where a sensitive area is above a less sensitive area.
(3) Or dining, or family, or recreation room.
(4) Special detailing is required for vibration isolation of plumbing in kitchens and bathrooms.
(5) The airborne STC criteria in this table apply as well to vertical partitions between these two spaces.
(6) This arrangement requires equivalent airborne sound insulation and perhaps less impact sound insulation than the converse.
(7) Special detailing required for proper treatment of staircase halls and corridors.

Source: *"A Guide to Airborne, Impact, and Structureborne Noise Control in Multifamily Dwellings," U.S. Dept. of Housing and Urban Development, HUD-TS-24 (1974).*

Table 2G-9
SUGGESTED CRITERIA FOR AIRBORNE SOUND INSULATION WITHIN A DWELLING UNIT AND OTHER CRITERIA

Partition Function Between Rooms			Grade I		Grade II		Grade III	
			STC	IIC	STC	IIC	STC	IIC
Bedroom	to	Bedroom (1),(2)	48		44		40	
Living room	to	Bedroom (1),(2)	50		46		42	
Bathroom	to	Bedroom (1),(2),(3)	52		48		45	
Kitchen	to	Bedroom (1),(2),(3)	52		48		45	
Bathroom	to	Living room (2),(3)	52		48		45	
Mechanical rooms	to	Sensitive areas	65		62		58	
Mechanical rooms	to	Less sensitive areas (kitchens, family rooms, etc.)	60		58		54	
Business areas	to	Sensitive areas	60		58		56	
Living areas	above	Business areas		60		58		56
Business areas	above	Living areas		65		63		61

(1) Closets may be profitably used as "buffer" zones, providing unlouvered doors are used.
(2) Doors leading to bedrooms and bathrooms preferably should be of solid-core construction and gasketed to assure a comfortable degree of privacy.
(3) Special detailing is required for vibration isolation of plumbing in kitchens and bathrooms.

Source: *"A Guide to Airborne, Impact, and Structureborne Noise Control in Multifamily Dwellings," U.S. Dept. of Housing and Urban Development, HUD-TS-24 (1974).*

HOW TO CALCULATE NOISE REDUCTION WITHIN A SPACE

In addition to controlling sound transmission between spaces, controlling undesirable sound within a space is also important. Control of sound within a space is primarily dependent on the absorption of the various surfaces and objects in the room; the amount of the absorptive surfaces; and, in many cases, the size of the room itself. All of these factors can be designed to control noise reduction in the space; reverberation time; and, to a certain extent, total noise reduction through a barrier, as discussed in the previous section, "How to Calculate Noise Reduction Between Spaces."

The absorption of a material is the amount of incident sound energy that it absorbs instead of reflects. It is defined as a coefficient of absorption (a) and is the ratio of the sound intensity absorbed by a material to the total intensity reaching the material. The maximum absorption possible, therefore, is 1, that of free space. Generally, a material with a coefficient below 0.2 is considered to be reflective, and one with a coefficient above 0.2 is considered sound-absorbing. The coefficient of absorption varies with the frequency of the sound, some materials being better at absorbing some frequencies rather than others. For critical applications, all frequencies should be checked, but for convenience the single-number noise reduction coefficient (NRC) is used. The NRC is the average of a material's absorption coefficients at the four frequencies of 250, 500, 1000, and 2000 Hz, rounded to the nearest multiple of 0.05. Representative coefficients of absorption and NRC values are given in Table 2G–10.

The total absorption of a material is dependent on its coefficient of absorption and the area of the material.

FORMULA: $A = Sa$

where:

A = total absorption in *sabins*
S = surface area in sq. ft. (or sq. m)
a = coefficient of absorption

Since most rooms have several materials of different areas, the total absorption in a room is the sum of the various individual material absorptions.

Increasing sound absorption within a space will result in a noise reduction according to the following formula.

FORMULA:

$$NR = 10 \log \frac{a(2)}{a(1)}$$

where:

NR = noise reduction in decibels
a(1) = total original room absorption in sabins
a(2) = total room absorption after increase of absorption

Note that this formula relates to overall reverberant noise level in a room and does not affect noise level very near the source.

Example

A room 15 ft. by 20 ft. with a 9 ft. ceiling has a carpeted floor with 44 oz. carpet on pad, gypsum board walls, and a gypsum board ceiling. What would be the noise reduction possible by directly attaching acoustical tile to the ceiling with a given NRC of 0.70?

Original total absorption of room:

Floor: 15 ft. × 20 ft. = 300 × 0.40 = 120
Walls: 2 × 15 ft. × 9 ft. = 270 × 0.05 = 14
2 × 20 ft. × 9 ft. = 360 × 0.05 = 18
Ceiling: 15 ft. × 20 ft. = 300 × 0.05 = 15
Total = 167 sabins

Absorption after treatment:
Ceiling = 15 ft. × 20 ft. = 300 × 0.70 = 210 sabins
Subtracting 15 from old value and adding 210 new value, net total is 362 sabins.

$$\text{Noise reduction} = 10 \log \frac{362}{167}$$

$$NR = 10 \log 2.17$$
$$NR = 3.36 \text{ dB}$$

Increasing the absorption by this amount produces a just perceptible reduction in noise as shown in Table 2G-4. However, increasing the absorption even more would result in a clearly noticeable noise reduction.

Table 2G-10
COEFFICIENTS OF ABSORPTION OF SELECTED MATERIALS

Material	NRC	125	250	500	1000	2000	4000
Floors							
Carpet, direct glue to concrete	0.30	0.02	0.06	0.14	0.37	0.60	0.65
Carpet, on 40 oz. hair pad over concrete	0.55	0.08	0.24	0.57	0.69	0.71	0.73
Carpet, 44 oz., 1/4 in. pile ht. laid directly on concrete	0.30						
Carpet, 43 oz., 1/2 in. pile ht. laid directly on concrete	0.50						
Carpet, 44 oz., 0.25 in. pile ht. coated backing on 40 oz. hair pad	0.40						
Carpet, 43. oz., 0.50 in. pile ht. coated backing on 40 oz. hair pad	0.70						
Concrete or Terrazzo	0.00	0.01	0.01	0.02	0.02	0.02	0.02
Vinyl tile, cork, linoleum, on concrete	0.05	0.02	0.03	0.03	0.03	0.03	0.02
Wood	0.10	0.15	0.11	0.10	0.07	0.06	0.07
Wood parquet on concrete	0.05	0.04	0.04	0.07	0.06	0.06	0.07

Table 2G-10 (Continued)

Material	NRC	125	250	500	1000	2000	4000
Walls							
Brick	0.05	0.03	0.03	0.03	0.04	0.05	0.07
Concrete block, standard, two coats latex paint	0.05	0.10	0.05	0.06	0.07	0.09	0.08
Concrete block, lightweight, two coats latex paint	0.20						
Concrete block, lightweight, medium texture, unpainted	0.45						
Concrete block, standard, medium texture, unpainted	0.27						
Glass, heavy plate	0.05	0.18	0.06	0.04	0.03	0.02	0.02
Glass, standard window	0.15	0.35	0.25	0.18	0.12	0.07	0.04
Gpysum board	0.05	0.10	0.08	0.05	0.03	0.03	0.03
Marble or glazed tile	0.00	0.01	0.01	0.01	0.01	0.02	0.02
Plaster or lath	0.05	0.14	0.10	0.06	0.05	0.04	0.03
Plywood paneling, 3/8 in.	0.15	0.28	0.22	0.17	0.09	0.10	0.11
Carpet, 35 oz., 0.175 in. cut loop, uncoated backing, mounted on 5/8 in. furring strips with rockwool filler	0.55						
Carpet, 23 oz., 1/4 in. cut loop, coated backing, same mounting as above	0.75						
Sound-Absorbing Material							
7/16 in. fiberglass with fabric cover, 9.75 lb./cu. ft.	0.95	0.20	0.79	1.17	1.17	1.05	1.04
1 in. fiberglass with fabric cover, 7.5 lb./cu. ft.	0.80	0.10	0.29	0.81	0.99	1.04	0.99
2 in. fiberglass with fabric cover, 7 lb/cu. ft.	0.95	0.20	0.79	1.17	1.17	1.05	1.04
1 in. porous acoustic foam, 1.8 lb/cu. ft.	0.85	0.11	0.48	1.04	0.90	0.89	0.97
2 in. foam with aluminized Mylar cover	0.70	0.10	0.24	0.77	0.80	0.91	0.51
Fabric, medium velour, 14 oz. draped to half area	0.55	0.07	0.31	0.49	0.75	0.70	0.60
Fabric, heavy velour, 18 oz. draped to half area	0.60	0.14	0.35	0.55	0.72	0.70	0.65
1 in. acoustical fiberglass	0.65	0.06	0.20	0.64	0.90	0.95	0.97
2 in. acoustical fiberglass	0.75	0.16	0.34	0.72	0.97	0.97	0.97
1 1/4 in., spray-on cellulose fiber, fire resistant, applied on 1/2 in. plywood	0.75	0.10	0.30	0.73	0.92	0.98	0.98
Ceilings							
Acoustical tile, 3/4 in. mounted directly to gypsum board	0.70	0.10	0.20	0.77	0.84	0.81	0.80
Suspended acoustical tile, 5/8 in., finely perforated	0.60	0.29	0.29	0.55	0.75	0.73	0.57
Suspended acoustical tile, 1 in., textured	0.90	0.58	0.86	0.75	0.99	1.00	0.96
Suspended acoustical tile, 5/8 in. with vinyl acrylic coating	0.55	0.35	0.31	0.42	0.63	0.75	0.75

Table 2G-10 (Continued)

Material	NRC	125	250	500	1000	2000	4000
Miscellaneous							
Air, sabins per 1000 cu. ft. at 50% relative humidity					0.9	2.3	7.2
Audience in upholstered seats, sabins per person		2.5–4.0		4.0–5.5		5.0–7.0	
Seat, heavily upholstered, sabins per seat		1.5–3.5		4.0–5.0		3.5–5.5	
Water surface	0.00	0.01	0.01	0.01	0.01	0.02	0.03

Note: These are representative values only. Refer to the manufacturer's literature for values of specific products. Values of products specifically designed for acoustical purposes can vary widely in their NRC values.

HOW TO CALCULATE REVERBERATION TIME

Reverberation is an important quality of the acoustical environment of a space. It is the one quality that affects the intelligibility of speech and the quality of the conditions for music of all types. Reverberation time is the time it takes the sound level to decrease 60 dB after the source has stopped producing the sound. Reverberation time is found by the following formula.

FORMULA:

$$T = \frac{0.05V}{A}$$

where:

T = reverberation time in sec.
V = volume of the room in cu. ft.
A = room absorption in sabins

Each type of use has its own preferred range of reverberation time—shorter times being best for smaller spaces and longer reverberation times working best for larger spaces. See Table 2G–11 for recommended reverberation times.

Table 2G-11
RECOMMENDED REVERBERATION TIMES

Auditoriums (speech and music)	1.5–1.8
Broadcast studios (speech only)	0.4–0.6
Churches	1.4–3.4
Elementary classrooms	0.6–0.8
Lecture/conference rooms	0.9–1.1
Movie theaters	0.8–1.2
Offices, small rooms for speech	0.3–0.6
Opera halls	1.5–1.8
Symphony concert halls	1.6–2.1
Theaters (small dramatic)	0.9–1.4

RULES OF THUMB

- The normal human ear can hear sounds in the range of 20 to 20,000 Hz and is most sensitive to frequencies in the 3000 to 4000 Hz range.
- For sounds of equal energy, the human ear is less sensitive to low frequencies than to middle or high frequencies.
- Outside, in an ideal "free" field (no reflections), sound intensity decreases by 6 dB for each doubling of distance from the sound source. Inside, beyond 1 to 4 ft. from a source, sound decay depends on the absorption of the room, not distance.
- By reducing the loudness of continuous room noise by one third, a person talking in that room at close range needs only to use about one fourth as much voice power to be understood; or, with the same power, that person can move away from the listener twice as far.
- The average absorption coefficient of a room should be *at least* 0.20. Average absorption above 0.50 is usually not desirable, nor is it economically justified. A lower value is suitable for large rooms; larger values for small or noisy rooms.
- Each doubling of the amount of absorption in a room results in a noise deduction of only 3 dB.
- If additional absorptive material is being added to a room to improve it, the total absorption should be increased at least three times (amounting to a change in about 5 dB, which is clearly noticeable). The increase may need to be more or less than three times to bring absorption to between 0.20 and 0.50.
- In adding extra absorption, an increase of ten times is about the practical limit. Beyond this (representing a reverberant noise reduction of 10 dB) more absorption results in a decreasing amount of noise reduction and the reaching of the practical limit of 0.50 total average absorption coefficient.
- Each doubling of the absorption in a room reduces reverberation time by one half.
- If a corridor is appreciably higher than its width, some absorptive material should be placed on the walls as well as the ceiling, especially if the floor is hard-surfaced. If the corridor is wider than it is high, ceiling treatment is usually enough.
- Although absorptive materials can be placed anywhere, ceiling treatment for sound absorption is more effective in large rooms, while wall treatment is more effective in small rooms.
- Generally, absorption increases with an increase in thickness of a porous absorber, except for low-frequency situations, which require special design treatment.
- In general, transmission loss through a barrier tends to increase with frequency.
- A wall with 0.1% open area (from cracks, holes, undercut doors, and so on) can have only a maximum transmission loss of about 30 dB. A wall with 1% open area can have only a maximum of 20 dB.
- A hairline crack will decrease a partition's transmission loss by about 6 dB. A one square inch opening in a 100 square foot gypsum board partition can transmit as much sound as the entire partition.

- Although placing fibrous insulation in a wall cavity increases its STC rating, the *density* of the insulation is not a significant variable.
- In determining the required STC rating of a barrier, the following rough guidelines may be used:

Table 2G-12
EFFECT OF BARRIER STC ON HEARING
(assuming NC-25 background level on receiving side of barrier)

STC	Effect on Hearing
25	Normal speech can clearly be heard through barrier.
30	Loud speech can be heard and understood fairly well.
	Normal speech can be heard but barely understood.
35	Loud speech is not intelligible but can be heard.
42–45	Loud speech can be heard only faintly. Normal speech cannot be heard.
46–50	Loud speech not audible. Loud sounds other than speech can be heard only faintly, if at all.

PART 2H

Vertical Transportation

ELEVATOR SELECTION

At the preliminary planning stage, it is useful to have a rough idea of the number of elevators required for the building and the approximate floor space they will require. Selection of the capacity, speed, and number of elevators for a particular building type is dependent on many interrelated factors. Detailed calculations can become quite complex, as the final solution is a balance between level of service, floor space required, and cost. The following procedure simplifies making preliminary estimates, based on information that is usually known early in the schematic design process. It can be used for relatively simple building types such as low-rise office buildings, residential buildings, and hotels. Complex occupancies such as hospitals, mixed-use facilities, high-rise buildings, and the like will require the assistance of an elevator consultant.

1. Find the desired handling capacity of the system.

For most occupancies this is expressed as a percentage of the total building population that the elevators should be able to accommodate during a certain peak period, usually a five-minute period at the busiest time of the day.

FORMULA: $HC = r \times D$

where:

HC = handling capacity in numbers of people for a five-minute period
r = recommended percentage of building population (Table 2H-1)
D = building population

Various recommended percentages are given in Table 2H-1. Using a lower percentage in a given range will result in fewer elevators being required, with a lower level of service; that is, people may have to wait longer in the lobby for the elevator to arrive, or travel times may be longer than recommended.

The building population, D, can be estimated if it is not known. Table 2H-2 gives some typical density factors based on net square feet per person or people per room for residential occupancies. Net square feet includes the usable portion of the building above the lobby, not including toilet rooms, service rooms, shaft space, and similar non-usable areas.

Table 2H-1
MINIMUM HANDLING CAPACITIES AS PERCENT OF BUILDING POPULATION TO BE CARRIED UP DURING FIVE MINUTES AT PEAK PERIOD

Building Type	Up at Peak Period with 10% Down Traffic (in percent)
Offices	
Diversified	11%-12
Diversified single purpose	12%-15
Single purpose	13%-20
Residential	
Hotels	12%-15
Apartments	5%-7
Dormitories	11%-15
Senior citizen housing	5%-6

Note: The percentages above do not include special population-generating areas such as cafeteria floors, meeting room floors in hotels, and similar areas.

Table 2H-2
TYPICAL POPULATION FACTORS

Building Type	Net Square Feet per Person
Offices	
Diversified	150
Diversified single purpose	135
Single purpose	120
Residential	*People per room*
Hotel, normal	1.3-1.5
Hotel, convention	1.5-1.9
Apartment, high rent	1.5-1.75
Apartment, moderate rent	1.8-2
Apartment, low rent	2.5-3
Senior citizen housing	1.2-1.5
Dormitories	200 sq. ft. per person

Notes: Net area of offices 1 to 20 floors is about 75% to 80% of gross area.

The percentages above do not include special population-generating areas such as cafeteria floors, meeting room floors in hotels, and similar areas.

2. Make a tentative selection of elevator capacity and speed and find the round-trip time.

Knowing the building type you are designing and the number of floors, select a recommended elevator capacity and speed from Tables 2H-3 and 2H-4. With this information, find the average round-trip time in seconds from Table 2H-5.

Table 2H-3
RECOMMENDED ELEVATOR CAPACITIES

Building Type	Building Size			Service Elevator
	Small	Medium	Large	
Offices	2500/3000	3000/3500	3500/4000	4000–6500
Garages	2500	3000	3500	—
Retail	3500	3500	4000	4000–8000
Hotels	3000	3500	3500	4000
Apartments	2000/2500	2500	2500	4000
Dormitories	3000	3000	3000	—
Senior citizen	2500	2500	2500	4000

Table 2H-4
RECOMMENDED ELEVATOR SPEEDS

Offices	Small	Medium	Large	Service
Number of floors				
2–5	250	300/400	400	200
5–10	400	400	500	300
10–15	400	400/500	500/700	400
15–25	500	500/700	700	500
25–35	—	800/1000	1000	500
35–45	—	1000/1200	1200	700
45–60	—	1200/1400	1400/1600	800
over 60	—	—	1800	800
Garages				
2–5	200			
5–10	200–400			
10–15	300–500			
Hotels				
2–6	150–300			200
6–12	200–500			300
12–20	400–500			400
20–25	500/700			500
25–30	700/800			500
30–40	700–1000			700
40–50	1000–1200			800
Apartments/Dormitories/Senior Citizen Housing				
2–6	100/150			200
6–12	200/250			200
12–20	300–500			200
20–25	400/500			300
25–30	500			300

Table 2H-5
ROUND-TRIP TIMES FOR VARIOUS CAR CAPACITIES AND SPEEDS

	Car Capacity (in pounds)													
	2500				3000			3500				4000		
	Car Speeds													
Floors*	250	300	400	500	300	400	500	300	400	500	700	400	500	700
20				180	228	213	199	246	231	218	212	261	247	241
19				176	221	207	194	238	225	212	207	254	241	235
18				171	214	201	189	231	219	206	201	246	234	229
17				166	207	195	184	223	212	200	196	239	227	222
16				162	200	189	178	215	205	194	190	231	220	216
15			167	157	192	183	173	207	198	188	184	222	212	208
14			161	151	184	176	167	198	190	181	177	214	204	201
13			154	146	176	169	160	189	182	173	170	204	196	192
12			148	140	168	161	153	180	174	166	163	195	187	184
11			141	134	159	153	146	170	165	157	155	184	177	175
10			133	127	149	144	138	160	155	149	146	174	167	165
9			125	119	139	135	129	149	145	139	137	162	156	155
8		119	116	111	128	125	120	137	134	129	128	150	145	144
7		109	107	102	117	115	110	125	123	118	117	137	133	132
6		98	96	92	104	103	99	112	111	107	106	124	120	120
5	87	85	84	82	91	91	88	98	98	95	94	110	107	107
4	73	72	72	70	78	78	75	84	84	82	82	96	94	94
3	58	58	58	57	64	64	63	70	71	69	70	82	80	80

*Includes lobby floor

Note: The round-trip times are based on the following assumptions:

	Capacity			
	2500	3000	3500	4000
Passengers	13	16	19	22
Lobby loading time (sec.)	12	14	17	20
Door opening time	4.6	4.6	4.6	5.3

Acceleration: 3.5 ft. per second/second for 250, 300, and 400 fpm cars
4.5 ft. per second/second for 500 and 700 fpm cars

Unload time: 2 seconds

Landing call time, down: 4 seconds

Probable down stops = 10% of peak up traffic

Highest average stop = highest floor less one

$$\text{Probable stops, up} = N - N\left(\frac{N-1}{N}\right)^{p}$$

where:

N = maximum number of floors

p = number of passengers

3. Find the handling capacity of one car for a five-minute period.

FORMULA:

$$h = \frac{300P}{RT}$$

where:

h = single-car handling capacity for five minutes
P = individual car loading; use the following values:

2500 lb. capacity:	13 people
3000 lb.	16
3500 lb.	19
4000 lb.	22

RT = round-trip time, found from Table 2H–5
Note: 5 min. × 60 sec./min. = 300 sec.
This value can be calculated or you can use Table 2H–6.

4. Find the number of elevator cars required.

FORMULA:

$$N = \frac{HC}{h}$$

where:

N = number of cars
HC = handling capacity calculated in step 1
h = handling capacity of one car

5. Check the interval against suggested interval times.

The interval is the average time between departure of cars from the lobby. If the interval is too long, people complain about the elevator service. Although the allowable interval time is a subjective measure, some recommended times have been developed. (See Table 2H–7.)

To calculate interval use the following formula.

FORMULA:

$$I = \frac{RT}{N}$$

where:

I = interval
RT = round-trip time
N = number of cars

If the calculated interval exceeds the recommended interval by a significant amount, either the number of cars needs to be increased (an obvious cost and space factor) or a higher capacity and/or faster elevators need to be selected to decrease the individual car round-trip time.

Table 2H-6
FIVE-MINUTE SINGLE-CAR CAPACITY

Round-Trip Time	Car Capacities and Passengers			
	2500 13	3000 16	3500 19	4000 22
60	65	80	95	110
65	60	74	88	102
70	56	69	81	94
75	52	64	76	88
80	49	60	71	83
85	46	56	67	78
90	43	53	63	73
95	41	51	60	69
100	39	48	57	66
105	37	46	54	63
110	35	44	52	60
115	34	42	50	57
120	33	40	48	55
125	31	38	46	53
130	30	37	44	51
135	29	36	42	49
140	28	34	41	47
145	27	33	39	46
150	26	32	38	44
155	25	31	37	43
160	24	30	36	41
165	24	29	35	40
170	23	28	34	39
175	22	27	33	38
180	22	27	32	37
185	21	26	31	36
190	21	25	30	35
195	20	25	29	34
200	20	24	29	33
205	19	23	28	32
210	19	23	27	31
215	18	22	27	31
220	18	22	26	30
225	17	21	25	29
230	17	21	25	29
235	17	20	24	28
240	16	20	24	28
245	16	20	23	27
250	16	19	23	26
255	15	19	22	26
260	15	18	22	25

Example

Estimate the number of elevators required for an eleven-story diversified office building if there will be 18,000 sq. ft. of net area per floor above the lobby.

Table 2H-7
RECOMMENDED INTERVALS

Building Type	Interval (in seconds)
Offices	(with 10% down traffic)
Diversified	30-35
Diversified, single purpose	28-33
Single purpose	25-30
Suburban	35-40
Hotels	40-60
Apartment, high rent	50-70
Apartment, moderate to low rent	60-90
Dormitories	50-70
Senior citizen housing	50-90

10 floors × 18,000 = 180,000 sq. ft. total
From Table 2H-2, population = 180,000/150 = 1200 people
Handling capacity, HC = 11% (from Table 2H-1) × 1200 = 132
From Tables 2H-3 and 2H-4, try a 3500 lb. elevator at 500 fpm. (capacity of 19 people)
From Table 2H-5, the round-trip time is 157 sec.
Handling capacity of one car:

$$h = \frac{300 \times 19}{157} = 36.3 \text{ people}$$

(From Table 2H-6, capacity is also 36 people.)
Number of cars:

$$N = \frac{132}{36} = 3.67 \text{ cars (use 4)}$$

Check interval:

$$I = \frac{157}{4} = 39 \text{ sec.}$$

Comparing this with Table 2H-7, this is too long. Using five cars would give an acceptable interval of 31 seconds but at the cost of another elevator. Try a 3000 lb. car at 500 fpm. This gives a round-trip time of 146 sec. (shorter because there are fewer people on it, resulting in fewer probable stops). Capacity on one car is then:

$$h = \frac{300 \times 16}{146} = 32.88 \text{ (use 33)}$$

N = 132/33, or 4 cars
Interval is then 36.5 sec.

This is still a little over the recommended time, but probably close enough, considering the cost of another elevator.

RULES OF THUMB

1. Assuming 125 sq. ft. per person, there should be one elevator for each 225 to 250 occupants.
2. Assuming 150 sq. ft. per person, there should be one elevator for each 275 to 300 occupants.

Table 2H-8
ELECTRIC ELEVATOR HOISTWAY SIZES

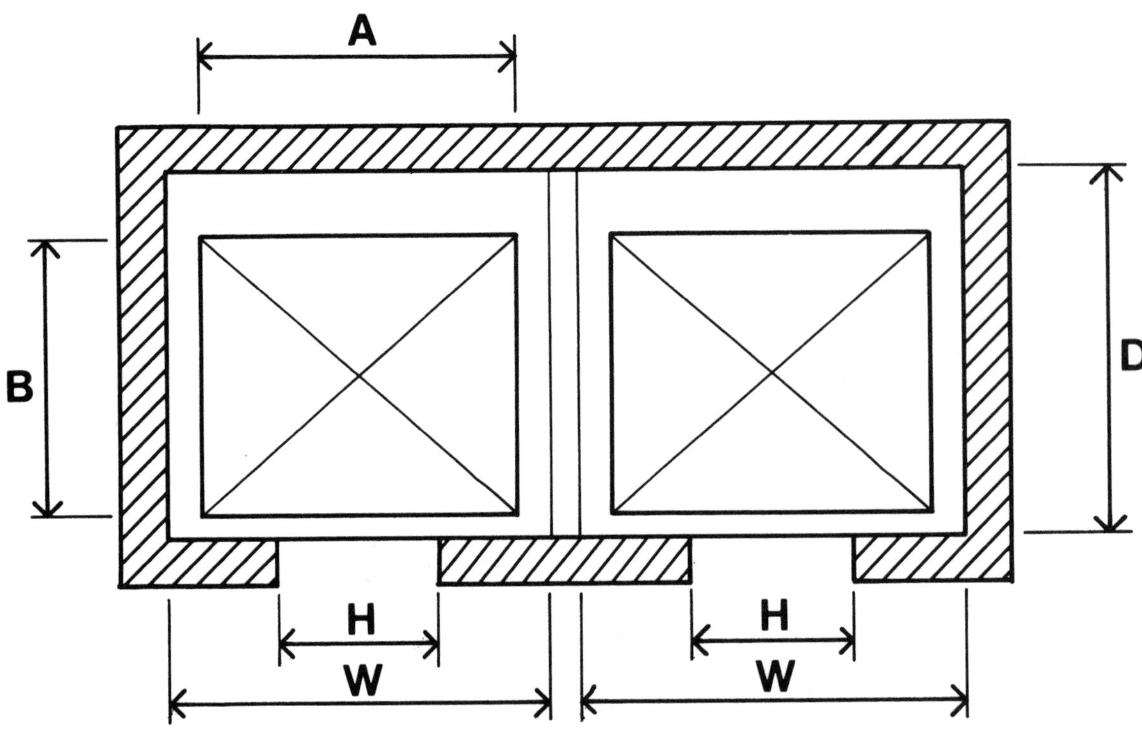

Car Capacity (in lbs.)	Car Size		Hoistway						Door
			100-350 fpm		500-750 fpm		800-1200 fpm		
	A	B	W(1)	D	W(1)	D	W(1)	D	H
2000	5-8	4-3	7-4	6-10	7-5	6-11			3-0
2500	6-8	4-3	8-4	6-10	8-6	6-11	8-6	7-0	3-6
3000	6-8	4-7	8-4	7-2	8-6	7-4	8-6	7-4	3-6
3500	6-8	5-3	8-4	7-10	8-6	8-0	8-6	8-1	3-6
3500(2)	7-8	4-7	—	—	9-6	7-4	—	—	4-2
4000	7-8	5-3	9-4	7-10	9-6	8-0	9-6	8-1	4-0
5000(2)	8-8	5-1	—	—	10-6	8-1	—	—	6-0

(Dimensions given are in feet-inches format.)
(1) Does not include any allowance for rail backing.
(2) Department and retail stores.

Reprinted with permission from Vertical Transportation Standards 1983 edition, Copyright 1983, National Elevator Industry, Inc., 630 Third Avenue, New York, NY 10017. This reprinted material is not the complete and official position of the National Elevator Industry, Inc., which is represented only by the standard in its entirety.

These assume a building with less than 20 floors and with floor areas greater than 10,000 sq. ft.

3. There should be one service elevator for each 300,000 sq. ft. of office space.
4. The ratio of service elevators to passenger elevators in hotels should be 0.5 : 1 to 0.6 : 1.

Table 2H-9
HYDRAULIC PASSENGER ELEVATOR HOISTWAY SIZES

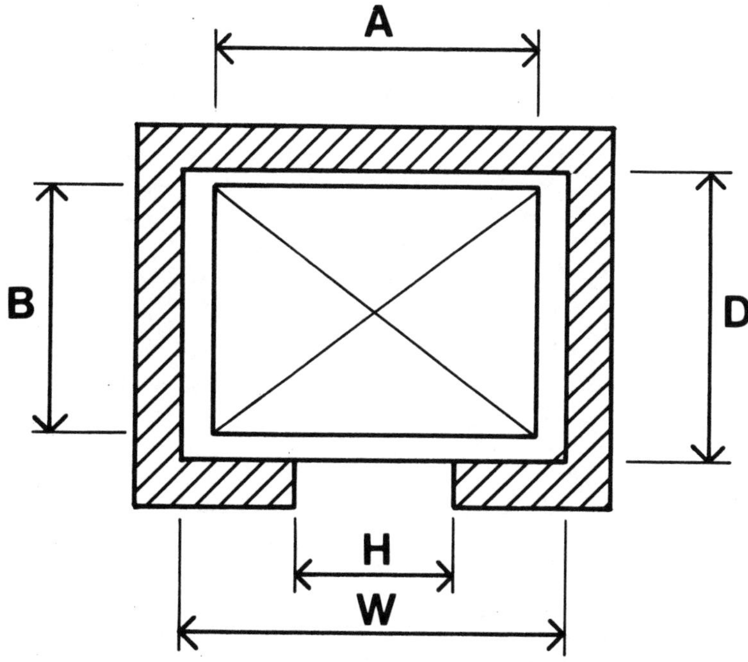

Car Capacity (in lbs.)	A	B	W	D	H
1500	4-6	4-3	6-8	5-11	2-8
2000	5-8	4-3	7-4	5-11	3-0
2500	6-8	4-3	8-4	5-11	3-6
3000	6-8	4-7	8-4	6-3	3-6
3500	6-8	5-3	8-4	6-11	3-6
3500	7-8	4-7	9-4	6-6	5-0
4000	7-8	5-3	9-4	6-11	4-0
5000	8-8	5-1	10-4	7-0	6-0

(Dimensions given are in feet-inches format.)

Reprinted with permission from Vertical Transportation Standards 1983 edition, Copyright 1983, National Elevator Industry, Inc., 630 Third Avenue, New York, NY 10017. This reprinted material is not the complete and official position of the National Elevator Industry, Inc., which is represented only by the standard in its entirety.

Table 2H-10
ELECTRIC FREIGHT ELEVATOR HOISTWAY SIZES FOR COMMERCIAL USE

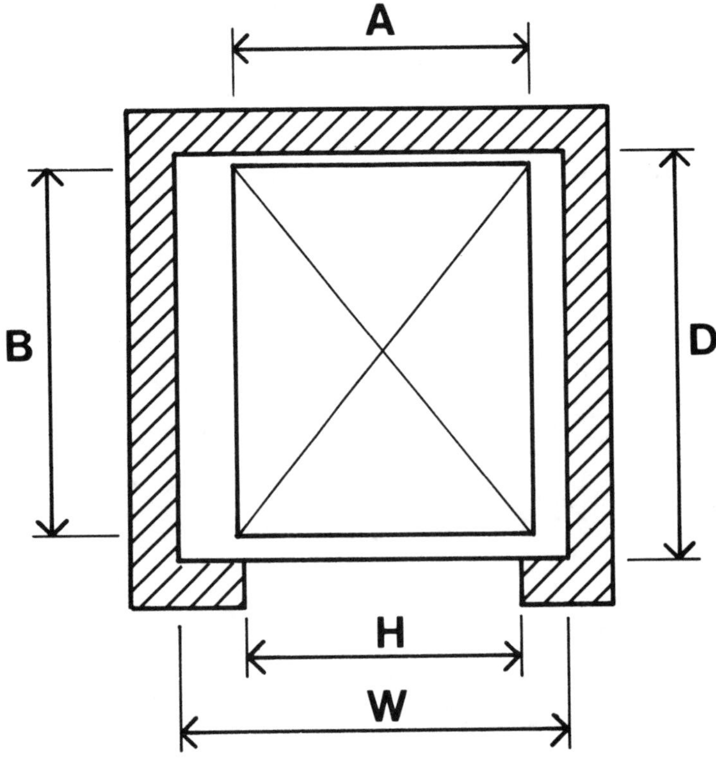

Rated Load (in lbs.)	A	B	W	H
2500	5-0	6-5	7-5	5-0
4000	8-0	9-11	10-7	8-0
6000	10-0	11-5	12-11	10-0
8000	11-8	9-5	14-7	11-8

(Dimensions given are in feet-inches format.)

Reprinted with permission from Vertical Transporation Standards 1983 edition, Copyright 1983, National Elevator Industry, Inc., 630 Third Avenue, New York, NY 10017. This reprinted material is not the complete and official position of the National Elevator Industry, Inc., which is represented only by the standard in its entirety.

DETERMINING ESCALATOR SPACE REQUIREMENTS

During the early design stages of a project, it is necessary to know the space requirements of escalators, if they will be used. Since the angle of escalators is fixed at 30 degrees, it is a simple procedure to determine horizontal space requirements. To do this, use the following method.

1. Decide on the required capacity of the escalator. This is dependent on the number of people you need to move in a given time period, usually per hour or per five-minute peak period.

Table 2H-11
ESCALATOR CAPACITIES

Width:	32 in.		48 in.	
Speed:	90 fpm	120 fpm	90 fpm	120 fpm
Maximum capacity/hour	5000	6700	8000	10700
Normal capacity/hour	3600	4200	5400	6500
Observed capacity/hour	2040	2700	4080	5400
Normal capacity/5 min.	300	350	450	540
Observed capacity/5 min.	170	225	340	450

2. Based on the required capacity, select the speed and width of the escalator. Use Table 2H-11 to do this. Several capacities are given. The maximum is theoretical and seldom reached, so it is better to use the "Normal Capacity" figures.
3. Knowing the tread width gives the approximate overall width of the escalator assembly. For 32 inch tread widths, this is 5 feet 0 inches; for 40 inch tread widths, it is 5 feet 8 inches; and for 48 inch widths, it is 6 feet 4 inches.
4. Determine the total length required. To do this you only need to know, in addition to the speed, the total rise of the escalator and whether the landing will have 1 1/3 or 2 1/3 flat steps. (See Figure 2H-1.) Knowing the rise, landing step type, and speed, look in Table 2H-12 to find the support-to-support dimension. This is the actual required length of the escalator assembly without landing areas. For safety reasons, there needs to be a minimum landing area to avoid bunching of people. This dimension also is given in Table 2H-12.

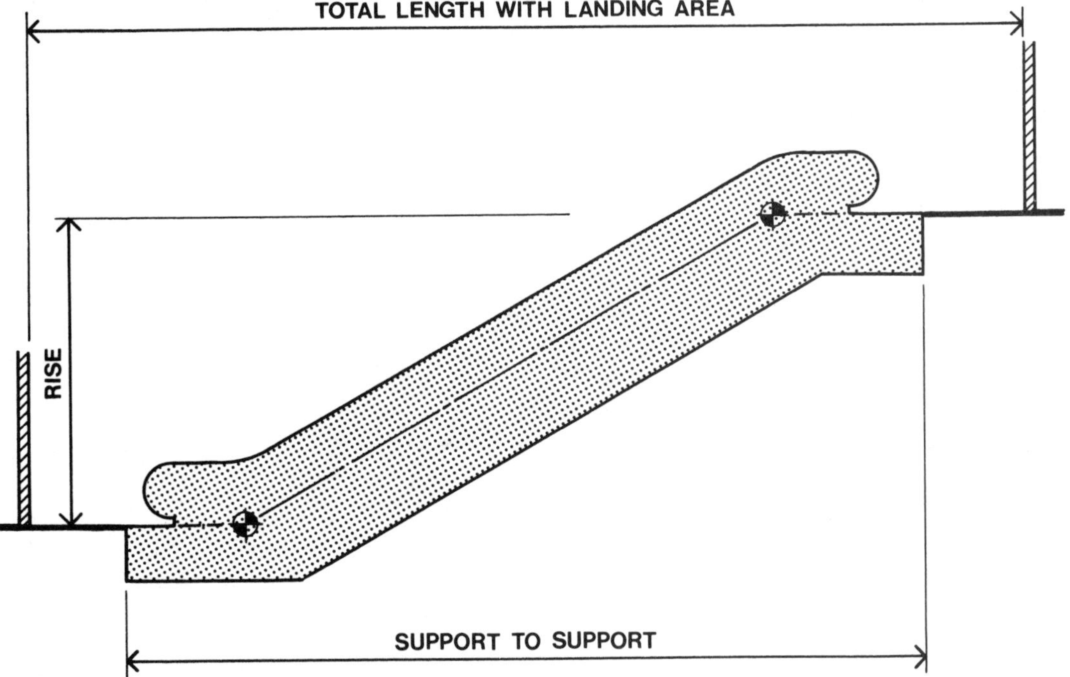

Figure 2H-1: Horizontal Space Requirements for Escalators

Table 2H-12
HORIZONTAL SPACE REQUIREMENTS FOR ESCALATORS
(See also Figure 2H-1.)

Support Edge to Support Edge			Total Length, with Landing Areas			
			1 1/3 flat steps		2 1/3 flat steps	
Rise (in. ft.)	1 1/3 flat steps	2 1/3 flat steps	90 fpm	120 fpm	90 fpm	120 fpm
12	35.6	38.3	48.9	52.9	51.6	55.6
13	37.3	40.0	50.7	54.7	53.3	57.3
14	39.1	41.7	52.4	56.4	55.1	59.1
15	40.8	43.5	54.1	58.1	56.8	60.8
16	42.5	45.2	55.9	59.9	58.5	62.5
17	44.3	46.9	57.6	61.6	60.3	64.3
18	46.0	48.7	59.3	63.3	62.0	66.0
19	47.7	50.4	61.1	65.1	63.7	67.7
20	49.5	52.1	62.8	66.8	65.5	69.5
21	51.2	53.9	64.5	68.5	67.2	71.2
22	52.9	55.6	66.3	70.3	68.9	72.9
23	54.7	57.3	68.0	72.0	70.7	74.7
24	56.4	59.1	69.7	73.7	72.4	76.4
25	58.1	60.8	71.5	75.5	74.1	78.1
26	59.9	62.5	73.2	77.2	75.9	79.9
27	61.6	64.3	74.9	78.9	77.6	81.6
28	63.3	66.0	76.7	80.7	79.3	83.3
29	65.1	67.7	78.4	82.4	81.1	85.1
30	66.8	69.5	80.1	84.1	82.8	86.8
31	68.5	71.2	81.9	85.9	84.5	88.5
32	70.3	72.9	83.6	87.6	86.3	90.3
33	72.0	74.7	85.3	89.3	88.0	92.0
34	73.7	76.4	87.0	91.0	89.7	93.7
35	75.5	78.1	88.8	92.8	91.5	95.5

SECTION 3

Energy Standards

PART 3A

Heat Loss Calculations

COMMON HEAT LOSS TERMS

Conductivity (k): the number of British thermal units per hour that pass through one square foot of homogeneous material one inch thick when the temperature differential is one degree Fahrenheit. The units are Btu/h ft F.

Conductance (C): the number of British thermal units per hour that pass through one square foot of homogeneous material of a given thickness when the temperature differential is one degree Fahrenheit. The units are Btu/hr ft^2 F.

Resistance (R): the number of hours needed for one Btu to pass through a given thickness of a solid when the temperature differential is one degree Fahrenheit.

FORMULA:

$$R = \frac{1}{C}$$

Overall coefficient of heat transmission (U): the overall rate of heat flow through any combination of materials, including air spaces and air layers on the interior and exterior of a building assembly. It is the reciprocal of the sum of all the resistances in the building assembly.

FORMULA:

$$U = \frac{1}{\Sigma R}$$

HEAT LOSS THROUGH THE BUILDING ENVELOPE

Heat loss for an entire assembly of the building envelope is calculated by the following formula.

FORMULA:

$$q = (U \times A) \times \Delta t$$

where:

q = total heat loss through the building assembly in Btu/hr
U = overall coefficient of heat transmission through the building assembly
A = the area in sq. ft. of the building assembly with coefficient of heat transmission, U
Δt = temperature differential between inside and outside design temperatures (outside design temperatures for selected areas are given in Table 3A–22.)

Note: To find the total heat loss, individual heat losses of each assembly (walls, windows, doors, and so on) are calculated and then added together.

Thermal properties of various building materials, surface air films, air spaces, glazing, doors, and other construction components are given in Tables 3A–1 through 3A–8.

Table 3A–9 gives U values resulting from adding insulation to wall assemblies. If you already know the U value for a particular assembly, these tables allow you to determine the new U value without additional calculation.

Formula That Includes Framing Members and Insulated Areas

For building assemblies that include framing members and insulated areas, the average U value can be calculated with the following formula.

FORMULA:

$$U_{ave} = \frac{S}{100}(U_s) + 1 - \frac{S}{100}(U_i)$$

where:

U_{ave} = average U value for building section
U_s = U value for area backed by framing member
U_i = U value for area between framing members
S = percentage of area backed by framing members

HOW TO CALCULATE HEAT LOSS THROUGH INFILTRATION

Calculation for sensible heat loss (or gain) through infiltration is given by the following formula.

FORMULA:

$$q_v = V \times 1.08 \times \Delta t$$

where:

q_v = sensible heat loss (or gain) due to ventilation in Btu/h
V = volume flow rate of outside air, in cu. ft. per min.
Δt = temperature difference between outdoor and indoor air

Table 3A-1
THERMAL PROPERTIES OF TYPICAL BUILDING AND INSULATING MATERIALS—DESIGN VALUES[a]

Description	Density lb/ft³	Conductivity[b] λ Btu•in./h•ft²•F	Conductance (C) Btu/h•ft²•F	Resistance[c] (R) Per inch thickness (1/λ) h•ft²•F/Btu	Resistance[c] (R) For thickness listed (1/C) h•ft²•F/Btu	Specific Heat Btu/lb • deg F
BUILDING BOARD						
Boards, Panels, Subflooring, Sheathing Woodboard Panel Products						
Asbestos-cement board	120	4.0	—	0.25	—	0.24
Asbestos-cement board 0.125 in.	120	—	33.00	—	0.03	
Asbestos-cement board 0.25 in.	120	—	16.50	—	0.06	
Gypsum or plaster board 0.375 in.	50	—	3.10	—	0.32	0.26
Gypsum or plaster board 0.5 in.	50	—	2.22	—	0.45	
Gypsum or plaster board 0.625 in.	50	—	1.78	—	0.56	
Plywood (Douglas Fir)°	34	0.80	—	1.25	—	0.29
Plywood (Douglas Fir) 0.25 in.	34	—	3.20	—	0.31	
Plywood (Douglas Fir) 0.375 in.	34	—	2.13	—	0.47	
Plywood (Douglas Fir) 0.5 in.	34	—	1.60	—	0.62	
Plywood (Douglas Fir) 0.625 in.	34	—	1.29	—	0.77	
Plywood or wood panels 0.75 in.	34	—	1.07	—	0.93	0.29
Vegetable Fiber Board						
Sheathing, regular density 0.5 in.	18	—	0.76	—	1.32	0.31
0.78125 in.	18	—	0.49	—	2.06	
Sheathing intermediate density 0.5 in.	22	—	0.82	—	1.22	0.31
Nail-base sheathing 0.5 in.	25	—	0.88	—	1.14	0.31
Shingle backer 0.375 in.	18	—	1.06	—	0.94	0.31
Shingle backer 0.3125 in.	18	—	1.28	—	0.78	
Sound deadening board 0.5 in.	15	—	0.74	—	1.35	0.30
Tile and lay-in panels, plain or acoustic	18	0.40	—	2.50	—	0.14
0.5 in.	18	—	0.80	—	1.25	
0.75 in.	18	—	0.53	—	1.89	
Laminated paperboard	30	0.50	—	2.00	—	0.33
Homogeneous board from repulped paper	30	0.50	—	2.00	—	0.28
Hardboard						
Medium density	50	0.73	—	1.37	—	0.31
High density, service temp. service underlay	55	0.82	—	1.22	—	0.32
High density, std. tempered	63	1.00	—	1.00	—	0.32
Particleboard						
Low density	37	0.54	—	1.85	—	0.31
Medium density	50	0.94	—	1.06	—	0.31
High density	62.5	1.18	—	0.85	—	0.31
Underlayment 0.625 in.	40	—	1.22	—	0.82	0.29
Wood subfloor 0.75 in.		—	1.06	—	0.94	0.33
BUILDING MEMBRANE						
Vapor—permeable felt	—	—	16.70	—	0.06	
Vapor—seal, 2 layers of mopped 15-lb felt	—	—	8.35	—	0.12	
Vapor—seal, plastic film	—	—	—	—	Negl.	
FINISH FLOORING MATERIALS						
Carpet and fibrous pad	—	—	0.48	—	2.08	0.34
Carpet and rubber pad	—	—	0.81	—	1.23	0.33
Cork tile 0.125 in.	—	—	3.60	—	0.28	0.48
Terrazzo 1 in.	—	—	12.50	—	0.08	0.19
Tile—asphalt, linoleum, vinyl, rubber	—	—	20.00	—	0.05	0.30
vinyl asbestos						0.24
ceramic						0.19
Wood, hardwood finish 0.75 in.	—	—	1.47	—	0.68	
INSULATING MATERIALS						
Blanket and Batt[d]						
Mineral Fiber, fibrous form processed from rock, slag, or glass						
approx.[e] 3–4 in.	0.3-2.0	—	0.091	—	11[d]	
approx.[e] 3.5 in.	0.3-2.0	—	0.077	—	13[d]	
approx.[e] 5.5–6.5 in.	0.3-2.0	—	0.053	—	19[d]	
approx.[e] 6–7.5 in.	0.3-2.0	—	0.045	—	22[d]	
approx.[e] 9–10 in.	0.3-2.0	—	0.033	—	30[d]	
approx.[e] 12–13 in.	0.3-2.0	—	0.026	—	38[d]	

Description	Density lb/ft³	Conductivity[b] λ Btu•in./h•ft²•F	Conductance (C) Btu/h•ft²•F	Resistance[c] (R) Per inch thickness (1/λ) h•ft²•F/Btu	Resistance[c] (R) For thickness listed (1/C) h•ft²•F/Btu	Specific Heat, Btu/lb • deg F
Board and Slabs						
Cellular glass	8.5	0.35	—	*2.86*	—	0.18
Glass fiber, organic bonded	4-9	0.25	—	*4.00*	—	0.23
Expanded perlite, organic bonded	1.0	0.36	—	*2.78*	—	0.30
Expanded rubber (rigid)	4.5	0.22	—	*4.55*	—	0.40
Expanded polystyrene extruded						
Cut cell surface	1.8	0.25	—	*4.00*	—	0.29
Smooth skin surface	1.8-3.5	0.20	—	*5.00*	—	0.29
Expanded polystyrene, molded beads	1.0	0.26	—	*3.85*	—	—
	1.25	0.25	—	*4.00*	—	—
	1.5	0.24	—	*4.17*	—	—
	1.75	0.24	—	*4.17*	—	—
	2.0	0.23	—	*4.35*	—	—
Cellular polyurethane[f] (R-11 exp.)(unfaced)	1.5	0.16	—	*6.25*	—	0.38
Cellular polyisocyanurate[n] (R-11 exp.) (foil faced, glass fiber-reinforced core)	2.0	0.14	—	*7.20*	—	0.22
Nominal 0.5 in.		—	0.278	—	*3.6*	
Nominal 1.0 in.		—	0.139	—	*7.2*	
Nominal 2.0 in.		—	0.069	—	*14.4*	
Mineral fiber with resin binder	15.0	0.29	—	*3.45*	—	0.17
Mineral fiberboard, wet felted						
Core or roof insulation	16-17	0.34	—	*2.94*	—	
Acoustical tile	18.0	0.35	—	*2.86*	—	0.19
Acoustical tile	21.0	0.37	—	*2.70*	—	
Mineral fiberboard, wet molded						
Acoustical tile[h]	23.0	0.42	—	*2.38*	—	0.14
Wood or cane fiberboard						
Acoustical tile[g] 0.5 in.	—	—	0.80	—	*1.25*	0.31
Acoustical tile[g] 0.75 in.	—	—	0.53	—	*1.89*	
Interior finish (plank, tile)	15.0	0.35	—	*2.86*	—	0.32
Cement fiber slabs (shredded wood with Portland cement binder	25-27.0	0.50-0.53	—	*2.0-1.89*	—	—
Cement fiber slabs (shredded wood with magnesia oxysulfide binder)	22.0	0.57	—	*1.75*	—	0.31
LOOSE FILL						
Cellulosic insulation (milled paper or wood pulp)	2.3-3.2	0.27-0.32	—	*3.70-3.13*	—	0.33
Sawdust or shavings	8.0-15.0	0.45	—	*2.22*	—	0.33
Wood fiber, softwoods	2.0-3.5	0.30	—	*3.33*	—	0.33
Perlite, expanded	2.0-4.1	0.27-0.31	—	*3.7-3.3*	—	0.26
	4.1-7.4	0.31-0.36	—	*3.3-2.8*	—	
	7.4-11.0	0.36-0.42	—	*2.8-2.4*	—	
Mineral fiber (rock, slag or glass)						
approx.[e] 3.75-5 in.	0.6-2.0	—	—		11.0	0.17
approx.[e] 6.5-8.75 in.	0.6-2.0	—	—		19.0	
approx.[e] 7.5-10 in.	0.6-2.0	—	—		22.0	
approx.[e] 10.25-13.75 in.	0.6-2.0	—	—		30.0	
Mineral fiber (rock, slag or glass) approx.[e] 3.5 in. (closed sidewall application)	2.0-3.5	—	—	—	12.0-14.0	
Vermiculite, exfoliated	7.0-8.2	0.47	—	*2.13*	—	0.32
	4.0-6.0	0.44	—	*2.27*	—	
FIELD APPLIED[q]						
Polyurethane foam	1.5-2.5	0.16-0.18	—	6.25-5.26	—	
Ureaformaldehyde foam	0.7-1.6	0.22-028	—	3.57-4.55	—	
Spray cellulosic fiber base	2.0-6.0	0.24-0.30	—	3.33-4.17	—	
PLASTERING MATERIALS						
Cement plaster, sand aggregate	116	5.0	—	*0.20*	—	0.20
Sand aggregate 0.375 in.	—	—	13.3	—	*0.08*	0.20
Sand aggregate 0.75 in.	—	—	6.66	—	*0.15*	0.20
Gypsum plaster:						
Lightweight aggregate 0.5 in.	45	—	3.12	—	*0.32*	
Lightweight aggregate 0.625 in.	45	—	2.67	—	*0.39*	
Lightweight agg. on metal lath 0.75 in.	—	—	2.13	—	*0.47*	
Perlite aggregate	45	1.5	—	*0.67*	—	0.32

Table 3A-1 (Continued)

Description	Density lb/ft³	Conductivity[b] λ Btu·in./h·ft²·F	Conductance (C) Btu/h·ft²·F	Resistance[c] (R) Per inch thickness (1/λ) h·ft²·F/Btu	Resistance[c] (R) For thickness listed (1/C) h·ft²·F/Btu	Specific Heat, Btu/lb·deg F
PLASTERING MATERIALS						
Sand aggregate	105	5.6	—	*0.18*	—	0.20
Sand aggregate ... 0.5 in.	105	—	11.10	—	*0.09*	
Sand aggregate ... 0.625 in.	105	—	9.10	—	*0.11*	
Sand aggregate on metal lath ... 0.75 in.	—	—	7.70	—	*0.13*	
Vermiculite aggregate	45	1.7	—	*0.59*	—	
MASONRY MATERIALS						
Concretes						
Cement mortar	116	5.0	—	*0.20*	—	
Gypsum-fiber concrete 87.5% gypsum, 12.5% wood chips	51	1.66	—	*0.60*	—	0.21
Lightweight aggregates including expanded shale, clay or slate; expanded slags; cinders; pumice; vermiculite; also cellular concretes	120	5.2	—	*0.19*	—	
	100	3.6	—	*0.28*	—	
	80	2.5	—	*0.40*	—	
	60	1.7	—	*0.59*	—	
	40	1.15	—	*0.86*	—	
	30	0.90	—	*1.11*	—	
	20	0.70	—	*1.43*	—	
Perlite, expanded	40	0.93	—	*1.08*	—	
	30	0.71	—	*1.41*	—	
	20	0.50	—	*2.00*	—	0.32
Sand and gravel or stone aggregate (oven dried)	140	9.0	—	*0.11*	—	0.22
Sand and gravel or stone aggregate (not dried)	140	12.0	—	*0.08*	—	
Stucco	116	5.0	—	*0.20*	—	
MASONRY UNITS						
Brick, common[i]	120	5.0	—	*0.20*	—	0.19
Brick, face[i]	130	9.0	—	*0.11*	—	
Clay tile, hollow:						
1 cell deep ... 3 in.	—	—	1.25	—	*0.80*	0.21
1 cell deep ... 4 in.	—	—	0.90	—	*1.11*	
2 cells deep ... 6 in.	—	—	0.66	—	*1.52*	
2 cells deep ... 8 in.	—	—	0.54	—	*1.85*	
2 cells deep ... 10 in.	—	—	0.45	—	*2.22*	
3 cells deep ... 12 in.	—	—	0.40	—	*2.50*	
Concrete blocks, three oval core:						
Sand and gravel aggregate ... 4 in.	—	—	1.40	—	*0.71*	0.22
... 8 in.	—	—	0.90	—	*1.11*	
... 12 in.	—	—	0.78	—	*1.28*	
Cinder aggregate ... 3 in.	—	—	1.16	—	*0.86*	0.21
... 4 in.	—	—	0.90	—	*1.11*	
... 8 in.	—	—	0.58	—	*1.72*	
... 12 in.	—	—	0.53	—	*1.89*	
Lightweight aggregate ... 3 in.	—	—	0.79	—	*1.27*	0.21
(expanded shale, clay, slate ... 4 in.	—	—	0.67	—	*1.50*	
or slag; pumice): ... 8 in.	—	—	0.50	—	*2.00*	
... 12 in.	—	—	0.44	—	*2.27*	
Concrete blocks, rectangular core.[j,k]						
Sand and gravel aggregate						
2 core, 8 in. 36 lb.	—	—	0.96	—	*1.04*	0.22
Same with filled cores[l]	—	—	0.52	—	*1.93*	0.22
Lightweight aggregate (expanded shale, clay, slate or slag, pumice):						
3 core, 6 in. 19 lb.	—	—	0.61	—	*1.65*	0.21
Same with filled cores[l]	—	—	0.33	—	*2.99*	
2 core, 8 in. 24 lb.	—	—	0.46	—	*2.18*	
Same with filled cores[l]	—	—	0.20	—	*5.03*	
3 core, 12 in. 38 lb.	—	—	0.40	—	*2.48*	
Same with filled cores[l]	—	—	0.17	—	*5.82*	
Stone, lime or sand	—	12.50	—	*0.08*	—	0.19
Gypsum partition tile:						
3 • 12 • 30 in. solid	—	—	0.79	—	*1.26*	0.19
3 • 12 • 30 in. 4-cell	—	—	0.74	—	*1.35*	
4 • 12 • 30 in. 3-cell	—	—	0.60	—	*1.67*	

Description	Density lb/ft³	Conductivity[b] λ Btu•in./h•ft²•F	Conductance (C) Btu/h•ft²•F	Resistance[c] (R) Per inch thickness (1/λ) h•ft²•F/Btu	For thickness listed (1/C) h•ft²•F/Btu	Specific Heat, Btu/lb•deg F
ROOFING[h]						
Asbestos-cement shingles	120	—	4.76	—	*0.21*	0.24
Asphalt roll roofing	70	—	6.50	—	*0.15*	0.36
Asphalt shingles	70	—	2.27	—	*0.44*	0.30
Built-up roofing ... 0.375 in.	70	—	3.00	—	*0.33*	0.35
Slate ... 0.5 in.	—	—	20.00	—	*0.05*	0.30
Wood shingles, plain and plastic film faced	—	—	1.06	—	*0.94*	0.31
SIDING MATERIALS (on flat surface)						
Shingles						
Asbestos-cement	120	—	4.75	—	*0.21*	
Wood, 16 in., 7.5 exposure	—	—	1.15	—	*0.87*	0.31
Wood, double, 16-in., 12-in. exposure	—	—	0.84	—	*1.19*	0.28
Wood, plus insul. backer board, 0.3125 in.	—	—	0.71	—	*1.40*	0.31
Siding						
Asbestos-cement, 0.25 in., lapped	—	—	4.76	—	*0.21*	0.24
Asphalt roll siding	—	—	6.50	—	*0.15*	0.35
Asphalt insulating siding (0.5 in. bed.)	—	—	0.69	—	*1.46*	0.35
Hardboard siding, 0.4375 in.	40	1.49	—	*0.67*		0.28
Wood, drop, 1 • 8 in.	—	—	1.27	—	*0.79*	0.28
Wood, bevel, 0.5 • 8 in., lapped	—	—	1.23	—	*0.81*	0.28
Wood, bevel, 0.75 • 10 in., lapped	—	—	0.95	—	*1.05*	0.28
Wood, plywood, 0.375 in., lapped	—	—	1.59	—	*0.59*	0.29
Aluminum or Steel[m], over sheathing						
Hollow-backed	—	—	1.61	—	*0.61*	0.29
Insulating-board backed nominal 0.375 in.	—	—	0.55	—	*1.82*	0.32
Insulating-board backed nominal 0.375 in., foil backed			0.34		*2.96*	
Architectural glass	—	—	10.00	—	*0.10*	0.20
WOODS (12% Moisture Content)[o,p]						
Hardwoods						0.39
Oak	41.2-46.8	1.12-1.25	—	*0.89-0.80*	—	
Birch	42.6-45.4	1.16-1.22	—	*0.87-0.82*	—	
Maple	39.8-44.0	1.09-1.19	—	*0.94-0.88*	—	
Ash	38.4-41.9	1.06-1.14	—	*0.94-0.88*	—	
Softwoods						0.39
Southern Pine	35.6-41.2	1.00-1.12	—	*1.00-0.89*	—	
Douglas Fir-Larch	33.5-36.3	0.95-1.01	—	*1.06-0.99*	—	
Southern Cypress	31.4-32.1	0.90-0.92	—	*1.11-1.09*	—	
Hem-Fir, Spruce-Pine-Fir	24.5-31.4	0.74-0.90	—	*1.35-1.11*	—	
West Coast Woods, Cedars	21.7-31.4	0.68-0.90	—	*1.48-1.11*	—	
California Redwood	24.5-28.0	0.74-0.82	—	*1.35-1.22*	—	

Notes for Table 3A

[a]Except where otherwise noted, all values are for a mean temperature of 75 F. Representative values for dry materials, selected by ASHRAE TC 4.4, are intended as design (not specification) values for materials in normal use. Insulation materials in actual service may have thermal values that vary from design values depending on their in-situ properties (e.g., density and moisture content). For properties of a particular product, use the value supplied by the manufacturer or by unbiased tests.

[b]To obtain thermal conductivities in But/h•ft²•F, divide the λ value by 12 in./ft.

[c]Resistance values are the reciprocals of C before rounding off C to two decimal places.

[d]Does not include paper backing and facing, if any. Where insulation forms a boundary (reflective or otherwise) of an air space, see Tables 2A and 2B for the insulating value of an air space with the appropriate effective emittance and temperature conditions of the space.

[e]Conductivity varies with fiber diameter. (See Chapter 20, Thermal Conductivity section.) Insulation is produced in different densities, therefore, there is a wide variation in thickness for the same R-value among manufacturers. No effort should be made to relate any specific R-value to any specific density or thickness.

[f]Values are for aged, unfaced, board stock. For change in conductivity with age of expanded urethane, see Chapter 20, Factors Affecting Thermal Conductivity.

[g]Insulating values of acoustical tile vary, depending on density of the board and on type, size and depth of perforations.

[h]ASTM C 855-77 recognizes the specification of roof insulation on the basis of the C-values shown. Roof insulation is made in thickness to meet these values.

[i]Face brick and common brick do not always have these specific densities. When density differs from that shown, there will be a change in thermal conductivity.

[j]At 45 F mean temperature. Data on rectangular core concrete blocks differ from the above data on oval core blocks, due to core configuration, different mean temperatures, and possibly differences in unit weights. Weight data on the oval core blocks tested are not available.

[k]Weights of units approximately 7.625 in. high and 15.75 in. long. These weights are given as a means of describing the blocks tested, but conductance values are all for 1 ft² of area.

[l]Vermiculite, perlite, or mineral wool insulation. Where insulation is used, vapor barriers or other precautions must be considered to keep insulation dry.

[m]Values for metal siding applied over flat surfaces vary widely, depending on amount of ventilation of air space beneath the siding; whether air space is reflective or nonreflective; and on thickness, type, and application of insulating backing-board used. Values given are averages for use as design guides, and were obtained from several guarded hotbox tests (ASTM C236) or calibrated hotbox (ASTM C 976) on hollow-backed types and types made using backing-boards of wood fiber, foamed plastic, and glass fiber. Departures of±50% or more from the values given may occur.

[n]Time-aged values for board stock with gas-barrier quality (0.001 in. thickness or greater) aluminum foil facers on tow major surfaces.

[o]See Ref. 5.

[p]See Ref. 6, 7, 8 and 9. The conductivity values listed are for heat transfer across the grain. The thermal conductivity of wood varies linearly with the density and the density ranges listed are those normally found for the wood species given. If the density of the wood species is not known, use the mean conductivity value.

Source: 1985 Handbook of Fundamentals, *ASHRAE*.
Reproduced with permission.

Table 3A-2
SURFACE CONDUCTANCES AND RESISTANCES FOR AIR[a,b,c]

Position of Surface	Direction of Heat Flow	Surface Emittance: Non-reflective ε = 0.90		Reflective ε = 0.20		Reflective ε = 0.05	
		h_i	R	h_i	R	h_i	R
STILL AIR							
Horizontal	Upward	1.63	*0.61*	0.91	*1.10*	0.76	*1.32*
Sloping—45 deg	Upward	1.60	*0.62*	0.88	*1.14*	0.73	*1.37*
Vertical........	Horizontal	1.46	*0.68*	0.74	*1.35*	0.59	*1.70*
Sloping—45 deg	Downward	1.32	*0.76*	0.60	*1.67*	0.45	*2.22*
Horizontal	Downward	1.08	*0.92*	0.37	*2.70*	0.22	*4.55*
MOVING AIR		h_o	R	h_o	R	h_o	R
(Any Position)							
15-mph Wind (for winter)	Any	6.00	0.17				
7.5-mph Wind (for summer)	Any	4.00	0.25				

[a]No surface has both an air space resistance value and a surface resistance value. No air space value exists for any surface facing an air space of less than 0.5 in.

[b]For ventilated attics or spaces above ceilings under summer conditions (heat flow down) see Table 3-A-6

[c]Conductances are for surfaces of the stated emittance facing virtual blackbody surroundings at the same temperature as the ambient air. Values are based on a surface-air temperature difference of 10 deg F and for surface temperature of 70 F.

Source: 1985 Handbook of Fundamentals, *ASHRAE. Reproduced with permission.*

Table 3A-3
THERMAL RESISTANCES OF PLANE[a] AIR SPACES[b,c]

Position of Air Space	Direction of Heat Flow	Air Space Mean Temp,[d] (F)	Air Space Temp Diff,[d] (deg F)	0.5-in. Air Space[c] Value of $E^{d,e}$ 0.03	0.05	0.2	0.5	0.82	0.75-in. Air Space[c] Value of $E^{d,e}$ 0.03	0.05	0.2	0.5	0.82
Horiz.	Up ↑	90	10	2.13	2.03	1.51	0.99	0.73	2.34	2.22	1.61	1.04	0.75
		50	30	1.62	1.57	1.29	0.96	0.75	1.71	1.66	1.35	0.99	0.77
		50	10	2.13	2.05	1.60	1.11	0.84	2.30	2.21	1.70	1.16	0.87
		0	20	1.73	1.70	1.45	1.12	0.91	1.83	1.79	1.52	1.16	0.93
		0	10	2.10	2.04	1.70	1.27	1.00	2.23	2.16	1.78	1.31	1.02
		−50	20	1.69	1.66	1.49	1.23	1.04	1.77	1.74	1.55	1.27	1.07
		−50	10	2.04	2.00	1.75	1.40	1.16	2.16	2.11	1.84	1.46	1.20
45° Slope	Up ↗	90	10	2.44	2.31	1.65	1.06	0.76	2.96	2.78	1.88	1.15	0.81
		50	30	2.06	1.98	1.56	1.10	0.83	1.99	1.92	1.52	1.08	0.82
		50	10	2.55	2.44	1.83	1.22	0.90	2.90	2.75	2.00	1.29	0.94
		0	20	2.20	2.14	1.76	1.30	1.02	2.13	2.07	1.72	1.28	1.00
		0	10	2.63	2.54	2.03	1.44	1.10	2.72	2.62	2.08	1.47	1.12
		−50	20	2.08	2.04	1.78	1.42	1.17	2.05	2.01	1.76	1.41	1.16
		−50	10	2.62	2.56	2.17	1.66	1.33	2.53	2.47	2.10	1.62	1.30
Vertical	Horiz. →	90	10	2.47	2.34	1.67	1.06	0.77	3.50	3.24	2.08	1.22	0.84
		50	30	2.57	2.46	1.84	1.23	0.90	2.91	2.77	2.01	1.30	0.94
		50	10	2.66	2.54	1.88	1.24	0.91	3.70	3.46	2.35	1.43	1.01
		0	20	2.82	2.72	2.14	1.50	1.13	3.14	3.02	2.32	1.58	1.18
		0	10	2.93	2.82	2.20	1.53	1.15	3.77	3.59	2.64	1.73	1.26
		−50	20	2.90	2.82	2.35	1.76	1.39	2.90	2.83	2.36	1.77	1.39
		−50	10	3.20	3.10	2.54	1.87	1.46	3.72	3.60	2.87	2.04	1.56
45° Slope	Down ↘	90	10	2.48	2.34	1.67	1.06	0.77	3.53	3.27	2.10	1.22	0.84
		50	30	2.64	2.52	1.87	1.24	0.91	3.43	3.23	2.24	1.39	0.99
		50	10	2.67	2.55	1.89	1.25	0.92	3.81	3.57	2.40	1.45	1.02
		0	20	2.91	2.80	2.19	1.52	1.15	3.75	3.57	2.63	1.72	1.26
		0	10	2.94	2.83	2.21	1.53	1.15	4.12	3.91	2.81	1.80	1.30
		−50	20	3.16	3.07	2.52	1.86	1.45	3.78	3.65	2.90	2.05	1.57
		−50	10	3.26	3.16	2.58	1.89	1.47	4.35	4.18	3.22	2.21	1.66
Horiz.	Down ↓	90	10	2.48	2.34	1.67	1.06	0.77	3.55	3.29	2.10	1.22	0.85
		50	30	2.66	2.54	1.88	1.24	0.91	3.77	3.52	2.38	1.44	1.02
		50	10	2.67	2.55	1.89	1.25	0.92	3.84	3.59	2.41	1.45	1.02
		0	20	2.94	2.83	2.20	1.53	1.15	4.18	3.96	2.83	1.81	1.30
		0	10	2.96	2.85	2.22	1.53	1.16	4.25	4.02	2.87	1.82	1.31
		−50	20	3.25	3.15	2.58	1.89	1.47	4.60	4.41	3.36	2.28	1.69
		−50	10	3.28	3.18	2.60	1.90	1.47	4.71	4.51	3.42	2.30	1.71

Position of Air Space	Direction of Heat Flow	Air Space Mean Temp,[d] (F)	Temp Diff,[d] (deg F)	1.5-in. Air Space[c] Value of $E^{d,e}$ 0.03	0.05	0.2	0.5	0.82	3.5-in. Air Space[c] Value of $E^{d,e}$ 0.03	0.05	0.2	0.5	0.82
		90	10	2.55	2.41	1.71	1.08	0.77	2.84	2.66	1.83	1.13	0.80
		50	30	1.87	1.81	1.45	1.04	0.80	2.09	2.01	1.58	1.10	0.84
		50	10	2.50	2.40	1.81	1.21	0.89	2.80	2.66	1.95	1.28	0.93
Horiz	Up ↑	0	20	2.01	1.95	1.63	1.23	0.97	2.25	2.18	1.79	1.32	1.03
		0	10	2.43	2.35	1.90	1.38	1.06	2.71	2.62	2.07	1.47	1.12
		−50	20	1.94	1.91	1.68	1.36	1.13	2.19	2.14	1.86	1.47	1.20
		−50	10	2.37	2.31	1.99	1.55	1.26	2.65	2.58	2.18	1.67	1.33
		90	10	2.92	2.73	1.86	1.14	0.80	3.18	2.96	1.97	1.18	0.82
		50	30	2.14	2.06	1.61	1.12	0.84	2.26	2.17	1.67	1.15	0.86
45° Slope	Up ↗	50	10	2.88	2.74	1.99	1.29	0.94	3.12	2.95	2.10	1.34	0.96
		0	20	2.30	2.23	1.82	1.34	1.04	2.42	2.35	1.90	1.38	1.06
		0	10	2.79	2.69	2.12	1.49	1.13	2.98	2.87	2.23	1.54	1.16
		−50	20	2.22	2.17	1.88	1.49	1.21	2.34	2.29	1.97	1.54	1.25
		−50	10	2.71	2.64	2.23	1.69	1.35	2.87	2.79	2.33	1.75	1.39
		90	10	3.99	3.66	2.25	1.27	0.87	3.69	3.40	2.15	1.24	0.85
		50	30	2.58	2.46	1.84	1.23	0.90	2.67	2.55	1.89	1.25	0.91
		50	10	3.79	3.55	2.39	1.45	1.02	3.63	3.40	2.32	1.42	1.01
Vertical	Horiz. →	0	20	2.76	2.66	2.10	1.48	1.12	2.88	2.78	2.17	1.51	1.14
		0	10	3.51	3.35	2.51	1.67	1.23	3.49	3.33	2.50	1.67	1.23
		−50	20	2.64	2.58	2.18	1.66	1.33	2.82	2.75	2.30	1.73	1.37
		−50	10	3.31	3.21	2.62	1.91	1.48	3.40	3.30	2.67	1.94	1.50
		90	10	5.07	4.55	2.56	1.36	0.91	4.81	4.33	2.49	1.34	0.90
		50	30	3.58	3.36	2.31	1.42	1.00	3.51	3.30	2.28	1.40	1.00
45° Slope	Down ↘	50	10	5.10	4.66	2.85	1.60	1.09	4.74	4.36	2.73	1.57	1.08
		0	20	3.85	3.66	2.68	1.74	1.27	3.81	3.63	2.66	1.74	1.27
		0	10	4.92	4.62	3.16	1.94	1.37	4.59	4.32	3.02	1.88	1.34
		−50	20	3.62	3.50	2.80	2.01	1.54	3.77	3.64	2.90	2.05	1.57
		−50	10	4.67	4.47	3.40	2.29	1.70	4.50	4.32	3.31	2.25	1.68
		90	10	6.09	5.35	2.79	1.43	0.94	10.07	8.19	3.41	1.57	1.00
		50	30	6.27	5.63	3.18	1.70	1.14	9.60	8.17	3.86	1.88	1.22
		50	10	6.61	5.90	3.27	1.73	1.15	11.15	9.27	4.09	1.93	1.24
Horiz.	Down ↓	0	20	7.03	6.43	3.91	2.19	1.49	10.90	9.52	4.87	2.47	1.62
		0	10	7.31	6.66	4.00	2.22	1.51	11.97	10.32	5.08	2.52	1.64
		−50	20	7.73	7.20	4.77	2.85	1.99	11.64	10.49	6.02	3.25	2.18
		−50	10	8.09	7.52	4.91	2.89	2.01	12.98	11.56	6.36	3.34	2.22

[a] See Chapter 20, section on Factors Affecting Heat Transfer across Air Spaces. Thermal resistance values were determined from the relation, $R = 1/C$, where $C = h_c + Eh_r$; h_c is the conduction-convection coefficient, Eh_r is the radiation coefficient $\cong 0.00686E\,[(t_m + 460)/100]^3$, and t_m is the mean temperature of the air space. Values for h_c were determined from research data; see Ref. 4. For interpolation from Table 2A and 2B to air spaces less than 0.5 in. (as in insulating window glass), assume

$$h_c = 0.159\,(1 + 0.0016\,t_m)/l$$

where l is the air space thickness in in., and h_c is heat transfer through air conduction only.

[b] Values are based on data presented in Ref. 4; see also Chapter 3, Tables 3 and 4, and Chapter 39. Values apply for ideal conditions, i.e., air spaces of uniform thickness bounded by plane, smooth, parallel surfaces with no leakage of air to or from the space. When accurate values are required, use overall U-factors determined through calibrated hot box (ASTM C-976) or guarded hot box (ASTM C-236) testing. Thermal resistance values for multiple air spaces must be based on careful estimates of mean temperature differences for each air space.

[c] A single resistance value cannot account for multiple air spaces; each air space requies a separate resistance calculation that applies only for the established boundary conditions. Resistances of horizontal spaces with heat flow downward are substantially independent of temperature difference.

[d] Interpolation is permissible for other values of mean temperature, temperature difference and effective emittance E. Interpolation and moderate extrapolation for air spaces greater than 3.5 in. are also permissible.

[e] Effective emittance of space E is given by $1/E = 1/e_1 + 1/e_2 - 1$, where e_1 and e_2 are the emittances of the surfaces of the air space. See Table 2B.

TABLE 2B Reflectivity and Emittance Values of Various Surfaces and Effective Emittances of Air Spaces

Surface	Reflectivity in Percent	Average *Emittance* ε	Effective *Emittance E* of Air Space: One surface emittance ε; the other 0.90	Both surfaces emittances ε
Aluminum foil, bright	92 to 97	0.05	0.05	0.03
Aluminum sheet	80 to 95	0.12	0.12	0.06
Aluminum coated paper, polished	75 to 84	0.20	0.20	0.11
Steel, galvanized, bright. . .	70 to 80	0.25	0.24	0.15
Aluminum paint	30 to 70	0.50	0.47	0.35
Building materials: wood, paper, masonry, nonmetallic paints	5 to 15	0.90	0.82	0.82
Regular glass	5 to 15	0.84	0.77	0.72

Source: 1985 Handbook of Fundamentals, *ASHRAE*. *Reproduced with permission.*

Table 3A-4
COEFFICIENTS FOR TRANSMISSION (U) FOR GLAZING

Overall Coefficients of Heat Transmission (*U*-Factor) of Windows, Sliding Patio Doors, and Skylights for Use in Peak Load Determination and Mechanical Equipment Sizing Only and Not in Any Analysis of Annual Energy Usage, Btu/h·ft²·F

Part A. Exterior[a] Vertical Panels

	No Storm Sash				Glass Outdoor Storm Sash 1-in. Air Space[b] Added to Described Product			
	No Shade		Indoor Shade		No Shade		Indoor Shade	
	Winter*	Summer**	Winter*	Summer**	Winter*	Summer**	Winter*	Summer**
Flat Glass[c]								
Single Glass, Clear	1.10	1.04	0.83	0.81	0.50	0.50	0.44	0.49
Single Glass, Low Emittance Coating[d]								
$e = 0.60$	1.02	1.00	0.76	0.80	0.47	0.60	0.39	0.55
$e = 0.40$	0.91	0.90	0.68	0.70	0.44	0.60	0.37	0.55
$e = 0.20$	0.79	0.75	0.59	0.55	0.40	0.50	0.33	0.45
Insulating Glass, Double[e]								
3/16-in. air space[f]	0.62	0.65	0.52	0.58	0.37	0.40	0.29	0.37
1/4-in. air space[f]	0.58	0.61	0.48	0.55	0.35	0.39	0.28	0.36
1/2-in. air space[g]	0.49	0.56	0.42	0.52	0.32	0.39	0.25	0.37
1/2-in. air space low emittance coating[h]								
$e = 0.60$	0.43	0.53	0.38	0.49	0.41	0.30	0.24	0.37
$e = 0.40$	0.38	0.47	0.36	0.43	0.27	0.39	0.22	0.35
$e = 0.20$	0.32	0.39	0.30	0.36	0.24	0.33	0.20	0.30
Insulating Glass, Triple[e]								
1/4-in. air space[f]	0.39	0.44	0.31	0.40	0.27	0.32	0.22	0.30
1/2-in. air space[i]	0.31	0.39	0.26	0.36	0.23	0.31	0.19	0.29

	Glass Indoor Storm Sash 1-in. Air Space[b] Added to Described Product				Acrylic Indoor Storm Sash 1-in. Air Space[b] Added to Described Product			
	No Shade		Indoor Shade		No Shade		Indoor Shade	
	Winter*	Summer**	Winter*	Summer**	Winter*	Summer**	Winter*	Summer**
Flat Glass[c]								
Single Glass, Clear	0.50	0.50	0.44	0.49	0.48	0.48	0.42	0.47
Single Glass, Low Emittance Coating[d]								
$e = 0.60$	0.47	0.50	0.39	0.45	0.45	0.50	0.38	0.45
$e = 0.40$	0.42	0.45	0.36	0.40	0.41	0.45	0.35	0.40
$e = 0.20$	0.37	0.35	0.32	0.30	0.36	0.35	0.31	0.30
Insulating Glass, Double[e]								
3/16-in. air space[f]	0.37	0.40	0.29	0.36	0.35	0.39	0.28	0.35
1/4-in. air space[f]	0.35	0.39	0.28	0.36	0.34	0.38	0.27	0.34
1/2-in. air space[g]	0.31	0.38	0.25	0.35	0.30	0.37	0.24	0.33
1/2-in. air space, Low emittance coating[h]								
$e = 0.60$	0.29	0.37	0.24	0.33	0.28	0.35	0.23	0.31
$e = 0.40$	0.27	0.33	0.22	0.30	0.26	0.32	0.22	0.29
$e = 0.20$	0.25	0.29	0.20	0.26	0.24	0.28	0.20	0.25
Insulating Glass, Triple[e]								
1/4-in. air space[f]	0.27	0.32	0.22	0.30	0.26	0.31	0.22	0.29
1/2-in. air space[i]	0.23	0.30	0.19	0.28	0.22	0.29	0.18	0.28

Part B. Exterior[a] Horizontal Panels (Skylights)

Description	Winter[j]	Summer[k]
Flat Glass[g]		
Single Glass	1.23	0.83
Insulating Glass; Double[e]		
3/16-in. air space[f]	0.70	0.57
1/4-in. air space[f]	0.65	0.54
1/2-in. air space[g]	0.59	0.49
1/2-in. air space, low emittance coating[h]		
$e = 0.60$	0.56	0.46
$e = 0.40$	0.52	0.42
$e = 0.20$	0.48	0.36
Plastic Domes[l]		
Single Walled	1.15	0.80
Double Walled	0.70	0.46

Part C. Adjustment Factors for Various Window, Sliding Patio Door, and Skylight Types (Multiply *U*-Factors in Parts A and B by These Factors)

Product Description	Single Glass	Double Insulating Glass	Triple Insulating Glass	Storm Sash Applied Over Single Glass	Storm Sash Applied Over Double or Triple Insulating Glass
All Glass[m]	1.00	1.00	1.00	1.00	1.00
Wood Frame	0.85 - 0.95	0.90 - 1.00	0.95 - 1.00	0.90 - 1.00	0.95 - 1.00
Metal Frame	1.10 - 1.00	1.30 - 1.20	1.50 - 1.30	1.40 - 1.20	1.50 - 1.30
Thermally-Improved Metal Frame	0.90 - 1.00	0.95 - 1.15	1.00 - 1.25	0.90 - 1.20	0.95 - 1.25

[a] See Part C for appropriate adjustments for various windows and sliding patio doors. Window manufacturers should be consulted for specific data.
[b] 1/8-in. glass or Acrylic as noted, 1 to 4-in. air space.
[c] Hemispherical emittance of uncoated glass surface = 0.84, coated glass surface as specified.
[d] Coating on second surface, i.e., room side of glass.
[e] Double and triple refer to number of lights of glass.
[f] 1/8-in. glass.
[g] 1/4-in. glass.
[h] Coating on either glass surface 2 or 3 for winter, and for surface 2 for summer *U*-factors.
[i] Window design 1/4-in. glass, 1/8-in. glass and 1/4-in. glass.
[j] For heat flow up.
[k] For heat flow down.
[l] Based on area of opening, not total surface area.
[m] Refers to windows with negligible opaque areas.
*15 mph outdoor air velocity; 0 F outdoor air; 70 F inside air temperature, natural convection.
**7.5 mph outdoor air velocity; 89 F outdoor air; 75 F inside air, natural convection; solar radiation 248.3 Btu/h·ft^2.

The reciprocal of the above *U*-factors is the thermal resistance, *R*, for each type of glazing. If tightly drawn drapes (heavy close weave), closed Venetian blinds or closely fitted roller shades are used internally, the additional *R* is approximately 0.29 ft^2·h·F/Btu. If miniature louvered solar screens are used in close proximity to the outer fenestration surface, the additional *R* is approximately 0.24 ft^2·h·F/Btu.

Example: Find the winter *U*-factor for uncoated double insulating glass 0.5-in. air space when (1) external miniature louvered sun screens are used, and (2) tightly woven drapes are added.

Solution: Winter *R* for 0.5-in. air space double insulating glass = 1/.49 = 2.04, added resistance for the miniature louvered sun screen = 0.24; so total *R* = 2.28 and *U*-factor = 0.44 Btu/h·ft^2·F. Adding the tightly woven drape *R* = 0.29, total *R* = 2.57, so *U* = 0.39 Btu/h·ft^2·F.

Source: 1985 Handbook of Fundamentals, *ASHRAE. Reproduced with permission.*

Table 3A-5
COEFFICIENTS OF TRANSMISSION (U) FOR WOOD AND STEEL DOORS

Coefficients of Transmission (*U*) for Wood Doors[a], Btu/h·ft^2·F

Door Thickness, in.[d]	Description	Winter[b] No Storm Door	Winter[b] Wood Storm Door[e]	Winter[b] Metal Storm Door[f]	Summer[c] No Storm Door
1-3/8	Hollow core flush door	0.47	0.30	0.32	0.45
1-3/8	Solid core flush door	0.39	0.26	0.28	0.38
1-3/8	Panel door with 7/16-in. panels	0.57	0.33	0.37	0.54
1-3/4	Hollow core flush door	0.46	0.29	0.32	0.44
	with single glazing[g]	0.56	0.33	0.36	0.54
1-3/4	Solid core flush door	0.33	0.28	0.25	0.32
	With single glazing[g]	0.46	0.29	0.32	0.44
	With insulating glass[g]	0.37	0.25	0.27	0.36
1-3/4	Panel door with 7/16-in. panels[h]	0.54	0.32	0.36	0.52
	With single glazing[i]	0.67	0.36	0.41	0.63
	With insulating glass[i]	0.50	0.31	0.34	0.48
1-3/4	Panel door with 1-1/8-in. panels[h]	0.39	0.26	0.28	0.38
	With single glazing[i]	0.61	0.34	0.38	0.58
	With insulating glass[i]	0.44	0.28	0.31	0.42
2-1/4	Solid core flush door	0.27	0.20	0.21	0.26
	With single glazing[g]	0.41	0.27	0.29	0.40
	With insulating glass[g]	0.33	0.23	0.25	0.32

Coefficients of Transmission (*U*) for Steel Doors[a], Btu/h·ft^2·F

Door Thickness, in.[d]	Description	Winter[b] No Storm Door	Winter[b] Wood Storm Door[e]	Winter[b] Metal Storm Door[f]	Summer[c] No Storm Door
1-3/4	Solid urethane foam core with thermal break[11]	0.19	0.16	0.17	0.18
1-3/4	Solid urethane foam core without thermal break[12]	0.40	—	—	0.39

[a] Values for doors are based on nominal 3'8" by 6'8" door size. Interpolation and moderate extrapolation are permitted for glazing areas and door thicknesses other than those specified.
[b] 15 mph outdoor air velocity; 0 F outdoor air; 70 F inside air temp, natural convection.
[c] 7.5 mph outdoor air velocity; 89 F outdoor air; 75 F inside air temp., natural convection.
[d] Nominal thickness.
[e] Values for wood storm door are approximately 50% glass area.
[f] Values for metal storm door are for any percent of glass area.
[g] 17% exposed glass area; insulating glass contains 0.25 inch air space.
[h] 55% panel area.
[i] 33% glass area; 22% panel area; insulating glass contains 0.25 inch air space.

Source: 1985 Handbook of Fundamentals, *ASHRAE. Reproduced with permission.*

Table 3A-6
EFFECTIVE RESISTANCE OF VENTILATED ATTICS

PART A. NONREFLECTIVE SURFACES

Ventilation Air Temp., F	Sol-Air[e] Temp., F	No Ventilation		Natural Ventilation		Power Ventilation[b]					
		Ventilation Rate, cfm/ft²									
		0		0.1[c]		0.5		1.0		1.5	
		1/U Ceiling Resistance, R[d]									
		10	20	10	20	10	20	10	20	10	20
	120	1.9	1.9	2.8	3.4	6.3	9.3	9.6	16	11	20
80	140	1.9	1.9	2.8	3.5	6.5	10	9.8	17	12	21
	160	1.9	1.9	2.8	3.6	6.7	11	10	18	13	22
	120	1.9	1.9	2.5	2.8	4.6	6.7	6.1	10	6.9	13
90	140	1.9	1.9	2.6	3.1	5.2	7.9	7.6	12	8.6	15
	160	1.9	1.9	2.7	3.4	5.8	9.0	8.5	14	10	17
	120	1.9	1.9	2.2	2.3	3.3	4.4	4.0	6.0	4.1	6.9
100	140	1.9	1.9	2.4	2.7	4.2	6.1	5.8	8.7	6.5	10
	160	1.9	1.9	2.6	3.2	5.0	7.6	7.2	11	8.3	13
PART B. REFLECTIVE SURFACES[f]											
	120	6.5	6.5	8.1	8.8	13	17	17	25	19	30
80	140	6.5	6.5	8.2	9.0	14	18	18	26	20	31
	160	6.5	6.5	8.3	9.2	15	18	19	27	21	32
	120	6.5	6.5	7.5	8.0	10	13	12	17	13	19
90	140	6.5	6.5	7.7	8.3	12	15	14	20	16	22
	160	6.5	6.5	7.9	8.6	13	16	16	22	18	25
	120	6.5	6.5	7.0	7.4	8.0	10	8.5	12	8.8	12
100	140	6.5	6.5	7.3	7.8	10	12	11	15	12	16
	160	6.5	6.5	7.6	8.2	11	14	13	18	15	20

[a] Although the term effective resistance is commonly used when there is attic ventilation, this table includes values for situations with no ventilation. The effective resistance of the attic, added to the resistance (1/U) of the ceiling yields the effective resistance of this combination based on sol-air (Chapter 26) and room temperatures. These values apply to wood frame construction with a roof deck and roofing that has a conductance of 1.0 Btu/h • ft² • F.

[b] Based on air discharging outward from attic.

[c] When attic ventilation meets the requirements stated in Chapter 22, 0.1 cfm/ft² is assumed as the natural summer ventilation rate for design purposes.

[d] Resistance in h • ft² • F/Btu. When determining ceiling resistance, do not add the effect of a reflective surface facing the attic, as it is accounted for in Table 4, Part B.

[e] Roof surface temperature rather than sol-air temperature (see Chapter 26) can be used if 0.25 is subtracted from the attic resistance shown.

[f] Surfaces with effective emittance *E* of 0.05 between ceiling joists facing the attic space.

Source: 1985 Handbook of Fundamentals, *ASHRAE. Reproduced with permission.*

Table 3A-7
HEAT LOSS COEFFICIENT OF SLAB FLOOR CONSTRUCTION

Heat Loss Coefficient of Slab Floor Construction, F_2 (Btu/h·F per ft of perimeter)

Construction	Insulated	Degree Days (65 F Base)		
		2950	5350	7433
8-in. block wall, brick facing	Uninsulated	0.62	0.68	0.72
	R = 5.4 from edge to footer	0.48	0.50	0.56
4-in block wall, brick facing	Uninsulated	0.80	0.84	0.93
	R = 5.4 from edge to footer	0.47	0.49	0.54
Metal stud wall, stucco	Uninsulated	1.15	1.20	1.34
	R = 5.4 from edge to footer	0.51	0.53	0.58
Poured concrete wall, with duct near perimeter[a]	Uninsulated	1.84	2.12	2.73
	R = 5.4 from edge to footer, 3 ft under floor	0.64	0.72	0.90

[a] Weighted average temperature of the heating duct was assumed at 110 F during the heating season (outdoor air temperature less than 65 F).

Table 3A-8
HEAT LOSS BELOW GRADE IN BASEMENT WALLS AND FLOORS

Heat Loss Below Grade in Basement Walls

Depth ft	Path length through soil, ft	Heat Loss, Btu/h•ft•F Uninsulated		R = 4.17		R = 8.34		R = 12.5	
0-1	0.68	0.410		0.152		0.093		0.067	
1-2	2.27	0.222	0.632	0.116	0.268	0.079	0.172	0.059	0.126
2-3	3.88	0.155	0.787	0.094	0.362	0.068	0.240	0.053	0.179
3-4	5.52	0.119	0.906	0.079	0.441	0.060	0.300	0.048	0.227
4-5	7.05	0.096	1.002	0.069	0.510	0.053	0.353	0.044	0.271
5-6	8.65	0.079	1.081	0.060	0.570	0.048	0.401	0.040	0.311
6-7	10.28	0.069	1.150	0.054	0.624	0.044	0.445	0.037	0.348

Heat Loss Through Basement Floors
Btu/h•ft²•F

Depth of Foundation Wall Below Grade ft	Shortest Width of House, ft 20	24	28	32
5	0.032	0.029	0.026	0.023
6	0.030	0.027	0.025	0.022
7	0.029	0.026	0.023	0.021

Source: 1985 Handbook of Fundamentals, *ASHRAE. Reproduced with permission.*

Table 3A-9
DETERMINATION OF U VALUE RESULTING FROM ADDITION OF THERMAL INSULATION TO ANY GIVEN BUILDING SECTION

GIVEN BLDG SECTION PROPERTY U	R	ADDITIONAL THERMAL INSULATION, R[a, b], (hr•ft²•F)/Btu 1	2	3	4	5	6	7	9	11	13	15	17	19	30	38
0.08	12.5	0.074	0.069	0.065	0.061	0.057	0.054	0.051	0.047	0.043	0.039	0.036	0.034	0.032	0.024	0.020
0.10	10.0	0.091	0.083	0.077	0.071	0.067	0.063	0.059	0.053	0.048	0.043	0.040	0.037	0.034	0.025	0.021
0.12	8.3	0.107	0.097	0.088	0.081	0.075	0.070	0.065	0.058	0.052	0.047	0.043	0.039	0.037	0.026	0.022
0.14	7.1	0.123	0.109	0.099	0.090	0.082	0.076	0.071	0.062	0.055	0.050	0.045	0.041	0.038	0.027	0.022
0.16	6.3	0.138	0.121	0.108	0.098	0.089	0.082	0.075	0.066	0.058	0.052	0.047	0.043	0.040	0.028	0.023
0.18	5.6	0.153	0.132	0.117	0.105	0.095	0.087	0.080	0.069	0.060	0.054	0.049	0.044	0.041	0.028	0.023
0.20	5.0	0.167	0.143	0.125	0.111	0.100	0.091	0.083	0.071	0.063	0.056	0.050	0.045	0.042	0.029	0.023
0.22	4.5	0.180	0.153	0.133	0.117	0.105	0.095	0.087	0.074	0.064	0.057	0.051	0.046	0.042	0.029	0.024
0.24	4.2	0.194	0.162	0.140	0.122	0.109	0.098	0.090	0.076	0.066	0.058	0.052	0.047	0.043	0.029	0.024
0.26	3.8	0.206	0.171	0.146	0.127	0.113	0.102	0.092	0.078	0.067	0.059	0.053	0.048	0.044	0.030	0.024
0.28	3.6	0.219	0.179	0.152	0.132	0.117	0.104	0.095	0.080	0.069	0.060	0.054	0.049	0.044	0.030	0.024
0.30	3.3	0.231	0.188	0.158	0.136	0.120	0.107	0.097	0.081	0.070	0.061	0.055	0.049	0.045	0.030	0.024
0.40	2.5	0.286	0.222	0.182	0.154	0.133	0.118	0.105	0.087	0.074	0.065	0.057	0.051	0.047	0.031	0.025
0.50	2.0	0.333	0.250	0.200	0.167	0.143	0.125	0.111	0.091	0.077	0.067	0.059	0.053	0.048	0.031	0.025
0.60	1.7	0.375	0.273	0.214	0.176	0.150	0.130	0.115	0.094	0.079	0.068	0.060	0.054	0.048	0.032	0.025
0.70	1.4	0.412	0.292	0.226	0.184	0.156	0.135	0.119	0.096	0.080	0.069	0.061	0.054	0.049	0.032	0.025

[a] If the insulation occupies a previously considered air space, an adjustment must be made in the given building section *R*-value.
[b] Adjust for furring or framing sections as necessary, separately.

Source: ASHRAE Cooling and Heating Load Calculation Manual, *Dept. of Housing and Urban Development, 1980. Reproduced with permission.*

There are various ways to calculate V, but for preliminary estimating purposes, two methods can be used.

1. Air change method:

FORMULA:

$$V = \frac{ACH \times volume}{60 \text{ min./hr.}}$$

where ACH is the air changes per hour determined by Table 3A–10.

2. Tabulated estimate:

FORMULA:

$$q_v = f \times V$$

where:

q_v = estimated heat loss in Btu/hr. due to infiltration
f = factor from Table 3A–11
V = volume of room or building in cu. ft.

REQUIREMENTS FOR BUILDING ENVELOPE COMPONENTS

ASHRAE Standard 90A–1980 defines minimum requirements for building envelope construction to conserve energy. These can be used as guidelines for making decisions concerning the design and selection of materials for roofs, exterior walls, and fenestration.

Generally speaking, Standard 90A–1980 defines minimum U values for overall wall and roof assemblies based on degree days. For degree days, see Table 3C–4. The designer is then free to increase or decrease the value of individual U values of the various components (such as increasing glazing area, adding insulation, changing materials, and so on), as long as the overall value does not exceed that established in the criteria and as long as the overall heat gain or loss for the entire building envelope does not exceed the total resulting from conformance to the stated U values.

Although the calculation procedures outlined in the standard are relatively simple, changing one value in the formulas requires a lengthy recalculation to check the final answer. This is an application that is ideally suited for a "spreadsheet" type of program on a microcomputer. By simply entering the various individual U values, areas, and other factors, you can quickly study various alternatives.

Caution: Standard 90A–1980 gives criteria based on degree days to account for climatic variations, but local codes often establish their own criteria, which may differ from Standard 90A. Check your local energy conservation code for specific values.

Standard 90A–1980 gives criteria for two types of structures: Type A buildings and Type B buildings. Type A buildings consist of detached one- and two-family dwellings (A–1) and all other residential buildings three stories or less, including but not limited to multifamily dwellings and hotels and motels (A–2). Type B buildings consist of all others not covered by Type A.

1. Criteria for Type A buildings:

Walls: Any building that is heated and/or mechanically cooled shall have a combined thermal transmittance value, U_o, for the gross area of exterior walls that does not exceed the values shown in Figure 3A–1. The formula for determining this follows.

Table 3A-10
DESIGN INFILTRATION RATE IN AIR CHANGES PER HOUR FOR WINTER

Type of Construction	Winter Outdoor Design Temperature (in degrees F) Wind speed = 15 mph									
	50	40	30	20	10	0	−10	−20	−30	−40
Tight	0.4	0.5	0.6	0.6	0.7	0.8	0.8	0.9	0.9	1.0
Medium	0.6	0.7	0.8	0.9	1.0	1.1	1.2	1.2	1.3	1.4
Loose	0.8	0.9	1.0	1.2	1.3	1.4	1.5	1.6	1.8	1.9
	Summer Outdoor Design Temperature (in degrees F) **Wind speed = 7.5 mph**									
	85	90	95	100	105	110				
Tight	0.3	0.3	0.3	0.4	0.4	0.4				
Medium	0.4	0.4	0.5	0.5	0.5	0.6				
Loose	0.4	0.5	0.6	0.6	0.7	0.8				

Tight: New buildings where there is close supervision of workmanship and special precautions are taken to prevent infiltration. Windows weatherstripped with average gap of 1/64 in. crack. Doors perfect fit weatherstripping.

Medium: Building is constructed using conventional construction procedures. Windows weatherstripped if vertical and horizontal sliding type. Metal casement windows not weatherstripped. Doors with small perimeter gap having stop trip fitted properly.

Loose: Buildings constructed with poor workmanship or older buildings where joints have separated. Doors and windows not weatherstripped, with large gaps.

Source: ASHRAE Cooling and Heating Load Calculation Manual, *1980. Reproduced with permission.*

Table 3A-11
ESTIMATED HEAT LOSS FROM BUILDING BY INFILTRATION

Room or Building Type	No. of Walls with Windows	Temperature Difference (degrees F)			
		25	50	75	100
A	None	0.23	0.45	0.68	0.90
A	1	0.34	0.68	1.02	1.36
A	2	0.68	1.35	2.02	2.70
A	3 or 4	0.90	1.80	2.70	3.60
B	any	1.35	2.70	4.05	5.40
C	any	0.90–1.35	1.80–2.70	2.70–4.05	3.60–5.40
D	any	0.45–0.68	0.90–1.35	1.35–2.02	1.80–2.70
E	any	0.68–1.35	1.35–2.70	2.03–4.05	2.70–5.40

The tabulated factors, when multiplied by room or building volume, in cubic feet, will result in estimated heat loss (Btu/h) due to infiltration and does not include the heat needed to warm ventilated air.

A = Offices, apartments, hotels, multistory buildings in general.
B = Entrance halls or vestibules.
C = Industrial buildings.
D = Houses, all types, all rooms except vestibules.
E = Public or institutional buildings.

Source: ASHRAE Handbook of Fundamentals, *1981. Reproduced with permission.*

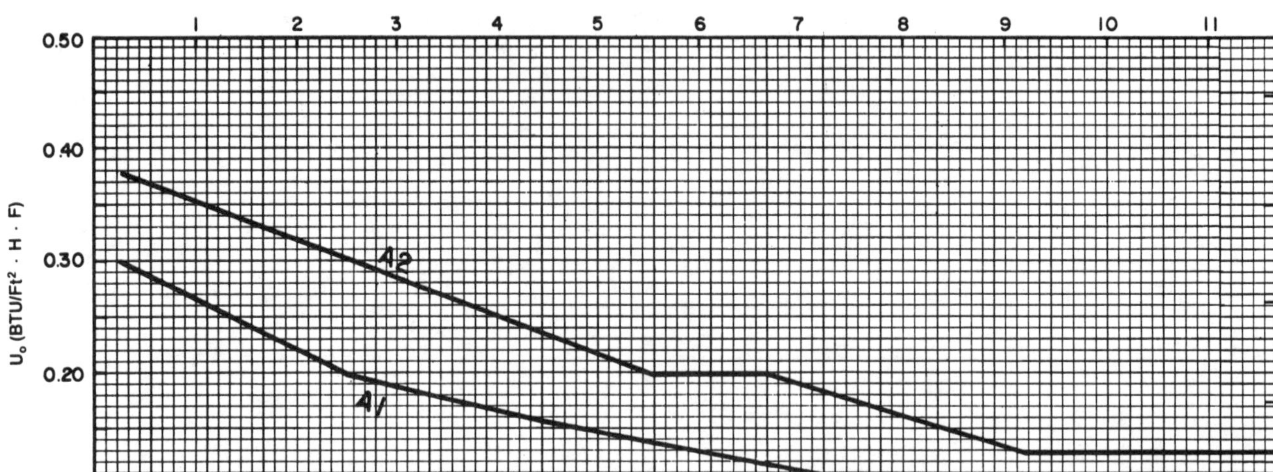

Figure 3A-1: U_o Walls—Type A Buildings—Heating

Source: ASHRAE Standard 90A. Reproduced with permission.

FORMULA:

$$U_o = \frac{[U_w \times A_w] + [U_g \times A_g] + [U_d \times A_d]}{A_o}$$

where:

U_o = average thermal transmittance of the gross wall area in Btu/ft^2 h F (maximum allowable values given in Figure 3A-1 for Type A buildings and Figure 3A-3 for Type B buildings)

A_o = the gross area of exterior walls in sq. ft.

U_w = the thermal transmittance of all opaque wall areas (the overall coefficient of heat transmission as described in the previous "Definitions" section)

A_w = the opaque wall area in sq. ft.

U_g = the thermal transmittance of the glazing area (See Table 3A-4.)

A_g = the glazing area in sq. ft.

U_d = the thermal transmittance of the door area (See Table 3A-5.)

A_d = the door area in sq. ft.

Where more than one type of wall, window, or door is used, each U × A term in the formula just given must be expanded and totaled to account for the different construction types.

Roof/ceilings: Any building that is heated and/or mechanically cooled shall have a combined thermal transmittance value, U_o, for the gross area of the roof assembly that does not exceed the values shown in Figure 3A-2. The formula for determining this follows.

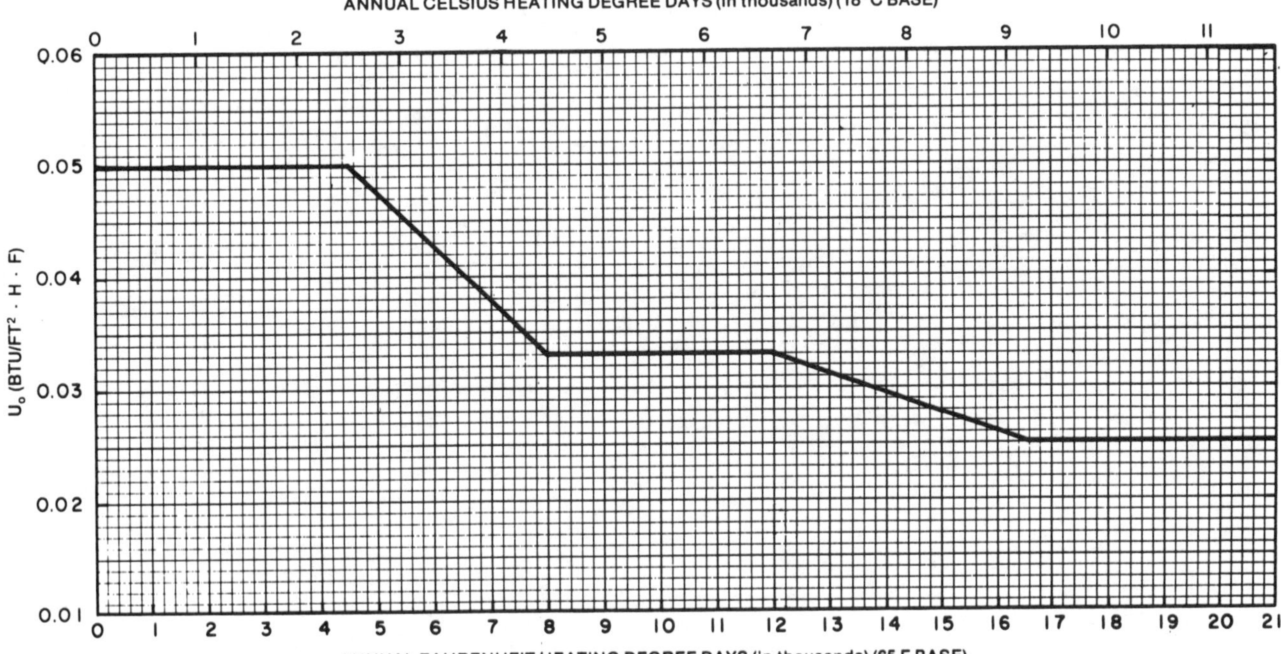

Figure 3A-2: U_o Roof/Ceilings—Type A and A_2 Buildings

Source: ASHRAE Standard 90A. Reproduced with permission.

FORMULA:

$$U_o = \frac{[U_r \times A_r] + [U_s \times A_s]}{A_o}$$

where:

U_o = average thermal transmittance of the gross roof/ceiling area in Btu/ft² h F (maximum allowable values given in Figure 3A–2)

A_o = the gross area of the roof/ceiling assembly in sq. ft. (The area is taken as the total interior surface area of the assembly.)

U_r = the thermal transmittance of all opaque roof/ceiling areas (the overall coefficient of heat transmission, as described in the previous "Definitions" section)

A_r = the opaque roof/ceiling area in sq. ft. (interior measurement)

U_s = the thermal transmittance of any skylight area (See Table 3A–4.)

A_s = the skylight area in sq. ft.

Where more than one type of roof/ceiling assembly or skylight is used, each U × A term in the formula just given must be expanded and totaled to account for the different construction types.

Floors over outdoor air (overhangs): U_o values shall be as shown in Figure 3A–2 for roof/ceilings.

2. Criteria for Type B buildings:

Walls, heating criteria: Any building that is heated and/or mechanically cooled shall have a combined thermal transmittance value, U_o, for the gross area of exterior walls that does not exceed the values shown in Figure 3A–3. The formula for determining this follows.

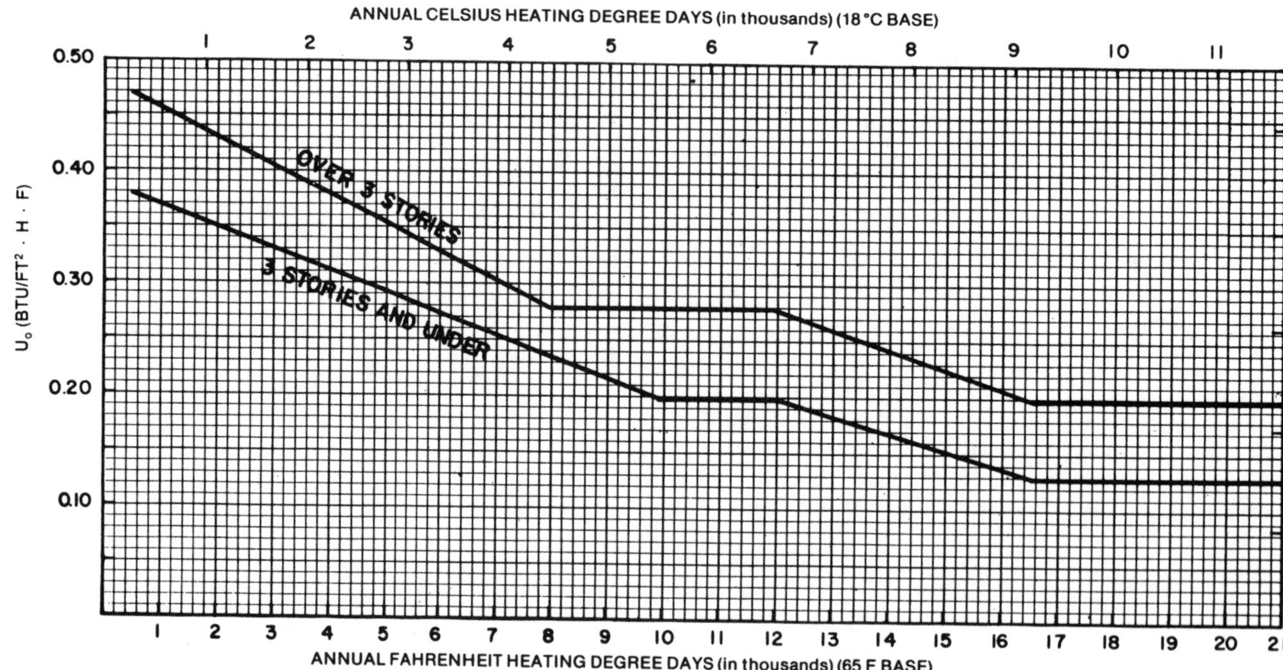

Figure 3A-3: U_o Walls—Type B Buildings—Heating

Source: ASHRAE Standard 90A. Reproduced with permission.

FORMULA:

$$U_o = \frac{[U_w \times A_w] + [U_g \times A_g] + [U_d \times A_d]}{A_o}$$

where:

U_o = average thermal transmittance of the gross wall area in Btu/ft² h F (maximum allowable values given in Figure 3A-3)

A_o = the gross area of exterior walls in sq. ft.

U_w = the thermal transmittance of all opaque wall areas (the overall coefficient of heat transmission, as described in the previous "Definitions" section)

A_w = the opaque wall area in sq. ft.

U_g = the thermal transmittance of the glazing area (See Table 3A-4.)

A_g = the glazing area in sq. ft.

U_d = the thermal transmittance of the door area (See Table 3A-5.)

A_d = the door area in sq. ft.

Where more than one type of wall, window, or door is used, each U × A term in the formula just given must be expanded and totaled to account for the different construction types.

Walls, cooling criteria: Any building that is mechanically cooled shall have an overall thermal transfer value, $OTTV_w$, for the gross area of exterior walls above grade that does not exceed the values shown in Figure 3A-4. The formula for calculating $OTTV_w$ follows.

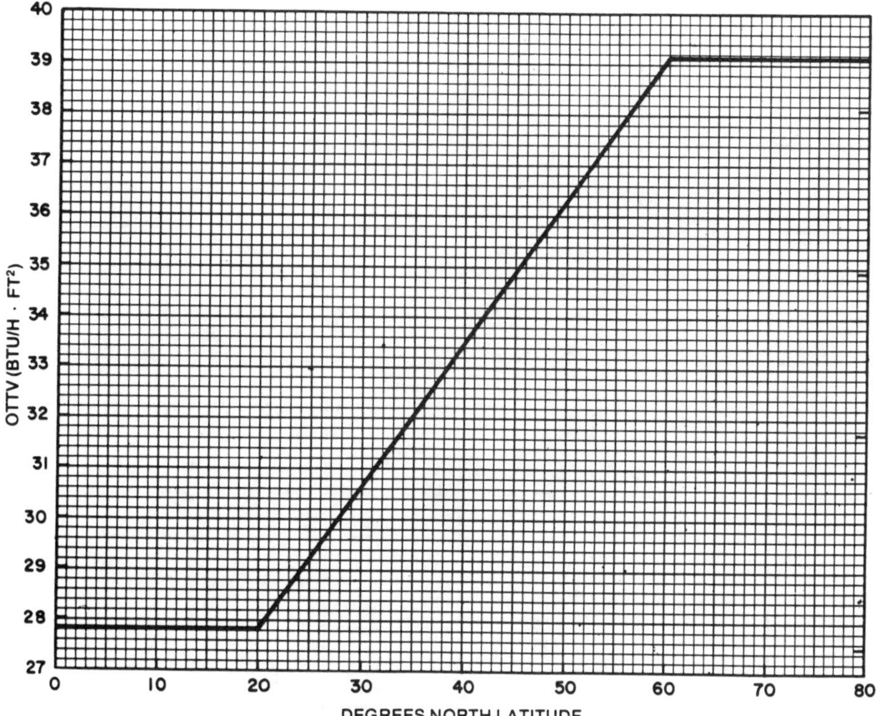

Figure 3A-4: Overall Thermal Transfer Values ($OTTV_w$) Walls—Cooling Type B Buildings

Source: ASHRAE Standard 90A. Reproduced with permission.

FORMULA:

$$OTTV_w = \frac{[U_w \times A_w \times TD_{eq}] + [A_g \times SF \times SC] + [U_g \times A_g \times \Delta t]}{A_o}$$

where:

$OTTV_w$ = overall thermal transfer value for walls (See Figure 3A-4 for minimum requirements.)

A_o = the gross area of exterior walls in sq. ft.

U_w = the thermal transmittance of all opaque wall areas (the overall coefficient of heat transmission, as described in the previous "Definitions" section)

A_w = the opaque wall area in sq. ft.

TD_{eq} = temperature difference factor accounting for the walls' thermal mass (See Figure 3A-5 for values.) The walls' thermal mass can be calculated from material weights given in Table 5-1.

U_g = the thermal transmittance of the glazing area (See Table 3A-4.)

A_g = the glazing area in sq. ft.

SF = solar factor value, as given in Figure 3A-6

SC = shading coefficient of the glass (See Tables 3A-13 and 4F-11.)

Δt = temperature difference between exterior and interior design conditions (For exterior design conditions, see Table 3A-12. Interior design condition for summer is 78° F.)

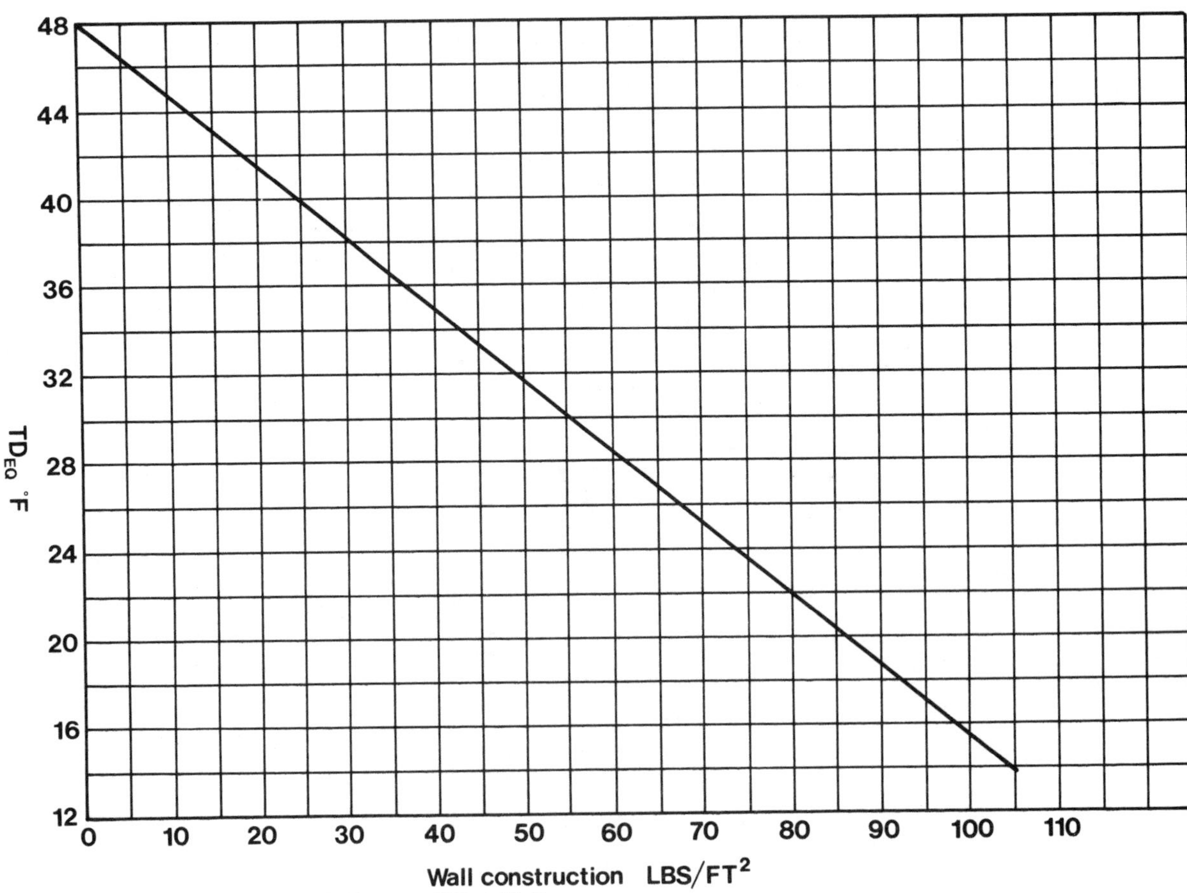

Figure 3A-5: For Temperature Difference (TD_{eq}) Walls

Source: ASHRAE Standard 90A. Reproduced with permission.

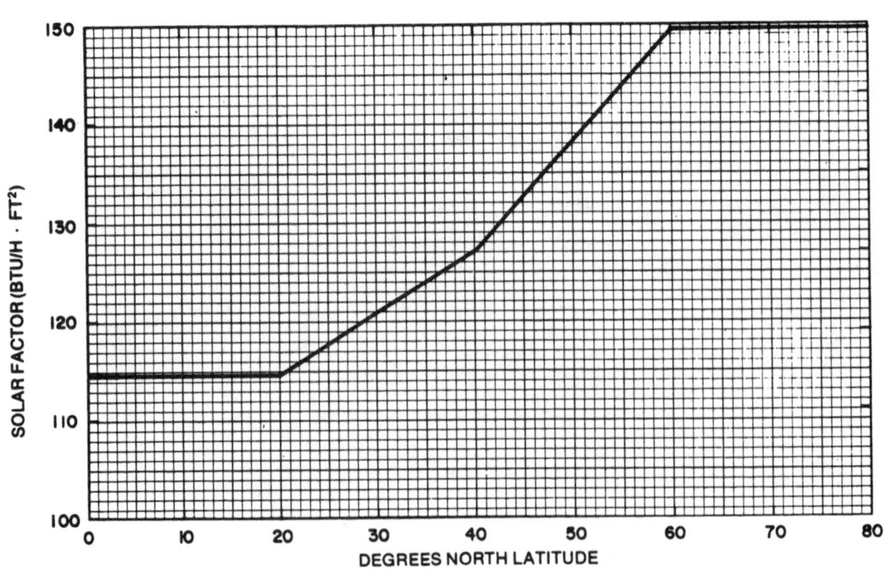

Figure 3A-6: Solar Factor (SF) Values

Source: ASHRAE Standard 90A. Reproduced with permission.

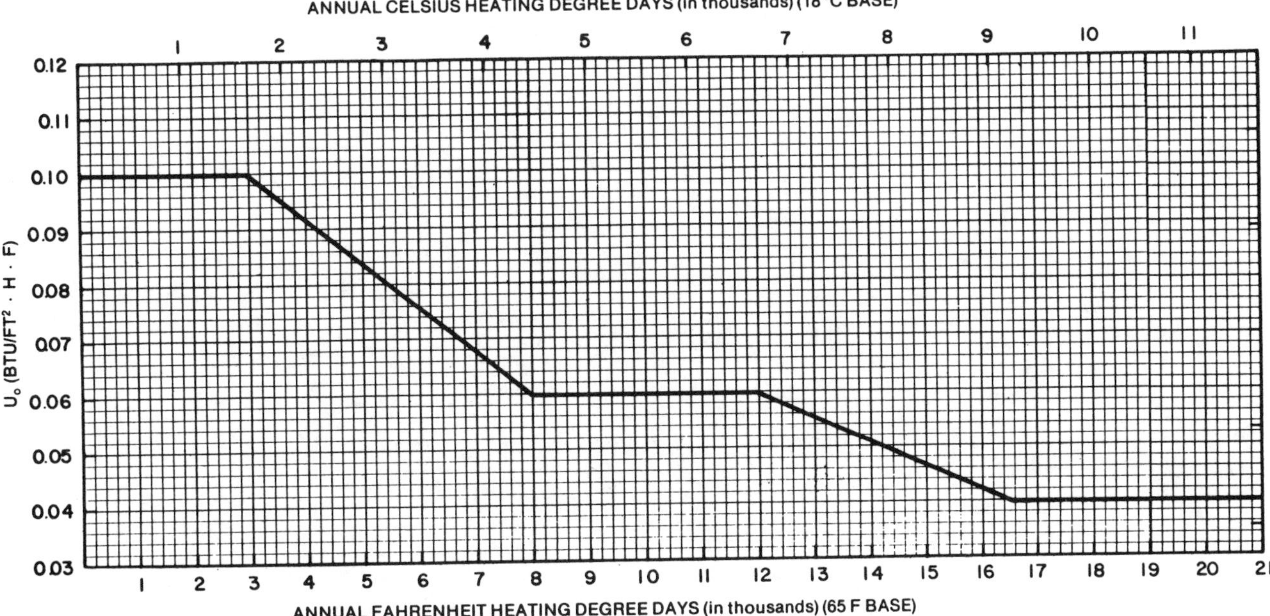

Figure 3A-7: U_o Roof/Ceilings—Type B Buildings

Source: ASHRAE Standard 90A. Reproduced with permission.

Where more than one type of wall or window is used, each U × A term in the formula just given must be expanded and totaled to account for the different construction types.

Roof/ceilings, heating: Any building that is heated shall have a combined thermal transmittance value, U_o, for the gross area of the roof assembly that does not exceed the values shown in Figure 3A-7. The formula for determining this follows.

FORMULA:

$$U_o = \frac{[U_r \times A_r] + [U_s \times A_s]}{A_o}$$

where:

U_o = average thermal transmittance of the gross roof/ceiling area in Btu/ft² h F (maximum allowable values given in Figure 3A-7)

A_o = the gross area of the roof/ceiling assembly in sq. ft. (The area is taken as the total interior surface area of the assembly.)

U_r = the thermal transmittance of all opaque roof/ceiling areas (the overall coefficient of heat transmission, as described in the previous "Definitions" section)

A_r = the opaque roof/ceiling area in sq. ft. (interior measurement)

U_s = the thermal transmittance of any skylight area (See Table 3A-4.)

A_s = the skylight area in sq. ft.

Where more than one type of roof/ceiling assembly or skylight is used, each U × A term in the formula just given must be expanded and totaled to account for the different construction types.

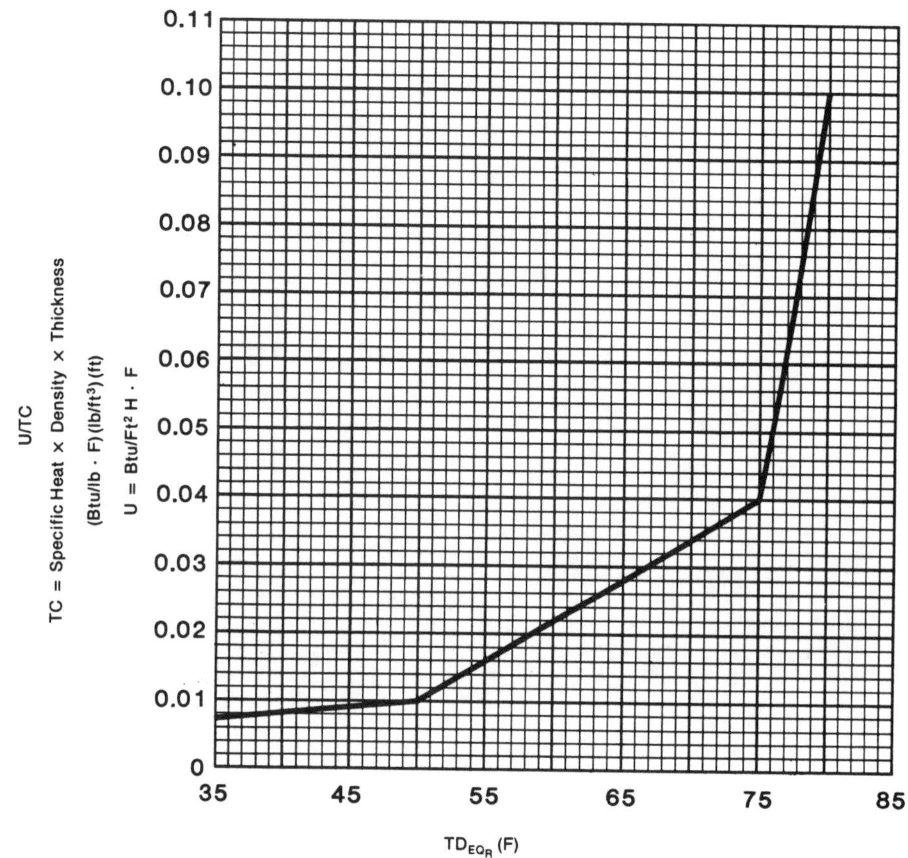

Note: TC is calculated as the sum of the TC's for each layer in the roof construction.

Figure 3A-8: TD_{eqr} Values

Source: ASHRAE Standard 90A. Reproduced with permission.

Roof/ceilings, cooling: Any building that is mechanically cooled shall have an Overall Thermal Transfer Value, $OTTV_r$, for the gross area of a roof assembly that does not exceed 8.5 Btu/h ft^2. (Verify this figure with local energy conservation codes.) The formula for determining this follows.

FORMULA:

$$8.5 \geq \frac{[U_r \times A_r \times TD_{eqr}] + [138 \times A_s \times SC] + [U_s \times A_s \times \Delta t]}{A_o}$$

where:

A_o = the gross area of the roof/ceiling assembly in sq. ft. (The area is taken as the total interior surface area of the assembly.)

U_r = the thermal transmittance of all opaque roof/ceiling areas (the overall coefficient of heat transmission, as described in the previous "Definitions" section)

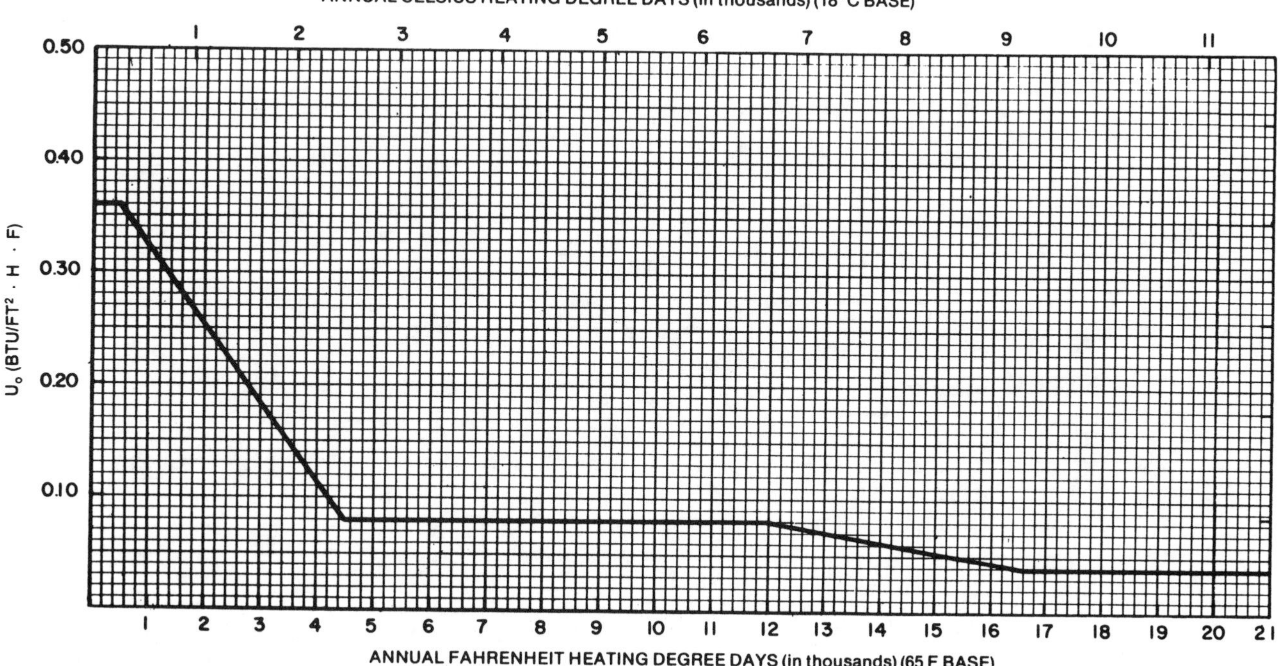

Figure 3A-9: U_o Floors Over Unheated Spaces—All Buildings

Source: ASHRAE Standard 90A. Reproduced with permission.

A_r = the opaque roof/ceiling area in sq. ft. (interior measurement)

TD_{eqr} = temperature difference factor accounting for the roof's thermal mass (See Figure 3A-8 for values.) The roof's thermal mass can be calculated from material weights given in Table 5-1.

A_s = the skylight area in sq. ft.

SC = shading coefficient of the skylight (See Tables 3A-13 and 4F-11.)

U_s = the thermal transmittance of any skylight area (See Table 3A-4.)

Δt = temperature difference between exterior and interior design conditions (For exterior design conditions, see Table 3A-12.) Interior design condition for summer is 78° F.

Where more than one type of roof/ceiling assembly or skylight is used, each U × A term in the formula just given must be expanded and totaled to account for the different construction types.

Floors over outdoor air (overhangs): U_o values shall be as shown in Figure 3A-7 for roof/ceilings.

3. Criteria for both Type A and B buildings:

Floors over unheated spaces: U_o value shall not exceed those given in Figure 3A-9.

Slab-on-grade floors: R values shall be no less than those shown in Figure 3A-10.

Air leakage: Window leakage shall not exceed 0.5 cubic feet per minute per foot of sash crack. Entrance swinging and sliding doors for residential use shall be designed to limit air leakage to no more than 0.5 cubic feet per minute per square foot of door area. Entrance swinging, sliding, and other types of doors for non-residential use shall be designed to limit air leakage to no more than 11 cubic feet per minute per linear foot of door crack.

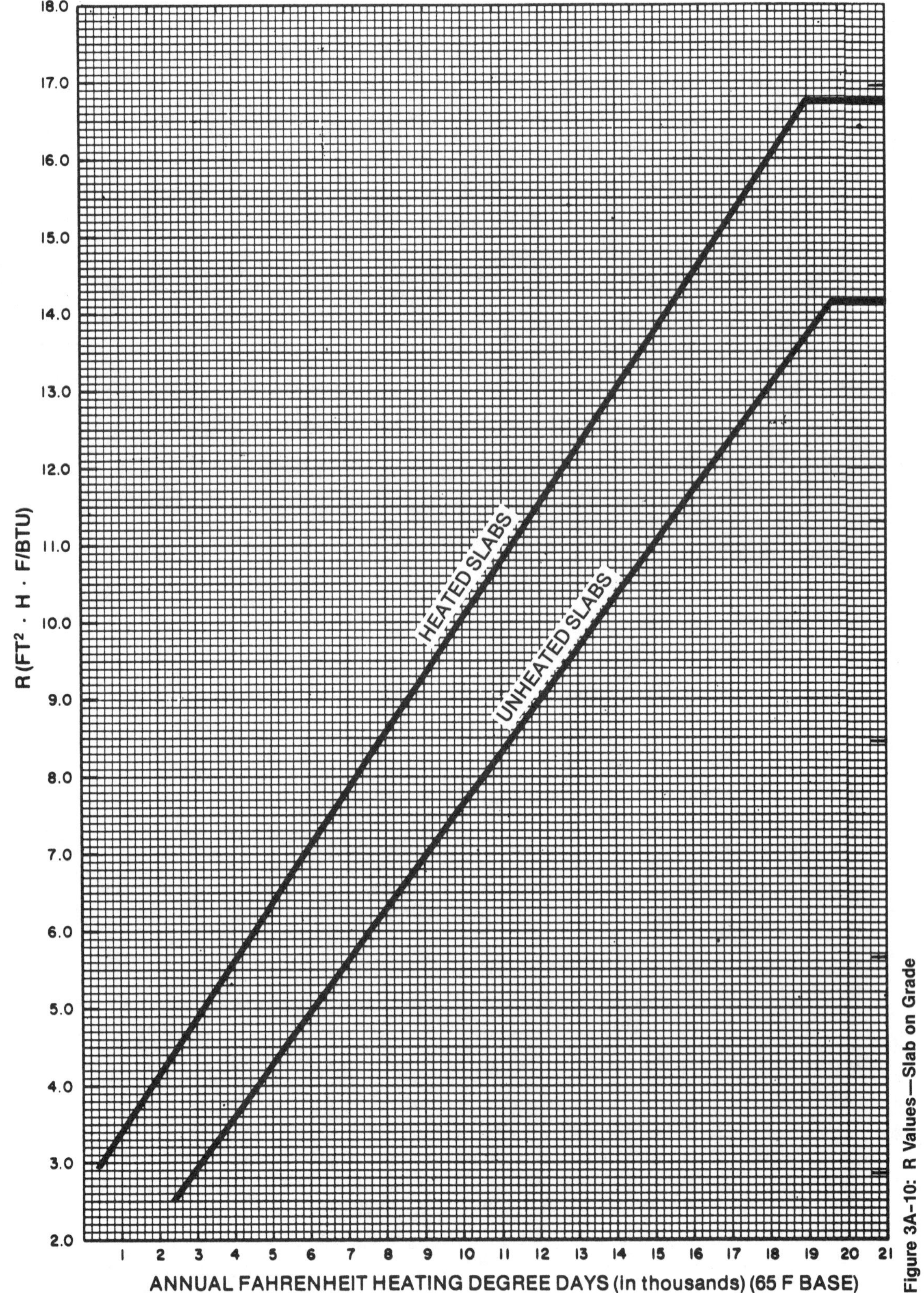

Figure 3A-10: R Values—Slab on Grade

Source: ASHRAE Standard 90A. Reproduced with permission.

Table 3A-12
CLIMATIC DESIGN CONDITIONS FOR THE UNITED STATES[a]

Col. 1	Col. 2		Col. 3		Col. 4	Winter,[d] F Col. 5		Summer,[e] F Col. 6			Col. 7	Col. 8		
State and Station	Latitude[b]		Longitude[b]		Elevation[c]	Design Dry-Bulb		Design Dry-Bulb and Mean Coincident Wet-Bulb			Mean Daily Range	Design Wet-Bulb		
	°	′	°	′	Ft	99%	97.5%	1%	2.5%	5%		1%	2.5%	5%
ALABAMA														
Alexander City	33	0	86	0	660	18	22	96/77	93/76	91/76	21	79	78	78
Anniston AP	33	4	85	5	599	18	22	97/77	94/76	92/76	21	79	78	78
Auburn	32	4	85	3	730	18	22	96/77	93/76	91/76	21	79	78	78
Birmingham AP	33	3	86	5	610	17	21	96/74	94/75	92/74	21	78	77	76
Decatur	34	4	87	0	580	11	16	95/75	93/74	91/74	22	78	77	76
Dothan AP	31	2	85	2	321	23	27	94/76	92/76	91/76	20	80	79	78
Florence AP	34	5	87	4	528	17	21	97/74	94/74	92/74	22	78	77	76
Gadsden	34	0	86	0	570	16	20	96/75	94/75	92/74	22	78	77	76
Huntsville AP	34	4	86	4	619	11	16	95/75	93/74	91/74	23	78	77	76
Mobile AP	30	4	88	2	211	25	29	95/77	93/77	91/76	18	80	79	78
Mobile CO	30	4	88	1	119	25	29	95/77	93/77	91/76	16	80	79	78
Montgomery AP	32	2	86	2	195	22	25	96/76	95/76	93/76	21	79	79	78
Selma-Craig AFB	32	2	87	0	207	22	26	97/78	95/77	93/77	21	81	80	79
Talladega	33	3	86	1	565	18	22	97/77	94/76	92/76	21	79	78	78
Tuscaloosa AP	33	1	87	4	170r	20	23	98/75	96/76	94/76	22	79	78	77
ALASKA														
Anchorage AP	61	1	150	0	90	−23	−18	71/59	68/58	66/56	15	60	59	57
Barrow (S)	71	2	156	5	22	−45	−41	57/53	53/50	49/47	12	54	50	47
Fairbanks AP (S)	64	5	147	5	436	−51	−47	82/62	78/60	75/59	24	64	62	60
Juneau AP	58	2	134	4	17	−4	1	74/60	70/58	67/57	15	61	59	58
Kodiak	57	3	152	3	21	10	13	69/58	65/56	62/55	10	60	58	56
Nome AP	64	3	165	3	13	−31	−27	66/57	62/55	59/54	10	58	56	55
ARIZONA														
Douglas AP	31	3	109	3	4098	27	31	98/63	95/63	93/63	31	70	69	68
Flagstaff AP	35	1	111	4	6973	−2	4	84/55	82/55	80/54	31	61	60	59
Fort Huachuca AP (S)	31	3	110	2	4664	24	28	95/62	92/62	90/62	27	69	68	67
Kingman AP	35	2	114	0	3446	18	25	103/65	100/64	97/64	30	70	69	69
Nogales	31	2	111	0	3800	28	32	99/64	96/64	94/64	31	71	70	69
Phoenix AP(S)	33	3	112	0	1117	31	34	109/71	107/71	105/71	27	76	75	75
Prescott AP	34	4	112	3	5014	4	9	96/61	94/60	92/60	30	66	65	64
Tucson AP (S)	32	1	111	0	2584	28	32	104/66	102/66	100/66	26	72	71	71
Winslow AP	35	0	110	4	4880	5	10	97/61	95/60	93/60	32	66	65	64
Yuma AP	32	4	114	4	199	36	39	111/72	109/72	107/71	27	79	78	77

[a] Table 1 was prepared by ASHRAE Technical Committee 4.2, Weather Data, from data compiled from official weather stations where hourly weather observations are made by trained observers. See also Ref. 3, 4, 5, 7, and 10.

[b] Latitude, for use in calculating solar loads, and longitude are given to the nearest 10minutes. For example, the latitude and longitude for Anniston, Alabama are given as 33 34 and 85 55 respectively, or 33° 40 and 85° 50.

[c] Elevations are ground elevations for each station. Temperature readings are generally made at an elevation of 5 ft above ground, except for locations marked r, indicating roof exposure of thermometer.

[d] Percentage of winter design data shows the percent of the 3-month period, December through February.

[e] Percentage of summer design data shows the percent of 4-month period, June through September.

Table 3A-12 (Continued)

Col. 1	Col. 2		Col. 3		Col. 4	Col. 5 Winter,[d] F		Col. 6 Summer,[e] F			Col. 7	Col. 8		
State and Station	**Latitude[b]**		**Longitude[b]**		**Elevation[c]**	**Design Dry-Bulb**		**Design Dry-Bulb and Mean Coincident Wet-Bulb**			**Mean Daily**	**Design Wet-Bulb**		
	°	'	°	'	**Ft**	**99%**	**97.5%**	**1%**	**2.5%**	**5%**	**Range**	**1%**	**2.5%**	**5%**
ARKANSAS														
Blytheville AFB	36	0	90	0	264	10	15	96/78	94/77	91/76	21	81	80	78
Camden	33	4	92	5	116	18	23	98/76	96/76	94/76	21	80	79	78
El Dorado AP	33	1	92	5	252	18	23	98/76	96/76	94/76	21	80	79	78
Fayetteville AP	36	0	94	1	1253	7	12	97/72	94/73	92/73	23	77	76	75
Fort Smith AP	35	2	94	2	449	12	17	101/75	98/76	95/76	24	80	79	78
Hot Springs	34	3	93	1	535	17	23	101/77	97/77	94/77	22	80	79	78
Jonesboro	35	5	90	4	345	10	15	96/78	94/77	91/76	21	81	80	78
Little Rock AP (S)	34	4	92	1	257	15	20	99/76	96/77	94/77	22	80	79	78
Pine Bluff AP	34	1	92	0	204	16	22	100/78	97/77	95/78	22	81	80	80
Texarkana AP	33	3	94	0	361	18	23	98/76	96/77	93/76	21	80	79	78
CALIFORNIA														
Bakersfield AP	35	2	119	0	495	30	32	104/70	101/69	98/68	32	73	71	70
Barstow AP	34	5	116	5	2142	26	29	106/68	104/68	102/67	37	73	71	70
Blythe AP	33	4	114	3	390	30	33	112/71	110/71	108/70	28	75	75	74
Burbank AP	34	1	118	2	699	37	39	95/68	91/68	88/67	25	71	70	69
Chico	39	5	121	5	205	28	30	103/69	101/68	98/67	36	71	70	68
Concord	38	0	122	0	195	24	27	100/69	97/68	94/67	32	71	70	68
Covina	34	0	117	5	575	32	35	98/69	95/68	92/67	31	73	71	70
Crescent City AP	41	5	124	0	50	31	33	68/60	65/59	63/58	18	62	60	59
Downey	34	0	118	1	116	37	40	93/70	89/70	86/69	22	72	71	70
El Cajon	32	4	117	0	525	42	44	83/69	80/69	78/68	30	71	70	68
El Centro AP (S)	32	5	115	4	−30	35	38	112/74	110/74	108/74	34	81	80	78
Escondido	33	0	117	1	660	39	41	89/68	85/68	82/68	30	71	70	69
Eureka/ Arcata AP	41	0	124	1	217	31	33	68/60	65/59	63/58	11	62	60	59
Fairfield- Travis AFB	38	2	122	0	72	29	32	99/68	95/67	91/66	34	70	68	67
Fresno AP (S)	36	5	119	4	326	28	30	102/70	100/69	97/68	34	72	71	70
Hamilton AFB	38	0	122	3	3	30	32	89/68	84/66	80/65	28	72	69	67
Laguna Beach	33	3	117	5	35	41	43	83/68	80/68	77/67	18	70	69	68
Livermore	37	4	122	0	545	24	27	100/69	97/68	93/67	24	71	70	68
Lompoc, Vandenburg AFB	34	4	120	3	552	35	38	75/61	70/61	67/60	20	63	61	60
Long Beach AP	33	5	118	1	34	41	43	83/68	80/68	77/67	22	70	69	68
Los Angeles AP (S)	34	0	118	2	99	41	43	83/68	80/68	77/67	15	70	69	68
Los Angeles CO (S)	34	0	118	1	312	37	40	93/70	89/70	86/69	20	72	71	70
Merced-Castle AFB	37	2	120	3	178	29	31	102/70	99/69	96/68	36	72	71	70
Modesto	37	4	121	0	91	28	30	101/69	98/68	95/67	36	71	70	69
Monterey	36	4	121	5	38	35	38	75/63	71/61	68/61	20	64	62	61
Napa	38	2	122	2	16	30	32	100/69	96/68	92/67	30	71	69	68
Needles AP	34	5	114	4	913	30	33	112/71	110/71	108/70	27	75	75	74
Oakland AP	37	4	122	1	3	34	36	85/64	80/63	75/62	19	66	64	63
Oceanside	33	1	117	2	30	41	43	83/68	80/68	77/67	13	70	69	68
Ontario	34	0	117	36	995	31	33	102/70	99/69	96/67	36	74	72	71
Obhard	34	1	119	1	43	34	36	83/66	80/64	77/63	19	70	68	67
Palmdale AP	34	4	118	1	2517	18	22	103/65	101/65	98/64	35	69	67	66
Palm Springs	33	5	116	4	411	33	35	112/71	110/70	108/70	35	76	74	73
Pasadena	34	1	118	1	864	32	35	98/69	95/68	92/67	29	73	71	70
Petaluma	38	1	122	4	27	26	29	94/68	90/66	87/65	31	72	70	68
Pomona CO	34	0	117	5	871	28	30	102/70	99/69	95/68	36	74	72	71
Redding AP	40	3	122	1	495	29	31	105/68	102/67	100/66	32	71	69	68
Redlands	34	0	117	1	1318	31	33	102/70	99/69	96/68	33	74	72	71
Richmond	38	0	122	2	55	34	36	85/64	80/63	75/62	17	66	64	63
Riverside- March AFB (S)	33	5	117	2	1511	29	32	100/68	98/68	95/67	37	72	71	70

Col. 1	Col. 2		Col. 3		Col. 4	Winter,[d] F Col. 5		Summer,[e] F Col. 6			Col. 7	Col. 8		
State and Station	Latitude[b]		Longitude[c]		Elevation[c]	Design Dry-Bulb		Design Dry-Bulb and Mean Coincident Wet-Bulb			Mean Daily	Design Wet-Bulb		
	°	′	°	′	Ft	99%	97.5%	1%	2.5%	5%	Range	1%	2.5%	5%
Sacramento AP	38	3	121	3	17	30	32	101/70		94/69	36	72	71	98/70
Salinas AP	36	4	121	4	74	30	32	74/61	70/60	67/59	24	62	61	59
San Bernardino, Norton AFB	34	1	117	1	1125	31	33	102/70	99/69	96/68	38	74	72	71
San Diego AP	32	4	117	1	19	42	44	83/69	80/69	78/68	12	71	70	68
San Fernando	34	1	118	3	977	37	39	95/68	91/68	88/67	38	71	70	69
San Francisco AP	37	4	122	2	8	35	38	82/64	77/63	73/62	20	65	64	62
San Francisco CO	37	5	122	3	52	38	40	74/63	71/62	69/61	14	64	62	61
San Jose AP	37	2	122	0	70r	34	36	85/66	81/65	77/64	26	68	67	65
San Luis Obispo	35	2	120	4	315	33	35	92/69	88/70	84/69	26	73	71	70
Santa Ana AP	33	4	117	5	115r	37	39	89/69	85/68	82/68	28	71	70	69
Santa Barbara MAP	34	3	119	5	10	34	36	81/67	77/66	75/65	24	68	67	66
Santa Cruz	37	0	122	0	125	35	38	75/63	71/61	68/61	28	64	62	61
Santa Maria AP (S)	34	5	120	3	238	31	33	81/64	76/63	73/62	23	65	64	63
Santa Monica CO	34	0	118	3	57	41	43	83/68	80/68	77/67	16	70	69	68
Santa Paula	34	2	119	0	263	33	35	90/68	86/67	84/66	36	71	69	68
Santa Rosa	38	3	122	5	167	27	29	99/68	95/67	91/66	34	70	68	67
Stockton AP	37	5	121	2	28	28	30	100/69	97/68	94/67	37	71	70	68
Ukiah	39	1	122	4	620	27	29	99/69	95/68	91/67	40	70	68	67
Visalia	36	2	119	1	354	28	30	102/70	100/69	97/68	38	72	71	70
Yreka	41	4	122	4	2625	13	17	95/65	92/64	89/63	38	67	65	64
Yuba City	39	1	121	4	70	29	31	104/68	101/67	99/66	36	71	69	68
COLORADO														
Alamosa AP	37	3	105	5	7536	−21	−16	84/57	82/57	80/57	35	62	61	60
Boulder	40	0	105	2	5385	−2	8	93/59	91/59	89/59	27	64	63	62
Colorado Springs AP	38	5	104	4	6173	−3	2	91/58	88/57	86/57	30	63	62	61
Denver AP	39	5	104	5	5283	−5	1	93/59	91/59	89/59	28	64	63	62
Durango	37	1	107	5	6550	−1	4	89/59	87/59	85/59	30	64	63	62
Fort Collins	40	4	105	0	5001	−10	−4	93/59	91/59	89/59	28	64	63	62
Grand Junction AP (S)	39	1	108	3	4849	2	7	96/59	94/59	92/59	29	64	63	62
Greeley	40	3	104	4	4648	−11	−5	96/60	94/60	92/60	29	65	64	63
La Junta AP	38	0	103	3	4188	−3	3	100/68	98/68	95/67	31	72	70	69
Leadville	39	2	106	2	10177	−8	−4	84/52	81/51	78/50	30	56	55	54
Pueblo AP	38	2	104	2	4639	−7	0	97/61	95/61	92/61	31	67	66	65
Sterling	40	4	103	1	3939	−7	−2	95/62	93/62	90/62	30	67	66	65
Trinidad AP	37	2	104	2	5746	−2	3	93/61	91/61	89/61	32	66	65	64
CONNECTICUT														
Bridgeport AP	41	1	73	1	7	6	9	86/73	84/71	81/70	18	75	74	73
Hartford, Brainard Field	41	5	72	4	15	3	7	91/74	88/73	85/72	22	77	75	74
New Haven AP	41	2	73	0	6	3	7	88/75	84/73	82/72	17	76	75	74
New London	41	2	72	1	60	5	9	88/73	85/72	83/71	16	76	75	74
Norwalk	41	1	73	3	37	6	9	86/73	84/71	81/70	19	75	74	73
Norwich	41	3	72	0	20	3	7	89/75	86/73	83/72	18	76	75	74
Waterbury	41	3	73	0	605	−4	2	88/73	85/71	82/70	21	75	74	72
Windsor Locks, Bradley Field (S)	42	0	72	4	169	0	4	91/74	88/72	85/71	22	76	75	73
DELAWARE														
Dover AFB	39	0	75	3	38	11	15	92/75	90/75	87/74	18	79	77	76
Wilmington AP	39	4	75	3	78	10	14	92/74	89/74	87/73	20	77	76	75
DISTRICT OF COLUMBIA														
Andrews AFB	38	5	76	5	279	10	14	92/75	90/74	87/73	18	78	76	75
Washington National AP	38	5	77	0	14	14	17	93/75	91/74	89/74	18	78	77	76
FLORIDA														
Belle Glade	26	4	80	4	16	41	44	92/76	91/76	89/76	16	79	78	78

Table 3A-12 (Continued)

Col. 1	Col. 2		Col. 3		Col. 4	Winter,[d] F Col. 5		Summer,[e] F Col. 6			Col. 7	Col. 8		
State and Station	Latitude[b]		Longitude[c]		Elevation[c]	Design Dry-Bulb		Design Dry-Bulb and Mean Coincident Wet-Bulb			Mean Daily Range	Design Wet-Bulb		
	°	'	°	'	Ft	99%	97.5%	1%	2.5%	5%		1%	2.5%	5%
Cape Kennedy AP	28	3	80	3	16	35	38	90/78	88/78	87/78	15	80	79	79
Daytona Beach AP	29	1	81	0	31	32	35	92/78	90/77	88/77	15	80	79	78
Fort Lauderdale	26	0	80	1	13	42	46	92/78	91/78	90/78	15	80	79	79
Fort Myers AP	26	4	81	5	13	41	44	93/78	92/78	91/77	18	80	79	79
Fort Pierce	27	3	80	2	10	38	42	91/78	90/78	89/78	15	80	79	79
Gainesville AP (S)	29	4	82	2	155	28	31	95/77	93/77	92/77	18	80	79	78
Jacksonville AP	30	3	81	4	24	29	32	96/77	94/77	92/76	19	79	79	78
Key West AP	24	3	81	5	6	55	57	90/78	90/78	89/78	9	80	79	79
Lakeland CO (S)	28	0	82	0	214	39	41	93/76	91/76	89/76	17	79	78	78
Miami AP (S)	25	5	80	2	7	44	47	91/77	90/77	89/77	15	79	79	78
Miami Beach CO	25	5	80	1	9	45	48	90/77	89/77	88/77	10	79	79	78
Ocala	29	1	82	1	86	31	34	95/77	93/77	92/76	18	80	79	78
Orlando AP	28	3	81	2	106r	35	38	94/76	93/76	91/76	17	79	78	78
Panama City, Tyndall AFB	30	0	85	4	22	29	33	92/78	90/77	89/77	14	81	80	79
Pensacola CO	30	3	87	1	13	25	29	94/77	93/77	91/77	14	80	79	79
St. Augustine	29	5	81	2	15	31	35	92/78	89/78	87/78	16	80	79	79
St. Petersburg	28	0	82	4	35	36	40	92/77	91/77	90/76	16	79	79	78
Sanford	28	5	81	2	14	35	38	94/76	93/76	91/76	17	79	78	78
Sarasota	27	2	82	3	30	39	42	93/77	92/77	90/76	17	79	79	78
Tallahassee AP (S)	30	2	84	2	58	27	30	94/77	92/76	90/76	19	79	78	78
Tampa AP (S)	28	0	82	3	19	36	40	92/77	91/77	90/76	17	79	79	78
West Palm Beach AP	26	4	80	1	15	41	45	92/78	91/78	90/78	16	80	79	79
GEORGIA														
Albany, Turner AFB	31	3	84	1	224	25	29	97/77	95/76	93/76	20	80	79	78
Americus	32	0	84	2	476	21	25	97/77	94/76	92/75	20	79	78	77
Athens	34	0	83	2	700	18	22	94/74	92/74	90/74	21	78	77	76
Atlanta AP (S)	33	4	84	3	1005	17	22	94/74	92/74	90/73	19	77	76	75
Augusta AP	33	2	82	0	143	20	23	97/77	95/76	93/76	19	80	79	78
Brunswick	31	1	81	3	14	29	32	92/78	89/78	87/78	18	80	79	79
Columbus, Lawson AFB	32	3	85	0	242	21	24	95/76	93/76	91/75	21	79	78	77
Dalton	34	5	85	0	720	17	22	94/76	93/76	91/76	22	79	78	77
Dublin	32	3	83	0	215	21	25	96/77	93/76	91/75	20	79	78	77
Gainesville	34	2	83	5	1254	16	21	93/74	91/74	89/73	21	77	76	75
Griffin (S)	33	1	84	2	980	18	22	93/76	90/75	88/74	21	78	77	76
La Grange	33	0	85	0	715	19	23	94/76	91/75	89/74	21	78	77	76
Macon AP	32	4	83	4	356	21	25	96/77	93/76	91/75	22	79	78	77
Marietta, Dobbins AFB	34	0	84	3	1016	17	21	94/74	92/74	90/74	21	78	77	76
Moultrie	31	1	83	4	340	27	30	97/77	95/77	92/76	20	80	79	78
Rome AP	34	2	85	1	637	17	22	94/76	93/76	91/76	23	79	78	77
Savannah-Travis AP	32	1	81	1	52	24	27	96/77	93/77	91/77	20	80	79	78
Valdosta-Moody AFB	31	0	83	1	239	28	31	96/77	94/77	92/76	20	80	79	78
Waycross	31	2	82	2	140	26	29	96/77	94/77	91/76	20	80	79	78
HAWAII														
Hilo AP (S)	19	4	155	1	31	61	62	84/73	83/72	82/72	15	75	74	74
Honolulu AP	21	2	158	0	7	62	63	87/73	86/73	85/72	12	76	75	74
Kaneohe Bay MCAS	21	2	157	5	18	65	66	85/75	84/74	83/74	12	76	76	75
Wahiawa	21	3	158	0	900	58	59	86/73	85/72	84/72	14	75	74	73
IDAHO														
Boise AP(S)	43	3	116	1	2842	3	10	96/65	94/64	91/64	31	68	66	65
Burley	42	3	113	5	4180	−3	2	99/62	95/61	92/66	35	64	63	61
Coeur d'Alene AP	47	5	116	5	2973	−8	−1	89/62	86/61	83/60	31	64	63	61
Idaho Falls AP	43	3	112	0	4730r	−11	−6	89/61	87/61	84/59	38	65	63	61
Lewiston AP	46	2	117	0	1413	−1	6	96/65	93/64	90/63	32	67	66	64
Moscow	46	4	117	0	2660	−7	0	90/63	87/62	84/61	32	65	64	62
Mountain Home AFB	43	0	115	5	2992	6	12	99/64	97/63	94/62	36	66	65	63
Pocatello AP	43	0	112	4	4444	−8	−1	94/61	91/60	89/59	35	64	63	61
Twin Falls AP (S)	42	3	114	3	4148	−3	2	99/62	95/61	92/60	34	64	63	61

Col. 1	Col. 2		Col. 3		Col. 4	Winter,[d] F Col. 5		Summer,[e] F Col. 6			Col. 7	Col. 8		
State and Station	Latitude[b]		Longitude[b]		Elevation[c]	Design Dry-Bulb		Design Dry-Bulb and Mean Coincident Wet-Bulb			Mean Daily Range	Design Wet-Bulb		
	°	′	°	′	Ft	99%	97.5%	1%	2.5%	5%		1%	2.5%	5%
ILLINOIS														
Aurora	41	5	88	2	744	−6	−1	93/76	91/76	88/75	20	79	78	76
Belleville, Scott AFB	38	3	89	5	447	1	6	94/76	92/76	89/75	21	79	78	76
Bloomington	40	3	89	0	775	−6	−2	92/75	90/74	88/73	21	78	76	75
Carbondale	37	5	89	1	380	2	7	95/77	93/77	90/76	21	80	79	77
Champaign/Urbana	40	0	88	2	743	−3	2	95/75	92/74	90/73	21	78	77	75
Chicago, Midway AP	41	5	87	5	610	−5	0	94/74	91/73	88/72	20	77	75	74
Chicago, O'Hare AP	42	0	87	5	658	−8	−4	91/74	89/74	86/72	20	77	76	74
Chicago CO	41	5	87	4	594	−3	2	94/75	91/74	88/73	15	79	77	75
Danville	40	1	87	4	558	−4	1	93/75	90/74	88/73	21	78	77	75
Decatur	39	5	88	5	670	−3	2	94/75	91/74	88/73	21	78	77	75
Dixon	41	5	89	3	696	−7	−2	93/75	90/74	88/73	23	78	77	75
Elgin	42	0	88	2	820	−7	−2	91/75	88/74	86/73	21	78	77	75
Freeport	42	2	89	4	780	−9	−4	91/74	89/73	87/72	24	77	76	74
Galesburg	41	0	90	3	771	−7	−2	93/75	91/75	88/74	22	78	77	75
Greenville	39	0	89	2	563	−1	4	94/76	92/75	89/74	21	79	78	76
Joliet	41	3	88	1	588	−5	0	93/75	90/74	88/73	20	78	77	75
Kankakee	41	1	87	5	625	−4	1	93/75	90/74	88/73	21	78	77	75
La Salle/Peru	41	2	89	1	520	−7	−2	93/75	91/75	88/74	22	78	77	75
Macomb	40	3	90	4	702	−5	0	95/76	92/76	89/75	22	79	78	76
Moline AP	41	3	90	3	582	−9	−4	93/75	91/75	88/74	23	78	77	75
Mt Vernon	38	2	88	5	500	0	5	95/76	92/75	89/74	21	79	78	76
Peoria AP	40	4	89	4	652	−8	−4	91/75	89/74	87/73	22	78	76	75
Quincy AP	40	0	91	1	762	−2	3	96/76	93/76	90/76	22	80	78	77
Rantoul, Chanute AFB	40	2	88	1	740	−4	1	94/75	91/74	89/73	21	78	77	75
Rockford	42	1	89	0	724	−9	−4	91/74	89/73	87/72	24	77	76	74
Springfield AP	39	5	89	4	587	−3	2	94/75	92/74	89/74	21	79	77	76
Waukegan	42	2	87	5	680	−6	−3	92/76	89/74	87/73	21	78	76	75
INDIANA														
Anderson	40	0	85	4	847	0	6	95/76	92/75	89/74	22	79	78	76
Bedford	38	5	86	3	670	0	5	95/76	92/75	89/74	22	79	78	76
Bloomington	39	1	86	4	820	0	5	95/76	92/75	89/74	22	79	78	76
Columbus, Bakalar AFB	39	2	85	5	661	3	7	95/76	92/75	90/74	22	79	78	76
Crawfordsville	40	0	86	5	752	−2	3	94/75	91/74	88/73	22	79	77	76
Evansville AP	38	0	87	3	381	4	9	95/76	93/75	91/75	22	79	78	77
Fort Wayne AP	41	0	85	1	791	−4	1	92/73	89/72	87/72	24	77	75	74
Goshen AP	41	3	85	5	823	−3	1	91/73	89/73	86/72	23	77	75	74
Hobart	41	3	87	2	600	−4	2	91/73	88/73	85/72	21	77	75	74
Huntington	40	4	85	3	802	−4	1	92/73	89/72	87/72	23	77	75	74
Indianapolis AP (S)	39	4	86	2	793	−2	2	92/74	90/74	87/73	22	78	76	75
Jeffersonville	38	2	85	5	455	5	10	95/74	93/74	90/74	23	79	77	76
Kokomo	40	3	86	1	790	−4	0	91/74	90/73	88/73	22	77	75	74
Lafayette	40	2	86	5	600	−3	3	94/74	91/73	88/73	22	78	76	75
La Porte	41	3	86	4	810	−3	3	93/74	90/74	87/73	22	78	76	75
Marion	40	3	85	4	791	−4	0	91/74	90/73	88/73	23	77	75	74
Muncie	40	1	85	2	955	−3	2	92/74	90/73	87/73	22	78	76	75
Peru, Grissom AFB	40	4	86	1	804	−6	−1	90/74	88/73	86/73	22	77	75	74
Richmond AP	39	5	84	5	1138	−2	2	92/74	90/74	87/73	22	78	76	75
Shelbyville	39	3	85	5	765	−1	3	93/74	91/74	88/73	22	78	76	75
South Bend AP	41	4	86	2	773	−3	1	91/73	89/73	86/72	22	77	75	74
Terre Haute AP	39	3	87	2	601	−2	4	95/75	92/74	89/73	22	79	77	76
Valparaiso	41	2	87	0	801	−3	3	93/74	90/74	87/73	22	78	76	75
Vincennes	38	4	87	3	420	1	6	95/75	92/74	90/73	22	79	77	76
IOWA														
Ames (S)	42	0	93	4	1004	−11	−6	93/75	90/74	87/73	23	78	76	75
Burlington AP	40	5	91	1	694	−7	−3	94/74	91/75	88/73	22	78	77	75
Cedar Rapids AP	41	5	91	4	863	−10	−5	91/76	88/75	86/74	23	78	77	75
Clinton	41	5	90	1	595	−8	−3	92/75	90/75	87/74	23	78	77	75
Council Bluffs	41	2	95	5	1210	−8	−3	94/76	91/75	88/74	22	78	77	75

Table 3A-12 (Continued)

Col. 1	Col. 2		Col. 3		Col. 4	Winter,[d] F Col. 5		Summer,[e] F Col. 6			Col. 7	Col. 8		
State and Station	Latitude[b]		Longitude[c]		Elevation[c]	Design Dry-Bulb		Design Dry-Bulb and Mean Coincident Wet-Bulb			Mean Daily	Design Wet-Bulb		
	°	′	°	′	Ft	99%	97.5%	1%	2.5%	5%	Range	1%	2.5%	5%
Des Moines AP	41	3	93	4	948r	−10	−5	94/75	91/74	88/73	23	78	77	75
Dubuque	42	2	90	4	1065	−12	−7	90/74	88/73	86/72	22	77	75	74
Fort Dodge	42	3	94	1	1111	−12	−7	91/74	88/74	86/72	23	77	75	74
Iowa City	41	4	91	3	645	−11	−6	92/76	89/76	87/74	22	80	78	76
Keokuk	40	2	91	2	526	−5	0	95/75	92/75	89/74	22	79	77	76
Marshalltown	42	0	92	5	898	−12	−7	92/76	90/75	88/74	23	78	77	75
Mason City AP	43	1	93	2	1194	−15	−11	90/74	88/74	85/72	24	77	75	74
Newton	41	4	93	0	946	−10	−5	94/75	91/74	88/73	23	78	77	75
Ottumwa AP	41	1	92	2	842	−8	−4	94/75	91/74	88/73	22	78	77	75
Sioux City AP	42	2	96	2	1095	−11	−7	95/74	92/74	89/73	24	78	77	75
Waterloo	42	3	92	2	868	−15	−10	91/76	89/75	86/74	23	78	77	75
KANSAS														
Atchison	39	3	95	1	945	−2	2	96/77	93/76	91/76	23	81	79	77
Chanute AP	34	4	95	3	977	3	7	100/74	97/74	94/74	23	78	77	76
Dodge City AP (S)	37	5	100	0	2594	0	5	100/69	97/69	95/69	25	74	73	71
El Dorado	37	5	96	5	1282	3	7	101/72	98/73	96/73	24	77	76	75
Emporia	38	2	96	1	1209	1	5	100/74	97/74	94/73	25	78	77	76
Garden City AP	38	0	101	0	2882	−1	4	99/69	96/69	94/69	28	74	73	71
Goodland AP	39	2	101	4	3645	−5	0	99/66	96/65	93/66	31	71	70	68
Great Bend	38	2	98	5	1940	0	4	101/73	98/73	95/73	28	78	76	75
Hutchinson AP	38	0	97	5	1524	4	8	102/72	99/72	97/72	28	77	75	74
Liberal	37	0	101	0	2838	2	7	99/68	96/68	94/68	28	73	72	71
Manhattan, Fort Riley (S)	39	0	96	5	1076	−1	3	99/75	95/75	92/74	24	78	77	76
Parsons	37	2	95	3	908	5	9	100/74	97/74	94/74	23	79	77	76
Russell AP	38	5	98	5	1864	0	4	101/73	98/73	95/73	29	78	76	75
Salina	38	5	97	4	1271	0	5	103/74	100/74	97/73	26	78	77	75
Topeka AP	39	0	95	4	877	0	4	99/75	96/75	93/74	24	79	78	76
Wichita AP	37	4	97	3	1321	3	7	101/72	98/73	96/73	23	77	76	75
KENTUCKY														
Ashland	38	3	82	4	551	5	10	94/76	91/74	89/73	22	78	77	75
Bowling Green AP	37	0	86	3	535	4	10	94/77	92/75	89/74	21	79	77	76
Corbin AP	37	0	84	1	1175	4	9	94/73	92/73	89/72	23	77	76	75
Covington AP	39	0	84	4	869	1	6	92/73	90/72	88/72	22	77	75	74
Hopkinsville, Ft. Campbell	36	4	87	3	540	4	10	94/77	92/75	89/74	21	79	77	76
Lexington AP (S)	38	0	84	4	979	3	8	93/73	91/73	88/72	22	77	76	75
Louisville AP	38	1	85	4	474	5	10	95/74	93/74	90/74	23	79	77	76
Madisonville	37	2	87	3	439	5	10	96/76	93/75	90/75	22	79	78	77
Owensboro	37	5	87	1	420	5	10	97/76	94/75	91/75	23	79	78	77
Paducah AP	37	0	88	4	398	7	12	98/76	95/75	92/75	20	79	78	77
LOUISIANA														
Alexandria AP	31	2	92	2	92	23	27	95/77	94/77	92/77	20	80	79	78
Baton Rouge AP	30	3	91	1	64	25	29	95/77	93/77	92/77	19	80	80	79
Bogalusa	30	5	89	5	103	24	28	95/77	93/77	92/77	19	80	80	79
Houma	29	3	90	4	13	31	35	95/78	93/78	92/77	15	81	80	79
Lafayette AP	30	1	92	0	38	26	30	95/78	94/78	92/78	18	81	80	79
Lake Charles AP (S)	30	1	93	1	14	27	31	95/77	93/77	92/77	17	80	79	79
Minden	32	4	93	2	250	20	25	99/77	96/76	94/76	20	79	79	78
Monroe AP	32	3	92	0	78	20	25	99/77	96/76	94/76	20	79	79	78
Natchitoches	31	5	93	0	120	22	26	97/77	95/77	93/77	20	80	79	78
New Orleans AP	30	0	90	2	3	29	33	93/78	92/78	90/77	16	81	80	79
Shreveport AP(S)	32	3	93	5	252	20	25	99/77	96/76	94/76	20	79	79	78
MAINE														
Augusta AP	44	2	69	5	350	−7	−3	88/73	85/70	82/68	22	74	72	70
Bangor, Dow AFB	44	5	68	5	162	−11	−6	86/70	83/68	80/67	22	73	71	69
Caribou AP (S)	46	5	68	0	624	−18	−13	84/69	81/67	78/66	21	71	69	67
Lewiston	44	0	70	1	182	−7	−2	88/73	85/70	82/68	22	74	72	70
Millinocket AP	45	4	68	4	405	−13	−9	87/69	83/68	80/66	22	72	70	68
Portland (S)	43	4	70	2	61	−6	−1	87/72	84/71	81/69	22	74	72	70
Waterville	44	3	69	4	89	−8	−4	87/72	84/69	81/68	22	74	72	70

Col. 1	Col. 2		Col. 3		Col. 4	Winter,[d] F Col. 5		Summer,[e] F Col. 6			Col. 7	Col. 8		
State and Station	Latitude[b]		Longitude[c]		Elevation[c]	Design Dry-Bulb		Design Dry-Bulb and Mean Coincident Wet-Bulb			Mean Daily	Design Wet-Bulb		
	°	'	°	'	Ft	99%	97.5%	1%	2.5%	5%	Range	1%	2.5%	5%
MARYLAND														
Baltimore AP	39	1	76	4	146	10	13	94/75	91/75	89/74	21	78	77	76
Baltimore CO	39	2	76	3	14	14	17	92/77	89/76	87/75	17	80	78	76
Cumberland	39	4	78	5	945	6	10	92/75	89/74	87/74	22	77	76	75
Frederick AP	39	3	77	3	294	8	12	94/76	91/75	88/74	22	78	77	76
Hagerstown	39	4	77	4	660	8	12	94/75	91/74	89/74	22	77	76	75
Salisbury (S)	38	2	75	3	52	12	16	93/75	91/75	88/74	18	79	77	76
MASSACHUSETTS														
Boston AP (S)	42	2	71	0	15	6	9	91/73	88/71	85/70	16	75	74	72
Clinton	42	2	71	4	398	−2	2	90/72	87/71	84/69	17	75	73	72
Fall River	41	4	71	1	190	5	9	87/72	84/71	81/69	18	74	73	72
Framingham	42	2	71	3	170	3	6	89/72	86/71	83/69	17	74	73	71
Gloucester	42	3	70	4	10	2	5	89/73	86/71	83/70	15	75	74	72
Greenfield	42	3	72	4	205	−7	−2	88/72	85/71	82/69	23	74	73	71
Lawrence	42	4	71	1	57	−6	0	90/73	87/72	84/70	22	76	74	73
Lowell	42	3	71	2	90	−4	1	91/73	88/72	85/70	21	76	74	73
New Bedford	41	4	71	0	70	5	9	85/72	82/71	80/69	19	74	73	72
Pittsfield AP	42	3	73	2	1170	−8	−3	87/71	84/70	81/68	23	73	72	70
Springfield, Westover AFB	42	1	72	3	247	−5	0	90/72	87/71	84/69	19	75	73	72
Taunton	41	5	71	1	20	5	9	89/73	86/72	83/70	18	75	74	73
Worcester AP	42	2	71	5	986	0	4	87/71	84/70	81/68	18	73	72	70
MICHIGAN														
Adrian	41	5	84	0	754	−1	3	91/73	88/72	85/71	23	76	75	73
Alpena AP	45	0	83	3	689	−11	−6	89/70	85/70	83/69	27	73	72	70
Battle Creek AP	42	2	85	2	939	1	5	92/74	88/72	85/70	23	76	74	73
Benton Harbor AP	42	1	86	3	649	1	5	91/72	88/72	85/70	20	75	74	72
Detroit	42	2	83	0	633	3	6	91/73	88/72	86/71	20	76	74	73
Escanaba	45	4	87	0	594	−11	−7	87/70	83/69	80/68	17	73	71	69
Flint AP	42	0	83	4	766	−4	1	90/73	87/72	85/71	25	76	74	72
Grand Rapids AP	42	5	85	3	681	1	5	91/72	88/72	85/70	24	75	74	72
Holland	42	5	86	1	612	2	6	88/72	86/71	83/70	22	75	73	72
Jackson AP	42	2	84	2	1003	1	5	92/74	88/72	85/70	23	76	74	73
Kalamazoo	42	1	85	3	930	1	5	92/74	88/72	85/70	23	76	74	73
Lansing AP	42	5	84	4	852	−3	1	90/73	87/72	84/70	24	75	74	72
Marquette CO	46	3	87	3	677	−12	−8	84/70	81/69	77/66	18	72	70	68
Mt Pleasant	43	4	84	5	796	0	4	91/73	87/72	84/71	24	76	74	72
Muskegon AP	43	1	86	1	627	2	6	86/72	84/70	82/70	21	75	73	72
Pontiac	42	4	83	2	974	0	4	90/73	87/72	85/71	21	76	74	73
Port Huron	43	0	82	3	586	0	4	90/73	87/72	83/71	21	76	74	73
Saginaw AP	43	3	84	1	662	0	4	91/73	87/72	84/71	23	76	74	72
Sault Ste. Marie AP (S)	46	3	84	2	721	−12	−8	84/70	81/69	77/66	23	72	70	68
Traverse City AP	44	4	85	4	618	−3	1	89/72	86/71	83/69	22	75	73	71
Ypsilanti	42	1	83	3	777	1	5	92/72	89/71	86/70	22	75	74	72
MINNESOTA														
Albert Lea	43	4	93	2	1235	−17	−12	90/74	87/72	84/71	24	77	75	73
Alexandria AP	45	5	95	2	1421	−22	−16	91/72	88/72	85/70	24	76	74	72
Bemidji AP	47	3	95	0	1392	−31	−26	88/69	85/69	81/67	24	73	71	69
Brainerd	46	2	94	2	1214	−20	−16	90/73	87/71	84/69	24	75	73	71
Duluth AP	46	5	92	1	1426	−21	−16	85/70	82/68	79/66	22	72	70	68
Fairbault	44	2	93	2	1190	−17	−12	91/74	88/72	85/71	24	77	75	73
Fergus Falls	46	1	96	0	1210	−21	−17	91/72	88/72	85/70	24	76	74	72
International Falls AP	48	3	93	2	1179	−29	−25	85/68	83/68	80/66	26	71	70	68
Mankato	44	1	94	0	785	−17	−12	91/72	88/72	85/70	24	77	75	73
Minneapolis/ St Paul AP	44	5	93	1	822	−16	−12	92/75	89/73	86/71	22	77	75	73
Rochester AP	44	0	92	3	1297	−17	−12	90/74	87/72	84/71	24	77	75	73
St Cloud AP (S)	45	4	94	1	1034	−15	−11	91/74	88/72	85/70	24	76	74	72

Table 3A-12 (Continued)

Col. 1	Col. 2		Col. 3		Col. 4	Winter,[d] F Col. 5		Summer,[e] F Col. 6			Col. 7	Col. 8		
State and Station	Latitude[b] °	'	Longitude[b] °	'	Elevation[c] Ft	Design Dry-Bulb 99%	97.5%	Design Dry-Bulb and Mean Coincident Wet-Bulb 1%	2.5%	5%	Mean Daily Range	Design Wet-Bulb 1%	2.5%	5%
Virginia	47	3	92	3	1435	−25	−21	85/69	83/68	80/66	23	71	70	68
Willmar	45	1	95	0	1133	−15	−11	91/74	88/72	85/71	24	76	74	72
Winona	44	1	91	4	652	−14	−10	91/75	88/73	85/72	24	77	75	74
MISSISSIPPI														
Biloxi, Keesler AFB	30	2	89	0	25	28	31	94/79	92/79	90/78	16	82	81	80
Clarksdale	34	1	90	3	178	14	19	96/77	94/77	92/76	21	80	79	78
Columbus AFB	33	4	88	3	224	15	20	95/77	93/77	91/76	22	80	79	78
Greenville AFB	33	3	91	1	139	15	20	95/77	93/77	91/76	21	80	79	78
Greenwood	33	3	90	1	128	15	20	95/77	93/77	91/76	21	80	79	78
Hattiesburg	31	2	89	2	200	24	27	96/78	94/77	92/77	21	81	80	79
Jackson AP	32	2	90	1	330	21	25	97/76	95/76	93/76	21	79	78	78
Laurel	31	4	89	1	264	24	27	96/78	94/77	92/77	21	81	80	79
McComb AP	31	2	90	3	458	21	26	96/77	94/76	92/76	18	80	79	78
Meridian AP	32	2	88	5	294	19	23	97/77	95/76	93/76	22	80	79	78
Natchez	31	4	91	3	168	23	27	96/78	94/78	92/77	21	81	80	79
Tupelo	34	2	88	4	289	14	19	96/77	94/77	92/76	22	80	79	78
Vicksburg CO	32	2	91	0	234	22	26	97/78	95/78	93/77	21	81	80	79
MISSOURI														
Cape Girardeau	37	1	89	3	330	8	13	98/76	95/75	92/75	21	79	78	77
Columbia AP (S)	39	0	92	2	778	−1	4	97/74	94/74	91/73	22	78	77	76
Farmington AP	37	5	90	3	928	3	8	96/76	93/75	90/74	22	78	77	75
Hannibal	39	4	91	2	489	−2	3	96/76	93/76	90/76	22	80	78	77
Jefferson City	38	4	92	1	640	2	7	98/75	95/74	92/74	23	78	77	76
Joplin AP	37	1	94	3	982	6	10	100/73	97/73	94/73	24	78	77	76
Kansas City AP	39	1	94	4	742	2	6	99/75	96/74	93/74	20	78	77	76
Kirksville AP	40	1	92	4	966	−5	0	96/74	93/74	90/73	24	78	77	76
Mexico	39	1	92	0	775	−1	4	97/74	94/74	91/73	22	78	77	76
Moberly	39	3	92	3	850	−2	3	97/74	94/74	91/73	23	78	77	76
Poplar Bluff	36	5	90	3	322	11	16	98/78	95/76	92/76	22	81	79	78
Rolla	38	0	91	5	1202	3	9	94/77	91/75	89/74	22	78	77	76
St Joseph AP	39	5	95	0	809	−3	2	96/77	93/76	91/76	23	81	79	77
St Louis AP	38	5	90	2	535	2	6	97/75	94/75	91/74	21	78	77	76
St Louis CO	38	4	90	2	465	3	8	98/75	94/75	91/74	18	78	77	76
Sedalia, Whiteman AFB	38	4	93	3	838	−1	4	95/76	92/76	90/75	22	79	78	76
Sikeston	36	5	89	3	318	9	15	98/77	95/76	92/75	21	80	78	77
Springfield AP	37	1	93	2	1265	3	9	96/73	93/74	91/74	23	78	77	75
MONTANA														
Billings AP	45	5	108	3	3567	−15	−10	94/64	91/64	88/63	31	67	66	64
Bozeman	45	5	111	0	4856	−20	−14	90/61	87/60	84/59	32	63	62	60
Butte AP	46	0	112	3	5526r	−24	−17	86/58	83/56	80/56	35	60	58	57
Cut Bank AP	48	4	112	2	3838r	−25	−20	88/61	85/61	82/60	35	64	62	61
Glasgow AP (S)	48	1	106	4	2277	−22	−18	92/64	89/63	85/62	29	68	66	64
Glendive	47	1	104	4	2076	−18	−13	95/66	92/64	89/62	29	69	67	65
Great Falls AP (S)	47	3	111	2	3664r	−21	−15	91/60	88/60	85/59	28	64	62	60
Havre	48	3	109	4	2488	−18	−11	94/65	90/64	87/63	33	68	66	65
Helena AP	46	4	112	0	3893	−21	−16	91/60	88/60	85/59	32	64	62	61
Kalispell AP	48	2	114	2	2965	−14	−7	91/62	87/61	84/60	34	65	63	62
Lewiston AP	47	0	109	3	4132	−22	−16	90/62	87/61	83/60	30	65	63	62
Livingston AP	45	4	110	3	4653	−20	−14	90/61	87/60	84/59	32	63	62	60
Miles City AP	46	3	105	5	2629	−20	−15	98/66	95/66	92/65	30	70	68	67
Missoula AP	46	5	114	1	3200	−13	−6	92/62	88/61	85/60	36	65	63	62
NEBRASKA														
Beatrice	40	2	96	5	1235	−5	−2	99/75	95/74	92/74	24	78	77	76
Chadron AP	42	5	103	0	3300	−8	−3	97/66	94/65	91/65	30	71	69	68
Columbus	41	3	97	2	1442	−6	−2	98/74	95/73	92/73	25	77	76	75
Fremont	41	3	96	3	1203	−6	−2	98/75	95/74	92/74	22	78	77	76

Col. 1	Col. 2		Col. 3		Col. 4	Winter,[d] F Col. 5		Summer,[e] F Col. 6			Col. 7	Col. 8		
State and Station	Latitude[b]		Longitude[c]		Elevation[c]	Design Dry-Bulb		Design Dry-Bulb and Mean Coincident Wet-Bulb			Mean Daily	Design Wet-Bulb		
	°	′	°	′	Ft	99%	97.5%	1%	2.5%	5%	Range	1%	2.5%	5%
Grand Island AP	41	0	98	2	1841	−8	−3	97/72	94/71	91/71	28	75	74	73
Hastings	40	4	98	3	1932	−7	−3	97/72	94/71	91/71	27	75	74	73
Kearney	40	4	99	1	2146	−9	−4	96/71	93/70	90/70	28	74	73	72
Lincoln CO (S)	40	5	96	5	1150	−5	−2	99/75	95/74	92/74	24	78	77	76
McCook	40	1	100	4	2565	−6	−2	98/69	95/69	91/69	28	74	72	71
Norfolk	42	0	97	3	1532	−8	−4	97/74	93/74	90/73	30	78	77	75
North Platte AP (S)	41	1	100	4	2779	−8	−4	97/69	94/69	90/69	28	74	72	71
Omaha AP	41	2	95	5	978	−8	−3	94/76	91/75	88/74	22	78	77	75
Scottsbluff AP	41	5	103	4	3950	−8	−3	95/65	92/65	90/64	31	70	68	67
Sidney AP	41	1	103	0	4292	−8	−3	95/65	92/65	90/64	31	70	68	67
NEVADA														
Carson City	39	1	119	5	4675	4	9	94/60	91/59	89/58	42	63	61	60
Elko AP	40	5	115	5	5075	−8	−2	94/59	92/59	90/58	42	63	62	60
Ely AP (S)	39	1	114	5	6257	−10	−4	89/57	87/56	85/55	39	60	59	58
Las Vegas AP (S)	36	1	115	1	2162	25	28	108/66	106/65	104/65	30	71	70	69
Lovelock AP	40	0	118	3	.3900	8	12	98/63	96/63	93/62	42	66	65	64
Reno AP (S)	39	3	119	5	4404	5	10	95/61	92/60	90/59	45	64	62	61
Reno CO	39	3	119	5	4490	6	11	96/61	93/60	91/59	45	64	62	61
Tonopah AP	38	0	117	1	5426	5	10	94/60	92/59	90/58	40	64	62	61
Winnemucca AP	40	5	117	5	4299	−1	3	96/60	94/60	92/60	42	64	62	61
NEW HAMPSHIRE														
Berlin	44	3	71	1	1110	−14	−9	87/71	84/69	81/68	22	73	71	70
Claremont	43	2	72	2	420	−9	−4	89/72	86/70	83/69	24	74	73	71
Concord AP	43	1	71	3	339	−8	−3	90/72	87/70	84/69	26	74	73	71
Keene	43	0	72	2	490	−12	−7	90/72	87/70	83/69	24	74	73	71
Laconia	43	3	71	3	505	−10	−5	89/72	86/70	83/69	25	74	73	71
Manchester, Grenier AFB	43	0	71	3	253	−8	−3	91/72	88/71	85/70	24	75	74	72
Portsmouth, Pease AFB	43	1	70	5	127	−2	2	89/73	85/71	83/70	22	75	74	72
NEW JERSEY														
Atlantic City CO	39	3	74	3	11	10	13	92/74	89/74	86/72	18	78	77	75
Long Branch	40	2	74	0	20	10	13	93/74	90/73	87/72	18	78	77	75
Newark AP	40	4	74	1	11	10	14	94/74	91/73	88/72	20	77	76	75
New Brunswick	40	3	74	3	86	6	10	92/74	89/73	86/72	19	77	76	75
Paterson	40	5	74	1	100	6	10	94/74	91/73	88/72	21	77	76	75
Phillipsburg	40	4	75	1	180	1	6	92/73	89/72	86/71	21	76	75	74
Trenton CO	40	1	74	5	144	11	14	91/75	88/74	85/73	19	78	76	75
Vineland	39	3	75	0	95	8	11	91/75	89/74	86/73	19	78	76	75
NEW MEXICO														
Alamagordo, Holloman AFB	32	5	106	1	4070	14	19	98/64	96/64	94/64	30	69	68	67
Albuquerque AP (S)	35	0	106	4	5310	12	16	96/61	94/61	92/61	27	66	65	64
Artesia	32	5	104	2	3375	13	19	103/67	100/67	97/67	30	72	71	70
Carlsbad AP	32	2	104	2	3234	13	19	103/67	100/67	97/67	28	72	71	70
Clovis AP	34	3	103	1	4279	8	13	95/65	93/65	91/65	28	69	68	67
Farmington AP	36	5	108	1	5495	1	6	95/63	93/62	91/61	30	67	65	64
Gallup	35	3	108	5	6465	0	5	90/59	89/58	86/58	32	64	62	61
Grants	35	1	107	5	6520	−1	4	89/59	88/58	85/57	32	64	62	61
Hobbs AP	32	4	103	1	3664	13	18	101/66	99/66	97/66	29	71	70	69
Las Cruces	32	2	107	0	3900	15	20	99/64	96/64	94/64	30	69	68	67
Los Alamos	35	5	106	2	7410	5	9	89/60	87/60	85/60	32	62	61	60
Raton AP	36	5	104	3	6379	−4	1	91/60	89/60	87/60	34	65	64	63
Roswell, Walker AFB	33	2	104	3	3643	13	18	100/66	98/66	96/66	33	71	70	69
Santa Fe CO	35	4	106	0	7045	6	10	90/61	88/61	86/61	28	63	62	61
Silver City AP	32	4	108	2	5373	5	10	95/61	94/60	91/60	30	66	64	63
Socorro AP	34	0	106	5	4617	13	17	97/62	95/62	93/62	30	67	66	65
Tucumcari AP	35	1	103	4	4053	8	13	99/66	97/66	95/65	28	70	69	68
NEW YORK														
Albany AP (S)	42	5	73	5	277	−6	−1	91/73	88/72	85/70	23	75	74	72
Albany CO	42	5	73	5	19	−4	1	91/73	88/72	85/70	20	75	74	72
Auburn	43	0	76	3	715	−3	2	90/73	87/71	84/70	22	75	73	72
Batavia	43	0	78	1	900	1	5	90/72	87/71	84/70	22	75	73	72
Binghamton AP	42	1	76	0	1590	−2	1	86/71	83/69	81/68	20	73	72	70
Buffalo AP	43	0	78	4	705r	2	6	88/71	85/70	83/69	21	74	73	72
Cortland	42	4	76	1	1129	−5	0	88/71	85/71	82/70	23	74	73	71
Dunkirk	42	3	79	2	590	4	9	88/73	85/72	83/71	18	75	74	72

Table 3A-12 (Continued)

Col. 1	Col. 2		Col. 3		Col. 4	Winter,[d] F Col. 5		Summer,[e] F Col. 6			Col. 7	Col. 8		
State and Station	Latitude[b]		Longitude[c]		Elevation[c]	Design Dry-Bulb		Design Dry-Bulb and Mean Coincident Wet-Bulb			Mean Daily	Design Wet-Bulb		
	°	′	°	′	Ft	99%	97.5%	1%	2.5%	5%	Range	1%	2.5%	5%
Elmira AP	42	1	76	5	860	−4	1	89/71	86/71	83/70	24	74	73	71
Geneva (S)	42	5	77	0	590	−3	2	90/73	87/71	84/70	22	75	73	72
Glens Falls	42	2	73	4	321	−11	−5	88/72	85/71	82/69	23	74	73	71
Gloversville	43	1	74	2	790	−8	−2	89/72	86/71	83/69	23	75	74	72
Hornell	42	2	77	4	1325	−4	0	88/71	85/70	82/69	24	74	73	72
Ithaca (S)	42	3	76	3	950	−5	0	88/71	85/71	82/70	24	74	73	71
Jamestown	42	1	79	2	1390	−1	3	88/70	86/70	83/69	20	74	72	71
Kingston	42	0	74	0	279	−3	2	91/73	88/72	85/70	22	76	74	73
Lockport	43	1	78	4	520	4	7	89/74	86/72	84/71	21	76	74	73
Massena AP	45	0	75	0	202r	−13	−8	86/70	83/69	80/68	20	73	72	70
Newburg- Stewart AFB	41	3	74	1	460	−1	4	90/73	88/72	85/70	21	76	74	73
NYC-Central Park (S)	40	5	74	0	132	11	15	92/74	89/73	87/72	17	76	75	74
NYC- Kennedy AP	40	4	73	5	16	12	15	90/73	87/72	84/71	16	76	75	74
NYC- La Guardia AP	40	5	73	5	19	11	15	92/74	89/73	87/72	16	76	75	74
Niagra Falls AP	43	1	79	0	596	4	7	89/74	86/72	84/71	20	76	74	73
Olean	42	1	78	3	1420	−2	2	87/71	84/71	81/70	23	74	73	71
Oneonta	42	3	75	0	1150	−7	−4	86/71	83/69	80/68	24	73	72	70
Oswego CO	43	3	76	3	300	1	7	86/73	83/71	80/70	20	75	73	72
Plattsburg AFB	44	4	73	3	165	−13	−8	86/70	83/69	80/68	22	73	72	70
Poughkeepsie	41	4	73	5	103	0	6	92/74	89/74	86/72	21	77	75	74
Rochester AP	43	1	77	4	543	1	5	91/73	88/71	85/70	22	75	73	72
Rome- Griffiss AFB	43	1	75	3	515	−11	−5	88/71	85/70	83/69	22	75	73	71
Schenectady (S)	42	5	74	0	217	−4	1	90/73	87/72	84/70	22	75	74	72
Suffolk County AFB	40	5			57	7	10	86/72	83/71	80/70	16	76	74	73
Syracuse AP	43	1	76	1	424	−3	2	90/73	87/71	84/70	20	75	73	72
Utica	43	1	75	2	714	−12	−6	88/73	85/71	82/70	22	75	73	71
Watertown	44	0	76	0	497	−11	−6	86/73	83/71	81/70	20	75	73	72
NORTH CAROLINA														
Asheville AP	35	3	82	3	217r	10	14	89/73	87/72	85/71	21	75	74	72
Charlotte AP	35	0	81	0	735	18	22	95/74	93/74	91/74	20	77	76	76
Durham	36	0	78	5	406	16	20	94/75	92/75	90/75	20	78	77	76
Elizabeth City AP	36	2	76	1	10	12	19	93/78	91/77	89/76	18	80	78	78
Fayetteville, Pope AFB	35	1	79	0	95	17	20	95/76	92/76	90/75	20	79	78	77
Goldsboro, Seymour- Johnson AFB	35	2	78	0	88	18	21	94/77	91/76	89/75	18	79	78	77
Greensboro AP (S)	36	1	80	0	887	14	18	93/74	91/73	89/73	21	77	76	75
Greenville	35	4	77	2	25	18	21	93/77	91/76	89/75	19	79	78	77
Henderson	36	2	78	2	510	12	15	95/77	92/76	90/76	20	79	78	77
Hickory	35	4	81	2	1165	14	18	92/73	90/72	88/72	21	75	74	73
Jacksonville	34	5	77	3	24	20	24	92/78	90/78	88/77	18	80	79	78
Lumberton	34	4	79	0	132	18	21	95/76	92/76	90/75	20	79	78	77
New Bern AP	35	1	77	0	17	20	24	92/78	90/78	88/77	18	80	79	78
Raleigh/ Durham AP (S)	35	5	78	5	433	16	20	94/75	92/75	90/75	20	78	77	76
Rocky Mount	36	0	77	5	81	18	21	94/77	91/76	89/75	19	79	78	77
Wilmington AP	34	2	78	0	30	23	26	93/79	91/78	89/77	18	81	80	79
Winston-Salem AP	36	1	80	1	967	16	20	94/74	91/73	89/73	20	76	75	74
NORTH DAKOTA														
Bismarck AP (S)	46	5	100	5	1647	−23	−19	95/68	91/68	88/67	27	73	71	70
Devil's Lake	48	1	98	5	1471	−25	−21	91/69	88/68	85/66	25	73	71	69
Dickinson AP	46	5	102	5	2595	−21	−17	94/68	90/66	87/65	25	71	69	68
Fargo AP	46	5	96	5	900	−22	−18	92/73	89/71	85/69	25	76	74	72
Grand Forks AP	48	0	97	2	832	−26	−22	91/70	87/70	84/68	25	74	72	70
Jamestown AP	47	0	98	4	1492	−22	−18	94/70	90/69	87/68	26	74	74	71
Minot AP	48	2	101	2	1713	−24	−20	92/68	89/67	86/65	25	72	70	68
Williston	48	1	103	4	1877	−25	−21	91/68	88/67	85/65	25	72	70	68
OHIO														
Akron-Canton AP	41	0	81	3	1210	1	6	89/72	86/71	84/70	21	75	73	72
Ashtabula	42	0	80	5	690	4	9	88/73	85/72	83/71	18	75	74	72
Athens	39	2	82	1	700	0	6	95/75	92/74	90/73	22	78	76	74
Bowling Green	41	3	83	4	675	−2	2	92/73	89/73	86/71	23	76	75	73

Col. 1	Col. 2		Col. 3		Col. 4	Winter,[d] F Col. 5		Summer,[e] F Col. 6			Col. 7	Col. 8		
State and Station	Latitude[b]		Longitude[c]		Elevation[c]	Design Dry-Bulb		Design Dry-Bulb and Mean Coincident Wet-Bulb			Mean Daily Range	Design Wet-Bulb		
	°	′	°	′	Ft	99%	97.5%	1%	2.5%	5%		1%	2.5%	5%
Cambridge	40	0	81	4	800	1	7	93/75	90/74	87/73	23	78	76	75
Chillicothe	39	2	83	0	638	0	6	95/75	92/74	90/73	22	78	76	74
Cincinnati CO	39	1	84	4	761	1	6	92/73	90/72	88/72	21	77	75	74
Cleveland AP (S)	41	2	81	5	777r	1	5	91/73	88/72	86/71	22	76	74	73
Columbus AP (S)	40	0	82	5	812	0	5	92/73	90/73	87/72	24	77	75	74
Dayton AP	39	5	84	1	997	−1	4	91/73	89/72	86/71	20	76	75	73
Defiance	41	2	84	2	700	−1	4	94/74	91/73	88/72	24	77	76	74
Findlay AP	41	0	83	4	797	2	3	92/74	90/73	87/72	24	77	76	74
Fremont	41	2	83	1	600	−3	1	90/73	88/73	85/71	24	76	75	73
Hamilton	39	2	84	3	650	0	5	92/73	90/72	87/71	22	76	75	73
Lancaster	39	4	82	4	920	0	5	93/74	91/73	88/72	23	77	75	74
Lima	40	4	84	0	860	−1	4	94/74	91/73	88/72	24	77	76	74
Mansfield AP	40	5	82	3	1297	0	5	90/73	87/72	85/72	22	76	74	73
Marion	40	4	83	1	920	0	5	93/74	91/73	88/72	23	77	76	74
Middletown	39	3	84	3	635	0	5	92/73	90/72	87/71	22	76	75	73
Newark	40	1	82	3	825	−1	5	94/73	92/73	89/72	23	77	75	74
Norwalk	41	1	82	4	720	−3	1	90/73	88/73	85/71	22	76	75	73
Portsmouth	38	5	83	0	530	5	10	95/76	92/74	89/73	22	78	77	75
Sandusky CO	41	3	82	4	606	1	6	93/73	91/72	88/71	21	76	74	73
Springfield	40	0	83	5	1020	−1	3	91/74	89/73	87/72	21	77	76	74
Steubenville	40	2	80	4	992	1	5	89/72	86/71	84/70	22	74	73	72
Toledo AP	41	4	83	5	676r	−3	1	90/73	88/73	85/71	25	76	75	73
Warren	41	2	80	5	900	0	5	89/71	87/71	85/70	23	74	73	71
Wooster	40	5	82	0	1030	1	6	89/72	86/71	84/70	22	75	73	72
Youngstown AP	41	2	80	4	1178	−1	4	88/71	86/71	84/70	23	74	73	71
Zanesville AP	40	0	81	5	881	1	7	93/75	90/74	87/73	23	78	76	75
OKLAHOMA														
Ada	34	5	96	4	1015	10	14	100/74	97/74	95/74	23	77	76	75
Altus AFB	34	4	99	2	1390	11	16	102/73	100/73	98/73	25	77	76	75
Ardmore	34	2	97	1	880	13	17	100/74	98/74	95/74	23	77	77	76
Bartlesville	36	5	96	0	715	6	10	101/73	98/74	95/74	23	77	77	76
Chickasha	35	0	98	0	1085	10	14	101/74	98/74	95/74	24	78	77	76
Enid-Vance AFB	36	2	98	0	1287	9	13	103/74	100/74	97/74	24	79	77	76
Lawton AP	34	3	98	2	1108	12	16	101/74	99/74	96/74	24	78	77	76
Mc Alester	34	5	95	5	760	14	19	99/74	96/74	93/74	23	77	76	75
Muskogee AP	35	4	95	2	610	10	15	101/74	98/75	95/75	23	79	78	77
Norman	35	1	97	3	1109	9	13	99/74	96/74	94/74	24	77	76	75
Oklahoma City AP (S)	35	2	97	4	1280	9	13	100/74	97/74	95/73	23	78	77	76
Ponca City	36	4	97	0	996	5	9	100/74	97/74	94/74	24	77	76	76
Seminole	35	2	96	4	865	11	15	99/74	96/74	94/73	23	77	76	75
Stillwater (S)	36	1	97	1	884	8	13	100/74	96/74	93/74	24	77	76	75
Tulsa AP	36	1	95	5	650	8	13	101/74	98/75	95/75	22	79	78	77
Woodward	36	3	99	3	1900	6	10	100/73	97/73	94/73	26	78	76	75
OREGON														
Albany	44	4	123	1	224	18	22	92/67	89/66	86/65	31	69	67	66
Astoria AP (S)	46	1	123	5	8	25	29	75/65	71/62	68/61	16	65	63	62
Baker AP	44	5	117	5	3368	−1	6	92/63	89/61	86/60	30	65	63	61
Bend	44	0	121	2	3599	−3	4	90/62	87/60	84/59	33	64	62	60
Corvallis (S)	44	3	123	2	221	18	22	92/67	89/66	86/65	31	69	67	66
Eugene AP	44	1	123	1	364	17	22	92/67	89/66	86/65	31	69	67	66
Grants Pass	42	3	123	2	925	20	24	99/69	96/68	93/67	33	71	69	68
Klamath Falls AP	42	1	121	4	4091	4	9	90/61	87/60	84/59	36	63	61	60
Medford AP (S)	42	2	122	5	1298	19	23	98/68	94/67	91/66	35	70	68	67
Pendleton AP	45	4	118	5	1492	−2	5	97/65	93/64	90/62	29	66	65	63
Portland AP	45	4	122	4	21	17	23	89/68	85/67	81/65	23	69	67	66
Portland CO	45	3	122	4	57	18	24	90/68	86/67	82/65	21	69	67	66
Roseburg AP	43	1	123	2	505	18	23	93/67	90/66	87/65	30	69	67	66
Salem AP	45	0	123	0	195	18	23	92/68	88/66	84/65	31	69	68	66
The Dalles	45	4	121	1	102	13	19	93/69	89/68	85/66	28	70	68	67
PENNSYLVANIA														
Allentown AP	40	4	75	3	376	4	9	92/73	88/72	86/72	22	76	75	73
Altoona CO	40	2	78	2	1468	0	5	90/72	87/71	84/70	23	74	73	72
Butler	40	4	80	0	1100	1	6	90/73	87/72	85/71	22	75	74	73
Chambersburg	40	0	77	4	640	4	8	93/75	90/74	87/73	23	77	76	75
Erie AP	42	1	80	1	732	4	9	88/73	85/72	83/71	18	75	74	72

Table 3A-12 (Continued)

Col. 1	Col. 2		Col. 3		Col. 4	Winter,[d] F Col. 5		Summer,[e] F Col. 6			Col. 7	Col. 8		
State and Station	Latitude[b]		Longitude[c]		Elevation[c]	Design Dry-Bulb		Design Dry-Bulb and Mean Coincident Wet-Bulb			Mean Daily	Design Wet-Bulb		
	°	'	°	'	Ft	99%	97.5%	1%	2.5%	5%	Range	1%	2.5%	5%
Harrisburg AP	40	1	76	5	335	7	11	94/75	91/74	88/73	21	77	76	75
Johnstown	40	2	78	5	1214	−3	2	86/70	83/70	80/68	23	72	71	70
Lancaster	40	1	76	2	255	4	8	93/75	90/74	87/73	22	77	76	75
Meadville	41	4	80	1	1065	0	4	88/71	85/70	83/69	21	73	72	71
New Castle	41	0	80	2	825	2	7	91/73	88/72	86/71	23	75	74	73
Philadelphia AP	39	5	75	2	7	10	14	93/75	90/74	87/72	21	77	76	75
Pittsburgh AP	40	3	80	1	1137	1	5	89/72	86/71	84/70	22	74	73	72
Pittsburgh CO	40	3	80	0	749r	3	7	91/72	88/71	86/70	19	74	73	72
Reading CO	40	2	76	0	226	9	13	92/73	89/72	86/72	19	76	75	73
Scranton/ Wilkes-Barre	41	2	75	4	940	1	5	90/72	87/71	84/70	19	74	73	72
State College (S)	40	5	77	5	1175	3	7	90/72	87/71	84/70	23	74	73	72
Sunbury	40	5	76	5	480	2	7	92/73	89/72	86/70	22	75	74	73
Uniontown	39	5	79	4	1040	5	9	91/74	88/73	85/72	22	76	75	74
Warren	41	5	79	1	1280	−2	4	89/71	86/71	83/70	24	74	73	72
West Chester	40	0	75	4	440	9	13	92/75	89/74	86/72	20	77	76	75
Williamsport AP	41	1	77	0	527	2	7	92/73	89/72	86/70	23	75	74	73
York	40	0	76	4	390	8	12	94/75	91/74	88/73	22	77	76	75
RHODE ISLAND														
Newport (S)	41	3	71	2	20	5	9	88/73	85/72	82/70	16	76	75	73
Providence AP	41	4	71	3	55	5	9	89/73	86/72	83/70	19	75	74	73
SOUTH CAROLINA														
Anderson	34	3	82	4	764	19	23	94/74	92/74	90/74	21	77	76	75
Charleston AFB (S)	32	5	80	0	41	24	27	93/78	91/78	89/77	18	81	80	79
Charleston CO	32	5	80	0	9	25	28	94/78	92/78	90/77	13	81	80	79
Columbia AP	34	0	81	1	217	20	24	97/76	95/75	93/75	22	79	78	77
Florence AP	34	1	79	4	146	22	25	94/77	92/77	90/76	21	80	79	78
Georgetown	33	2	79	2	14	23	26	92/79	90/78	88/77	18	81	80	79
Greenville AP	34	5	82	1	957	18	22	93/74	91/74	89/74	21	77	76	75
Greenwood	34	1	82	1	671	18	22	95/75	93/74	91/74	21	78	77	76
Orangeburg	33	3	80	5	244	20	24	97/76	95/75	93/75	20	79	78	77
Rock Hill	35	0	81	0	470	19	23	96/75	94/74	92/74	20	78	77	76
Spartanburg AP	35	0	82	0	816	18	22	93/74	91/74	89/74	20	77	76	75
Sumter-Shaw AFB	34	0	80	3	291	22	25	95/77	92/76	90/75	21	79	78	77
SOUTH DAKOTA														
Aberdeen AP	45	3	98	3	1296	−19	−15	94/73	91/72	88/70	27	77	75	73
Brookings	44	2	96	5	1642	−17	−13	95/73	92/72	89/71	25	77	75	73
Huron AP	44	3	98	1	1282	−18	−14	96/73	93/72	90/71	28	77	75	73
Mitchell	43	5	98	0	1346	−15	−10	96/72	93/71	90/70	28	76	75	73
Pierre AP	44	2	100	2	1718r	−15	−10	99/71	95/71	92/69	29	75	74	72
Rapid City AP (S)	44	0	103	0	3165	−11	−7	95/66	92/65	89/65	28	71	69	67
Sioux Falls AP	43	4	96	4	1420	−15	−11	94/73	91/72	88/71	24	76	75	73
Watertown AP	45	0	97	0	1746	−19	−15	94/73	91/72	88/71	26	76	75	73
Yankton	43	0	97	2	1280	−13	−7	94/73	91/72	88/71	25	77	76	74
TENNESSEE														
Athens	33	3	84	4	940	13	18	95/74	92/73	90/73	22	77	76	75
Bristol- Tri City AP	36	3	82	2	1519	9	14	91/72	89/72	87/71	22	75	75	73
Chattanooga AP	35	0	85	1	670	13	18	96/75	93/74	91/74	22	78	77	76
Clarksville	36	4	87	2	470	6	12	95/76	93/74	90/74	21	78	77	76
Columbia	35	4	87	0	690	10	15	97/75	94/74	91/74	21	78	77	76
Dyersburg	36	0	89	3	334	10	15	96/78	94/77	91/76	21	81	80	78
Greenville	35	5	82	5	1320	11	16	92/73	90/72	88/72	22	76	75	74
Jackson AP	35	4	88	5	413	11	16	98/76	95/75	92/75	21	79	78	77
Knoxville AP	35	5	84	0	980	13	19	94/74	92/73	90/73	21	77	76	75
Memphis AP	35	0	90	0	263	13	18	98/77	95/76	93/76	21	80	79	78
Murfreesboro	35	5	86	2	608	9	14	97/75	94/74	91/74	22	78	77	76
Nashville AP (S)	36	1	86	4	577	9	14	97/75	94/74	91/74	21	78	77	76
Tullahoma	35	2	86	1	1075	8	13	96/74	93/73	91/73	22	77	76	75
TEXAS														
Abilene AP	32	3	99	4	1759	15	20	101/71	99/71	97/71	22	75	74	74
Alice AP	27	4	98	0	180	31	34	100/78	98/77	95/77	20	82	81	79
Amarillo AP	35	1	101	4	3607	6	11	98/67	95/67	93/67	26	71	70	70
Austin AP	30	2	97	4	597	24	28	100/74	98/74	97/74	22	78	77	77
Bay City	29	0	96	0	52	29	33	96/77	94/77	92/77	16	80	79	79
Beaumont	30	0	94	0	18	27	31	95/79	93/78	91/78	19	81	80	80
Beeville	28	2	97	4	225	30	33	99/78	97/77	95/77	18	82	81	79
Big Spring AP (S)	32	2	101	3	2537	16	20	100/69	97/69	95/69	26	74	73	72
Brownsville AP (S)	25	5	97	3	16	35	39	94/77	93/77	92/77	18	80	79	79

Col. 1	Col. 2		Col. 3		Col. 4	Winter,[d] F Col. 5		Summer,[e] F Col. 6			Col. 7	Col. 8		
State and Station	Latitude[b]		Longitude[c]		Elevation[c]	Design Dry-Bulb		Design Dry-Bulb and Mean Coincident Wet-Bulb			Mean Daily	Design Wet-Bulb		
	°	′	°	′	Ft	99%	97.5%	1%	2.5%	5%	Range	1%	2.5%	5%
Brownwood	31	5	99	0	1435	18	22	101/73	99/73	96/73	22	77	76	75
Bryan AP	30	4	96	2	275	24	29	98/76	96/76	94/76	20	79	78	78
Corpus Christi AP	27	5	97	3	43	31	35	95/78	94/78	92/78	19	80	80	79
Corsicana	32	0	96	3	425	20	25	100/75	98/75	96/75	21	79	78	77
Dallas AP	32	5	96	5	481	18	22	102/75	100/75	97/75	20	78	78	77
Del Rio, Laughlin AFB	29	2	101	0	1072	26	31	100/73	98/73	97/73	24	79	77	76
Denton	33	1	97	1	655	17	22	101/74	99/74	97/74	22	78	77	76
Eagle Pass	28	5	100	3	743	27	32	101/73	99/73	98/73	24	78	78	77
El Paso AP (S)	31	5	106	2	3918	20	24	100/64	98/64	96/64	27	69	68	68
Fort Worth AP (S)	32	5	97	0	544r	17	22	101/74	99/74	97/74	22	78	77	76
Galveston AP	29	2	94	5	5	31	36	90/79	89/79	88/78	10	81	80	80
Greenville	33	0	96	1	575	17	22	101/74	99/74	97/74	21	78	77	76
Harlingen	26	1	97	4	37	35	39	96/77	94/77	93/77	19	80	79	79
Houston AP	29	4	95	2	50	27	32	96/77	94/77	92/77	18	80	79	79
Houston CO	29	5	95	2	158r	28	33	97/77	95/77	93/77	18	80	79	79
Huntsville	30	4	95	3	494	22	27	100/75	98/75	96/75	20	78	78	77
Killeen-Gray AFB	31	0	97	4	1021	20	25	99/73	97/73	95/73	22	77	76	75
Lamesa	32	5	102	0	2965	13	17	99/69	96/69	94/69	26	73	72	71
Laredo AFB	27	3	99	3	503	32	36	102/73	101/73	99/74	23	78	78	77
Longview	32	2	94	4	345	19	24	99/76	97/76	95/76	20	80	79	78
Lubbock AP	33	4	101	5	3243	10	15	98/69	96/69	94/69	26	73	72	71
Lufkin AP	31	1	94	5	286	25	29	99/76	97/76	94/76	20	80	79	78
Mc Allen	26	1	98	1	122	35	39	97/77	95/77	94/77	21	80	79	79
Midland AP (S)	32	0	102	1	2815r	16	21	100/69	98/69	96/69	26	73	72	71
Mineral Wells AP	32	5	98	0	934	17	22	101/74	99/74	97/74	22	78	77	76
Palestine CO	31	5	95	4	580	23	27	100/76	98/76	96/76	20	79	79	78
Pampa	35	3	101	0	3230	7	12	99/67	96/67	94/67	26	71	70	70
Pecos	31	2	103	3	2580	16	21	100/69	98/69	96/69	27	73	72	71
Plainview	34	1	101	4	3400	8	13	98/68	96/68	94/68	26	72	71	70
Port Arthur AP	30	0	94	0	16	27	31	95/79	93/78	91/78	19	81	80	80
San Angelo, Goodfellow AFB	31	2	100	2	1878	18	22	101/71	99/71	97/70	24	75	74	73
San Antonio AP (S)	29	3	98	3	792	25	30	99/72	97/73	96/73	19	77	76	76
Sherman Perrin AFB	33	4	96	4	763	15	20	100/75	98/75	95/74	22	78	77	76
Snyder	32	4	101	0	2325	13	18	100/70	98/70	96/70	26	74	73	72
Temple	31	1	97	2	675	22	27	100/74	99/74	97/74	22	78	77	77
Tyler AP	32	2	95	2	527	19	24	99/76	97/76	95/76	21	80	79	78
Vernon	34	1	99	2	1225	13	17	102/73	100/73	97/73	24	77	76	75
Victoria AP	28	5	97	0	104	29	32	98/78	96/77	94/77	18	82	81	79
Waco AP	31	4	97	0	500	21	26	101/75	99/75	97/75	22	78	78	77
Wichita Falls AP	34	0	98	3	994	14	18	103/73	101/73	98/73	24	77	76	75
UTAH														
Cedar City AP	37	4	113	1	5613	−2	5	93/60	91/60	89/59	32	65	63	62
Logan	41	4	111	5	4775	−3	2	93/62	91/61	88/60	33	65	64	63
Moab	38	5	109	3	3965	6	11	100/60	98/60	96/60	30	65	64	63
Ogden AP	41	1	112	0	4455	1	5	93/63	91/61	88/61	33	66	65	64
Price	39	4	110	5	5580	−2	5	93/60	91/60	89/59	33	65	63	62
Provo	40	1	111	4	4470	1	6	98/62	96/62	94/61	32	66	65	64
Richfield	38	5	112	0	5300	−2	5	93/60	91/60	89/59	34	65	63	62
St George CO	37	1	113	4	2899	14	21	103/65	101/65	99/64	33	70	68	67
Salt Lake City AP (S)	40	5	112	0	4220	3	8	97/62	95/62	92/61	32	66	65	64
Vernal AP	40	3	109	3	5280	−5	0	91/61	89/60	86/59	32	64	63	62
VERMONT														
Barre	44	1	72	3	1120	−16	−11	84/71	81/69	78/68	23	73	71	70
Burlington AP (S)	44	3	73	1	331	−12	−7	88/72	85/70	82/69	23	74	72	71
Rutland	43	3	73	0	620	−13	−8	87/72	84/70	81/69	23	74	72	71
VIRGINIA														
Charlottsville	38	1	78	3	870	14	18	94/74	91/74	88/73	23	77	76	75
Danville AP	36	3	79	2	590	14	16	94/74	92/73	90/73	21	77	76	75
Fredericksburg	38	2	77	3	50	10	14	96/76	93/75	90/74	21	78	77	76
Harrisonburg	38	3	78	5	1340	12	16	93/72	91/72	88/71	23	75	74	73
Lynchburg AP	37	2	79	1	947	12	16	93/74	90/74	88/73	21	77	76	75
Norfolk AP	36	5	76	1	26	20	22	93/77	91/76	89/76	18	79	78	77
Petersburg	37	1	77	3	194	14	17	95/76	92/76	90/75	20	79	78	77
Richmond AP	37	3	77	2	162	14	17	95/76	92/76	90/75	21	79	78	77

Table 3A-12 (Continued)

Col. 1	Col. 2		Col. 3		Col. 4	Winter,[d] F Col. 5		Summer,[e] F Col. 6			Col. 7	Col. 8		
State and Station	Latitude[b]		Longitude[c]		Elevation[c]	Design Dry-Bulb		Design Dry-Bulb and Mean Coincident Wet-Bulb			Mean Daily Range	Design Wet-Bulb		
	°	'	°	'	Ft	99%	97.5%	1%	2.5%	5%		1%	2.5%	5%
Roanoke AP	37	2	80	0	1174r	12	16	93/72	91/72	88/71	23	75	74	73
Staunton	38	2	78	5	1480	12	16	93/72	91/72	88/71	23	75	74	73
Winchester	39	1	78	1	750	6	10	93/75	90/74	88/74	21	77	76	75
WASHINGTON														
Aberdeen	47	0	123	5	12	25	28	80/65	77/62	73/61	16	65	63	62
Bellingham AP	48	5	122	3	150	10	15	81/67	77/65	74/63	19	68	65	63
Bremerton	47	3	122	4	162	21	25	82/65	78/64	75/62	20	66	64	63
Ellensburg AP	47	0	120	3	1729	2	6	94/65	91/64	87/62	34	66	65	63
Everett-Paine AFB	47	5	122	2	598	21	25	80/65	76/64	73/62	20	67	64	63
Kennewick	46	0	119	1	392	5	11	99/68	96/67	92/66	30	70	68	67
Longview	46	1	123	0	12	19	24	88/68	85/67	81/65	30	69	67	66
Moses Lake, Larson AFB	47	1	119	2	1183	1	7	97/66	94/65	90/63	32	67	66	64
Olympia AP	47	0	122	5	190	16	22	87/66	83/65	79/64	32	67	66	64
Port Angeles	48	1	123	3	99	24	27	72/62	69/61	67/60	18	64	62	61
Seattle-Boeing Field	47	3	122	2	14	21	26	84/68	81/66	77/65	24	69	67	65
Seattle CO (S)	47	4	122	2	14	22	27	85/68	82/66	78/65	19	69	67	65
Seattle-Tacoma AP (S)	47	3	122	2	386	21	26	84/65	80/64	76/62	22	66	64	63
Spokane AP (S)	47	4	117	3	2357	−6	2	93/64	90/63	87/62	28	65	64	62
Tacoma-Mc Chord AFB	47	1	122	3	350	19	24	86/66	82/65	79/63	22	68	66	64
Walla Walla AP	46	1	118	2	1185	0	7	97/67	94/66	90/65	27	69	67	66
Wenatchee	47	2	120	2	634	7	11	99/67	96/66	92/64	32	68	67	65
Yakima AP	46	3	120	3	1061	−2	5	96/65	93/65	89/63	36	68	66	65
WEST VIRGINIA														
Beckley	37	5	81	1	2330	−2	4	83/71	81/69	79/69	22	73	71	70
Bluefield AP	37	2	81	2	2850	−2	4	83/71	81/69	79/69	22	73	71	70
Charleston AP	38	2	81	4	939	7	11	92/74	90/73	87/72	20	76	75	74
Clarksburg	39	2	80	2	977	6	10	92/74	90/73	87/72	21	76	75	74
Elkins AP	38	5	79	5	1970	1	6	86/72	84/70	82/70	22	74	72	71
Huntington CO	38	2	82	3	565r	5	10	94/76	91/74	89/73	22	78	77	75
Martinsburg AP	39	2	78	0	537	6	10	93/75	90/74	88/74	21	77	76	75
Morgantown AP	39	4	80	0	1245	4	8	90/74	87/73	85/73	22	76	75	74
Parkersburg CO	39	2	81	3	615r	7	11	93/75	90/74	88/73	21	77	76	75
Wheeling	40	1	80	4	659	1	5	89/72	86/71	84/70	21	74	73	72
WISCONSIN														
Appleton	44	2	88	2	742	−14	−9	89/74	86/72	83/71	23	76	74	72
Ashland	46	3	90	5	650	−21	−16	85/70	82/68	79/66	23	72	70	68
Beloit	42	3	89	0	780	−7	−3	92/75	90/75	88/74	24	78	77	75
Eau Claire AP	44	5	91	3	888	−15	−11	92/75	89/73	86/71	23	77	75	73
Fond du Lac	43	5	88	3	760	−12	−8	89/74	86/72	84/71	23	76	74	72
Green Bay AP	44	3	88	1	683	−13	−9	88/74	85/72	83/71	23	76	74	72
La Crosse AP	43	5	91	2	652	−13	−9	91/75	88/73	85/72	22	77	75	74
Madison AP (S)	43	1	89	2	858	−11	−7	91/74	88/73	85/71	22	77	75	73
Manitowoc	44	1	87	4	660	−11	−7	89/74	86/72	83/71	21	76	74	72
Marinette	45	0			605	−15	−11	87/73	84/71	82/70	20	75	73	71
Milwaukee AP	43	0	87	5	672	−8	−4	90/74	87/73	84/71	21	76	74	73
Racine	42	4	87	4	640	−6	−2	91/75	88/73	85/72	21	77	75	74
Sheboygan	43	4	87	4	648	−10	−6	89/75	86/73	83/72	20	77	75	74
Stevens Point	43	0	89	3	1079	−15	−11	92/75	89/73	86/71	23	77	75	73
Waukesha	43	0	88	1	860	−9	−5	90/74	87/73	84/71	22	76	74	73
Wausau AP	44	6	89	4	1196	−16	−12	91/74	88/72	85/70	23	76	74	72
WYOMING														
Casper AP	42	5	106	3	5319	−11	−5	92/58	90/57	87/57	31	63	61	60
Cheyene AP	41	1	104	5	6126	−9	−1	89/58	86/58	84/57	30	63	62	60
Cody AP	44	3	109	0	5090	−19	−13	89/60	86/60	83/59	32	64	63	61
Evanston	41	2	111	0	6860	−9	−3	86/55	84/55	82/54	32	59	58	57
Lander AP (S)	42	5	108	4	5563	−16	−11	91/61	88/61	85/60	32	64	63	61
Laramie AP (S)	41	2	105	3	7266	−14	−6	84/56	81/56	79/55	28	61	60	59
Newcastle	43	5	104	1	4480	−17	−12	91/64	87/63	84/63	30	69	68	66
Rawlins	41	5	107	1	6736	−12	−4	86/57	83/57	81/56	40	62	61	60
Rock Springs AP	41	4	109	0	6741	−9	−3	86/55	84/55	82/54	32	59	58	57
Sheridan AP	44	5	107	0	3942	−14	−8	94/62	91/62	88/61	32	66	65	63
Torrington	4	0	104	1	4098	−14	−8	94/62	91/62	88/61	30	66	65	63

Source: 1985 Handbook of Fundamentals, *ASHRAE. Reproduced with permission.*

Table 3A-13
SHADING COEFFICIENTS

Shading Coefficients for Single Glass with Indoor Shading by Venetian Blinds or Roller Shades

	Nominal Thickness[a] in.	Solar Trans.[b]	Type of Shading: Venetian Blinds, Medium	Venetian Blinds, Light	Roller Shade, Opaque, Dark	Roller Shade, Opaque, White	Roller Shade, Translucent, Light
Clear	3/32 to 1/4	0.87 to 0.80					
Clear	1/4 to 1/2	0.80 to 0.71					
Clear Pattern	1/8 to 1/2	0.87 to 0.79	0.64	0.55	0.59	0.25	0.39
Heat-Absorbing Pattern	1/8	—					
Tinted	3/16, 7/32	0.74, 0.71					
Heat-Absorbing[d]	3/16, 1/4	0.46					
Heat-Absorbing Pattern	3/16, 1/4	—	0.57	0.53	0.45	0.30	0.36
Tinted	1/8, 7/32	0.59, 0.45					
Heat-Absorbing or Pattern	—	0.44 to 0.30	0.54	0.52	0.40	0.28	0.32
Heat-Absorbing[d]	3/8	0.34					
Heat-Absorbing		0.29 to 0.15					
or Pattern	—	0.24	0.42	0.40	0.36	0.28	0.31
Reflective Coated Glass							
S.C.[c] = 0.30			0.25	0.23			
0.40			0.33	0.29			
0.50			0.42	0.38			
0.60			0.50	0.44			

[a] Refer to manufacturer's literature for values.
[b] For vertical blinds with opaque white and beige louvers in the tightly closed position, SC is 0.25 and 0.29 when used with glass of 0.71 to 0.80 transmittance.
[c] SC for glass with no shading device.
[d] Refers to gray, bronze, and green tinted heat-absorbing glass.

Shading Coefficients for Insulating Glass[a] with Indoor Shading by Venetian Blinds or Roller Shades

Type of Glass	Nominal Thickness, Each Light	Solar Trans.[b] Outer Pane	Solar Trans.[b] Inner Pane	Type of Shading: Venetian Blinds[c], Medium	Venetian Blinds[c], Light	Roller Shade, Opaque, Dark	Roller Shade, Opaque, White	Roller Shade, Translucent, Light
Clear Out	3/32, 1/8 in.	0.87	0.87					
Clear In				0.57	0.51	0.60	0.25	0.37
Clear Out								
Clear In	1/4 in.	0.80	0.80					
Heat-Absorbing[d] Out, Clear In	1/4 in.	0.46	0.80	0.39	0.36	0.40	0.22	0.30
Reflective Coated Glass								
SC[e] = 0.20				0.19	0.18			
0.30				0.27	0.26			
0.40				0.34	0.33			

[a] Refers to factory-fabricated units with 3/16, 1/4, or 1/2-in. air space, or to prime windows plus storm windows.
[b] Refer to manufacturer's literature for exact values.
[c] For vertical blinds with opaque white or beige louvers, tightly closed, SC is approximately the same as for opaque white roller shades.
[d] Refers to bronze, or green tinted, heat-absorbing glass.
[e] SC for glass with no shading device.

Shading Coefficients for Double Glazing with Between-Glass Shading

Type of Glass	Nominal Each Pane	Solar Trans.[a] Outer Pane	Solar Trans.[a] Inner Pane	Description of Air Space	Type of Shading: Venetian Blinds, Light	Venetian Blinds, Medium	Louvered Sun Screen
Clear Out, Clear In	3/32, 1/8 in.	0.87	0.87	Shade in contact with glass or shade separated from glass by air space.	0.33	0.36	0.43
Clear Out, Clear In	1/4 in.	0.80	0.80	Shade in contact with glass-voids filled with plastic.	—	—	0.49
Heat-Abs.[b] Out, Clear In				Shade in contact with glass or shade separated from glass by air space.	0.28	0.30	0.37
	1/4 in.	0.46	0.80	Shade in contact with glass-voids filled with plastic.	—	—	0.41

[a] Refer to manufacturer's literature for exact values.
[b] Refers to grey, bronze and green tinted heat-absorbing glass.

Source: 1985 Handbook of Fundamentals, *ASHRAE*. *Reproduced with permission.*

PART 3B

Heat Gain Calculations

The following simplified method can be used to calculate cooling loads for residential buildings and to approximate cooling loads for some small commercial buildings if their use patterns are somewhat similar to residential occupancy. The method makes the following assumptions:

1. Most heat gain is through the building envelope and ventilation (or infiltration) rather than from internal sources such as lighting, people, equipment, and so forth.
2. The building is occupied and air-conditioned 24 hours per day.
3. The building consists of a single zone with no way to redistribute cooling unit capacity.
4. The indoor temperature can vary up to 3°F on a design day.
5. The thermostat setting is 75°F.
6. Reasonable design features will be incorporated into the building, such as shading of windows and insulation.

The design method involves calculating sensible cooling loads from four sources: (1) through the building envelope, (2) through glazing, (3) from infiltration and ventilation, and (4) from people and equipment. The latent portion of the cooling load can be approximated by adding 0.3 times the calculated sensible cooling load in moist climates or 0.2 times the sensible cooling load in dry climates.

HOW TO CALCULATE HEAT GAINS THROUGH THE BUILDING ENVELOPE

Heat gain through roofs, walls, and floors can be calculated with the following formula.

FORMULA: $q = U \times A \times DETD$

where:

q = heat gain in Btu/hour through the building assembly under consideration
U = thermal transmittance value for summer conditions
A = area of the assembly under consideration, in sq. ft.
DETD = design equivalent temperature difference (Table 3B–1)

A separate calculation is made for each different building assembly and then added to get the total heat gain through the building envelope.

When selecting the appropriate DETD, use the mean daily ranges and summer design dry-bulb temperatures listed in Table 3A–12. For ceilings under naturally vented attics, or beneath vented flat roofs, use the combined U value for the roof, vented space, and ceiling. If the design temperature difference is not an even increment of 5°, as listed in Table 3B–1, the equivalent temperature difference should be corrected 1°F for each 1° difference in design values.

Table 3B-1
DESIGN EQUIVALENT TEMPERATURE DIFFERENCES

Design Temperature	85 F		90			95			100		105	110
Daily Temperature Range[a]	L	M	L	M	H	L	M	H	M	H	H	H
WALLS AND DOORS												
1. Frame and veneer-on-frame	17.6	13.6	22.6	18.6	13.6	27.6	23.6	18.6	28.6	23.6	28.6	33.6
2. Masonry walls, 8-in. block or brick	10.3	6.3	15.3	11.3	6.3	20.3	16.3	11.3	21.3	16.3	21.3	26.3
3. Partitions, frame	9.0	5.0	14.0	10.0	5.0	19.0	15.0	10.0	20.0	15.0	20.0	25.0
masonry	2.5	0	7.5	3.5	0	12.5	8.5	3.5	13.5	8.5	13.5	18.5
4. Wood doors	17.6	13.6	22.6	18.6	13.6	27.6	23.6	18.6	28.6	23.6	28.6	33.6
CEILINGS AND ROOFS[b]												
1. Ceilings under naturally vented attic or vented flat roof—deck	38.0	34.0	43.0	39.0	34.0	48.0	44.0	39.0	49.0	44.0	49.0	54.0
—light	30.0	26.0	35.0	31.0	26.0	40.0	36.0	31.0	41.0	36.0	41.0	46.0
2. Built-up roof, no ceiling—dark	38.0	34.0	43.0	39.0	34.0	48.0	44.0	39.0	49.0	44.0	49.0	54.0
—light	30.0	26.0	35.0	31.0	26.0	40.0	36.0	31.0	41.0	36.0	41.0	46.0
3. Ceilings under unconditioned rooms	9.0	5.0	14.0	10.0	5.0	19.0	15.0	10.0	20.0	15.0	20.0	25.0
FLOORS												
1. Over unconditioned rooms	9.0	5.0	14.0	10.0	5.0	19.0	15.0	10.0	20.0	15.0	20.0	25.0
2. Over basement, enclosed crawl space or concrete slab on ground	0	0	0	0	0	0	0	0	0	0	0	0
3. Over open crawl space	9.0	5.0	14.0	10.0	5.0	19.0	15.0	10.0	20.0	15.0	20.0	25.0

[a]Daily Temperature Range
L (Low) Calculation Value: 12 deg F. Applicable Range: Less than 15 deg F.
M (Medium) Calculation Value: 20 deg F. Applicable Range: 15 to 25 deg F.
H (High) Calculation Value: 30 deg F. Applicable Range: More than 25 deg F.

[b]Ceilings and Roofs: For roofs in shade, 18-h average = 11 deg F temperature differential. At 90 F design and medium daily range, equivalent temperature differential for light-colored roof equals 6.1 + (11 + (0.71) (39 − 11) = 31 deg F.

Source: 1985 Handbook of Fundamentals, *ASHRAE.*
Reproduced with permission.

HOW TO CALCULATE HEAT GAINS THROUGH GLAZING

Glazing heat gain is calculated with the following formula.

FORMULA: $q = A \times DCLF$

where:

A = area of glazing in sq. ft.
DCLF = design cooling load factor (Table 3B–2)

Table 3B-2
DESIGN COOLING LOAD FACTORS THROUGH GLASS

Outdoor Design Temp.	Regular Single Glass						Regular Double Glass						Heat Absorbing Double Glass						Clear Triple Glass		
	85	90	95	100	105	110	85	90	95	100	105	110	85	90	95	100	105	110	85	90	95
No Awnings or Inside Shading																					
North	23	27	31	35	39	44	19	21	24	26	28	30	12	14	17	19	21	23	17	19	20
NE and NW	56	60	64	68	72	77	46	48	51	53	55	57	27	29	32	34	36	38	42	43	44
East and West	81	85	89	93	97	102	68	70	73	75	77	79	42	44	47	49	51	53	62	63	64
SE and SW	70	74	78	82	86	91	59	61	64	66	68	70	35	37	40	42	44	46	53	55	56
South	40	44	48	52	56	61	33	35	38	40	42	44	19	21	24	26	28	30	30	31	33
Horiz. Skylight	160	164	168	172	176	181	139	141	144	146	148	150	89	91	94	96	98	100	126	127	129
Draperies or Venetian Blinds																					
North	15	19	23	27	31	36	12	14	17	19	21	23	9	11	14	16	18	20	11	12	14
NE and NW	32	36	40	44	48	53	27	29	32	34	36	38	20	22	25	27	29	31	24	26	27
East and West	48	52	56	60	64	69	42	44	47	49	51	53	30	32	35	37	39	41	38	39	41
SE and SW	40	44	48	52	56	61	35	37	40	42	44	46	24	26	29	31	33	35	32	33	34
South	23	27	31	35	39	44	20	22	25	27	29	31	15	17	20	22	24	26	18	19	21
Roller Shades Half-Drawn																					
North	18	22	26	30	34	39	15	17	20	22	24	26	10	12	15	17	19	21	13	14	15
NE and NW	40	44	48	52	56	61	38	40	43	45	47	49	24	26	29	31	33	35	34	35	35
East and West	61	65	69	73	77	82	54	56	59	61	63	65	35	37	40	42	44	46	49	49	50
SE and SW	52	56	60	64	68	73	46	48	51	53	55	57	30	32	35	37	39	41	41	42	43
South	29	33	37	41	45	50	27	29	32	34	36	38	18	20	23	25	27	29	25	26	26
Awnings																					
North	20	24	28	32	36	41	13	15	18	20	22	24	10	12	15	17	19	21	11	12	13
NE and NW	21	25	29	33	37	42	14	16	19	21	23	25	11	13	16	18	20	22	12	13	14
East and West	22	26	30	34	38	43	14	16	19	21	23	25	12	14	17	19	21	23	12	13	14
SE and SW	21	25	29	33	37	42	14	16	19	21	23	25	11	13	16	18	20	22	12	13	14
South	21	24	28	32	36	41	13	15	18	20	22	24	11	13	16	18	20	22	11	12	13

Source: 1985 Handbook of Fundamentals, *ASHRAE*.
Reproduced with permission.

The factors in Table 3B–2 are averages from 5:30 A.M. to 6:30 P.M. at 30° and 40° north latitude.

If permanent shading devices such as roof overhangs are used, their effect must be considered separately. Glazing protected by such shading devices is considered north-facing glass. In order to simplify determination of what portion of the glazing is in shade, the shade line factors in Table 3B–3 can be used. The factors are expressed as the distance the shade line falls beneath the edge of the overhang width. They represent the average of the shade line values for the five hours of maximum solar intensity on each wall orientation shown and for a solar declination of 18° north (August 1).

Table 3B-3
SHADE LINE FACTORS

Direction Window Faces	Latitude (in degrees)						
	25	30	35	40	45	50	55
E	0.8	0.8	0.8	0.8	0.8	0.8	0.8
SE	1.9	1.6	1.4	1.3	1.1	1.0	0.9
S	10.1	5.4	3.6	2.6	2.0	1.7	1.4
SW	1.9	1.6	1.4	1.3	1.1	1.0	0.9
W	0.8	0.8	0.8	0.8	0.8	0.8	0.8

Note: Distance shadow line falls below the edge of the overhang equals shade line factor multiplied by width of overhang. Values are averages for 5 hours of greatest solar intensity on August 1.

Source: 1985 Handbook of Fundamentals, *ASHRAE*.
Reproduced with permission.

HOW TO CALCULATE GAINS FROM INFILTRATION AND VENTILATION

Heat gain from infiltration is calculated with the following formula.

FORMULA: $q = A \times f$

where:

q = sensible heat gain in Btu/h
A = gross area of exposed wall area in sq. ft.
f = infiltration factor (Table 3B–4)

If mechanical ventilation is provided, the following formula is used.

FORMULA: $q = Q \times f_m$

where:

Q = volume of outdoor introduced into the space in cu. ft. per min. (See Table 2B–12 or use other volume as determined by design requirements.)
f_m = mechanical ventilation factor (Table 3B–4)

Table 3B-4
SENSIBLE COOLING LOAD FROM INFILTRATION AND VENTILATION

Design Temperature (in degrees F)	85	90	95	100	105	110
Infiltration of gross exposed wall area Btu/h • ft²	0.7	1.1	1.5	1.9	2.2	2.6
Mechanical ventilation (in Btu/h • cfm)	11.0	16.0	22.0	27.0	32.0	38.0

Source: 1985 Handbook of Fundamentals, *ASHRAE.*
Reproduced with permission.

HOW TO CALCULATE GAINS FROM OCCUPANCY

Sensible heat gain from occupants is assumed to be 225 Btu/h per person. Gain from appliances is assumed to be 1200 Btu/h.

PART 3C

Passive Solar Design

This part presents methods to assist in making decisions about passive solar design at two levels of detail: one for preliminary estimates during schematic design and one for more detailed design and calculation of system performance. The methods are those presented in *Passive Solar Design Handbook,* Volume 2, prepared for the U.S. Department of Energy by the Los Alamos Scientific Laboratory, January 1980. The primary author was J. Douglas Balcomb.

The methods are applicable for residential and small commercial buildings where the heating requirement is determined primarily by losses through the building envelope, with only a small contribution of internal gain from occupants, lighting, and equipment. Six variations of two basic types (direct gain and thermal storage wall) of passive design approaches are discussed—direct gain, Trombe wall, and water wall, each with and without night insulation. Additional data for 94 systems is given in *The Passive Solar Design Handbook,* Volume 3, by J. D Balcomb, et al., published by the American Solar Energy Society, Inc., 1983.

COMMON SOLAR FORMULAS AND THEIR TERMS

Solar Savings Fraction (SSF): The solar savings fraction is a measure of a building's passive solar performance. It compares the solar savings of the passive building to the thermal load of a reference building, one that is identical to the passive building but has the solar collection element replaced with a ''neutral'' wall that experiences neither solar gain nor heat loss.

FORMULA:

$$SSF = \frac{\text{solar savings}}{\text{net reference load}}$$

where:

solar savings is the reduction in backup heating requirements resulting from the presence of the solar collection element

It has meaning only with respect to the net reference load where the net reference load is the auxiliary heating requirement for a comparable non-solar building. It can also be viewed in terms of the following formula.

FORMULA:

$$SSF = 1 - \frac{\text{auxiliary heat supplied to solar building}}{\text{auxiliary heat in non-solar building}}$$

The SSF is not calculated by the designer; values of SSF are the result of complex calculations using different variables for different geographical locations. The values are given in tables and are used in other types of calculations.

Building Load Coefficient (BLC): The additional energy, in Btu/day, required to increase a building's temperature 1°F if the solar collection element were covered with a perfect insulator. It is similar in concept to the heating load described in the previous section on heat loss calculations but involves simplified methods of determining heat loss through the envelope and from infiltration. It is also based on a daily rate rather than an hourly rate. The method for calculating the BLC is described in the following section, "Design Procedures for Design Development Phase."

Load Collector Ratio (LCR): The LCR quantifies the relationship between energy conservation and the amount of solar gain as they relate to specific geographical locations and types of passive systems. The solar-savings fraction, SSF, can be calculated as a function of LCR. The actual procedure is very complex but can be represented in a table for each geographical location. (See Table 3C–3.) A complete set of tables is available in *The Passive Solar Design Handbook,* Volume 3.

FORMULA:

$$\text{LCR} = \frac{\text{building load coefficient (BLC)}}{\text{solar collection area}} \text{ or } \text{LCR} = \frac{\text{BLC}}{\text{A}}$$

where:

BLC is in Btu/degree days
solar collection area is in sq. ft.

SCHEMATIC DESIGN ESTIMATES OF COLLECTOR AREA AND THERMAL MASS

Table 3C–1 gives suggested ranges of solar collection area as a percentage of floor area for various geographical locations. It also gives a range of the solar savings (SSF) that might be expected for solar collection areas with and without R-9 night insulation. For this rough estimate, the glazing area does not depend on whether the passive system is direct gain, Trombe wall, or water wall, assuming that thermal storage is adequate.

To use the table, substitute the values under the six columns for any given city listed, in the following way:

"A solar collection area of [R1]% to [R2]% of the floor area can be expected to reduce the annual heating load of a building in [location] by [S1]% to [S2]%, or, if R-9 night insulation is used, by [S3]% to [S4]%.

In order to select what part of the range to use, the suggested starting points for SSF can be determined from Figure 3C–1.

This method makes the following assumptions:

1. The building uses double glazing and well-insulated walls.
2. Infiltration is minimized.
3. The upper limit of glazing was calculated on achieving an average inside temperature of 75°F during a series of clear January days when the average outside temperature is equal to the average January temperature for the location.

4. The design can take credit for any south-facing windows in addition to the "solar glazing."
5. Values in Table 3C–1 were derived assuming that the solar glazing was half direct gain and half water wall.

Once the size of the collector area is estimated, an approximate amount of thermal storage mass must be calculated. The rule of thumb is that there should be a storage mass of 0.6 times the SSF pounds of water or three times the SSF pounds of masonry for each square foot of south glazing where SSF is the desired solar savings in percent.

Table 3C-1
VALUES TO BE USED IN THE SOLAR GLAZING RULE OF THUMB

City	R1	R2	S1	S2	S3	S4
Birmingham, Alabama	0.09	0.18	22	37	34	58
Mobile, Alabama	0.06	0.12	26	44	34	60
Montgomery, Alabama	0.07	0.15	24	41	34	59
Phoenix, Arizona	0.06	0.12	37	60	48	75
Prescott, Arizona	0.10	0.20	29	48	44	72
Tucson, Arizona	0.06	0.12	35	57	45	73
Winslow, Arizona	0.12	0.24	30	47	48	74
Yuma, Arizona	0.04	0.09	43	66	51	78
Fort Smith, Arkansas	0.10	0.20	24	39	38	64
Little Rock, Arkansas	0.10	0.19	23	38	37	62
Bakersfield, California	0.08	0.15	31	50	42	67
Daggett, California	0.07	0.15	35	56	46	73
Fresno, California	0.09	0.17	29	46	41	65
Long Beach, California	0.05	0.10	35	58	44	72
Los Angeles, California	0.05	0.09	36	58	44	72
Mount Shasta, California	0.11	0.21	24	38	42	67
Needles, California	0.06	0.12	39	61	49	76
Oakland, California	0.07	0.15	35	55	46	72
Red Bluff, California	0.09	0.18	29	46	41	65
Sacramento, California	0.09	0.18	29	47	41	66
San Diego, California	0.04	0.09	37	61	46	74
San Francisco, California	0.06	0.13	34	54	45	71
Santa Maria, California	0.05	0.11	31	53	42	69
Colorado Springs, Colorado	0.12	0.24	27	42	47	74
Denver, Colorado	0.12	0.23	27	43	47	74
Eagle, Colorado	0.14	0.29	25	35	53	77
Grand Junction, Colorado	0.13	0.27	29	43	50	76
Pueblo, Colorado	0.11	0.23	29	45	48	75
Hartford, Connecticut	0.17	0.35	14	19	40	64
Wilmington, Delaware	0.15	0.29	19	30	39	63
Washington, DC	0.12	0.23	18	28	37	61
Apalachicola, Florida	0.05	0.10	28	47	36	61
Daytona Beach, Florida	0.04	0.08	30	51	36	63
Jacksonville, Florida	0.05	0.09	27	47	35	62
Miami, Florida	0.01	0.02	27	48	31	54
Orlando, Florida	0.03	0.06	30	52	37	63
Tallahassee, Florida	0.05	0.11	26	45	35	60
Tampa, Florida	0.03	0.06	30	52	36	63
West Palm Beach, Florida	0.01	0.03	30	51	34	59
Atlanta, Georgia	0.08	0.17	22	36	34	58
Augusta, Georgia	0.08	0.16	24	40	35	60

Note: –NR– means Not Recommended.

City	R1	R2	S1	S2	S3	S4
Macon, Georgia	0.07	0.15	25	41	35	59
Savannah, Georgia	0.06	0.13	25	43	35	60
Boise, Idaho	0.14	0.28	27	38	48	71
Lewiston, Idaho	0.15	0.29	22	29	44	65
Pocatello, Idaho	0.13	0.26	25	35	51	74
Chicago, Illinois	0.17	0.35	17	23	43	67
Moline, Illinois	0.20	0.39	17	22	46	70
Springfield, Illinois	0.15	0.30	19	28	42	67
Evansville, Indiana	0.14	0.27	19	29	37	61
Fort Wayne, Indiana	0.16	0.33	13	17	37	60
Indianapolis, Indiana	0.14	0.28	15	21	37	60
South Bend, Indiana	0.18	0.35	12	15	39	61
Burlington, Iowa	0.18	0.36	20	27	47	71
Des Moines, Iowa	0.21	0.43	19	25	50	75
Mason City, Iowa	0.22	0.44	18	19	56	79
Sioux City, Iowa	0.23	0.46	20	24	53	76
Dodge City, Kansas	0.12	0.23	27	42	46	73
Goodland, Kansas	0.13	0.27	26	39	47	74
Topeka, Kansas	0.14	0.28	24	35	45	71
Wichita, Kansas	0.14	0.28	26	41	45	72
Lexington, Kentucky	0.13	0.27	17	26	35	58
Louisville, Kentucky	0.13	0.27	18	27	35	59
Baton Rouge, Louisiana	0.06	0.12	26	43	34	59
Lake Charles, Louisiana	0.06	0.11	24	41	32	57
New Orleans, Louisiana	0.05	0.11	27	46	35	61
Shreveport, Louisiana	0.08	0.15	26	43	36	61
Caribou, Maine	0.25	0.50	– NR	–	53	74
Portland, Maine	0.17	0.34	14	17	45	69
Baltimore, Maryland	0.14	0.27	19	30	38	62
Boston, Massachusetts	0.15	0.29	17	25	40	64
Alpena, Michigan	0.21	0.42	– NR	–	47	69
Detroit, Michigan	0.17	0.34	13	17	39	61
Flint, Michigan	0.15	0.31	11	12	40	62
Grand Rapids, Michigan	0.19	0.38	12	13	39	61
Sault Ste. Marie, Michigan	0.25	0.50	– NR	–	50	70
Traverse City, Michigan	0.18	0.36	– NR	–	42	62
Duluth, Minnesota	0.25	0.50	– NR	–	50	70
International Falls, Minnesota	0.25	0.50	– NR	–	47	66
Minneapolis-St. Paul, Minnesota	0.25	0.50	– NR	–	55	76
Rochester, Minnesota	0.24	0.49	– NR	–	54	76
Jackson, Mississippi	0.08	0.15	24	40	34	59
Meridian, Mississippi	0.08	0.15	23	39	34	58
Columbia, Missouri	0.13	0.26	20	30	41	66
Kansas City, Missouri	0.14	0.29	22	32	44	70
Saint Louis, Missouri	0.15	0.29	21	33	41	65
Springfield, Missouri	0.13	0.26	22	34	40	65
Billings, Montana	0.16	0.32	24	31	53	76
Cut Bank, Montana	0.24	0.49	22	23	62	81
Dillon, Montana	0.16	0.32	24	32	54	77
Glasgow, Montana	0.25	0.50	– NR	–	55	75
Great Falls, Montana	0.18	0.37	23	28	56	77
Helena, Montana	0.20	0.39	21	25	55	77
Lewistown, Montana	0.19	0.38	21	25	54	76
Miles City, Montana	0.23	0.47	21	23	60	80

Note: –NR– means Not Recommended.

Table 3C-1 (Continued)

City	R1	R2	S1	S2	S3	S4
Missoula, Montana	0.18	0.36	15	16	47	68
Grand Island, Nebraska	0.18	0.36	24	33	51	76
North Omaha, Nebraska	0.20	0.40	21	29	51	76
North Platte, Nebraska	0.17	0.34	25	36	50	76
Scottsbluff, Nebraska	0.16	0.31	24	36	49	74
Elko, Nevada	0.12	0.25	27	39	52	76
Ely, Nevada	0.12	0.23	27	41	50	77
Las Vegas, Nevada	0.09	0.18	35	56	48	75
Lovelock, Nevada	0.13	0.25	32	48	53	78
Reno, Nevada	0.11	0.22	31	48	49	76
Tonopah, Nevada	0.11	0.23	31	48	51	77
Winnemucca, Nevada	0.13	0.26	28	42	49	75
Concord, New Hampshire	0.17	0.34	13	15	45	68
Newark, New Jersey	0.13	0.25	19	29	39	64
Albuquerque, New Mexico	0.11	0.22	29	47	46	73
Clayton, New Mexico	0.10	0.20	28	45	45	73
Farmington, New Mexico	0.12	0.24	29	45	49	76
Los Alamos, New Mexico	0.11	0.22	25	40	44	72
Roswell, New Mexico	0.10	0.19	30	49	45	73
Turth or Consequences, New Mexico	0.9	0.17	32	51	46	73
Tucumcari, New Mexico	0.10	0.20	30	48	45	73
Zuni, New Mexico	0.11	0.21	27	43	45	73
Albany, New York	0.21	0.41	13	15	43	66
Binghamton, New York	0.15	0.30	– NR	–	35	56
Buffalo, New York	0.19	0.37	– NR	–	36	57
Massena, New York	0.25	0.50	– NR	–	50	71
New York (Central Park), NY	0.15	0.30	16	25	36	59
Rochester, New York	0.18	0.37	– NR	–	37	58
Syracuse, New York	0.19	0.38	– NR	–	37	59
Asheville, North Carolina	0.10	0.20	21	35	36	61
Cape Hatteras, North Carolina	0.09	0.17	24	40	36	60
Charlotte, North Carolina	0.08	0.17	23	38	36	60
Greensboro, North Carolina	0.10	0.20	23	37	37	63
Raleigh-Durham, North Carolina	0.09	0.19	22	37	36	61
Bismarck, North Dakota	0.25	0.50	– NR	–	56	77
Fargo, North Dakota	0.25	0.50	– NR	–	51	72
Minot, North Dakota	0.25	0.50	– NR	–	52	72
Akron-Canton, Ohio	0.15	0.31	12	16	35	57
Cincinnati, Ohio	0.12	0.24	15	23	35	57
Cleveland, Ohio	0.15	0.31	11	14	34	55
Columbus, Ohio	0.14	0.28	13	18	35	57
Dayton, Ohio	0.14	0.28	14	20	36	59
Toledo, Ohio	0.17	0.34	13	17	38	61
Youngstown, Ohio	0.16	0.32	– NR	6	34	54
Oklahoma City, Oklahoma	0.11	0.22	25	41	41	67
Tulsa, Oklahoma	0.11	0.22	24	38	40	65
Astoria, Oregon	0.09	0.19	21	34	37	60
Burns, Oregon	0.13	0.25	23	32	47	71
Medford, Oregon	0.12	0.24	21	32	38	60
North Bend, Oregon	0.09	0.17	25	42	38	64
Pendleton, Oregon	0.14	0.27	22	30	43	64
Portland, Oregon	0.13	0.26	21	31	38	60
Redmond, Oregon	0.13	0.27	26	38	47	71

Note: –NR– means Not Recommended.

City	R1	R2	S1	S2	S3	S4
Salem, Oregon	0.12	0.24	21	32	37	59
Allentown, Pennsylvania	0.15	0.29	16	24	39	63
Erie, Pennsylvania	0.17	0.34	–	NR –	35	55
Harrisburg, Pennsylvania	0.13	0.26	17	26	38	62
Philadelphia, Pennsylvania	0.15	0.29	19	29	38	62
Pittsburgh, Pennsylvania	0.14	0.28	12	16	33	55
Wilkes-Barre-Scranton, Pennsylvania	0.16	0.32	13	18	37	60
Providence, Rhode Island	0.15	0.30	17	24	40	64
Charleston, South Carolina	0.07	0.14	25	41	34	59
Columbia, South Carolina	0.08	0.17	25	41	36	61
Greenville-Spartanburg, South Carolina	0.08	0.17	23	38	36	60
Huron, South Dakota	0.25	0.50	–	NR –	58	79
Pierre, South Dakota	0.22	0.43	21	23	58	80
Rapid City, South Dakota	0.15	0.30	23	32	51	76
Sioux Falls, South Dakota	0.22	0.45	18	19	57	79
Chattanooga, Tennessee	0.09	0.19	19	32	33	56
Knoxville, Tennessee	0.09	0.18	20	33	33	56
Memphis, Tennessee	0.09	0.19	22	36	36	60
Nashville, Tennessee	0.10	0.21	19	30	33	55
Abilene, Texas	0.09	0.18	29	47	41	68
Amarillo, Texas	0.11	0.22	29	46	45	72
Austin, Texas	0.06	0.13	27	46	37	63
Brownsville, Texas	0.03	0.06	27	46	32	57
Corpus Christi, Texas	0.05	0.09	29	49	36	63
Dallas, Texas	0.08	0.17	27	44	38	64
Del Rio, Texas	0.06	0.12	30	50	39	66
El Paso, Texas	0.09	0.17	32	53	45	72
Fort Worth, Texas	0.09	0.17	26	44	38	64
Houston, Texas	0.06	0.11	25	43	34	59
Laredo, Texas	0.05	0.09	31	52	39	64
Lubbock, Texas	0.09	0.19	30	49	44	72
Lufkin, Texas	0.07	0.14	26	43	35	61
Midland-Odessa, Texas	0.09	0.18	32	52	44	72
Port Arthur, Texas	0.06	0.11	26	44	34	60
San Angelo, Texas	0.08	0.15	29	48	40	67
San Antonio, Texas	0.06	0.12	28	48	38	64
Sherman, Texas	0.10	0.20	25	41	38	64
Waco, Texas	0.08	0.15	27	45	38	64
Wichita Falls, Texas	0.10	0.20	27	45	41	67
Bryce Canyon, Utah	0.13	0.25	26	39	52	78
Cedar City, Utah	0.12	0.24	28	43	48	75
Salt Lake City, Utah	0.13	0.26	27	39	48	72
Burlington, Vermont	0.22	0.43	–	NR –	46	68
Norfolk, Virginia	0.09	0.19	23	38	37	62
Richmond, Virginia	0.11	0.22	21	34	37	61
Roanoke, Virginia	0.11	0.23	21	34	37	61
Olympia, Washington	0.12	0.23	20	29	38	59
Seattle-Tacoma, Washington	0.11	0.22	21	30	39	59
Spokane, Washington	0.20	0.39	20	24	48	68
Yakima, Washington	0.18	0.36	24	31	49	70
Charleston, West Virginia	0.13	0.25	16	24	32	54
Huntington, West Virginia	0.13	0.25	17	27	34	57
Eau Claire, Wisconsin	0.25	0.50	–	NR –	53	75
Green Bay, Wisconsin	0.23	0.46	–	NR –	53	75

Note: –NR– means Not Recommended.

Table 3C-1 (Continued)

City	R1	R2	S1	S2	S3	S4
La Crosse, Wisconsin	0.21	0.43	-	NR -	52	75
Madison, Wisconsin	0.20	0.40	15	17	51	74
Milwaukee, Wisconsin	0.18	0.35	15	18	48	71
Casper, Wyoming	0.13	0.26	27	39	53	78
Cheyenne, Wyoming	0.11	0.21	25	39	47	74
Rock Springs, Wyoming	0.14	0.28	26	38	54	79
Sheridan, Wyoming	0.16	0.31	22	30	52	75
Canada						
Edmonton, Alberta	0.25	0.50	-	NR -	54	72
Suffield, Alberta	0.25	0.50	28	30	67	85
Nanaimo, British Columbia	0.13	0.26	26	35	45	66
Vancouver, British Columbia	0.13	0.26	20	28	40	60
Winnipeg, Manitoba	0.25	0.50	-	NR -	54	74
Dartmouth, Nova Scotia	0.14	0.28	17	24	45	70
Moosonee, Ontario	0.25	0.50	-	NR -	48	67
Ottawa, Ontario	0.25	0.50	-	NR -	59	80
Toronto, Ontario	0.18	0.36	17	23	44	68
Normandin, Quebec	0.25	0.50	-	NR -	54	74

Note: -NR- means Not Recommended.

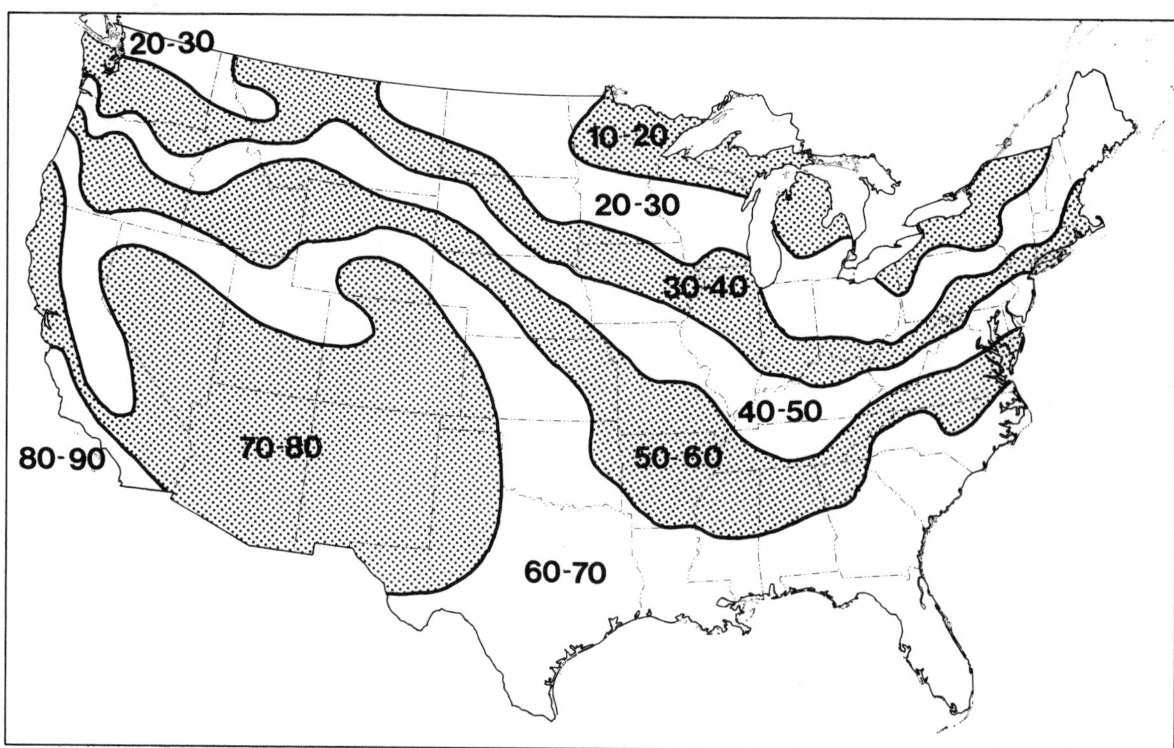

Source: Passive Solar Design Handbook, *Volume 3*

Figure 3C-1: Suggested Ranges of Solar Savings Fractions (SSF)

Table 3C–2 gives the tabular form.

Table 3C–2
RECOMMENDED THERMAL STORAGE PER SQUARE FOOT OF COLLECTION AREA

Desired or Expected SSF (in percent)	**Water** (in pounds)	**Masonry** (in pounds)
10	6	30
20	12	60
30	18	90
40	24	120
50	30	150
60	36	180
70	42	210
80	48	240
90	54	270

These guidelines make the following assumptions:

1. The mass is in direct sun all day. If the mass is located completely out of the sun, then about four times as much mass is needed.
2. The thermal storage for direct gain situations is within the direct gain space or encloses it.
3. The mass for direct gain has an exposed surface area equal to at least three times the glazed area.
4. If masonry is used, it is not effective beyond a depth of 4 inches to 6 inches.

RULE OF THUMB

Orientation of the solar glazing should lie between 20 degrees east and 32 degrees west of true south. More specifically, approximate decreases in performance can be expected on the following basis:

- 5% decrease at 18 degrees east or 30 degrees west.
- 10% decrease at 28 degrees east or 40 degrees west.
- 20% decrease at 42 degrees east or 54 degrees west.

DESIGN PROCEDURES FOR DESIGN DEVELOPMENT PHASE

Once more information is known about the construction materials and details of a proposed design, a more detailed review of solar performance is possible. The preliminary design decisions developed using the technique outlined in the previous section can also be verified and refined if necessary.

This section describes the LCR method of determining *annual* passive solar performance and energy needs. A more detailed method (the SLR method) is also available for calculating monthly performance. Several aspects of a passive solar building can be studied using this technique. However, only three will be summarized here: (1) verifying the solar collection area, the type of system to use, and the solar-savings fraction; (2) studying the tradeoff between construction, as reflected in the BLC, and solar contributions; and (3) estimating the annual auxiliary energy needed.

Calculating the Building Load Coefficient (BLC)

The first task is to calculate the building load coefficient, BLC. This is the additional heating required to maintain a 1°F increase in the building's inside temperature. It is the same as calculating the heat loss, as described in Part 3A, except that the solar collector is excluded (including any south-facing windows) and the heat losses are multiplied by 24 to convert Btu/hour to Btu/degree day. To calculate this, complete the following steps:

1. Determine the heat losses of the various opaque portions of the building envelope, using the following general equation.

FORMULA:

$$L = U \times A \times 24$$

where:

L = heat loss in Btu/DD
U = overall coefficient of heat transmission
A = area of the construction assembly in sq. ft.

since:

$$U = \frac{1}{R}$$

the equation can be rewritten:

$$L = 24 \times \frac{\text{Area}}{\text{R value}}$$

This calculation should be done for the roof and each wall section that has a different U value.

2. Determine the loss through the non-south glazing area. Use the detailed procedure in Part 3A or approximate using the following formula.

FORMULA:

$$L_g = 26 \times \frac{\text{non-south window area}}{\text{number of glazings}}$$

where:

the number of glazings is the number of layers of glass; for example, two for double glazing

The constant, 26, is derived from approximating the U value of glazing as 1.1 divided by the number of glazings (1.1 times 24 is about 26).

3. Determine losses through the perimeter for slab on grade construction, through floors over vented crawl spaces, or through basements. Follow the procedures outlined in Part 3A or use the following approximations.

PERIMETER SLAB:

$$L_p = 100 \times \frac{\text{length of perimeter foundation}}{\text{R value of perimeter insulation} + 5}$$

VENTED CRAWL SPACE:

$$L_f = 24 \times \frac{\text{area of ground floor}}{\text{R value of floor}}$$

BASEMENT:

$$L_b = 256 \times \frac{\text{length of wall}}{\text{R value of wall insulation} + 8}$$

4. Determine loss due to infiltration. This can be approximated by the following formula.

FORMULA: $L_i = 0.432 \times ACH \times ADR \times H_c \times A$

where:

ACH = average air changes per hour
ADR = air density ratio as shown in Figure 3C–2
H_c = height of ceiling
A = combined area of all floors in sq. ft.

For estimated air changes per hour, refer to Table 3A–13.

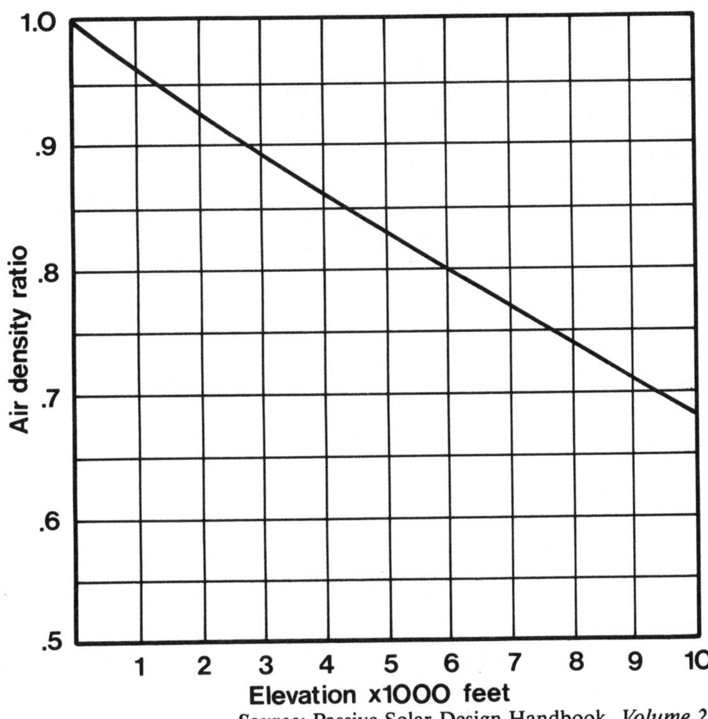

Source: Passive Solar Design Handbook, *Volume 2.*

Figure 3C–2: Air Density Ratios for Different Elevations

5. Add the components together to get the final BLC. Do not include the solar glazing or window area on the south side of the building.

At this point check the building's heat loss rate against the criteria given in Table 3C–3. Simply divide the BLC by the floor area of the building in square feet to get a Btu/DD ft^2 figure.

Table 3C–3
OVERALL HEAT LOSS CRITERIA

	Maximum Heat Loss (in Btu/DD/sq. ft.)	
Range of Heating Degree Days	**Passively Heated Solar Buildings, Exclusive of Solar Wall**	**Conventional Building**
less than 1000	7.6	9
1000–3000	6.6	8
3000–5000	5.6	7
5000–7000	4.6	6
over 7000	3.6	5

Source: Passive Solar Design Handbook, *Volume 2.*

Determining the Solar Collector Area

The next step is to determine the solar collector area. This is the net glazing area projected on a vertical plane. The net area does not include mullions or other framing members, only the glazing. If it is installed at an angle other than vertical, the projected area should be calculated.

Next, determine the load collector ratio.

FORMULA:

$$LCR = \frac{BLC}{A_c}$$

where:

BCL = building load coefficient
A_c = net projected south glazing area

Knowing the LCR for the building, its location, and the type of passive system being investigated, refer to the appropriate section of Table 3C–4 to find the solar savings fraction. Straight line interpolation is used for values between those listed. Table 3C–4 is an abbreviated table of LCR values, including the following six types of passive systems:

WW	Water wall
WWNI	Water wall with R-9 night insulation
TW	Trombe wall
TWNI	Trombe wall with R-9 night insulation
DG	Direct gain
DGNI	Direct gain with R-9 night insulation

The *Passive Solar Design Handbook,* Volume 3 contains expanded tables for 94 different variations of systems, including sun spaces. The variations include modifying such variables as thickness of masonry, number of glazings, vented or unvented Trombe walls, and so on.

The SSF value determined can be compared with Figure 3C–1 and the approximate values determined from Table 3C–1. If the SSF is too low or too high, either the design can be changed (insulation, infiltration rate, amount of non-south facing windows, and so on) to lower the BLC, or the amount of solar collector area can be increased. Both have the effect of lowering the LCR. You can also consider using another system. If, for example, using a Trombe wall without night insulation yields an SSF too low, using a direct gain system with night insulation might give a higher SSF without changing the LCR.

Annual auxiliary heat required for the system selected can also be calculated knowing the BLC and the SSF with the following formula.

FORMULA: $Q = (1 - SSF) \times BLC \times DD$

where:

Q = annual auxiliary heat required in Btu
SSF = solar savings fraction, as determined from Table 3C–4
BLC = building load coefficient in Btu/DD
DD = degree days, from Table 3C–4

EFFECT OF CHANGING SYSTEM VARIABLES ON PERFORMANCE

The LCR values in Table 3C–4 were calculated based on a "reference" design, making many assumptions about the construction details of the reference passive system. Changing these variables affects the performance of a passive building in various ways; some changes affect performance only slightly, while others—such as night insulation—have a great effect.

The following are features of the reference passive system design:

Thermal storage capacity: 45 Btu/F ft^2 of glazing.

Double glazing with transmittance of 0.747, spacing 1/4 in.

Room temperature control range: 65°F to 75°F.

Night insulation when calculated: R-9.

Thermal mass-to-room air conductance: 1.0 Btu/F hr ft^2.

Masonry thermal conductivity: k = 1.0 Btu/ft hr F.

Masonry density: 150 lb/ft^3.

Masonry specific heat: c = 0.2 Btu/lb F.

Infrared emittance of mass surface = 0.9.

No internal heat generation.

Trombe wall when calculated vented at top and bottom.

Trombe wall vent area = 3% of wall area.

Direct gain mass: 6 in. thick masonry.

Direct gain mass area three times glazing area.

Transmitted solar radiation uniformly distributed on mass.

Non-mass absorption fraction: 0.2.

Vertical, south-facing glass.

Ground reflectance: 0.3.

Mass absorptance for thermal storage walls: 1.0.

Mass absorptance for direct gain: 0.8.

One of the most significant variables is whether or not night insulation is used. As shown in the tables, this type of insulation is very important to the performance of passive solar systems. Since an R-9 value is often difficult (or expensive) to achieve in practice, the effectiveness of other R values has been calculated in terms of the fractional decrease in performance. This is shown in Figure 3C-3.

Sensitivity curves for each of the variables have been calculated for different representative climates, so the designer can evaluate the effect of changing variables on a particular design from those used to calculate the LCR tables. Refer to the *Passive Solar Design Handbook* Volume 2 or Volume 3 for detailed listings.

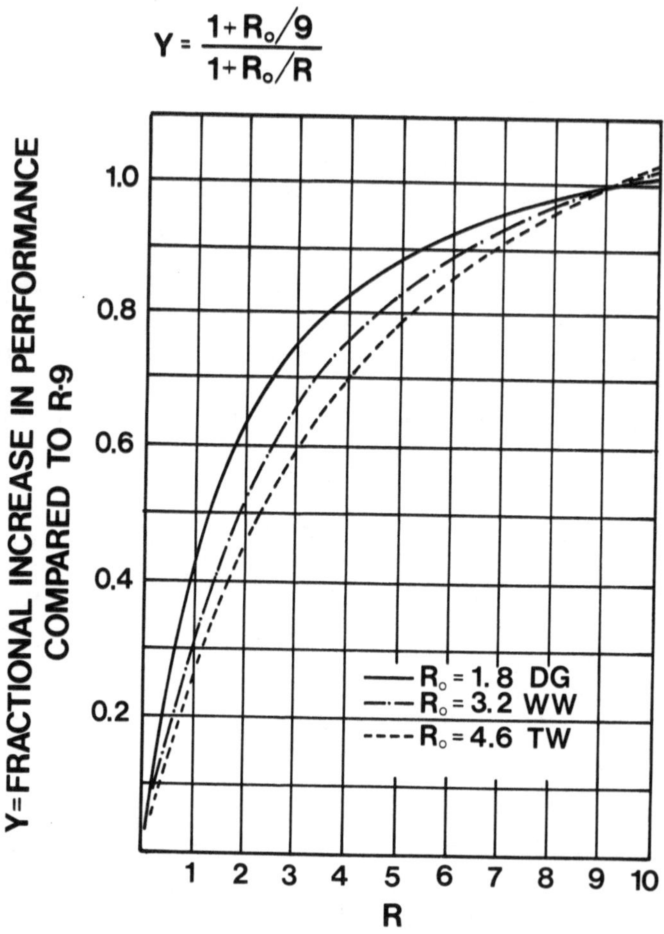

Source: Passive Solar Design Handbook, *Volume 2.*

Figure 3C-3: Variation of Performance Using Other Than R-9 Insulation

Table 3C-4
SOLAR SAVINGS FRACTIONS

Birmingham Alabama		**SSF =**	**0.1**	**0.2**	**0.3**	**0.4**	**0.5**	**0.6**	**0.7**	**0.8**	**0.9**
		WW	186	87	53	37	27	21	15	10	5
33.6 N	L	WWNI	281	134	85	60	45	36	29	23	16
2844 DD	C	TW	179	82	50	33	23	16	11	7	4
T(JAN)=44	R	TWNI	265	126	79	56	42	32	25	18	12
		DG	192	83	47	28	15	-	-	-	-
		DGNI	296	139	86	61	45	34	25	18	11

Mobile Alabama		**SSF =**	**0.1**	**0.2**	**0.3**	**0.4**	**0.5**	**0.6**	**0.7**	**0.8**	**0.9**
		WW	318	144	89	64	48	37	29	21	13
30.7 N	L	WWNI	441	205	127	92	71	56	45	36	25
1684 DD	C	TW	293	135	83	57	40	30	22	15	10
T(JAN) =51	R	TWNI	412	191	120	86	65	51	39	29	19
		DG	354	159	96	63	43	29	18	10	-
		DGNI	469	216	135	96	72	55	42	30	20

Montgomery Alabama		**SSF =**	**0.1**	**0.2**	**0.3**	**0.4**	**0.5**	**0.6**	**0.7**	**0.8**	**0.9**
		WW	236	111	68	48	36	27	21	15	8
32.3 N	L	WWNI	339	165	103	73	56	44	35	28	20
2269 DD	C	TW	224	103	63	43	30	22	15	11	7
T(JAN)=48	R	TWNI	320	153	96	68	51	40	30	23	15
		DG	257	115	67	42	27	16	7	-	-
		DGNI	362	171	107	75	56	42	32	23	15

Phoenix Arizona		**SSF =**	**0.1**	**0.2**	**0.3**	**0.4**	**0.5**	**0.6**	**0.7**	**0.8**	**0.9**
		WW	467	219	139	100	75	58	45	34	22
33.4 N	L	WWNI	620	293	188	136	104	82	65	51	36
1552 DD	C	TW	436	202	126	87	63	46	34	25	16
T(JAN)=51	R	TWNI	583	275	176	126	95	73	56	42	28
		DG	555	256	157	107	75	53	37	24	12
		DGNI	673	316	201	143	107	82	62	45	29

Prescott Arizona		**SSF =**	**0.1**	**0.2**	**0.3**	**0.4**	**0.5**	**0.6**	**0.7**	**0.8**	**0.9**
		WW	189	89	56	40	30	23	17	12	7
34.6 N	L	WWNI	286	135	88	63	48	39	31	25	18
4456 DD	C	TW	183	85	53	36	25	18	13	9	5
T(JAN)=37	R	TWNI	269	128	82	59	45	35	27	20	14
		DG	198	89	52	32	20	10	-	-	-
		DGNI	300	142	90	64	49	37	28	20	13

Tucson Arizona		**SSF =**	**0.1**	**0.2**	**0.3**	**0.4**	**0.5**	**0.6**	**0.7**	**0.8**	**0.9**
		WW	425	199	127	92	70	55	43	32	21
32.1 N	L	WWNI	571	268	172	125	97	77	62	49	36
1752 DD	C	TW	394	185	116	81	59	43	32	23	16
T(JAN)=51	R	TWNI	533	252	161	116	89	69	54	40	27
		DG	498	231	143	98	69	49	34	22	12
		DGNI	613	289	185	132	100	77	59	43	29

Table 3C-4 (Continued)

Winslow Arizona		**SSF =**	**0.1**	**0.2**	**0.3**	**0.4**	**0.5**	**0.6**	**0.7**	**0.8**	**0.9**
		WW	165	78	49	34	25	19	14	9	4
35.0 N	L	WWNI	255	123	79	57	43	34	27	21	15
4733 DD	C	TW	162	75	46	31	22	15	10	7	4
T(JAN)=33	R	TWNI	242	116	74	53	40	31	24	18	12
		DG	168	74	42	24	12	-	-	-	-
		DGNI	268	127	81	57	43	32	24	17	11

Yuma Arizona		**SSF =**	**0.1**	**0.2**	**0.3**	**0.4**	**0.5**	**0.6**	**0.7**	**0.8**	**0.9**
		WW	728	342	219	155	116	89	70	52	35
32.7 N	L	WWNI	932	442	283	204	154	119	94	74	53
1010 DD	C	TW	670	313	194	135	97	72	53	38	25
T(JAN)=55	R	TWNI	877	413	264	187	140	108	82	61	40
		DG	887	412	254	174	124	89	64	44	26
		DGNI	1021	481	305	215	160	122	92	67	44

Fort Smith Arkansas		**SSF =**	**0.1**	**0.2**	**0.3**	**0.4**	**0.5**	**0.6**	**0.7**	**0.8**	**0.9**
		WW	158	74	45	31	23	17	13	8	-
35.3 N	L	WWNI	246	119	75	53	40	32	26	20	14
3336 DD	C	TW	153	70	43	29	20	14	9	6	3
T(JAN)=39	R	TWNI	233	111	70	50	37	29	22	17	11
		DG	156	67	36	20	-	-	-	-	-
		DGNI	258	121	76	53	40	30	22	16	10

Little Rock Arkansas		**SSF =**	**0.1**	**0.2**	**0.3**	**0.4**	**0.5**	**0.6**	**0.7**	**0.8**	**0.9**
		WW	157	72	44	31	22	17	12	8	-
34.7 N	L	WWNI	246	117	74	52	40	31	25	20	14
3354 DD	C	TW	153	69	42	28	19	13	9	6	3
T(JAN)=39	R	TWNI	232	110	69	49	37	29	22	16	11
		DG	154	65	35	18	-	-	-	-	-
		DGNI	257	120	75	53	39	29	22	15	10

Bakersfield California		**SSF =**	**0.1**	**0.2**	**0.3**	**0.4**	**0.5**	**0.6**	**0.7**	**0.8**	**0.9**
		WW	323	143	89	63	46	35	26	18	10
35.4 N	L	WWNI	449	203	127	91	69	54	42	32	22
2185 DD	C	TW	297	135	81	55	39	28	20	14	8
T(JAN)=48	R	TWNI	418	191	119	85	63	48	36	27	17
		DG	359	158	93	60	40	26	15	-	-
		DGNI	475	216	135	94	69	52	39	27	17

Daggett California		**SSF =**	**0.1**	**0.2**	**0.3**	**0.4**	**0.5**	**0.6**	**0.7**	**0.8**	**0.9**
		WW	360	165	103	73	55	42	32	24	15
34.9 N	L	WWNI	491	228	144	103	79	62	49	39	27
2203 DD	C	TW	334	153	94	65	46	34	25	17	11
T(JAN)=47	R	TWNI	461	214	135	96	72	56	43	32	21
		DG	411	185	112	74	51	35	23	13	-
		DGNI	526	244	153	108	81	61	46	33	22

Fresno California		**SSF =**	**0.1**	**0.2**	**0.3**	**0.4**	**0.5**	**0.6**	**0.7**	**0.8**	**0.9**
		WW	272	122	74	51	37	27	20	13	7
36.8 N	L	WWNI	383	179	110	77	58	45	34	26	18
2650 DD	C	TW	252	114	68	45	31	22	15	10	5
T(JAN)=45	R	TWNI	361	166	102	72	53	40	30	22	14
		DG	295	128	72	44	27	15	-	-	-
		DGNI	408	186	114	79	57	42	31	22	13

Long Beach California		**SSF =**	**0.1**	**0.2**	**0.3**	**0.4**	**0.5**	**0.6**	**0.7**	**0.8**	**0.9**
		WW	527	249	156	112	85	67	53	40	27
33.8 N	L	WWNI	689	331	208	150	115	91	74	59	42
1606 DD	C	TW	488	228	142	99	72	53	39	29	19
T(JAN)=54	R	TWNI	650	307	195	139	106	83	64	48	32
		DG	630	291	180	123	87	63	44	30	17
		DGNI	753	354	224	159	120	92	70	52	34

Los Angeles California		**SSF =**	**0.1**	**0.2**	**0.3**	**0.4**	**0.5**	**0.6**	**0.7**	**0.8**	**0.9**
		WW	563	259	161	115	87	68	54	41	27
33.9 N	L	WWNI	737	342	215	153	117	93	75	60	43
1819 DD	C	TW	513	238	147	101	73	54	40	29	20
T(JAN)=54	R	TWNI	687	320	200	143	108	84	65	49	33
		DG	665	304	187	127	90	65	46	31	18
		DGNI	793	369	231	163	123	94	72	53	35

Mount Shasta California		**SSF =**	**0.1**	**0.2**	**0.3**	**0.4**	**0.5**	**0.6**	**0.7**	**0.8**	**0.9**
		WW	142	62	37	25	18	13	9	5	-
41.3 N	L	WWNI	230	106	66	46	35	27	21	16	11
5890 DD	C	TW	137	61	36	23	15	10	7	4	-
T(JAN)=34	R	TWNI	216	99	62	43	32	25	19	14	9
		DG	130	50	23	-	-	-	-	-	-
		DGNI	237	107	66	46	33	25	18	12	7

Needles California		**SSF =**	**0.1**	**0.2**	**0.3**	**0.4**	**0.5**	**0.6**	**0.7**	**0.8**	**0.9**
		WW	508	239	152	108	81	62	47	35	23
34.8 N	L	WWNI	668	317	202	147	111	86	68	53	37
1428 DD	C	TW	474	220	136	94	67	49	36	26	17
T(JAN)=52	R	TWNI	630	297	189	134	100	77	59	44	29
		DG	608	280	171	116	81	57	40	26	13
		DGNI	729	342	217	153	114	86	65	47	30

Oakland California		**SSF =**	**0.1**	**0.2**	**0.3**	**0.4**	**0.5**	**0.6**	**0.7**	**0.8**	**0.9**
		WW	348	170	107	75	56	42	32	23	14
37.7 N	L	WWNI	472	234	150	106	80	62	49	38	27
2909 DD	C	TW	327	155	96	66	47	34	24	17	11
T(JAN)=49	R	TWNI	446	219	139	98	73	56	43	31	20
		DG	405	189	115	76	51	35	22	12	-
		DGNI	512	249	157	110	82	61	46	33	21

Table 3C-4 (Continued)

Red Bluff California		**SSF =**	**0.1**	**0.2**	**0.3**	**0.4**	**0.5**	**0.6**	**0.7**	**0.8**	**0.9**
		WW	258	115	69	48	35	26	19	13	6
40.1 N	L	WWNI	365	170	104	74	56	43	33	26	18
2688 DD	C	TW	239	108	64	43	30	21	15	10	5
T(JAN)=45	R	TWNI	345	158	98	69	51	39	29	21	14
		DG	276	119	68	41	25	14	-	-	-
		DGNI	389	177	109	76	55	41	30	21	13
Sacramento California		**SSF =**	**0.1**	**0.2**	**0.3**	**0.4**	**0.5**	**0.6**	**0.7**	**0.8**	**0.9**
		WW	258	119	73	50	36	26	19	13	6
38.5 N	L	WWNI	368	174	108	76	57	44	34	26	18
2843 DD	C	TW	244	110	66	44	31	22	15	10	5
T(JAN)=45	R	TWNI	347	162	101	71	52	39	30	21	14
		DG	283	124	71	44	27	15	-	-	-
		DGNI	393	182	112	78	57	42	31	22	13
San Diego California		**SSF =**	**0.1**	**0.2**	**0.3**	**0.4**	**0.5**	**0.6**	**0.7**	**0.8**	**0.9**
		WW	612	284	179	129	98	77	61	46	31
32.7 N	L	WWNI	796	373	235	170	131	104	84	67	48
1507 DD	C	TW	562	261	163	113	82	61	46	33	23
T(JAN)=55	R	TWNI	744	348	220	158	120	94	73	54	37
		DG	734	338	210	144	103	75	53	37	22
		DGNI	864	403	255	181	137	105	80	59	40
San Francisco California		**SSF =**	**0.1**	**0.2**	**0.3**	**0.4**	**0.5**	**0.6**	**0.7**	**0.8**	**0.9**
		WW	332	163	103	72	53	40	31	22	13
37.6N	L	WWNI	453	225	145	103	77	60	47	37	26
3042 DD	C	TW	313	149	92	63	45	33	23	16	10
T(JAN)=48	R	TWNI	428	210	134	94	71	54	41	30	20
		DG	385	180	109	72	49	32	20	11	-
		DGNI	491	239	151	106	79	59	44	32	20
Santa Maria California		**SSF =**	**0.1**	**0.2**	**0.3**	**0.4**	**0.5**	**0.6**	**0.7**	**0.8**	**0.9**
		WW	327	164	107	77	58	46	35	26	17
34.9 N	L	WWNI	448	224	148	108	83	66	53	42	30
3053 DD	C	TW	311	152	97	67	49	36	27	19	12
T(JAN)=50	R	TWNI	423	211	138	100	76	59	46	34	23
		DG	383	185	116	79	55	38	26	16	7
		DGNI	485	241	156	112	85	65	50	36	24
Colorado Springs Colorado		**SSF =**	**0.1**	**0.2**	**0.3**	**0.4**	**0.5**	**0.6**	**0.7**	**0.8**	**0.9**
		WW	130	60	38	26	19	15	11	7	-
38.8 N	L	WWNI	211	102	65	47	36	29	23	18	13
6473 DD	C	TW	128	59	36	24	17	11	8	5	2
T(JAN)=29	R	TWNI	201	96	61	44	33	26	20	15	10
		DG	120	51	26	10	-	-	-	-	-
		DGNI	220	104	66	47	35	26	20	14	9

Denver Colorado		**SSF =**	**0.1**	**0.2**	**0.3**	**0.4**	**0.5**	**0.6**	**0.7**	**0.8**	**0.9**
		WW	136	63	39	27	20	15	11	7	–
39.7 N	L	WWNI	218	105	67	48	37	29	24	19	13
6016 DD	C	TW	132	61	38	25	17	12	8	5	3
T(JAN)=30	R	TWNI	207	99	63	45	34	27	21	15	10
		DG	127	54	28	13	–	–	–	–	–
		DGNI	227	108	68	48	36	27	20	14	9

Eagle Colorado		**SSF =**	**0.1**	**0.2**	**0.3**	**0.4**	**0.5**	**0.6**	**0.7**	**0.8**	**0.9**
		WW	95	43	26	17	12	8	5	–	–
39.6 N	L	WWNI	172	81	52	37	28	22	17	13	9
8426 DD	C	TW	96	43	25	16	10	7	4	–	–
T(JAN)=18	R	TWNI	163	77	49	34	26	20	15	11	7
		DG	72	22	–	–	–	–	–	–	–
		DGNI	174	81	51	35	26	19	14	9	5

Grand Junction Colorado		**SSF =**	**0.1**	**0.2**	**0.3**	**0.4**	**0.5**	**0.6**	**0.7**	**0.8**	**0.9**
		WW	135	61	37	25	18	13	9	5	–
39.1 N	L	WWNI	222	104	66	46	35	28	22	17	12
5605 DD	C	TW	133	60	36	23	16	11	7	4	1
T(JAN)=27	R	TWNI	210	98	61	43	33	25	19	14	9
		DG	125	50	24	–	–	–	–	–	–
		DGNI	229	106	66	46	34	25	18	13	8

Pueblo Colorado		**SSF =**	**0.1**	**0.2**	**0.3**	**0.4**	**0.5**	**0.6**	**0.7**	**0.8**	**0.9**
		WW	145	67	41	29	21	16	12	8	–
38.3 N	L	WWNI	234	109	70	50	38	30	24	19	14
5394 DD	C	TW	143	65	39	26	18	13	9	5	3
T(JAN)=30	R	TWNI	220	103	66	47	36	28	21	16	11
		DG	140	59	32	16	–	–	–	–	–
		DGNI	242	113	71	50	38	28	21	15	9

Hartford Connecticut		**SSF =**	**0.1**	**0.2**	**0.3**	**0.4**	**0.5**	**0.6**	**0.7**	**0.8**	**0.9**
		WW	62	26	14	9	5	–	–	–	–
41.9 N	L	WWNI	134	62	39	28	21	16	13	10	7
6350 DD	C	TW	66	28	16	9	5	–	–	–	–
T(JAN)=25	R	TWNI	127	59	37	26	19	15	11	8	5
		DG	–	–	–	–	–	–	–	–	–
		DGNI	131	60	37	25	18	13	9	6	3

Wilmington Delaware		**SSF =**	**0.1**	**0.2**	**0.3**	**0.4**	**0.5**	**0.6**	**0.7**	**0.8**	**0.9**
		WW	95	44	26	18	12	9	5	–	–
39.7 N	L	WWNI	171	83	52	37	28	22	18	14	9
4940 DD	C	TW	97	44	26	17	11	7	4	–	–
T(JAN)=32	R	TWNI	163	78	49	35	26	20	15	11	7
		DG	74	24	–	–	–	–	–	–	–
		DGNI	174	82	51	36	26	19	14	10	5

Table 3C-4 (Continued)

Washington DC		**SSF =**	**0.1**	**0.2**	**0.3**	**0.4**	**0.5**	**0.6**	**0.7**	**0.8**	**0.9**
		WW	92	42	25	17	11	8	4	–	–
38.9 N	L	WWNI	169	80	51	36	27	21	17	13	9
5010 DD	C	TW	94	42	25	16	10	6	3	–	–
T(JAN)=32	R	TWNI	160	76	48	34	25	19	15	11	7
		DG	69	19	–	–	–	–	–	–	–
		DGNI	171	80	50	35	25	19	13	9	5

Apalachicola Florida		**SSF =**	**0.1**	**0.2**	**0.3**	**0.4**	**0.5**	**0.6**	**0.7**	**0.8**	**0.9**
		WW	405	182	114	81	61	48	37	27	18
29.7 N	L	WWNI	547	249	156	113	87	68	55	44	31
1361 DD	C	TW	371	170	104	72	51	38	28	20	13
T(JAN)=54	R	TWNI	511	233	147	105	79	62	48	36	24
		DG	464	208	126	84	59	41	28	17	8
		DGNI	585	267	168	119	89	68	52	38	25

Daytona Beach Florida		**SSF =**	**0.1**	**0.2**	**0.3**	**0.4**	**0.5**	**0.6**	**0.7**	**0.8**	**0.9**
		WW	603	281	180	130	100	79	62	48	32
29.2 N	L	WWNI	784	367	235	172	133	106	86	69	49
902 DD	C	TW	556	260	164	114	83	62	47	34	23
T(JAN)=58	R	TWNI	735	344	221	159	122	96	74	56	38
		DG	725	337	211	146	105	76	55	38	23
		DGNI	852	399	256	183	139	107	82	61	41

Jacksonville Florida		**SSF =**	**0.1**	**0.2**	**0.3**	**0.4**	**0.5**	**0.6**	**0.7**	**0.8**	**0.9**
		WW	425	191	120	87	66	52	41	31	20
30.5 N	L	WWNI	573	260	164	119	92	74	60	47	34
1327 DD	C	TW	390	179	111	77	55	41	30	22	15
T(JAN)=55	R	TWNI	533	244	154	111	85	66	52	39	26
		DG	489	221	136	92	65	46	32	21	11
		DGNI	611	279	177	126	96	73	56	41	27

Miami Florida		**SSF =**	**0.1**	**0.2**	**0.3**	**0.4**	**0.5**	**0.6**	**0.7**	**0.8**	**0.9**
		WW	2285	1138	731	516	389	307	242	186	130
25.8 N	L	WWNI	2804	1401	906	641	483	382	307	242	174
206 DD	C	TW	2102	1013	641	449	329	245	184	135	94
T(JAN)=67	R	TWNI	2638	1304	832	589	446	344	265	198	133
		DG	2912	1403	886	620	452	336	249	181	121
		DGNI	3119	1534	975	692	520	398	303	224	151

Orlando Florida		**SSF =**	**0.1**	**0.2**	**0.3**	**0.4**	**0.5**	**0.6**	**0.7**	**0.8**	**0.9**
		WW	723	346	224	163	124	98	78	60	41
28.5 N	L	WWNI	927	446	289	211	163	130	105	84	60
733 DD	C	TW	663	319	202	142	104	78	58	43	30
T(JAN)=60	R	TWNI	867	418	270	195	149	117	91	68	46
		DG	879	421	265	185	134	99	72	51	32
		DGNI	1010	487	314	226	171	132	101	75	50

Tallahassee Florida

		SSF =	0.1	0.2	0.3	0.4	0.5	0.6	0.7	0.8	0.9
		WW	359	162	101	72	55	43	33	24	16
30.4 N	L	WWNI	491	226	141	102	79	62	50	40	28
1563 DD	C	TW	330	152	93	64	46	34	25	18	12
T(JAN)=53	R	TWNI	458	211	133	95	72	56	43	32	22
		DG	405	183	110	74	51	35	23	14	5
		DGNI	523	240	151	107	80	62	47	34	22

Tampa Florida

		SSF =	0.1	0.2	0.3	0.4	0.5	0.6	0.7	0.8	0.9
		WW	720	343	223	162	124	98	78	59	41
28.0 N	L	WWNI	926	441	288	211	162	129	105	83	60
718 DD	C	TW	663	317	201	141	104	78	58	43	30
T(JAN)=60	R	TWNI	866	415	269	195	149	117	90	68	46
		DG	878	418	264	184	134	98	72	50	32
		DGNI	1008	484	312	225	171	132	101	75	50

West Palm Beach Florida

		SSF =	0.1	0.2	0.3	0.4	0.5	0.6	0.7	0.8	0.9
		WW	1523	761	494	350	264	208	164	126	88
26.7 N	L	WWNI	1886	943	619	441	331	261	211	167	120
299 DD	C	TW	1407	682	433	304	223	167	125	91	63
T(JAN)=65	R	TWNI	1775	884	568	403	305	237	183	136	92
		DG	1930	935	592	415	302	224	165	119	79
		DGNI	2093	1038	663	471	355	272	207	153	103

Atlanta Georgia

		SSF =	0.1	0.2	0.3	0.4	0.5	0.6	0.7	0.8	0.9
		WW	172	79	48	33	25	19	14	9	4
33.6 N	L	WWNI	264	126	79	56	42	33	27	21	15
3095 DD	C	TW	166	75	46	31	21	15	10	7	4
T(JAN)=42	R	TWNI	249	118	74	52	39	30	23	17	11
		DG	173	74	41	23	10	-	-	-	-
		DGNI	276	129	80	56	42	32	23	17	10

Augusta Georgia

		SSF =	0.1	0.2	0.3	0.4	0.5	0.6	0.7	0.8	0.9
		WW	213	101	62	43	32	25	19	13	7
33.4 N	L	WWNI	312	152	95	67	51	41	33	26	18
2547 DD	C	TW	204	94	58	39	27	20	14	9	6
T(JAN)=46	R	TWNI	295	141	89	63	48	37	28	21	14
		DG	228	101	59	37	22	12	-	-	-
		DGNI	332	157	98	69	52	39	29	21	13

Macon Georgia

		SSF =	0.1	0.2	0.3	0.4	0.5	0.6	0.7	0.8	0.9
		WW	244	114	70	49	37	28	21	15	9
32.7 N	L	WWNI	349	169	105	74	57	45	36	28	20
2240 DD	C	TW	230	106	65	44	31	22	16	11	7
T(JAN)=48	R	TWNI	330	156	98	69	52	41	31	23	16
		DG	266	119	70	44	28	17	9	-	-
		DGNI	373	175	109	77	57	43	33	24	15

Table 3C-4 (Continued)

Savannah Georgia		**SSF =**	**0.1**	**0.2**	**0.3**	**0.4**	**0.5**	**0.6**	**0.7**	**0.8**	**0.9**
		WW	278	131	81	57	43	33	26	19	11
32.1 N	L	WWNI	389	189	118	84	65	51	41	32	23
1952 DD	C	TW	260	122	75	51	37	26	19	13	9
T(JAN)=50	R	TWNI	367	175	110	79	59	46	36	27	18
		DG	309	141	84	55	37	24	14	6	-
		DGNI	417	197	124	88	66	50	38	27	18
Boise Idaho		**SSF =**	**0.1**	**0.2**	**0.3**	**0.4**	**0.5**	**0.6**	**0.7**	**0.8**	**0.9**
		WW	132	58	34	22	15	10	5	-	-
43.6 N	L	WWNI	215	101	63	44	32	25	19	14	9
5833 DD	C	TW	127	56	32	20	13	8	4	-	-
T(JAN)=29	R	TWNI	203	95	59	41	30	22	16	12	7
		DG	117	42	-	-	-	-	-	-	-
		DGNI	221	102	62	42	30	22	15	10	5
Lewiston Idaho		**SSF =**	**0.1**	**0.2**	**0.3**	**0.4**	**0.5**	**0.6**	**0.7**	**0.8**	**0.9**
		WW	110	46	26	15	9	4	-	-	-
46.4 N	L	WWNI	192	88	54	37	27	20	15	11	7
5464 DD	C	TW	108	46	25	15	9	4	-	-	-
T(JAN)=31	R	TWNI	181	82	50	34	25	18	13	9	6
		DG	85	-	-	-	-	-	-	-	-
		DGNI	194	87	52	34	24	17	11	7	3
Pocatello Idaho		**SSF =**	**0.1**	**0.2**	**0.3**	**0.4**	**0.5**	**0.6**	**0.7**	**0.8**	**0.9**
		WW	105	47	28	18	12	8	3	-	-
42.9 N	L	WWNI	182	88	55	39	29	22	17	13	9
7063 DD	C	TW	104	47	27	17	11	6	3	-	-
T(JAN)=23	R	TWNI	173	82	51	36	26	20	15	11	7
		DG	84	27	-	-	-	-	-	-	-
		DGNI	186	87	54	37	26	19	14	9	5
Chicago Illinois		**SSF =**	**0.1**	**0.2**	**0.3**	**0.4**	**0.5**	**0.6**	**0.7**	**0.8**	**0.9**
		WW	73	31	17	11	6	-	-	-	-
41.8 N	L	WWNI	149	69	43	30	22	17	14	10	7
6127 DD	C	TW	78	33	18	11	6	-	-	-	-
T(JAN)=24	R	TWNI	141	65	40	28	21	16	12	9	5
		DG	34	-	-	-	-	-	-	-	-
		DGNI	148	67	41	28	20	14	10	7	3
Moline Illinois		**SSF =**	**0.1**	**0.2**	**0.3**	**0.4**	**0.5**	**0.6**	**0.7**	**0.8**	**0.9**
		WW	72	30	17	10	6	-	-	-	-
41.4 N	L	WWNI	147	68	42	30	22	17	13	10	7
6395 DD	C	TW	76	32	18	10	6	-	-	-	-
T(JAN)=21	R	TWNI	139	64	40	28	21	16	12	9	5
		DG	29	-	-	-	-	-	-	-	-
		DGNI	145	66	40	27	19	14	10	6	3

Springfield Illinois		**SSF =**	**0.1**	**0.2**	**0.3**	**0.4**	**0.5**	**0.6**	**0.7**	**0.8**	**0.9**
		WW	90	39	22	14	10	6	-	-	-
39.8 N	L	WWNI	168	78	49	34	25	20	16	12	8
5558 DD	C	TW	92	39	23	14	9	5	2	-	-
T(JAN)=27	R	TWNI	159	74	46	32	24	18	14	10	6
		DG	61	-	-	-	-	-	-	-	-
		DGNI	169	77	47	32	23	17	12	8	4

Evansville Indiana		**SSF =**	**0.1**	**0.2**	**0.3**	**0.4**	**0.5**	**0.6**	**0.7**	**0.8**	**0.9**
		WW	104	46	26	17	12	8	5	-	-
38.0 N	L	WWNI	182	86	54	37	28	22	17	13	9
4629 DD	C	TW	104	45	26	17	11	7	4	-	-
T(JAN)=33	R	TWNI	173	81	50	35	26	20	15	11	7
		DG	81	25	-	-	-	-	-	-	-
		DGNI	186	85	52	36	26	19	14	9	5

Fort Wayne Indiana		**SSF =**	**0.1**	**0.2**	**0.3**	**0.4**	**0.5**	**0.6**	**0.7**	**0.8**	**0.9**
		WW	62	25	13	8	-	-	-	-	-
41.0 N	L	WWNI	136	62	39	27	20	16	12	9	6
6209 DD	C	TW	67	28	15	8	4	-	-	-	-
T(JAN)=25	R	TWNI	128	59	37	25	19	14	11	8	5
		DG	-	-	-	-	-	-	-	-	-
		DGNI	132	60	36	24	17	12	9	5	2

Indianapolis Indiana		**SSF =**	**0.1**	**0.2**	**0.3**	**0.4**	**0.5**	**0.6**	**0.7**	**0.8**	**0.9**
		WW	74	31	17	11	7	-	-	-	-
39.7 N	L	WWNI	148	69	43	30	23	17	14	11	7
5577 DD	C	TW	77	33	18	11	6	2	-	-	-
T(JAN)=28	R	TWNI	141	65	41	28	21	16	12	9	6
		DG	35	-	-	-	-	-	-	-	-
		DGNI	147	67	41	28	20	14	10	7	3

South Bend Indiana		**SSF =**	**0.1**	**0.2**	**0.3**	**0.4**	**0.5**	**0.6**	**0.7**	**0.8**	**0.9**
		WW	60	24	12	6	-	-	-	-	-
41.7 N	L	WWNI	137	61	38	26	19	15	11	9	6
6462 DD	C	TW	66	26	14	7	-	-	-	-	-
T(JAN)=24	R	TWNI	129	58	36	25	18	13	10	7	5
		DG	-	-	-	-	-	-	-	-	-
		DGNI	132	58	35	23	16	12	8	5	-

Burlington Iowa		**SSF =**	**0.1**	**0.2**	**0.3**	**0.4**	**0.5**	**0.6**	**0.7**	**0.8**	**0.9**
		WW	83	36	20	13	8	5	-	-	-
40.8 N	L	WWNI	159	74	36	32	24	19	15	11	8
6149 DD	C	TW	85	36	21	13	7	4	-	-	-
T(JAN)=23	R	TWNI	151	70	43	30	22	17	13	9	6
		DG	50	-	-	-	-	-	-	-	-
		DGNI	159	72	44	30	22	16	11	7	4

Table 3C-4 (Continued)

Des Moines Iowa		**SSF =**	**0.1**	**0.2**	**0.3**	**0.4**	**0.5**	**0.6**	**0.7**	**0.8**	**0.9**
		WW	78	33	18	11	7	3	-	-	-
41.5 N	L	WWNI	155	71	44	31	23	18	14	11	7
6710 DD	C	TW	81	34	19	11	6	3	-	-	-
T(JAN)=19	R	TWNI	146	67	41	29	21	16	12	9	6
		DG	41	-	-	-	-	-	-	-	-
		DGNI	153	69	42	29	20	15	11	7	3

Mason City Iowa		**SSF =**	**0.1**	**0.2**	**0.3**	**0.4**	**0.5**	**0.6**	**0.7**	**0.8**	**0.9**
		WW	68	27	14	8	4	-	-	-	-
43.1 N	L	WWNI	143	65	40	28	21	16	12	9	6
7901 DD	C	TW	72	29	16	9	4	-	-	-	-
T(JAN)=14	R	TWNI	136	62	38	26	19	15	11	8	5
		DG	-	-	-	-	-	-	-	-	-
		DGNI	141	63	37	25	18	13	9	6	2

Sioux City Iowa		**SSF =**	**0.1**	**0.2**	**0.3**	**0.4**	**0.5**	**0.6**	**0.7**	**0.8**	**0.9**
		WW	77	32	17	11	7	-	-	-	-
42.4 N	L	WWNI	153	70	44	30	22	17	14	10	7
6953 DD	C	TW	80	33	18	11	6	-	-	-	-
T(JAN)=18	R	TWNI	144	66	41	28	21	16	12	9	6
		DG	37	-	-	-	-	-	-	-	-
		DGNI	151	68	41	28	20	14	10	7	3

Dodge City Kansas		**SSF =**	**0.1**	**0.2**	**0.3**	**0.4**	**0.5**	**0.6**	**0.7**	**0.8**	**0.9**
		WW	140	64	39	27	19	15	10	6	-
37.8 N	L	WWNI	228	107	67	48	36	29	23	18	13
5046 DD	C	TW	138	62	37	25	17	11	8	5	2
T(JAN)=31	R	TWNI	215	100	63	45	34	26	20	15	10
		DG	132	54	27	10	-	-	-	-	-
		DGNI	236	109	68	47	35	26	20	14	8

Goodland Kansas		**SSF =**	**0.1**	**0.2**	**0.3**	**0.4**	**0.5**	**0.6**	**0.7**	**0.8**	**0.9**
		WW	120	55	33	23	17	12	8	5	-
39.4 N	L	WWNI	202	95	61	43	33	26	21	16	12
6119 DD	C	TW	118	54	32	21	14	10	6	4	1
T(JAN)=28	R	TWNI	190	90	57	40	31	24	18	13	9
		DG	105	42	18	-	-	-	-	-	-
		DGNI	206	97	60	42	31	24	17	12	7

Topeka Kansas		**SSF =**	**0.1**	**0.2**	**0.3**	**0.4**	**0.5**	**0.6**	**0.7**	**0.8**	**0.9**
		WW	112	50	29	20	14	10	6	-	-
39.1 N	L	WWNI	194	91	57	40	30	23	19	14	10
5243 DD	C	TW	112	49	29	18	12	8	5	2	-
T(JAN)=28	R	TWNI	183	85	53	37	28	21	16	12	8
		DG	93	33	-	-	-	-	-	-	-
		DGNI	198	91	56	39	28	21	15	10	6

Wichita Kansas		**SSF =**	**0.1**	**0.2**	**0.3**	**0.4**	**0.5**	**0.6**	**0.7**	**0.8**	**0.9**
		WW	138	63	38	26	19	14	10	6	-
37.6 N	L	WWNI	224	106	66	47	35	28	22	17	12
4687 DD	C	TW	135	61	36	24	16	11	7	4	2
T(JAN)=31	R	TWNI	212	99	62	44	33	25	19	14	9
		DG	128	52	25	-	-	-	-	-	-
		DGNI	232	107	66	46	34	26	19	13	8

Lexington Kentucky		**SSF =**	**0.1**	**0.2**	**0.3**	**0.4**	**0.5**	**0.6**	**0.7**	**0.8**	**0.9**
		WW	96	42	24	16	11	7	4	-	-
38.0 N	L	WWNI	174	82	51	36	27	21	17	13	9
4729 DD	C	TW	98	42	25	15	10	6	3	-	-
T(JAN)=33	R	TWNI	165	77	48	34	25	19	15	11	7
		DG	71	17	-	-	-	-	-	-	-
		DGNI	177	81	50	34	25	18	13	9	5

Louisville Kentucky		**SSF =**	**0.1**	**0.2**	**0.3**	**0.4**	**0.5**	**0.6**	**0.7**	**0.8**	**0.9**
		WW	98	44	25	17	12	8	4	-	-
38.2 N	L	WWNI	176	84	52	37	27	21	17	13	9
4645 DD	C	TW	99	44	25	16	10	6	3	-	-
T(JAN)=33	R	TWNI	167	78	49	34	25	19	15	11	7
		DG	74	21	-	-	-	-	-	-	-
		DGNI	179	83	51	35	25	19	14	9	5

Baton Rouge Louisiana		**SSF =**	**0.1**	**0.2**	**0.3**	**0.4**	**0.5**	**0.6**	**0.7**	**0.8**	**0.9**
		WW	312	142	87	62	46	36	28	20	12
30.5 N	L	WWNI	430	203	125	90	69	54	43	34	24
1670 DD	C	TW	287	133	81	55	39	28	21	15	9
T(JAN)=51	R	TWNI	405	188	118	84	63	49	38	28	19
		DG	346	156	93	61	41	27	17	8	-
		DGNI	460	213	133	94	70	53	40	29	19

Lake Charles Louisiana		**SSF =**	**0.1**	**0.2**	**0.3**	**0.4**	**0.5**	**0.6**	**0.7**	**0.8**	**0.9**
		WW	330	144	89	63	48	37	28	21	13
30.1 N	L	WWNI	457	205	127	92	70	55	44	35	25
1498 DD	C	TW	301	136	83	56	40	29	21	15	10
T(JAN)=52	R	TWNI	425	192	120	85	64	50	39	29	19
		DG	364	160	95	62	42	28	18	9	-
		DGNI	482	218	136	96	71	54	41	30	19

New Orleans Louisiana		**SSF =**	**0.1**	**0.2**	**0.3**	**0.4**	**0.5**	**0.6**	**0.7**	**0.8**	**0.9**
		WW	374	169	104	74	56	44	34	25	16
30.0 N	L	WWNI	506	235	146	105	80	64	51	40	29
1465 DD	C	TW	342	158	97	66	47	35	25	18	12
T(JAN)=53	R	TWNI	474	219	137	98	74	57	44	33	22
		DG	423	191	115	76	52	36	24	14	6
		DGNI	542	249	156	110	83	63	48	35	23

Table 3C-4 (Continued)

Shreveport Louisiana		**SSF =**	**0.1**	**0.2**	**0.3**	**0.4**	**0.5**	**0.6**	**0.7**	**0.8**	**0.9**
		WW	250	115	70	50	37	29	22	15	9
32.5 N	L	WWNI	356	170	105	75	57	45	36	29	20
2167 DD	C	TW	234	108	66	45	32	23	16	11	7
T(JAN)=47	R	TWNI	336	158	99	70	53	41	32	23	16
		DG	271	120	71	45	29	18	9	-	-
		DGNI	380	177	110	78	58	44	33	24	15

Caribou Maine		**SSF =**	**0.1**	**0.2**	**0.3**	**0.4**	**0.5**	**0.6**	**0.7**	**0.8**	**0.9**
		WW	48	18	8	-	-	-	-	-	-
46.9 N	L	WWNI	119	55	34	24	18	13	10	7	5
9632 DD	C	TW	54	21	10	3	-	-	-	-	-
T(JAN)=11	R	TWNI	113	52	32	22	16	12	9	6	4
		DG	-	-	-	-	-	-	-	-	-
		DGNI	114	51	31	20	14	10	6	4	-

Portland Maine		**SSF =**	**0.1**	**0.2**	**0.3**	**0.4**	**0.5**	**0.6**	**0.7**	**0.8**	**0.9**
		WW	60	24	13	7	-	-	-	-	-
43.6 N	L	WWNI	133	61	38	27	20	15	12	9	6
7498 DD	C	TW	65	27	14	8	3	-	-	-	-
T(JAN)=21	R	TWNI	126	58	36	25	19	14	11	8	5
		DG	-	-	-	-	-	-	-	-	-
		DGNI	130	58	35	24	17	12	8	5	2

Baltimore Maryland		**SSF =**	**0.1**	**0.2**	**0.3**	**0.4**	**0.5**	**0.6**	**0.7**	**0.8**	**0.9**
		WW	101	46	28	19	13	9	6	-	-
39.2 N	L	WWNI	178	86	55	39	29	23	18	14	10
4729 DD	C	TW	102	46	27	18	12	7	4	2	-
T(JAN)=33	R	TWNI	169	81	51	36	27	21	16	12	8
		DG	81	29	-	-	-	-	-	-	-
		DGNI	182	86	54	37	27	20	15	10	6

Boston Massachusetts		**SSF =**	**0.1**	**0.2**	**0.3**	**0.4**	**0.5**	**0.6**	**0.7**	**0.8**	**0.9**
		WW	81	35	20	13	9	5	-	-	-
42.4 N	L	WWNI	159	73	46	32	24	19	15	11	8
5621 DD	C	TW	85	36	21	13	8	4	-	-	-
T(JAN)=29	R	TWNI	150	69	43	30	23	17	13	10	6
		DG	49	-	-	-	-	-	-	-	-
		DGNI	158	72	44	30	22	16	11	8	4

Alpena Michigan		**SSF =**	**0.1**	**0.2**	**0.3**	**0.4**	**0.5**	**0.6**	**0.7**	**0.8**	**0.9**
		WW	53	19	8	-	-	-	-	-	-
45.1 N	L	WWNI	126	57	35	24	17	13	10	7	5
8518 DD	C	TW	58	22	10	-	-	-	-	-	-
T(JAN)=18	R	TWNI	119	54	33	22	16	12	9	6	4
		DG	-	-	-	-	-	-	-	-	-
		DGNI	121	53	31	20	14	10	6	3	-

Detroit Michigan		SSF =	0.1	0.2	0.3	0.4	0.5	0.6	0.7	0.8	0.9
		WW	62	26	14	8	-	-	-	-	-
42.4 N	L	WWNI	137	63	39	27	20	16	12	9	6
6228 DD	C	TW	68	28	15	8	3	-	-	-	-
T(JAN)=25	R	TWNI	130	60	37	26	19	14	11	8	5
		DG	-	-	-	-	-	-	-	-	-
		DGNI	134	60	36	25	17	12	9	5	2

Flint Michigan		SSF =	0.1	0.2	0.3	0.4	0.5	0.6	0.7	0.8	0.9
		WW	54	21	10	-	-	-	-	-	-
43.0 N	L	WWNI	129	58	36	25	18	14	11	8	5
7041 DD	C	TW	60	24	12	5	-	-	-	-	-
T(JAN)=22	R	TWNI	122	55	34	23	17	13	9	7	4
		DG	-	-	-	-	-	-	-	-	-
		DGNI	124	54	32	21	15	10	7	4	-

Grand Rapids Michigan		SSF =	0.1	0.2	0.3	0.4	0.5	0.6	0.7	0.8	0.9
		WW	57	22	10	-	-	-	-	-	-
42.9 N	L	WWNI	133	59	37	25	19	14	11	8	5
6801 DD	C	TW	63	25	12	6	-	-	-	-	-
T(JAN)=23	R	TWNI	125	56	34	24	17	13	10	7	4
		DG	-	-	-	-	-	-	-	-	-
		DGNI	128	56	33	22	15	11	7	4	-

Sault Ste. Marie Michigan		SSF =	0.1	0.2	0.3	0.4	0.5	0.6	0.7	0.8	0.9
		WW	45	15	-	-	-	-	-	-	-
46.5 N	L	WWNI	116	53	33	22	16	12	9	6	4
9193 DD	C	TW	51	19	8	-	-	-	-	-	-
T(JAN)=14	R	TWNI	110	50	31	21	15	11	8	6	3
		DG	-	-	-	-	-	-	-	-	-
		DGNI	110	49	29	19	12	8	5	2	-

Traverse City Michigan		SSF =	0.1	0.2	0.3	0.4	0.5	0.6	0.7	0.8	0.9
		WW	51	18	-	-	-	-	-	-	-
44.7 N	L	WWNI	127	56	34	23	17	13	9	7	4
7698 DD	C	TW	58	21	9	-	-	-	-	-	-
T(JAN)=21	R	TWNI	120	53	32	22	16	11	8	6	4
		DG	-	-	-	-	-	-	-	-	-
		DGNI	121	52	30	20	13	9	6	3	-

Duluth Minnesota		SSF =	0.1	0.2	0.3	0.4	0.5	0.6	0.7	0.8	0.9
		WW	42	15	-	-	-	-	-	-	-
46.8 N	L	WWNI	113	52	32	22	16	12	9	7	4
9756 DD	C	TW	49	18	8	-	-	-	-	-	-
T(JAN)=9	R	TWNI	107	49	30	21	15	11	8	6	3
		DG	-	-	-	-	-	-	-	-	-
		DGNI	107	48	28	18	12	8	5	3	-

Table 3C-4 (Continued)

International Falls Minnesota		**SSF =**	**0.1**	**0.2**	**0.3**	**0.4**	**0.5**	**0.6**	**0.7**	**0.8**	**0.9**
		WW	38	10	-	-	-	-	-	-	-
48.6 N	L	WWNI	109	49	30	21	15	11	8	6	4
10547 DD	C	TW	45	16	-	-	-	-	-	-	-
T(JAN)=2	R	TWNI	104	47	28	19	14	10	7	5	3
		DG	-	-	-	-	-	-	-	-	-
		DGNI	103	45	26	16	11	7	4	-	-
Minneapolis Minnesota		**SSF =**	**0.1**	**0.2**	**0.3**	**0.4**	**0.5**	**0.6**	**0.7**	**0.8**	**0.9**
		WW	54	21	10	-	-	-	-	-	-
44.9 N	L	WWNI	126	58	36	25	18	14	11	8	5
8159 DD	C	TW	59	24	12	5	-	-	-	-	-
T(JAN)=12	R	TWNI	120	55	34	23	17	13	9	7	4
		DG	-	-	-	-	-	-	-	-	-
		DGNI	122	54	32	22	15	10	7	4	-
Rochester Minnesota		**SSF =**	**0.1**	**0.2**	**0.3**	**0.4**	**0.5**	**0.6**	**0.7**	**0.8**	**0.9**
		WW	53	20	9	-	-	-	-	-	-
43.9 N	L	WWNI	126	57	35	24	18	14	11	8	5
8227 DD	C	TW	59	23	12	5	-	-	-	-	-
T(JAN)=13	R	TWNI	120	54	33	23	17	13	9	7	4
		DG	-	-	-	-	-	-	-	-	-
		DGNI	121	54	32	21	15	10	7	4	-
Jackson Mississippi		**SSF =**	**0.1**	**0.2**	**0.3**	**0.4**	**0.5**	**0.6**	**0.7**	**0.8**	**0.9**
		WW	230	108	66	46	34	26	20	14	8
32.3 N	L	WWNI	331	161	100	71	54	43	34	27	19
2300 DD	C	TW	218	101	62	42	29	21	15	10	6
T(JAN)=47	R	TWNI	313	149	94	66	50	39	30	22	15
		DG	248	111	65	41	26	15	5	-	-
		DGNI	354	167	104	73	55	41	31	22	14
Meridian Mississippi		**SSF =**	**0.1**	**0.2**	**0.3**	**0.4**	**0.5**	**0.6**	**0.7**	**0.8**	**0.9**
		WW	216	103	63	44	33	25	19	13	7
32.3 N	L	WWNI	315	154	97	69	53	41	33	26	19
2388 DD	C	TW	206	96	59	40	28	20	14	10	6
T(JAN)=47	R	TWNI	298	144	90	64	48	38	29	21	14
		DG	233	104	61	38	24	13	-	-	-
		DGNI	335	160	100	71	53	40	30	21	14
Columbia Missouri		**SSF =**	**0.1**	**0.2**	**0.3**	**0.4**	**0.5**	**0.6**	**0.7**	**0.8**	**0.9**
		WW	102	45	26	17	12	8	5	-	-
38.8 N	L	WWNI	182	85	53	37	28	22	17	13	9
5083 DD	C	TW	103	45	26	16	10	6	3	-	-
T(JAN)=29	R	TWNI	173	80	50	35	26	20	15	11	7
		DG	79	23	-	-	-	-	-	-	-
		DGNI	185	84	51	36	26	19	14	9	5

Kansas City Missouri		SSF =	**0.1**	**0.2**	**0.3**	**0.4**	**0.5**	**0.6**	**0.7**	**0.8**	**0.9**
		WW	102	45	26	17	12	8	5	-	-
39.3 N	L	WWNI	182	85	53	37	28	22	17	14	9
5357 DD	C	TW	103	45	26	17	11	7	4	-	-
T(JAN)=27	R	TWNI	172	80	50	35	26	20	15	11	7
		DG	79	25	-	-	-	-	-	-	-
		DGNI	184	84	52	36	26	19	14	10	5

Saint Louis Missouri		SSF =	**0.1**	**0.2**	**0.3**	**0.4**	**0.5**	**0.6**	**0.7**	**0.8**	**0.9**
		WW	113	50	29	19	14	10	6	-	-
38.7 N	L	WWNI	194	91	57	40	30	23	18	14	10
4750 DD	C	TW	113	49	29	18	12	8	4	2	-
T(JAN)=31	R	TWNI	184	86	53	37	28	21	16	12	8
		DG	94	32	-	-	-	-	-	-	-
		DGNI	199	91	56	38	28	21	15	10	6

Springfield Missouri		SSF =	**0.1**	**0.2**	**0.3**	**0.4**	**0.5**	**0.6**	**0.7**	**0.8**	**0.9**
		WW	123	55	33	22	16	11	8	4	-
37.2 N	L	WWNI	207	97	61	43	32	25	20	16	11
4570 DD	C	TW	122	54	32	21	14	9	6	3	-
T(JAN)=33	R	TWNI	196	91	57	40	30	23	18	13	8
		DG	108	41	16	-	-	-	-	-	-
		DGNI	213	97	60	42	31	23	17	12	7

Billings Montana		SSF =	**0.1**	**0.2**	**0.3**	**0.4**	**0.5**	**0.6**	**0.7**	**0.8**	**0.9**
		WW	91	41	23	15	9	6	-	-	-
45.8 N	L	WWNI	165	80	50	35	26	20	15	12	8
7265 DD	C	TW	92	40	23	14	9	5	-	-	-
T(JAN)=22	R	TWNI	158	75	47	32	24	18	14	10	6
		DG	64	-	-	-	-	-	-	-	-
		DGNI	168	78	48	33	23	17	12	8	4

Cut Bank Montana		SSF =	**0.1**	**0.2**	**0.3**	**0.4**	**0.5**	**0.6**	**0.7**	**0.8**	**0.9**
		WW	77	33	18	10	5	-	-	-	-
48.6 N	L	WWNI	153	71	44	31	23	17	13	9	6
9033 DD	C	TW	80	34	18	11	5	-	-	-	-
T(JAN)=16	R	TWNI	144	67	42	29	21	15	11	8	5
		DG	40	-	-	-	-	-	-	-	-
		DGNI	151	69	42	28	20	14	9	6	-

Dillon Montana		SSF =	**0.1**	**0.2**	**0.3**	**0.4**	**0.5**	**0.6**	**0.7**	**0.8**	**0.9**
		WW	90	40	24	15	10	6	-	-	-
45.2 N	L	WWNI	168	78	50	35	26	20	16	12	8
8354 DD	C	TW	92	40	23	15	9	5	-	-	-
T(JAN)=20	R	TWNI	158	74	47	33	24	18	14	10	6
		DG	64	-	-	-	-	-	-	-	-
		DGNI	168	78	48	33	24	17	12	8	4

Table 3C-4 (Continued)

Glasgow Montana		SSF =	0.1	0.2	0.3	0.4	0.5	0.6	0.7	0.8	0.9
		WW	60	23	10	–	–	–	–	–	–
48.2 N	L	WWNI	130	61	38	26	19	14	10	8	5
8969 DD	C	TW	64	25	13	5	–	–	–	–	–
T(JAN)=9	R	TWNI	124	58	35	24	17	13	9	7	4
		DG	–	–	–	–	–	–	–	–	–
		DGNI	128	58	34	22	15	10	7	4	–

Great Falls Montana		SSF =	0.1	0.2	0.3	0.4	0.5	0.6	0.7	0.8	0.9
		WW	86	38	21	13	7	–	–	–	–
47.5 N	L	WWNI	161	77	48	33	25	19	14	10	7
7652 DD	C	TW	88	38	21	13	7	3	–	–	–
T(JAN)=20	R	TWNI	153	72	45	31	23	17	12	9	5
		DG	56	–	–	–	–	–	–	–	–
		DGNI	163	75	46	31	22	15	11	7	3

Helena Montana		SSF =	0.1	0.2	0.3	0.4	0.5	0.6	0.7	0.8	0.9
		WW	77	34	19	11	6	–	–	–	–
46.6 N	L	WWNI	151	71	45	31	23	17	13	10	6
8190 DD	C	TW	80	34	19	11	6	–	–	–	–
T(JAN)=18	R	TWNI	144	67	42	29	21	16	12	8	5
		DG	41	–	–	–	–	–	–	–	–
		DGNI	151	69	42	29	20	14	10	6	2

Lewistown Montana		SSF =	0.1	0.2	0.3	0.4	0.5	0.6	0.7	0.8	0.9
		WW	76	33	19	11	6	–	–	–	–
47.0 N	L	WWNI	153	71	45	31	23	18	13	10	7
8586 DD	C	TW	80	34	19	11	6	–	–	–	–
T(JAN)=19	R	TWNI	144	67	42	29	21	16	12	9	5
		DG	41	–	–	–	–	–	–	–	–
		DGNI	151	69	42	29	20	14	10	6	3

Miles City Montana		SSF =	0.1	0.2	0.3	0.4	0.5	0.6	0.7	0.8	0.9
		WW	78	33	18	10	5	–	–	–	–
46.4 N	L	WWNI	151	72	44	31	22	17	13	10	6
7889 DD	C	TW	80	34	18	10	5	–	–	–	–
T(JAN)=15	R	TWNI	144	67	41	28	21	15	11	8	5
		DG	39	–	–	–	–	–	–	–	–
		DGNI	151	69	41	28	19	14	9	6	2

Missoula Montana		SSF =	0.1	0.2	0.3	0.4	0.5	0.6	0.7	0.8	0.9
		WW	66	27	13	–	–	–	–	–	–
46.9 N	L	WWNI	140	65	40	28	20	15	11	8	5
7931 DD	C	TW	71	28	15	7	–	–	–	–	–
T(JAN)=21	R	TWNI	133	61	38	26	18	13	10	7	4
		DG	–	–	–	–	–	–	–	–	–
		DGNI	138	62	37	24	16	11	7	4	–

Grand Island Nebraska		SSF =	0.1	0.2	0.3	0.4	0.5	0.6	0.7	0.8	0.9
		WW	98	43	25	16	11	7	4	-	-
41.0 N	L	WWNI	178	82	52	36	27	21	17	13	9
6425 DD	C	TW	99	43	25	16	10	6	3	-	-
T(JAN)=22	R	TWNI	168	78	48	34	25	19	15	11	7
		DG	73	18	-	-	-	-	-	-	-
		DGNI	179	82	50	34	25	18	13	9	5

North Omaha Nebraska		SSF =	0.1	0.2	0.3	0.4	0.5	0.6	0.7	0.8	0.9
		WW	85	36	20	13	9	5	-	-	-
41.4 N	L	WWNI	163	75	47	33	24	19	15	12	8
6601 DD	C	TW	87	37	21	13	8	4	-	-	-
T(JAN)=20	R	TWNI	154	71	44	30	23	17	13	10	6
		DG	52	-	-	-	-	-	-	-	-
		DGNI	162	73	44	31	22	16	12	8	4

North Platte Nebraska		SSF =	0.1	0.2	0.3	0.4	0.5	0.6	0.7	0.8	0.9
		WW	103	46	27	18	13	9	5	-	-
41.1 N	L	WWNI	181	85	54	38	29	22	18	14	10
6743 DD	C	TW	103	46	27	17	11	7	4	1	-
T(JAN)=23	R	TWNI	172	80	50	35	27	20	16	11	7
		DG	81	27	-	-	-	-	-	-	-
		DGNI	184	85	53	37	27	20	14	10	6

Scottsbluff Nebraska		SSF =	0.1	0.2	0.3	0.4	0.5	0.6	0.7	0.8	0.9
		WW	103	47	28	19	13	9	6	-	-
41.9 N	L	WWNI	180	86	55	39	29	23	18	14	10
6774 DD	C	TW	103	46	28	18	12	7	4	2	-
T(JAN)=25	R	TWNI	171	81	51	36	27	21	16	12	8
		DG	82	29	-	-	-	-	-	-	-
		DGNI	183	86	54	37	27	20	15	10	6

Elko Nevada		SSF =	0.1	0.2	0.3	0.4	0.5	0.6	0.7	0.8	0.9
		WW	113	52	31	21	15	10	7	-	-
40.8 N	L	WWNI	195	92	58	42	31	24	19	15	10
7483 DD	C	TW	114	51	30	20	13	8	5	2	-
T(JAN) = 23	R	TWNI	184	87	55	39	29	22	17	12	8
		DG	97	36	-	-	-	-	-	-	-
		DGNI	199	93	58	40	29	22	16	11	6

Ely Nevada		SSF =	0.1	0.2	0.3	0.4	0.5	0.6	0.7	0.8	0.9
		WW	111	52	32	22	16	12	8	4	-
39.3 N	L	WWNI	191	91	59	42	32	26	20	16	11
7814 DD	C	TW	111	51	31	20	14	9	6	3	1
T(JAN)=24	R	TWNI	180	86	55	39	30	23	18	13	9
		DG	96	38	16	-	-	-	-	-	-
		DGNI	195	92	58	41	31	23	17	12	7

Table 3C-4 (Continued)

Las Vegas Nevada		**SSF =**	**0.1**	**0.2**	**0.3**	**0.4**	**0.5**	**0.6**	**0.7**	**0.8**	**0.9**
		WW	311	144	90	64	48	37	28	20	12
36.1 N	L	WWNI	430	204	129	92	70	56	44	35	24
2601 DD	C	TW	291	134	83	56	40	29	21	15	9
T(JAN)=44	R	TWNI	405	191	120	86	64	50	38	28	19
		DG	350	158	95	62	42	28	17	9	-
		DGNI	461	216	136	96	71	54	41	29	19

Lovelock Nevada		**SSF =**	**0.1**	**0.2**	**0.3**	**0.4**	**0.5**	**0.6**	**0.7**	**0.8**	**0.9**
		WW	160	73	45	31	22	16	12	7	-
40.1 N	L	WWNI	248	118	74	53	40	31	25	19	13
5990 DD	C	TW	153	70	42	28	19	13	9	5	3
T(JAN)=29	R	TWNI	235	110	70	49	37	28	22	16	10
		DG	156	66	35	18	-	-	-	-	-
		DGNI	259	121	75	53	39	29	21	15	9

Reno Nevada		**SSF =**	**0.1**	**0.2**	**0.3**	**0.4**	**0.5**	**0.6**	**0.7**	**0.8**	**0.9**
		WW	166	77	47	33	24	18	13	8	-
39.5 N	L	WWNI	258	122	77	55	42	33	26	20	14
6022 DD	C	TW	161	74	45	30	21	14	10	6	3
T(JAN)=32	R	TWNI	243	115	73	51	39	30	23	17	11
		DG	166	71	39	22	-	-	-	-	-
		DGNI	269	126	79	56	41	31	23	16	10

Tonopah Nevada		**SSF =**	**0.1**	**0.2**	**0.3**	**0.4**	**0.5**	**0.6**	**0.7**	**0.8**	**0.9**
		WW	163	75	47	33	24	18	13	9	4
38.1 N	L	WWNI	251	120	76	55	42	33	26	21	15
5900 DD	C	TW	156	72	44	30	21	14	10	6	3
T(JAN)=30	R	TWNI	238	113	72	51	39	30	23	17	11
		DG	161	70	39	22	9	-	-	-	-
		DGNI	263	124	78	55	41	31	23	16	10

Winnemucca Nevada		**SSF =**	**0.1**	**0.2**	**0.3**	**0.4**	**0.5**	**0.6**	**0.7**	**0.8**	**0.9**
		WW	131	60	37	25	18	13	9	5	-
40.9 N	L	WWNI	214	103	65	47	35	28	22	17	12
6629 DD	C	TW	129	59	35	23	16	11	7	4	1
T(JAN)=28	R	TWNI	203	96	61	43	32	25	19	14	9
		DG	121	49	24	-	-	-	-	-	-
		DGNI	222	104	65	46	34	25	18	13	7

Concord New Hampshire		**SSF =**	**0.1**	**0.2**	**0.3**	**0.4**	**0.5**	**0.6**	**0.7**	**0.8**	**0.9**
		WW	56	23	12	6	-	-	-	-	-
43.2 N	L	WWNI	129	59	37	26	19	15	12	9	6
7360 DD	C	TW	62	25	13	7	-	-	-	-	-
T(JAN)=21	R	TWNI	123	56	35	24	18	14	10	7	5
		DG	-	-	-	-	-	-	-	-	-
		DGNI	125	56	34	23	16	12	8	5	-

Newark New Jersey		**SSF =**	**0.1**	**0.2**	**0.3**	**0.4**	**0.5**	**0.6**	**0.7**	**0.8**	**0.9**
		WW	91	42	25	16	11	8	4	–	–
40.7 N	L	WWNI	167	80	51	36	27	21	17	13	9
5034 DD	C	TW	93	42	25	16	10	6	3	–	–
T(JAN) = 31	R	TWNI	158	76	48	34	25	19	15	11	7
		DG	67	18	–	–	–	–	–	–	–
		DGNI	169	79	49	34	25	19	13	9	5

Albuquerque New Mexico		**SSF =**	**0.1**	**0.2**	**0.3**	**0.4**	**0.5**	**0.6**	**0.7**	**0.8**	**0.9**
		WW	178	84	53	37	28	21	16	11	6
35.0 N	L	WWNI	270	130	83	60	46	37	30	23	17
4292 DD	C	TW	171	80	50	34	24	17	12	8	5
T(JAN) = 35	R	TWNI	255	122	78	56	43	33	26	19	13
		DG	183	82	47	29	16	–	–	–	–
		DGNI	283	135	86	61	46	35	26	19	12

Clayton New Mexico		**SSF =**	**0.1**	**0.2**	**0.3**	**0.4**	**0.5**	**0.6**	**0.7**	**0.8**	**0.9**
		WW	160	73	46	32	24	18	14	9	4
36.4 N	L	WWNI	251	117	75	54	41	33	27	21	15
5212 DD	C	TW	154	71	43	29	20	14	10	6	4
T(JAN) = 33	R	TWNI	235	111	70	50	38	30	23	17	11
		DG	157	68	38	21	9	–	–	–	–
		DGNI	260	122	77	54	41	31	23	17	10

Farmington New Mexico		**SSF =**	**0.1**	**0.2**	**0.3**	**0.4**	**0.5**	**0.6**	**0.7**	**0.8**	**0.9**
		WW	145	66	41	29	21	16	11	7	–
36.7 N	L	WWNI	234	108	70	50	38	30	24	19	13
5713 DD	C	TW	142	64	39	26	18	13	8	5	3
T(JAN) = 29	R	TWNI	220	103	65	47	35	27	21	16	10
		DG	138	58	31	15	–	–	–	–	–
		DGNI	241	112	70	50	37	28	21	15	9

Los Alamos New Mexico		**SSF =**	**0.1**	**0.2**	**0.3**	**0.4**	**0.5**	**0.6**	**0.7**	**0.8**	**0.9**
		WW	128	58	36	26	19	14	10	7	–
35.9 N	L	WWNI	210	100	64	46	35	28	23	18	13
6359 DD	C	TW	125	58	35	24	16	11	8	5	2
T(JAN) = 29	R	TWNI	199	94	60	43	33	26	20	15	10
		DG	116	49	25	–	–	–	–	–	–
		DGNI	217	102	64	46	34	26	19	14	9

Roswell New Mexico		**SSF =**	**0.1**	**0.2**	**0.3**	**0.4**	**0.5**	**0.6**	**0.7**	**0.8**	**0.9**
		WW	200	95	59	42	32	24	18	13	7
33.4 N	L	WWNI	299	142	92	66	50	40	32	25	18
3697 DD	C	TW	194	89	55	38	27	19	14	9	6
T(JAN) = 38	R	TWNI	283	134	86	61	47	36	28	21	14
		DG	214	95	56	35	22	12	–	–	–
		DGNI	316	149	95	67	51	38	29	21	13

Table 3C-4 (Continued)

Truth or Consequences New Mexico		**SSF =**	**0.1**	**0.2**	**0.3**	**0.4**	**0.5**	**0.6**	**0.7**	**0.8**	**0.9**
		WW	229	109	69	49	37	29	22	16	9
33.2 N	L	WWNI	332	160	103	74	57	45	37	29	21
3392 DD	C	TW	220	102	64	44	31	23	16	11	7
T(JAN)=40	R	TWNI	314	150	96	69	53	41	32	24	16
		DG	251	114	69	44	29	18	9	-	-
		DGNI	354	168	107	76	58	44	33	24	15

Tucumcari New Mexico		**SSF =**	**0.1**	**0.2**	**0.3**	**0.4**	**0.5**	**0.6**	**0.7**	**0.8**	**0.9**
		WW	194	90	56	40	30	23	17	12	7
35.2 N	L	WWNI	291	138	88	63	48	39	31	25	18
4047 DD	C	TW	187	86	53	36	25	18	13	9	5
T(JAN)=37	R	TWNI	274	130	82	59	45	35	27	20	13
		DG	203	90	53	32	20	10	-	-	-
		DGNI	306	144	91	65	49	37	28	20	13

Zuni New Mexico		**SSF =**	**0.1**	**0.2**	**0.3**	**0.4**	**0.5**	**0.6**	**0.7**	**0.8**	**0.9**
		WW	144	66	41	29	22	16	12	8	-
35.1 N	L	WWNI	231	109	69	50	38	31	25	19	14
5815 DD	C	TW	140	64	39	26	18	13	9	6	3
T(JAN)=30	R	TWNI	218	103	65	47	36	28	21	16	11
		DG	137	59	32	16	-	-	-	-	-
		DGNI	238	112	71	50	38	28	21	15	9

Albany New York		**SSF =**	**0.1**	**0.2**	**0.3**	**0.4**	**0.5**	**0.6**	**0.7**	**0.8**	**0.9**
		WW	56	23	12	6	-	-	-	-	-
42.7 N	L	WWNI	129	59	37	26	19	15	11	9	6
6888 DD	C	TW	62	25	13	7	-	-	-	-	-
T(JAN)=21	R	TWNI	123	56	35	24	18	14	10	7	5
		DG	-	-	-	-	-	-	-	-	-
		DGNI	125	56	34	23	16	12	8	5	-

Binghamton New York		**SSF =**	**0.1**	**0.2**	**0.3**	**0.4**	**0.5**	**0.6**	**0.7**	**0.8**	**0.9**
		WW	42	15	-	-	-	-	-	-	-
42.2 N	L	WWNI	115	52	32	22	16	12	10	7	5
7285 DD	C	TW	50	19	8	-	-	-	-	-	-
T(JAN)=22	R	TWNI	109	49	30	21	15	11	8	6	4
		DG	-	-	-	-	-	-	-	-	-
		DGNI	109	48	28	19	13	9	6	3	-

Buffalo New York		**SSF =**	**0.1**	**0.2**	**0.3**	**0.4**	**0.5**	**0.6**	**0.7**	**0.8**	**0.9**
		WW	46	17	6	-	-	-	-	-	-
42.9 N	L	WWNI	121	54	33	23	17	13	10	7	5
6927 DD	C	TW	54	20	9	-	-	-	-	-	-
T(JAN)=24	R	TWNI	115	51	31	21	16	12	9	6	4
		DG	-	-	-	-	-	-	-	-	-
		DGNI	115	50	29	20	13	9	6	3	-

Massena New York

		SSF =	0.1	0.2	0.3	0.4	0.5	0.6	0.7	0.8	0.9
		WW	42	14	-	-	-	-	-	-	-
44.9 N	L	WWNI	115	51	32	22	16	12	9	7	5
8237 DD	C	TW	50	18	8	-	-	-	-	-	-
T(JAN)=14	R	TWNI	109	49	30	21	15	11	8	6	4
		DG	-	-	-	-	-	-	-	-	-
		DGNI	109	47	28	18	13	9	6	3	-

NYC (Central Park) New York

		SSF =	0.1	0.2	0.3	0.4	0.5	0.6	0.7	0.8	0.9
		WW	85	37	22	14	10	6	-	-	-
40.8 N	L	WWNI	159	76	48	34	25	20	16	12	8
4848 DD	C	TW	87	38	22	14	8	5	2	-	-
T(JAN)=32	R	TWNI	151	72	45	32	24	18	14	10	6
		DG	56	-	-	-	-	-	-	-	-
		DGNI	161	74	46	32	23	17	12	8	4

Rochester New York

		SSF =	0.1	0.2	0.3	0.4	0.5	0.6	0.7	0.8	0.9
		WW	50	18	8	-	-	-	-	-	-
43.1 N	L	WWNI	124	55	34	24	17	13	10	8	5
6719 DD	C	TW	56	22	10	-	-	-	-	-	-
T(JAN)=24	R	TWNI	117	53	32	22	16	12	9	6	4
		DG	-	-	-	-	-	-	-	-	-
		DGNI	118	52	31	20	14	10	6	4	-

Syracuse New York

		SSF =	0.1	0.2	0.3	0.4	0.5	0.6	0.7	0.8	0.9
		WW	50	18	8	-	-	-	-	-	-
43.1 N	L	WWNI	124	55	34	24	17	13	10	8	5
6678 DD	C	TW	56	22	11	4	-	-	-	-	-
T(JAN)=24	R	TWNI	117	53	32	22	16	12	9	6	4
		DG	-	-	-	-	-	-	-	-	-
		DGNI	118	52	31	20	14	10	7	4	-

Asheville North Carolina

		SSF =	0.1	0.2	0.3	0.4	0.5	0.6	0.7	0.8	0.9
		WW	138	64	39	27	20	15	11	7	-
35.4 N	L	WWNI	225	106	68	49	37	29	23	18	13
4237 DD	C	TW	136	62	38	25	17	12	8	5	2
T(JAN)=38	R	TWNI	212	100	64	45	34	26	20	15	10
		DG	131	55	28	12	-	-	-	-	-
		DGNI	232	109	68	48	36	27	20	14	9

Cape Hatteras North Carolina

		SSF =	0.1	0.2	0.3	0.4	0.5	0.6	0.7	0.8	0.9
		WW	214	97	60	42	31	23	18	12	7
35.3 N	L	WWNI	312	148	93	66	50	39	31	25	18
2731 DD	C	TW	200	92	56	38	26	19	13	9	5
T(JAN)=45	R	TWNI	294	138	87	61	46	36	27	20	13
		DG	223	98	56	34	21	10	-	-	-
		DGNI	329	154	96	67	50	38	28	20	13

Table 3C-4 (Continued)

Charlotte North Carolina		**SSF =**	**0.1**	**0.2**	**0.3**	**0.4**	**0.5**	**0.6**	**0.7**	**0.8**	**0.9**
		WW	177	82	50	35	25	19	14	9	4
35.2 N	L	WWNI	270	129	81	57	43	34	27	21	15
3218 DD	C	TW	170	78	47	31	22	15	10	7	4
T(JAN)=42	R	TWNI	255	121	76	53	40	31	24	18	12
		DG	180	77	43	24	12	-	-	-	-
		DGNI	283	133	82	58	43	32	24	17	11

Greensboro North Carolina		**SSF =**	**0.1**	**0.2**	**0.3**	**0.4**	**0.5**	**0.6**	**0.7**	**0.8**	**0.9**
		WW	151	70	43	29	22	16	12	7	-
36.1 N	L	WWNI	239	113	72	51	39	31	24	19	14
3825 DD	C	TW	147	67	41	27	19	13	9	5	3
T(JAN)=39	R	TWNI	226	107	67	48	36	28	21	16	10
		DG	147	62	33	16	-	-	-	-	-
		DGNI	249	117	73	51	38	28	21	15	9

Raleigh-Durham North Carolina		**SSF =**	**0.1**	**0.2**	**0.3**	**0.4**	**0.5**	**0.6**	**0.7**	**0.8**	**0.9**
		WW	155	73	45	31	23	17	12	8	-
35.9 N	L	WWNI	244	117	75	53	40	31	25	20	14
3514 DD	C	TW	151	69	42	28	19	13	9	6	3
T(JAN)=40	R	TWNI	230	110	69	49	37	29	22	16	11
		DG	153	65	36	19	-	-	-	-	-
		DGNI	254	120	75	53	39	29	22	15	9

Bismarck North Dakota		**SSF =**	**0.1**	**0.2**	**0.3**	**0.4**	**0.5**	**0.6**	**0.7**	**0.8**	**0.9**
		WW	60	24	11	5	-	-	-	-	-
46.8 N	L	WWNI	132	61	38	26	19	14	11	8	5
9044 DD	C	TW	64	26	13	7	-	-	-	-	-
T(JAN)=8	R	TWNI	125	58	36	24	18	13	10	7	4
		DG	-	-	-	-	-	-	-	-	-
		DGNI	129	58	34	23	16	11	7	4	-

Fargo North Dakota		**SSF =**	**0.1**	**0.2**	**0.3**	**0.4**	**0.5**	**0.6**	**0.7**	**0.8**	**0.9**
		WW	48	17	-	-	-	-	-	-	-
46.9 N	L	WWNI	119	55	34	23	17	12	9	7	5
9271 DD	C	TW	54	20	9	-	-	-	-	-	-
T(JAN)=6	R	TWNI	114	52	31	21	15	11	8	6	4
		DG	-	-	-	-	-	-	-	-	-
		DGNI	114	51	29	19	13	9	6	3	-

Minot North Dakota		**SSF =**	**0.1**	**0.2**	**0.3**	**0.4**	**0.5**	**0.6**	**0.7**	**0.8**	**0.9**
		WW	54	19	7	-	-	-	-	-	-
48.3 N	L	WWNI	126	58	35	24	17	13	10	7	5
9407 DD	C	TW	59	22	10	-	-	-	-	-	-
T(JAN)=8	R	TWNI	120	55	33	22	16	12	9	6	4
		DG	-	-	-	-	-	-	-	-	-
		DGNI	122	54	31	20	14	9	6	3	-

Akron-Canton Ohio

		SSF =	0.1	0.2	0.3	0.4	0.5	0.6	0.7	0.8	0.9
		WW	61	25	13	7	–	–	–	–	–
40.9 N	L	WWNI	137	62	39	27	20	15	12	9	6
6224 DD	C	TW	67	27	14	8	–	–	–	–	–
T(JAN)=26	R	TWNI	130	59	36	25	18	14	10	7	5
		DG	–	–	–	–	–	–	–	–	–
		DGNI	133	59	35	24	17	12	8	5	2

Cincinnati Ohio

		SSF =	0.1	0.2	0.3	0.4	0.5	0.6	0.7	0.8	0.9
		WW	81	36	20	13	8	5	–	–	–
39.1 N	L	WWNI	156	74	46	32	24	19	15	11	8
5070 DD	C	TW	84	36	21	13	8	4	–	–	–
T(JAN)=31	R	TWNI	148	70	43	30	22	17	13	9	6
		DG	49	–	–	–	–	–	–	–	–
		DGNI	157	72	44	30	22	16	11	8	4

Cleveland Ohio

		SSF =	0.1	0.2	0.3	0.4	0.5	0.6	0.7	0.8	0.9
		WW	59	23	11	5	–	–	–	–	–
41.4 N	L	WWNI	135	60	37	26	19	14	11	8	6
6154 DD	C	TW	65	26	13	7	–	–	–	–	–
T(JAN)=27	R	TWNI	128	57	35	24	18	13	10	7	4
		DG	–	–	–	–	–	–	–	–	–
		DGNI	130	57	34	23	16	11	8	5	–

Columbus Ohio

		SSF =	0.1	0.2	0.3	0.4	0.5	0.6	0.7	0.8	0.9
		WW	67	28	15	9	5	–	–	–	–
40.0 N	L	WWNI	141	65	41	29	21	16	13	10	7
5702 DD	C	TW	71	30	16	9	5	–	–	–	–
T(JAN)=28	R	TWNI	133	62	38	27	20	15	11	8	5
		DG	–	–	–	–	–	–	–	–	–
		DGNI	138	63	38	26	19	13	9	6	3

Dayton Ohio

		SSF =	0.1	0.2	0.3	0.4	0.5	0.6	0.7	0.8	0.9
		WW	72	30	17	10	6	–	–	–	–
39.9 N	L	WWNI	146	68	43	30	22	17	13	10	7
5641 DD	C	TW	76	32	18	10	6	–	–	–	–
T(JAN)=28	R	TWNI	139	64	40	28	21	16	12	9	6
		DG	30	–	–	–	–	–	–	–	–
		DGNI	145	66	40	27	20	14	10	7	3

Toledo Ohio

		SSF =	0.1	0.2	0.3	0.4	0.5	0.6	0.7	0.8	0.9
		WW	62	25	13	7	–	–	–	–	–
41.6 N	L	WWNI	138	62	39	27	20	15	12	9	6
6381 DD	C	TW	68	27	15	8	3	–	–	–	–
T(JAN)=25	R	TWNI	130	59	36	25	19	14	10	8	5
		DG	–	–	–	–	–	–	–	–	–
		DGNI	134	60	36	24	17	12	8	5	2

Table 3C-4 (Continued)

Youngstown Ohio		**SSF =**	**0.1**	**0.2**	**0.3**	**0.4**	**0.5**	**0.6**	**0.7**	**0.8**	**0.9**
		WW	52	20	9	-	-	-	-	-	-
41.3 N	L	WWNI	126	57	35	24	18	14	10	8	5
6426 DD	C	TW	58	23	11	5	-	-	-	-	-
T(JAN)=26	R	TWNI	120	54	33	23	17	12	9	7	4
		DG	-	-	-	-	-	-	-	-	-
		DGNI	121	53	32	21	15	10	7	4	-

Oklahoma City Oklahoma		**SSF =**	**0.1**	**0.2**	**0.3**	**0.4**	**0.5**	**0.6**	**0.7**	**0.8**	**0.9**
		WW	161	74	45	31	23	17	13	8	-
35.4 N	L	WWNI	251	119	75	53	40	32	26	20	14
3695 DD	C	TW	156	71	43	28	20	14	9	6	3
T(JAN)=37	R	TWNI	237	111	70	50	37	29	22	16	11
		DG	158	67	36	19	-	-	-	-	-
		DGNI	262	122	76	53	40	30	22	16	10

Tulsa Oklahoma		**SSF =**	**0.1**	**0.2**	**0.3**	**0.4**	**0.5**	**0.6**	**0.7**	**0.8**	**0.9**
		WW	147	67	41	28	21	15	11	7	-
36.2 N	L	WWNI	235	111	70	49	38	30	24	19	13
3680 DD	C	TW	144	65	39	26	18	12	8	5	3
T(JAN)=37	R	TWNI	222	104	65	46	35	27	21	15	10
		DG	141	58	30	14	-	-	-	-	-
		DGNI	245	113	70	49	37	28	20	14	9

Astoria Oregon		**SSF =**	**0.1**	**0.2**	**0.3**	**0.4**	**0.5**	**0.6**	**0.7**	**0.8**	**0.9**
		WW	122	59	36	24	17	11	7	-	-
46.1 N	L	WWNI	201	100	64	46	34	26	20	15	10
5295 DD	C	TW	121	56	34	22	14	9	6	2	-
T(JAN)=41	R	TWNI	191	94	60	42	31	23	17	13	8
		DG	112	46	19	-	-	-	-	-	-
		DGNI	208	101	64	44	32	23	17	11	6

Burns Oregon		**SSF =**	**0.1**	**0.2**	**0.3**	**0.4**	**0.5**	**0.6**	**0.7**	**0.8**	**0.9**
		WW	100	44	26	17	11	7	-	-	-
43.6 N	L	WWNI	179	84	52	37	28	21	16	12	8
7212 DD	C	TW	101	44	25	16	10	6	2	-	-
T(JAN)=25	R	TWNI	170	79	49	34	25	19	14	10	6
		DG	76	19	-	-	-	-	-	-	-
		DGNI	182	83	51	35	25	18	13	8	4

Medford Oregon		**SSF =**	**0.1**	**0.2**	**0.3**	**0.4**	**0.5**	**0.6**	**0.7**	**0.8**	**0.9**
		WW	134	57	34	22	15	9	5	-	-
42.4 N	L	WWNI	222	100	62	44	32	25	19	14	9
4930 DD	C	TW	130	56	32	20	13	8	4	-	-
T(JAN)=37	R	TWNI	209	94	58	40	29	22	16	12	7
		DG	118	42	-	-	-	-	-	-	-
		DGNI	227	102	62	42	30	21	15	10	5

North Bend Oregon		**SSF =**	**0.1**	**0.2**	**0.3**	**0.4**	**0.5**	**0.6**	**0.7**	**0.8**	**0.9**
		WW	172	86	55	39	29	21	15	10	5
43.4 N	L	WWNI	260	130	86	63	48	37	29	23	16
4688 DD	C	TW	168	81	51	34	24	17	12	8	4
T(JAN) = 45	R	TWNI	247	123	80	58	44	33	25	19	12
		DG	181	84	49	30	17	-	-	-	-
		DGNI	275	137	88	63	47	35	26	18	11

Pendleton Oregon		**SSF =**	**0.1**	**0.2**	**0.3**	**0.4**	**0.5**	**0.6**	**0.7**	**0.8**	**0.9**
		WW	117	49	28	17	10	5	-	-	-
45.7 N	L	WWNI	204	90	56	39	28	21	15	11	7
5240 DD	C	TW	115	48	26	16	9	5	-	-	-
T(JAN) = 32	R	TWNI	190	85	52	35	25	19	14	10	6
		DG	94	22	-	-	-	-	-	-	-
		DGNI	205	91	54	36	25	17	12	8	3

Portland Oregon		**SSF =**	**0.1**	**0.2**	**0.3**	**0.4**	**0.5**	**0.6**	**0.7**	**0.8**	**0.9**
		WW	135	56	32	20	13	8	-	-	-
45.6 N	L	WWNI	223	100	61	42	31	23	17	13	8
4792 DD	C	TW	130	55	31	19	12	7	3	-	-
T(JAN) = 38	R	TWNI	209	94	57	39	28	21	15	11	7
		DG	117	38	-	-	-	-	-	-	-
		DGNI	228	100	60	40	28	20	14	9	4

Redmond Oregon		**SSF =**	**0.1**	**0.2**	**0.3**	**0.4**	**0.5**	**0.6**	**0.7**	**0.8**	**0.9**
		WW	125	56	33	22	15	10	6	-	-
44.3 N	L	WWNI	209	98	61	43	32	25	19	15	10
6643 DD	C	TW	122	54	32	20	13	9	5	2	-
T(JAN) = 30	R	TWNI	196	92	57	40	30	22	17	12	8
		DG	110	41	12	-	-	-	-	-	-
		DGNI	213	98	61	42	30	22	16	11	6

Salem Oregon		**SSF =**	**0.1**	**0.2**	**0.3**	**0.4**	**0.5**	**0.6**	**0.7**	**0.8**	**0.9**
		WW	137	57	34	22	15	9	5	-	-
44.9 N	L	WWNI	226	101	62	43	32	24	18	14	9
4852 DD	C	TW	133	56	32	20	13	8	4	-	-
T(JAN) = 39	R	TWNI	212	95	58	40	29	22	16	11	7
		DG	121	41	-	-	-	-	-	-	-
		DGNI	231	102	62	42	30	21	15	10	5

Allentown Pennsylvania		**SSF =**	**0.1**	**0.2**	**0.3**	**0.4**	**0.5**	**0.6**	**0.7**	**0.8**	**0.9**
		WW	76	33	19	12	8	5	-	-	-
40.6 N	L	WWNI	152	71	45	32	24	18	15	11	8
5827 DD	C	TW	80	35	20	12	7	4	-	-	-
T(JAN) = 28	R	TWNI	143	67	42	30	22	17	13	9	6
		DG	43	-	-	-	-	-	-	-	-
		DGNI	150	69	43	29	21	16	11	7	4

Table 3C-4 (Continued)

Erie Pennsylvania		**SSF =**	**0.1**	**0.2**	**0.3**	**0.4**	**0.5**	**0.6**	**0.7**	**0.8**	**0.9**
		WW	53	19	8	-	-	-	-	-	-
42.1 N	L	WWNI	129	57	35	24	17	13	10	7	5
6851 DD	C	TW	59	22	11	4	-	-	-	-	-
T(JAN)=25	R	TWNI	122	54	33	22	16	12	9	6	4
		DG	-	-	-	-	-	-	-	-	-
		DGNI	124	53	31	21	14	10	6	4	-

Harrisburg Pennsylvania		**SSF =**	**0.1**	**0.2**	**0.3**	**0.4**	**0.5**	**0.6**	**0.7**	**0.8**	**0.9**
		WW	83	37	22	14	10	6	-	-	-
40.2 N	L	WWNI	158	75	47	34	25	20	16	12	8
5224 DD	C	TW	86	38	22	14	8	5	2	-	-
T(JAN)=30	R	TWNI	150	71	44	31	23	18	14	10	6
		DG	55	-	-	-	-	-	-	-	-
		DGNI	158	74	46	32	23	17	12	8	4

Philadelphia Pennsylvania		**SSF =**	**0.1**	**0.2**	**0.3**	**0.4**	**0.5**	**0.6**	**0.7**	**0.8**	**0.9**
		WW	95	43	26	17	12	8	5	-	-
39.9 N	L	WWNI	171	82	52	37	28	22	17	13	9
4865 DD	C	TW	96	43	25	16	10	6	4	-	-
T(JAN)=32	R	TWNI	162	77	49	34	26	20	15	11	7
		DG	72	22	-	-	-	-	-	-	-
		DGNI	174	81	51	35	26	19	14	9	5

Pittsburgh Pennsylvania		**SSF =**	**0.1**	**0.2**	**0.3**	**0.4**	**0.5**	**0.6**	**0.7**	**0.8**	**0.9**
		WW	62	25	13	7	-	-	-	-	-
40.5 N	L	WWNI	137	62	39	27	20	15	12	9	6
5930 DD	C	TW	68	28	15	8	3	-	-	-	-
T(JAN)=28	R	TWNI	130	59	37	25	19	14	11	8	5
		DG	-	-	-	-	-	-	-	-	-
		DGNI	134	60	36	24	17	12	8	5	2

Scranton Pennsylvania		**SSF =**	**0.1**	**0.2**	**0.3**	**0.4**	**0.5**	**0.6**	**0.7**	**0.8**	**0.9**
		WW	63	26	14	8	4	-	-	-	-
41.3 N	L	WWNI	137	63	40	28	20	16	12	9	6
6277 DD	C	TW	68	28	15	9	4	-	-	-	-
T(JAN)=26	R	TWNI	130	60	37	26	19	14	11	8	5
		DG	-	-	-	-	-	-	-	-	-
		DGNI	134	61	37	25	18	13	9	6	2

Providence Rhode Island		**SSF =**	**0.1**	**0.2**	**0.3**	**0.4**	**0.5**	**0.6**	**0.7**	**0.8**	**0.9**
		WW	77	34	20	13	8	5	-	-	-
41.7 N	L	WWNI	153	71	45	32	24	19	15	11	8
5972 DD	C	TW	81	35	20	12	7	4	-	-	-
T(JAN)=28	R	TWNI	145	67	42	30	22	17	13	9	6
		DG	44	-	-	-	-	-	-	-	-
		DGNI	152	69	43	30	22	16	11	8	4

Charleston South Carolina		SSF =	0.1	0.2	0.3	0.4	0.5	0.6	0.7	0.8	0.9
		WW	252	118	72	51	38	29	22	16	9
32.9 N	L	WWNI	358	173	108	76	58	46	37	29	21
2146 DD	C	TW	238	110	67	46	32	23	17	11	7
T(JAN) = 49	R	TWNI	339	161	101	71	54	42	32	24	16
		DG	276	124	73	47	30	19	10	-	-
		DGNI	384	180	113	79	59	45	34	24	16

Columbia South Carolina		SSF =	0.1	0.2	0.3	0.4	0.5	0.6	0.7	0.8	0.9
		WW	215	102	62	43	32	25	19	13	7
33.9 N	L	WWNI	315	153	96	68	52	41	33	26	18
2598 DD	C	TW	206	95	58	39	28	20	14	9	6
T(JAN) = 45	R	TWNI	298	142	89	63	48	37	28	21	14
		DG	231	102	60	37	23	12	-	-	-
		DGNI	335	158	99	69	52	39	29	21	13

Greenville South Carolina		SSF =	0.1	0.2	0.3	0.4	0.5	0.6	0.7	0.8	0.9
		WW	178	83	51	35	26	20	14	10	4
34.9 N	L	WWNI	272	129	82	58	44	35	28	22	15
3163 DD	C	TW	172	78	48	32	22	16	11	7	4
T(JAN) = 42	R	TWNI	257	121	76	54	41	31	24	18	12
		DG	182	78	44	25	13	-	-	-	-
		DGNI	285	134	83	58	43	33	24	17	11

Huron South Dakota		SSF =	0.1	0.2	0.3	0.4	0.5	0.6	0.7	0.8	0.9
		WW	63	25	12	6	-	-	-	-	-
44.4 N	L	WWNI	136	62	39	27	19	15	11	9	6
8054 DD	C	TW	67	27	14	7	-	-	-	-	-
T(JAN) = 13	R	TWNI	129	59	36	25	18	14	10	7	5
		DG	-	-	-	-	-	-	-	-	-
		DGNI	133	59	35	24	16	12	8	5	-

Pierre South Dakota		SSF =	0.1	0.2	0.3	0.4	0.5	0.6	0.7	0.8	0.9
		WW	77	32	17	10	6	-	-	-	-
44.4 N	L	WWNI	153	70	44	30	22	17	13	10	7
7677 DD	C	TW	80	33	18	10	6	-	-	-	-
T(JAN) = 16	R	TWNI	144	67	41	28	21	16	12	8	5
		DG	36	-	-	-	-	-	-	-	-
		DGNI	151	68	41	28	20	14	10	6	3

Rapid City South Dakota		SSF =	0.1	0.2	0.3	0.4	0.5	0.6	0.7	0.8	0.9
		WW	91	40	23	15	10	6	-	-	-
44.0 N	L	WWNI	166	79	50	35	26	20	16	12	8
7324 DD	C	TW	92	40	23	14	9	5	2	-	-
T(JAN) = 22	R	TWNI	158	75	47	33	24	18	14	10	6
		DG	64	-	-	-	-	-	-	-	-
		DGNI	168	78	48	33	24	17	12	8	4

Table 3C-4 (Continued)

Sioux Falls South Dakota		**SSF =**	**0.1**	**0.2**	**0.3**	**0.4**	**0.5**	**0.6**	**0.7**	**0.8**	**0.9**
		WW	68	28	15	8	4	-	-	-	-
43.6 N	L	WWNI	143	66	41	28	21	16	12	9	6
7838 DD	C	TW	72	30	16	9	4	-	-	-	-
T(JAN)=14	R	TWNI	135	62	38	26	19	15	11	8	5
		DG	-	-	-	-	-	-	-	-	-
		DGNI	140	63	38	25	18	13	9	6	2

Chattanooga Tennessee		**SSF =**	**0.1**	**0.2**	**0.3**	**0.4**	**0.5**	**0.6**	**0.7**	**0.8**	**0.9**
		WW	136	63	38	26	19	14	10	6	-
35.0 N	L	WWNI	220	106	67	47	35	28	22	17	12
3505 DD	C	TW	133	61	36	24	16	11	7	4	2
T(JAN)=40	R	TWNI	208	99	62	44	33	25	19	14	9
		DG	127	52	25	-	-	-	-	-	-
		DGNI	228	108	67	47	34	26	19	13	8

Knoxville Tennessee		**SSF =**	**0.1**	**0.2**	**0.3**	**0.4**	**0.5**	**0.6**	**0.7**	**0.8**	**0.9**
		WW	143	66	39	27	20	14	10	6	-
35.8 N	L	WWNI	230	110	69	48	37	29	23	18	13
3478 DD	C	TW	140	63	38	25	17	11	8	5	2
T(JAN)=41	R	TWNI	217	103	64	45	34	26	20	15	10
		DG	136	56	28	10	-	-	-	-	-
		DGNI	238	111	69	48	35	26	19	14	8

Memphis Tennessee		**SSF =**	**0.1**	**0.2**	**0.3**	**0.4**	**0.5**	**0.6**	**0.7**	**0.8**	**0.9**
		WW	161	74	44	31	22	17	12	8	-
35.0 N	L	WWNI	251	119	75	52	40	31	25	20	14
3227 DD	C	TW	156	70	42	28	19	13	9	6	3
T(JAN)=40	R	TWNI	237	112	70	49	37	28	22	16	11
		DG	159	66	35	18	-	-	-	-	-
		DGNI	263	122	75	53	39	29	22	15	9

Nashville Tennessee		**SSF =**	**0.1**	**0.2**	**0.3**	**0.4**	**0.5**	**0.6**	**0.7**	**0.8**	**0.9**
		WW	124	56	32	22	16	11	8	4	-
36.1 N	L	WWNI	207	98	61	42	32	25	20	16	11
3696 DD	C	TW	122	54	32	21	14	9	6	3	-
T(JAN)=38	R	TWNI	195	92	57	40	30	23	17	13	8
		DG	108	41	15	-	-	-	-	-	-
		DGNI	212	98	60	42	31	23	17	11	7

Abilene Texas		**SSF =**	**0.1**	**0.2**	**0.3**	**0.4**	**0.5**	**0.6**	**0.7**	**0.8**	**0.9**
		WW	236	111	69	49	37	28	22	15	9
32.4 N	L	WWNI	339	164	104	74	57	45	36	29	20
2610 DD	C	TW	224	104	64	44	31	22	16	11	7
T(JAN)=44	R	TWNI	321	153	97	69	52	41	31	23	16
		DG	257	116	69	44	29	18	9	-	-
		DGNI	362	171	108	77	57	44	33	24	15

Amarillo
Texas

		SSF =	0.1	0.2	0.3	0.4	0.5	0.6	0.7	0.8	0.9
		WW	178	83	52	36	27	21	16	11	5
35.2 N	L	WWNI	271	130	83	59	45	36	29	23	16
4183 DD	C	TW	173	79	49	33	23	16	11	8	5
T(JAN)=36	R	TWNI	256	122	77	55	42	33	25	19	12
		DG	183	80	46	27	15	-	-	-	-
		DGNI	285	134	85	60	45	34	25	18	12

Austin
Texas

		SSF =	0.1	0.2	0.3	0.4	0.5	0.6	0.7	0.8	0.9
		WW	311	143	89	63	48	37	28	21	13
30.3 N	L	WWNI	432	203	127	91	70	55	45	35	25
1737 DD	C	TW	288	134	82	56	40	29	21	15	10
T(JAN)=50	R	TWNI	404	189	119	85	64	50	39	29	19
		DG	348	157	95	62	42	28	18	9	-
		DGNI	460	214	135	95	71	54	41	30	19

Brownsville
Texas

		SSF =	0.1	0.2	0.3	0.4	0.5	0.6	0.7	0.8	0.9
		WW	656	308	192	137	105	82	65	49	33
25.9 N	L	WWNI	846	402	252	180	138	111	89	70	50
650 DD	C	TW	609	280	175	121	88	65	48	35	24
T(JAN)=60	R	TWNI	797	373	235	168	128	99	77	57	38
		DG	799	365	226	155	111	80	58	40	24
		DGNI	929	432	272	194	146	112	85	63	42

Corpus Christi
Texas

		SSF =	0.1	0.2	0.3	0.4	0.5	0.6	0.7	0.8	0.9
		WW	469	225	146	105	80	62	49	37	24
27.8 N	L	WWNI	621	299	195	141	109	86	69	55	39
930 DD	C	TW	442	208	131	92	67	50	37	26	18
T(JAN)=56	R	TWNI	586	282	182	131	100	78	60	45	30
		DG	564	264	165	113	81	58	41	27	15
		DGNI	677	325	208	149	113	87	66	48	32

Dallas
Texas

		SSF =	0.1	0.2	0.3	0.4	0.5	0.6	0.7	0.8	0.9
		WW	237	109	68	48	36	28	21	15	9
32.8 N	L	WWNI	343	162	102	73	56	45	36	28	20
2290 DD	C	TW	223	103	64	43	31	22	16	11	7
T(JAN)=45	R	TWNI	321	151	95	68	52	40	31	23	15
		DG	255	114	68	43	28	17	8	-	-
		DGNI	362	169	106	75	57	43	32	23	15

Del Rio
Texas

		SSF =	0.1	0.2	0.3	0.4	0.5	0.6	0.7	0.8	0.9
		WW	375	167	105	75	57	44	34	25	16
29.4 N	L	WWNI	512	232	146	106	81	64	51	40	29
1523 DD	C	TW	343	158	97	66	48	35	26	18	12
T(JAN)=51	R	TWNI	476	218	138	98	74	58	44	33	22
		DG	424	189	115	77	53	36	24	14	5
		DGNI	543	248	157	111	83	63	48	35	23

Table 3C-4 (Continued)

El Paso Texas		**SSF =**	**0.1**	**0.2**	**0.3**	**0.4**	**0.5**	**0.6**	**0.7**	**0.8**	**0.9**
		WW	274	131	82	58	44	34	26	19	12
31.8 N	L	WWNI	384	189	119	85	65	52	42	33	24
2678 DD	C	TW	258	122	76	52	37	27	19	14	9
T(JAN)=44	R	TWNI	363	175	111	79	60	47	36	27	18
		DG	307	141	85	56	37	25	15	7	-
		DGNI	413	197	125	89	66	51	38	28	18

Fort Worth Texas		**SSF =**	**0.1**	**0.2**	**0.3**	**0.4**	**0.5**	**0.6**	**0.7**	**0.8**	**0.9**
		WW	225	104	65	46	34	26	20	14	8
32.8 N	L	WWNI	328	155	98	71	54	43	34	27	19
2382 DD	C	TW	212	99	61	41	29	21	15	10	6
T(JAN)=45	R	TWNI	307	146	92	66	50	39	30	22	15
		DG	240	108	64	40	25	15	6	-	-
		DGNI	345	162	102	73	54	41	31	22	14

Houston Texas		**SSF =**	**0.1**	**0.2**	**0.3**	**0.4**	**0.5**	**0.6**	**0.7**	**0.8**	**0.9**
		WW	336	148	93	66	50	39	30	22	14
30.0 N	L	WWNI	466	209	131	95	73	58	46	36	26
1434 DD	C	TW	309	140	86	59	42	31	22	16	10
T(JAN)=52	R	TWNI	433	196	124	88	67	52	40	30	20
		DG	375	166	99	66	45	30	19	11	-
		DGNI	492	223	140	99	74	57	43	31	20

Laredo Texas		**SSF =**	**0.1**	**0.2**	**0.3**	**0.4**	**0.5**	**0.6**	**0.7**	**0.8**	**0.9**
		WW	528	252	163	115	87	67	52	39	26
27.5 N	L	WWNI	693	331	216	156	117	92	74	58	41
876 DD	C	TW	495	231	145	101	73	54	40	28	19
T(JAN)=56	R	TWNI	652	312	200	143	108	83	64	48	32
		DG	639	297	184	126	89	64	45	30	17
		DGNI	756	360	230	163	122	93	70	51	34

Lubbock Texas		**SSF =**	**0.1**	**0.2**	**0.3**	**0.4**	**0.5**	**0.6**	**0.7**	**0.8**	**0.9**
		WW	206	97	61	43	32	25	19	13	8
33.6 N	L	WWNI	306	146	94	67	51	41	33	26	19
3545 DD	C	TW	198	92	57	39	28	20	14	10	6
T(JAN)=39	R	TWNI	288	137	87	63	48	37	29	21	14
		DG	220	99	58	37	23	13	-	-	-
		DGNI	323	153	97	69	52	39	30	21	14

Lufkin Texas		**SSF =**	**0.1**	**0.2**	**0.3**	**0.4**	**0.5**	**0.6**	**0.7**	**0.8**	**0.9**
		WW	273	125	78	55	42	32	25	18	11
31.2 N	L	WWNI	385	182	113	81	63	50	40	32	22
1940 DD	C	TW	254	118	73	49	35	25	18	13	8
T(JAN)=49	R	TWNI	361	170	107	76	58	45	35	26	17
		DG	299	135	80	52	34	22	13	-	-
		DGNI	409	191	120	85	63	48	36	26	17

Midland-Odessa Texas		**SSF =**	**0.1**	**0.2**	**0.3**	**0.4**	**0.5**	**0.6**	**0.7**	**0.8**	**0.9**
		WW	265	127	79	56	43	33	26	19	11
31.9 N	L	WWNI	373	182	115	83	64	51	41	32	23
2621 DD	C	TW	249	118	74	50	36	26	19	13	9
T(JAN)=44	R	TWNI	352	170	108	77	59	46	35	27	18
		DG	294	136	82	54	36	24	14	6	-
		DGNI	400	191	121	86	65	50	37	27	18

Port Arthur Texas		**SSF =**	**0.1**	**0.2**	**0.3**	**0.4**	**0.5**	**0.6**	**0.7**	**0.8**	**0.9**
		WW	339	153	95	67	51	40	31	22	14
29.9 N	L	WWNI	466	215	134	96	74	59	47	37	27
1518 DD	C	TW	311	143	88	60	43	31	23	16	11
T(JAN)=52	R	TWNI	435	201	126	90	68	53	41	30	20
		DG	380	170	102	68	46	31	20	11	-
		DGNI	496	228	143	101	76	58	44	32	21

San Angelo Texas		**SSF =**	**0.1**	**0.2**	**0.3**	**0.4**	**0.5**	**0.6**	**0.7**	**0.8**	**0.9**
		WW	269	129	80	57	43	33	26	19	11
31.4 N	L	WWNI	377	185	117	84	65	51	41	33	23
2240 DD	C	TW	253	120	75	51	36	26	19	13	9
T(JAN)=46	R	TWNI	357	172	109	78	59	46	36	27	18
		DG	300	138	84	55	37	24	15	6	-
		DGNI	405	194	123	87	66	50	38	27	18

San Antonio Texas		**SSF =**	**0.1**	**0.2**	**0.3**	**0.4**	**0.5**	**0.6**	**0.7**	**0.8**	**0.9**
		WW	345	156	97	70	52	41	31	23	14
29.5 N	L	WWNI	474	219	137	99	76	60	48	38	27
1570 DD	C	TW	318	146	90	62	44	32	24	17	11
T(JAN)=51	R	TWNI	443	204	129	92	70	54	42	31	21
		DG	389	175	105	70	48	33	21	12	-
		DGNI	505	232	146	103	78	59	45	33	21

Sherman Texas		**SSF =**	**0.1**	**0.2**	**0.3**	**0.4**	**0.5**	**0.6**	**0.7**	**0.8**	**0.9**
		WW	191	88	54	38	28	21	16	11	6
33.7 N	L	WWNI	286	136	85	61	47	37	30	23	17
2864 DD	C	TW	182	83	51	34	24	17	12	8	5
T(JAN)=42	R	TWNI	271	127	80	57	43	33	26	19	13
		DG	197	86	49	29	17	-	-	-	-
		DGNI	302	141	88	62	46	35	26	19	12

Waco Texas		**SSF =**	**0.1**	**0.2**	**0.3**	**0.4**	**0.5**	**0.6**	**0.7**	**0.8**	**0.9**
		WW	263	121	75	53	40	31	24	17	10
31.6 N	L	WWNI	373	176	110	79	61	48	39	30	22
2058 DD	C	TW	245	114	70	47	34	24	18	12	8
T(JAN)=47	R	TWNI	350	164	103	74	56	43	33	25	17
		DG	287	129	77	49	32	21	12	-	-
		DGNI	396	185	116	82	61	47	35	25	16

Table 3C-4 (Continued)

Wichita Falls Texas		SSF =	0.1	0.2	0.3	0.4	0.5	0.6	0.7	0.8	0.9
		WW	207	96	59	41	31	24	18	13	7
34.0 N	L	WWNI	304	145	91	65	50	40	32	25	18
2904 DD	C	TW	197	90	55	37	26	19	13	9	5
T(JAN)=41	R	TWNI	288	136	85	61	46	36	28	21	14
		DG	217	96	56	34	21	11	-	-	-
		DGNI	322	151	94	67	50	38	28	20	13

Bryce Canyon Utah		SSF =	0.1	0.2	0.3	0.4	0.5	0.6	0.7	0.8	0.9
		WW	98	47	29	20	15	11	7	3	-
37.7 N	L	WWNI	171	85	55	40	30	24	19	15	11
9133 DD	C	TW	99	46	28	19	12	8	5	3	-
T(JAN)=20	R	TWNI	163	80	52	37	28	22	17	12	8
		DG	80	32	-	-	-	-	-	-	-
		DGNI	175	85	54	39	29	22	16	11	7

Cedar City Utah		SSF =	0.1	0.2	0.3	0.4	0.5	0.6	0.7	0.8	0.9
		WW	139	64	39	27	20	15	11	7	-
37.7 N	L	WWNI	223	106	68	49	37	29	23	18	13
6137 DD	C	TW	135	62	38	25	17	12	8	5	2
T(JAN)=29	R	TWNI	211	100	64	45	34	27	20	15	10
		DG	130	55	29	12	-	-	-	-	-
		DGNI	231	109	68	48	36	27	20	14	9

Salt Lake City Utah		SSF =	0.1	0.2	0.3	0.4	0.5	0.6	0.7	0.8	0.9
		WW	131	59	35	23	16	11	7	3	-
40.8 N	L	WWNI	215	101	64	45	33	26	20	15	11
5983 DD	C	TW	127	57	34	22	14	9	6	3	-
T(JAN)=28	R	TWNI	203	95	59	42	31	23	18	13	8
		DG	118	45	18	-	-	-	-	-	-
		DGNI	221	102	63	44	32	23	17	11	6

Burlington Vermont		SSF =	0.1	0.2	0.3	0.4	0.5	0.6	0.7	0.8	0.9
		WW	42	14	-	-	-	-	-	-	-
44.5 N	L	WWNI	115	51	32	22	16	12	9	7	5
7876 DD	C	TW	50	18	8	-	-	-	-	-	-
T(JAN)=17	R	TWNI	109	49	30	21	15	11	8	6	4
		DG	-	-	-	-	-	-	-	-	-
		DGNI	109	47	28	19	13	9	6	3	-

Norfolk Virginia		SSF =	0.1	0.2	0.3	0.4	0.5	0.6	0.7	0.8	0.9
		WW	162	75	46	32	23	17	13	8	-
36.9 N	L	WWNI	251	120	76	54	41	32	26	20	14
3488 DD	C	TW	156	72	43	29	20	14	9	6	3
T(JAN)=40	R	TWNI	237	113	71	50	38	29	22	17	11
		DG	160	68	37	20	-	-	-	-	-
		DGNI	263	123	77	54	40	30	22	16	10

Richmond Virginia		**SSF =**	**0.1**	**0.2**	**0.3**	**0.4**	**0.5**	**0.6**	**0.7**	**0.8**	**0.9**
		WW	132	61	37	25	18	13	9	5	-
37.5 N	L	WWNI	216	103	65	46	35	27	22	17	12
3939 DD	C	TW	130	59	35	23	16	11	7	4	2
T(JAN)=37	R	TWNI	205	97	61	43	32	25	19	14	9
		DG	122	49	24	-	-	-	-	-	-
		DGNI	223	105	65	45	34	25	18	13	8

Roanoke Virginia		**SSF =**	**0.1**	**0.2**	**0.3**	**0.4**	**0.5**	**0.6**	**0.7**	**0.8**	**0.9**
		WW	124	58	35	24	18	13	9	5	-
37.3 N	L	WWNI	206	99	63	45	34	27	21	17	12
4307 DD	C	TW	123	56	34	22	15	10	7	4	1
T(JAN)=36	R	TWNI	195	93	59	42	32	24	19	14	9
		DG	113	46	21	-	-	-	-	-	-
		DGNI	212	100	63	44	33	24	18	13	7

Olympia Washington		**SSF =**	**0.1**	**0.2**	**0.3**	**0.4**	**0.5**	**0.6**	**0.7**	**0.8**	**0.9**
		WW	112	48	28	17	10	5	-	-	-
47.0 N	L	WWNI	191	90	55	38	28	21	16	11	7
5530 DD	C	TW	109	48	27	16	10	5	-	-	-
T(JAN)=37	R	TWNI	181	84	52	36	26	19	14	10	6
		DG	90	23	-	-	-	-	-	-	-
		DGNI	195	89	54	36	25	18	12	8	3

Seattle-Tacoma Washington		**SSF =**	**0.1**	**0.2**	**0.3**	**0.4**	**0.5**	**0.6**	**0.7**	**0.8**	**0.9**
		WW	128	54	30	19	11	6	-	-	-
47.4 N	L	WWNI	213	98	59	41	30	22	16	11	7
5185 DD	C	TW	123	53	29	18	11	6	-	-	-
T(JAN)=38	R	TWNI	199	91	55	38	27	20	14	10	6
		DG	108	33	-	-	-	-	-	-	-
		DGNI	217	97	58	38	27	19	13	8	3

Spokane Washington		**SSF =**	**0.1**	**0.2**	**0.3**	**0.4**	**0.5**	**0.6**	**0.7**	**0.8**	**0.9**
		WW	91	37	20	10	-	-	-	-	-
47.6 N	L	WWNI	169	78	47	32	23	17	12	9	6
6835 DD	C	TW	92	38	20	11	5	-	-	-	-
T(JAN)=25	R	TWNI	161	73	44	30	21	15	11	8	4
		DG	56	-	-	-	-	-	-	-	-
		DGNI	171	75	45	29	20	13	9	5	-

Yakima Washington		**SSF =**	**0.1**	**0.2**	**0.3**	**0.4**	**0.5**	**0.6**	**0.7**	**0.8**	**0.9**
		WW	117	48	26	15	8	-	-	-	-
46.6 N	L	WWNI	201	90	55	38	27	20	14	10	7
6009 DD	C	TW	114	47	25	15	8	4	-	-	-
T(JAN)=28	R	TWNI	190	85	51	35	25	18	13	9	5
		DG	92	-	-	-	-	-	-	-	-
		DGNI	205	89	53	35	24	16	11	7	3

Table 3C-4 (Continued)

Charleston West Virginia		**SSF =**	**0.1**	**0.2**	**0.3**	**0.4**	**0.5**	**0.6**	**0.7**	**0.8**	**0.9**
		WW	93	41	23	15	10	7	3	–	–
38.4 N	L	WWNI	170	80	50	35	26	20	16	12	9
4590 DD	C	TW	94	41	24	15	9	5	2	–	–
T(JAN)=34	R	TWNI	161	75	47	33	24	19	14	10	7
		DG	66	–	–	–	–	–	–	–	–
		DGNI	172	79	48	33	24	18	13	8	5

Huntington West Virginia		**SSF =**	**0.1**	**0.2**	**0.3**	**0.4**	**0.5**	**0.6**	**0.7**	**0.8**	**0.9**
		WW	99	44	26	17	12	8	4	–	–
38.4 N	L	WWNI	178	84	53	37	28	21	17	13	9
4624 DD	C	TW	101	44	26	16	10	6	3	–	–
T(JAN)=34	R	TWNI	169	79	49	34	26	20	15	11	7
		DG	76	22	–	–	–	–	–	–	–
		DGNI	181	83	51	35	26	19	14	9	5

Eau Claire Wisconsin		**SSF =**	**0.1**	**0.2**	**0.3**	**0.4**	**0.5**	**0.6**	**0.7**	**0.8**	**0.9**
		WW	50	19	8	–	–	–	–	–	–
44.9 N	L	WWNI	121	56	34	24	17	13	10	8	5
8388 DD	C	TW	56	22	11	4	–	–	–	–	–
T(JAN)=12	R	TWNI	115	53	32	22	16	12	9	6	4
		DG	–	–	–	–	–	–	–	–	–
		DGNI	117	52	31	20	14	10	7	4	–

Green Bay Wisconsin		**SSF =**	**0.1**	**0.2**	**0.3**	**0.4**	**0.5**	**0.6**	**0.7**	**0.8**	**0.9**
		WW	57	22	11	5	–	–	–	–	–
44.5 N	L	WWNI	132	59	37	26	19	14	11	8	5
8098 DD	C	TW	63	25	13	6	–	–	–	–	–
T(JAN)=15	R	TWNI	125	56	35	24	17	13	10	7	4
		DG	–	–	–	–	–	–	–	–	–
		DGNI	127	56	34	22	16	11	7	4	–

La Crosse Wisconsin		**SSF =**	**0.1**	**0.2**	**0.3**	**0.4**	**0.5**	**0.6**	**0.7**	**0.8**	**0.9**
		WW	59	23	12	6	–	–	–	–	–
43.9 N	L	WWNI	133	61	37	26	19	15	11	9	6
7417 DD	C	TW	64	26	13	7	–	–	–	–	–
T(JAN)=16	R	TWNI	126	57	35	24	18	13	10	7	5
		DG	–	–	–	–	–	–	–	–	–
		DGNI	129	57	34	23	16	11	8	5	–

Madison Wisconsin		**SSF =**	**0.1**	**0.2**	**0.3**	**0.4**	**0.5**	**0.6**	**0.7**	**0.8**	**0.9**
		WW	62	25	13	7	–	–	–	–	–
43.1 N	L	WWNI	137	62	39	27	20	15	12	9	6
7730 DD	C	TW	67	27	15	8	3	–	–	–	–
T(JAN)=17	R	TWNI	130	59	36	25	19	14	11	8	5
		DG	–	–	–	–	–	–	–	–	–
		DGNI	133	59	36	24	17	12	8	5	2

Milwaukee Wisconsin		**SSF =**	**0.1**	**0.2**	**0.3**	**0.4**	**0.5**	**0.6**	**0.7**	**0.8**	**0.9**
		WW	64	26	14	8	-	-	-	-	-
42.9 N	L	WWNI	140	63	39	27	20	16	12	9	6
7444 DD	C	TW	69	28	15	8	4	-	-	-	-
T(JAN) = 19	R	TWNI	132	60	37	26	19	14	11	8	5
		DG	-	-	-	-	-	-	-	-	-
		DGNI	136	60	36	25	17	12	9	5	2

Casper Wyoming		**SSF =**	**0.1**	**0.2**	**0.3**	**0.4**	**0.5**	**0.6**	**0.7**	**0.8**	**0.9**
		WW	107	49	30	20	14	10	7	-	-
42.9 N	L	WWNI	184	90	57	41	31	24	19	15	10
7555 DD	C	TW	107	49	29	19	12	8	5	2	-
T(JAN) = 23	R	TWNI	175	84	53	38	28	22	17	12	8
		DG	90	34	-	-	-	-	-	-	-
		DGNI	190	90	56	39	29	21	16	11	6

Cheyenne Wyoming		**SSF =**	**0.1**	**0.2**	**0.3**	**0.4**	**0.5**	**0.6**	**0.7**	**0.8**	**0.9**
		WW	111	52	32	22	16	12	8	5	-
41.1 N	L	WWNI	190	91	58	42	32	25	21	16	11
7255 DD	C	TW	112	51	31	20	14	9	6	3	1
T(JAN) = 27	R	TWNI	181	86	55	39	30	23	18	13	9
		DG	96	38	16	-	-	-	-	-	-
		DGNI	195	92	58	41	31	23	17	12	7

Rock Springs Wyoming		**SSF =**	**0.1**	**0.2**	**0.3**	**0.4**	**0.5**	**0.6**	**0.7**	**0.8**	**0.9**
		WW	98	45	28	19	13	9	6	-	-
41.6 N	L	WWNI	176	84	54	38	29	23	18	14	10
8410 DD	C	TW	100	45	27	17	11	7	4	2	-
T(JAN) = 19	R	TWNI	167	79	50	36	27	21	16	12	8
		DG	78	28	-	-	-	-	-	-	-
		DGNI	179	84	53	37	27	20	15	10	6

Canada

Edmonton Alberta		**SSF =**	**0.1**	**0.2**	**0.3**	**0.4**	**0.5**	**0.6**	**0.7**	**0.8**	**0.9**
		WW	66	26	10	-	-	-	-	-	-
53.6 N	L	WWNI	139	65	39	27	19	13	10	7	4
10268 DD	C	TW	69	27	13	-	-	-	-	-	-
T(JAN) = 7	R	TWNI	132	61	37	25	17	12	9	6	3
		DG	-	-	-	-	-	-	-	-	-
		DGNI	136	61	35	23	15	10	6	3	-

Vancouver British Columbia		**SSF =**	**0.1**	**0.2**	**0.3**	**0.4**	**0.5**	**0.6**	**0.7**	**0.8**	**0.9**
		WW	111	47	26	15	9	4	-	-	-
49.3 N	L	WWNI	193	89	54	37	27	20	15	11	7
5515 DD	C	TW	109	46	25	15	8	4	-	-	-
T(JAN) = 37	R	TWNI	181	83	50	34	24	18	13	9	6
		DG	86	-	-	-	-	-	-	-	-
		DGNI	195	88	52	34	24	17	11	7	3

Table 3C-4 (Continued)

Winnipeg Manitoba		**SSF =**	**0.1**	**0.2**	**0.3**	**0.4**	**0.5**	**0.6**	**0.7**	**0.8**	**0.9**
		WW	53	21	9	-	-	-	-	-	-
49.9 N	L	WWNI	125	58	36	25	18	13	10	7	5
10679 DD	C	TW	59	23	11	4	-	-	-	-	-
T(JAN) = -	R	TWNI	119	55	34	23	17	12	9	6	4
		DG	-	-	-	-	-	-	-	-	-
		DGNI	121	54	32	21	15	10	6	3	-

Dartmouth Nova Scotia		**SSF =**	**0.1**	**0.2**	**0.3**	**0.4**	**0.5**	**0.6**	**0.7**	**0.8**	**0.9**
		WW	73	31	18	11	7	4	-	-	-
44.6 N	L	WWNI	148	68	43	30	23	18	14	11	7
7361 DD	C	TW	76	33	18	11	6	3	-	-	-
T(JAN)=26	R	TWNI	140	64	40	28	21	16	12	9	6
		DG	34	-	-	-	-	-	-	-	-
		DGNI	146	66	41	28	20	15	11	7	3

Ottawa Ontario		**SSF =**	**0.1**	**0.2**	**0.3**	**0.4**	**0.5**	**0.6**	**0.7**	**0.8**	**0.9**
		WW	65	26	14	8	-	-	-	-	-
45.5 N	L	WWNI	140	63	39	27	20	16	12	9	6
8735 DD	C	TW	69	28	15	8	3	-	-	-	-
T(JAN)=13	R	TWNI	133	60	37	26	19	14	11	8	5
		DG	-	-	-	-	-	-	-	-	-
		DGNI	137	60	36	25	17	12	9	5	2

Toronto Ontario		**SSF =**	**0.1**	**0.2**	**0.3**	**0.4**	**0.5**	**0.6**	**0.7**	**0.8**	**0.9**
		WW	73	31	17	11	7	-	-	-	-
43.7 N	L	WWNI	148	68	43	30	22	17	14	10	7
6827 DD	C	TW	76	32	18	11	6	2	-	-	-
T(JAN)=25	R	TWNI	140	65	40	28	21	16	12	9	6
		DG	32	-	-	-	-	-	-	-	-
		DGNI	146	66	40	28	20	14	10	7	3

Normandin Quebec		**SSF =**	**0.1**	**0.2**	**0.3**	**0.4**	**0.5**	**0.6**	**0.7**	**0.8**	**0.9**
		WW	49	19	9	-	-	-	-	-	-
48.8 N	L	WWNI	118	56	35	24	18	13	10	7	5
10528 DD	C	TW	54	22	11	4	-	-	-	-	-
T(JAN)=4	R	TWNI	112	52	33	23	16	12	9	6	4
		DG	-	-	-	-	-	-	-	-	-
		DGNI	113	52	31	21	14	10	6	4	-

PRELIMINARY DESIGN, SUMMARY GUIDELINES RELATED TO SEVERAL VARIABLES

DIRECT GAIN SYSTEMS

- The best performance/cost balance for masonry thickness is between 2 inches and 4 inches, with 4 inches providing a good balance. The highest solar savings can be obtained by spreading the mass over as large an area as possible.
- Surface absorptance (or the area-weighted average of all surfaces) should not drop below 0.5. Some common solar absorptances are given below.

Flat black paint	0.98
Brown concrete	0.85
Medium light-brown paint	0.80
Red bricks	0.70
Uncolored concrete	0.65
Medium-yellow paint	0.57
Medium-blue paint	0.51
White semigloss paint	0.30

- Absorption by non-mass surfaces such as furniture, wall hangings, and so on should be minimized and should not exceed 0.5. In general, keep lightweight objects, especially dark ones, out of direct sunlight; use light colors on low-mass surfaces; and keep furnishings, wall coverings, and floor coverings to a minimum in direct gain zones.
- For most climates, double glazing is required for the solar collector, with very little performance gain in adding a third or fourth glazing layer.
- Increasing the air gap between double glazing in direct gain buildings from 1/4 inch to 1/2 inch can raise the SSF by 12% to 15%.

THERMAL STORAGE WALL SYSTEMS

- The presence of vents in the wall becomes important for either thick walls or walls of low thermal conductivity.
- The optimum thickness of a Trombe wall depends on the wall material's thermal conductivity; the higher the conductivity, the thicker the wall can be.
- Compared to water walls of the same heat capacity, an *unvented* Trombe wall is much more effective in reducing temperature swings within the space.
- The recommended vent area (lower vents, which should be equal in area to the upper vents) as a percentage of total Trombe wall area depends on the SSF, as follows:

SSF (in percent)	**Recommended Vent Area** (in percent)
25	3
50	1
75	1/2

- Using a Trombe wall with a selective surface to reduce the infrared radiation transmitted from the wall to the glass significantly improves the SSF.

PART 3D

Daylighting

There are several methods to predict daylighting in buildings. The following is based on a procedure adopted by the Illuminating Engineering Society, which was developed under the sponsorship of the Libbey Owens Ford Company. It is often referred to as the Lumen Method.

This prediction method makes the following assumptions:

1. Illumination is calculated for three points in a room, all on the center line of the window: one 5 feet from the window, one 5 feet from the back wall, and one in the midpoint of the room.
2. The prediction points and the windowsill are 30 inches above the floor.
3. The top of the window extends to the ceiling.
4. No account is made for reflections from neighboring buildings.
5. The windows are vertical and rooms are rectangular.

For any given situation, daylighting calculations should be made for several conditions, to represent differing sky conditions, times of the year, and times of day. Because the calculation procedure is repetitive for different variables, this application is well suited for using a simple spreadsheet program on a microcomputer. Geographical variables of the area in which you practice can be used with other variables' input as required to yield tables useful for studying different design alternatives. There are also special daylighting application programs for microcomputers for detailed analysis.

DAYLIGHTING WITH SIDELIGHTING CALCULATIONS

Step 1. Determine the solar altitude and azimuth of the sun on the day and for the time under study. This information is available from Table 3D–1 or from standard sun charts. You can also calculate the exact position following the procedures given later in this part.

Step 2. Determine the illumination on the window from the *sky.* This is a combination of illumination from the sky itself and directly from the sun (if any). It varies with the sky conditions, time of day, time of year, and altitude of the sun above the horizon. First, find the solar illumination, E_{uw}, on the window resulting from direct sunlight. Obviously, on cloudy days or where the window faces away from the sun, this value will be zero. It is assumed that some type of shading will keep direct sunlight from entering the room. Knowing the solar altitude and azimuth, read the values from Figure 3D–1. Second, find the illumination from the sky, E_{kw}. Knowing the solar altitude and azimuth of the sun relative to true south, read the values from Figures 3D–2 through 3D–5, depending on the sky conditions and time of year. Add the two values to get the total illumination from the sky on the window.

Step 3. Determine the illumination on the window from the *ground.* This depends on the direct and indirect illumination from the sun and sky as well as the reflectance of the ground. Knowing the solar altitude, find the solar illumination (direct sun) on a horizontal surface (if any) from Figure 3D–1. Add this to the skylight illumination on a horizontal surface from Figures 3D–2, 3D–4, or 3D–5, depending on sky conditions and time of year.

Table 3D-1
SOLAR ALTITUDE AND AZIMUTH FOR DIFFERENT LATITUDES

		Date	Solar Time*						
			AM: 6 PM: 6	7 5	8 4	9 3	10 2	11 1	Noon
	ALTITUDE	June 21	12	24	37	50	63	75	83
		Mar.–Sept. 21	—	13	26	38	49	57	60
		Dec. 21	—	—	12	21	29	35	37
	AZIMUTH	June 21	111	104	99	92	84	67	0
		Mar.–Sept. 21	90	83	74	64	49	28	0
		Dec. 21	—	60	54	44	32	17	0
	ALTITUDE	June 21	13	25	37	50	62	74	79
		Mar.–Sept. 21	—	12	25	36	46	53	56
		Dec. 21	—	—	9	18	26	31	33
	AZIMUTH	June 21	110	103	95	90	78	58	0
		Mar.–Sept. 21	90	82	72	61	46	26	0
		Dec. 21	—	—	54	43	30	16	0
	ALTITUDE	June 21	14	26	37	49	61	71	75
		Mar.–Sept. 21	—	12	23	34	43	50	52
		Dec. 21	—	—	7	16	23	27	28
	AZIMUTH	June 21	109	101	90	83	70	46	0
		Mar.–Sept. 21	90	81	71	58	43	24	0
		Dec. 21	—	—	54	43	30	16	0
	ALTITUDE	June 21	16	26	38	49	60	68	71
		Mar.–Sept. 21	—	11	22	32	40	46	48
		Dec. 21	—	—	4	13	19	23	25
	AZIMUTH	June 21	108	99	89	78	63	39	0
		Mar.–Sept. 21	90	80	69	56	41	22	0
		Dec. 21	—	—	53	42	29	15	0
	ALTITUDE	June 21	17	27	37	48	57	65	67
		Mar.–Sept. 21	—	10	20	30	37	42	44
		Dec. 21	—	—	2	10	15	20	21
	AZIMUTH	June 21	107	97	88	74	58	34	0
		Mar.–Sept. 21	90	79	67	54	39	21	0
		Dec. 21	—	—	52	41	28	14	0
	ALTITUDE	June 21	17	27	37	47	56	63	65
		Mar.–Sept. 21	—	10	20	29	36	40	42
		Dec. 21	—	—	1	8	14	17	19
	AZIMUTH	June 21	106	95	85	72	55	31	0
		Mar.–Sept. 21	90	79	67	53	38	20	0
		Dec. 21	—	—	52	41	28	14	0

* Time measured by the daily motion of the sun. Noon is taken as the instant in which the center of the sun passes the observer's meridian.

Source: IES Lighting Handbook.

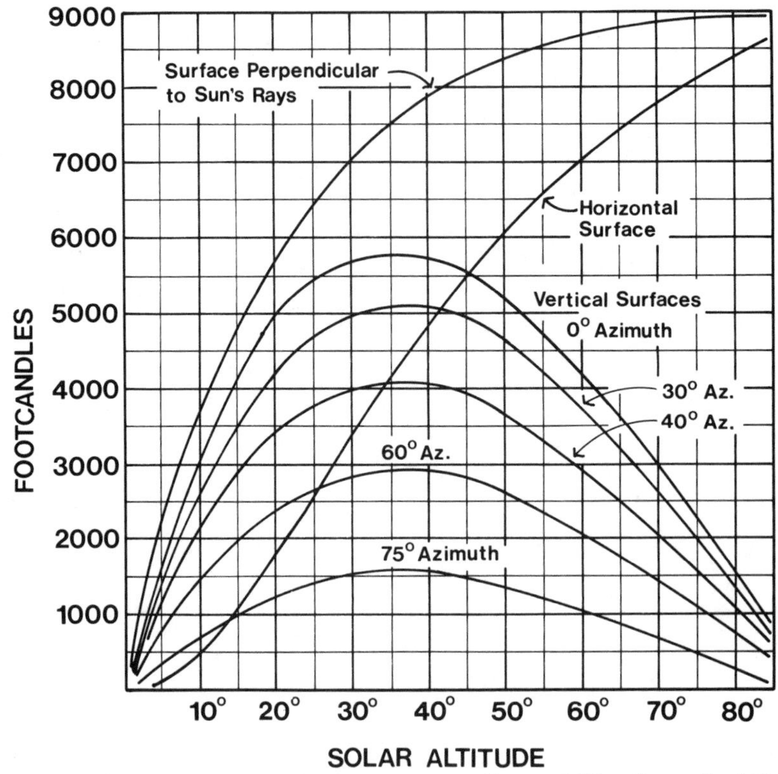

Source: Libbey Owens Ford Co.

Figure 3D-1: Solar Illumination from Direct Rays

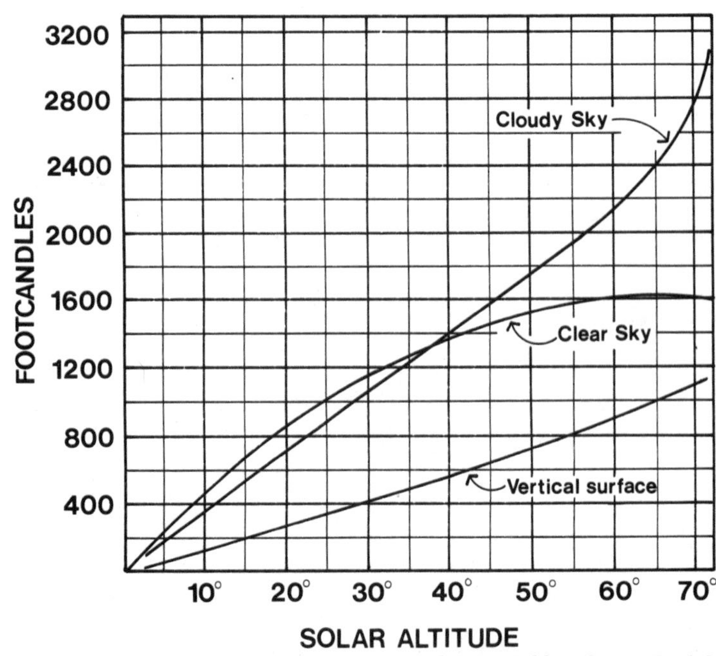

Source: Libbey Owens Ford Co.

Figure 3D-2: Clear and Cloudy Sky Illuminance on Horizontal Surfaces and Overcast Sky Illuminance on Vertical Surfaces

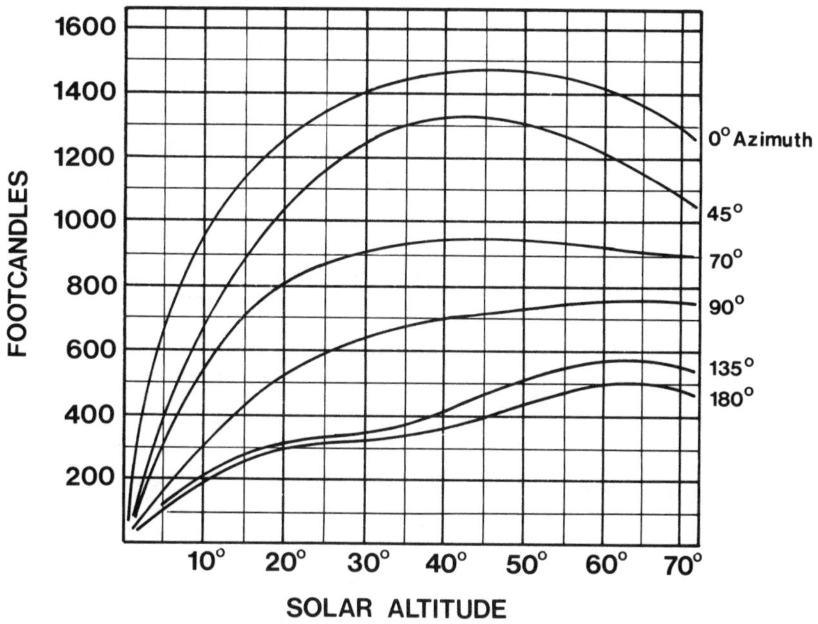

Azimuth bearings are from sun's position

Source: IES Lighting Handbook.

Figure 3D-3: Clear Summer Skylight Illuminance on Vertical Surfaces

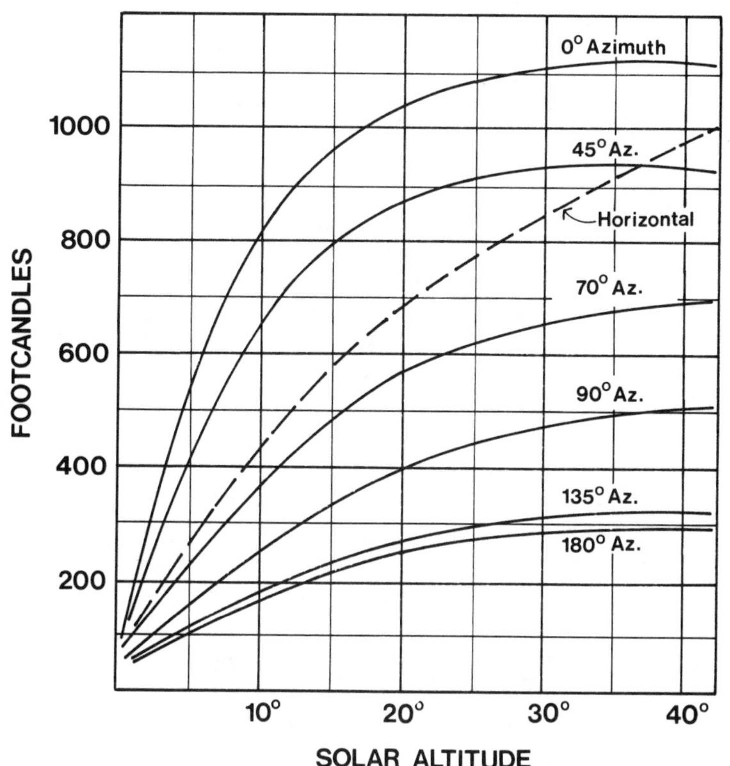

Azimuth bearings are from sun's position

Source: IES Lighting Handbook.

Figure 3D-4: Clear Winter Skylight Illuminance on Vertical Surfaces

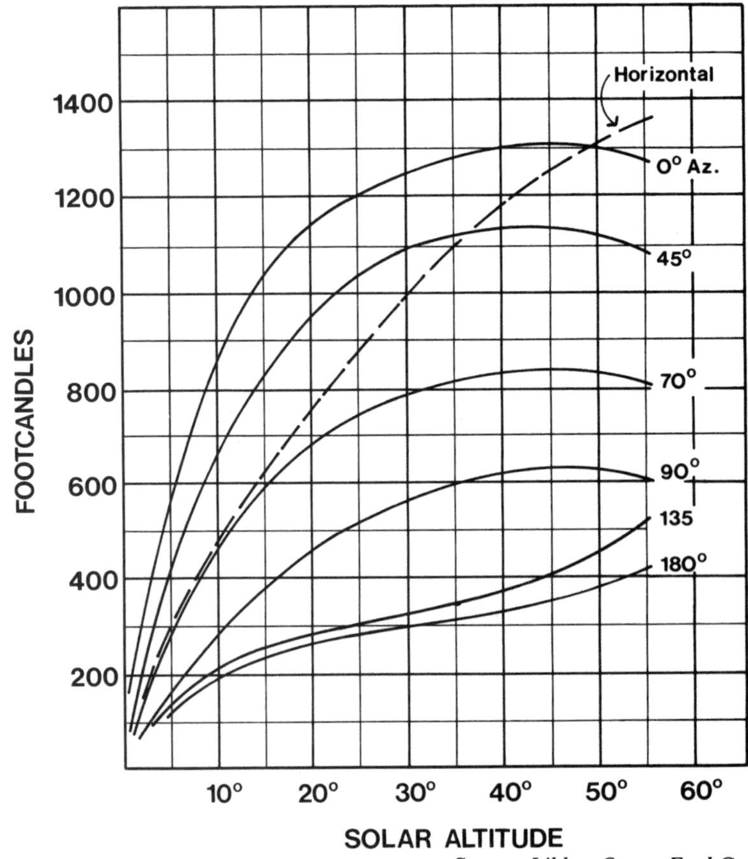

Source: Libbey Owens Ford Co.

Figure 3D-5: Clear Autumn/Spring Skylight on Vertical Surfaces

Multiply the result by the reflectance factors given in Table 3D-2 and by a proportion factor of 0.5.

Step 4. Determine the total transmitting area of the glass, A_g. This excludes mullions and other solid obstructions. Find the transmittance factor, T_g, of the glass from the manufacturer's literature or use representative values from Table 3D-3.

Step 5. Determine coefficients of utilization for illumination from the sky. This takes into account the characteristics of the room and involves two factors: the C factor for room length and width, and the K factor for room width and ceiling height. Both vary with the reflectance of the walls and are calculated assuming reflectance factors of 80% for the ceiling and 30% for the floor. Values are given for each of the three calculation points previously mentioned.

Note that in these calculations, room width is defined as the distance, in feet, from the window to the wall opposite the window and room length is the distance parallel to the window. Refer to Tables 3D-4 and 3D-5 for values. Interpolate as necessary.

When a diffuse window shade is used, add the illumination from the ground and the sky at the window and divide by two. Then use this value in the equation when finding illumination on the work plane. Do the same to find the illumination on the window from the ground. Use Table 3D-6 to find the coefficient of utilization.

If horizontal blinds are used, determine or assume the tilt angle and obtain coefficients of utilization from Tables 3D-8 and 3D-9. A third factor, V, must be included in the final calculation formula if horizontal blinds are used.

Table 3D-2
REFLECTANCES OF BUILDING MATERIALS AND OUTSIDE SURFACES

Material	Reflectance	Material	Reflectance
Bluestone, sandstone	0.18	Asphalt (free from dirt)	0.07
Brick		Earth (moist cultivated)	0.07
Light buff	0.48	Granolite pavement	0.17
Dark buff	0.40	Grass (dark green)	0.06
Dark-red (glazed)	0.30	Gravel	0.13
Cement	0.27	Macadam	0.18
Concrete	0.40	Slate (dark clay)	0.08
Paint (white)		Snow	
New	0.75	New	0.74
Old	0.55	Old	0.64
Glass		Vegetation (mean)	0.25
Clear	0.07		
Reflective	0.20–0.30		
Tinted	0.07		

Source: IES Lighting Handbook.

Table 3D-3
TRANSMITTANCE DATA OF GLASS AND PLASTIC MATERIALS

Material	Approximate Transmittance
Polished plate/float glass	0.80–0.90
Sheet glass	0.85–0.91
Heat-absorbing plate glass	0.70–0.80
Heat-absorbing sheet glass	0.70–0.85
Tinted polished plate	0.40–0.50
Figure glass	0.70–0.90
Corrugated glass	0.80–0.85
Glass block	0.60–0.80
Clear plastic sheet	0.80–0.92
Tinted plastic sheet	0.90–0.42
Colorless patterned plastic	0.80–0.90
White translucent plastic	0.10–0.80
Glass fiber reinforced plastic	0.05–0.80
Double glazed—2 clear lights	0.77
Tinted plus clear	0.37–0.45
Reflective glass[1]	0.05–0.60

[1]Includes single glass, double-glazed units, and laminated assemblies. Consult manufacturer's material for specific values.

Source: IES Lighting Handbook.

Step 6. Determine coefficients of utilization for illuminations from the ground. Use Table 3D–7 to obtain these values. Interpolate as necessary.

If horizontal blinds are used, determine or assume the tilt angle and obtain coefficients of utilization from Table 3D–9.

Step 7. Calculate the illumination on the work plane from light from the sky and light from the ground. Both calculations are performed for each of the three reference points: MAX, MID, and MIN, in the room.

TABLES SHOWING COEFFICIENTS OF UTILIZATION

(Ceiling reflectance = 80 percent; Floor reflectance = 30 percent)

Table 3D-4
ILLUMINANCE FROM AN OVERCAST SKY, WITHOUT WINDOW CONTROLS

			C									K							
Room Length			6.1 M (20 FT)		9.1 M (30 FT)		12.2 M (40 FT)		Ceiling Height			2.4 M (8 FT)		3 M (10 FT)		3.7 M (12 FT)		4.3 M (14 FT)	
Wall Reflectance (per cent)			70	30	70	30	70	30	Wall Reflectance (per cent)			70	30	70	30	70	30	70	30
	Room Width M	FT								Room Width M	FT								
	6.1	20	.0276	.0251	.0191	.0173	.0143	.0137		6.1	20	.125	.129	.121	.123	.111	.111	.0991	.0973
MAX	9.1	30	.0272	.0248	.0188	.0172	.0137	.0131	MAX	9.1	30	.122	.131	.122	.121	.111	.111	.0945	.0973
	12.2	40	.0269	.0246	.0182	.0171	.0133	.0130		12.2	40	.145	.133	.131	.126	.111	.111	.0973	.0982
	6.1	20	.0159	.0117	.0101	.0087	.0081	.0071		6.1	20	.0908	.0982	.107	.115	.111	.111	.105	.122
MID	9.1	30	.0058	.0050	.0054	.0040	.0034	.0033	MID	9.1	30	.156	.102	.0939	.113	.111	.111	.121	.134
	12.2	40	.0039	.0027	.0030	.0023	.0022	.0019		12.2	40	.106	.0948	.123	.107	.111	.111	.135	.127
	6.1	20	.0087	.0053	.0063	.0043	.0050	.0037		6.1	20	.0908	.102	.0951	.114	.111	.111	.118	.134
MIN	9.1	30	.0032	.0019	.0029	.0017	.0020	.0014	MIN	9.1	30	.0924	.119	.101	.114	.111	.111	.125	.126
	12.2	40	.0019	.0009	.0016	.0009	.0012	.0008		12.2	40	.111	.0926	.125	.109	.111	.111	.133	.130

Table 3D-5
ILLUMINANCE FROM A CLEAR SKY, WITHOUT WINDOW CONTROLS

			C									K							
	Room Width M	FT								Room Width M	FT								
	6.1	20	.0206	.0173	.0143	.0123	.0110	.0098		6.1	20	.145	.155	.129	.132	.111	.111	.101	.0982
MAX	9.1	30	.0203	.0173	.0137	.0120	.0098	.0092	MAX	9.1	30	.141	.149	.125	.130	.111	.111	.0954	.101
	12.2	40	.0200	.0168	.0131	.0119	.0096	.0091		12.2	40	.157	.157	.135	.134	.111	.111	.0964	.0991
	6.1	20	.0153	.0104	.0100	.0079	.0083	.0067		6.1	20	.110	.128	.116	.126	.111	.111	.103	.108
MID	9.1	30	.0082	.0054	.0062	.0043	.0046	.0037	MID	9.1	30	.106	.125	.110	.129	.111	.111	.112	.120
	12.2	40	.0052	.0032	.0040	.0028	.0029	.0023		12.2	40	.117	.118	.122	.118	.111	.111	.123	.122
	6.1	20	.0106	.0060	.0079	.0049	.0067	.0043		6.1	20	.105	.129	.112	.130	.111	.111	.111	.116
MIN	9.1	30	.0054	.0028	.0047	.0023	.0032	.0021	MIN	9.1	30	.0994	.144	.107	.126	.111	.111	.107	.124
	12.2	40	.0031	.0014	.0027	.0013	.0021	.0012		12.2	40	.119	.116	.130	.118	.111	.111	.120	.118

Table 3D-6
ILLUMINANCE FROM THE "UNIFORM SKY," WITHOUT DIFFUSE WINDOW SHADES

			C									K							
	Room Width M	FT								Room Width M	FT								
	6.1	20	.0247	.0217	.0174	.0152	.0128	.0120		6.1	20	.145	.154	.123	.128	.111	.111	.0991	.0964
MAX	9.1	30	.0241	.0214	.0166	.0151	.0120	.0116	MAX	9.1	30	.141	.151	.126	.128	.111	.111	.0945	.0964
	12.2	40	.0237	.0212	.0161	.0150	.0118	.0113		12.2	40	.159	.157	.137	.127	.111	.111	.0973	.0964
	6.1	20	.0169	.0122	.0110	.0092	.0089	.0077		6.1	20	.101	.116	.115	.125	.111	.111	.101	.110
MID	9.1	30	.0078	.0060	.0067	.0048	.0044	.0041	MID	9.1	30	.0952	.113	.105	.122	.111	.111	.110	.122
	12.2	40	.0053	.0033	.0039	.0028	.0029	.0024		12.2	40	.111	.105	.124	.107	.111	.111	.130	.124
	6.1	20	.0108	.0066	.0080	.0052	.0063	.0047		6.1	20	.0974	.111	.107	.121	.111	.111	.112	.119
MIN	9.1	30	.0047	.0026	.0042	.0023	.0029	.0020	MIN	9.1	30	.0956	.125	.103	.117	.111	.111	.115	.125
	12.2	40	.0027	.0013	.0022	.0012	.0018	.0011		12.2	40	.111	.105	.125	.111	.111	.111	.133	.124

Table 3D-7
ILLUMINANCE FROM A UNIFORM GROUND, WITHOUT WINDOW CONTROLS

			C									K							
	Room Width M	FT								Room Width M	FT								
	6.1	20	.0147	.0112	.0102	.0088	.0081	.0071		6.1	20	.124	.206	.140	.135	.111	.111	.0909	.0859
MAX	9.1	30	.0141	.0112	.0098	.0088	.0077	.0070	MAX	9.1	30	.182	.188	.140	.143	.111	.111	.0918	.0878
	12.2	40	.0137	.0112	.0093	.0086	.0072	.0069		12.2	40	.124	.182	.140	.142	.111	.111	.0936	.0879
	6.1	20	.0128	.0090	.0094	.0071	.0073	.0060		6.1	20	.123	.145	.122	.129	.111	.111	.100	.0945
MID	9.1	30	.0083	.0057	.0062	.0048	.0050	.0041	MID	9.1	30	.0966	.104	.107	.112	.111	.111	.110	.105
	12.2	40	.0055	.0037	.0044	.0033	.0042	.0026		12.2	40	.0790	.0786	.0999	.106	.111	.111	.118	.118
	6.1	20	.0106	.0071	.0082	.0054	.0067	.0044		6.1	20	.0994	.108	.110	.114	.111	.111	.107	.104
MIN	9.1	30	.0051	.0026	.0041	.0023	.0033	.0021	MIN	9.1	30	.0816	.0822	.0984	.105	.111	.111	.121	.116
	12.2	40	.0029	.0018	.0026	.0012	.0022	.0011		12.2	40	.0700	.0656	.0946	.0986	.111	.111	.125	.132

Source: IES Lighting Handbook

TABLES SHOWING COEFFICIENTS OF UTILIZATION AND V FACTORS FOR VENETIAN BLINDS

(Ceiling reflectance = 80 percent; Floor reflectance = 30 percent)

Table 3D-8
ILLUMINANCE FROM THE SKY, WITH VENETIAN BLINDS

C

Room Length			6.1M (20FT)		9.1M (30FT)		12.2M (40FT)	
Wall Reflectance (per cent)			70	30	70	30	70	30
	Room Width M	FT						
MAX	6.1	20	.0556	.0556	.0392	.0397	.0298	.0317
	9.1	30	.0522	.0533	.0367	.0389	.0278	.0311
	12.2	40	.0506	.0528	.0359	.0381	.0270	.0306
MID	6.1	20	.0556	.0556	.0418	.0411	.0320	.0364
	9.1	30	.0372	.0339	.0278	.0286	.0220	.0256
	12.2	40	.0217	.0211	.0192	.0186	.0139	.0164
MIN	6.1	20	.0556	.0556	.0422	.0456	.0320	.0409
	9.1	30	.0294	.0233	.0222	.0203	.0189	.0194
	12.2	40	.0139	.0110	.0133	.0108	.0120	.0100

K

Ceiling Height			2.4M (8FT)		3M (10FT)		3.7M (12FT)		4.3M (14FT)	
Wall Reflectance (per cent)			70	30	70	30	70	30	70	30
	Room Width M	FT								
MAX			.154	.170	.129	.131	.107	.112	.091	.091
MID	6.1	20	.100	.106	.101	.106	.099	.102	.091	.091
	9.1	30	.074	.080	.086	.090	.091	.093	.091	.091
	12.2	40	.070	.074	.079	.084	.088	.091	.091	.091
MIN	6.1	20	.080	.080	.091	.091	.093	.093	.091	.091
	9.1	30	.068	.068	.079	.079	.087	.087	.091	.091
	12.2	40	.064	.064	.076	.076	.084	.084	.091	.091

V

Venetian Blind Setting		30°		45°		60°	
Wall Reflectance (per cent)		70	30	70	30	70	30
15° SUN ALT.	MAX	.0687	.0554	.0426	.0346	.0218	.0162
	MID	.0488	.0341	.0371	.0218	.0195	.0110
	MIN	.0376	.0228	.0276	.0156	.0142	.0078
30° SUN ALT	MAX	.0630	.050	.0394	.0312	.0208	.0156
	MID	.0462	.0324	.0337	.0216	.0176	.0110
	MIN	.0342	.0204	.0250	.0143	.0130	.0071
45° SUN ALT.	MAX	.0553	.0434	.0345	.0274	.0198	.0141
	MID	.0416	.0301	.0304	.0211	.0158	.0105
	MIN	.0308	.0182	.0225	.0127	.0117	.0064
60° SUN ALT.	MAX	.0464	.0362	.0313	.0236	.0190	.0135
	MID	.0370	.0264	.0270	.0185	.0140	.0092
	MIN	.0274	.0159	.0199	.0111	.0104	.0056

Table 3D-9
ILLUMINANCE FROM THE GROUND, WITH VENETIAN BLINDS

C

	Room Width M	FT	6.1M (20FT) 70	6.1M (20FT) 30	9.1M (30FT) 70	9.1M (30FT) 30	12.2M (40FT) 70	12.2M (40FT) 30
MAX	6.1	20	.0556	.0556	.0392	.0426	.0303	.0348
	9.1	30	.0528	.0539	.0370	.0433	.0289	.0337
	12.2	40	.0506	.0544	.0359	.0426	.0278	.0344
MID	6.1	20	.0556	.0556	.0414	.0459	.0320	.0381
	9.1	30	.0367	.0356	.0274	.0308	.0217	.0270
	12.2	40	.0239	.0233	.0192	.0222	.0153	.0181
MIN	6.1	20	.0556	.0556	.0430	.0486	.0328	.0398
	9.1	30	.0261	.0228	.0214	.0211	.0170	.0192
	12.2	40	.0128	.0108	.0119	.0107	.0098	.0097

K

	Room Width M	FT	2.4M (8FT) 70	2.4M (8FT) 30	3M (10FT) 70	3M (10FT) 30	3.7M (12FT) 70	3.7M (12FT) 30	4.3M (14FT) 70	4.3M (14FT) 30
MAX			.174	.200	.142	.157	.117	.123	.091	.091
MID	6.1	20	.104	.116	.110	.121	.106	.112	.091	.091
	9.1	30	.074	.082	.092	.099	.099	.106	.091	.091
	12.2	40	.058	.062	.079	.083	.092	.096	.091	.091
MIN	6.1	20	.078	.082	.093	.097	.099	.102	.091	.091
	9.1	30	.058	.060	.074	.076	.090	.092	.091	.091
	12.2	40	.052	.056	.070	.071	.086	.087	.091	.091

V

	30° 70	30° 30	45° 70	45° 30	60° 70	60° 30
MAX	.150	.108	.141	.102	.087	.063
MID	.141	.094	.118	.077	.067	.043
MIN	.124	.072	.096	.056	.049	.028

Source: IES Lighting Handbook

FORMULA:

$$E_{kwp} = E_{kuw} \times A_g \times T_g \times LLF \times C \times K$$

and

$$E_{gwp} = E_{gw} \times A_g \times T_g \times LLD \times C \times K$$

where:

E_{kwp} = illumination from the sky on the work plane
E_{gwp} = illumination from the ground on the work plane
E_{kuw} = illumination from the sun and sky on the window
E_{gw} = illumination from the ground on the window
A_g = net area of the window glass
T_g = transmittance of the glass
LLF = light loss factor due to dirt (For vertical glass in office or retail situations, use 0.82 for a 3-month cleaning cycle or 0.73 for a 6-month cleaning cycle.)
C = coefficient of utilization for room length and width
K = coefficient of utilization for room width and ceiling height

Step 8. Add the illuminations from the sky and ground on the work plane to get total illumination on the work plane at the three reference points.

HOW TO FACTOR IN OVERHANGS

Illumination calculations for rooms with overhangs are made the same as those without except that the overhang dimensions are used to "increase" the size of the room to an "equivalent room." Calculations are then made for this equivalent room and graphically charted to find the illumination in the actual room.

The method of establishing the size of the equivalent room is shown in Figure 3D–6. The width of the overhang is added to the width of the room as though the glazing were located at the outer edge of the overhang. The length of the room is found by projecting lines from the center of the three calculation points to the edge of the side walls out to the edge of the extended line of the overhang. This "new" room length is then used when finding the coefficients of utilization from the tables. If the "new" room length exceeds 40 feet, then 40 feet is used as the length.

The length of the equivalent room is also used in determining the length of the glazing when calculating window area, A_g, with the maximum length also being 40 feet. The windowsill is disregarded when calculating the window area for ground illumination; therefore, the height of the window is assumed to extend from floor to ceiling. For calculating window area for sky illumination, the distance from the windowsill to the ceiling is used.

Two assumptions are made with this technique. First, it is assumed that the glazing extends to the ceiling. This is important because the availability and depth of penetration of daylight into a room depends on the height of the window head. Second, the reflectance of the overhang is the same as the ceiling.

All the other calculations are made as outlined before except that instead of adding the illumination from the sky and the ground to get total illumination at the three prediction points, the results are plotted graphically on a cross section of the room. This is because the illumination calculated is for a larger "equivalent" room where the points of maximum and midpoint illumination are not the same as in the actual room.

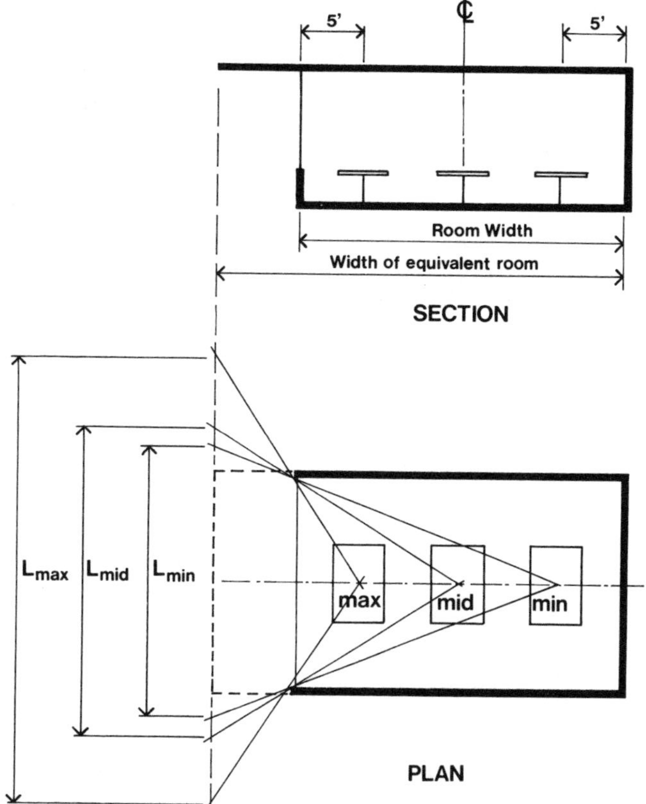

Figure 3D-6: Determining Equivalent Room Sizes for Rooms with Overhangs

Graph the results of the calculations on a piece of graph paper for the three points and connect them with a smooth curve. The horizontal ordinate is in feet and the vertical ordinate is in footcandles. Then, read the footcandle values for the MAX and MID points in the actual room and add them together to get the total illumination. The MIN point, of course, will be the same in both the actual room and the "equivalent" room. (See Figure 3D-7(b).)

If direct sunlight falls under the overhang, an additional factor must be added to account for the extra light reflected into the room. Determine where the sunlight falls on the ground under the overhang. This depends on the angle of the sun at the time for which you are making the calculation and the width of the overhang. This "profile angle" can be calculated following the procedures given later in this section. Next, determine the distance from each of the three calculation points to the edge of the shaded area. (See Figure 3D-7(a).)

Use the following formula to determine the factor X_e for each of the three points.

FORMULA:

$$X_e = \frac{A - B}{C + 20}$$

With the value of X_e, use the graphs in Figures 3D-8 through 3D-10 to find the multiplying factor, X_f. This factor is then multiplied by the ground illumination on the work surface, E_{gwp}, found by the formulas and graphically adjusting for the overhang, to get the final illumination from the ground on the work surface. This is then added to the sky illumination to arrive at the total illumination on the work surfaces at the three calculation points.

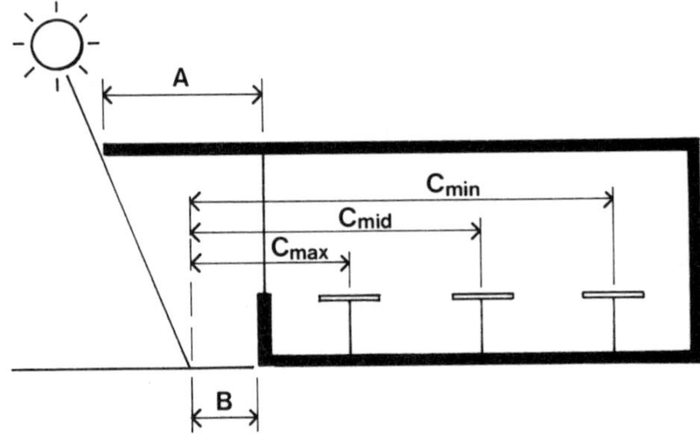

(a) Dimensions for calculating X_e

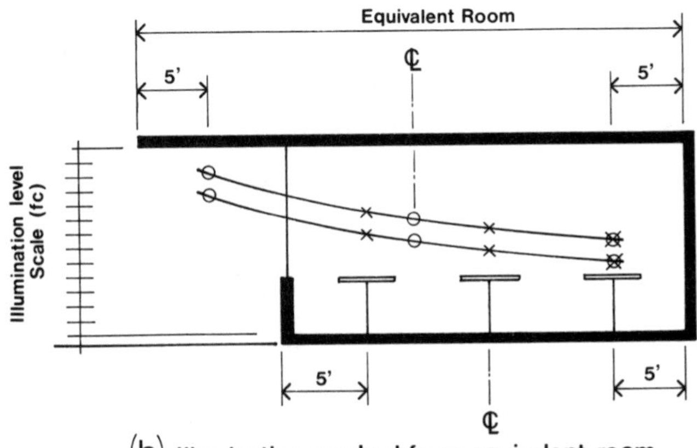

(b) Illumination graphed from equivalent room

Figure 3D-7: Daylighting Calculation Procedures for Overhangs

HOW TO CALCULATE SUN POSITION

There are many times during the design when the position of the sun is required. Some of these include:

- Calculating daylighting when overhangs are involved.
- Determining required dimensions of overhangs and other shading devices.
- Calculating solar radiation on a surface when the surface is not in the position given in reference tables.

For most applications, sun charts provide enough accuracy to determine the solar altitude (degrees above the horizon) and solar azimuth (degrees east or west of south) for given geographical locations, time of day, and time of year. When more accuracy is required, the following procedures and formulas can be used.

The position of the sun anywhere in the world as described by the solar altitude and solar azimuth depends on the latitude of the site under consideration, the declination of the sun (degrees north or south of the equator), and the solar hour angle.

Latitude, L, can be determined from a map or from values given for representative cities in Table 3C-3 or Table 3E-1.

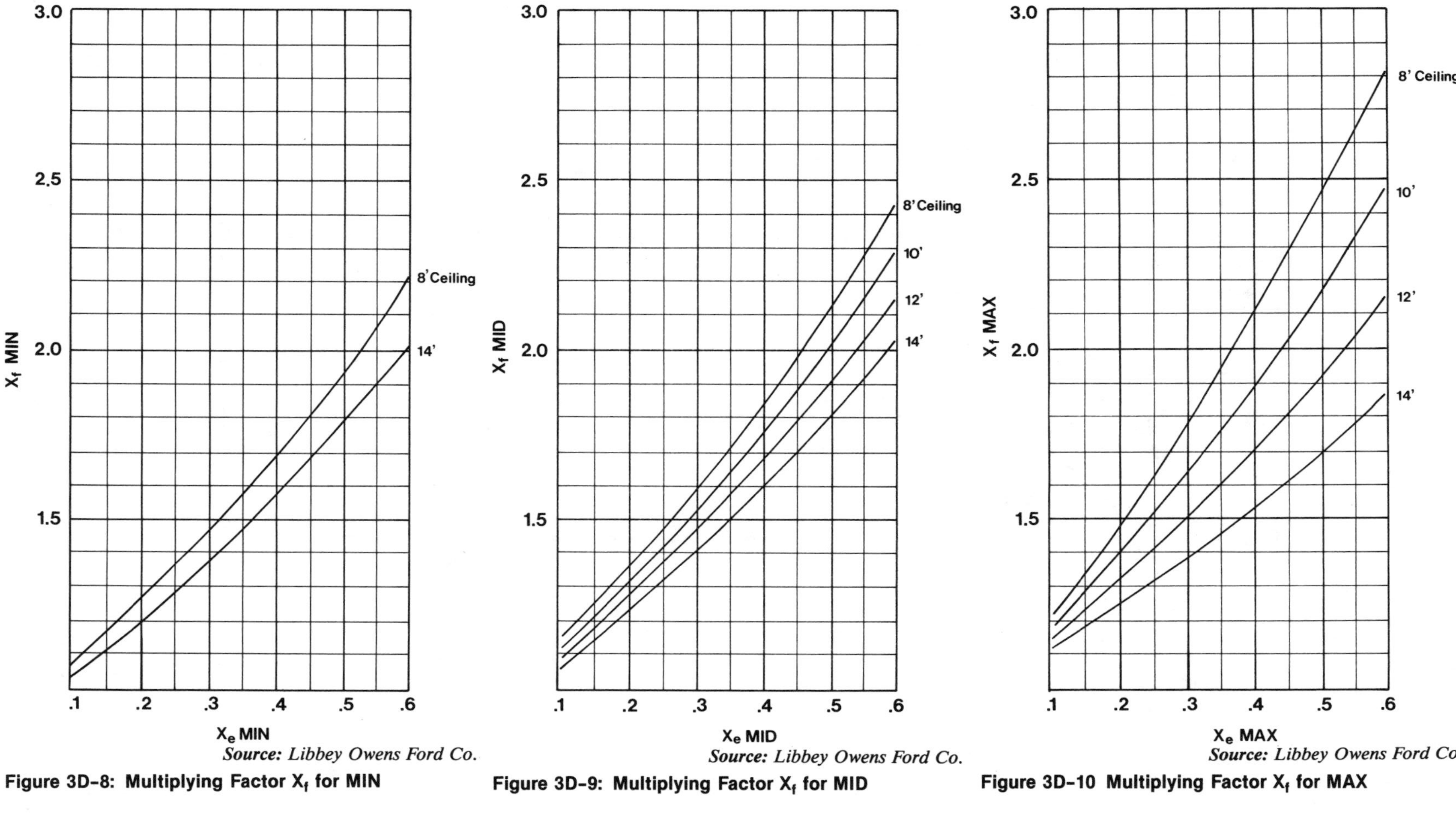

Source: Libbey Owens Ford Co.

Figure 3D-8: Multiplying Factor X_f for MIN

Source: Libbey Owens Ford Co.

Figure 3D-9: Multiplying Factor X_f for MID

Source: Libbey Owens Ford Co.

Figure 3D-10 Multiplying Factor X_f for MAX

Solar declination, D, can be calculated from the following formula.

FORMULA: $D = 23.45 \times \sin[0.9863013 \times (284 + N)]$

where:

D = solar declination in degrees (decimal format)
N = number of Julian day of the year
(e.g., February 15 = 46th day of the year)

Some representative solar declinations are given in Table 3D–10.

Table 3D–10
SOLAR DECLINATIONS

Dates		Declination
June 22		+23.45
15	June 29	+23.25
8	July 6	+22.75
1	13	+21.92
May 25	20	+20.83
18	27	+19.42
11	Aug 3	+17.67
4	10	+15.75
Apr 26	18	+13.33
19	25	+11.00
12	Sep 1	+8.50
5	8	+5.92
Mar 28	16	+2.83
21	23	0.00
14	Oct 1	−2.83
7	8	−5.58
Feb 28	15	−8.25
21	22	−10.83
14	29	−13.25
7	Nov 5	−15.50
Jan 31	12	−17.50
24	19	−19.33
17	26	−20.83
10	Dec 3	−22.00
3	10	−22.83
Dec 27	17	−23.33
	Dec 22	−23.45

Note: Declinations are given to the nearest 5 minutes in decimal format except for June 22 and December 22, which are exact.

The solar hour angle depends on local solar time, which is measured from solar noon—the time when the sun is highest in the sky at a given location and when the center of the sun passes the meridian of the location. This, of course, depends on the longitude of the site under consideration. Local solar time also varies with the time of the year; the length of solar days vary from actual uniform clock time.

The formula for finding the solar hour angle follows.

FORMULA: H = 0.25 × number of minutes from local solar noon

or

H = 15 × number of hours from local solar noon

To find the number of minutes or hours from solar noon, standard time must be converted to solar time. The equation for this follows.

FORMULA: Solar time = T + 4 (SM − L) + ET

where:

T = standard time in hours and minutes
(if daylight savings time, subtract one hour)
SM = standard meridian of the time zone of the site
For most of the western hemisphere these are

Time Zones	Standard Meridian
Atlantic	60
Eastern	75
Central	90
Mountain	105
Pacific	120
Yukon	135
Alaska/Hawaii	150

L = longitude of site (See Table 3E–1.)
ET = equation of time, from Figure 3D–11. This accounts for the varying length of solar days during the year. It is either a positive or negative value.

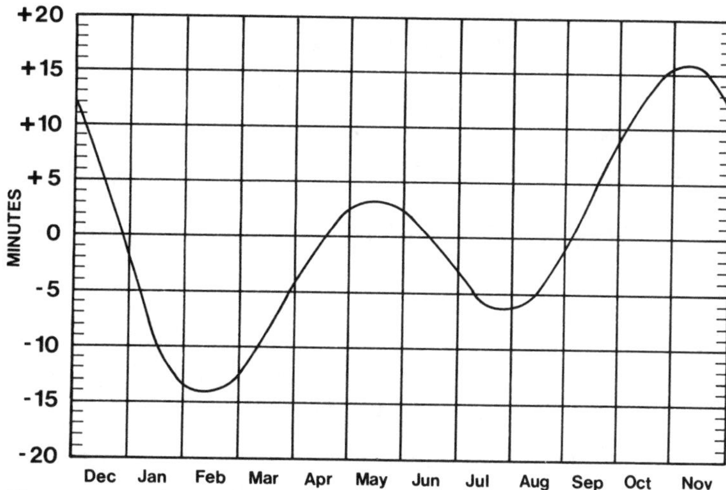

Figure 3D–11: Equation of Time Chart

Note that when the latitude of the site is east of the standard meridian, the value will be positive, resulting in the addition of time to standard time; if west of standard meridian, the value will be negative, and the effect will be to subtract time.

Example

Find the solar hour angle for a position in Flagstaff, Arizona, on October 1 at 4:30 P.M.

Longitude of Flagstaff, Airzona: 111° 40′, round off to 112°

Equation of time for October 1: +9 min.

Standard meridian for mountain time zone: 105°

Daylight savings time: not applicable since Arizona does not use daylight savings time

Solar time = 4:30 + 4(105 − 112) + (+9)
= 4:30 − :28 + :09
= 4:11 P.M.

Minutes from solar noon = 4(60) + 11 = 251 min.

Hours from solar noon = 4 + 11/60 = 4.183 hr.

Solar hour angle, H = 0.25 × 251 = 62.75

or

H = 15 × 4.183 = 62.75

Calculating solar altitude and azimuth:

$$\sin S_{al} = [(\sin L)(\sin D)] + [(\cos L)(\cos D)(\cos H)]$$
$$\sin S_{az} = (\cos D)(\sin H)/\cos S_{al}$$

where:

S_{al} = solar altitude
S_{az} = solar azimuth
L = latitude of site
D = solar declination
H = solar hour angle

Example

Find the solar altitude and azimuth of the same site in Phoenix at the same time as in the previous example.

Latitude of Phoenix: 33.4° (from Table 3C–3)

Declination of October 1: −2.83 (from Table 3D–10)

$$\begin{aligned}\sin S_{al} &= [(\sin 33.4)(\sin -2.83)] + [(\cos 33.4)(\cos -2.83)(\cos 62.74)] \\ &= [-0.03] + [0.38] \\ S_{al} &= \arcsin 0.35 \\ &= 20.5°\end{aligned}$$

$$\begin{aligned}\sin S_{az} &= (\cos -2.83)(\sin 62.75)/\cos 20.5 \\ S_{az} &= \arcsin 0.95 \\ &= 71.4°\end{aligned}$$

SHADING DEVICES

The amount of window shaded from an overhang (or the required overhang for a required amount of shading) can be calculated from the following formula.

FORMULA: $h = D_{ov} \times \sec (S_{az} - W_{az}) \times \tan S_{al}$

where:

h = height of the shadow below the overhang
D_{ov} = depth of window overhang from window surface
S_{az} = solar azimuth
W_{az} = azimuth from south to line perpendicular to window surface
S_{al} = solar altitude
(See Figure 3D–12.)

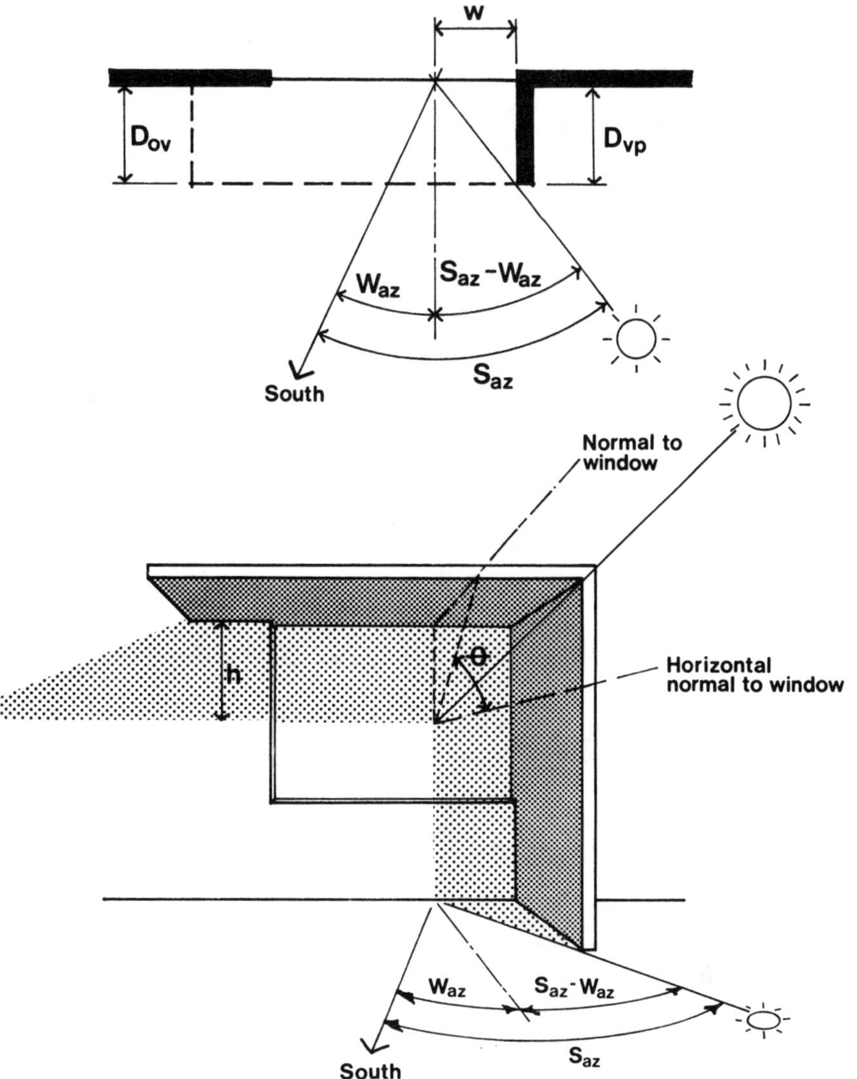

Figure 3D–12: Calculating Shading from Overhangs

Note that if W_{az} is on the opposite side of zero degree azimuth from the sun, its value should be negative, so the difference is the total angle between the sun and a line perpendicular to the window.

Since the secant of an angle is the inverse of the cosine, the formula can also be written as follows.

FORMULA:

$$h = \frac{D_{ov} \times \tan S_{al}}{\cos (S_{az} - W_{az})}$$

The amount of window shaded from a vertical projection (or the required projection for a required amount of shading) can be calculated from the following formula.

FORMULA:

$$w = D_{vp} \times \tan (S_{az} - W_{az})$$

where:

w = width of the shadow from the side projection
D_{vp} = depth of the vertical projection
(See Figure 3D–12.)

The angle of sunlight perpendicular to the window (profile angle) can be calculated from the following formula.

FORMULA:

$$\theta = \arctan \frac{\tan S_{al}}{\cos (S_{az} - W_{az})}$$

where:

θ = angle of shadow cast from overhang measured from horizontal
S_{al} = solar altitude
S_{az} = solar azimuth
W_{az} = azimuth from south of line perpendicular to window surface

If h has been calculated, then: $\theta = \arctan (h/D_{ov})$

SOURCES FOR MORE INFORMATION

Bennett, Robert. *Sun Angles for Design.* Bala Cynwyd, PA: Robert Bennett, 1978.

Evans, Benjamin H. *Daylighting in Architecture.* New York: Architectural Record Books, 1981.

Illuminating Engineering Society. *IES Lighting Handbook,* 5th ed. New York: Illuminating Engineering Society of North America, 1981.

Libbey Owens Ford Company. *How to Predict Interior Daylight Illumination.* Toledo, OH: Libbey Owens Ford Company, 1976. (Includes the "Sun Angle Calculator.")

Moore, Fuller. *Concepts and Practice of Architectural Daylighting.* New York: Van Nostrand Reinhold Company, 1985.

Robbins, Claude. *Daylighting, Design and Analysis.* New York: Van Nostrand Reinhold Company, 1986.

PART 3E

Climate

CLIMATIC DATA FOR SELECTED CITIES IN THE U.S.

Basic climatic data is needed for a wide variety of applications. Values for temperatures, rainfall, snow, and wind are required for initial site analysis. Other information is useful for heat loss calculations, passive solar design, and daylighting. The following table summarizes most of the climate information you need on a day-to-day basis for a wide spectrum of locations across the United States. Refer to Table 3.12 for additional data.

Table 3E-1
CLIMATIC DATA FOR SELECTED CITIES IN THE UNITED STATES

STATION NO. 13876

LATITUDE: 33° 34′ N
LONGITUDE: 86° 45′ W
ELEVATION: 192 meters (629.8 feet)

Birmingham, Alabama

	Maximum Daily Temp. °F	Minimum Daily Temp. °F	Average Monthly Temp. °F	Heating Degree Days Base 65 °F	Cooling Degree Days Base 65 °F	Total Global Radiation Btu/ft²	Total Global Radiation Langleys
Jan	54.3	34.1	44.2	653	9	706.6	191.7
Feb	57.7	36.1	46.9	517	9	967.1	262.3
Mar	64.8	41.8	53.3	389	25	1296.1	351.6
Apr	75.3	51.0	63.2	115	61	1673.5	454.0
May	82.5	58.4	70.5	20	189	1856.9	503.7
June	88.4	66.4	77.4	0	371	1918.5	520.4
July	90.3	69.5	79.9	0	461	1809.8	490.9
Aug	89.7	68.7	79.2	0	439	1723.8	467.6
Sept	84.7	63.0	73.9	5	272	1454.6	394.6
Oct	75.8	50.8	63.3	137	83	1210.8	328.4
Nov	64.0	40.1	52.1	391	0	857.9	232.7
Dec	55.5	34.9	45.2	614	0	661.4	179.4
Ann	73.6	51.2	62.4	2844	1928	1344.7	364.8

STATION NO. 13894

LATITUDE: 30° 41′ N
LONGITUDE: 88° 15′ W
ELEVATION: 67 meters (219.8 feet)

Mobile, Alabama

	Maximum Daily Temp. °F	Minimum Daily Temp. °F	Average Monthly Temp. °F	Heating Degree Days Base 65 °F	Cooling Degree Days Base 65 °F	Total Global Radiation Btu/ft²	Total Global Radiation Langleys
Jan	61.1	41.3	51.2	450	22	828.2	224.6
Feb	64.1	43.9	54.0	337	29	1099.6	298.3
Mar	69.5	49.2	59.4	220	47	1407.5	381.8
Apr	78.0	57.7	67.9	40	126	1721.7	467.0
May	85.0	64.5	74.8	0	302	1872.1	507.8
June	89.8	70.7	80.3	0	459	1868.5	506.8
July	90.5	72.6	81.6	0	515	1715.3	465.3
Aug	90.6	72.3	81.5	0	511	1641.5	445.3
Sept	86.5	68.4	77.5	0	374	1449.4	393.1
Oct	79.7	58.0	68.9	38	158	1298.7	352.3
Nov	69.5	47.5	58.5	211	14	955.1	259.1
Dec	63.0	42.8	52.9	383	9	759.2	205.9
Ann	77.3	57.4	67.4	1683	2576	1384.7	375.6

STATION NO. 13895

LATITUDE: 32° 18′ N
LONGITUDE: 86° 24′ W
ELEVATION: 62 meters (203.4 feet)

Montgomery, Alabama

	Maximum Daily Temp. °F	Minimum Daily Temp. °F	Average Monthly Temp. °F	Heating Degree Days Base 65 °F	Cooling Degree Days Base 65 °F	Total Global Radiation Btu/ft²	Total Global Radiation Langleys
Jan	57.9	37.1	47.5	554	13	751.7	203.9
Feb	61.4	39.7	50.6	418	14	1013.0	274.8
Mar	67.7	45.2	56.5	299	34	1340.6	363.6
Apr	76.8	53.6	65.2	76	81	1728.9	469.0
May	83.6	61.2	72.4	7	236	1897.4	514.7
June	89.2	68.6	78.9	0	416	1972.3	535.0
July	90.5	71.5	81.0	0	495	1841.0	499.4
Aug	90.7	70.7	80.7	0	486	1745.7	473.5
Sept	86.5	65.5	76.0	0	329	1467.7	398.1
Oct	78.0	53.5	65.8	92	117	1261.6	342.2
Nov	67.2	42.7	55.0	306	5	915.4	248.3
Dec	59.3	37.7	48.5	511	0	719.4	195.1
Ann	75.7	53.9	64.8	2268	2237	1387.9	376.5

STATION NO. 27502

Barrow, Alaska

LATITUDE: 71° 18′ N
LONGITUDE: 156° 47′ W
ELEVATION: 4 meters (13.1 feet)

	Maximum Daily Temp. °F	Minimum Daily Temp. °F	Average Monthly Temp. °F	Heating Degree Days Base 65 °F	Cooling Degree Days Base 65 °F	Total Global Radiation Btu/ft²	Total Global Radiation Langleys
Jan	−8.0	−21.3	−14.7	2470	0	0.0	0.0
Feb	−12.6	−24.6	−18.6	2340	0	73.8	20.0
Mar	−8.6	−21.8	−15.2	2486	0	490.5	133.1
Apr	6.5	−8.2	−0.9	1976	0	1050.2	284.9
May	24.2	14.0	19.1	1422	0	1140.0	309.2
June	37.1	28.9	33.0	959	0	1527.5	414.3
July	44.3	33.0	38.7	814	0	1459.1	395.8
Aug	42.0	33.1	37.6	848	0	855.8	232.1
Sept	33.4	27.2	30.3	1040	0	414.3	112.4
Oct	20.2	10.4	15.3	1541	0	125.7	34.1
Nov	5.4	−6.4	−0.5	1964	0	3.6	1.0
Dec	−6.4	−18.1	−12.3	2396	0	0.0	0.0
Ann	14.8	3.8	9.3	20264	0	595.0	161.4

STATION NO. 26615

Bethel, Alaska

LATITUDE: 60° 47′ N
LONGITUDE: 161° 48′ W
ELEVATION: 46 meters (150.9 feet)

	Maximum Daily Temp. °F	Minimum Daily Temp. °F	Average Monthly Temp. °F	Heating Degree Days Base 65 °F	Cooling Degree Days Base 65 °F	Total Global Radiation Btu/ft²	Total Global Radiation Langleys
Jan	12.3	−2.2	5.1	1856	0	96.8	26.3
Feb	15.8	0.5	8.2	1589	0	316.7	85.9
Mar	20.3	2.5	11.4	1661	0	738.5	200.3
Apr	32.7	16.3	24.5	1215	0	1200.4	325.6
May	48.5	31.7	40.1	770	0	1453.2	394.2
June	60.2	43.0	51.6	401	0	1518.4	411.9
July	61.9	47.4	54.7	319	0	1289.7	349.8
Aug	58.5	46.0	52.3	392	0	920.0	249.6
Sept	51.8	38.2	45.0	599	0	700.7	190.1
Oct	36.1	24.3	30.2	1078	0	370.3	100.5
Nov	23.6	10.8	17.2	1433	0	135.2	36.7
Dec	11.3	−2.5	4.4	1877	0	48.7	13.2
Ann	36.1	21.3	28.7	13203	0	732.4	198.7

STATION NO. 26533

Bettles, Alaska

LATITUDE: 66° 55′ N
LONGITUDE: 151° 31′ W
ELEVATION: 205 meters (672.4 feet)

	Maximum Daily Temp. °F	Minimum Daily Temp. °F	Average Monthly Temp. °F	Heating Degree Days Base 65 °F	Cooling Degree Days Base 65 °F	Total Global Radiation Btu/ft²	Total Global Radiation Langleys
Jan	−5.3	−21.1	−13.2	2423	0	10.0	2.7
Feb	1.0	−16.5	−7.8	2038	0	172.3	46.7
Mar	12.9	−10.0	1.5	1967	0	615.6	167.0
Apr	31.7	9.2	20.5	1334	0	1228.3	333.2
May	51.6	31.7	41.7	722	0	1698.7	460.8
June	67.2	45.1	56.2	270	5	1857.2	503.8
July	68.2	47.5	57.9	230	11	1562.6	423.9
Aug	60.9	42.9	51.9	405	0	1075.1	291.6
Sept	48.2	31.7	40.0	749	0	672.2	182.3
Oct	26.6	13.3	20.0	1395	0	252.1	68.4
Nov	5.8	−8.6	−1.4	1991	0	40.3	10.9
Dec	−4.3	−20.0	−12.2	2392	0	0.0	0.0
Ann	30.4	12.1	21.3	15925	16	765.4	207.6

STATION NO. 26411

Fairbanks, Alaska

LATITUDE: 64° 49′ N
LONGITUDE: 147° 52′ W
ELEVATION: 138 meters (452.6 feet)

	Maximum Daily Temp. °F	Minimum Daily Temp. °F	Average Monthly Temp. °F	Heating Degree Days Base 65 °F	Cooling Degree Days Base 65 °F	Total Global Radiation Btu/ft²	Total Global Radiation Langleys
Jan	−2.2	−21.6	−11.9	2383	0	30.1	8.2
Feb	9.3	−14.3	−2.5	1890	0	221.4	60.1
Mar	23.3	−4.3	9.5	1719	0	674.2	182.9
Apr	40.4	17.3	28.9	1082	0	1193.9	323.8
May	58.8	35.7	47.3	549	0	1603.6	435.0
June	70.7	47.2	59.0	211	31	1751.9	475.2
July	71.8	49.6	60.7	148	14	1542.5	418.4
Aug	65.8	44.9	55.4	302	5	1118.0	303.3
Sept	54.4	34.4	44.4	617	0	709.4	192.4
Oct	33.5	16.9	25.2	1233	0	292.6	79.4
Nov	11.7	−6.2	2.8	1865	0	74.1	20.1
Dec	−1.5	−19.3	−10.4	2336	0	2.5	0.7
Ann	36.3	15.0	25.7	14342	50	767.8	208.3

STATION NO. 25507

Homer, Alaska

LATITUDE: 59° 38′ N
LONGITUDE: 151° 30′ W
ELEVATION: 22 meters (72.2 feet)

	Maximum Daily Temp. °F	Minimum Daily Temp. °F	Average Monthly Temp. °F	Heating Degree Days Base 65 °F	Cooling Degree Days Base 65 °F	Total Global Radiation Btu/ft²	Total Global Radiation Langleys
Jan	28.0	14.7	21.4	1352	0	121.6	33.0
Feb	31.8	17.9	24.9	1121	0	333.9	90.6
Mar	35.0	20.2	27.6	1157	0	759.3	206.0
Apr	42.3	27.7	35.0	900	0	1248.3	338.6
May	50.3	34.2	42.3	704	0	1582.6	429.3
June	56.7	40.7	48.7	488	0	1750.6	474.8
July	60.1	44.5	52.3	392	0	1598.0	433.5
Aug	60.1	44.6	52.4	391	0	1188.7	322.4
Sept	54.8	39.2	47.0	540	0	791.4	214.7
Oct	44.4	30.3	37.4	855	0	437.1	118.6
Nov	34.5	21.8	28.2	1103	0	175.3	47.6
Dec	27.6	15.2	21.4	1352	0	64.0	17.4
Ann	43.8	29.2	36.5	10363	0	837.6	227.2

STATION NO. 25309

Juneau, Alaska

LATITUDE: 58° 22′ N
LONGITUDE: 134° 35′ W
ELEVATION: 7 meters (23.0 feet)

	Maximum Daily Temp. °F	Minimum Daily Temp. °F	Average Monthly Temp. °F	Heating Degree Days Base 65 °F	Cooling Degree Days Base 65 °F	Total Global Radiation Btu/ft²	Total Global Radiation Langleys
Jan	29.1	17.8	23.5	1287	0	116.3	31.5
Feb	33.9	22.1	28.0	1035	0	282.4	76.6
Mar	38.2	25.6	31.9	1026	0	610.0	165.5
Apr	46.5	31.3	38.9	783	0	1045.9	283.7
May	55.4	38.2	46.8	563	0	1291.3	350.3
June	62.0	44.4	53.2	353	0	1414.4	383.7
July	63.6	47.7	55.7	288	0	1278.4	346.8
Aug	62.3	46.2	54.3	331	0	984.5	267.0
Sept	56.1	42.3	49.2	473	0	638.8	173.3
Oct	47.2	36.4	41.8	718	0	320.4	86.9
Nov	37.3	27.6	32.5	974	0	148.6	40.3
Dec	32.0	22.5	27.3	1168	0	61.9	16.8
Ann	47.0	33.5	40.3	9005	0	682.7	185.2

STATION NO. 25501

Kodiak, Alaska

LATITUDE: 57° 45′ N
LONGITUDE: 152° 20′ W
ELEVATION: 34 meters (111.5 feet)

	Maximum Daily Temp. °F	Minimum Daily Temp. °F	Average Monthly Temp. °F	Heating Degree Days Base 65 °F	Cooling Degree Days Base 65 °F	Total Global Radiation Btu/ft²	Total Global Radiation Langleys
Jan	34.5	26.3	30.4	1073	0	149.3	40.5
Feb	35.7	27.0	31.4	940	0	355.9	96.5
Mar	36.9	27.2	32.1	1019	0	781.9	212.1
Apr	41.6	32.2	36.9	842	0	1207.8	327.6
May	47.9	38.5	43.2	675	0	1376.3	373.3
June	54.6	44.7	49.7	459	0	1529.9	415.0
July	59.1	49.1	54.1	337	0	1408.2	382.0
Aug	60.1	49.7	54.9	311	0	1164.2	315.8
Sept	54.9	45.0	50.0	450	0	794.0	215.4
Oct	45.6	35.8	40.7	752	0	489.2	132.7
Nov	39.0	30.5	34.8	905	0	206.5	56.0
Dec	34.3	25.5	29.9	1087	0	97.1	26.3
Ann	45.4	36.0	40.7	8860	0	796.7	216.1

STATION NO. 26510

McGrath, Alaska

LATITUDE: 62° 58′ N
LONGITUDE: 155° 37′ W
ELEVATION: 103 meters (337.8 feet)

	Maximum Daily Temp. °F	Minimum Daily Temp. °F	Average Monthly Temp. °F	Heating Degree Days Base 65 °F	Cooling Degree Days Base 65 °F	Total Global Radiation Btu/ft²	Total Global Radiation Langleys
Jan	0.5	−18.2	−8.9	2290	0	57.9	15.7
Feb	10.9	−11.2	−0.2	1825	0	258.5	70.1
Mar	22.0	−4.3	8.9	1739	0	692.7	187.9
Apr	37.7	15.3	26.5	1154	0	1187.8	322.2
May	54.5	33.6	44.1	648	0	1488.2	403.7
June	66.1	45.2	55.7	284	5	1586.7	430.4
July	67.7	48.7	58.2	218	7	1379.7	374.2
Aug	62.1	44.9	53.5	356	0	1019.1	276.4
Sept	52.3	35.2	43.8	635	0	695.0	188.5
Oct	32.4	18.2	25.3	1229	0	317.0	86.0
Nov	12.9	−2.9	5.0	1800	0	100.2	27.2
Dec	−0.8	−17.6	−9.2	2299	0	19.5	5.3
Ann	34.8	15.6	25.2	14486	13	733.5	199.0

STATION NO. 26617

Nome, Alaska

LATITUDE: 64° 30′ N
LONGITUDE: 165° 26′ W
ELEVATION: 7 meters (23.0 feet)

	Maximum Daily Temp. °F	Minimum Daily Temp. °F	Average Monthly Temp. °F	Heating Degree Days Base 65 °F	Cooling Degree Days Base 65 °F	Total Global Radiation Btu/ft²	Total Global Radiation Langleys
Jan	13.5	−1.6	6.0	1829	0	29.8	8.1
Feb	13.7	−3.3	5.2	1674	0	223.9	60.7
Mar	16.6	−1.9	7.4	1786	0	631.2	171.2
Apr	27.0	10.8	18.9	1382	0	1185.7	321.6
May	41.4	28.1	34.8	936	0	1573.0	426.7
June	52.2	38.8	45.5	585	0	1753.3	475.6
July	55.8	44.4	50.1	461	0	1414.1	383.6
Aug	54.6	43.7	49.2	490	0	993.0	269.3
Sept	48.2	35.9	42.1	686	0	673.3	182.6
Oct	34.4	22.6	28.5	1130	0	305.8	83.0
Nov	22.1	9.1	15.6	1481	0	64.9	17.6
Dec	11.7	−3.0	4.4	1877	0	2.9	0.8
Ann	32.6	18.6	25.6	14324	0	737.6	200.1

SOLMET STATION NO. 23183

LATITUDE: 33° 26′ N
LONGITUDE: 112° 1′ W
ELEVATION: 339 meters (1111.9 feet)

Phoenix, Arizona

	Maximum Daily Temp. °F	Minimum Daily Temp. °F	Average Monthly Temp. °F	Heating Degree Days Base 65 °F	Cooling Degree Days Base 65 °F	Total Global Radiation Btu/ft²	Total Global Radiation Langleys
Jan	64.8	37.6	51.2	427	0	1021.3	277.0
Feb	69.3	40.8	55.1	292	13	1374.1	372.7
Mar	74.5	44.8	59.7	184	20	1814.1	492.1
Apr	83.6	51.8	67.7	59	140	2354.8	638.8
May	92.9	59.6	76.3	0	355	2676.5	726.0
June	101.5	67.7	84.6	0	587	2739.2	743.0
July	104.8	77.5	91.2	0	812	2486.5	674.5
Aug	102.2	76.0	89.1	0	747	2292.6	621.9
Sept	98.4	69.1	83.8	0	563	2015.4	546.7
Oct	87.6	56.8	72.2	16	239	1576.5	427.6
Nov	74.7	44.8	59.8	182	25	1150.5	312.1
Dec	66.4	38.5	52.5	387	0	932.0	252.8
Ann	85.1	55.4	70.3	1552	3506	1869.4	507.1

STATION NO. 23160

LATITUDE: 32° 7′ N
LONGITUDE: 110° 56′ W
ELEVATION: 779 meters (2555.1 feet)

Tucson, Arizona

	Maximum Daily Temp. °F	Minimum Daily Temp. °F	Average Monthly Temp. °F	Heating Degree Days Base 65 °F	Cooling Degree Days Base 65 °F	Total Global Radiation Btu/ft²	Total Global Radiation Langleys
Jan	63.5	38.2	50.9	441	0	1099.0	298.1
Feb	67.0	39.9	53.5	333	11	1432.0	388.4
Mar	71.5	43.6	57.6	243	13	1864.3	505.7
Apr	80.7	50.3	65.5	81	95	2363.0	641.0
May	89.6	57.5	73.6	0	272	2671.4	724.6
June	97.9	66.2	82.1	0	513	2729.6	740.4
July	98.3	74.2	86.3	0	659	2341.1	635.0
Aug	95.3	72.3	83.8	0	581	2182.9	592.1
Sept	93.1	67.1	80.1	0	452	1978.8	536.7
Oct	83.8	56.4	70.1	29	185	1601.9	434.5
Nov	72.2	44.8	58.5	220	25	1208.4	327.8
Dec	64.8	39.1	52.0	401	0	995.8	270.1
Ann	81.5	54.1	67.8	1751	2813	1872.3	507.9

STATION NO. 23194

LATITUDE: 35° 1′ N
LONGITUDE: 110° 44′ W
ELEVATION: 1488 meters (4880.6 feet)

Winslow, Arizona

	Maximum Daily Temp. °F	Minimum Daily Temp. °F	Average Monthly Temp. °F	Heating Degree Days Base 65 °F	Cooling Degree Days Base 65 °F	Total Global Radiation Btu/ft²	Total Global Radiation Langleys
Jan	45.6	19.6	32.6	1003	0	984.6	267.1
Feb	53.3	24.8	39.1	724	0	1327.0	359.9
Mar	60.2	29.4	44.8	625	0	1780.0	482.8
Apr	70.1	37.3	53.7	347	9	2283.3	619.3
May	79.9	45.5	62.7	122	50	2594.6	703.8
June	89.8	53.7	71.8	13	218	2711.6	735.5
July	93.6	62.9	78.3	0	410	2346.9	636.6
Aug	90.6	61.5	76.1	0	344	2140.6	580.6
Sept	85.4	53.5	69.5	18	153	1927.8	522.9
Oct	73.2	41.3	57.3	252	13	1512.8	410.4
Nov	58.2	28.2	43.2	653	0	1119.3	303.6
Dec	46.7	20.9	33.8	967	0	894.4	242.6
Ann	70.6	39.9	55.3	4732	1202	1801.9	488.8

STATION NO. 23195

Yuma, Arizona

LATITUDE: 32° 40′ N
LONGITUDE: 114° 36′ W
ELEVATION: 63 meters (206.6 feet)

	Maximum Daily Temp. °F	Minimum Daily Temp. °F	Average Monthly Temp. °F	Heating Degree Days Base 65 °F	Cooling Degree Days Base 65 °F	Total Global Radiation Btu/ft²	Total Global Radiation Langleys
Jan	67.4	43.3	55.4	308	9	1096.1	297.3
Feb	72.6	46.1	59.4	191	36	1443.2	391.5
Mar	77.6	50.2	63.9	95	63	1919.2	520.6
Apr	85.6	56.7	71.2	23	209	2412.8	654.5
May	93.4	63.9	78.7	0	425	2728.3	740.0
June	100.8	70.8	85.8	0	623	2813.9	763.3
July	106.0	81.4	93.7	0	889	2453.4	665.5
Aug	104.4	81.2	92.8	0	860	2329.3	631.8
Sept	100.3	73.9	87.1	0	662	2051.0	556.3
Oct	89.8	62.0	75.9	4	342	1622.8	440.2
Nov	76.5	50.5	63.5	108	63	1214.7	329.5
Dec	68.2	44.4	56.3	275	5	1000.1	271.3
Ann	86.9	60.4	73.7	1010	4194	1923.7	521.8

STATION NO. 13964

Fort Smith, Arkansas

LATITUDE: 35° 20′ N
LONGITUDE: 94° 22′ W
ELEVATION: 141 meters (462.5 feet)

	Maximum Daily Temp. °F	Minimum Daily Temp. °F	Average Monthly Temp. °F	Heating Degree Days Base 65 °F	Cooling Degree Days Base 65 °F	Total Global Radiation Btu/ft²	Total Global Radiation Langleys
Jan	49.9	28.0	39.0	805	0	743.7	201.7
Feb	54.6	32.0	43.3	607	0	998.9	271.0
Mar	62.1	38.5	50.3	470	14	1311.7	355.8
Apr	74.2	50.2	62.2	131	47	1615.9	438.3
May	81.3	58.8	70.1	16	175	1912.1	518.7
June	89.0	67.0	78.0	0	389	2089.4	566.8
July	93.8	70.5	82.2	0	533	2065.3	560.2
Aug	93.5	69.3	81.4	0	508	1877.4	509.3
Sept	86.3	61.7	74.0	0	274	1501.5	407.3
Oct	76.5	49.9	63.2	135	77	1200.7	325.7
Nov	62.7	38.0	50.4	437	0	851.4	231.0
Dec	52.2	30.8	41.5	729	0	681.6	184.9
Ann	73.0	49.6	61.3	3335	2021	1404.1	380.9

STATION NO. 13963

Little Rock, Arkansas

LATITUDE: 34° 44′ N
LONGITUDE: 92° 14′ W
ELEVATION: 81 meters (265.7 feet)

	Maximum Daily Temp. °F	Minimum Daily Temp. °F	Average Monthly Temp. °F	Heating Degree Days Base 65 °F	Cooling Degree Days Base 65 °F	Total Global Radiation Btu/ft²	Total Global Radiation Langleys
Jan	50.1	28.9	39.5	790	0	731.3	198.4
Feb	53.8	31.9	42.9	617	0	1002.8	272.0
Mar	61.8	38.7	50.3	470	13	1312.7	356.1
Apr	73.5	49.9	61.7	139	40	1610.7	436.9
May	81.4	58.1	69.8	20	167	1929.3	523.3
June	89.3	66.8	78.1	0	392	2106.5	571.4
July	92.6	70.1	81.4	0	508	2032.3	551.3
Aug	92.6	68.6	80.6	0	482	1860.5	504.7
Sept	85.8	60.8	73.3	4	254	1518.0	411.8
Oct	76.0	48.7	62.4	142	63	1228.3	333.2
Nov	62.4	38.1	50.3	441	0	847.2	229.8
Dec	52.1	31.1	41.6	724	0	673.7	182.7
Ann	72.6	49.3	61.0	3353	1924	1404.4	381.0

STATION NO. 23155

LATITUDE: 35° 25′ N
LONGITUDE: 119° 3′ W
ELEVATION: 150 meters (492.0 feet)

Bakersfield, California

	Maximum Daily Temp. °F	Minimum Daily Temp. °F	Average Monthly Temp. °F	Heating Degree Days Base 65 °F	Cooling Degree Days Base 65 °F	Total Global Radiation Btu/ft²	Total Global Radiation Langleys
Jan	57.5	37.4	47.5	542	0	766.4	207.9
Feb	63.3	41.4	52.4	353	0	1101.9	298.9
Mar	68.6	44.5	56.6	265	5	1594.8	432.6
Apr	75.5	49.9	62.7	139	70	2094.7	568.2
May	83.6	56.0	69.8	22	171	2509.1	680.6
June	91.5	62.3	76.9	0	362	2749.3	745.8
July	99.1	68.7	83.9	0	585	2683.5	727.9
Aug	96.5	66.6	81.6	0	515	2420.7	656.6
Sept	91.1	62.1	76.6	0	347	1991.8	540.3
Oct	80.5	53.3	66.9	54	113	1458.3	395.6
Nov	67.8	44.2	56.0	275	5	942.3	255.6
Dec	57.4	38.4	47.9	529	0	677.4	183.8
Ann	77.7	52.1	64.9	2183	2178	1749.2	474.5

STATION NO. 23161

LATITUDE: 34° 52′ N
LONGITUDE: 116° 47′ W
ELEVATION: 588 meters (1928.6 feet)

Daggett, California

	Maximum Daily Temp. °F	Minimum Daily Temp. °F	Average Monthly Temp. °F	Heating Degree Days Base 65 °F	Cooling Degree Days Base 65 °F	Total Global Radiation Btu/ft²	Total Global Radiation Langleys
Jan	0.0 ND	0.0 ND	47.3	549	0	958.2	259.9
Feb	0.0 ND	0.0 ND	52.0	371	5	1280.7	347.4
Mar	0.0 ND	0.0 ND	56.7	270	13	1772.3	480.7
Apr	0.0 ND	0.0 ND	64.3	117	95	2274.1	616.9
May	0.0 ND	0.0 ND	72.3	13	239	2591.2	702.9
June	0.0 ND	0.0 ND	80.1	0	452	2766.3	750.3
July	0.0 ND	0.0 ND	87.3	0	689	2603.4	706.2
Aug	0.0 ND	0.0 ND	85.5	0	635	2382.6	646.3
Sept	0.0 ND	0.0 ND	79.2	0	425	2007.9	544.7
Oct	0.0 ND	0.0 ND	68.1	56	153	1515.6	411.1
Nov	0.0 ND	0.0 ND	55.5	295	11	1085.1	294.3
Dec	0.0 ND	0.0 ND	48.0	526	0	876.0	237.6
Ann	0.0 ND	0.0 ND	66.4	2201	2729	1842.8	499.9

SOLMET STATION NO. 93193

LATITUDE: 36° 46′ N
LONGITUDE: 119° 43′ W
ELEVATION: 100 meters (328.0 feet)

Fresno, California

	Maximum Daily Temp. °F	Minimum Daily Temp. °F	Average Monthly Temp. °F	Heating Degree Days Base 65 °F	Cooling Degree Days Base 65 °F	Total Global Radiation Btu/ft²	Total Global Radiation Langleys
Jan	54.8	35.8	45.3	610	0	656.7	178.1
Feb	60.8	39.0	49.9	423	0	1012.3	274.6
Mar	66.6	41.2	53.9	344	0	1565.8	424.7
Apr	74.3	46.2	60.3	182	40	2092.6	567.6
May	82.9	51.9	67.4	50	124	2483.8	673.7
June	90.3	57.5	73.9	9	275	2732.8	741.3
July	98.2	62.9	80.6	0	482	2685.1	728.3
Aug	96.0	60.6	78.3	0	410	2423.3	657.3
Sept	91.0	56.5	73.8	0	266	1985.1	538.5
Oct	79.8	48.6	64.2	90	65	1429.2	387.7
Nov	66.1	40.8	53.5	344	0	888.5	241.0
Dec	54.6	36.9	45.8	594	0	574.2	155.7
Ann	76.3	48.2	62.3	2650	1670	1710.8	464.1

STATION NO. 23129

LATITUDE: 33° 49′ N
LONGITUDE: 118° 9′ W
ELEVATION: 17 meters (55.8 feet)

Long Beach, California

	Maximum Daily Temp. °F	Minimum Daily Temp. °F	Average Monthly Temp. °F	Heating Degree Days Base 65 °F	Cooling Degree Days Base 65 °F	Total Global Radiation Btu/ft²	Total Global Radiation Langleys
Jan	65.2	43.2	54.2	338	0	927.7	251.6
Feb	66.2	44.8	55.5	272	5	1215.0	329.6
Mar	67.7	46.7	57.2	247	0	1609.9	436.7
Apr	70.5	50.6	60.6	148	14	1937.7	525.6
May	73.8	54.3	64.1	70	41	2064.5	560.0
June	76.8	57.8	67.3	22	92	2139.9	580.5
July	82.8	61.6	72.2	0	225	2299.9	623.8
Aug	84.0	62.5	73.3	0	259	2099.8	569.6
Sept	83.3	60.2	71.8	5	211	1701.0	461.4
Oct	78.3	55.5	66.9	47	106	1326.4	359.8
Nov	72.7	48.4	60.6	155	22	1003.5	272.2
Dec	66.9	44.1	55.5	293	0	846.8	229.7
Ann	74.0	52.5	63.3	1606	985	1597.7	433.4

STATION NO. 23174

LATITUDE: 33° 56′ N
LONGITUDE: 118° 24′ W
ELEVATION: 32 meters (105.0 feet)

Los Angeles, California

	Maximum Daily Temp. °F	Minimum Daily Temp. °F	Average Monthly Temp. °F	Heating Degree Days Base 65 °F	Cooling Degree Days Base 65 °F	Total Global Radiation Btu/ft²	Total Global Radiation Langleys
Jan	63.5	45.4	54.5	329	4	926.1	251.2
Feb	64.1	47.0	55.6	270	5	1214.0	329.3
Mar	64.3	48.6	56.5	266	0	1618.7	439.1
Apr	65.9	51.7	58.8	194	9	1950.9	529.2
May	68.4	55.3	61.9	113	16	2059.6	558.7
June	70.3	58.6	64.5	70	56	2119.1	574.8
July	74.8	62.1	68.5	18	126	2307.5	625.9
Aug	75.8	63.2	69.5	14	153	2079.5	564.1
Sept	75.7	61.6	68.7	22	133	1681.4	456.1
Oct	72.9	57.5	65.2	76	83	1317.0	357.2
Nov	69.6	51.3	60.5	157	22	1003.9	272.3
Dec	66.5	47.3	56.9	279	0	848.5	230.2
Ann	69.2	54.1	61.7	1818	614	1593.8	432.3

STATION NO. 24215

LATITUDE: 41° 19′ N
LONGITUDE: 122° 19′ W
ELEVATION: 1093 meters (3585.0 feet)

Mount Shasta, California

	Maximum Daily Temp. °F	Minimum Daily Temp. °F	Average Monthly Temp. °F	Heating Degree Days Base 65 °F	Cooling Degree Days Base 65 °F	Total Global Radiation Btu/ft²	Total Global Radiation Langleys
Jan	41.8	25.4	33.6	972	0	560.8	152.1
Feb	47.3	28.3	37.8	761	0	857.4	232.6
Mar	51.0	29.8	40.4	761	0	1250.0	339.1
Apr	58.5	34.0	46.3	560	0	1756.0	476.3
May	66.6	40.0	53.3	371	7	2186.0	593.0
June	74.0	46.0	60.0	176	27	2436.1	660.8
July	84.9	50.6	67.8	36	122	2577.5	699.2
Aug	83.4	48.6	66.0	63	94	2213.0	600.3
Sept	77.8	44.5	61.2	144	31	1735.3	470.7
Oct	64.9	37.9	51.4	421	0	1155.1	313.3
Nov	51.6	31.7	41.7	698	0	659.3	178.8
Dec	43.7	27.3	35.5	914	0	504.9	137.0
Ann	62.1	37.0	49.6	5890	284	1491.0	404.4

STATION NO. 23230

Oakland, California

LATITUDE: 37° 44′ N
LONGITUDE: 122° 12′ W
ELEVATION: 2 meters (6.6 feet)

	Maximum Daily Temp. °F	Minimum Daily Temp. °F	Average Monthly Temp. °F	Heating Degree Days Base 65 °F	Cooling Degree Days Base 65 °F	Total Global Radiation Btu/ft²	Total Global Radiation Langleys
Jan	54.5	42.7	48.6	508	0	707.8	192.0
Feb	58.0	45.7	51.9	365	0	1017.5	276.0
Mar	60.2	47.2	53.7	349	0	1456.3	395.0
Apr	62.8	49.4	56.1	270	0	1922.1	521.4
May	65.4	52.4	58.9	193	0	2211.3	599.8
June	68.5	55.2	61.9	113	20	2350.0	637.4
July	69.7	56.4	63.1	79	20	2322.5	630.0
Aug	70.2	56.8	63.5	74	27	2052.6	556.8
Sept	72.3	56.6	64.5	58	43	1701.1	461.4
Oct	68.7	53.4	61.1	135	13	1212.0	328.8
Nov	62.0	48.5	55.3	290	0	822.1	223.0
Dec	55.5	44.2	49.9	468	0	647.0	175.5
Ann	64.0	50.7	57.4	2909	128	1535.2	416.4

STATION NO. 24216

Red Bluff, California

LATITUDE: 40° 9′ N
LONGITUDE: 122° 15′ W
ELEVATION: 108 meters (354.2 feet)

	Maximum Daily Temp. °F	Minimum Daily Temp. °F	Average Monthly Temp. °F	Heating Degree Days Base 65 °F	Cooling Degree Days Base 65 °F	Total Global Radiation Btu/ft²	Total Global Radiation Langleys
Jan	53.6	36.7	45.2	614	0	570.2	154.7
Feb	59.5	40.4	50.0	419	0	892.5	242.1
Mar	63.8	42.5	53.2	365	0	1354.2	367.3
Apr	71.6	47.3	59.5	218	52	1910.0	518.1
May	80.6	54.2	67.4	63	139	2374.9	644.2
June	89.3	61.7	75.5	7	322	2599.8	705.2
July	98.0	66.6	82.3	0	535	2671.6	724.7
Aug	95.7	64.1	79.9	0	461	2310.7	626.8
Sept	90.6	60.0	75.3	0	308	1845.2	500.5
Oct	78.3	51.7	65.0	81	81	1227.5	333.0
Nov	64.0	43.3	53.7	338	0	706.4	191.6
Dec	54.7	38.1	46.4	576	0	510.7	138.5
Ann	75.0	50.6	62.8	2687	1903	1581.1	428.9

STATION NO. 23232

Sacramento, California

LATITUDE: 38° 31′ N
LONGITUDE: 121° 30′ W
ELEVATION: 8 meters (26.2 feet)

	Maximum Daily Temp. °F	Minimum Daily Temp. °F	Average Monthly Temp. °F	Heating Degree Days Base 65 °F	Cooling Degree Days Base 65 °F	Total Global Radiation Btu/ft²	Total Global Radiation Langleys
Jan	53.0	37.1	45.1	616	0	596.9	161.9
Feb	59.1	40.4	49.8	425	0	939.4	254.8
Mar	64.1	41.9	53.0	371	0	1458.4	395.6
Apr	71.3	45.3	58.3	227	25	2003.6	543.5
May	78.8	49.8	64.3	119	97	2434.8	660.4
June	86.4	54.6	70.5	20	184	2683.8	728.0
July	92.9	57.5	75.2	0	315	2688.0	729.1
Aug	91.3	56.9	74.1	0	284	2368.3	642.4
Sept	87.7	55.3	71.5	4	200	1906.7	517.2
Oct	77.1	49.5	63.3	101	47	1314.9	356.7
Nov	63.6	42.4	53.0	360	0	781.9	212.1
Dec	53.3	38.3	45.8	594	0	538.4	146.0
Ann	73.2	47.4	60.3	2842	1157	1642.9	445.6

STATION NO. 23188

LATITUDE: 32° 44′ N
LONGITUDE: 117° 10′ W
ELEVATION: 9 meters (29.5 feet)

San Diego, California

	Maximum Daily Temp. °F	Minimum Daily Temp. °F	Average Monthly Temp. °F	Heating Degree Days Base 65 °F	Cooling Degree Days Base 65 °F	Total Global Radiation Btu/ft²	Total Global Radiation Langleys
Jan	64.6	45.8	55.2	313	9	975.7	264.7
Feb	65.6	47.8	56.7	236	0	1266.3	343.5
Mar	66.0	50.1	58.0	218	0	1631.6	442.6
Apr	67.6	53.8	60.7	144	14	1936.7	525.3
May	69.4	57.2	63.3	77	25	2002.8	543.3
June	71.1	59.9	65.5	50	67	2062.2	559.4
July	75.3	63.9	69.6	5	148	2186.5	593.1
Aug	77.3	65.4	71.4	0	200	2057.3	558.0
Sept	76.5	63.2	69.9	14	162	1717.4	465.9
Oct	73.8	58.4	66.1	41	76	1373.3	372.5
Nov	70.1	51.5	60.8	139	13	1062.7	288.2
Dec	66.1	47.2	56.7	256	0	903.8	245.2
Ann	70.3	55.4	62.9	1507	722	1598.0	433.5

STATION NO. 23234

LATITUDE: 37° 37′ N
LONGITUDE: 122° 23′ W
ELEVATION: 5 meters (16.4 feet)

San Francisco, California

	Maximum Daily Temp. °F	Minimum Daily Temp. °F	Average Monthly Temp. °F	Heating Degree Days Base 65 °F	Cooling Degree Days Base 65 °F	Total Global Radiation Btu/ft²	Total Global Radiation Langleys
Jan	55.3	41.2	48.3	517	0	707.6	191.9
Feb	58.6	43.8	51.2	385	0	1009.3	273.8
Mar	61.0	44.9	53.0	371	0	1455.1	394.7
Apr	63.5	47.0	55.3	290	0	1920.0	520.8
May	66.6	49.9	58.3	209	0	2225.6	603.7
June	70.2	53.0	61.6	119	18	2376.9	644.7
July	70.9	54.0	62.5	92	14	2391.6	648.7
Aug	71.6	54.3	63.0	83	22	2116.5	574.1
Sept	73.6	54.5	64.1	65	38	1742.0	472.5
Oct	70.3	51.6	61.0	137	13	1226.1	332.6
Nov	63.3	47.2	55.3	290	0	821.4	222.8
Dec	56.3	42.9	49.7	473	0	642.4	174.2
Ann	65.1	48.7	56.9	3042	108	1552.8	421.2

STATION NO. 93037

LATITUDE: 38° 49′ N
LONGITUDE: 104° 43′ W
ELEVATION: 1881 meters (6169.7 feet)

Colorado Springs, Colorado

	Maximum Daily Temp. °F	Minimum Daily Temp. °F	Average Monthly Temp. °F	Heating Degree Days Base 65 °F	Cooling Degree Days Base 65 °F	Total Global Radiation Btu/ft²	Total Global Radiation Langleys
Jan	41.0	16.1	28.6	1127	0	890.7	241.6
Feb	43.6	18.9	31.3	943	0	1178.2	319.6
Mar	47.7	22.8	35.3	920	0	1550.0	420.4
Apr	59.2	33.1	46.2	563	0	1931.2	523.8
May	68.4	42.6	55.5	301	5	2128.7	577.4
June	78.1	51.1	64.6	103	90	2368.9	642.6
July	84.4	57.0	70.7	9	185	2211.8	600.0
Aug	82.4	55.8	69.1	13	139	2025.4	549.4
Sept	74.9	46.9	60.9	155	31	1759.1	477.2
Oct	64.2	36.8	50.5	455	5	1358.6	368.5
Nov	49.8	25.1	37.5	824	0	944.2	256.1
Dec	43.1	18.9	31.0	1053	0	781.9	212.1
Ann	61.4	35.4	48.4	6473	461	1594.1	432.4

STATION NO. 23062

Denver, Colorado

LATITUDE: 39° 45′ N
LONGITUDE: 104° 52′ W
ELEVATION: 1625 meters (5330.0 feet)

	Maximum Daily Temp. °F	Minimum Daily Temp. °F	Average Monthly Temp. °F	Heating Degree Days Base 65 °F	Cooling Degree Days Base 65 °F	Total Global Radiation Btu/ft²	Total Global Radiation Langleys
Jan	43.5	16.2	29.9	1087	0	840.1	227.9
Feb	46.2	19.4	32.8	902	0	1127.0	305.7
Mar	50.1	23.8	37.0	868	0	1530.4	415.1
Apr	61.0	33.9	47.5	524	0	1879.3	509.8
May	70.3	43.6	57.0	252	0	2134.9	579.1
June	80.1	51.9	66.0	79	110	2350.7	637.6
July	87.4	58.6	73.0	0	247	2272.6	616.5
Aug	85.8	57.4	71.6	0	207	2044.1	554.5
Sept	77.7	47.8	62.8	119	54	1726.8	468.4
Oct	66.8	37.2	52.0	407	4	1300.5	352.8
Nov	53.3	25.4	39.4	767	0	883.5	239.7
Dec	46.2	18.9	32.6	1003	0	731.8	198.5
Ann	64.0	36.2	50.1	6016	625	1568.4	425.4

STATION NO. 23063

Eagle, Colorado

LATITUDE: 39° 39′ N
LONGITUDE: 106° 55′ W
ELEVATION: 1985 meters (6510.8 feet)

	Maximum Daily Temp. °F	Minimum Daily Temp. °F	Average Monthly Temp. °F	Heating Degree Days Base 65 °F	Cooling Degree Days Base 65 °F	Total Global Radiation Btu/ft²	Total Global Radiation Langleys
Jan	0.0 ND	0.0 ND	18.0	1456	0	754.2	204.6
Feb	0.0 ND	0.0 ND	23.3	1166	0	1078.0	292.4
Mar	0.0 ND	0.0 ND	31.1	1049	0	1501.7	407.3
Apr	0.0 ND	0.0 ND	41.9	693	0	1932.6	524.2
May	0.0 ND	0.0 ND	51.3	425	0	2255.3	611.7
June	0.0 ND	0.0 ND	58.9	189	5	2508.9	680.5
July	0.0 ND	0.0 ND	65.9	41	70	2384.5	646.8
Aug	0.0 ND	0.0 ND	63.7	77	38	2083.8	565.2
Sept	0.0 ND	0.0 ND	55.6	284	0	1766.8	479.2
Oct	0.0 ND	0.0 ND	44.8	625	0	1307.2	354.6
Nov	0.0 ND	0.0 ND	30.9	1022	0	868.6	235.6
Dec	0.0 ND	0.0 ND	20.3	1386	0	690.9	187.4
Ann	0.0 ND	0.0 ND	42.2	8426	117	1594.3	432.5

STATION NO. 23066

Grand Junction, Colorado

LATITUDE: 39° 7′ N
LONGITUDE: 108° 32′ W
ELEVATION: 1475 meters (4838.0 feet)

	Maximum Daily Temp. °F	Minimum Daily Temp. °F	Average Monthly Temp. °F	Heating Degree Days Base 65 °F	Cooling Degree Days Base 65 °F	Total Global Radiation Btu/ft²	Total Global Radiation Langleys
Jan	36.7	16.5	26.6	1190	0	791.3	214.6
Feb	44.0	23.2	33.6	878	0	1119.0	303.5
Mar	52.8	29.6	41.2	738	0	1553.5	421.4
Apr	64.6	38.8	51.7	403	0	1986.4	538.8
May	75.8	48.5	62.2	131	47	2379.8	645.5
June	85.9	56.6	71.3	20	209	2598.5	704.8
July	93.1	64.2	78.7	0	425	2465.2	668.7
Aug	89.1	61.6	75.4	0	320	2182.0	591.9
Sept	81.3	53.0	67.2	59	126	1834.4	497.6
Oct	67.9	41.9	54.9	324	11	1345.0	364.8
Nov	50.9	28.6	39.8	756	0	918.1	249.0
Dec	39.4	19.6	29.5	1100	0	731.3	198.4
Ann	65.1	40.2	52.7	5603	1139	1658.7	449.9

STATION NO. 93058

Pueblo, Colorado

LATITUDE: 38° 17′ N
LONGITUDE: 104° 31′ W
ELEVATION: 1439 meters (4719.9 feet)

	Maximum Daily Temp. °F	Minimum Daily Temp. °F	Average Monthly Temp. °F	Heating Degree Days Base 65 °F	Cooling Degree Days Base 65 °F	Total Global Radiation Btu/ft²	Total Global Radiation Langleys
Jan	45.5	14.7	30.1	1082	0	894.3	242.6
Feb	49.8	19.6	34.7	848	0	1171.6	317.8
Mar	54.9	25.0	40.0	774	0	1563.8	424.2
Apr	66.4	36.9	51.7	405	5	1956.0	530.6
May	75.5	46.6	61.1	148	27	2162.5	586.6
June	85.8	55.6	70.7	27	198	2434.2	660.3
July	91.1	61.6	76.4	0	353	2311.6	627.0
Aug	88.8	60.1	74.5	0	293	2102.0	570.2
Sept	81.5	50.8	66.2	54	90	1779.5	482.7
Oct	70.7	38.2	54.5	335	9	1360.9	369.2
Nov	56.5	25.1	40.8	725	0	953.8	258.7
Dec	48.2	17.7	33.0	992	0	782.2	212.2
Ann	67.9	37.7	52.8	5393	981	1622.7	440.2

STATION NO. 14740

Hartford, Connecticut

LATITUDE: 41° 56′ N
LONGITUDE: 72° 41′ W
ELEVATION: 55 meters (180.4 feet)

	Maximum Daily Temp. °F	Minimum Daily Temp. °F	Average Monthly Temp. °F	Heating Degree Days Base 65°F	Cooling Degree Days Base 65 °F	Total Global Radiation Btu/ft²	Total Global Radiation Langleys
Jan	33.4	16.1	24.8	1246	0	477.5	129.5
Feb	35.7	17.9	26.8	1069	0	714.7	193.9
Mar	44.6	26.6	35.6	911	0	978.5	265.4
Apr	58.9	36.5	47.7	518	0	1315.0	356.7
May	70.3	46.2	58.3	225	18	1568.5	425.5
June	79.5	56.0	67.8	23	108	1685.6	457.2
July	84.1	61.2	72.7	0	238	1649.0	447.3
Aug	81.9	58.9	70.4	11	178	1421.7	385.6
Sept	74.5	51.0	62.8	104	40	1154.5	313.2
Oct	64.3	40.8	52.6	383	0	852.9	231.3
Nov	50.6	31.9	41.3	711	0	497.3	134.9
Dec	36.8	19.6	28.2	1139	0	385.1	104.4
Ann	59.6	38.6	49.1	6349	583	1058.3	287.1

STATION NO.13781

Wilmington, Delaware

LATITUDE: 39° 40′ N
LONGITUDE: 75° 36′ W
ELEVATION: 24 meters (78.7 feet)

	Maximum Daily Temp. °F	Minimum Daily Temp. °F	Average Monthly Temp. °F	Heating Degree Days Base 65 °F	Cooling Degree Days Base 65 °F	Total Global Radiation Btu/ft²	Total Global Radiation Langleys
Jan	40.2	23.8	32.0	1022	0	571.4	155.0
Feb	42.2	24.9	33.6	878	0	827.0	224.3
Mar	51.1	32.0	41.6	724	0	1149.2	311.7
Apr	63.0	41.5	52.3	380	0	1480.1	401.5
May	73.1	51.6	62.4	128	47	1710.2	463.9
June	81.6	61.1	71.4	0	194	1882.6	510.6
July	85.5	66.1	75.8	0	335	1822.8	494.4
Aug	83.9	64.3	74.1	0	281	1614.6	438.0
Sept	78.2	57.6	67.9	31	119	1317.7	357.4
Oct	67.8	46.5	57.2	254	11	983.9	266.9
Nov	55.2	36.2	45.7	578	0	644.6	174.8
Dec	43.0	26.3	34.7	938	0	488.6	132.5
Ann	63.7	44.3	54.0	4939	992	1207.7	327.6

SOLMET STATION NO. 93734

LATITUDE: 38° 57′ N
LONGITUDE: 77° 27′ W
ELEVATION: 88 meters (288.6 feet)

Washington / Sterling, District of Columbia

	Maximum Daily Temp. °F	Minimum Daily Temp. °F	Average Monthly Temp. °F	Heating Degree Days Base 65 °F	Cooling Degree Days Base 65 °F	Total Global Radiation Btu/ft²	Total Global Radiation Langleys
Jan	41.2	23.0	32.1	1019	0	572.0	155.2
Feb	43.4	24.1	33.8	873	0	815.3	221.2
Mar	52.7	30.9	41.8	718	0	1125.0	305.2
Apr	65.0	41.1	53.1	356	0	1458.9	395.7
May	74.5	50.6	62.6	130	56	1718.1	466.0
June	82.7	59.4	71.1	4	187	1900.9	515.6
July	86.4	64.1	75.3	0	319	1817.5	493.0
Aug	85.0	62.1	73.6	0	266	1617.4	438.7
Sept	78.7	55.0	66.9	41	99	1340.0	363.5
Oct	68.2	43.5	55.9	290	9	1003.8	272.3
Nov	55.6	33.7	44.7	608	0	650.9	176.6
Dec	43.3	24.7	34.0	959	0	481.1	130.5
Ann	64.7	42.7	53.7	5009	940	1208.4	327.8

STATION NO. 13889

LATITUDE: 30° 30′ N
LONGITUDE: 81° 42′ W
STATION ELEVATION: 9 meters (29.5 feet)

Jacksonville, Florida

	Maximum Daily Temp. °F	Minimum Daily Temp. °F	Average Monthly Temp. °F	Heating Degree Days Base 65 °F	Cooling Degree Days Base 65 °F	Total Global Radiation Btu/ft²	Total Global Radiation Langleys
Jan	64.6	44.5	54.6	347	23	899.9	244.1
Feb	66.9	45.7	56.3	281	38	1164.3	315.8
Mar	72.2	50.1	61.2	175	58	1521.7	412.8
Apr	79.0	57.1	68.1	23	117	1855.7	503.4
May	84.6	63.9	74.3	0	288	1956.3	530.7
June	88.3	70.0	79.2	0	425	1885.2	511.4
July	90.0	72.0	81.0	0	495	1802.0	488.8
Aug	89.7	72.3	81.0	0	495	1694.2	459.5
Sept	86.0	70.4	78.2	0	396	1442.3	391.2
Oct	79.2	61.7	70.5	18	189	1223.1	331.8
Nov	71.4	51.0	61.2	160	47	996.0	270.2
Dec	65.6	45.1	55.4	317	18	817.6	221.8
Ann	78.1	58.7	68.4	1327	2596	1438.2	390.1

SOLMET STATION NO. 12839

LATITUDE: 25° 48′ N
LONGITUDE: 80° 16′ W
STATION ELEVATION: 2 meters (6.6 feet)

Miami, Florida

	Maximum Daily Temp. °F	Minimum Daily Temp. °F	Average Monthly Temp. °F	Heating Degree Days Base 65 °F	Cooling Degree Days Base 65 °F	Total Global Radiation Btu/ft²	Total Global Radiation Langleys
Jan	75.6	58.7	67.2	52	121	1057.4	286.8
Feb	76.6	59.0	67.8	67	144	1314.0	356.4
Mar	79.5	63.0	71.3	16	211	1603.3	434.9
Apr	82.7	67.3	75.0	0	299	1859.0	504.3
May	85.3	70.7	78.0	0	401	1843.6	500.1
June	88.0	73.9	81.0	0	479	1707.9	463.3
July	89.1	75.5	82.3	0	535	1763.4	478.3
Aug	89.9	75.8	82.9	0	554	1629.8	442.1
Sept	88.3	75.0	81.7	0	500	1456.3	395.0
Oct	84.6	71.0	77.8	0	396	1302.7	353.4
Nov	79.9	64.5	72.2	13	229	1118.6	303.4
Dec	76.6	60.0	68.3	56	158	1019.1	276.4
Ann	83.0	67.9	75.5	205	4037	1472.9	399.5

STATION NO. 12841

Orlando, Florida

LATITUDE: 28° 33′ N
LONGITUDE: 81° 20′ W
STATION ELEVATION: 36 meters (118.1 feet)

	Maximum Daily Temp. °F	Minimum Daily Temp. °F	Average Monthly Temp. °F	Heating Degree Days Base 65 °F	Cooling Degree Days Base 65 °F	Total Global Radiation Btu/ft²	Total Global Radiation Langleys
Jan	70.5	50.0	60.3	196	50	999.3	271.1
Feb	71.8	51.2	61.5	184	85	1243.5	337.3
Mar	76.0	55.7	65.9	94	121	1582.3	429.2
Apr	81.5	61.1	71.3	13	202	1898.1	514.9
May	86.7	66.1	76.4	0	353	1989.0	539.5
June	89.3	71.1	80.2	0	455	1831.3	496.7
July	89.8	72.9	81.4	0	508	1801.3	488.6
Aug	90.0	73.5	81.8	0	520	1673.2	453.9
Sept	87.9	72.3	80.1	0	452	1496.6	406.0
Oct	82.5	66.0	74.3	0	288	1304.4	353.8
Nov	76.2	56.9	66.6	74	122	1096.1	297.3
Dec	71.5	51.5	61.5	169	61	926.1	251.2
Ann	81.1	62.4	71.8	733	3226	1486.7	403.3

STATION NO. 93805

Tallahassee, Florida

LATITUDE: 30° 23′ N
LONGITUDE: 84° 22′ W
STATION ELEVATION: 21 meters (68.9 feet)

	Maximum Daily Temp. °F	Minimum Daily Temp. °F	Average Monthly Temp. °F	Heating Degree Days Base 65 °F	Cooling Degree Days Base 65 °F	Total Global Radiation Btu/ft²	Total Global Radiation Langleys
Jan	64.2	41.0	52.6	407	22	876.6	237.8
Feb	66.5	43.0	54.8	322	38	1137.6	308.6
Mar	72.1	48.4	60.3	185	40	1479.5	401.3
Apr	80.1	55.7	67.9	32	121	1823.0	494.5
May	86.7	62.8	74.8	0	302	1935.9	525.1
June	90.4	69.6	80.0	0	450	1882.7	510.7
July	90.6	71.6	81.1	0	499	1748.3	474.2
Aug	90.5	71.7	81.1	0	499	1675.4	454.5
Sept	87.4	68.7	78.1	0	392	1493.0	405.0
Oct	80.6	57.9	69.3	31	164	1317.7	357.4
Nov	71.4	46.4	58.9	203	20	1008.5	273.5
Dec	65.1	41.3	53.2	374	9	812.9	220.5
Ann	78.8	56.5	67.7	1562	2561	1432.6	388.6

STATION NO. 12842

Tampa, Florida

LATITUDE: 27° 58′ N
LONGITUDE: 82° 32′ W
STATION ELEVATION: 3 meters (9.8 feet)

	Maximum Daily Temp. °F	Minimum Daily Temp. °F	Average Monthly Temp. °F	Heating Degree Days Base 65 °F	Cooling Degree Days Base 65 °F	Total Global Radiation Btu/ft²	Total Global Radiation Langleys
Jan	70.6	50.1	60.4	202	59	1010.7	274.1
Feb	71.9	51.7	61.8	175	86	1259.4	341.6
Mar	76.1	55.9	66.0	90	121	1593.7	432.3
Apr	82.4	61.6	72.0	9	218	1908.5	517.7
May	87.5	66.9	77.2	0	378	1998.2	542.0
June	89.9	72.0	81.0	0	479	1847.4	501.1
July	90.1	73.7	81.9	0	524	1752.7	475.4
Aug	90.4	74.0	82.2	0	533	1653.1	448.4
Sept	89.0	72.6	80.8	0	473	1492.0	404.7
Oct	83.9	65.5	74.7	0	301	1346.4	365.2
Nov	77.1	56.4	66.8	70	124	1107.8	300.5
Dec	72.0	51.2	61.6	167	63	935.4	253.7
Ann	81.7	62.6	72.2	716	3366	1492.1	404.7

STATION NO. 12844

West Palm Beach, Florida

LATITUDE: 26° 41′ N
LONGITUDE: 80° 6′ W
ELEVATION: 6 meters (19.7 feet)

	Maximum Daily Temp. °F	Minimum Daily Temp. °F	Average Monthly Temp. °F	Heating Degree Days Base 65 °F	Cooling Degree Days Base 65 °F	Total Global Radiation Btu/ft²	Total Global Radiation Langleys
Jan	75.0	55.9	65.5	83	97	999.8	271.2
Feb	76.0	56.2	66.1	90	121	1232.7	334.4
Mar	79.3	60.2	69.8	23	173	1556.2	422.1
Apr	82.9	64.9	73.9	0	270	1814.5	492.2
May	86.1	68.9	77.5	0	387	1844.6	500.3
June	88.3	72.7	80.5	0	464	1706.3	462.8
July	89.6	74.1	81.9	0	524	1778.7	482.5
Aug	90.2	74.4	82.3	0	535	1663.3	451.2
Sept	88.3	74.7	81.5	0	495	1418.6	384.8
Oct	84.3	70.1	77.2	0	378	1223.8	332.0
Nov	79.5	62.5	71.0	22	202	1060.0	287.5
Dec	76.1	57.4	66.8	77	133	958.2	259.9
Ann	83.0	66.0	74.5	299	3785	1438.1	390.1

STATION NO. 13874

Atlanta, Georgia

LATITUDE: 33° 39′ N
LONGITUDE: 84° 26′ W
ELEVATION: 315 meters (1033.2 feet)

	Maximum Daily Temp. °F	Minimum Daily Temp. °F	Average Monthly Temp. °F	Heating Degree Days Base 65 °F	Cooling Degree Days Base 65 °F	Total Global Radiation Btu/ft²	Total Global Radiation Langleys
Jan	51.4	33.4	42.4	700	0	717.6	194.6
Feb	54.5	35.5	45.0	560	0	968.9	262.8
Mar	61.1	41.1	51.1	443	11	1303.6	353.6
Apr	71.4	50.7	61.1	144	27	1686.2	457.4
May	79.0	59.2	69.1	27	153	1853.8	502.9
June	84.6	66.6	75.6	0	320	1913.8	519.1
July	86.5	69.4	78.0	0	401	1812.2	491.5
Aug	86.4	68.6	77.5	0	387	1708.5	463.4
Sept	81.2	63.4	72.3	7	227	1422.0	385.7
Oct	72.5	52.3	62.4	137	56	1199.9	325.5
Nov	61.9	40.8	51.4	407	0	882.9	239.5
Dec	52.7	34.3	43.5	666	0	674.2	182.9
Ann	70.3	51.3	60.8	3094	1588	1345.3	364.9

STATION NO. 3813

Macon, Georgia

LATITUDE: 32° 42′ N
LONGITUDE: 83° 39′ W
ELEVATION: 110 meters (360.8 feet)

	Maximum Daily Temp. °F	Minimum Daily Temp. °F	Average Monthly Temp. °F	Heating Degree Days Base 65 °F	Cooling Degree Days Base 65 °F	Total Global Radiation Btu/ft²	Total Global Radiation Langleys
Jan	58.7	36.9	47.8	542	9	768.9	208.6
Feb	61.8	39.0	50.4	423	13	1019.7	276.6
Mar	68.4	44.6	56.5	297	34	1363.3	369.8
Apr	78.3	53.2	65.8	65	90	1736.2	470.9
May	86.0	60.9	73.5	5	268	1885.1	511.3
June	90.9	68.2	79.6	0	437	1919.4	520.6
July	92.1	70.7	81.4	0	508	1785.3	484.3
Aug	91.8	70.0	80.9	0	491	1717.8	465.9
Sept	86.6	64.9	75.8	0	324	1438.8	390.3
Oct	78.2	53.2	65.7	81	103	1247.1	338.3
Nov	67.9	42.4	55.2	302	9	939.6	254.9
Dec	59.6	37.0	48.3	517	0	729.0	197.7
Ann	76.7	53.4	65.1	2239	2293	1379.2	374.1

STATION NO. 3822

Savannah, Georgia

LATITUDE: 32° 8′ N
LONGITUDE: 81° 12′ W
ELEVATION: 16 meters (52.5 feet)

	Maximum Daily Temp. °F	Minimum Daily Temp. °F	Average Monthly Temp. °F	Heating Degree Days Base 65 °F	Cooling Degree Days Base 65 °F	Total Global Radiation Btu/ft²	Total Global Radiation Langleys
Jan	61.1	38.7	49.9	482	14	794.7	215.6
Feb	63.6	40.5	52.1	378	18	1043.8	283.1
Mar	69.5	46.4	58.0	256	38	1398.5	379.3
Apr	77.8	54.3	66.1	63	95	1761.4	477.8
May	84.8	61.8	73.3	0	259	1852.3	502.4
June	89.3	68.8	79.1	0	423	1844.3	500.3
July	90.8	71.3	81.1	0	499	1783.5	483.8
Aug	90.3	70.9	80.6	0	482	1620.9	439.7
Sept	85.4	66.9	76.2	0	335	1363.7	369.9
Oct	78.2	55.9	67.1	59	124	1216.7	330.0
Nov	69.3	44.9	57.1	252	14	941.1	255.3
Dec	62.1	38.7	50.4	457	5	753.7	204.4
Ann	76.8	54.9	65.9	1951	2317	1364.5	370.1

STATION NO. 21504

Hilo, Hawaii

LATITUDE: 19° 43′ N
LONGITUDE: 155° 4′ W
ELEVATION: 11 meters (36.1 feet)

	Maximum Daily Temp. °F	Minimum Daily Temp. °F	Average Monthly Temp. °F	Heating Degree Days Base 65 °F	Cooling Degree Days Base 65 °F	Total Global Radiation Btu/ft²	Total Global Radiation Langleys
Jan	79.6	62.8	71.2	0	191	1119.8	303.7
Feb	79.4	62.6	71.0	0	169	1246.2	338.0
Mar	78.8	63.3	71.1	0	191	1348.6	365.8
Apr	79.8	64.6	72.2	0	216	1434.8	389.2
May	81.3	65.6	73.5	0	263	1553.0	421.3
June	82.7	66.5	74.6	0	288	1658.5	449.9
July	83.0	67.5	75.3	0	319	1624.5	440.6
Aug	83.5	68.2	75.9	0	337	1592.4	431.9
Sept	83.6	67.6	75.6	0	317	1546.8	419.6
Oct	83.2	66.7	75.0	0	310	1372.1	372.2
Nov	81.3	65.6	73.5	0	254	1104.9	299.7
Dec	79.4	63.7	71.6	0	203	1019.3	276.5
Ann	81.3	65.4	73.4	0	3065	1385.1	375.7

STATION NO. 22521

Honolulu, Hawaii

LATITUDE: 21° 20′ N
LONGITUDE: 157° 55′ W
ELEVATION: 5 meters (16.4 feet)

	Maximum Daily Temp. °F	Minimum Daily Temp. °F	Average Monthly Temp. °F	Heating Degree Days Base 65 °F	Cooling Degree Days Base 65 °F	Total Global Radiation Btu/ft²	Total Global Radiation Langleys
Jan	79.3	65.3	72.3	0	225	1179.8	320.0
Feb	79.2	65.3	72.3	0	203	1396.3	378.8
Mar	79.7	66.3	73.0	0	247	1621.7	439.9
Apr	81.4	68.1	74.8	0	293	1795.8	487.1
May	83.6	70.2	76.9	0	369	1949.3	528.8
June	85.6	72.2	78.9	0	416	2004.4	543.7
July	86.8	73.4	80.1	0	468	2002.2	543.1
Aug	87.4	74.0	80.7	0	486	1966.5	533.4
Sept	87.4	73.4	80.4	0	461	1810.1	491.0
Oct	85.8	72.0	78.9	0	430	1540.3	417.8
Nov	83.2	69.8	76.5	0	344	1266.1	343.4
Dec	80.3	67.1	73.7	0	270	1132.5	307.2
Ann	83.3	69.8	76.6	0	4221	1638.7	444.5

STATION NO. 24131

LATITUDE: 43° 34′ N
LONGITUDE: 116° 13′ W
ELEVATION: 874 meters (2866.7 feet)

Boise, Idaho

	Maximum Daily Temp. °F	Minimum Daily Temp. °F	Average Monthly Temp. °F	Heating Degree Days Base 65 °F	Cooling Degree Days Base 65 °F	Total Global Radiation Btu/ft²	Total Global Radiation Langleys
Jan	36.5	21.4	29.0	1116	0	485.3	131.6
Feb	43.8	27.2	35.5	824	0	839.7	227.8
Mar	51.6	30.5	41.1	740	0	1304.1	353.7
Apr	61.4	36.5	49.0	479	0	1826.9	495.5
May	70.6	44.1	57.4	252	16	2276.7	617.6
June	78.3	51.2	64.8	95	90	2463.2	668.2
July	90.5	58.5	74.5	0	293	2612.7	708.7
Aug	87.6	56.7	72.2	11	234	2196.5	595.8
Sept	77.6	48.5	63.1	126	68	1737.2	471.2
Oct	64.7	39.4	52.1	405	5	1137.8	308.6
Nov	48.9	30.7	39.8	756	0	628.3	170.4
Dec	39.1	25.0	32.1	1019	0	437.2	118.6
Ann	62.6	39.1	50.9	5832	713	1495.5	405.6

STATION NO. 24149

LATITUDE: 46° 23′ N
LONGITUDE: 117° 1′ W
ELEVATION: 438 meters (1436.6 feet)

Lewiston, Idaho

	Maximum Daily Temp. °F	Minimum Daily Temp. °F	Average Monthly Temp. °F	Heating Degree Days Base 65 °F	Cooling Degree Days Base 65 °F	Total Global Radiation Btu/ft²	Total Global Radiation Langleys
Jan	37.9	24.4	31.2	1048	0	339.7	92.1
Feb	46.0	30.1	38.1	752	0	609.0	165.2
Mar	52.9	32.9	42.9	684	0	1019.6	276.6
Apr	62.0	38.6	50.3	441	0	1435.0	389.3
May	70.6	45.5	58.1	230	18	1842.5	499.8
June	77.9	52.1	65.0	83	83	2014.8	546.5
July	89.2	57.6	73.4	0	263	2335.8	633.6
Aug	87.1	55.9	71.5	16	218	1931.3	523.9
Sept	77.6	48.9	63.3	122	72	1434.6	389.1
Oct	63.2	40.3	51.8	409	0	859.8	233.2
Nov	48.0	32.9	40.5	734	0	412.8	112.0
Dec	41.0	28.6	34.8	936	0	286.1	77.6
Ann	62.8	40.6	51.7	5463	657	1210.1	328.2

STATION NO. 24156

LATITUDE: 42° 55′ N
LONGITUDE: 112° 36′ W
ELEVATION: 1365 meters (4477.2 feet)

Pocatello, Idaho

	Maximum Daily Temp. °F	Minimum Daily Temp. °F	Average Monthly Temp. °F	Heating Degree Days Base 65 °F	Cooling Degree Days Base 65 °F	Total Global Radiation Btu/ft²	Total Global Radiation Langleys
Jan	32.4	14.0	23.2	1296	0	539.2	146.3
Feb	38.6	20.1	29.4	995	0	882.0	239.2
Mar	45.8	24.9	35.4	918	0	1371.4	372.0
Apr	57.7	32.8	45.3	590	0	1820.3	493.8
May	68.1	40.7	54.4	335	5	2280.2	618.5
June	76.5	47.1	61.8	137	41	2479.8	672.6
July	88.8	54.1	71.5	0	203	2599.8	705.2
Aug	86.4	52.5	69.5	20	158	2239.4	607.4
Sept	75.7	43.1	59.4	191	23	1769.3	479.9
Oct	63.0	33.8	48.4	515	0	1203.2	326.4
Nov	45.9	25.5	35.7	878	0	688.7	186.8
Dec	35.5	18.3	26.9	1181	0	477.1	129.4
Ann	59.5	33.9	46.7	7061	436	1529.2	414.8

STATION NO. 14819

LATITUDE: 41° 47′ N
LONGITUDE: 87° 45′ W
ELEVATION: 190 meters (623.2 feet)

Chicago, Illinois

	Maximum Daily Temp. °F	Minimum Daily Temp. °F	Average Monthly Temp. °F	Heating Degree Days Base 65 °F	Cooling Degree Days Base 65 °F	Total Global Radiation Btu/ft²	Total Global Radiation Langleys
Jan	31.5	17.0	24.3	1262	0	507.0	137.5
Feb	34.6	20.2	27.4	1053	0	759.5	206.0
Mar	44.6	29.0	36.8	873	0	1106.9	300.2
Apr	59.3	40.4	49.9	452	0	1459.0	395.8
May	70.3	49.7	60.0	207	52	1788.9	485.2
June	80.6	60.3	70.5	25	191	2007.0	544.4
July	84.4	65.0	74.7	0	301	1943.8	527.3
Aug	83.3	64.1	73.7	7	275	1719.4	466.4
Sept	75.8	56.0	65.9	56	83	1353.9	367.2
Oct	65.0	45.6	55.4	315	18	968.9	262.8
Nov	48.1	32.6	40.4	738	0	565.6	153.4
Dec	35.3	21.6	28.5	1130	0	401.5	108.9
Ann	59.4	41.8	50.6	6125	923	1215.1	329.6

STATION NO. 93822

LATITUDE: 39° 50′ N
LONGITUDE: 89° 40′ W
ELEVATION: 187 meters (613.4 feet)

Springfield, Illinois

	Maximum Daily Temp. °F	Minimum Daily Temp. °F	Average Monthly Temp. °F	Heating Degree Days Base 65 °F	Cooling Degree Days Base 65 °F	Total Global Radiation Btu/ft²	Total Global Radiation Langleys
Jan	34.8	18.6	26.7	1186	0	584.7	158.6
Feb	38.9	21.8	30.4	968	0	860.9	233.5
Mar	48.7	30.1	39.4	794	0	1143.0	310.0
Apr	63.6	42.6	53.1	362	5	1515.0	411.0
May	74.1	52.6	63.4	131	81	1865.5	506.0
June	83.3	62.5	72.9	11	248	2096.7	568.7
July	86.6	65.6	76.1	0	344	2058.2	558.3
Aug	85.0	63.7	74.4	7	299	1805.8	489.8
Sept	78.7	55.6	67.2	47	113	1453.9	394.4
Oct	68.1	45.0	56.6	281	20	1068.3	289.8
Nov	51.0	32.7	41.9	693	0	676.6	183.5
Dec	38.2	22.7	30.5	1069	0	490.1	132.9
Ann	62.6	42.8	52.7	5557	1116	1301.5	353.0

STATION NO. 93817

LATITUDE: 38° 3′ N
LONGITUDE: 87° 32′ W
ELEVATION: 118 meters (387.0 feet)

Evansville, Indiana

	Maximum Daily Temp. °F	Minimum Daily Temp. °F	Average Monthly Temp. °F	Heating Degree Days Base 65 °F	Cooling Degree Days Base 65 °F	Total Global Radiation Btu/ft²	Total Global Radiation Langleys
Jan	41.5	23.7	32.6	1003	0	574.1	155.7
Feb	45.4	26.4	35.9	814	0	823.2	223.3
Mar	54.6	34.0	44.3	652	11	1151.0	312.2
Apr	67.9	45.5	56.7	263	13	1500.8	407.1
May	77.0	54.4	65.7	94	117	1782.8	483.6
June	86.0	63.4	74.7	4	295	1982.7	537.8
July	88.9	66.7	77.8	0	396	1920.3	520.9
Aug	88.0	64.4	76.2	0	346	1735.1	470.6
Sept	81.4	56.7	69.1	32	157	1403.3	380.6
Oct	71.2	45.2	58.2	236	23	1087.0	294.8
Nov	55.2	34.5	44.9	603	0	682.5	185.1
Dec	44.0	26.5	35.3	920	0	498.7	135.3
Ann	66.8	45.1	56.0	4628	1363	1261.8	342.3

STATION NO. 14827

Fort Wayne, Indiana

LATITUDE: 41° 0′ N
LONGITUDE: 85° 12′ W
ELEVATION: 252 meters (826.6 feet)

	Maximum Daily Temp. °F	Minimum Daily Temp. °F	Average Monthly Temp. °F	Heating Degree Days Base 65 °F	Cooling Degree Days Base 65 °F	Total Global Radiation Btu/ft²	Total Global Radiation Langleys
Jan	32.6	17.9	25.3	1229	0	455.2	123.5
Feb	35.5	19.7	27.6	1046	0	697.6	189.2
Mar	45.1	27.9	36.5	884	0	982.0	266.4
Apr	59.5	39.0	49.3	470	0	1360.7	369.1
May	70.2	48.9	59.6	216	47	1671.9	453.5
June	80.1	58.8	69.5	22	157	1841.7	499.6
July	83.6	62.4	73.0	0	250	1787.0	484.7
Aug	82.2	60.4	71.3	11	207	1594.3	432.5
Sept	75.9	53.0	64.5	90	74	1273.6	345.5
Oct	64.6	42.5	53.6	362	9	924.2	250.7
Nov	48.3	32.0	40.2	743	0	516.3	140.1
Dec	35.7	21.4	28.6	1127	0	369.5	100.2
Ann	59.4	40.3	49.9	6208	747	1122.7	304.5

STATION NO. 93819

Indianapolis, Indiana

LATITUDE: 39° 44′ N
LONGITUDE: 86° 17′ W
ELEVATION: 246 meters (806.9 feet)

	Maximum Daily Temp. °F	Minimum Daily Temp. °F	Average Monthly Temp. °F	Heating Degree Days Base 65 °F	Cooling Degree Days Base 65 °F	Total Global Radiation Btu/ft²	Total Global Radiation Langleys
Jan	36.0	19.7	27.9	1148	0	495.6	134.4
Feb	39.3	22.1	30.7	959	0	746.9	202.6
Mar	49.0	30.3	39.7	783	0	1037.4	281.4
Apr	62.8	41.8	52.3	387	5	1398.4	379.3
May	72.9	51.5	62.2	158	72	1688.0	457.9
June	82.3	61.1	71.7	11	211	1868.1	506.7
July	85.4	64.6	75.0	0	310	1806.3	490.0
Aug	84.0	62.4	73.2	4	257	1643.5	445.8
Sept	77.7	54.9	66.3	63	101	1324.0	359.1
Oct	67.0	44.3	55.7	301	13	977.0	265.0
Nov	50.5	32.8	41.7	698	0	579.1	157.1
Dec	38.7	23.1	30.9	1057	0	416.6	113.0
Ann	62.2	42.4	52.3	5576	974	1165.0	316.0

STATION NO. 14931

Burlington, Iowa

LATITUDE: 40° 47′ N
LONGITUDE: 91° 7′ W
ELEVATION: 214 meters (701.9 feet)

	Maximum Daily Temp. °F	Minimum Daily Temp. °F	Average Monthly Temp. °F	Heating Degree Days Base 65 °F	Cooling Degree Days Base 65 °F	Total Global Radiation Btu/ft²	Total Global Radiation Langleys
Jan	31.7	14.1	22.9	1305	0	579.2	157.1
Feb	36.2	18.4	27.3	1055	0	858.6	232.9
Mar	46.6	27.1	36.9	869	0	1165.1	316.0
Apr	62.1	40.5	51.3	416	4	1537.9	417.2
May	72.7	50.9	61.8	171	72	1875.6	508.8
June	81.9	60.9	71.4	14	207	2121.0	575.3
July	86.1	64.6	75.4	0	320	2084.9	565.5
Aug	84.6	63.1	73.9	7	283	1828.1	495.9
Sept	76.7	54.1	65.4	68	81	1416.5	384.2
Oct	66.7	43.9	55.3	319	20	1060.8	287.7
Nov	49.2	30.3	39.8	756	0	663.7	180.0
Dec	35.9	19.3	27.6	1157	0	480.7	130.4
Ann	60.9	40.6	50.8	6149	994	1306.0	354.3

STATION NO. 14933

Des Moines, Iowa

LATITUDE: 41° 32′ N
LONGITUDE: 93° 39′ W
ELEVATION: 294 meters (964.3 feet)

	Maximum Daily Temp. °F	Minimum Daily Temp. °F	Average Monthly Temp. °F	Heating Degree Days Base 65 °F	Cooling Degree Days Base 65 °F	Total Global Radiation Btu/ft²	Total Global Radiation Langleys
Jan	27.5	11.3	19.4	1413	0	580.7	157.5
Feb	32.5	15.8	24.2	1141	0	860.7	233.5
Mar	42.5	25.2	33.9	963	0	1180.5	320.2
Apr	59.7	39.2	49.5	464	0	1556.6	422.2
May	70.9	50.9	60.9	185	58	1867.5	506.6
June	79.8	61.1	70.5	25	191	2124.8	576.3
July	84.9	65.3	75.1	0	317	2096.8	568.7
Aug	83.2	63.4	73.3	13	270	1827.9	495.8
Sept	74.6	54.0	64.3	94	72	1433.9	388.9
Oct	64.9	43.6	54.3	349	18	1067.8	289.6
Nov	46.4	29.2	37.8	815	0	658.3	178.6
Dec	32.8	17.2	25.0	1238	0	486.9	132.1
Ann	58.3	39.7	49.0	6709	927	1311.8	355.8

STATION NO. 14943

Sioux City, Iowa

LATITUDE: 42° 24′ N
LONGITUDE: 96° 23′ W
ELEVATION: 336 meters (1102.1 feet)

	Maximum Daily Temp. °F	Minimum Daily Temp. °F	Average Monthly Temp. °F	Heating Degree Days Base 65 °F	Cooling Degree Days Base 65 °F	Total Global Radiation Btu/ft²	Total Global Radiation Langleys
Jan	28.2	7.7	18.0	1456	0	568.6	154.2
Feb	33.3	13.4	23.4	1165	0	841.6	228.3
Mar	42.9	23.4	33.2	985	0	1170.4	317.5
Apr	61.3	37.4	49.4	473	5	1577.8	428.0
May	72.5	49.3	60.9	189	61	1901.1	515.7
June	81.3	59.3	70.3	32	191	2123.6	576.0
July	86.7	63.9	75.3	0	324	2122.1	575.6
Aug	84.8	62.1	73.5	9	274	1845.2	500.5
Sept	75.3	51.4	63.4	112	65	1421.4	385.5
Oct	65.8	40.4	53.1	378	9	1038.1	281.6
Nov	47.0	25.6	36.3	860	0	642.6	174.3
Dec	33.3	13.6	23.5	1287	0	469.3	127.3
Ann	59.4	37.3	48.4	6952	931	1310.2	355.4

SOLMET STATION NO. 13985

Dodge City, Kansas

LATITUDE: 37° 46′ N
LONGITUDE: 99° 58′ W
ELEVATION: 787 meters (2581.4 feet)

	Maximum Daily Temp. °F	Minimum Daily Temp. °F	Average Monthly Temp. °F	Heating Degree Days Base 65 °F	Cooling Degree Days Base 65 °F	Total Global Radiation Btu/ft²	Total Global Radiation Langleys
Jan	42.6	19.0	30.8	1058	0	826.6	224.2
Feb	47.1	23.2	35.2	833	0	1122.0	304.4
Mar	53.9	28.4	41.2	738	0	1476.4	400.5
Apr	66.9	41.1	54.0	344	13	1885.8	511.5
May	76.2	51.7	64.0	113	83	2089.7	566.8
June	86.0	61.4	73.7	20	281	2358.2	639.7
July	91.4	66.9	79.2	0	439	2295.5	622.6
Aug	90.4	65.7	78.1	0	405	2055.3	557.5
Sept	81.4	56.3	68.9	40	157	1686.7	457.5
Oct	70.7	45.0	57.9	247	27	1300.7	352.8
Nov	55.2	30.4	42.8	666	0	893.7	242.4
Dec	44.6	22.2	33.4	979	0	731.9	198.5
Ann	67.2	42.6	54.9	5045	1409	1560.2	423.2

STATION NO. 3928

Wichita, Kansas

LATITUDE: 37° 39′ N
LONGITUDE: 97° 25′ W
ELEVATION: 408 meters (1338.2 feet)

	Maximum Daily Temp. °F	Minimum Daily Temp. °F	Average Monthly Temp. °F	Heating Degree Days Base 65 °F	Cooling Degree Days Base 65 °F	Total Global Radiation Btu/ft²	Total Global Radiation Langleys
Jan	41.4	21.2	31.3	1044	0	783.9	212.6
Feb	47.1	25.4	36.3	803	0	1058.2	287.1
Mar	55.0	32.1	43.6	670	7	1405.5	381.2
Apr	68.1	45.1	56.6	274	22	1782.5	483.5
May	77.1	55.0	66.1	90	122	2035.8	552.2
June	86.5	65.0	75.8	5	329	2264.3	614.2
July	91.7	69.6	80.7	0	486	2238.5	607.2
Aug	91.0	68.3	79.7	0	455	2031.6	551.1
Sept	81.9	59.2	70.6	31	200	1616.1	438.4
Oct	71.3	47.9	59.6	211	43	1249.8	339.0
Nov	55.8	33.8	44.8	605	0	870.8	236.2
Dec	44.3	24.6	34.5	945	0	689.9	187.1
Ann	67.6	45.6	56.6	4685	1672	1502.3	407.5

STATION NO. 93821

Louisville, Kentucky

LATITUDE: 38° 11′ N
LONGITUDE: 85° 44′ W
ELEVATION: 149 meters (488.7 feet)

	Maximum Daily Temp. °F	Minimum Daily Temp. °F	Average Monthly Temp. °F	Heating Degree Days Base 65 °F	Cooling Degree Days Base 65 °F	Total Global Radiation Btu/ft²	Total Global Radiation Langleys
Jan	42.0	24.5	33.3	983	0	545.5	148.0
Feb	45.0	26.5	35.8	817	0	789.3	214.1
Mar	54.0	34.0	44.0	661	9	1102.0	298.9
Apr	66.9	44.8	55.9	284	13	1466.7	397.9
May	75.6	53.9	64.8	104	99	1719.8	466.5
June	83.7	62.9	73.3	4	254	1903.5	516.3
July	87.3	66.4	76.9	0	369	1837.5	498.4
Aug	86.8	64.9	75.9	0	337	1680.2	455.8
Sept	80.5	57.7	69.1	34	157	1361.2	369.2
Oct	70.3	45.9	58.1	239	27	1042.2	282.7
Nov	54.9	35.1	45.0	599	0	652.8	177.1
Dec	44.1	27.1	35.6	911	0	487.9	132.3
Ann	65.9	45.3	55.6	4644	1267	1215.7	329.8

STATION NO. 13970

Baton Rouge, Louisiana

LATITUDE: 30° 32′ N
LONGITUDE: 91° 9′ W
ELEVATION: 23 meters (75.4 feet)

	Maximum Daily Temp. °F	Minimum Daily Temp. °F	Average Monthly Temp. °F	Heating Degree Days Base 65 °F	Cooling Degree Days Base 65 °F	Total Global Radiation Btu/ft²	Total Global Radiation Langleys
Jan	61.5	40.5	51.0	450	16	785.1	213.0
Feb	64.5	43.2	53.9	335	23	1054.1	285.9
Mar	70.6	48.7	59.7	207	43	1379.4	374.2
Apr	79.0	57.7	68.4	32	135	1681.2	456.0
May	85.2	64.3	74.8	0	302	1871.2	507.6
June	90.3	70.3	80.3	0	459	1926.3	522.5
July	91.2	72.7	82.0	0	526	1745.7	473.5
Aug	91.1	72.1	81.6	0	515	1676.8	454.8
Sept	87.2	67.7	77.5	0	374	1464.4	397.2
Oct	80.4	56.6	68.5	54	162	1301.1	352.9
Nov	70.3	46.9	58.6	207	14	920.4	249.6
Dec	63.7	42.0	52.9	380	5	736.8	199.9
Ann	77.9	56.9	67.4	1669	2585	1378.5	373.9

SOLMET STATION NO. 3937

LATITUDE: 30° 7′ N
LONGITUDE: 93° 13′ W
ELEVATION: 3 meters (9.8 feet)

Lake Charles, Louisiana

	Maximum Daily Temp. °F	Minimum Daily Temp. °F	Average Monthly Temp. °F	Heating Degree Days Base 65 °F	Cooling Degree Days Base 65 °F	Total Global Radiation Btu/ft²	Total Global Radiation Langleys
Jan	61.6	42.9	52.3	414	20	728.4	197.6
Feb	64.6	45.5	55.1	306	29	1009.8	273.9
Mar	70.0	50.5	60.3	200	54	1313.4	356.3
Apr	78.2	59.5	68.9	25	142	1570.4	426.0
May	84.3	66.0	75.2	0	315	1849.4	501.7
June	89.6	71.8	80.7	0	470	1970.3	534.5
July	91.2	73.6	82.4	0	538	1787.7	484.9
Aug	91.2	73.2	82.2	0	533	1657.4	449.6
Sept	87.9	68.8	78.4	0	401	1485.2	402.9
Oct	81.6	58.4	70.0	36	191	1381.1	374.6
Nov	71.1	49.2	60.2	176	32	916.6	248.6
Dec	64.2	44.3	54.3	337	5	705.6	191.4
Ann	78.0	58.6	68.3	1498	2738	1364.6	370.2

STATION NO. 12916

LATITUDE: 29° 59′ N
LONGITUDE: 90° 15′ W
ELEVATION: 3 meters (9.8 feet)

New Orleans, Louisiana

	Maximum Daily Temp. °F	Minimum Daily Temp. °F	Average Monthly Temp. °F	Heating Degree Days Base 65 °F	Cooling Degree Days Base 65 °F	Total Global Radiation Btu/ft²	Total Global Radiation Langleys
Jan	62.3	43.5	52.9	401	27	834.6	226.4
Feb	65.1	46.0	55.6	299	34	1111.9	301.6
Mar	70.4	50.9	60.7	187	54	1414.8	383.8
Apr	78.4	58.8	68.6	29	137	1780.3	482.9
May	84.9	65.3	75.1	0	311	1967.7	533.7
June	89.6	71.2	80.4	0	461	2003.8	543.5
July	90.4	73.3	81.9	0	524	1813.5	491.9
Aug	90.6	73.1	81.9	0	524	1716.6	465.6
Sept	86.6	69.7	78.2	0	396	1513.6	410.6
Oct	79.9	59.6	69.8	40	189	1335.0	362.1
Nov	70.3	49.8	60.1	178	31	972.6	263.8
Dec	64.2	45.3	54.8	326	11	779.4	211.4
Ann	77.7	58.9	68.3	1463	2705	1437.0	389.8

SOLMET STATION NO. 14607

LATITUDE: 46° 52′ N
LONGITUDE: 68° 1′ W
ELEVATION: 190 meters (623.2 feet)

Caribou, Maine

	Maximum Daily Temp. °F	Minimum Daily Temp. °F	Average Monthly Temp. °F	Heating Degree Days Base 65 °F	Cooling Degree Days Base 65 °F	Total Global Radiation Btu/ft²	Total Global Radiation Langleys
Jan	19.8	1.5	10.7	1683	0	419.3	113.7
Feb	23.0	2.7	12.9	1458	0	724.0	196.4
Mar	32.8	14.4	23.6	1282	0	1133.1	307.4
Apr	45.5	27.9	36.7	848	0	1414.2	383.6
May	60.3	39.0	49.7	473	0	1577.8	428.0
June	70.3	48.8	59.6	169	7	1757.4	476.7
July	75.6	54.1	64.9	83	81	1762.4	478.0
Aug	73.1	51.5	62.3	121	38	1500.7	407.1
Sept	64.7	43.4	54.1	326	0	1102.6	299.1
Oct	52.8	34.8	43.8	657	0	688.3	186.7
Nov	38.2	24.6	31.4	1008	0	366.4	99.4
Dec	23.9	8.2	16.1	1516	0	310.5	84.2
Ann	48.3	29.2	38.8	9632	128	1063.1	288.4

STATION NO. 14764

LATITUDE: 43° 39′ N
LONGITUDE: 70° 19′ W
ELEVATION: 19 meters (62.3 feet)

Portland, Maine

	Maximum Daily Temp. °F	Minimum Daily Temp. °F	Average Monthly Temp. °F	Heating Degree Days Base 65 °F	Cooling Degree Days Base 65 °F	Total Global Radiation Btu/ft²	Total Global Radiation Langleys
Jan	31.2	11.7	21.5	1348	0	450.3	122.1
Feb	33.3	12.5	22.9	1179	0	681.9	185.0
Mar	40.8	22.8	31.8	1028	0	969.6	263.0
Apr	52.8	32.5	42.7	668	0	1303.9	353.7
May	63.6	41.7	52.7	380	0	1567.4	425.2
June	73.2	51.1	62.2	104	22	1711.6	464.3
July	79.1	56.9	68.0	27	119	1659.1	450.0
Aug	77.6	55.2	66.4	54	99	1460.9	396.3
Sept	69.9	47.4	58.7	200	11	1157.8	314.1
Oct	60.2	38.0	49.1	491	0	822.4	223.1
Nov	47.5	29.7	38.6	792	0	459.3	124.6
Dec	34.9	16.4	25.7	1217	0	362.9	98.4
Ann	55.3	34.7	45.0	7497	252	1050.6	285.0

SOLMET STATION NO. 94701

LATITUDE: 42° 22′ N
LONGITUDE: 71° 2′ W
ELEVATION: 5 meters (16.4 feet)

Boston, Massachusetts

	Maximum Daily Temp. °F	Minimum Daily Temp. °F	Average Monthly Temp. °F	Heating Degree Days Base 65 °F	Cooling Degree Days Base 65 °F	Total Global Radiation Btu/ft²	Total Global Radiation Langleys
Jan	35.9	22.5	29.2	1109	0	475.5	129.0
Feb	37.5	23.3	30.4	968	0	709.6	192.5
Mar	44.6	31.5	38.1	833	0	1016.4	275.7
Apr	56.3	40.8	48.6	491	0	1325.8	359.6
May	67.1	50.1	58.6	218	20	1620.5	439.6
June	76.6	59.3	68.0	27	117	1817.1	492.9
July	81.4	65.1	73.3	0	259	1749.2	474.5
Aug	79.3	63.3	71.3	7	202	1486.5	403.2
Sept	72.2	56.7	64.5	76	59	1259.9	341.7
Oct	63.2	47.5	55.4	301	0	889.6	241.3
Nov	51.7	38.7	45.2	594	0	502.9	136.4
Dec	39.3	26.6	33.0	992	0	403.0	109.3
Ann	58.7	43.8	51.3	5620	661	1104.7	299.6

STATION NO. 14822

LATITUDE: 42° 25′ N
LONGITUDE: 83° 1′ W
ELEVATION: 191 meters (626.5 feet)

Detroit, Michigan

	Maximum Daily Temp. °F	Minimum Daily Temp. °F	Average Monthly Temp. °F	Heating Degree Days Base 65 °F	Cooling Degree Days Base 65 °F	Total Global Radiation Btu/ft²	Total Global Radiation Langleys
Jan	31.7	19.2	25.5	1224	0	417.4	113.2
Feb	33.7	20.1	26.9	1066	0	680.4	184.6
Mar	43.1	27.6	35.4	918	0	1000.2	271.3
Apr	57.6	38.6	48.1	506	0	1399.0	379.5
May	68.5	48.3	58.4	238	32	1715.9	465.4
June	79.1	59.1	69.1	25	148	1866.1	506.2
July	83.1	63.4	73.3	0	261	1835.4	497.9
Aug	81.6	62.1	71.9	11	225	1575.5	427.3
Sept	74.2	54.8	64.5	79	65	1253.2	339.9
Oct	63.4	45.2	54.3	342	9	876.1	237.6
Nov	47.7	34.4	41.1	716	0	477.8	129.6
Dec	35.4	23.8	29.6	1096	0	343.5	93.2
Ann	58.3	41.4	49.9	6228	742	1120.0	303.8

STATION NO. 94860

LATITUDE: 42° 53′ N
LONGITUDE: 85° 31′ W
ELEVATION: 245 meters (803.6 feet)

Grand Rapids, Michigan

	Maximum Daily Temp. °F	Minimum Daily Temp. °F	Average Monthly Temp. °F	Heating Degree Days Base 65 °F	Cooling Degree Days Base 65 °F	Total Global Radiation Btu/ft²	Total Global Radiation Langleys
Jan	30.3	16.0	23.2	1296	0	369.6	100.2
Feb	32.6	16.4	24.5	1134	0	648.3	175.8
Mar	42.0	24.2	33.1	988	0	1014.4	275.1
Apr	57.3	35.6	46.5	554	0	1411.9	383.0
May	68.8	45.4	57.1	270	23	1755.2	476.1
June	79.1	55.6	67.4	43	115	1956.5	530.7
July	83.3	59.6	71.5	7	209	1914.4	519.3
Aug	81.9	58.1	70.0	27	182	1676.3	454.7
Sept	73.9	50.8	62.4	113	36	1262.1	342.4
Oct	63.1	40.8	52.0	409	5	857.8	232.7
Nov	46.2	31.1	38.7	788	0	445.7	120.9
Dec	33.9	20.8	27.4	1165	0	310.7	84.3
Ann	57.7	37.9	47.8	6800	574	1135.3	307.9

STATION NO. 14850

LATITUDE: 44° 44′ N
LONGITUDE: 85° 35′ W
ELEVATION: 192 meters (629.8 feet)

Traverse City, Michigan

	Maximum Daily Temp. °F	Minimum Daily Temp. °F	Average Monthly Temp. °F	Heating Degree Days Base 65 °F	Cooling Degree Days Base 65 °F	Total Global Radiation Btu/ft²	Total Global Radiation Langleys
Jan	0.0 ND	0.0 ND	20.8	1370	0	310.8	84.3
Feb	0.0 ND	0.0 ND	20.7	1238	0	567.5	153.9
Mar	0.0 ND	0.0 ND	28.7	1125	0	1001.0	271.5
Apr	0.0 ND	0.0 ND	42.7	668	0	1405.2	381.2
May	0.0 ND	0.0 ND	52.8	387	9	1729.1	469.0
June	0.0 ND	0.0 ND	63.7	103	65	1912.4	518.7
July	0.0 ND	0.0 ND	68.7	32	148	1909.8	518.0
Aug	0.0 ND	0.0 ND	67.5	65	144	1609.3	436.5
Sept	0.0 ND	0.0 ND	59.4	176	9	1165.3	316.1
Oct	0.0 ND	0.0 ND	49.8	470	0	753.9	204.5
Nov	0.0 ND	0.0 ND	36.9	842	0	376.8	102.2
Dec	0.0 ND	0.0 ND	25.9	1211	0	256.8	69.6
Ann	0.0 ND	0.0 ND	44.8	7697	374	1083.2	293.8

STATION NO. 14913

LATITUDE: 46° 50′ N
LONGITUDE: 92° 11′ W
ELEVATION: 432 meters (1417.0 feet)

Duluth, Minnesota

	Maximum Daily Temp. °F	Minimum Daily Temp. °F	Average Monthly Temp. °F	Heating Degree Days Base 65 °F	Cooling Degree Days Base 65 °F	Total Global Radiation Btu/ft²	Total Global Radiation Langleys
Jan	17.6	−0.6	8.5	1750	0	388.6	105.4
Feb	22.1	2.0	12.1	1480	0	672.8	182.5
Mar	32.6	14.4	23.5	1287	0	1034.5	280.6
Apr	47.8	29.3	38.6	792	0	1372.8	372.4
May	60.0	38.8	49.4	482	0	1642.6	445.6
June	69.7	48.3	59.0	193	13	1767.2	479.4
July	76.4	54.7	65.6	67	85	1854.3	503.0
Aug	74.4	53.7	64.1	103	76	1546.9	419.6
Sept	64.0	44.8	54.4	317	0	1095.0	297.0
Oct	54.3	36.2	45.3	610	0	724.8	196.6
Nov	35.3	21.4	28.4	1098	0	380.7	103.3
Dec	22.5	6.3	14.4	1568	0	291.7	79.1
Ann	48.1	29.1	38.6	9756	175	1064.3	288.7

STATION NO. 14918

LATITUDE: 48° 34′ N
LONGITUDE: 93° 23′ W
ELEVATION: 361 meters (1184.1 feet)

International Falls, Minnesota

	Maximum Daily Temp. °F	Minimum Daily Temp. °F	Average Monthly Temp. °F	Heating Degree Days Base 65 °F	Cooling Degree Days Base 65 °F	Total Global Radiation Btu/ft²	Total Global Radiation Langleys
Jan	12.8	−9.1	1.9	1955	0	355.7	96.5
Feb	19.4	−5.5	7.0	1624	0	662.5	179.7
Mar	32.3	8.9	20.6	1375	0	1045.9	283.7
Apr	49.1	27.3	38.2	803	0	1443.7	391.6
May	62.5	37.7	50.1	461	0	1716.2	465.5
June	72.4	48.3	60.4	167	29	1853.3	502.7
July	78.2	53.4	65.8	65	90	1921.0	521.1
Aug	75.5	50.9	63.2	112	56	1618.3	439.0
Sept	64.2	41.7	53.0	364	0	1121.3	304.1
Oct	54.0	32.9	43.5	666	0	703.9	190.9
Nov	32.5	17.3	24.9	1202	0	345.5	93.7
Dec	18.1	−0.8	8.7	1744	0	271.7	73.7
Ann	47.6	25.3	36.5	10546	175	1088.2	295.2

STATION NO. 14922

LATITUDE: 44° 53′ N
LONGITUDE: 93° 13′ W
ELEVATION: 255 meters (836.4 feet)

Minneapolis / St. Paul, Minnesota

	Maximum Daily Temp. °F	Minimum Daily Temp. °F	Average Monthly Temp. °F	Heating Degree Days Base 65 °F	Cooling Degree Days Base 65 °F	Total Global Radiation Btu/ft²	Total Global Radiation Langleys
Jan	21.2	3.2	12.2	1636	0	464.0	125.9
Feb	25.9	7.1	16.5	1357	0	763.9	207.2
Mar	36.9	19.6	28.3	1138	0	1103.5	299.3
Apr	55.5	34.7	45.1	596	0	1441.9	391.1
May	67.9	46.3	57.1	270	25	1737.3	471.2
June	77.1	56.7	66.9	65	121	1927.5	522.8
July	82.4	61.4	71.9	11	225	1970.0	534.4
Aug	80.8	59.6	70.2	20	182	1687.0	457.6
Sept	70.7	49.3	60.0	173	22	1254.7	340.3
Oct	60.7	39.2	50.0	472	5	859.6	233.2
Nov	40.6	24.2	32.4	977	0	480.4	130.3
Dec	26.6	10.6	18.6	1436	0	353.3	95.8
Ann	53.8	34.3	44.1	8158	585	1170.2	317.4

STATION NO. 3940

LATITUDE: 32° 19′ N
LONGITUDE: 90° 5′ W
ELEVATION: 101 meters (331.3 feet)

Jackson, Mississippi

	Maximum Daily Temp. °F	Minimum Daily Temp. °F	Average Monthly Temp. °F	Heating Degree Days Base 65 °F	Cooling Degree Days Base 65 °F	Total Global Radiation Btu/ft²	Total Global Radiation Langleys
Jan	58.4	35.8	47.1	569	13	753.5	204.4
Feb	61.7	37.8	49.8	441	16	1026.4	278.4
Mar	68.7	43.4	56.1	311	36	1369.1	371.4
Apr	78.2	53.1	65.7	74	94	1708.4	463.4
May	85.0	60.4	72.7	5	245	1940.8	526.4
June	91.0	67.7	79.4	0	432	2024.2	549.1
July	92.7	70.6	81.7	0	517	1909.0	517.8
Aug	92.6	69.8	81.2	0	500	1780.5	483.0
Sept	88.0	64.0	76.0	0	329	1509.2	409.4
Oct	80.1	51.5	65.8	90	115	1271.4	344.9
Nov	68.5	42.0	55.3	301	9	901.6	244.6
Dec	60.5	37.3	48.9	504	4	708.8	192.3
Ann	77.1	52.8	65.0	2299	2320	1408.6	382.1

SOLMET STATION NO. 3945

Columbia, Missouri

LATITUDE: 38° 49′ N
LONGITUDE: 92° 13′ W
ELEVATION: 270 meters (885.6 feet)

	Maximum Daily Temp. °F	Minimum Daily Temp. °F	Average Monthly Temp. °F	Heating Degree Days Base 65 °F	Cooling Degree Days Base 65 °F	Total Global Radiation Btu/ft²	Total Global Radiation Langleys
Jan	38.0	20.6	29.3	1107	0	611.5	165.9
Feb	42.7	24.5	33.6	878	0	874.8	237.3
Mar	51.3	32.0	41.7	729	7	1178.8	319.7
Apr	65.3	44.6	55.0	313	13	1525.9	413.9
May	74.5	54.3	64.4	117	97	1879.8	509.9
June	82.7	63.3	73.0	11	250	2089.5	566.8
July	87.4	67.1	77.3	0	380	2116.1	574.0
Aug	86.4	65.5	76.0	4	346	1877.9	509.4
Sept	79.4	57.2	68.3	41	140	1450.4	393.4
Oct	69.2	46.7	58.0	247	29	1100.8	298.6
Nov	53.6	34.2	43.9	632	0	702.7	190.6
Dec	41.1	24.5	32.8	997	0	522.5	141.7
Ann	64.3	44.5	54.4	5081	1269	1327.6	360.1

STATION NO. 3947

Kansas City, Missouri

LATITUDE: 39° 18′ N
LONGITUDE: 94° 43′ W
ELEVATION: 315 meters (1033.2 feet)

	Maximum Daily Temp. °F	Minimum Daily Temp. °F	Average Monthly Temp. °F	Heating Degree Days Base 65 °F	Cooling Degree Days Base 65 °F	Total Global Radiation Btu/ft²	Total Global Radiation Langleys
Jan	35.7	18.4	27.1	1174	0	647.9	175.7
Feb	41.4	23.1	32.3	914	0	894.7	242.7
Mar	50.7	30.6	40.7	752	0	1202.9	326.3
Apr	64.7	43.7	54.2	335	11	1575.0	427.2
May	74.2	54.0	64.1	126	99	1872.6	507.9
June	82.8	63.2	73.0	14	254	2079.6	564.1
July	88.0	66.9	77.5	0	387	2102.1	570.2
Aug	87.2	65.8	76.5	0	360	1862.4	505.2
Sept	78.8	57.1	68.0	49	139	1452.4	394.0
Oct	68.2	46.9	57.6	257	29	1092.3	296.3
Nov	51.4	33.1	42.3	680	0	737.3	200.0
Dec	39.3	23.3	31.3	1044	0	561.5	152.3
Ann	63.5	43.8	53.7	5357	1283	1340.0	363.5

STATION NO. 13994

St. Louis, Missouri

LATITUDE: 38° 45′ N
LONGITUDE: 90° 23′ W
ELEVATION: 172 meters (564.2 feet)

	Maximum Daily Temp. °F	Minimum Daily Temp. °F	Average Monthly Temp. °F	Heating Degree Days Base 65 °F	Cooling Degree Days Base 65 °F	Total Global Radiation Btu/ft²	Total Global Radiation Langleys
Jan	39.9	22.6	31.3	1044	0	627.4	170.2
Feb	44.2	26.0	35.1	837	0	885.5	240.2
Mar	53.0	33.5	43.3	680	9	1204.7	326.8
Apr	67.0	46.0	56.5	272	16	1564.2	424.3
May	76.0	55.5	65.8	103	128	1871.3	507.6
June	84.9	64.8	74.9	9	306	2092.5	567.6
July	88.4	68.8	78.6	0	421	2049.5	555.9
Aug	87.2	67.1	77.2	0	378	1816.5	492.7
Sept	80.1	59.1	69.6	34	173	1459.2	395.8
Oct	69.8	48.4	59.1	223	40	1099.8	298.3
Nov	54.1	35.9	45.0	599	0	718.3	194.8
Dec	42.7	26.5	34.6	941	0	530.6	143.9
Ann	65.6	46.2	55.9	4748	1474	1326.6	359.9

STATION NO. 24033

Billings, Montana

LATITUDE: 45° 48′ N
LONGITUDE: 108° 32′ W
ELEVATION: 1088 meters (3568.6 feet)

	Maximum Daily Temp. °F	Minimum Daily Temp. °F	Average Monthly Temp. °F	Heating Degree Days Base 65 °F	Cooling Degree Days Base 65 °F	Total Global Radiation Btu/ft²	Total Global Radiation Langleys
Jan	31.2	12.5	21.9	1336	0	486.0	131.8
Feb	37.1	17.7	27.4	1053	0	763.2	207.0
Mar	42.1	23.1	32.6	1003	0	1189.5	322.6
Apr	55.8	33.4	44.6	612	0	1526.3	414.0
May	65.7	43.3	54.5	333	7	1912.8	518.8
June	73.7	51.5	62.6	130	58	2173.7	589.6
July	85.6	58.0	71.8	9	220	2383.7	646.6
Aug	83.8	56.3	70.1	14	173	2022.4	548.6
Sept	71.3	46.5	58.9	220	38	1470.0	398.7
Oct	61.0	37.5	49.3	486	0	986.8	267.7
Nov	45.0	26.4	35.7	878	0	561.4	152.3
Dec	35.8	17.7	26.8	1183	0	421.2	114.2
Ann	57.3	35.3	46.3	7265	497	1324.7	359.3

SOLMET STATION NO. 24143

Great Falls, Montana

LATITUDE: 47° 29′ N
LONGITUDE: 111° 22′ W
ELEVATION: 1116 meters (3660.5 feet)

	Maximum Daily Temp. °F	Minimum Daily Temp. °F	Average Monthly Temp. °F	Heating Degree Days Base 65 °F	Cooling Degree Days Base 65 °F	Total Global Radiation Btu/ft²	Total Global Radiation Langleys
Jan	29.3	11.6	20.5	1379	0	420.5	114.1
Feb	35.9	17.2	26.6	1075	0	720.2	195.3
Mar	40.4	20.6	30.5	1069	0	1170.4	317.5
Apr	54.5	32.3	43.4	648	0	1488.7	403.8
May	65.0	41.5	53.3	365	0	1847.6	501.2
June	72.1	49.5	60.8	162	36	2101.4	570.0
July	83.7	54.9	69.3	18	149	2329.0	631.8
Aug	81.8	53.0	67.4	41	115	1933.0	524.3
Sept	70.0	44.6	57.3	259	29	1378.5	373.9
Oct	59.4	37.1	48.3	524	5	924.6	250.8
Nov	43.4	25.7	34.6	911	0	497.6	135.0
Dec	34.7	18.2	26.5	1193	0	336.2	91.2
Ann	55.9	33.8	44.9	7652	338	1262.3	342.4

STATION NO. 24144

Helena, Montana

LATITUDE: 46° 36′ N
LONGITUDE: 112° 0′ W
ELEVATION: 1188 meters (3896.6 feet)

	Maximum Daily Temp. °F	Minimum Daily Temp. °F	Average Monthly Temp. °F	Heating Degree Days Base 65 °F	Cooling Degree Days Base 65 °F	Total Global Radiation Btu/ft²	Total Global Radiation Langleys
Jan	28.3	7.8	18.1	1453	0	419.4	113.8
Feb	35.8	14.9	25.4	1109	0	708.8	192.3
Mar	41.7	19.4	30.6	1066	0	1145.5	310.7
Apr	55.2	30.2	42.7	668	0	1486.8	403.3
May	64.8	39.5	52.2	400	0	1860.2	504.6
June	71.6	46.7	59.2	193	20	2039.8	553.3
July	83.7	52.1	67.9	32	122	2333.8	633.0
Aug	82.0	50.4	66.2	56	94	1930.2	523.6
Sept	70.0	40.9	55.5	302	18	1412.5	383.1
Oct	58.7	31.9	45.3	610	0	926.3	251.2
Nov	42.6	20.8	31.7	999	0	521.2	141.4
Dec	33.2	13.3	23.3	1292	0	364.4	98.8
Ann	55.6	30.7	43.2	8190	256	1262.4	342.4

North Platte, Nebraska

LATITUDE: 41° 22′ N
LONGITUDE: 96° 3 1′ W
ELEVATION: 404 meters (1325.1 feet)

	Maximum Daily Temp. °F	Minimum Daily Temp. °F	Average Monthly Temp. °F	Heating Degree Days Base 65 °F	Cooling Degree Days Base 65 °F	Total Global Radiation Btu/ft²	Total Global Radiation Langleys
Jan	29.1	11.2	20.2	1388	0	634.0	172.0
Feb	34.8	16.1	25.5	1105	0	892.1	242.0
Mar	44.1	25.1	34.6	941	0	1222.5	331.6
Apr	61.0	38.9	50.0	455	5	1558.4	422.7
May	71.4	50.4	60.9	185	58	1872.6	507.9
June	80.2	60.2	70.2	32	189	2122.5	575.7
July	85.4	64.8	75.1	5	319	2106.5	571.4
Aug	84.0	63.4	73.7	9	279	1858.5	504.1
Sept	75.2	53.6	64.4	99	81	1373.2	372.5
Oct	65.9	42.8	54.4	342	13	1049.8	284.8
Nov	47.4	28.3	37.9	812	0	644.1	174.7
Dec	34.3	17.0	25.7	1217	0	511.2	138.7
Ann	59.4	39.3	49.4	6601	949	1320.5	358.2

STATION NO. 24028

Scottsbluff, Nebraska

LATITUDE: 41° 52′ N
LONGITUDE: 103° 36′ W
ELEVATION: 1206 meters (3955.7 feet)

	Maximum Daily Temp. °F	Minimum Daily Temp. °F	Average Monthly Temp. °F	Heating Degree Days Base 65 °F	Cooling Degree Days Base 65 °F	Total Global Radiation Btu/ft²	Total Global Radiation Langleys
Jan	38.5	11.3	24.9	1242	0	675.7	183.3
Feb	43.1	15.9	29.5	994	0	950.5	257.8
Mar	48.0	20.6	34.3	950	0	1307.4	354.6
Apr	60.4	32.0	46.2	563	0	1668.0	452.4
May	70.2	42.8	56.5	279	14	1933.2	524.4
June	79.7	52.0	65.9	90	117	2236.6	606.7
July	88.8	58.6	73.7	0	272	2283.7	619.5
Aug	86.9	56.3	71.6	7	212	1999.5	542.4
Sept	77.1	45.2	61.2	158	45	1598.9	433.7
Oct	66.0	34.3	50.2	459	0	1145.0	310.6
Nov	50.4	21.9	36.2	864	0	723.2	196.2
Dec	40.8	14.4	27.6	1157	0	575.1	156.0
Ann	62.5	33.8	48.2	6773	666	1424.7	386.5

STATION NO. 24121

Elko, Nevada

LATITUDE: 40° 50′ N
LONGITUDE: 115° 47′ W
ELEVATION: 1547 meters (5074.2 feet)

	Maximum Daily Temp. °F	Minimum Daily Temp. °F	Average Monthly Temp. °F	Heating Degree Days Base 65 °F	Cooling Degree Days Base 65 °F	Total Global Radiation Btu/ft²	Total Global Radiation Langleys
Jan	36.0	10.4	23.2	1296	0	688.9	186.9
Feb	41.6	16.8	29.2	1001	0	1034.4	280.6
Mar	48.4	21.5	35.0	929	0	1463.0	396.9
Apr	58.8	28.1	43.5	644	0	1899.7	515.3
May	68.5	35.2	51.9	405	0	2303.3	624.8
June	77.5	41.6	59.6	189	27	2533.7	687.3
July	90.4	48.6	69.5	27	166	2622.9	711.5
Aug	88.2	45.8	67.0	59	121	2315.9	628.2
Sept	78.8	36.4	57.6	247	25	1892.6	513.4
Oct	65.8	28.0	46.9	560	0	1322.5	358.7
Nov	49.0	20.6	34.8	905	0	812.1	220.3
Dec	38.2	13.5	25.9	1211	0	617.0	167.4
Ann	61.8	28.9	45.4	7483	342	1625.5	440.9

STATION NO. 23169

LATITUDE: 36° 5′ N
LONGITUDE: 115° 10′ W
ELEVATION: 664 meters (2177.9 feet)

Las Vegas, Nevada

	Maximum Daily Temp. °F	Minimum Daily Temp. °F	Average Monthly Temp. °F	Heating Degree Days Base 65 °F	Cooling Degree Days Base 65 °F	Total Global Radiation Btu/ft²	Total Global Radiation Langleys
Jan	55.7	32.6	44.2	644	0	978.0	265.3
Feb	61.3	36.9	49.1	450	5	1339.5	363.3
Mar	67.8	41.7	54.8	324	7	1823.5	494.6
Apr	77.5	50.0	63.8	126	90	2319.0	629.0
May	87.5	59.0	73.3	9	266	2646.3	717.8
June	97.2	67.4	82.3	0	518	2777.8	753.5
July	103.9	75.3	89.6	0	761	2588.4	702.1
Aug	101.5	73.3	87.4	0	693	2354.8	638.8
Sept	94.8	65.4	80.1	0	452	2037.3	552.6
Oct	81.0	53.1	67.1	74	139	1539.8	417.7
Nov	65.7	40.8	53.3	356	5	1085.5	294.4
Dec	56.7	33.7	45.2	614	0	880.5	238.8
Ann	79.2	52.4	65.8	2601	2945	1864.2	505.7

STATION NO. 23185

LATITUDE: 39° 30′ N
LONGITUDE: 119° 47′ W
ELEVATION: 1341 meters (4398.5 feet)

Reno, Nevada

	Maximum Daily Temp. °F	Minimum Daily Temp. °F	Average Monthly Temp. °F	Heating Degree Days Base 65 °F	Cooling Degree Days Base 65 °F	Total Global Radiation Btu/ft²	Total Global Radiation Langleys
Jan	45.4	18.3	31.9	1026	0	800.4	217.1
Feb	51.1	23.0	37.1	779	0	1149.9	311.9
Mar	56.0	24.6	40.3	765	0	1649.4	447.4
Apr	64.0	29.6	46.8	545	0	2159.3	585.7
May	72.2	37.0	54.6	328	5	2523.1	684.4
June	80.4	42.5	61.5	144	40	2701.4	732.8
July	91.1	47.4	69.3	16	149	2692.1	730.2
Aug	89.0	44.8	66.9	49	108	2405.7	652.5
Sept	81.8	38.6	60.2	167	23	1997.7	541.9
Oct	70.0	30.5	50.3	455	0	1431.0	388.2
Nov	56.3	23.9	40.1	747	0	912.3	247.5
Dec	46.4	19.6	33.0	992	0	705.5	191.4
Ann	67.0	31.7	49.4	6021	328	1760.7	477.6

STATION NO. 23153

LATITUDE: 38° 4′ N
LONGITUDE: 117° 8′ W
ELEVATION: 1653 meters (5421.8 feet)

Tonopah, Nevada

	Maximum Daily Temp. °F	Minimum Daily Temp. °F	Average Monthly Temp. °F	Heating Degree Days Base 65 °F	Cooling Degree Days Base 65 °F	Total Global Radiation Btu/ft²	Total Global Radiation Langleys
Jan	0.0 ND	0.0 ND	30.2	1078	0	917.9	249.0
Feb	0.0 ND	0.0 ND	34.6	850	0	1274.1	345.6
Mar	0.0 ND	0.0 ND	39.6	787	0	1776.9	482.0
Apr	0.0 ND	0.0 ND	48.1	511	0	2250.9	610.6
May	0.0 ND	0.0 ND	56.9	268	18	2577.4	699.1
June	0.0 ND	0.0 ND	65.3	92	101	2788.0	756.3
July	0.0 ND	0.0 ND	73.0	0	250	2702.8	733.1
Aug	0.0 ND	0.0 ND	70.7	13	189	2437.9	661.3
Sept	0.0 ND	0.0 ND	63.5	108	63	2042.7	554.1
Oct	0.0 ND	0.0 ND	52.1	407	7	1520.5	412.4
Nov	0.0 ND	0.0 ND	39.8	756	0	1030.7	279.6
Dec	0.0 ND	0.0 ND	31.9	1026	0	826.8	224.3
Ann	0.0 ND	0.0 ND	50.5	5899	630	1845.5	500.6

STATION NO. 14745

Concord, New Hampshire

LATITUDE: 43° 12′ N
LONGITUDE: 71° 30′ W
ELEVATION: 105 meters (344.4 feet)

	Maximum Daily Temp. °F	Minimum Daily Temp. °F	Average Monthly Temp. °F	Heating Degree Days Base 65 °F	Cooling Degree Days Base 65 °F	Total Global Radiation Btu/ft²	Total Global Radiation Langleys
Jan	31.3	9.9	20.6	1375	0	459.5	124.6
Feb	33.8	11.3	22.6	1186	0	686.1	186.1
Mar	42.4	22.1	32.3	1013	0	973.6	264.1
Apr	56.7	31.7	44.2	623	0	1317.1	357.3
May	68.6	41.5	55.1	315	7	1582.2	429.2
June	77.7	51.6	64.7	58	49	1704.6	462.4
July	82.6	56.7	69.7	14	162	1674.6	454.2
Aug	80.1	54.2	67.2	45	112	1455.3	394.7
Sept	72.4	46.5	59.5	182	16	1140.2	309.3
Oct	62.3	36.3	49.3	486	0	817.1	221.6
Nov	47.9	28.1	38.0	810	0	462.7	125.5
Dec	34.6	14.9	24.8	1246	0	362.1	98.2
Ann	57.5	33.7	45.6	7358	347	1053.0	285.6

STATION NO. 14734

Newark, New Jersey

LATITUDE: 40° 42′ N
LONGITUDE: 74° 10′ W
ELEVATION: 9 meters (29.5 feet)

	Maximum Daily Temp. °F	Minimum Daily Temp. °F	Average Monthly Temp. °F	Heating Degree Days Base 65 °F	Cooling Degree Days Base 65 °F	Total Global Radiation Btu/ft²	Total Global Radiation Langleys
Jan	38.5	24.3	31.4	1040	0	551.7	149.6
Feb	40.2	24.9	32.6	905	0	793.0	215.1
Mar	48.8	32.4	40.6	756	0	1108.7	300.7
Apr	61.2	42.2	51.7	398	0	1448.6	392.9
May	71.6	52.1	61.9	142	47	1687.1	457.6
June	81.1	61.6	71.4	0	196	1795.3	487.0
July	85.6	67.2	76.4	0	353	1759.9	477.4
Aug	83.7	65.5	74.6	0	297	1564.8	424.5
Sept	77.0	58.6	67.8	32	117	1272.9	345.3
Oct	66.9	48.1	57.5	243	11	950.9	257.9
Nov	54.2	38.2	46.2	563	0	596.2	161.7
Dec	41.5	27.4	34.5	945	0	454.4	123.3
Ann	62.5	45.2	53.9	5033	1022	1165.3	316.1

SOLMET STATION NO. 23050

Albuquerque, New Mexico

LATITUDE: 35° 3′ N
LONGITUDE: 106° 37′ W
ELEVATION: 1619 meters (5310.3 feet)

	Maximum Daily Temp. °F	Minimum Daily Temp. °F	Average Monthly Temp. °F	Heating Degree Days Base 65 °F	Cooling Degree Days Base 65 °F	Total Global Radiation Btu/ft²	Total Global Radiation Langleys
Jan	46.9	23.5	35.2	923	0	1016.5	275.7
Feb	52.6	27.4	40.0	698	0	1342.0	364.0
Mar	59.2	32.3	45.8	594	0	1767.6	479.5
Apr	70.1	41.4	55.8	281	5	2228.4	604.5
May	79.9	50.7	65.3	58	67	2538.1	688.5
June	89.5	59.7	74.6	0	290	2678.9	726.7
July	92.2	65.2	78.7	0	425	2488.6	675.0
Aug	89.7	63.4	76.6	0	360	2290.1	621.2
Sept	83.4	56.7	70.1	5	158	1971.7	534.8
Oct	71.7	44.7	58.2	218	5	1546.7	419.5
Nov	57.1	31.8	44.5	614	0	1133.7	307.5
Dec	47.5	24.9	36.2	893	0	927.7	251.6
Ann	70.0	43.5	56.8	4291	1316	1827.5	495.7

STATION NO. 93045

Truth or Consequences, New Mexico

LATITUDE: 33° 14′ N
LONGITUDE: 107° 16′ W
ELEVATION: 1481 meters (4857.7 feet)

	Maximum Daily Temp. °F	Minimum Daily Temp. °F	Average Monthly Temp. °F	Heating Degree Days Base 65 °F	Cooling Degree Days Base 65 °F	Total Global Radiation Btu/ft²	Total Global Radiation Langleys
Jan	0.0 ND	0.0 ND	40.0	774	0	1117.7	303.2
Feb	0.0 ND	0.0 ND	44.9	562	0	1451.5	393.7
Mar	0.0 ND	0.0 ND	50.2	459	0	1886.4	511.7
Apr	0.0 ND	0.0 ND	59.5	187	22	2337.8	634.1
May	0.0 ND	0.0 ND	68.2	18	119	2556.9	693.6
June	0.0 ND	0.0 ND	76.9	0	356	2649.6	718.7
July	0.0 ND	0.0 ND	79.3	0	443	2364.8	641.5
Aug	0.0 ND	0.0 ND	77.4	0	383	2215.9	601.1
Sept	0.0 ND	0.0 ND	71.6	4	202	1940.2	526.3
Oct	0.0 ND	0.0 ND	61.3	144	29	1578.7	428.2
Nov	0.0 ND	0.0 ND	48.7	488	0	1216.6	330.0
Dec	0.0 ND	0.0 ND	40.8	749	0	1002.6	271.9
Ann	0.0 ND	0.0 ND	59.9	3391	1557	1859.9	504.5

STATION NO. 14735

Albany, New York

LATITUDE: 42° 45′ N
LONGITUDE: 73° 48′ W
ELEVATION: 89 meters (291.9 feet)

	Maximum Daily Temp. °F	Minimum Daily Temp. °F	Average Monthly Temp. °F	Heating Degree Days Base 65 °F	Cooling Degree Days Base 65 °F	Total Global Radiation Btu/ft²	Total Global Radiation Langleys
Jan	30.4	12.5	21.5	1348	0	456.5	123.8
Feb	32.7	14.3	23.5	1161	0	688.4	186.7
Mar	42.6	24.2	33.4	979	0	985.9	267.4
Apr	58.0	35.7	46.9	542	0	1335.2	362.2
May	69.7	45.7	57.7	252	27	1569.9	425.8
June	79.4	55.6	67.5	38	113	1729.9	469.2
July	83.9	60.1	72.0	9	225	1724.9	467.9
Aug	81.4	57.8	69.6	22	164	1498.9	406.6
Sept	73.7	50.1	61.9	135	41	1170.3	317.5
Oct	62.8	40.0	51.4	421	0	817.3	221.7
Nov	48.1	31.1	39.6	761	0	457.1	124.0
Dec	34.1	17.7	25.9	1211	0	355.9	96.5
Ann	58.1	37.1	47.6	6887	572	1065.8	289.1

STATION NO. 14733

Buffalo, New York

LATITUDE: 42° 56′ N
LONGITUDE: 78° 44′ W
ELEVATION: 215 meters (705.2 feet)

	Maximum Daily Temp. °F	Minimum Daily Temp. °F	Average Monthly Temp. °F	Heating Degree Days Base 65 °F	Cooling Degree Days Base 65 °F	Total Global Radiation Btu/ft²	Total Global Radiation Langleys
Jan	29.8	17.6	23.7	1280	0	348.9	94.6
Feb	31.0	17.7	24.4	1136	0	546.4	148.2
Mar	39.0	25.2	32.1	1019	0	888.5	241.0
Apr	53.3	36.4	44.9	603	0	1314.9	356.7
May	64.3	45.9	55.1	320	13	1596.5	433.1
June	75.1	56.3	65.7	58	77	1803.7	489.3
July	79.5	60.7	70.1	11	169	1776.4	481.8
Aug	77.6	59.1	68.4	32	137	1513.2	410.5
Sept	70.8	52.3	61.6	137	36	1151.8	312.4
Oct	60.2	42.7	51.5	418	0	784.4	212.8
Nov	46.1	33.5	39.8	756	0	403.4	109.4
Dec	33.6	22.2	27.9	1148	0	283.3	76.8
Ann	55.0	39.1	47.1	6926	436	1034.3	280.5

SOLMET STATION NO. 94728

LATITUDE: 40° 47′ N
LONGITUDE: 73° 58′ W
ELEVATION: 57 meters (187.0 feet)

New York City (Central Park), New York

	Maximum Daily Temp. °F	Minimum Daily Temp. °F	Average Monthly Temp. °F	Heating Degree Days Base 65 °F	Cooling Degree Days Base 65 °F	Total Global Radiation Btu/ft²	Total Global Radiation Langleys
Jan	38.5	25.9	32.2	1017	0	500.4	135.7
Feb	40.2	26.5	33.4	884	0	721.0	195.6
Mar	48.4	33.7	41.1	740	0	1037.1	281.3
Apr	60.7	43.5	52.1	387	0	1363.9	370.0
May	71.4	53.1	62.3	137	54	1636.2	443.8
June	80.5	62.6	71.6	0	202	1710.3	463.9
July	85.2	68.0	76.6	0	360	1687.8	457.8
Aug	83.4	66.4	74.9	0	306	1483.3	402.3
Sept	76.8	59.9	68.4	29	130	1213.7	329.2
Oct	66.8	50.6	58.7	209	13	895.3	242.9
Nov	54.0	40.8	47.4	527	0	532.9	144.6
Dec	41.4	29.5	35.5	914	0	404.0	109.6
Ann	62.3	46.7	54.5	4847	1067	1098.9	298.1

STATION NO. 14732

LATITUDE: 40° 46′ N
LONGITUDE: 73° 54′ W
ELEVATION: 16 meters (52.5 feet)

New York City (La Guardia), New York

	Maximum Daily Temp. °F	Minimum Daily Temp. °F	Average Monthly Temp. °F	Heating Degree Days Base 65 °F	Cooling Degree Days Base 65 °F	Total Global Radiation Btu/ft²	Total Global Radiation Langleys
Jan	37.7	26.4	32.1	1019	0	547.6	148.5
Feb	39.2	27.0	33.1	893	0	794.5	215.5
Mar	47.1	34.1	40.6	756	0	1117.6	303.1
Apr	59.3	44.0	51.7	398	0	1456.6	395.1
May	69.8	53.7	61.8	144	45	1690.4	458.5
June	79.4	63.6	71.5	0	198	1801.9	488.8
July	84.1	69.3	76.7	0	362	1784.1	483.9
Aug	82.1	67.6	74.9	0	306	1583.2	429.5
Sept	75.2	60.9	68.1	29	122	1280.1	347.2
Oct	65.1	51.0	58.1	223	9	950.6	257.8
Nov	53.2	41.3	47.3	531	0	593.0	160.9
Dec	41.0	30.1	35.6	911	0	456.8	123.9
Ann	61.1	47.4	54.3	4909	1048	1171.4	317.7

STATION NO. 14768

LATITUDE: 43° 7′ N
LONGITUDE: 77° 40′ W
ELEVATION: 169 meters (554.3 feet)

Rochester, New York

	Maximum Daily Temp. °F	Minimum Daily Temp. °F	Average Monthly Temp. °F	Heating Degree Days Base 65 °F	Cooling Degree Days Base 65 °F	Total Global Radiation Btu/ft²	Total Global Radiation Langleys
Jan	31.3	16.7	24.0	1271	0	364.3	98.8
Feb	32.6	16.9	24.0	1125	0	559.5	151.8
Mar	41.1	24.9	33.0	992	0	903.4	245.1
Apr	56.0	36.1	46.1	567	0	1339.2	363.2
May	67.2	45.7	56.5	284	22	1606.4	435.7
June	78.0	55.8	66.9	45	103	1816.8	492.8
July	82.2	60.2	71.2	9	202	1780.8	483.0
Aug	80.1	58.5	69.3	25	158	1519.0	412.0
Sept	73.1	51.5	62.3	126	45	1159.7	314.6
Oct	62.4	42.2	52.3	398	0	781.9	212.1
Nov	47.9	33.1	40.5	734	0	403.9	109.6
Dec	34.9	21.7	28.3	1138	0	280.9	76.2
Ann	57.2	38.6	47.9	6718	531	1043.0	282.9

STATION NO. 3812

LATITUDE: 35° 26′ N
LONGITUDE: 82° 32′ W
ELEVATION: 661 meters (2168.1 feet)

Asheville, North Carolina

	Maximum Daily Temp. °F	Minimum Daily Temp. °F	Average Monthly Temp. °F	Heating Degree Days Base 65 °F	Cooling Degree Days Base 65 °F	Total Global Radiation Btu/ft²	Total Global Radiation Langleys
Jan	48.4	27.3	37.9	839	0	721.7	195.7
Feb	50.6	28.2	39.4	716	0	971.4	263.5
Mar	58.3	33.5	45.9	590	0	1306.0	354.3
Apr	69.4	42.4	55.9	279	5	1667.6	452.3
May	76.8	50.6	63.7	99	59	1804.4	489.4
June	82.5	58.7	70.6	13	182	1854.5	503.0
July	84.3	62.6	73.5	0	263	1776.1	481.8
Aug	83.8	61.8	72.8	0	243	1626.7	441.2
Sept	78.0	55.4	66.7	49	101	1360.8	369.1
Oct	69.1	44.5	56.8	268	14	1147.4	311.2
Nov	58.2	34.3	46.3	560	0	848.8	230.2
Dec	49.3	28.1	38.7	814	0	657.6	178.4
Ann	67.4	44.0	55.7	4235	871	1311.9	355.9

SOLMET STATION NO. 93729

LATITUDE: 35° 16′ N
LONGITUDE: 75° 33′ W
ELEVATION: 2 meters (6.6 feet)

Cape Hatteras, North Carolina

	Maximum Daily Temp. °F	Minimum Daily Temp. °F	Average Monthly Temp. °F	Heating Degree Days Base 65 °F	Cooling Degree Days Base 65 °F	Total Global Radiation Btu/ft²	Total Global Radiation Langleys
Jan	52.3	38.2	45.3	610	0	685.6	186.0
Feb	53.1	38.5	45.8	536	0	952.2	258.3
Mar	57.9	43.2	50.6	457	11	1326.4	359.8
Apr	66.3	51.5	58.9	187	4	1773.9	481.2
May	73.8	60.2	67.0	47	108	1961.8	532.1
June	80.5	68.1	74.3	0	283	2035.9	552.2
July	83.8	72.1	78.0	0	401	1920.6	521.0
Aug	83.4	71.5	77.5	0	387	1705.4	462.6
Sept	79.5	67.8	73.7	0	261	1470.4	398.9
Oct	71.3	59.1	65.2	76	81	1136.6	308.3
Nov	63.1	48.8	56.0	275	5	872.9	236.8
Dec	54.8	40.5	47.7	535	0	658.7	178.7
Ann	68.3	55.0	61.7	2731	1550	1375.0	373.0

STATION NO. 13722

LATITUDE: 35° 52′ N
LONGITUDE: 78° 47′ W
ELEVATION: 134 meters (439.5 feet)

Raleigh / Durham, North Carolina

	Maximum Daily Temp. °F	Minimum Daily Temp. °F	Average Monthly Temp. °F	Heating Degree Days Base 65 °F	Cooling Degree Days Base 65 °F	Total Global Radiation Btu/ft²	Total Global Radiation Langleys
Jan	51.0	30.0	40.5	760	0	693.9	188.2
Feb	53.2	31.1	42.2	637	0	943.1	255.8
Mar	61.0	37.4	49.2	500	11	1275.7	346.0
Apr	72.2	46.7	59.5	180	14	1644.3	446.0
May	79.4	55.4	67.4	47	122	1808.3	490.5
June	85.6	63.1	74.4	0	281	1864.1	505.6
July	87.7	67.2	77.5	0	387	1775.6	481.6
Aug	86.8	66.2	76.5	0	356	1611.3	437.1
Sept	81.5	59.7	70.6	11	180	1377.1	373.5
Oct	72.4	48.0	60.2	185	36	1105.4	299.8
Nov	62.1	37.8	50.0	450	0	812.1	220.3
Dec	51.9	30.5	41.2	738	0	635.6	172.4
Ann	70.4	47.8	59.1	3514	1393	1295.5	351.4

SOLMET STATION NO. 24011

LATITUDE: 46° 46′ N
LONGITUDE: 100° 45′ W
ELEVATION: 502 meters (1646.6 feet)

Bismarck, North Dakota

	Maximum Daily Temp. °F	Minimum Daily Temp. °F	Average Monthly Temp. °F	Heating Degree Days Base 65 °F	Cooling Degree Days Base 65 °F	Total Global Radiation Btu/ft²	Total Global Radiation Langleys
Jan	19.1	−2.8	8.2	1760	0	466.8	126.6
Feb	24.5	2.4	13.5	1442	0	775.7	210.4
Mar	35.4	14.7	25.1	1237	0	1168.1	316.9
Apr	54.8	31.1	43.0	659	0	1459.3	395.8
May	67.1	41.7	54.4	338	11	1848.1	501.3
June	75.8	51.8	63.8	121	85	2059.8	558.7
July	84.3	57.3	70.8	18	198	2183.6	592.3
Aug	83.5	54.9	69.2	34	164	1876.7	509.0
Sept	71.3	43.7	57.5	252	27	1354.5	367.4
Oct	60.3	33.2	46.8	563	0	907.8	246.2
Nov	39.4	18.3	28.9	1082	0	507.3	137.6
Dec	26.0	5.2	15.6	1530	0	372.9	101.1
Ann	53.5	29.3	41.4	9043	486	1248.4	338.6

STATION NO. 14914

LATITUDE: 46° 54′ N
LONGITUDE: 96° 48′ W
ELEVATION: 274 meters (898.7 feet)

Fargo, North Dakota

	Maximum Daily Temp. °F	Minimum Daily Temp. °F	Average Monthly Temp. °F	Heating Degree Days Base 65 °F	Cooling Degree Days Base 65 °F	Total Global Radiation Btu/ft²	Total Global Radiation Langleys
Jan	15.4	−3.6	5.9	1831	0	414.9	112.5
Feb	20.6	0.8	10.7	1519	0	705.7	191.4
Mar	33.5	14.9	24.2	1264	0	1097.9	297.8
Apr	52.6	31.9	42.3	680	0	1475.7	400.3
May	66.8	42.3	54.6	333	11	1834.7	497.7
June	75.9	53.4	64.7	95	86	1993.9	540.9
July	82.8	58.6	70.7	13	189	2119.9	575.0
Aug	81.6	56.8	69.2	32	162	1825.3	495.1
Sept	69.6	46.2	57.9	234	20	1303.7	353.6
Oct	58.4	35.5	47.0	558	0	873.8	237.0
Nov	37.2	20.0	28.6	1091	0	457.3	124.0
Dec	21.9	4.1	13.0	1611	0	337.3	91.5
Ann	51.4	30.1	40.8	9270	472	1203.4	326.4

STATION NO. 14895

LATITUDE: 40° 55′ N
LONGITUDE: 81° 26′ W
ELEVATION: 377 meters (1236.6 feet)

Akron / Canton, Ohio

	Maximum Daily Temp. °F	Minimum Daily Temp. °F	Average Monthly Temp. °F	Heating Degree Days Base 65 °F	Cooling Degree Days Base 65 °F	Total Global Radiation Btu/ft²	Total Global Radiation Langleys
Jan	33.9	18.6	26.3	1199	0	428.2	116.2
Feb	36.0	19.4	27.7	1044	0	649.5	176.2
Mar	45.4	26.9	36.2	893	0	964.1	261.5
Apr	59.3	37.7	48.5	495	0	1357.0	368.1
May	69.8	47.5	58.7	230	36	1667.8	452.4
June	79.4	57.1	68.3	32	131	1839.1	498.9
July	82.6	60.8	71.7	9	216	1786.9	484.7
Aug	81.3	59.3	70.3	14	180	1595.7	432.8
Sept	74.7	52.7	63.7	101	61	1271.8	345.0
Oct	63.7	42.8	53.3	369	5	907.6	246.2
Nov	48.6	32.7	40.7	729	0	504.7	136.9
Dec	36.5	22.2	29.4	1103	0	353.2	95.8
Ann	59.3	39.8	49.6	6223	634	1110.5	301.2

STATION NO. 93814

Cincinnati (Covington, KY), Ohio

LATITUDE: 39° 4′ N
LONGITUDE: 84° 40′ W
ELEVATION: 271 meters (888.9 feet)

	Maximum Daily Temp. °F	Minimum Daily Temp. °F	Average Monthly Temp. °F	Heating Degree Days Base 65 °F	Cooling Degree Days Base 65 °F	Total Global Radiation Btu/ft²	Total Global Radiation Langleys
Jan	39.7	22.4	31.1	1049	0	500.5	135.8
Feb	42.7	23.8	33.3	887	0	738.4	200.3
Mar	51.8	31.6	41.7	722	0	1027.3	278.7
Apr	65.0	42.7	53.9	340	7	1398.5	379.4
May	74.4	51.9	63.2	137	81	1672.4	453.6
June	83.2	61.0	72.1	9	221	1837.1	498.3
July	86.5	64.6	75.6	0	328	1770.9	480.4
Aug	85.8	63.0	74.4	0	293	1634.4	443.3
Sept	79.7	55.9	67.8	43	128	1311.6	355.8
Oct	68.5	45.0	56.8	270	16	989.8	268.5
Nov	53.2	34.3	43.8	635	0	588.5	159.6
Dec	42.0	25.3	33.7	968	0	432.5	117.3
Ann	64.4	43.5	54.0	5069	1080	1158.5	314.3

STATION NO. 14820

Cleveland, Ohio

LATITUDE: 41° 24′ N
LONGITUDE: 81° 51′ W
ELEVATION: 245 meters (803.6 feet)

	Maximum Daily Temp. °F	Minimum Daily Temp. °F	Average Monthly Temp. °F	Heating Degree Days Base 65 °F	Cooling Degree Days Base 65 °F	Total Global Radiation Btu/ft²	Total Global Radiation Langleys
Jan	33.4	20.3	26.9	1181	0	388.4	105.4
Feb	35.0	20.8	27.9	1039	0	601.1	163.1
Mar	44.1	28.1	36.1	895	0	922.3	250.2
Apr	58.0	38.5	48.3	500	0	1349.5	366.0
May	68.4	48.1	58.3	243	36	1681.1	456.0
June	78.2	57.5	67.9	40	126	1843.3	500.0
July	81.6	61.2	71.4	9	207	1827.9	495.8
Aug	80.4	59.6	70.0	16	171	1582.6	429.3
Sept	74.2	53.5	63.9	94	61	1239.5	336.2
Oct	63.6	43.9	53.8	353	5	867.0	235.2
Nov	48.8	34.4	41.6	702	0	466.1	126.4
Dec	36.4	24.1	30.3	1075	0	317.9	86.2
Ann	58.5	40.8	49.7	6152	612	1090.6	295.8

STATION NO. 14821

Columbus, Ohio

LATITUDE: 40° 0′ N
LONGITUDE: 82° 53′ W
ELEVATION: 254 meters (833.1 feet)

	Maximum Daily Temp. °F	Minimum Daily Temp. °F	Average Monthly Temp. °F	Heating Degree Days Base 65 °F	Cooling Degree Days Base 65 °F	Total Global Radiation Btu/ft²	Total Global Radiation Langleys
Jan	36.4	20.4	28.4	1134	0	459.3	124.6
Feb	39.2	21.4	30.3	972	0	676.8	183.6
Mar	49.3	29.1	39.2	799	0	979.6	265.7
Apr	62.8	39.5	51.2	418	0	1352.9	367.0
May	72.9	49.3	61.1	175	54	1646.9	446.7
June	81.9	58.9	70.4	13	175	1812.7	491.7
July	84.8	62.4	73.6	0	266	1754.9	476.0
Aug	83.7	60.1	71.9	7	221	1640.6	445.0
Sept	77.6	52.7	65.2	76	81	1281.6	347.6
Oct	66.4	42.0	54.2	342	7	945.1	256.4
Nov	50.9	32.4	41.7	698	0	537.8	145.9
Dec	38.7	22.7	30.7	1062	0	387.2	105.0
Ann	62.1	40.9	51.5	5701	808	1122.9	304.6

STATION NO. 13967

LATITUDE: 35° 24′ N
LONGITUDE: 97° 36′ W
ELEVATION: 397 meters (1302.2 feet)

Oklahoma City, Oklahoma

	Maximum Daily Temp. °F	Minimum Daily Temp. °F	Average Monthly Temp. °F	Heating Degree Days Base 65 °F	Cooling Degree Days Base 65 °F	Total Global Radiation Btu/ft²	Total Global Radiation Langleys
Jan	47.6	26.0	36.8	873	0	800.9	217.2
Feb	52.6	30.0	41.3	662	0	1055.0	286.2
Mar	59.8	36.5	48.2	531	11	1400.1	379.8
Apr	71.6	49.1	60.4	180	41	1725.4	468.0
May	78.7	57.9	68.3	36	137	1918.1	520.3
June	87.0	66.6	76.8	0	353	2143.9	581.5
July	92.6	70.4	81.5	0	511	2128.4	577.3
Aug	92.5	69.6	81.1	0	499	1950.3	529.0
Sept	84.7	61.3	73.0	11	252	1554.2	421.6
Oct	74.2	50.6	62.4	148	67	1232.6	334.4
Nov	60.9	37.4	49.2	473	0	901.0	244.4
Dec	50.7	29.2	40.0	774	0	725.4	196.8
Ann	71.1	48.7	59.9	3694	1876	1461.3	396.4

STATION NO. 13968

LATITUDE: 36° 12′ N
LONGITUDE: 95° 54′ W
ELEVATION: 206 meters (675.7 feet)

Tulsa, Oklahoma

	Maximum Daily Temp. °F	Minimum Daily Temp. °F	Average Monthly Temp. °F	Heating Degree Days Base 65 °F	Cooling Degree Days Base 65 °F	Total Global Radiation Btu/ft²	Total Global Radiation Langleys
Jan	47.0	26.1	36.6	878	0	731.7	198.5
Feb	52.2	30.2	41.2	666	0	978.2	265.3
Mar	59.7	36.9	48.3	527	9	1305.5	354.1
Apr	71.8	49.7	60.8	175	49	1602.7	434.7
May	79.2	58.4	68.8	27	144	1822.2	494.3
June	87.3	67.3	77.3	0	369	2020.6	548.1
July	92.8	71.4	82.1	0	529	2030.5	550.8
Aug	92.7	70.0	81.4	0	508	1865.4	506.0
Sept	84.8	61.7	73.3	9	257	1472.7	399.5
Oct	75.0	50.8	62.9	142	77	1163.8	315.7
Nov	60.8	38.0	49.4	468	0	827.4	224.4
Dec	50.1	29.5	39.8	779	0	659.3	178.8
Ann	71.1	49.2	60.2	3679	1948	1373.3	372.5

STATION NO. 24134

LATITUDE: 43° 35′ N
LONGITUDE: 119° 3′ W
ELEVATION: 1271 meters (4168.9 feet)

Burns, Oregon

	Maximum Daily Temp. °F	Minimum Daily Temp. °F	Average Monthly Temp. °F	Heating Degree Days Base 65 °F	Cooling Degree Days Base 65 °F	Total Global Radiation Btu/ft²	Total Global Radiation Langleys
Jan	35.4	15.0	25.2	1233	0	490.0	132.9
Feb	41.5	20.4	31.0	950	0	792.0	214.8
Mar	47.9	24.2	36.1	895	0	1187.1	322.0
Apr	58.1	30.2	44.2	623	0	1648.6	447.2
May	66.5	37.8	52.2	401	4	2052.4	556.7
June	73.9	44.1	59.0	203	23	2279.7	618.4
July	85.6	51.1	68.4	29	135	2460.0	667.3
Aug	83.4	48.8	66.1	67	101	2082.7	564.9
Sept	75.4	40.9	58.2	225	22	1620.1	439.4
Oct	62.6	32.0	47.3	549	0	1042.6	282.8
Nov	47.2	24.3	35.8	875	0	593.5	161.0
Dec	37.5	18.3	27.9	1148	0	430.5	116.8
Ann	59.6	32.3	46.0	7211	288	1389.9	377.0

SOLMET STATION NO. 24225

Medford, Oregon

LATITUDE: 42° 22′ N
LONGITUDE: 122° 52′ W
ELEVATION: 396 meters (1298.9 feet)

	Maximum Daily Temp. °F	Minimum Daily Temp. °F	Average Monthly Temp. °F	Heating Degree Days Base 65 °F	Cooling Degree Days Base 65 °F	Total Global Radiation Btu/ft²	Total Global Radiation Langleys
Jan	44.2	29.0	36.6	878	0	406.9	110.4
Feb	51.8	30.7	41.3	662	0	737.4	200.0
Mar	56.7	32.8	44.8	625	0	1132.6	307.2
Apr	63.8	36.6	50.2	443	0	1638.7	444.5
May	71.7	42.8	57.3	248	11	2033.7	551.6
June	79.4	49.1	64.3	94	72	2277.8	617.9
July	89.5	53.8	71.7	11	218	2475.5	671.5
Aug	87.8	52.9	70.4	20	189	2120.6	575.2
Sept	82.1	46.7	64.4	88	70	1589.0	431.0
Oct	67.4	39.4	53.4	360	0	981.9	266.4
Nov	52.7	34.2	43.5	644	0	504.3	136.8
Dec	44.2	31.1	37.7	846	0	336.7	91.3
Ann	66.0	39.9	53.0	4928	562	1352.9	367.0

STATION NO. 24155

Pendleton, Oregon

LATITUDE: 45° 41′ N
LONGITUDE: 118° 51′ W
ELEVATION: 456 meters (1495.7 feet)

	Maximum Daily Temp. °F	Minimum Daily Temp. °F	Average Monthly Temp. °F	Heating Degree Days Base 65 °F	Cooling Degree Days Base 65 °F	Total Global Radiation Btu/ft²	Total Global Radiation Langleys
Jan	38.6	25.3	32.0	1022	0	348.1	94.4
Feb	46.5	31.3	38.9	731	0	613.6	166.4
Mar	53.2	34.3	43.8	657	0	1043.6	283.1
Apr	61.9	39.8	50.9	423	0	1502.7	407.6
May	70.4	46.5	58.5	220	18	1925.5	522.3
June	78.3	52.8	65.6	68	86	2144.3	581.6
July	88.2	58.8	73.5	5	268	2395.7	649.8
Aug	85.5	57.5	71.5	13	212	1994.0	540.9
Sept	76.9	51.1	64.0	95	67	1502.2	407.5
Oct	63.4	41.8	52.6	383	0	908.1	246.3
Nov	48.9	33.8	41.4	707	0	438.4	118.9
Dec	41.8	29.6	35.7	907	0	293.0	79.5
Ann	62.8	41.9	52.4	5240	655	1259.1	341.5

STATION NO. 24229

Portland, Oregon

LATITUDE: 45° 36′ N
LONGITUDE: 122° 36′ W
ELEVATION: 12 meters (39.4 feet)

	Maximum Daily Temp. °F	Minimum Daily Temp. °F	Average Monthly Temp. °F	Heating Degree Days Base 65 °F	Cooling Degree Days Base 65 °F	Total Global Radiation Btu/ft²	Total Global Radiation Langleys
Jan	43.6	32.5	38.1	833	0	310.0	84.1
Feb	50.1	35.5	42.8	621	0	554.1	150.3
Mar	54.3	37.0	45.7	598	0	895.0	242.8
Apr	60.3	40.8	50.6	432	0	1307.7	354.7
May	67.0	46.3	56.7	263	5	1663.2	451.2
June	72.1	51.8	62.0	128	38	1772.5	480.8
July	79.0	55.2	67.1	47	113	2037.3	552.6
Aug	78.1	55.0	66.6	56	104	1673.7	454.0
Sept	73.9	50.5	62.2	119	34	1216.7	330.0
Oct	62.9	44.7	53.8	346	0	723.6	196.3
Nov	52.1	38.5	45.3	590	0	387.5	105.1
Dec	46.0	35.3	40.7	752	0	259.8	70.5
Ann	61.6	43.6	52.6	4792	299	1066.8	289.4

STATION NO. 14737

Allentown, Pennsylvania

LATITUDE: 40° 39′ N
LONGITUDE: 75° 26′ W
ELEVATION: 117 meters (383.8 feet)

	Maximum Daily Temp. °F	Minimum Daily Temp. °F	Average Monthly Temp. °F	Heating Degree Days Base 65 °F	Cooling Degree Days Base 65 °F	Total Global Radiation Btu/ft²	Total Global Radiation Langleys
Jan	35.7	19.8	27.8	1152	0	527.5	143.1
Feb	37.9	20.9	29.4	995	0	763.5	207.1
Mar	47.7	28.5	38.1	833	0	1078.3	292.5
Apr	61.3	38.5	49.9	452	0	1409.6	382.4
May	71.7	48.4	60.1	189	38	1636.8	444.0
June	81.0	57.9	69.5	20	155	1776.9	482.0
July	85.4	62.7	74.1	0	281	1764.9	478.7
Aug	82.8	60.6	71.7	5	212	1546.0	419.4
Sept	75.9	53.4	64.7	85	76	1238.1	335.8
Oct	65.6	42.5	54.1	344	5	926.0	251.2
Nov	51.7	32.8	42.3	680	0	568.2	154.1
Dec	38.7	22.6	30.7	1062	0	430.4	116.8
Ann	61.3	40.7	51.0	5827	770	1138.9	308.9

STATION NO. 14860

Erie, Pennsylvania

LATITUDE: 42° 5′ N
LONGITUDE: 80° 11′ W
ELEVATION: 225 meters (738.0 feet)

	Maximum Daily Temp. °F	Minimum Daily Temp. °F	Average Monthly Temp. °F	Heating Degree Days Base 65 °F	Cooling Degree Days Base 65 °F	Total Global Radiation Btu/ft²	Total Global Radiation Langleys
Jan	31.7	18.5	25.1	1237	0	345.6	93.7
Feb	32.5	17.9	25.2	1112	0	576.8	156.5
Mar	40.4	25.4	32.9	994	0	920.4	249.6
Apr	53.5	36.1	44.8	605	0	1359.0	368.6
May	63.7	45.5	54.6	335	13	1646.3	446.6
June	73.5	55.6	64.6	79	67	1846.6	500.9
July	77.4	60.0	68.7	23	139	1832.8	497.1
Aug	76.0	58.9	67.5	41	119	1454.9	394.7
Sept	70.2	52.6	61.4	140	32	1201.3	325.8
Oct	60.2	43.0	51.6	414	0	827.1	224.4
Nov	46.5	33.7	40.1	747	0	416.2	112.9
Dec	34.8	23.3	29.1	1112	0	277.6	75.3
Ann	55.0	39.2	47.1	6851	373	1058.7	287.2

STATION NO. 14751

Harrisburg, Pennsylvania

LATITUDE: 40° 13′ N
LONGITUDE: 76° 51′ W
ELEVATION: 106 meters (347.7 feet)

	Maximum Daily Temp. °F	Minimum Daily Temp. °F	Average Monthly Temp. °F	Heating Degree Days Base 65 °F	Cooling Degree Days Base 65 °F	Total Global Radiation Btu/ft²	Total Global Radiation Langleys
Jan	37.7	22.5	30.1	1082	0	535.6	145.3
Feb	40.5	24.0	32.3	914	0	771.0	209.1
Mar	50.7	31.2	41.0	743	0	1083.0	293.8
Apr	64.1	41.5	52.8	369	0	1410.5	382.6
May	74.5	51.6	63.1	128	68	1652.3	448.2
June	83.0	61.0	72.0	0	212	1804.6	489.5
July	86.8	65.4	76.1	0	344	1763.6	478.4
Aug	84.6	63.2	73.9	0	279	1550.5	420.6
Sept	78.0	56.0	67.0	50	110	1266.6	343.6
Oct	66.9	44.6	55.8	292	7	934.2	253.4
Nov	52.9	34.7	43.8	635	0	578.6	157.0
Dec	40.1	25.0	32.6	1003	0	447.3	121.3
Ann	63.3	43.4	53.4	5224	1024	1149.8	311.9

STATION NO. 13739

Philadelphia, Pennsylvania

LATITUDE: 39° 53′ N
LONGITUDE: 75° 15′ W
ELEVATION: 9 meters (29.5 feet)

	Maximum Daily Temp. °F	Minimum Daily Temp. °F	Average Monthly Temp. °F	Heating Degree Days Base 65 °F	Cooling Degree Days Base 65 °F	Total Global Radiation Btu/ft²	Total Global Radiation Langleys
Jan	40.1	24.4	32.3	1013	0	555.3	150.6
Feb	42.2	25.5	33.9	869	0	794.5	215.5
Mar	51.2	32.5	41.9	715	0	1108.2	300.6
Apr	63.5	42.3	52.9	365	0	1433.9	388.9
May	74.1	52.3	63.2	121	67	1659.9	450.2
June	83.0	61.6	72.3	0	221	1811.2	491.3
July	86.8	66.7	76.8	0	365	1758.1	476.9
Aug	84.8	64.7	74.8	0	302	1574.5	427.1
Sept	78.4	57.8	68.1	38	130	1281.4	347.6
Oct	67.9	46.9	57.4	248	13	958.5	260.0
Nov	55.5	36.9	46.2	563	0	619.3	168.0
Dec	43.2	27.2	35.2	923	0	470.4	127.6
Ann	64.2	44.9	54.6	4864	1103	1168.7	317.0

STATION NO. 94823

Pittsburgh, Pennsylvania

LATITUDE: 40° 30′ N
LONGITUDE: 80° 13′ W
ELEVATION: 373 meters (1223.4 feet)

	Maximum Daily Temp. °F	Minimum Daily Temp. °F	Average Monthly Temp. °F	Heating Degree Days Base 65 °F	Cooling Degree Days Base 65 °F	Total Global Radiation Btu/ft²	Total Global Radiation Langleys
Jan	35.3	20.8	28.1	1143	0	424.4	115.1
Feb	37.3	21.3	29.3	999	0	625.3	169.6
Mar	47.2	29.0	38.1	833	0	942.6	255.7
Apr	60.9	39.4	50.2	443	0	1316.6	357.1
May	70.8	48.7	59.8	207	45	1601.7	434.5
June	79.5	57.7	68.6	25	133	1761.6	477.8
July	82.5	61.3	71.9	5	220	1689.2	458.2
Aug	80.9	59.4	70.2	14	176	1510.4	409.7
Sept	74.9	52.7	63.8	97	61	1208.9	327.9
Oct	63.9	42.4	53.2	371	5	895.0	242.8
Nov	49.3	33.3	41.3	711	0	504.7	136.9
Dec	37.3	23.6	30.5	1069	0	346.8	94.1
Ann	60.0	40.8	50.4	5929	646	1068.9	289.9

STATION NO. 14765

Providence, Rhode Island

LATITUDE: 41° 44′ N
LONGITUDE: 71° 26′ W
ELEVATION: 19 meters (62.3 feet)

	Maximum Daily Temp. °F	Minimum Daily Temp. °F	Average Monthly Temp. °F	Heating Degree Days Base 65 °F	Cooling Degree Days Base 65 °F	Total Global Radiation Btu/ft²	Total Global Radiation Langleys
Jan	36.2	20.6	28.4	1134	0	506.2	137.3
Feb	37.6	21.2	29.4	995	0	738.5	200.3
Mar	44.7	29.0	36.9	869	0	1031.8	279.9
Apr	56.7	37.8	47.3	531	0	1373.9	372.7
May	66.8	46.9	56.9	257	7	1655.1	449.0
June	76.3	56.5	66.4	36	77	1775.5	481.6
July	81.1	63.0	72.1	0	223	1695.4	459.9
Aug	79.8	61.0	70.4	9	176	1498.6	406.5
Sept	73.1	53.6	63.4	92	45	1208.8	327.9
Oct	63.9	43.4	53.7	349	0	906.7	245.9
Nov	52.0	34.6	43.3	650	0	537.5	145.8
Dec	39.6	23.4	31.5	1039	0	418.5	113.5
Ann	59.0	40.9	50.0	5971	531	1112.2	301.7

SOLMET STATION NO. 13880

LATITUDE: 32° 54′ N
LONGITUDE: 80° 2′ W
ELEVATION: 12 meters (39.4 feet)

Charleston, South Carolina

	Maximum Daily Temp. °F	Minimum Daily Temp. °F	Average Monthly Temp. °F	Heating Degree Days Base 65 °F	Cooling Degree Days Base 65 °F	Total Global Radiation Btu/ft²	Total Global Radiation Langleys
Jan	59.8	37.3	48.6	520	11	744.2	201.9
Feb	61.9	39.0	50.5	418	13	995.3	270.0
Mar	67.8	45.1	56.5	299	36	1338.6	363.1
Apr	76.2	53.0	64.6	68	56	1732.3	469.9
May	83.1	61.1	72.1	4	225	1860.2	504.6
June	87.7	68.1	77.9	0	387	1843.9	500.2
July	89.1	71.2	80.2	0	470	1798.9	488.0
Aug	88.6	70.6	79.6	0	452	1585.3	430.0
Sept	84.5	65.9	75.2	0	306	1394.1	378.2
Oct	77.1	55.1	66.1	74	108	1192.7	323.5
Nov	68.4	44.1	56.3	270	9	934.1	253.4
Dec	60.8	37.7	49.3	486	0	720.7	195.5
Ann	75.4	54.0	64.7	2146	2077	1345.1	364.8

STATION NO. 13883

LATITUDE: 33° 57′ N
LONGITUDE: 81° 7′ W
ELEVATION: 69 meters (226.3 feet)

Columbia, South Carolina

	Maximum Daily Temp. °F	Minimum Daily Temp. °F	Average Monthly Temp. °F	Heating Degree Days Base 65 °F	Cooling Degree Days Base 65 °F	Total Global Radiation Btu/ft²	Total Global Radiation Langleys
Jan	56.9	33.9	45.4	607	0	761.7	206.6
Feb	59.7	35.5	47.6	491	4	1020.5	276.8
Mar	66.5	41.9	54.2	360	23	1355.0	367.5
Apr	76.9	51.3	64.1	83	56	1746.8	473.8
May	84.5	59.6	72.1	11	232	1894.9	514.0
June	90.3	67.2	78.8	0	414	1946.9	528.1
July	92.0	70.3	81.2	0	500	1841.8	499.6
Aug	91.0	69.4	80.2	0	470	1702.7	461.9
Sept	85.4	63.5	74.5	0	288	1439.3	390.4
Oct	77.1	51.3	64.2	112	86	1211.4	328.6
Nov	66.9	40.6	53.8	340	4	921.2	249.9
Dec	57.9	34.1	46.0	589	0	722.1	195.9
Ann	75.4	51.5	63.5	2597	2086	1380.4	374.4

STATION NO. 24090

LATITUDE: 44° 3′ N
LONGITUDE: 103° 4′ W
ELEVATION: 966 meters (3168.5 feet)

Rapid City, South Dakota

	Maximum Daily Temp. °F	Minimum Daily Temp. °F	Average Monthly Temp. °F	Heating Degree Days Base 65 °F	Cooling Degree Days Base 65 °F	Total Global Radiation Btu/ft²	Total Global Radiation Langleys
Jan	34.2	9.6	21.9	1336	0	542.3	147.1
Feb	37.6	13.9	25.8	1098	0	826.5	224.2
Mar	42.7	19.7	31.2	1048	0	1228.8	333.3
Apr	57.2	32.0	44.6	612	0	1589.1	431.1
May	67.4	42.9	55.2	319	14	1887.0	511.8
June	76.3	52.0	64.2	133	110	2131.2	578.1
July	86.3	58.8	72.6	13	248	2223.0	603.0
Aug	85.9	57.2	71.6	16	221	1962.7	532.4
Sept	74.7	46.3	60.5	191	56	1517.9	411.7
Oct	63.6	36.4	50.0	473	9	1063.6	288.5
Nov	47.5	23.2	35.4	887	0	646.7	175.4
Dec	38.0	14.9	26.5	1193	0	476.4	129.2
Ann	59.3	33.9	46.6	7322	661	1341.3	363.8

STATION NO. 14944

LATITUDE: 43° 34′ N
LONGITUDE: 96° 44′ W
ELEVATION: 435 meters (1426.8 feet)

Sioux Falls, South Dakota

	Maximum Daily Temp. °F	Minimum Daily Temp. °F	Average Monthly Temp. °F	Heating Degree Days Base 65 °F	Cooling Degree Days Base 65 °F	Total Global Radiation Btu/ft^2	Total Global Radiation Langleys
Jan	24.6	3.7	14.2	1575	0	532.6	144.5
Feb	29.7	9.0	19.4	1276	0	802.1	217.6
Mar	39.7	20.2	30.0	1084	0	1152.2	312.5
Apr	57.8	34.4	46.1	567	0	1542.9	418.5
May	69.7	45.7	57.7	257	31	1893.7	513.7
June	78.9	56.3	67.6	65	142	2099.9	569.6
July	85.1	61.5	73.3	9	266	2149.6	583.1
Aug	83.8	59.8	71.8	18	229	1844.5	500.3
Sept	73.0	48.7	60.9	164	41	1409.8	382.4
Oct	62.7	37.6	50.2	464	5	1005.3	272.7
Nov	43.5	22.7	33.1	956	0	607.5	164.8
Dec	29.6	10.4	20.0	1395	0	441.1	119.6
Ann	56.5	34.2	45.4	7837	718	1290.1	349.9

STATION NO. 13882

LATITUDE: 35° 2′ N
LONGITUDE: 85° 12′ W
ELEVATION: 210 meters (688.8 feet)

Chattanooga, Tennessee

	Maximum Daily Temp. °F	Minimum Daily Temp. °F	Average Monthly Temp. °F	Heating Degree Days Base 65 °F	Cooling Degree Days Base 65 °F	Total Global Radiation Btu/ft^2	Total Global Radiation Langleys
Jan	49.9	30.5	40.2	769	0	630.5	171.0
Feb	53.4	32.3	42.9	625	5	858.6	232.9
Mar	61.2	38.4	49.8	482	11	1176.2	319.1
Apr	72.9	48.1	60.5	164	29	1549.7	420.4
May	81.0	56.0	68.5	50	158	1731.9	469.8
June	87.5	64.5	76.0	0	329	1831.4	496.8
July	89.5	68.1	78.8	0	427	1735.2	470.7
Aug	89.0	67.0	78.0	0	401	1630.0	442.1
Sept	83.4	60.4	71.9	9	216	1335.5	362.2
Oct	73.5	48.1	60.8	182	50	1108.2	300.6
Nov	60.7	37.1	48.9	482	0	772.9	209.7
Dec	50.9	31.4	41.2	738	0	580.4	157.4
Ann	71.1	48.5	59.8	3505	1634	1245.1	337.7

STATION NO. 13893

LATITUDE: 35° 3′ N
LONGITUDE: 89° 59′ W
ELEVATION: 87 meters (285.4 feet)

Memphis, Tennessee

	Maximum Daily Temp. °F	Minimum Daily Temp. °F	Average Monthly Temp. °F	Heating Degree Days Base 65 °F	Cooling Degree Days Base 65 °F	Total Global Radiation Btu/ft^2	Total Global Radiation Langleys
Jan	49.4	31.6	40.5	760	0	682.7	185.2
Feb	53.1	34.4	43.0	594	0	944.8	256.3
Mar	60.8	41.1	51.0	455	22	1278.1	346.7
Apr	72.7	52.3	62.5	130	56	1638.7	444.5
May	81.2	60.6	70.9	22	203	1884.9	511.3
June	88.7	68.5	78.6	0	407	2044.6	554.6
July	91.6	71.5	81.6	0	515	1972.0	534.9
Aug	90.6	70.1	80.4	0	477	1824.0	494.8
Sept	84.3	62.8	73.6	5	265	1470.9	399.0
Oct	74.9	51.1	63.0	140	79	1204.5	326.7
Nov	61.5	40.3	50.9	423	0	816.7	221.5
Dec	51.7	33.7	42.7	689	0	628.6	170.5
Ann	71.7	51.5	61.6	3226	2029	1365.9	370.5

SOLMET STATION NO. 13897

LATITUDE: 36° 7′ N
LONGITUDE: 86° 41′ W
ELEVATION: 180 meters (590.4 feet)

Nashville, Tennessee

	Maximum Daily Temp. °F	Minimum Daily Temp. °F	Average Monthly Temp. °F	Heating Degree Days Base 65 °F	Cooling Degree Days Base 65 °F	Total Global Radiation Btu/ft²	Total Global Radiation Langleys
Jan	47.6	29.0	38.3	828	0	579.6	157.2
Feb	50.9	31.0	41.0	671	0	823.8	223.5
Mar	59.2	38.1	48.7	524	18	1129.8	306.5
Apr	71.3	48.8	60.1	175	29	1543.6	418.7
May	79.8	57.3	68.5	45	153	1824.8	495.0
June	87.5	65.7	76.6	0	347	1963.0	532.5
July	90.2	69.0	79.6	0	452	1891.1	513.0
Aug	89.2	67.7	78.5	0	418	1736.9	471.1
Sept	83.5	60.5	72.0	9	220	1397.9	379.2
Oct	73.2	48.6	60.9	180	52	1113.8	302.1
Nov	59.0	37.7	48.4	497	0	711.3	192.9
Dec	49.6	31.1	40.4	761	0	520.6	141.2
Ann	70.1	48.7	59.4	3695	1694	1269.7	344.4

STATION NO. 13962

LATITUDE: 32° 26′ N
LONGITUDE: 99° 41′ W
ELEVATION: 534 meters (1751.5 feet)

Abilene, Texas

	Maximum Daily Temp. °F	Minimum Daily Temp. °F	Average Monthly Temp. °F	Heating Degree Days Base 65 °F	Cooling Degree Days Base 65 °F	Total Global Radiation Btu/ft²	Total Global Radiation Langleys
Jan	55.7	31.7	43.7	659	0	923.8	250.6
Feb	59.9	35.9	47.9	479	0	1182.6	320.8
Mar	67.3	41.7	54.5	353	29	1576.1	427.5
Apr	77.7	52.7	65.2	103	110	1843.4	500.0
May	83.9	60.8	72.4	11	239	2037.4	552.6
June	91.6	69.0	80.3	0	459	2208.7	599.1
July	95.3	72.4	83.9	0	585	2139.1	580.2
Aug	95.3	71.9	83.6	0	576	1956.1	530.6
Sept	87.5	64.6	76.1	0	333	1597.6	433.3
Oct	78.0	54.2	66.1	88	122	1315.5	356.8
Nov	66.2	42.0	54.1	335	9	1007.9	273.4
Dec	58.2	34.5	46.4	576	0	863.3	234.2
Ann	76.4	52.6	64.5	2610	2466	1554.3	421.6

STATION NO. 23047

LATITUDE: 35° 14′ N
LONGITUDE: 101° 42′ W
ELEVATION: 1098 meters (3601.4 feet)

Amarillo, Texas

	Maximum Daily Temp. °F	Minimum Daily Temp. °F	Average Monthly Temp. °F	Heating Degree Days Base 65 °F	Cooling Degree Days Base 65 °F	Total Global Radiation Btu/ft²	Total Global Radiation Langleys
Jan	49.4	22.5	36.0	898	0	960.2	260.4
Feb	53.0	26.4	39.7	707	0	1243.5	337.3
Mar	60.0	31.2	45.6	599	0	1630.8	442.4
Apr	70.9	42.1	56.5	274	20	2019.1	547.7
May	79.2	51.9	65.6	81	99	2211.7	599.9
June	88.0	61.2	74.6	9	297	2393.1	649.1
July	91.4	65.9	78.7	0	425	2280.5	618.6
Aug	90.4	64.7	77.6	0	391	2103.1	570.5
Sept	82.9	56.7	69.8	20	164	1760.5	477.5
Oct	72.9	46.1	59.5	205	36	1403.5	380.7
Nov	60.0	32.5	46.3	560	0	1032.9	280.2
Dec	51.5	25.5	38.5	821	0	871.6	236.4
Ann	70.8	43.9	57.4	4181	1433	1659.2	450.1

STATION NO. 13958

LATITUDE: 30°18′ N
LONGITUDE: 97° 42′ W
ELEVATION: 189 meters (619.9 feet)

Austin, Texas

	Maximum Daily Temp. °F	Minimum Daily Temp. °F	Average Monthly Temp. °F	Heating Degree Days Base 65 °F	Cooling Degree Days Base 65 °F	Total Global Radiation Btu/ft²	Total Global Radiation Langleys
Jan	60.0	39.3	49.7	482	7	864.5	234.5
Feb	63.8	42.8	53.3	344	14	1124.6	305.0
Mar	70.7	48.2	59.5	221	50	1428.9	387.6
Apr	79.0	58.2	68.6	43	151	1605.1	435.4
May	85.2	65.1	75.2	0	315	1833.6	497.4
June	91.7	71.4	81.6	0	497	2072.0	562.0
July	95.4	73.7	84.6	0	607	2105.5	571.1
Aug	95.9	73.5	84.7	0	610	1931.3	523.9
Sept	89.4	68.4	78.9	0	416	1606.1	435.6
Oct	81.3	58.9	70.1	38	196	1333.3	361.6
Nov	70.2	48.0	59.1	203	27	986.7	267.6
Dec	63.0	41.6	52.3	398	4	825.1	223.8
Ann	78.8	57.4	68.1	1737	2907	1476.4	400.5

STATION NO. 12924

LATITUDE: 27° 46′ N
LONGITUDE: 97° 30′ W
ELEVATION: 13 meters (42.6 feet)

Corpus Christi, Texas

	Maximum Daily Temp. °F	Minimum Daily Temp. °F	Average Monthly Temp. °F	Heating Degree Days Base 65 °F	Cooling Degree Days Base 65 °F	Total Global Radiation Btu/ft²	Total Global Radiation Langleys
Jan	66.5	46.1	56.3	302	32	898.1	243.6
Feb	69.8	49.3	59.6	198	47	1147.4	311.2
Mar	75.5	54.2	64.9	119	117	1429.9	387.9
Apr	82.1	63.4	72.8	0	238	1642.4	445.5
May	86.6	69.1	77.9	0	400	1866.4	506.3
June	91.2	73.6	82.4	0	522	2093.8	567.9
July	94.4	75.2	84.8	0	614	2186.1	593.0
Aug	94.8	75.4	85.1	0	623	1990.8	540.0
Sept	90.0	72.0	81.0	0	479	1687.0	457.6
Oct	84.1	63.7	73.9	5	283	1416.3	384.2
Nov	75.2	54.6	64.9	81	77	1042.7	282.8
Dec	69.3	48.9	59.1	218	36	844.7	229.1
Ann	81.6	62.1	71.9	929	3474	1520.5	412.4

STATION NO. 13960

LATITUDE: 32° 51′ N
LONGITUDE: 96° 51′ W
ELEVATION: 149 meters (488.7 feet)

Dallas, Texas

	Maximum Daily Temp. °F	Minimum Daily Temp. °F	Average Monthly Temp. °F	Heating Degree Days Base 65 °F	Cooling Degree Days Base 65 °F	Total Global Radiation Btu/ft²	Total Global Radiation Langleys
Jan	55.1	35.7	45.4	607	0	821.5	222.8
Feb	59.2	39.5	49.4	436	0	1071.1	290.5
Mar	66.4	45.2	55.8	313	29	1421.8	385.7
Apr	76.3	56.4	66.4	70	112	1626.8	441.3
May	83.1	64.4	73.8	0	272	1888.5	512.3
June	90.6	72.6	81.6	0	497	2134.9	579.1
July	95.1	76.3	85.7	0	641	2122.1	575.6
Aug	95.7	75.9	85.8	0	644	1950.2	529.0
Sept	88.0	68.3	78.2	0	396	1587.1	430.5
Oct	78.4	57.5	68.0	54	148	1276.1	346.1
Nov	66.4	45.4	55.9	283	11	936.4	254.0
Dec	57.8	38.6	48.2	520	0	780.1	211.6
Ann	76.0	56.3	66.2	2290	2754	1468.1	398.2

STATION NO. 22010

Del Rio, Texas

LATITUDE: 29° 22′ N
LONGITUDE: 100° 55′ W
ELEVATION: 313 meters (1026.6 feet)

	Maximum Daily Temp. °F	Minimum Daily Temp. °F	Average Monthly Temp. °F	Heating Degree Days Base 65 °F	Cooling Degree Days Base 65 °F	Total Global Radiation Btu/ft²	Total Global Radiation Langleys
Jan	63.4	38.1	50.8	448	7	958.3	259.9
Feb	68.6	42.8	55.7	283	22	1205.8	327.1
Mar	76.4	48.8	62.6	162	86	1580.0	428.6
Apr	85.1	58.9	72.0	14	225	1699.5	461.0
May	90.2	66.1	78.2	0	409	1827.1	495.6
June	96.1	72.4	84.3	0	578	2023.9	549.0
July	99.2	74.2	86.7	0	671	2054.3	557.2
Aug	98.5	73.6	86.1	0	653	1936.5	525.3
Sept	91.9	68.5	80.2	0	455	1584.2	429.7
Oct	83.1	59.2	71.2	32	225	1359.6	368.8
Nov	72.2	46.9	59.6	184	22	1059.5	287.4
Dec	65.0	39.5	52.3	392	0	902.6	244.8
Ann	82.5	57.4	70.0	1523	3362	1515.9	411.2

SOLMET STATION NO. 3927

Fort Worth, Texas

LATITUDE: 32° 50′ N
LONGITUDE: 97° 3′ W
ELEVATION: 164 meters (537.9 feet)

	Maximum Daily Temp. °F	Minimum Daily Temp. °F	Average Monthly Temp. °F	Heating Degree Days Base 65 °F	Cooling Degree Days Base 65 °F	Total Global Radiation Btu/ft²	Total Global Radiation Langleys
Jan	55.7	33.9	44.8	625	0	805.3	218.4
Feb	59.8	37.6	48.7	455	0	1069.4	290.1
Mar	66.6	43.3	55.0	335	23	1409.2	382.2
Apr	76.3	54.1	65.2	86	94	1616.5	438.5
May	82.8	62.1	72.5	0	236	1890.4	512.8
June	90.8	70.3	80.6	0	468	2153.0	584.0
July	95.5	74.0	84.8	0	614	2155.2	584.6
Aug	96.1	73.7	84.9	0	616	1982.7	537.8
Sept	88.5	66.8	77.7	0	380	1621.3	439.8
Oct	79.2	56.0	67.6	59	140	1292.9	350.7
Nov	67.5	44.1	55.8	286	11	938.0	254.4
Dec	58.7	37.0	47.9	529	0	765.7	207.7
Ann	76.5	54.4	65.5	2381	2587	1474.9	400.1

STATION NO. 12960

Houston, Texas

LATITUDE: 29° 59′ N
LONGITUDE: 95° 22′ W
ELEVATION: 33 meters (108.2 feet)

	Maximum Daily Temp. °F	Minimum Daily Temp. °F	Average Monthly Temp. °F	Heating Degree Days Base 65 °F	Cooling Degree Days Base 65 °F	Total Global Radiation Btu/ft²	Total Global Radiation Langleys
Jan	62.6	41.5	52.1	416	14	772.4	209.5
Feb	66.0	44.6	55.3	293	22	1034.2	280.5
Mar	71.8	49.8	60.8	189	58	1297.4	351.9
Apr	79.4	59.3	69.4	22	155	1522.3	412.9
May	85.9	65.6	75.8	0	335	1774.9	481.4
June	91.3	70.9	81.1	0	482	1898.1	514.9
July	93.8	72.8	83.3	0	567	1828.1	495.9
Aug	94.3	72.4	83.4	0	569	1686.2	457.4
Sept	90.1	68.2	79.2	0	425	1471.0	399.0
Oct	83.5	58.3	70.9	23	207	1275.6	346.0
Nov	73.0	49.1	61.1	155	38	924.0	250.6
Dec	65.8	43.4	54.6	333	11	729.6	197.9
Ann	79.8	58.0	68.9	1433	2889	1351.1	366.5

STATION NO. 23042

Lubbock, Texas

LATITUDE: 33° 39′ N
LONGITUDE: 101° 49′ W
ELEVATION: 988 meters (3240.6 feet)

	Maximum Daily Temp. °F	Minimum Daily Temp. °F	Average Monthly Temp. °F	Heating Degree Days Base 65 °F	Cooling Degree Days Base 65 °F	Total Global Radiation Btu/ft²	Total Global Radiation Langleys
Jan	53.4	24.8	39.1	803	0	1030.9	279.6
Feb	57.0	28.3	42.7	623	0	1331.7	361.2
Mar	63.8	34.0	48.9	508	9	1762.0	477.9
Apr	74.8	45.1	60.0	189	40	2167.8	588.0
May	82.5	54.5	68.5	29	137	2395.9	649.9
June	90.6	63.6	77.1	0	362	2544.4	690.2
July	92.4	66.9	79.7	0	455	2411.8	654.2
Aug	91.3	65.5	78.4	0	414	2208.4	599.0
Sept	83.8	58.2	71.0	7	187	1820.1	493.7
Oct	74.7	47.3	61.0	162	38	1468.2	398.2
Nov	63.1	34.4	48.8	486	0	1116.1	302.7
Dec	55.2	27.4	41.3	734	0	934.5	253.5
Ann	73.6	45.8	59.7	3544	1647	1766.0	479.0

STATION NO. 93987

Lufkin, Texas

LATITUDE: 31° 14′ N
LONGITUDE: 94° 45′ W
ELEVATION: 96 meters (314.9 feet)

	Maximum Daily Temp. °F	Minimum Daily Temp. °F	Average Monthly Temp. °F	Heating Degree Days Base 65 °F	Cooling Degree Days Base 65 °F	Total Global Radiation Btu/ft²	Total Global Radiation Langleys
Jan	0.0 ND	0.0 ND	48.8	508	5	793.9	215.3
Feb	0.0 ND	0.0 ND	52.2	371	13	1069.2	290.0
Mar	0.0 ND	0.0 ND	58.0	256	38	1376.1	373.3
Apr	0.0 ND	0.0 ND	67.3	56	124	1623.9	440.5
May	0.0 ND	0.0 ND	74.1	0	281	1866.7	506.3
June	0.0 ND	0.0 ND	80.3	0	459	2055.3	557.5
July	0.0 ND	0.0 ND	83.0	0	558	2006.4	544.2
Aug	0.0 ND	0.0 ND	83.1	0	560	1864.1	505.6
Sept	0.0 ND	0.0 ND	77.5	0	374	1530.7	415.2
Oct	0.0 ND	0.0 ND	68.2	50	149	1348.7	365.8
Nov	0.0 ND	0.0 ND	57.2	256	22	963.3	261.3
Dec	0.0 ND	0.0 ND	50.8	439	0	767.6	208.2
Ann	0.0 ND	0.0 ND	66.7	1939	2592	1438.8	390.3

STATION NO. 23023

Midland / Odessa, Texas

LATITUDE: 31° 56′ N
LONGITUDE: 102° 12′ W
ELEVATION: 871 meters (2856.9 feet)

	Maximum Daily Temp. °F	Minimum Daily Temp. °F	Average Monthly Temp. °F	Heating Degree Days Base 65 °F	Cooling Degree Days Base 65 °F	Total Global Radiation Btu/ft²	Total Global Radiation Langleys
Jan	57.8	29.4	43.6	662	0	1081.2	293.3
Feb	62.1	33.5	47.[illegible]	481	0	1382.6	375.0
Mar	69.4	39.2	54.3	347	16	1838.8	498.8
Apr	79.1	49.4	64.3	97	76	2192.3	594.7
May	86.5	58.1	72.3	0	229	2430.1	659.2
June	92.8	66.9	79.9	0	446	2562.4	695.1
July	95.0	69.5	82.3	0	535	2389.3	648.1
Aug	94.4	69.1	81.8	0	520	2210.1	599.5
Sept	87.9	62.8	75.4	0	311	1843.9	500.2
Oct	79.2	52.4	65.8	81	104	1521.6	412.7
Nov	67.5	39.1	53.3	355	4	1176.1	319.0
Dec	60.1	31.6	45.9	590	0	999.7	271.2
Ann	77.7	50.1	63.9	2621	2250	1802.4	488.9

STATION NO. 12921

LATITUDE: 29° 32′ N
LONGITUDE: 98° 28′ W
ELEVATION: 242 meters (793.8 feet)

San Antonio, Texas

	Maximum Daily Temp. °F	Minimum Daily Temp. °F	Average Monthly Temp. °F	Heating Degree Days Base 65 °F	Cooling Degree Days Base 65 °F	Total Global Radiation Btu/ft²	Total Global Radiation Langleys
Jan	61.6	39.8	50.7	450	7	895.4	242.9
Feb	65.6	43.4	54.5	310	14	1154.0	313.0
Mar	72.5	49.1	60.8	193	63	1450.0	393.3
Apr	80.3	58.8	69.6	31	167	1612.3	437.3
May	86.2	65.7	76.0	0	340	1894.5	513.9
June	92.4	72.0	82.2	0	515	2069.0	561.2
July	95.6	73.8	84.7	0	610	2121.1	575.3
Aug	95.9	73.4	84.7	0	610	1947.1	528.2
Sept	89.8	68.8	79.3	0	428	1638.0	444.3
Oct	81.8	59.2	70.5	31	202	1350.1	366.2
Nov	71.1	48.2	59.7	178	20	1008.9	273.7
Dec	64.6	41.8	53.2	373	5	847.1	229.8
Ann	79.8	57.8	68.8	1570	2993	1499.0	406.6

STATION NO. 13966

LATITUDE: 33° 58′ N
LONGITUDE: 98° 29′ W
ELEVATION: 314 meters (1029.9 feet)

Wichita Falls, Texas

	Maximum Daily Temp. °F	Minimum Daily Temp. °F	Average Monthly Temp. °F	Heating Degree Days Base 65 °F	Cooling Degree Days Base 65 °F	Total Global Radiation Btu/ft²	Total Global Radiation Langleys
Jan	53.5	29.4	41.5	729	0	862.0	233.8
Feb	58.1	33.6	45.9	535	0	1122.9	304.6
Mar	65.8	39.2	52.5	409	22	1471.9	399.2
Apr	77.4	51.1	64.3	112	90	1762.8	478.2
May	84.7	59.8	72.3	13	238	2017.3	547.2
June	93.9	68.6	81.3	0	488	2221.4	602.5
July	99.2	72.3	85.8	0	644	2166.5	587.7
Aug	99.4	71.6	85.5	0	635	1969.2	534.1
Sept	90.3	63.6	77.0	0	360	1601.8	434.5
Oct	79.2	52.7	66.0	92	122	1291.4	350.3
Nov	66.0	39.7	52.9	369	5	957.3	259.7
Dec	56.2	32.2	44.2	644	0	798.8	216.7
Ann	77.0	51.2	64.1	2903	2610	1520.2	412.4

STATION NO. 93129

LATITUDE: 37° 42′ N
LONGITUDE: 113° 6′ W
ELEVATION: 1712 meters (5615.4 feet)

Cedar City, Utah

	Maximum Daily Temp. °F	Minimum Daily Temp. °F	Average Monthly Temp. °F	Heating Degree Days Base 65 °F	Cooling Degree Days Base 65 °F	Total Global Radiation Btu/ft²	Total Global Radiation Langleys
Jan	0.0 ND	0.0 ND	28.7	1125	0	882.4	239.3
Feb	0.0 ND	0.0 ND	33.1	893	0	1179.8	320.0
Mar	0.0 ND	0.0 ND	38.4	824	0	1635.6	443.7
Apr	0.0 ND	0.0 ND	47.1	536	0	2092.4	567.6
May	0.0 ND	0.0 ND	56.2	281	7	2467.3	669.3
June	0.0 ND	0.0 ND	65.0	85	85	2705.8	734.0
July	0.0 ND	0.0 ND	73.2	0	254	2503.3	679.0
Aug	0.0 ND	0.0 ND	71.3	5	200	2241.3	607.9
Sept	0.0 ND	0.0 ND	63.2	113	59	1968.4	533.9
Oct	0.0 ND	0.0 ND	51.5	423	5	1459.7	395.9
Nov	0.0 ND	0.0 ND	38.8	785	0	992.4	269.2
Dec	0.0 ND	0.0 ND	30.8	1058	0	785.5	213.1
Ann	0.0 ND	0.0 ND	49.8	6136	614	1742.8	472.7

STATION NO. 24127

Salt Lake City, Utah

LATITUDE: 40° 46′ N
LONGITUDE: 111° 58′ W
ELEVATION: 1288 meters (4224.6 feet)

	Maximum Daily Temp. °F	Minimum Daily Temp. °F	Average Monthly Temp. °F	Heating Degree Days Base 65 °F	Cooling Degree Days Base 65 °F	Total Global Radiation Btu/ft²	Total Global Radiation Langleys
Jan	37.4	18.5	28.0	1147	0	639.1	173.4
Feb	43.4	23.3	33.4	884	0	988.7	268.2
Mar	50.8	28.3	39.6	787	0	1454.3	394.5
Apr	61.8	36.6	49.2	473	0	1894.3	513.8
May	72.4	44.2	58.3	236	29	2362.4	640.8
June	81.3	51.1	66.2	86	122	2560.9	694.6
July	92.8	60.5	76.7	0	362	2590.1	702.6
Aug	90.2	58.7	74.5	4	299	2253.6	611.3
Sept	80.3	49.3	64.8	104	99	1843.3	500.0
Oct	66.4	38.4	52.4	401	11	1293.3	350.8
Nov	50.0	28.1	39.1	776	0	787.9	213.7
Dec	39.0	21.5	30.3	1075	0	569.8	154.6
Ann	63.8	38.2	51.0	5981	927	1603.1	434.9

STATION NO. 14742

Burlington, Vermont

LATITUDE: 44° 28′ N
LONGITUDE: 73° 9′ W
ELEVATION: 104 meters (341.1 feet)

	Maximum Daily Temp. °F	Minimum Daily Temp. °F	Average Monthly Temp. °F	Heating Degree Days Base 65 °F	Cooling Degree Days Base 65 °F	Total Global Radiation Btu/ft²	Total Global Radiation Langleys
Jan	25.9	7.6	16.8	1494	0	385.3	104.5
Feb	28.2	8.9	18.6	1298	0	606.8	164.6
Mar	38.0	20.1	29.1	1112	0	940.2	255.0
Apr	53.3	32.6	43.0	659	0	1296.2	351.6
May	66.1	43.5	54.8	329	14	1574.1	427.0
June	76.5	53.9	65.2	63	68	1728.9	469.0
July	81.0	58.5	69.8	20	167	1721.1	466.9
Aug	78.3	56.4	67.4	49	122	1475.0	400.1
Sept	70.0	48.6	59.3	191	20	1122.2	304.4
Oct	58.7	38.8	48.8	500	0	740.5	200.9
Nov	44.3	29.7	37.0	839	0	374.6	101.6
Dec	30.3	14.8	22.6	1314	0	283.2	76.8
Ann	54.2	34.5	44.4	7875	396	1020.7	276.9

STATION NO. 13737

Norfolk, Virginia

LATITUDE: 36° 54′ N
LONGITUDE: 76° 12′ W
ELEVATION: 9 meters (29.5 feet)

	Maximum Daily Temp. °F	Minimum Daily Temp. °F	Average Monthly Temp. °F	Heating Degree Days Base 65 °F	Cooling Degree Days Base 65 °F	Total Global Radiation Btu/ft²	Total Global Radiation Langleys
Jan	48.8	32.2	40.5	760	0	678.3	184.0
Feb	50.0	32.7	41.4	661	0	931.9	252.8
Mar	57.3	38.9	48.1	531	7	1280.9	347.4
Apr	67.7	47.9	57.8	225	9	1676.7	454.8
May	76.2	57.2	66.7	52	104	1887.5	512.0
June	83.5	65.5	74.5	0	284	2000.3	542.6
July	86.6	69.9	78.3	0	410	1853.2	502.7
Aug	84.9	68.9	76.9	0	369	1680.2	455.8
Sept	79.6	63.9	71.8	9	212	1395.6	378.6
Oct	70.1	53.3	61.7	140	38	1083.0	293.8
Nov	60.5	42.6	51.6	401	0	811.3	220.1
Dec	50.6	34.0	42.3	704	0	623.8	169.2
Ann	68.0	50.6	59.3	3487	1440	1325.2	359.5

STATION NO. 13741

Roanoke, Virginia

LATITUDE: 37° 19′ N
LONGITUDE: 79° 58′ W
ELEVATION: 358 meters (1174.2 feet)

	Maximum Daily Temp. °F	Minimum Daily Temp. °F	Average Monthly Temp. °F	Heating Degree Days Base 65 °F	Cooling Degree Days Base 65 °F	Total Global Radiation Btu/ft²	Total Global Radiation Langleys
Jan	45.6	27.2	36.4	886	0	660.5	179.2
Feb	47.9	28.3	38.1	752	0	899.4	244.0
Mar	56.3	34.3	45.3	610	0	1236.1	335.3
Apr	67.9	43.9	55.9	283	9	1581.5	429.0
May	76.1	52.7	64.4	101	83	1763.9	478.5
June	83.0	60.4	71.7	0	203	1881.9	510.5
July	85.9	64.4	75.2	0	315	1796.2	487.2
Aug	84.9	63.3	74.1	0	281	1620.2	439.5
Sept	79.5	56.5	68.0	31	121	1358.2	368.4
Oct	69.9	45.6	57.8	234	11	1080.2	293.0
Nov	57.6	35.8	46.7	549	0	764.7	207.4
Dec	46.6	28.1	37.4	855	0	590.8	160.3
Ann	66.8	45.0	55.9	4306	1030	1269.5	344.3

STATION NO. 24227

Olympia, Washington

LATITUDE: 46° 58′ N
LONGITUDE: 122° 54′ W
ELEVATION: 61 meters (200.1 feet)

	Maximum Daily Temp. °F	Minimum Daily Temp. °F	Average Monthly Temp. °F	Heating Degree Days Base 65 °F	Cooling Degree Days Base 65 °F	Total Global Radiation Btu/ft²	Total Global Radiation Langleys
Jan	44.0	30.4	37.2	860	0	268.8	72.9
Feb	49.6	32.4	41.0	671	0	502.9	136.4
Mar	53.6	32.8	43.2	675	0	845.0	229.2
Apr	59.9	36.5	48.2	504	0	1255.2	340.5
May	67.2	40.8	54.0	340	0	1631.9	442.6
June	71.9	45.9	58.9	196	13	1693.3	459.3
July	78.4	48.7	63.6	88	45	1912.7	518.8
Aug	77.2	48.4	62.8	103	34	1548.8	420.1
Sept	72.1	45.0	58.6	198	5	1156.9	313.8
Oct	61.2	40.0	50.6	445	0	636.3	172.6
Nov	51.3	35.2	43.3	650	0	339.3	92.0
Dec	45.8	33.1	39.5	790	0	221.5	60.1
Ann	61.0	39.1	50.1	5530	101	1001.1	271.5

STATION NO. 24233

Seattle / Tacoma, Washington

LATITUDE: 47° 27′ N
LONGITUDE: 122° 18′ W
ELEVATION: 122 meters (400.2 feet)

	Maximum Daily Temp. °F	Minimum Daily Temp. °F	Average Monthly Temp. °F	Heating Degree Days Base 65 °F	Cooling Degree Days Base 65 °F	Total Global Radiation Btu/ft²	Total Global Radiation Langleys
Jan	43.4	33.0	38.2	830	0	261.7	71.0
Feb	48.5	36.0	42.3	635	0	495.0	134.3
Mar	51.5	36.6	44.1	648	0	849.4	230.4
Apr	57.0	40.3	48.7	488	0	1293.5	350.9
May	64.1	45.6	54.9	311	0	1713.9	464.9
June	69.0	50.6	59.8	166	11	1801.8	488.8
July	75.1	53.8	64.5	79	65	2248.2	609.8
Aug	73.8	53.7	63.8	81	45	1616.3	438.4
Sept	68.7	50.4	59.6	169	7	1147.7	311.3
Oct	59.4	44.9	52.2	396	0	656.2	178.0
Nov	50.4	38.8	44.6	612	0	337.2	91.5
Dec	45.4	35.5	40.5	760	0	211.1	57.3
Ann	58.8	43.3	51.1	5184	128	1052.7	285.5

STATION NO. 24157

Spokane, Washington

LATITUDE: 47° 38′ N
LONGITUDE: 117° 32′ W
ELEVATION: 721 meters (2364.9 feet)

	Maximum Daily Temp. °F	Minimum Daily Temp. °F	Average Monthly Temp. °F	Heating Degree Days Base 65 °F	Cooling Degree Days Base 65 °F	Total Global Radiation Btu/ft²	Total Global Radiation Langleys
Jan	31.1	19.6	25.4	1228	0	315.0	85.4
Feb	39.0	25.3	32.2	918	0	605.9	164.3
Mar	46.2	28.8	37.5	851	0	1040.6	282.3
Apr	57.0	35.2	46.1	567	0	1494.9	405.5
May	66.5	42.8	54.7	326	7	1918.0	520.3
June	73.6	49.4	61.5	144	38	2082.8	565.0
July	84.3	55.1	69.7	20	166	2357.4	639.4
Aug	81.9	54.0	68.0	47	139	1942.0	526.8
Sept	72.5	46.7	59.6	194	32	1435.3	389.3
Oct	58.1	37.5	47.8	533	0	840.9	228.1
Nov	41.8	29.2	35.5	884	0	397.7	107.9
Dec	33.9	24.0	29.0	1116	0	255.2	69.2
Ann	57.2	37.3	47.3	6835	387	1223.8	332.0

STATION NO. 24243

Yakima, Washington

LATITUDE: 46° 34′ N
LONGITUDE: 120° 32′ W
ELEVATION: 325 meters (1066.0 feet)

	Maximum Daily Temp. °F	Minimum Daily Temp. °F	Average Monthly Temp. °F	Heating Degree Days Base 65 °F	Cooling Degree Days Base 65 °F	Total Global Radiation Btu/ft²	Total Global Radiation Langleys
Jan	36.4	18.6	27.5	1163	0	365.1	99.0
Feb	46.1	25.2	35.7	819	0	666.2	180.7
Mar	54.8	28.8	41.8	718	0	1122.3	304.4
Apr	64.1	34.8	49.5	464	0	1597.7	433.4
May	73.1	42.6	57.9	238	18	2008.5	544.8
June	79.7	49.3	64.5	94	77	2168.8	588.3
July	88.1	53.3	70.7	20	196	2358.1	639.6
Aug	85.9	51.2	68.6	36	148	1974.7	535.6
Sept	78.3	44.3	61.3	146	36	1483.3	402.3
Oct	64.7	35.4	50.1	461	0	890.7	241.6
Nov	48.5	28.3	38.4	797	0	444.3	120.5
Dec	39.1	23.5	31.3	1044	0	294.8	80.0
Ann	63.2	36.3	49.8	6008	479	1281.2	347.5

STATION NO. 13866

Charleston, West Virginia

LATITUDE: 38° 22′ N
LONGITUDE: 81° 36′ W
ELEVATION: 290 meters (951.2 feet)

	Maximum Daily Temp. °F	Minimum Daily Temp. °F	Average Monthly Temp. °F	Heating Degree Days Base 65 °F	Cooling Degree Days Base 65 °F	Total Global Radiation Btu/ft²	Total Global Radiation Langleys
Jan	43.6	25.3	34.5	945	0	498.4	135.2
Feb	46.2	26.8	36.5	797	0	706.5	191.6
Mar	55.2	33.8	44.5	641	5	1009.5	273.8
Apr	67.9	43.8	55.9	286	13	1355.7	367.7
May	76.6	52.3	64.5	112	95	1639.4	444.7
June	83.4	60.6	72.0	9	220	1775.9	481.7
July	85.6	64.3	75.0	0	310	1682.5	456.4
Aug	84.4	62.8	73.6	0	266	1514.3	410.8
Sept	79.0	55.9	67.5	45	121	1272.0	345.0
Oct	69.1	44.8	57.0	266	18	972.3	263.7
Nov	55.8	35.0	45.4	587	0	613.1	166.3
Dec	45.2	27.2	36.2	893	0	440.1	119.4
Ann	66.0	44.4	55.2	4590	1055	1123.3	304.7

STATION NO. 14991

LATITUDE: 44°52′ N
LONGITUDE: 91° 29′ W
ELEVATION: 273 meters (895.4 feet)

Eau Claire, Wisconsin

	Maximum Daily Temp. °F	Minimum Daily Temp. °F	Average Monthly Temp. °F	Heating Degree Days Base 65 °F	Cooling Degree Days Base 65 °F	Total Global Radiation Btu/ft²	Total Global Radiation Langleys
Jan	0.0 ND	0.0 ND	11.7	1651	0	451.7	122.5
Feb	0.0 ND	0.0 ND	15.4	1388	0	746.4	202.5
Mar	0.0 ND	0.0 ND	27.3	1168	0	1090.2	295.7
Apr	0.0 ND	0.0 ND	44.5	614	0	1425.9	386.8
May	0.0 ND	0.0 ND	56.2	292	20	1680.8	455.9
June	0.0 ND	0.0 ND	66.1	65	97	1871.9	507.8
July	0.0 ND	0.0 ND	70.5	13	184	1886.3	511.7
Aug	0.0 ND	0.0 ND	68.4	36	142	1620.7	439.6
Sept	0.0 ND	0.0 ND	58.7	202	13	1196.1	324.5
Oct	0.0 ND	0.0 ND	48.7	504	0	826.1	224.1
Nov	0.0 ND	0.0 ND	32.0	990	0	450.5	122.2
Dec	0.0 ND	0.0 ND	18.0	1456	0	340.8	92.4
Ann	0.0 ND	0.0 ND	43.1	8388	459	1132.3	307.1

STATION NO. 14898

LATITUDE: 44° 29′ N
LONGITUDE: 88° 8′ W
ELEVATION: 214 meters (701.9 feet)

Green Bay, Wisconsin

	Maximum Daily Temp. °F	Minimum Daily Temp. °F	Average Monthly Temp. °F	Heating Degree Days Base 65 °F	Cooling Degree Days Base 65 °F	Total Global Radiation Btu/ft²	Total Global Radiation Langleys
Jan	23.9	6.9	15.4	1537	0	451.2	122.4
Feb	27.2	8.8	18.0	1316	0	724.9	196.6
Mar	37.1	20.1	28.6	1127	0	1104.2	299.5
Apr	54.1	33.5	43.8	635	0	1438.6	390.2
May	65.8	43.1	54.5	337	11	1719.3	466.4
June	75.8	53.2	64.5	90	76	1907.8	517.5
July	80.7	57.7	69.2	22	151	1888.5	512.2
Aug	79.1	56.3	67.7	54	137	1621.8	439.9
Sept	69.8	48.0	58.9	191	7	1218.0	330.4
Oct	59.6	38.7	49.2	490	0	820.6	222.6
Nov	41.8	26.4	34.1	927	0	465.1	126.1
Dec	28.6	13.2	20.9	1366	0	349.7	94.9
Ann	53.6	33.8	43.7	8096	385	1142.5	309.9

STATION NO. 14839

LATITUDE: 42° 57′ N
LONGITUDE: 87° 54′ W
ELEVATION: 211 meters (692.1 feet)

Milwaukee, Wisconsin

	Maximum Daily Temp. °F	Minimum Daily Temp. °F	Average Monthly Temp. °F	Heating Degree Days Base 65 °F	Cooling Degree Days Base 65 °F	Total Global Radiation Btu/ft²	Total Global Radiation Langleys
Jan	27.3	11.4	19.4	1413	0	479.4	130.0
Feb	30.3	14.6	22.5	1190	0	736.5	199.8
Mar	39.4	23.4	31.4	1040	0	1088.8	295.3
Apr	54.6	34.7	44.7	608	0	1442.7	391.3
May	65.0	43.3	54.2	347	13	1768.4	479.7
June	75.3	53.6	64.5	90	74	1977.1	536.3
July	80.4	59.3	69.9	14	166	1961.8	532.1
Aug	79.7	58.7	69.2	36	166	1719.0	466.3
Sept	71.5	50.7	61.1	139	22	1310.3	355.4
Oct	61.4	40.6	51.0	439	5	907.9	246.3
Nov	44.4	28.5	36.5	855	0	524.6	142.3
Dec	31.5	16.8	24.2	1264	0	378.4	102.7
Ann	55.1	36.3	45.7	7443	450	1191.2	323.1

STATION NO. 24089

LATITUDE: 42° 55′ N
LONGITUDE: 106° 28′ W
ELEVATION: 1612 meters (5287.4 feet)

Casper, Wyoming

	Maximum Daily Temp. °F	Minimum Daily Temp. °F	Average Monthly Temp. °F	Heating Degree Days Base 65 °F	Cooling Degree Days Base 65 °F	Total Global Radiation Btu/ft²	Total Global Radiation Langleys
Jan	33.6	12.7	23.2	1296	0	683.2	185.3
Feb	37.7	15.9	26.8	1069	0	1013.5	274.9
Mar	42.6	19.4	31.0	1053	0	1441.1	390.9
Apr	55.5	29.9	42.7	668	0	1846.8	500.9
May	66.1	39.3	52.7	387	5	2203.6	597.7
June	76.3	47.4	61.9	146	54	2501.3	678.5
July	87.1	54.9	71.0	13	198	2534.6	687.5
Aug	85.6	53.5	69.6	16	158	2225.4	603.6
Sept	74.1	43.3	58.7	229	40	1749.5	474.6
Oct	61.4	33.9	47.7	535	0	1218.7	330.6
Nov	44.8	22.9	33.9	932	0	765.2	207.6
Dec	36.2	16.2	26.2	1202	0	594.2	161.2
Ann	58.4	32.4	45.4	7555	457	1564.7	424.4

STATION NO. 24018

LATITUDE: 41° 9′ N
LONGITUDE: 104° 49′ W
ELEVATION: 1872 meters (6140.2 feet)

Cheyenne, Wyoming

	Maximum Daily Temp. °F	Minimum Daily Temp. °F	Average Monthly Temp. °F	Heating Degree Days Base 65 °F	Cooling Degree Days Base 65 °F	Total Global Radiation Btu/ft²	Total Global Radiation Langleys
Jan	38.2	14.9	26.6	1190	0	765.8	207.7
Feb	40.7	17.3	29.0	1008	0	1067.8	289.6
Mar	43.5	19.6	31.6	1035	0	1433.1	388.7
Apr	55.4	30.0	42.7	668	0	1770.5	480.2
May	65.1	39.7	52.4	392	0	1994.6	541.0
June	74.4	48.1	61.3	155	45	2258.0	612.5
July	83.7	54.5	69.1	22	148	2229.9	604.9
Aug	81.9	53.2	67.6	31	112	1965.6	533.2
Sept	72.8	43.5	58.2	225	20	1667.4	452.3
Oct	61.8	33.9	47.9	529	0	1241.8	336.8
Nov	47.5	23.5	35.5	884	0	822.8	223.2
Dec	40.3	18.1	29.2	1109	0	671.0	182.0
Ann	58.8	33.0	45.9	7254	326	1490.7	404.4

STATION NO. 24029

LATITUDE: 44° 46′ N
LONGITUDE: 106° 58′ W
ELEVATION: 1209 meters (3965.5 feet)

Sheridan, Wyoming

	Maximum Daily Temp. °F	Minimum Daily Temp. °F	Average Monthly Temp. °F	Heating Degree Days Base 65 °F	Cooling Degree Days Base 65 °F	Total Global Radiation Btu/ft²	Total Global Radiation Langleys
Jan	33.5	8.5	21.0	1363	0	517.5	140.4
Feb	38.0	13.8	25.9	1094	0	788.2	213.8
Mar	43.1	18.9	31.0	1053	0	1204.8	326.8
Apr	56.3	30.9	43.6	641	0	1537.2	417.0
May	66.0	40.2	53.1	374	5	1882.7	510.7
June	74.3	47.8	61.1	167	50	2156.2	584.9
July	86.1	54.6	70.4	27	194	2329.0	631.8
Aug	85.3	53.0	69.2	31	160	2006.0	544.1
Sept	72.9	42.9	57.9	245	31	1501.8	407.4
Oct	62.5	33.1	47.8	533	0	1005.3	272.7
Nov	46.0	20.8	33.4	947	0	590.8	160.3
Dec	37.6	13.4	25.5	1224	0	441.4	119.7
Ann	58.5	31.5	45.0	7708	445	1330.1	360.8

SECTION 4

Building Components

PART 4A

Concrete

When concrete is the finish material in a building or serves as the substrate for other work, it is one of the primary concerns of architects. The tables in this part provide useful information for specifying and inspecting both structural and finished concrete work.

STANDARDS FOR CONCRETE TOLERANCES

Understanding industry standard tolerances for concrete work is critical not only for inspecting structural work but also for developing appropriate details and specifications for other construction that uses concrete as a substrate. The following tolerances are considered "industry standard" and are typically made a part of most specifications by reference to ACI-301. If more exact tolerances are required, they must be specifically called out in the specifications.

The standards appearing in Table 4A–1 are based on ACI-117, published by the American Concrete Institute, and include the types of concrete construction typically encountered in architectural and interior design work. Refer to ACI-117 for the complete text and for special structures not included here.

Table 4A–1
CONCRETE TOLERANCES

CAST-IN-PLACE	
Tolerance Applying to Concrete Dimensions and Locations Only	
Plumb (allowable variation):	
In the lines and surfaces of columns, piers, walls, and in arrises:	
In any 10 ft.	1/4 in.
Maximum for the total height of the structure (1)	1 in.
For exposed corner columns, control-joint grooves, and other conspicuous lines:	
In any 20 ft.	1/4 in.
Maximum for the total height of the structure (1)	1/2 in.
For slipformed walls or columns with respect to a reference point at the base of the structure, including both translational and rotational components:	
In any 5 ft. of height	1/8 in.
In any 50 ft. of height	1 in.
Maximum in total height structure (up to 600 ft.)	3 in.
Level or from the grades and elevations specified in the contract documents:	
In slab soffits, ceilings, beam soffits, and in arrises measured before removal of supporting shores:	
In any 10 ft.	±1/4 in.
In any bay or in any 20 ft.	±3/8 in.
Maximum for the total length of the structure	±3/4 in.

In exposed lintels, sills, parapets, horizontal grooves, and other conspicuous lines:	
In any bay or in 20 ft.	±1/4 in.
Maximum for the total length of the structure	±1/2 in.
Elevation control points for slabs on grade:	
In any bay for 20 ft.	±3/8 in.
Maximum for the total length of the structure	±3/4 in.
Linear building lines from the basic dimension in plan and related position of columns, walls, beams, and partitions:	
In any bay	±1/2 in.
In any 20 ft.	±1/2 in.
Maximum for the structure	±1 in.
Size of sleeves, floor openings, and wall openings:	±1/4 in.
Location of the center lines of sleeves, floor openings, and wall openings	±1/2 in.
Cross-sectional dimensions of columns, beams, walls, and slab thickness (including walls and columns constructed using slipforms):	
Up to 12 in.	+3/8 in. −1/4 in.
More than 12 in.	+1/2 in. −3/8 in.
Footings:	
Horizontal dimensions:	
Formed	+2 in. −1/2 in.
(Unformed excavation)	+3 in.
Misplacement or eccentricity:	
2% of the footing width in the direction of misplacement but not more than	±2 in.
Cross-sectional thickness	+no limit −5%
To receive masonry construction:	
Alignment in 10 ft.	±1/4 in.
Maximum for entire length 50 ft.	±1/2 in.
Level in 10 ft.	±1/4 in.
Maximum for entire length 50 ft.	±1/2 in.
Level—footings for construction other than that just shown for masonry (but not to exceed limits for cross-sectional thickness):	+1/2 in. −2 in.
Stairs:	
For an individual step:	
Riser	±1/8 in.
Tread	±1/4 in.
In a flight of stairs:	
Rise	±1/8 in.
Run	±1/4 in.

Tolerances for Finished Slab Surfaces

Class of tolerance (Specifier shall designate class to be used.):

- Class AA Surface Finish Tolerance. Depressions in floors between high spots shall not be greater than 1/8 in. below a 10 ft. long straightedge. (2)
- Class AX Surface Finish Tolerance. Depressions in floors between high spots shall not be greater than 3/16 in. below a 10 ft. long straightedge. (2)

Table 4A-1 (Continued)

- Class BX Surface Finish Tolerance. Depressions in floors between high spots shall not be greater than 5/16 in. below a 10 ft. long straightedge. (2)
- Class CX Surface Finish Tolerance. Depressions in floors between high spots shall not be greater than 1/2 in. below a 10 ft. long straightedge. (2)

Floor tolerance measurements should be made the day after a concrete floor is finished and before the shoring is removed, in order to eliminate any effects of shrinkage, curling, and deflection.

Cost of Achievability Factors

- Class AA or closer finish tolerances are extremely difficult and expensive to achieve on large areas. They should be specified only for critical areas where such tolerances are vital for the operations that will take place in the areas. Specifications for bidding contractors should thoroughly cover the:
  1. Importance of achieving the tolerance specified.
  2. Exact areas involved.
  3. Minimum joint spacing permitted.
  4. Precise method of measurement using a 10 ft. long straightedge that will be used to approve or reject the floors involved.
- Class BX finish tolerances are generally practical for floors over metal decking or precast beams if proper compensation has been made for deflection. The lack of planeness usual in the decking or precast beams makes closer tolerances quite difficult.
- Class BX finish tolerances are generally suitable for Class 1, 2, and 3 floors. They may also be suitable for Class 4, 5, 6, and 7 floors where traffic and other use considerations do not require closer surface tolerances. (See Table 4A-5 for definitions of floor classes.)

Tolerances for floors cast on metal decks or other easily deflected material shall not be less than the calculable deflection anticipated.

SLIPFORMED CONSTRUCTION

Variation from prescribed inside dimension for noncircular structures between opposite walls shall not exceed:	
Per 10 ft. of prescribed dimension	±1/2 in.
Maximum	±2 in.

PAVEMENTS

Mainline pavements (from specified slope):	
Longitudinal direction, as measured with 10 ft. straightedge	1/8 in.
Transverse direction, as measured with 10 ft. straightedge	1/4 in.
Ramps and intersections (from specified slope):	
As measured with 10 ft. straightedge	1/4 in.

PRECAST CONCRETE

Tolerances for precast non-prestressed elements

Length of element:	
Per 10 ft. of length	±1/8 in.
Maximum for entire length	±3/4 in.
Cross-sectional dimensions:	
Sections less than 6 in.	±1/8 in.
Sections 6 in. and less than 18 in.	±3/16 in.
Sections 18 in. to 36 in.	±1/4 in.
Sections over 36 in.	±3/8 in.

Variation from straight line:	
In any 10 ft. of length	±1/8 in.
Maximum for the entire length	±3/4 in.
Camber (variation from specified):	
Per 10 ft. of span	±1/8 in.
But not greater than	±1/2 in.
Differential in camber between adjacent units in erected position:	
Per 10 ft. of span	±1/8 in.
But not greater than	±1/2 in.
Tolerances for precast prestressed elements	
Length of element:	
Per 10 ft. of length	±1/8 in.
Maximum for entire length	±3/4 in.
Cross-sectional dimension:	
Sections less than 6 in.	±1/8 in.
Sections 6 in. and less than 18 in.	±3/16 in.
Sections 18 in. to 36 in.	±1/4 in.
Sections over 36 in.	±3/8 in.
Variation from straight line:	
In any 10 ft. of length	±1/8 in.
Maximum for the entire length	±3/4 in.
Camber (variation from specified):	
Per 10 ft. of span	±1/8 in.
But no greater than	±1 in.
Differential in camber between adjacent units in erected position:	
Per 10 ft. of span	±1/8 in.
But not greater than	±1 in.
Precast panels	
Casting tolerances:	
Height and width of panel, basic dimensions	
Under 10 ft.	±1/8 in.
10 ft. to 20 ft.	+1/8 in. −3/16 in.
Over 20 ft. to 30 ft.	+1/8 in. −1/4 in.
Each additional 10 ft. increment in excess of 30 ft.	±1/16 in.
Thickness	+1/4 in. −1/8 in.
Skew-measured by the difference in length of the two diagonals	
Per 6 ft. of diagonal length	−1/8 in. +1/4 in.
Openings cast into panels	
Size of opening	±1/4 in.
Location of center line of opening	±1/4 in.
Location of embedded items	
Inserts, bolts, pip sleeves, and so on	±3/8 in.
Flashing reglets at panel edge	±1/4 in.
Reglets for glazing gaskets	±1/8 in.
Electrical outlets, hose bibs, and so on	±1/2 in.
After casting tolerances (monolithically cast panels):	
With intermediate support	
Bowing and warpage	$\pm\dfrac{\text{Panel dim.}}{360}$
Without intermediate support	
Bowing and warpage	$\pm\dfrac{\text{Panel dim.}}{240}$

Table 4A-1 (Continued)

Erection tolerance:	
Distance between panels at face of panels, for panels with dimensions (normal to the joint)	
Of under 10 ft.	±3/16 in.
Of 10 ft. to 20 ft.	+3/16 in. −1/4 in.
For each 10 ft. increment in excess of 20 ft.	±1/16 in.
Joint taper (panel edges not parallel)	
Per lineal foot of joint	1/40 in.
Minimum allowable	1/16 in.
Maximum for entire length	3/8 in.
Panel alignment	
Alignment of horizontal and vertical joints	1/4 in.
Offset in exterior face of adjacent panels	1/4 in.
Location of openings in wall panels	±1/4 in.
EMBEDDED MATERIALS	
Tolerance from specified clearance relative to reinforcing:	±1 in. (3)
Tolerance from specified location:	±1/4 in.

(1) Total height is taken to be less than 100 ft. Structures with heights in excess of these values are to be considered special cases and other overall tolerances should be considered and/or specified.

(2) Compliance with the designated limits in four of five consecutive measurements should generally be satisfactory unless obvious faults are observed.

(3) But not less than diameter of the reinforcing bar.

Source: American Concrete Institute.

Table 4A-2
CONCRETE FINISHES—VERTICAL SURFACES

Type	Appearance	Technique
As-Cast Finishes		
Rough form	Texture left by forms; tie holes and defects patched.	Surface left as is after forms are removed.
Smooth form	Smooth, hard, uniform texture; joints symmetrical; seams minimized; fins removed.	Forms of plywood, metal, hardboard, or other smooth material.
Architectural		
Form liner	Appearance of type of form used; joints and form tie holes treated as desired.	Liners of plastic, wood, metal, as specified.
Scrubbed	Exposed aggregate with surface mortar removed; uniform appearance.	Surface wetted and scrubbed with wire or fiber brush.
Acid wash	Exposed aggregate with full color of aggregate brought out.	Surface wetted with muriatic acid; not recommended for vertical surfaces.
Water jet	Exposed aggregate.	High-pressure water jets in combination with air.

Sandblast		
Brush	Fine aggregate exposed but no projection of coarse aggregate.	
Light	Fine aggregate exposed with occasional exposure of coarse aggregate no more than 1/16 in.	
Medium	Coarse aggregate exposed no more than 1/4 in.	
Heavy	Rugged and uneven; coarse aggregate exposed 3/8 in.–1/2 in.	
Tooled		
Bushhammer	Rugged, heavy texture; can depend on type of form liner used, if any.	Pneumatic tools with various attachments removes a portion of exterior finish.
Grinding	Similar to terrazzo appearance.	Surfaces power-ground to match sample.
Manual	Projections produced by form liners broken off by hand or by removal of form at proper age of concrete.	
Applied	Stucco or similar troweled materials applied to concrete.	
Rubbed Finishes		
Smooth	Smooth, uniform color and texture.	Surfaces wetted and rubbed with carborundum brick.
Grout cleaned	Smooth, uniform, with bubbles and defects concealed.	Surface covered with grout and smoothed.
Cork floated	Smooth, "floated" appearance.	Surface covered with grout compressed into voids with slow-speed grinder or stone.

Source: American Concrete Institute.

Table 4A-3
CONCRETE FINISHES—FLOORS

Type	Class	Description
Scratched	C	Surface roughened with stiff brushes or rakes.
Floated	B	Surface floated and refloated to uniform sandy texture.
Troweled	A	Surface float finished, power troweled, and hand troweled to be unifrom in texture and appearance.
	B	Concrete on metal deck shall be Class B tolerance.
Broom or belt	B	Float finish followed by coarse transverse scored texture by broom or burlap belt.
Dry shake	B/A	Float finish followed by application of selected metallic or mineral aggregate; second floating followed by broom, floated, or troweled finish.
Non-slip	B	Dry shake finish using crushed ceramically bonded aluminum oxide or other specified abrasive.
Exposed aggregate	B	Selected aggregate (usually 3/8 in.–5/8 in.) spread uniformly over surface to provide complete coverage to depth of a single stone.

Source: American Concrete Institute.

Table 4A-4
FINISHING TOLERANCES OF CONCRETE SLABS

Class	Description
Class A	True planes within 1/8 in. in 10 ft., as determined by a 10 ft. straightedge placed anywhere on the slab in any direction.
Class B	True planes within 1/4 in. in 10 ft., as determined by a 10 ft. straightedge placed anywhere on the slab in any direction.
Class C	True planes within 1/4 in. in 2 ft., as determined by a 2 ft. straightedge placed anywhere on the slab in any direction.

Source: American Concrete Institute.

Table 4A-5
CLASSIFICATION OF CONCRETE FLOORS

Class	Use	Usual Traffic	Finishing Technique	Minimum Compressive Strength
1	Residential or tile covered	Light foot	Medium steel trowel	3500
2	Offices, churches, schools, hospitals, residential	Foot	Steel trowel; special finish for non-slip steel trowel; color-exposed aggregate	3500
3	Drives, garage floors, sidewalks for residences	Light foot and pneumatic wheels	Float, trowel, and broom	3500
4	Light industrial, commercial	Foot and pneumatic wheels	Hard steel trowel and brush for non-slip	4000
5	Single-course industrial, integral topping	Foot and wheels—abrasive wear	Special hard aggregate, float, and trowel	4500
6	Bonded, two-course heavy industrial	Foot and steel-tire vehicles—severe abrasion	Base: surface leveled by screeding Topping: special power floating	3500 (base) 5000–8000
7	Unbonded topping	Classes 3,4,5,6	—	

Source: American Concrete Institute.

Table 4A-6
CONCRETE AGGREGATE VISIBILITY

Aggregate size (in in.)	**Distance at which texture is visible** (in ft.)
1/4–1/2	20–30
1/2–1	30–75
1–2	75–125
2–3	125–175

PART 4B

Masonry

PROPERTIES AND COURSING OF BRICK

The tables included in this part provide a variety of reference data for unit masonry and stone. In addition to basic physical properties and sizes, there is information to help you design and detail proper dimensions, select finishes, and understand tolerances. For concrete masonry units, the tables give a quick and easy way to select the proper construction assemblies for thermal and fire resistance. Finally, there is a table to help determine the correct dimensions for fireplaces.

Table 4B-1
TYPICAL MATERIAL PROPERTIES OF BRICK

Material	Face Brick, ASTM C 216	Building Brick ASTM C 62	Paving Brick, ASTM C 902	Hollow Brick, ASTM C 652[b]	Mortar or Grout
Specific Heat[c] c Btu/lb/°F	0.24	0.22	0.24	0.22	0.20
Density ρ lb/cu ft	130	120	135	126	120
Thermal Conductivity k Btu/hr/°F/ft² per inch	9.00	5.00	9.00	10.00	12.00
Thermal Resistivity r (hr · °F · ft²)/Btu per inch	0.11	0.20	0.11	0.10	0.08
Thermal Conductance C_a (Btu/hr/°F/ft²)/ft	0.758	0.417	0.758	0.833	1.042
Heat Capacity β Btu/cu ft/°F	31.2	26.4	32.4	27.7	24.0
Thermal Diffusivity δ ft²/hr	0.024	0.016	0.023	0.030	0.043
Emissivity ϵ	0.93	0.93	0.93	0.93	—

[a] These values are representative of the information available to the Brick Institute of America, and are typical for brick being manufactured today. These values may vary by plus or minus 10% depending on the specific brick being considered.

[b] Hollow brick are assumed to be 60% solid and the core space fully grouted.

[c] Source is Reference 3.

[d] The thermal conductivity of grouted hollow brick should be determined by dual path analysis. Typically grouted hollow brick, 60% solid, fully grouted will have a thermal conductivity of approximately 10 Btu/hr/°F/ft² per inch.

Source: Brick Institute of America.

Table 4B-2
SIZES OF MODULAR BRICK[1]

Unit Designation	Nominal Dimensions, in.			Joint Thickness in.	Manufactured Dimensions in.			Modular Coursing in.
	t	*h*	*l*		*t*	*h*	*l*	
Standard Modular	4	2⅔	8	⅜	3⅝	2¼	7⅝	3C = 8
				½	3½	2¼	7½	
Engineer	4	3⅕	8	⅜	3⅝	2 13/16	7⅝	5C = 16
				½	3½	2 11/16	7½	
Economy 8 or Jumbo Closure	4	4	8	⅜	3⅝	3⅝	7⅝	1C = 4
				½	3½	3½	7½	
Double	4	5⅓	8	⅜	3⅝	4 15/16	7⅝	3C = 16
				½	3½	4 13/16	7½	
Roman	4	2	12	⅜	3⅝	1⅝	11⅝	2C = 4
				½	3½	1½	11½	
Norman	4	2⅔	12	⅜	3⅝	2¼	11⅝	3C = 8
				½	3½	2¼	11½	
Norwegian	4	3⅕	12	⅜	3⅝	2 13/16	11⅝	5C = 16
				½	3½	2 11/16	11½	
Economy 12 or Jumbo Utility	4	4	12	⅜	3⅝	3⅝	11⅝	1C = 4
				½	3½	3½	11½	
Triple	4	5⅓	12	⅜	3⅝	4 15/16	11⅝	3C = 16
				½	3½	4 13/16	11½	
SCR brick[2]	6	2⅔	12	⅜	5⅝	2¼	11⅝	3C = 8
				½	5½	2¼	11½	
6-in. Norwegian	6	3⅕	12	⅜	5⅝	2 13/16	11⅝	5C = 16
				½	5½	2 11/16	11½	
6-in. Jumbo	6	4	12	⅜	5⅝	3⅝	11⅝	1C = 4
				½	5½	3½	11½	
8-in. Jumbo	8	4	12	⅜	7⅝	3⅝	11⅝	1C = 4
				½	7½	3½	11½	

[1] Available as solid units conforming to ASTM C 216- or ASTM C 62-, or, in a number of cases, as hollow brick conforming to ASTM C 652-.

[2] Reg. U.S. Pat. Off., SCPI.

Source: Brick Institute of America.

Table 4B-3
VERTICAL COURSING TABLE FOR MODULAR BRICK[1]

No. of Courses	*Nominal Height (h) of Unit*[2]				
	2"	2⅔"	3⅕"	4"	5⅓"
1	0'- 2"	0'- 2 11/16"	0'- 3 3/16"	0'-4"	0'- 5 5/16"
2	0'- 4"	0'- 5 5/16"	0'- 6⅜"	0'-8"	0'-10 11/16"
3	0'- 6"	0'- 8"	0'- 9⅝"	1'-0"	1'- 4"
4	0'- 8"	0'-10 11/16"	1'- 0 13/16"	1'-4"	1'- 9 5/16"
5	0'-10"	1'- 1 5/16"	1'- 4"	1'-8"	2'- 2 11/16"
6	1'- 0"	1'- 4"	1'- 7 3/16"	2'-0"	2'- 8"
7	1'- 2"	1'- 6 11/16"	1'-10⅜"	2'-4"	3'- 1 5/16"
8	1'- 4"	1'- 9 5/16"	2'- 1⅝"	2'-8"	3'- 6 11/16"
9	1'- 6"	2'- 0"	2'- 4 13/16"	3'-0"	4'- 0"
10	1'- 8"	2'- 2 11/16"	2'- 8"	3'-4"	4'- 5 5/16"
11	1'-10"	2'- 5 5/16"	2'-11 3/16"	3'-8"	4'-10 11/16"
12	2'- 0"	2'- 8"	3'- 2⅜"	4'-0"	5'- 4"
13	2'- 2"	2'-10 11/16"	3'- 5⅝"	4'-4"	5'- 9 5/16"
14	2'- 4"	3'- 1 5/16"	3'- 8 13/16"	4'-8"	6'- 2 11/16"
15	2'- 6"	3'- 4"	4'- 0"	5'-0"	6'- 8"
16	2'- 8"	3'- 6 11/16"	4'- 3 3/16"	5'-4"	7'- 1 5/16"
17	2'-10"	3'- 9 5/16"	4'- 6⅜"	5'-8"	7'- 6 11/16"
18	3'- 0"	4'- 0"	4'- 9⅝"	6'-0"	8'- 0"
19	3'- 2"	4'- 2 11/16"	5'- 0 13/16"	6'-4"	8'- 5 5/16"
20	3'- 4"	4'- 5 5/16"	5'- 4"	6'-8"	8'-10 11/16"
21	3'- 6"	4'- 8"	5'- 7 3/16"	7'-0"	9'- 4"
22	3'- 8"	4'-10 11/16"	5'-10⅜"	7'-4"	9'- 9 5/16"
23	3'-10"	5'- 1 5/16"	6'- 1⅝"	7'-8"	10'- 2 11/16"
24	4'- 0"	5'- 4"	6' 4 13/16"	8'-0"	10'- 8"
25	4'- 2"	5'- 6 11/16"	6'- 8"	8'-4"	11'- 1 5/16"
26	4'- 4"	5'- 9 5/16"	6'-11 3/16"	8'-8"	11'- 6 11/16"
27	4'- 6"	6'- 0"	7'- 2⅜"	9'-0"	12'- 0"
28	4'- 8"	6'- 2 11/16"	7'- 5⅝"	9'-4"	12'- 5 5/16"
29	4'-10"	6'- 5 5/16"	7'- 8 13/16"	9'-8"	12'-10 11/16"
30	5'- 0"	6'- 8"	8'- 0"	10'-0"	13'- 4"
31	5'- 2"	6'-10 11/16"	8'- 3 3/16"	10'-4"	13'- 9 5/16"
32	5'- 4"	7'- 1 5/16"	8'- 6⅜"	10'-8"	14' 2 11/16"
33	5'- 6"	7'- 4"	8'- 9⅝"	11'-0"	14'- 8"
34	5'- 8"	7'- 6 11/16"	9'- 0 13/16"	11'-4"	15'- 1 5/16"
35	5'-10"	7'- 9 5/16"	9'- 4"	11'-8"	15'- 6 11/16"
36	6'- 0"	8'- 0"	9'- 7 3/16"	12'-0"	16'- 0"
37	6'- 2"	8'- 2 11/16"	9'-10⅜"	12'-4"	16'- 5 5/16"
38	6'- 4"	8'- 5 5/16"	10'- 1⅝"	12'-8"	16'-10 11/16"
39	6'- 6"	8'- 8"	10'- 4 13/16"	13'-0"	17'- 4"
40	6'- 8"	8'- 10 11/16"	10'- 8"	13'-4"	17'- 9 5/16"
41	6'-10"	9'- 1 5/16"	10'-11 3/16"	13'-8"	18'- 2 11/16"
42	7'- 0"	9'- 4"	11'- 2⅜"	14'-0"	18'- 8"
43	7'- 2"	9'- 6 11/16"	11'- 5⅝"	14'-4"	19'- 1 5/16"
44	7'- 4"	9'- 9 5/16"	11'- 8 13/16"	14'-8"	19'- 6 11/16"
45	7'- 6"	10'- 0"	12'- 0"	15'-0"	20'- 0"
46	7'- 8"	10'- 2 11/16"	12'- 3 3/16"	15'-4"	20'- 5 5/16"
47	7'-10"	10'- 5 5/16"	12'- 6⅜"	15'-8"	20'-10 11/16"
48	8'- 0"	10'- 8"	12'- 9⅝"	16'-0"	21'- 4"
49	8'- 2"	10'-10 11/16"	13'- 0 13/16"	16'-4"	21'- 9 5/16"
50	8'- 4"	11'- 1 5/16"	13'- 4"	16'-8"	22'- 2 11/16"
100	16'- 8"	22'- 2 11/16"	26'- 8"	33'-4"	44'- 5 5/16"

[1] Brick positioned in wall as stretchers.

[2] For convenience in using table, nominal ⅓", ⅔" and ⅕" heights of units have been changed to nearest 1/16". Vertical dimensions are from bottom of mortar joint to bottom of mortar joint.

Source: Brick Institute of America.

Table 4B-4
VERTICAL COURSING TABLE FOR NON-MODULAR BRICK[1]

No. of Courses	2¼-in. High Units		2⅝-in. High Units		2¾-in. High Units	
	⅜″ Joint	½″ Joint	⅜″ Joint	½″ Joint	⅜″ Joint	½″ Joint
1	0′- 2⅝″	0′- 2¾″	0′-3″	0′- 3⅛″	0′- 3⅛″	0′- 3¼″
2	0′- 5¼″	0′- 5½″	0′-6″	0′- 6¼″	0′- 6¼″	0′- 6½″
3	0′- 7⅞″	0′- 8¼″	0′-9″	0′- 9⅜″	0′- 9⅜″	0′- 9¾″
4	0′-10½″	0′-11″	1′-0″	1′- 0½″	1′- 0½″	1′- 1″
5	1′- 1⅛″	1′- 1¾″	1′-3″	1′- 3⅝″	1′- 3⅝″	1′- 4¼″
6	1′- 3¾″	1′- 4½″	1′-6″	1′- 6¾″	1′- 6¾″	1′- 7½″
7	1′- 6⅜″	1′- 7¼″	1′-9″	1′- 9⅞″	1′- 9⅞″	1′-10¾″
8	1′- 9″	1′-10″	2′-0″	2′- 1″	2′- 1″	2′- 2″
9	1′-11⅝″	2′- 0¾″	2′-3″	2′- 4⅛″	2′- 4⅛″	2′- 5¼″
10	2′- 2¼″	2′- 3½″	2′-6″	2′- 7¼″	2′- 7¼″	2′- 8½″
11	2′- 4⅞″	2′- 6¼″	2′-9″	2′-10⅜″	2′-10⅜″	2′-11¾″
12	2′- 7½″	2′- 9″	3′-0″	3′- 1½″	3′- 1½″	3′- 3″
13	2′-10⅛″	2′-11¾″	3′-3″	3′- 4⅝″	3′- 4⅝″	3′- 6¼″
14	3′- 0¾″	3′- 2½″	3′-6″	3′- 7¾″	3′- 7¾″	3′- 9½″
15	3′- 3⅜″	3′- 5¼″	3′-9″	3′-10⅞″	3′-10⅞″	4′- 0¾″
16	3′- 6″	3′- 8″	4′-0″	4′- 2″	4′- 2″	4′- 4″
17	3′- 8⅝″	3′-10¾″	4′-3″	4′- 5⅛″	4′- 5⅛″	4′- 7¼″
18	3′-11¼″	4′- 1½″	4′-6″	4′- 8¼″	4′- 8¼″	4′-10½″
19	4′- 1⅞″	4′- 4¼″	4′-9″	4′-11⅜″	4′-11⅜″	5′- 1¾″
20	4′- 4½″	4′- 7″	5′-0″	5′- 2½″	5′- 2½″	5- 5″
21	4′- 7⅛″	4′- 9¾″	5′-3″	5′- 5⅝″	5′- 5⅝″	5′- 8¼″
22	4′- 9¾″	5′- 0½″	5′-6″	5′- 8¾″	5′- 8¾″	5′-11½″
23	5′- 0⅜″	5′- 3¼″	5′-9″	5′-11⅞″	5′-11⅞″	6′- 2¾″
24	5′- 3″	5′- 6″	6′-0″	6′- 3″	6′- 3″	6′- 6″
25	5′- 5⅝″	5′- 8¾″	6′-3″	6′- 6⅛″	6′- 6⅛″	6′- 9¼″
26	5′- 8¼″	5′-11½″	6′-6″	6′- 9¼″	6′- 9¼″	7′- 0½″
27	5′-10⅞″	6′- 2¼″	6′-9″	7′- 0⅜″	7′- 0⅜″	7′- 3¾″
28	6′- 1½″	6′- 5″	7′-0″	7′- 3½″	7′- 3½″	7′- 7″
29	6′- 4⅛″	6′- 7¾″	7′-3″	7′- 6⅝″	7′- 6⅝″	7′-10¼″
30	6′- 6¾″	6′-10½″	7′-6″	7′- 9¾″	7′- 9¾″	8′- 1½″
31	6′- 9⅜″	7′- 1¼″	7′-9″	8′- 0⅞″	8′- 0⅞″	8′- 4¾″
32	7′- 0″	7′- 4″	8′-0″	8′- 4″	8′- 4″	8′- 8″
33	7′- 2⅝″	7′- 6¾″	8′-3″	8′- 7⅛″	8′- 7⅛″	8′-11¼″
34	7′- 5¼″	7′- 9½″	8′-6″	8′-10¼″	8′-10¼″	9′- 2½″
35	7′- 7⅞″	8′- 0¼″	8′-9″	9′- 1⅜″	9′- 1⅜″	9′- 5¾″
36	7′-10½″	8′- 3″	9′-0″	9′- 4½″	9′- 4½″	9′- 9″
37	8′- 1⅛″	8′- 5¾″	9′-3″	9′- 7⅝″	9′- 7⅝″	10- 0¼″
38	8′- 3¾″	8′- 8½″	9′-6″	9′-10¾″	9′-10¾″	10′- 3½″
39	8′- 6⅜″	8′-11¼″	9′-9″	10′- 1⅞″	10′- 1⅞″	10′- 6¾″
40	8′- 9″	9′- 2″	10′-0″	10′- 5″	10′- 5″	10′-10″
41	8′-11⅝″	9′- 4¾″	10′-3″	10′- 8⅛″	10′- 8⅛″	11′- 1¼″
42	9′- 2¼″	9′- 7½″	10′-6″	10′-11¼″	10′-11¼″	11′- 4½″
43	9′- 4⅞″	9′-10¼″	10′-9″	11′- 2⅜″	11′- 2⅜″	11′- 7¾″
44	9′- 7½″	10′- 1″	11′-0″	11′- 5½″	11′- 5½″	11′-11″
45	9′-10⅛″	10′- 3¾″	11′-3″	11′- 8⅝″	11′- 8⅝″	12′- 2¼″
46	10′- 0¾″	10′- 6½″	11′-6″	11′-11¾″	11′-11¾″	12′- 5½″
47	10′- 3⅜″	10′- 9¼″	11′-9″	12′- 2⅞″	12′- 2⅞″	12′- 8¾″
48	10′- 6″	11′- 0″	12′-0″	12′- 6″	12′- 6″	13′- 0″
49	10′- 8⅝″	11′- 2¾″	12′-3″	12′- 9⅛″	12′- 9⅛″	13′- 3¼″
50	10′-11¼″	11′- 5½″	12′-6″	13′- 0¼″	13′- 0¼″	13′- 6½″
100	21′-10½″	22′-11″	25′-0″	26′- 0½″	26′- 0½″	27′- 1″

[1] Brick positioned in wall as stretchers. Vertical dimensions are from bottom of mortar joint to bottom of mortar joint.

Source: Brick Institute of America.

TABLES SHOWING PROPERTIES OF LIMESTONE AND MARBLE

Table 4B-5
PHYSICAL PROPERTIES OF LIMESTONE

Property	Value
Coefficient of thermal expansion	0.0000024 in./in./°F to 0.0000030 in./in./°F
Modulus of elasticity	3,300,000 psi min. to 5,400,000 psi max.
Modulus of rupture	700 psi min. (some limestone available with higher values)
Ultimate compression	4000 psi min. (some limestone available with higher values)
Ultimate shear strength	900 psi min. to 1800 psi max.
Ultimate tensile strength	300 psi min. to 715 psi max.
Thermal conductivity (k)	6.5 Btu h/sq. ft./in./°F
Abrasion resistance	6 min. to 17 max. (ASTM C241)
Absorption	7 1/2% maximum (some limestone available with lower values)
Fire resistance	1 hr. 12 min. with ASTM E119 hose stream test
Weight	144 lbs./cu. ft.
Light reflectance	50–55%

Table 4B-6
PHYSICAL PROPERTIES OF MARBLE

Property	Value
Coefficient of thermal expansion	0.00000369 in./in./°F to 0.000001230 in./in./°F
Modulus of elasticity	1,970,000 psi to 14,850,000 psi
Modulus of rupture	1095 to 2709 psi
Ultimate compression	6012 to 16,750 psi
Ultimate shear strength	1638 to 4812 psi
Thermal conductivity (k)	10.45 to 15.65 Btu h/sq. ft./in./°F
Absorption	0.069 to 0.609%
Fire resistance	10 min. for 7/8 in. thickness
Weight	163–172 lbs./cu. ft.

TABLES FOR SELECTING MASONRY BASED ON WEATHERING REQUIREMENTS

Table 4B-7
GRADE REQUIREMENTS FOR FACE EXPOSURES OF MASONRY

Exposure	**Weathering Index** (See Figure 4B-1.) Less than 50	50-500	500 and greater
In vertical surfaces:			
In contact with earth	MW	SW	SW
Not in contact with earth	MW	SW	SW
In other than vertical surfaces:			
In contact with earth	SW	SW	SW
Not in contact with earth	MW	SW	SW

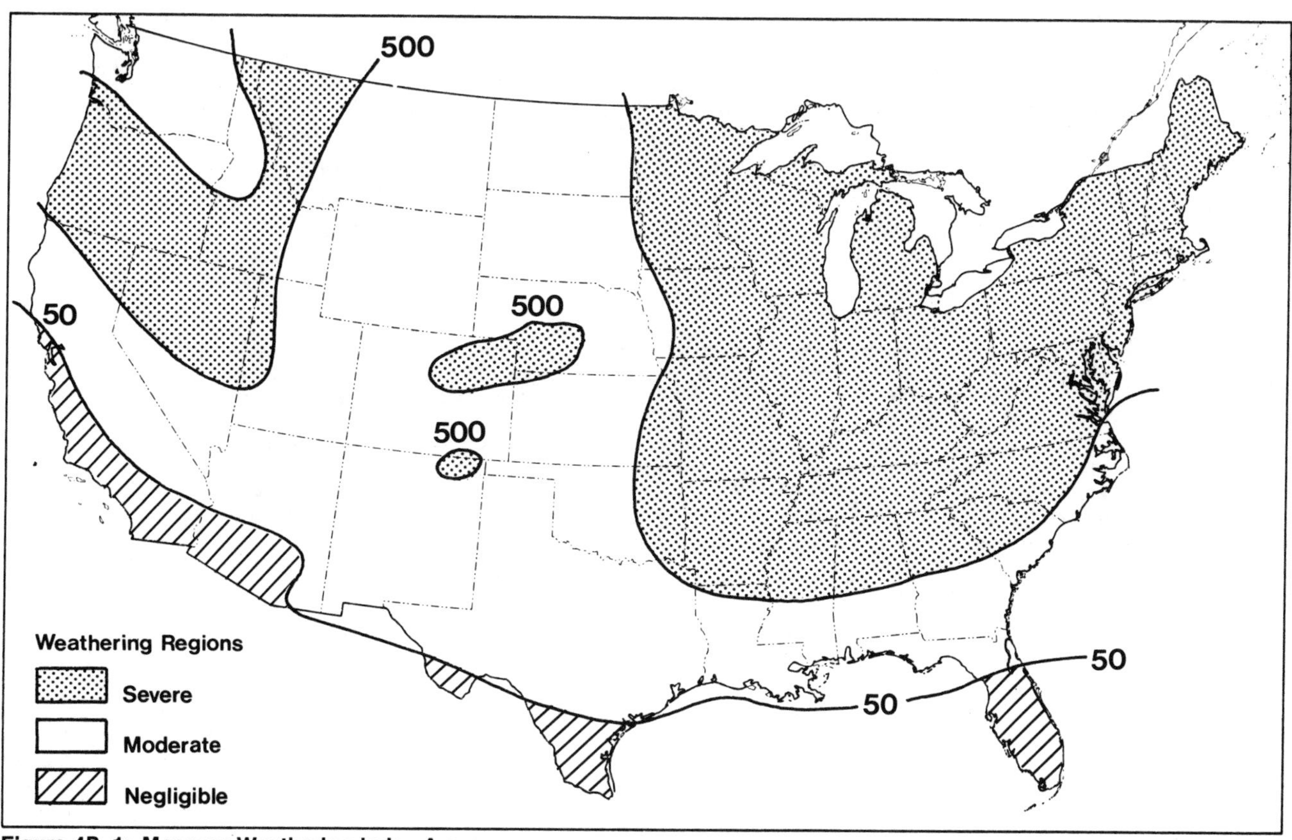

Figure 4B-1: Masonry Weathering Index Areas

TABLES SHOWING SIZES, TOLERANCES, AND FINISHES OF BUILDING STONE

Table 4B-8
TYPICAL MAXIMUM SIZES OF BUILDING STONE

Type		Maximum Size	Thickness
Marble	Group A	5 ft.–0 in. × 7 ft. × 0 in.	
	Group B	2 ft.–6 in. to 4 ft.–0 in. wide 4 ft.–0 in. to 7 ft.–0 in. long	
	Group C	2 ft.–6 in. to 4 ft.–0 in. wide 4 ft.–0 in. to 7 ft. 0 in. long	3/4 in., 7/8 in., 1 1/4 in., 2 in.
	Group D	2 ft.–6 in. to 4 ft.–0 in. wide 4 ft.–0 in. to 7 ft.–0 in. long	
	Max. 20 sq. ft. per piece recommended for Groups C and D		
	Marble tile	1 ft. × 1 ft. 2 ft. × 2 ft.	3/8 in. ±
Granite		4 ft. × 10 ft.	
Slate	Panels	4 ft.–0 in. × 6 ft.–6 in.	1 in., 1 1/4 in., 1 1/2 in.
Slate Flooring Natural Finish	Blue black	10 in. × 20 in.	3/8 in.
	Green or Gray	8 in. × 16 in.	3/8 in.
	Blue black	18 in. × 30 in.	3/4 in.
	Green or Gray	15 in. × 24 in.	3/4 in.
Slate Flooring Honed or sanded	Blue black	24 in. × 36 in.	1/2 in. or 3/4 in.
	Green or Gray	3 ft. × 5 ft.	2 in.
Limestone		4 ft. × 9 ft. 5 ft. × 18 ft.	3 in. 6 in.

Notes: These dimensions are general guidelines. Maximum sizes will depend on the type of stone, the quarry, and the quantities needed. Check with the quarry and the local supplier before deciding on final sizes for your application.

For interior uses, cut stone is usually 3/4 inch or 7/8 inch thick except for smaller marble tiles.

Thickness used often depends on the size and type of stone being used.

Thin tiles are available for thin-set application on floors and walls. These are generally 3/8 inch thick and 12 inches by 12 inches or 24 inches by 24 inches. Check with individual suppliers for exact sizes and stone types available.

Table 4B-9
TOLERANCES OF BUILDING STONE

Stone	Size and Squareness	Flatness and/or Thickness	
Marble, thin stock	±1/16 in.	+1/8 in. to −1/16 in.	
Marble tile		+1/32 in. to −1/32 in.	
		At bed or joint line a maximum of 3/64 in. or 1/6th of the joint width, whichever is greater for polished, honed, and fine-rubbed finishes.	
Granite	Max. 1/4 of the specified joint width	At other parts of the face surface:	
		Polished, honed, or fine-rubbed:	3/64 in.
		Rubbed or fine-stippled and sandblasted:	1/16 in.
		Shot ground, 8- and 6-cut finishes:	3/32 in.
		4-cut finish:	1/8 in.
		Thermal and coarse stippled sand blasted:	3/16 in.
		Note: Flatness is determined by use of a 4 ft. straightedge applied in any direction on the surface.	
Limestone	±1/16 in.	Smooth finish:	+1/16 in. to -1/16 in.
		Diamond gang finish:	+1/4 in. to -1/4 in.

Note: Verify other critical dimensions with fabricator.

Table 4B-10
TYPES OF STONE FINISHES

Marble Finishes	
Polished:	A glossy surface, which brings out the full color and character of the marble (not recommended for floor finishes).
Honed:	A satin-smooth surface, with little or no gloss (recommended for commercial floors).
Sandblasted:	A matte-textured surface with no gloss (recommended for exterior use).
Abrasive:	A flat, non-reflective surface suitable for exterior use, stair treads, and other non-slip surfaces (see note below).
Wet-sand:	A smooth surface suitable for stair treads and other non-slip surfaces (see note below).
Granite Finishes	
Polished:	Mirror gloss, with sharp reflections.
Honed:	Dull sheen, without reflections.
Fine-rubbed:	Smooth and free from scratches; no sheen.
Rubbed:	Plane surface with occasional slight "trails" or scratches.
Shot-ground:	Plane surface with pronounced circular markings or trails having no regular pattern.
Thermal: (flame)	Plane surface with flame finish applied by mechanically controlled means to ensure uniformity; surface coarseness varies, depending upon grain structure of granite.
Sandblasted: fine stipple	Plane surface, slightly pebbled, with occasional slight trails or scratches.

Table 4B-10 (Continued)

Sandblasted: coarse stipple	Coarse plane surface produced by blasting with an abrasive; coarseness varies with type of preparatory finish and grain structure of granite.
8-cut:	Fine bush-hammered; interrupted parallel markings not over 3/32 in. apart; a corrugated finish.
6-cut:	Medium bush-hammered; markings not more than 1/8 in. apart.
4-cut:	Coarse bush-hammered; markings not more than 7/32 in. apart.
Sawn:	Relatively plane surface, with texture ranging from wire sawn (a close approximation of rubbed finish) to shot sawn, with scorings 3/32 in. in depth; gang saws produce parallel scorings, rotary or circular saws make circular scorings; shot-sawn surfaces are sandblasted to remove all rust stains and iron particles.
Limestone Finishes	
Smooth finish:	Machine finish producing a uniform honed finish; use only select grade or standard grade.
Plucked:	Rough texture produced by rough planing the surface of the stone.
Machine tooled:	Finish made by cutting parallel, concave grooves in the stone with 4, 6, or 8 grooves to the inch; depth of the grooves range from 1/32 in.–1/16 in.
Chat-sawed:	Coarse, pebbled surface that closely resembles the appearance of sandblasting; sometimes contains shallow saw marks or parallel scores; direction of score or saw marks will be vertical and/or horizontal in the wall unless the direction is specified.
Shot-sawed:	Coarse, uneven finish ranging from a pebbled surface to one rippled with irregular, roughly parallel grooves; steel shot used during gang-sawing rusts during process, adding permanent brown tones to the natural color variations.
Split face:	Rough, uneven, concave-convex finish produced by splitting action; limits stone sizes to 1 ft. 4 in. high by 4 ft. 0 in. long; available in ashlar stone veneer only.
Rock face:	Similar to split face except the face of the stone has been dressed by machine or by hand to produce a bold convex projection along the face of the stone.
Limestone Appearance Grades	
Classifications are based on the degree of fineness of the grain particles and other natural characteristics that make up the stone. The structural soundness of each grade is essentially identical.	
Select:	Sound, durable stone embracing the average finer grained stone; in texture ranging from the finest, most uniform grained stock to stone having an average grain, as designating the range of this type; pore spaces not exceeding 1 mm; calcite streaks or veins not exceeding 1 mm; pit holes not exceeding 6 mm in diameter, with a maximum of one to any 10 sq. ft. of slab area.
Standard:	Sound, durable stone that is the average of the moderately large-grained product of the quarries that constitute the bulk of the total output of stone; allows certain variations in density, color-tone, and texture not allowable in select grade.
Rustic:	Includes the coarser, more or less open shelly-grained stone, having a varying amount of calcite streaks or veins, including stone having a decidedly coarse, somewhat honeycomb formation.
Variegated:	Includes stone with the irregular mixture of the buff and gray color tones that occur in the blocks that are quarried where the buff and gray color tones adjoin in the quarry ledges.

Note: The terms *polished* and *honed* are generally recognized in the industry with precise meaning. Some suppliers and fabricating shops may have their own terms for the other finishes. Verify that you are using the term that will give you what you want from the supplier.

TABLES SHOWING PROPERTIES AND THERMAL VALUES OF MASONRY WALLS

Table 4B-11
R AND U VALUES OF TYPICAL 6 INCH HOLLOW CONCRETE MASONRY WALLS

Construction	Cores Empty		Loose-Fill Insulation		Foamed-in-Place Insulation		Grout Fill 100 lb./cu. ft.		Grout Fill 130 lb./ft.^{3}		Density of Block lb./cu. ft.
	R	U	R	U	R	U	R	U	R	U	
Exposed Block, Both Sides	2.64	.38	6.98	.14	9.72	.10	2.69	.37	2.22	.45	80
	2.43	.41	6.09	.16	7.54	.13	2.46	.41	2.02	.50	95
	2.30	.43	5.77	.17	6.58	.15	2.33	.43	1.91	.52	105
	2.19	.46	5.21	.19	5.93	.17	2.22	.45	1.81	.55	115
	2.06	.49	4.39	.23	5.02	.20	2.09	.48	1.70	.59	125
	1.93	.52	3.76	.27	4.18	.24	1.96	.51	1.61	.62	135
½" Gypsum Board on Furring Strips	4.06	.25	8.40	.12	11.14	.09	4.11	.24	3.64	.27	80
	3.85	.26	7.51	.13	8.96	.11	3.88	.26	3.44	.29	95
	3.72	.27	7.19	.14	8.00	.125	3.75	.27	3.33	.30	105
	3.61	.28	6.63	.15	7.35	.14	3.64	.27	3.23	.31	115
	3.48	.29	5.81	.17	6.44	.16	3.51	.28	3.12	.32	125
	3.35	.30	5.18	.19	5.60	.18	3.38	.30	3.03	.33	135
½" Foil-Backed Gypsum Board on Furring Strips	6.17	.16	10.51	.10	13.25	.08	6.22	.16	5.75	.17	80
	5.96	.17	9.62	.10	11.07	.09	5.99	.17	5.55	.18	95
	5.83	.17	9.30	.11	10.00	.10	5.86	.17	5.44	.18	105
	5.72	.17	8.74	.11	9.46	.11	5.75	.17	5.34	.19	115
	5.59	.18	7.92	.13	8.55	.12	5.62	.18	5.23	.19	125
	5.45	.18	7.29	.14	7.71	.13	5.49	.18	5.14	.19	135
1" Rigid Glass Fiber plus ½" Gypsum Board	7.09	.14	11.43	.09	14.17	.07	7.14	.14	6.67	.15	80
	6.88	.15	10.54	.09	11.99	.08	6.91	.14	6.47	.15	95
	6.75	.15	10.22	.10	11.03	.09	6.78	.15	6.36	.16	105
	6.64	.15	9.66	.10	10.38	.10	6.67	.15	6.26	.16	115
	6.51	.15	8.84	.11	9.47	.11	6.54	.15	6.15	.16	125
	6.38	.16	8.21	.12	8.63	.12	6.41	.16	6.06	.17	135
1" Expanded Polystyreme plus ½" Gypsum Board	8.09	.12	12.43	.08	15.17	.07	8.14	.12	7.67	.13	80
	7.88	.13	11.54	.09	12.99	.08	7.91	.13	7.47	.13	95
	7.75	.13	11.22	.09	12.03	.08	7.78	.13	7.36	.14	105
	7.64	.13	10.66	.09	11.38	.09	7.67	.13	7.26	.14	115
	7.51	.13	9.84	.10	10.47	.10	7.54	.13	7.15	.14	125
	7.38	.14	9.21	.11	9.63	.10	7.41	.13	7.06	.14	135
1" Expanded Polyurethane plus ½" Gypsum Board	9.34	.11	13.68	.07	16.42	.06	9.39	.11	8.92	.11	80
	9.13	.11	12.79	.08	14.24	.07	9.16	.11	8.72	.11	95
	9.00	.11	12.47	.08	13.28	.08	9.03	.11	8.61	.12	105
	8.89	.11	11.91	.08	12.63	.08	8.92	.11	8.51	.12	115
	8.76	.11	11.09	.09	11.72	.09	8.79	.11	8.40	.12	125
	8.63	.12	10.46	.10	10.88	.09	8.66	.12	8.31	.12	135

Source: *National Concrete Masonry Association.*

Table 4B-12
R AND U VALUES OF TYPICAL 8 INCH HOLLOW CONCRETE MASONRY WALLS

Construction	Cores Empty		Loose-Fill Insulation		Foamed-in-Place Insulation		Grout Fill 100 lb./cu. ft.		Grout Fill 130 lb./ft.^{3}		Density of Block, lb./cu. ft.
	R	U	R	U	R	U	R	U	R	U	
Exposed Block, Both Sides	2.92	.34	8.92	.11	11.27	.09	3.33	.30	2.68	.37	80
	2.64	.38	7.67	.13	9.33	.11	3.03	.33	2.41	.41	95
	2.49	.40	6.91	.14	8.21	.12	2.86	.35	2.27	.44	105
	2.36	.42	6.21	.16	7.22	.14	2.71	.37	2.15	.47	115
	2.20	.45	5.34	.19	6.04	.17	2.53	.40	2.00	.50	125
	2.06	.49	4.51	.22	4.97	.20	2.34	.43	1.87	.53	135
½" Gypsum Board on Furring Strips	4.34	.23	10.34	.10	12.69	.08	4.75	.21	4.10	.24	80
	4.06	.25	9.09	.11	10.75	.09	4.45	.22	3.83	.26	95
	3.91	.26	8.33	.12	9.63	.10	4.28	.23	3.69	.27	105
	3.78	.26	7.63	.13	8.64	.12	4.13	.24	3.57	.28	115
	3.62	.28	6.76	.15	7.46	.13	3.95	.25	3.42	.29	125
	3.48	.29	5.93	.17	6.39	.16	3.29	.27	3.29	.30	135
½" Foil-Backed Gypsum Board on Furring Strips	6.45	.16	12.45	.08	14.80	.07	6.86	.15	6.21	.16	80
	6.17	.16	11.20	.09	12.86	.08	6.56	.15	5.94	.17	95
	6.02	.17	10.44	.10	11.74	.09	6.39	.16	5.80	.17	105
	5.89	.17	9.74	.10	10.75	.09	6.24	.16	5.68	.18	115
	5.73	.17	8.87	.11	9.57	.10	6.06	.17	5.53	.18	125
	5.59	.18	8.04	.12	8.50	.12	5.87	.17	5.40	.19	135
1" Rigid Glass Fiber plus ½" Gypsum Board	7.37	.14	13.37	.07	15.72	.06	7.78	.13	7.13	.14	80
	7.09	.14	12.12	.08	13.78	.07	7.48	.13	6.86	.15	95
	6.94	.14	11.36	.09	12.66	.08	7.31	.14	6.72	.15	105
	6.81	.15	10.66	.09	11.67	.09	7.16	.14	6.60	.15	115
	6.65	.15	9.79	.10	10.49	.10	6.98	.14	6.45	.16	125
	6.51	.15	8.96	.11	9.42	.11	6.79	.15	6.32	.16	135
1" Expanded Polystyrene plus ½" Gypsum Board	8.37	.12	14.37	.07	16.72	.06	8.78	.11	8.13	.12	80
	8.09	.12	13.12	.08	14.78	.07	8.48	.12	7.86	.13	95
	7.94	.13	12.36	.08	13.66	.07	8.31	.12	7.72	.13	105
	7.81	.13	11.66	.09	12.67	.08	8.16	.12	7.60	.13	115
	7.65	.13	10.79	.09	11.49	.09	7.98	.13	7.45	.13	125
	7.51	.13	9.96	.10	10.42	.10	7.79	.13	7.32	.14	135
1" Expanded Polyurethane plus ½" Gypsum Board	9.62	.10	15.62	.06	17.97	.06	10.03	.10	9.38	.11	80
	9.34	.11	14.37	.07	16.03	.06	9.73	.10	9.11	.11	95
	9.19	.11	13.61	.07	14.91	.07	9.56	.10	8.97	.11	105
	9.06	.11	12.91	.08	13.92	.07	9.41	.11	8.85	.11	115
	8.90	.11	12.04	.08	12.74	.08	9.23	.11	8.70	.11	125
	8.76	.11	11.21	.09	11.67	.09	9.04	.11	8.57	.12	135

Source: *National Concrete Masonry Association.*

Table 4B-13
VOLUMETRIC CHARACTERISTICS OF TYPICAL HOLLOW CONCRETE MASONRY UNITS

Width (in in.)	Gross Volume (in cu. in.) (cu. ft. indicated by parens.)	Minimum Thicknesses		3-Core Units		2-Core Units	
		Shell (in in.)	Web (in in.)	Percent Solid Volume	Equivalent Solid Thickness (in in.)	Percent Solid Volume	Equivalent Solid Thickness (in in.)
3 5/8	423	0.75	0.75	63	2.28	64	2.32
	(0.25)	1.00	1.00	73	2.66	73	2.66
5 5/8	670	1.00	1.00	59	3.32	57	3.21
	(0.388)	1.12	1.00	63	3.54	61	3.43
		1.25	1.00	66	3.71	64	3.60
		1.37	1.12	70	3.94	68	3.82
7 5/8	908	1.25	1.00	56	4.27	53	4.04
	(0.526)	1.37	1.12	60	4.57	57	4.35
		1.50	1.12	62	4.73	59	4.50
9 5/8	1145	1.25	1.12	53	5.10	48	4.62
	(0.664)	1.37	1.12	55	5.29	51	4.91
		1.50	1.25	58	5.58	54	5.20
11 5/8	1385	1.25	1.12	49	5.70	44	5.12
	(0.803)	1.37	1.12	51	5.93	46	5.35
		1.50	1.25	54	6.28	49	5.70
		1.75	1.25	57	6.63	52	6.05

Note: Data are based on units 7 5/8 in. high by 15 5/8 in. long.

Source: National Concrete Masonry Association.

Table 4B-14
PROPERTIES OF HOLLOW BLOCK WITH MINIMUM FACE SHELL AND WEB THICKNESS PERMITTED BY ASTM C-90

Nominal Block Thickness (in in.)	Net Area of Block (in sq. in. per ft. of length)	**Wall Weight**, in lbs. per sq. ft. where density of concrete in block, lb. per cu. ft. is:					Moment of Inertia, I, and Section Modulus, S, Where Mortar Is:			
							Face Shell Bedded		Fully Bedded	
		60	80	100	120	140	I	S	I	S
4	28	14	18	22	27	31	38	21	45	25
6	37	20	26	33	40	46	130	46	139	50
8	48	24	32	40	47	55	309	81	334	88
10	60	28	37	47	56	65	567	118	634	132
12	68	34	45	55	67	78	929	160	1063	183

Moment of Inertia, I, is in in.^{4}/ft.
Section Modulus, S, is in in.^{3}/ft.

Source: National Concrete Masonry Association.

Table 4B-15
R VALUES OF WALLS CONSTRUCTED OF 6 INCH HOLLOW CMU

	Density (in lb./cu. ft.)				
Details of Construction	60	80	100	120	140
1. No insulation	3.2	2.7	2.4	2.1	1.9
2. Cores filled with Vermiculite	7.1	5.7	4.5	3.6	2.8
3. Cores filled with Perlite	7.8	6.1	4.8	3.7	2.9
4. No insulation, 1/2 in. gypsum board on furring	4.6	4.1	3.8	3.5	3.3
5. No insulation, 1/2 in. foil back gypsum board on furring	6.2	5.7	5.4	5.1	4.9
6. Same as #4 with 1 in. extruded polystyrene	8.2	7.7	7.4	7.1	6.9
7. Same as #4 with 2 in. expanded polystyrene	11.2	10.7	10.4	10.1	9.9
8. Same as #4 with 2 in. extruded polystyrene	13.2	12.7	12.4	12.1	11.9
9. Same as #4 with 2 in. polyisocyanurate	17.6	17.1	16.8	16.5	16.3
10. Same as #4 R-11 fibrous batt 2 × 3 studs set out from wall	14.2	13.7	13.4	13.1	12.9
11. Same as #4 R-13 fibrous batt 2 × 3 studs set out from wall	16.2	15.7	15.4	15.1	14.9
12. Same as #4 R-19 fibrous batt 2 × 4 studs set out from wall	22.2	21.7	21.4	21.1	20.9

Source: *National Concrete Masonry Association.*

Table 4B-16
R VALUES OF WALLS CONSTRUCTED OF 8 INCH HOLLOW CMU

	Density (in lb./cu. ft.)				
Details of Construction	60	80	100	120	140
1. No insulation	3.6	3.0	2.6	2.3	2.0
2. Cores filled with Vermiculite	9.6	7.6	6.0	4.7	3.6
3. Cores filled with Perlite	10.4	8.2	6.3	4.8	3.7
4. No insulation, 1/2 in. gypsum board on furring	5.0	4.4	4.0	3.7	3.4
5. No insulation, 1/2 in. foil back gypsum board on furring	6.6	6.0	5.6	5.3	5.0
6. Same as #4 with 1 in. extruded polystyrene	8.6	8.0	7.6	7.3	7.0
7. Same as #4 with 2 in. expanded polystyrene	11.6	11.0	10.6	10.3	10.0
8. Same as #4 with 2 in. extruded polystyrene	13.6	13.0	12.6	12.3	12.0
9. Same as #4 with 2 in. polyisocyanurate	18.0	17.4	17.0	16.7	16.4
10. Same as #4 R-11 fibrous batt 2 × 3 studs set out from wall	14.6	14.0	13.6	13.3	13.0
11. Same as #4 R-13 fibrous batt 2 × 3 studs set out from wall	16.6	16.0	15.6	15.3	15.0
12. Same as #4 R-19 fibrous batt 2 × 4 studs set out from wall	22.6	22.0	21.6	21.3	21.0

Source: *National Concrete Masonry Association.*

TABLE SHOWING FIREPLACE OPENING RECOMMENDATIONS

Table 4B-17
RECOMMENDED DIMENSIONS FOR SINGLE-OPENING WOOD-BURNING FIREPLACES

Fireplace Opening		Firebox					
			Rear Wall				
Width	Ht.	Depth	Width	Vertical Wall Ht.	Splayed Ht.	Throat Depth	Flue Size (W × D)
24	24	16	11	14	18	8 3/4	12 × 8
26	24	16	13	14	18	8 3/4	12 × 8
28	24	16	15	14	18	8 3/4	12 × 8
30	29	16	17	14	23	8 3/4	12 × 12
32	29	16	19	14	23	8 3/4	12 × 12
36	29	16	23	14	23	8 3/4	12 × 12
40	29	16	27	14	23	8 3/4	16 × 12
42	32	16	29	14	26	8 3/4	16 × 16
48	32	18	33	14	26	8 3/4	16 × 16
54	37	20	37	16	29	13	16 × 16
60	37	22	42	16	29	13	20 × 16
60	40	22	42	16	31	13	20 × 16

PART 4C

Metals

The tables included in this part provide hard-to-find information on the composition and use of many finish metals as well as basic data on metal gages and the galvanic series.

The tables concerning stainless steel give guidelines for the proper selection of stainless steel types, finishes, and thicknesses. Following these are tables to help you understand the composition of the many available copper alloys and show you how to select the best one for your design needs.

Table 4C-1
COMPARATIVE METAL GAGES

	Aluminum, Copper, Brass, Bronze Sheets, Strips, and Wire; Small Copper and Brass Tubing	Stainless Steel Sheets	Stainless Steel, Aluminum, Bronze, and Large Copper and Brass Tubing; Stainless Strip	Steel Sheets
Gage No.	*B&S & AWG*	*USG*	*BWG*	*MSG*
3	0.2294	0.2500	0.259	0.2391
4	0.2043	0.2344	0.238	0.2242
5	0.1819	0.2187	0.220	0.2092
6	0.1620	0.2031	0.203	0.1943
7	0.1443	0.1875	0.180	0.1793
8	0.1285	0.1719	0.165	0.1644
9	0.1144	0.1562	0.148	0.1495
10	0.1019	0.1406	0.134	0.1345
11	0.0907	0.1250	0.120	0.1196
12	0.0808	0.1094	0.109	0.1046
13	0.0719	0.0938	0.095	0.0897
14	0.0640	0.0781	0.083	0.0747
15	0.0571	0.0703	0.072	0.0673
16	0.0508	0.0625	0.065	0.0598
17	0.0453	0.0562	0.058	0.0538
18	0.0403	0.0500	0.049	0.0478
19	0.0359	0.0437	0.042	0.0418
20	0.0320	0.0375	0.035	0.0359
21	0.0285	0.0344	0.032	0.0329
22	0.0253	0.0312	0.028	0.0299
23	0.0226	0.0281	0.025	0.0269
24	0.0201	0.0250	0.022	0.0239
25	0.0179	0.0219	0.020	0.0209
26	0.0159	0.0187	0.018	0.0179

27	0.0142	0.0172	0.016	0.0164
28	0.0126	0.0156	0.014	0.0149
29	0.0113	0.0141	0.013	0.0135
30	0.0100	0.0125	0.012	0.0120

B & S = Brown and Sharp
AWG = American Wire Gage
USG = United States Standard Gage
BWG = Birmingham Wire Gage
MSG = Manufacturer's Standard Gage

Table 4C-2
GALVANIC SERIES

Zinc
Galvanized steel
Aluminum alloys: 5052, 3004, 3003, 1100, 6053
Aluminum alloys: 2117, 2017, 2024
Low-carbon steel
Wrought iron
Cast iron
Type 410 stainless steel, active
Type 304 stainless steel, active
Type 316 stainless steel, active
Lead
Tin
Copper alloys:
280
675
404, 465, 466, 467
Nickel 200
Copper alloys:
270
443, 444, 445
708, 614
230
110
651, 665
715
923, cast
Monel alloy 400
Type 410 stainless steel, passive
Type 304 stainless steel, passive
Type 316 stainless steel, passive

Note: The farther apart the metals are from each other in the table, the greater the possibility for corrosion, with the metals listed on the top being the most susceptible to corrosion.

Table 4C-3
PROPERTIES AND USES OF ARCHITECTURAL STAINLESS STEEL

		Composition (in %)						
AISI Type	**Properties and Uses**	**Chromium**	**Nickel**	**Manganese**	**Molybdenum**	**Carbon** (max.)	**Thermal Conductivity**	**Coefficient of Thermal Expansion** (in./in./deg F × 10^{-6})
201	Similar to 301/302 but stronger and harder.	16–18	3.5–5.5	5.5–7.5	—	0.15	9.4	9.7
301	Can be cold-rolled to very high tensile strengths; structural members; roof drainage products.	16–18	6–8	2 max.	—	0.15	9.4	9.4
302	Traditional type used in architectural applications; resistant to atmospheric corrosion; strong and hard.	17–19	8–10	2 max.	—	0.15	9.4	9.6
304	Similar to 302 but with improved weldability; has largely replaced type 302 for architectural work—curtain walls, store fronts, facias, doors, railings, column covers, food preparation equip., sinks, countertops.	18–20	8–12	2 max.	—	0.08	9.4	9.6
316	Improved corrosion resistance for marine or extremely corrosive industrial environments.	16–18	10–14	2 max.	2–3	0.08	9.4	8.6
430	Less corrosion resistant than 200 and 300 series; used primarily for interior applications—trim, column covers, appliances, sometimes gutters and downspouts.	14–18	—	1 max.	—	0.12	15.1	5.8

Table 4C-4
TYPES OF STAINLESS STEEL PRODUCT FORMS

Item	Description	Thickness	Width	Diameter or Size
Sheet	Coils and cut lengths:			
	Mill finishes # 1, 2D, and 2B	Under 3/16 in.	24 in. and over	—
	Pol. finishes # 3, 4, 6, 7, and 8	Under 3/16 in.	All widths	—
Plates	Flat-rolled or forged	3/16 in. and over	Over 10 in.	—
Bars	Hot-finished rounds, squares, octagons, and hexagons	—	—	1/4 in. and over
	Hot-finished flats	1/8 in. and over	1/4 in. to 10 in. incl.	—
	Cold-finished rounds, squares, octagons, and hexagons	—	—	Over 1/2 in.
	Cold-finished flats	—	3/8 in. and over	—
Strip	Cold-finished coils or cut lengths	Under 3/16 in.	Under 24 in.	—
Wire	Cold finished only:			
	Round, square, octagon, hexagon, flat wire	0.010 in. to under 3/16 in.	1/16 in. to under 3/8 in.	1/2 in. and under

Table 4C-5
ARCHITECTURAL APPLICATIONS OF STAINLESS STEEL THICKNESSES

Gage	**Thickness** (in in.)	**Weight** (in lbs. per sq. ft.)	**Typical Applications** (verify with fabricator)
11	0.1250	5.250	Door bumpers, thresholds, cover plates
12	0.1094	4.594	Kick plates, large flush panels, elevator panels, escalator panels
14	0.0781	3.281	Column covers, convector covers
16	0.0625	2.625	Large mullions, unbacked fascia
18	0.0500	2.100	Corner guards, door sections, handrails
20	0.0375	1.575	Windowsills
22	0.0312	1.312	Light mullions, stiffeners
24	0.0250	1.050	Window framing, louvers
26	0.0187	0.787	Cleat and clips, industrial roofing
28	0.0156	0.656	Gravel stops, roofing gutters
30	0.0125	0.525	Laminated panels, exposed flashing
32	0.0100	0.426	Concealed flashing

Table 4C-6
COMPOSITION AND DESCRIPTION OF COPPER ALLOYS

Alloy #	Name	Nominal Composition	Color	Weathering
110	Copper	99.9% copper	Salmon-red	From reddish-brown to gray-green
122	Copper	99.9% copper 0.02% phosphorous	Salmon-red	From reddish-brown to gray-green
220	Commercial bronze	90% copper 10% zinc	Red-gold	From brown to gray-green
230	Red brass	85% copper 15% zinc	Reddish-yellow	From chocolate-brown to gray-green
260	Cartridge brass	70% copper 30% zinc	Yellow	Primarily for interior work; natural color usually retained through use of clear coatings
280	Muntz metal	60% copper 40% zinc	Reddish-yellow	From red-brown to gray-brown
385	Architectural bronze	57% copper 3% lead 40% zinc	Reddish-yellow	From russet-brown to dark-brown
655	Silicon bronze	97% copper 3% silicon	Reddish-old gold	From russet-brown to finely mottled dark gray-brown
745	Nickel silver	65% copper 25% zinc 10% nickel	Warm silver	From gray-brown to finely mottled gray-green
796	Leaded nickel silver	45% copper 42% zinc 10% nickel 2% manganese 1% lead	Warm silver	From gray-brown to finely mottled gray-green

Note: Alloy numbers are the current common number designations. The numbers are being replaced by the Unified Numbering System for Metals and Alloys (UNS) managed jointly by ASTM and the Society of Automotive Engineers. The UNS is an expansion of the current system. The number is preceded by the letter designation C and followed by two additional digits. For example, alloy 655 becomes alloy C65500.

Source: *Copper Development Association, Inc., Greenwich, CT.*

Color matching: Alloys to be used in various forms, for best color match with certain sheet and plate alloys. Color of surfaces compared after identical grinding or polishing. (See Table 4C–8 for forms to be matched in color.)

Table 4C-7
COPPER ALLOYS—SUMMARY OF TYPICAL ARCHITECTURAL USES BY ALLOY

Use	Alloy Number									
	110	122	220	230	260	280	385	655	745	796
Art works	●		●	●	●	●	●	●	●	●
Bank equipment	●	●	●	●		●	●		●	●
Builders' hardware			●	●	●		●		●	●
Curtain walls, store fronts			●	●		●	●		●	●
Ecclesiastical equipment	●		●	●	●	●				
Elevators, escalators			●	●		●	●		●	●
Entrance doors and frames	●	●	●	●		●	●		●	●
Firefighting devices			●	●		●				
Flag poles			●	●						
Floor tile	●	●	●	●						
Food service equipment	●	●		●		●		●		
Furniture	●		●	●	●	●		●	●	
Grilles, screens	●		●	●	●		●		●	●
Gutters, downspouts	●	●								
Identifying devices	●	●	●	●	●	●	●			
Lighting fixtures	●	●	●		●		●			
Louvers	●	●	●	●			●			
Mansards	●	●	●	●		●				
Plumbing fixtures			●	●	●					
Postal specialties	●	●	●	●	●	●				
Railings		●	●	●	●	●	●		●	●
Roofing, flashing	●	●								
Skylights	●	●					●			
Solar collector panels	●	●								
Sun control devices	●	●	●	●			●		●	●
Thresholds							●			●
Toilet and bath accessories			●	●	●		●			●
Wall coverings	●	●	●	●	●					
Wall panels	●	●	●	●		●				
Weatherstripping			●	●						
Windows	●	●	●	●		●	●	●	●	●

Source: *Copper Development Association, Inc., Greenwich, CT.*

Table 4C–8
COLOR MATCHING OF COPPER ALLOYS

Sheet and Plate Alloys	Extrusions	Castings	Fasteners	Tube and Pipe	Rod and Wire	Filler Metals
Alloy 110 Alloy 122 copper	Alloy 110 copper (simple shapes)	Copper (99.9 min)	Alloy 651 low silicon bronze (fair)	Alloy 122 copper	Alloy 110 copper	Alloy 189 copper
Allow 220 commercial bronze, 90%	Alloy 314 leaded commercial bronze	Alloy 834	Alloy 651 low silicon bronze	Alloy 220 commercial bronze, 90%	Alloy 220 commercial bronze, 90%	Alloy 655 high silicon bronze
Alloy 230 red brass, 85%	Alloy 385 architectural bronze	Alloy 836 (1)	Alloy 651 low silicon bronze (fair) Alloy 280	Alloy 230 red brass, 85%	Alloy 230 red brass, 85%	Alloy 655 high silicon bronze (fair)
Alloy 260 cartridge brass, 70%	Alloy 260 cartridge brass, 70% (simple shapes)	Alloys 852, 853	Alloy 260 cartridge brass, 70% Alloys 360, 464, 465	Alloy 260 cartridge brass, 70%	Alloy 260 cartridge brass, 70%	Alloy 681 low fuming bronze (poor)
Alloy 280 Muntz metal	Alloy 385 architectural bronze	Alloys 855 (1), 857	Alloy 651 low silicon bronze (fair) Alloy 280	Alloy 230, red brass, 85%	Alloy 280, Muntz metal	Alloy 681 low fuming bronze
Alloy 655 high silicon bronze	Alloy 655 (simple shapes)	Alloy 875	Alloy 651 low silicon bronze Alloy 655	Alloy 651 low silicon bronze Alloy 655	Alloy 651 low silicon bronze Alloy 655	Alloy 655 high silicon bronze
Alloy 745 nickel-silver	Alloy 796 leaded nickel-silver	Alloy 973	Alloy 745 nickel-silver	Alloy 745 nickel-silver	Alloy 745 nickel-silver	Alloy 773 nickel-silver

(1) There is a color-matching casting alloy occasionally used by architectural metals fabricators in lieu of Alloys 836 and 855. It has a nominal composition of 82.0% copper, 2.5% tin, 2.5% lead, and 13.0% zinc.

Source: *Copper Development Association, Inc., Greenwich, CT.*

Table 4C-9
MECHANICAL FASTENERS FOR COPPER ALLOYS

Fasteners	Characteristics
Alloy 260 (cartridge brass, 70%)	Used for full range of medium strength, cold-headed, roll-threaded (coarse thread) screws, bolts, and nuts; color matches Alloy 260 sheet, tube, and rod.
Alloy 280 (Muntz metal, 60%)	Used for screws, nuts, and bolts of relatively low strength where color match is critical; excellent color match with Alloy 385.
Alloy 360 (free-cutting brass)	Used for full range of medium to low strength, machine screws, bolts, and nuts; good color match with Alloy 260.
Alloy 464 through 467 (naval brass)	Used for full range of medium strength screws, bolts, and nuts; fair to good color match; slightly yellower than Alloy 385.
Alloy 485 (naval brass—high leaded)	Used for machine screws, bolts, and nuts of medium to low strength; color is yellow; color match with Alloys 280 and 385 is fair to good.
Alloy 651 (low silicon bronze)	Used for full range of medium to high strength nails, screws, bolts, and nuts where color match is not critical; color is slightly redder than that of Alloy 385.
Alloy 655 (high silicon bronze)	Used for special hot-headed bolts or bolts of large diameter or long lengths where color match is not critical; color is slightly redder than that of Alloy 385.
Alloy 745 (nickel-silver 65-10)	Used for full range of medium to high strength, cold-headed, roll-threaded (coarse thread) screws, bolts, and nuts; color matches Alloy 745 sheet, tube, and rod as well as Alloy 796 extrusions.

Copper alloys may be fastened to other metals with the following metal fasteners.

Other Metals	Fastener Material
Stainless steel	Stainless steel, copper alloy
Carbon steel	Metallic-coated carbon steel, copper alloy
Aluminum	Non-magnetic stainless steel

Source: *Copper Development Association, Inc., Greenwich, CT.*

Table 4C-10
SELECTED STANDARD COPPER ALLOY FINISHES

NAAMM Number	Name	Description
		MECHANICAL FINISHES
As Fabricated:		
M11	Specular as fabricated	Finish imparted through normal production processes such as rolling, extrusion, or casting.
M12	Matte finish as fabricated	
Buffed:		
M21	Smooth specular (**)	Buffed finishes are a result of grinding, polishing, and buffing operations; suitable for hardware and similar small products or surfaces; because of their high reflectivity, they should not be used on broad, flat surfaces; smooth specular is the brightest mechanical finish available; it has a smooth, mirrorlike appearance.
M22	Specular (**)	Obtained by grinding and polishing with only a light buffing to remove scratches or other surface imperfections.
Directional Textured:		
M31	Fine satin (**)	Fine, medium, and coarse satin produced by wheel- or belt-polishing with grits of varying degrees of fineness; produces soft velvety texture with tiny nearly parallel scratches in the surface of the metal.
M32	Medium satin (*)	
M33	Coarse satin (*)	
M34	Hand rubbed (*)	Rubbing with No. 0 pumice and solvent or a non-woven abrasive pad or a fine brass wire brush; relatively expensive; also used to even out and blend in satin finishes produced by other techniques.
M35	Brushed (**)	Coarser directional textured finishes achieved by the use of various types of power-driven wheel brushes.
M36	Uniform (*)	Produced by a single pass of a No. 80 grit belt.
Non-directional Textured:		
M42	Fine matte (*) (**)	Non-directional textures are produced by spraying sand or metal shot against the metal; primarily used on castings; since distortion can result, their use is limited to metals at least 1/4 in. thick; texture produced is rough, shows fingerprints, and holds dirt; clear protective organic coatings are used to retain a natural appearance.
M43	Medium matte	
M44	Coarse matte	
M45	Fine shot blast	
M46	Medium shot blast	
M47	Coarse shot blast	

NAAMM Number	Name	Description
		CHEMICAL FINISHES

A wide range of colored finishes may be produced on architectural copper-base alloys by conversion coatings that are chemical in nature. The metal at the surface is converted into a protective film, usually an oxide or sulfide of the metal involved, or a compound is precipitated which forms a surface film. The purpose is to hasten the natural weathered effect that generally results from exposure to the elements.

Several conversion treatments that produce the patinas (verde antiques) and statuary (oxidized) finishes are in general use. Because of the number of variables involved, chemically induced patinas are prone to such problems as lack of adhesion, excessive staining of adjacent materials, and inability to achieve reasonable color uniformity over large surface areas.

NAAMM Number	Name	Description
C50	Ammonium chloride (patina) (*)	
C51	Cuprous chloride-hydrochloric acid (patina) (*)	
C52	Ammonium sulfate (patina) (*)	
C55	Sulfide (statuary) (*)	

COATINGS

Coatings over architectural copper alloys can be described as (1) transparent coatings to preserve the natural color, warmth, and metallic tones inherent in these alloys or (2) as opaque coatings that utilize the basic properties of the alloy as a substrate to achieve corrosion resistance, longevity, and forming capabilities.

Clear Organic (O):
Clear organic coatings are designed to preserve the distinctive colors of the copper alloys and to prevent superficial discoloration tarnish, which results from weathering and handling.

NAAMM Number	Name	Description
06x	Air dry coatings	For general architectural work.
07x	Thermoset	For hardware.
08x	Chemical cure	
	Types of clear organic coatings:	
	Alkyd	Unmodified alkyd coatings have limited serviceability and tend to yellow under exterior exposure; modified with melamine resins, these coatings are low in cost and durable enough for exterior applications.

Table 4C-10 (Continued)

NAAMM Number	Name	Description
	Acrylic	Good color retention and resistance to chemicals, impact, and abrasion; available in air-drying or thermosetting compositions, acrylics are relatively high-cost materials; air drying is popular for exterior applications, while thermosetting types are useful for interior applications requiring high resistance to heat and abrasion.
	Cellulose acetate butyrate	Usually considered for interior applications, these are air drying; moderate in cost and have fair to good performance properties; have a tendency to darken under exterior exposure conditions.
	Epoxy	Excellent resistance to impact, abrasion, and chemicals; relatively expensive and are only available in thermosetting or two-part compositions; good for severe indoor applications but tend to chalk and darken in exterior service.
	Nitrocellulose	Least expensive and most common air-drying coatings for interior use; do not have high resistance to chemicals but are fast drying and easy to use.
	Silicone	Silicones provide the best potential for coatings that must operate at elevated temperatures or under severe exposure conditions; expensive.
	Urethane	Excellent resistance to chemicals and abrasion even for the air-drying coatings; new color-stable types available for exterior use; relatively high cost.
Laminated (L):		
L91	Clear polyvinyl fluoride	1 mil sheet of polyvinyl fluoride adhesively bonded to the copper alloy surface; film coating can be used for both interior and exterior applications; chemically inert, mechanically strong, and resists impact, abrasion, and weathering; used to preserve the natural appearance of sheet and strip alloys.

(*) Indicates finishes most frequently used for architectural work.

(**) Indicates finishes commonly used for hardware items.

Note: For a complete list of finishes refer to the *Metal Finishes Manual* published by the National Association of Architectural Metal Manufacturers.

Source: Copper Development Association, Inc., Greenwich, CT.

PART 4D

Non-Structural Wood Applications

The tables in this part give some commonly needed reference data for non-structural uses of wood. First, there is a method of calculating deflection so the correct size and thickness of shelving can be determined. This is especially important in interior design applications. A table is also provided for quick determination of shelving dimensions for common construction types.

In addition Table 4D–3 can assist you in preliminary selection of hardwood for various interior finish applications. From this table you can determine what species of wood is appropriate for common uses and its availability, appearance, and relative cost.

Finally, a method is presented to determine the dimensional changes of wood based on moisture content, and recommendations are given for installed moisture content of wood in various locations of the United States. These guidelines can help you avoid shrinkage problems with both rough framing and finish carpentry.

SHELF DEFLECTION

Table 4D–1 gives uniformly distributed loads necessary to cause a deflection of 1/8 inch for different shelf constructions and spans. Deflections other than 1/8 inch can be estimated by direct proportion. For example, for a deflection of 1/4 inch, twice the listed load can be applied. Table 4D–2 gives the modulus of elasticity for various shelving types. These can be used to calculate shelf deflection for any size, span, and loading according to the following formula.

FORMULA:

$$D = \frac{5Wl^3}{384EI}$$

where:

D = deflection in inches
W = total uniform load in pounds
l = span in inches
E = modulus of elasticity
I = moment of inertia

Table 4D-1
MAXIMUM ALLOWABLE TOTAL LOAD FOR SHELF DEFLECTION OF 1/8 INCH FOR SHELVES OF DIFFERENT MATERIALS, WIDTHS, AND SPANS

Shelf Length (in inches)		30			36			42		
Shelf Width (in inches)		8	10	12	8	10	12	8	10	12
	Shelf Thickness (in inches)									
Medium density particle-board (E = 400,000) faced with 0.05 plastic laminate	3/4 1 1/2	58 388	73 485	87 583	34 225	42 281	51 337	21 142	27 177	32 212
Medium density particle-board (E = 700,000) faced with 0.05 plastic laminate	3/4 1 1/2	102 680	127 850	153 1019	59 393	74 492	88 590	37 248	46 310	56 372
High density particle-board (E = 1,000,000) faced with 0.05 plastic laminate	3/4 1 1/2	146 971	182 1214	218 1456	84 562	105 702	126 843	53 354	66 442	80 531
Birch-faced plywood with 3/4 in. × 3/4 in. soft-wood edge strip	3/4	180	225	270	104	130	156	66	82	98
Birch-faced plywood with 3/4 in. × 1 1/2 in. soft-wood dropped edge strip	3/4	366	412	458	212	238	265	133	150	167
Douglas fir, coast	3/4	195	244	293	113	141	169	71	89	107
White oak	3/4	178	223	267	103	129	155	65	81	97
Red oak, black cherry	3/4	149	186	224	86	108	129	54	68	81
Redwood	3/4	134	168	201	78	97	116	49	61	73
Walnut	3/4	168	210	252	97	122	146	61	77	92

Since the moment of inertia for a simple rectangular section is

$$I = \frac{bh^3}{12}$$

the formula can be rewritten:

$$D = \frac{0.1563wl^4}{Ebh^3}$$

where:

w = load *per inch* of span in lbs.
l = span in in.
b = shelf width in in.
h = thickness of shelf in in.

Table 4D-2
MODULUS OF ELASTICITY OF WOOD USED FOR SHELVING (X 1000)
(at 12% moisture content)

Hardwoods	
Ash, white	1740
Aspen, quaking	1180
Basswood, American	1460
Beech, American	1720
Birch, yellow	2010
Cherry, black	1490
Chestnut, American	1230
Elm, American	1340
Hickory, pecan	1730
Hickory, shagbark	2160
Mahogany	1510
Maple, red	1640
Maple, sugar	1830
Oak, northern red	1820
Oak, southern red	1490
Oak, white	1780
Poplar, yellow	1580
Rosewood, Indian	1780
Sweetgum	1640
Teak	1590
Walnut, black	1680
Softwoods	
Cedar, Alaska	1420
Cedar, western red	1110
Douglas fir, coast	1950
Douglas fir, interior south	1490
Douglas fir, interior north	1790
Fir, California red	1490
Fir, white	1490
Hemlock, eastern	1200
Hemlock, western	1640
Larch, western	1870
Pine, eastern white	1240
Pine, ponderosa	1290
Pine, southern yellow, longleaf	1980
Pine, southern yellow, shortleaf	1750
Pine, sugar	1190
Pine, western white	1460
Redwood	1340
Spruce, Englemann	1300
Spruce, sitka	1570
Particleboard, medium density	250–700
Particleboard, high density	350–1000
Plywood, group 1 face ply	1800

Source: Wood Handbook, *Forest Products Laboratory.*

TABLE SHOWING SELECTION OF WOOD FOR INTERIOR APPLICATIONS

Table 4D-3
COMPARATIVE SELECTION TABLE OF HARDWOOD SPECIES

Common Trade Name	Botanical Name	Common Uses	Veneer Availability	Lumber Availability	Cost Range	Color
Afrormosia	*Pericopsis elata*	P F	L	L	3	Yellow to warm-brown; similar to teak
Amazaque	*Guibourtia ehie*	P F	A	A	2	Golden-brown
Ash						
Olive burl	*Fraxinus excelsior*	F	A		3	White and brown burly pattern
White ash	*F. americana*	T C F	A	A	2	Cream to light-brown
Avodire	*Turraeanthus africanus*	P C F	L		3	White to creamy gold
Beech	*Fagus grandifolia*	F	A	A	1	White to reddish-brown
Birch						
Yellow birch	*Betula alleghaniensis*	P T C F	A	A	1	Cream/light-brown tinged with red
Select red (heartwood)	*B. alleghaniensis*	P T C F	A	A	2	Light-brown to reddish-brown
Select white (sapwood)	*B. alleghaniensis*	P T C F	A	A	2	Creamy-white
Bubinga	*Guibourtia demeusii*	T C	L	A	3	Red with streaks of purple
Butternut	*Juglans cinerea*	P T C F	L	L	2	Warm buttery tan
Cherry	*Prunus serotina*	P T C F	A	A	2	Reddish-brown
Chestnut	*Castanea dentata*	P T	R	R	3	Light-brown
Cypress, yellow	*Taxodium distichum*	P F	L	A	2	Yellowish-brown/red
Ebony, Macassar	*Diospyros celebica*	P F	A	L	3	Dark-brown to black; streaked with yellowish-brown
Elm						
American elm (gray elm)	*Ulmus americana*	P F	A	A	2	Light grayish-brown
Slippery elm (red elm)	*U. rubra*	P F	A	A	2	Reddish-brown heartwood Light-brown sapwood

Table 4D-3 (Continued)

Common Trade Name	Botanical Name	Common Uses	Veneer Availability	Lumber Availability	Cost Range	Color
Gum: Sweetgum	*Liquidambar styraciflua*					
Red gum (heartwood)	*L. styraciflua*	C	A	A	2	Reddish-brown, dark streaks
Sap gum (sapwood)	*L. styraciflua*	P C F	A	A	1	Pinkish-white
Hackberry	*Celtis occidentalis*	F	L	A	1	Yellowish
Hickory shagbark	*C. ovata*	F	A	A	2	Creamy to reddish heartwood
Lauan						
Red lauan	*Shorea negrosensis*	P C F	A	A	1	Red to brown
Tanguile (dark-red Philippine mahogany)	*S. polysperma*	P T C F	A	A	1	Dark reddish-brown
White lauan (light-red Philippine mahogany)	*Pentacme contorta*	C F	A	A	1	Light to grayish-brown to light reddish-brown
Limba	*Terminalia superba*	P T C F	L	L	2	Pale-yellow to light-brown
Mahogany						
African	*Khaya ivorensis*	P T C F	L	L	2	Reddish-brown to tannish-brown
Honduran	*Swietenia macrophylla*	P T C F	A	A	2	Reddish-brown to tannish-brown
Maple						
Hard	*Acer saccharum*	C F	L	A	2	Cream to light reddish-brown
Select white (sapwood)	*A. saccharum*	C F	L	A	2	Creamy
Birdseye	*A. saccharum*	C F	L	A	3	Highly figured
Soft	*A. saccharinum*	C F	A	A	1	May contain dark streaks

Table 4D-3 (Continued)

Common Trade Name	Botanical Name	Common Uses	Veneer Availability	Lumber Availability	Cost Range	Color
Oak						
Red, northern	*Q. rubra*	P T C F	A	A	2	Light-brown with reddish tinge
White	*Q. alba*	P T C F	A	A	2	Light-brown with shades of ochre
English brown	*Q. robur*	P T C	L	L	3	Light-tan to deep-brown
Orientalwood	*Endiandro palmerstoni*	C F	L	L	3	Pinkish-gray to brown
Paldao	*Dracontomelum dao*	P T C F	L	L	2	Gray to reddish-brown
Pecan	*Carya illinoenis*	P F	A	A	2	Reddish-brown heartwood, creamy sapwood
Persimmon	*Diospyros virginiana*	F	L	L	2	Light-brown with dark stripes
Poplar, yellow	*Liriodendron tulipifera*	C	A	A	1	Yellowish with slight greenish cast
Primavera	*Cybistax donnellsmithii*	C F	L	L	2	Yellowish-brown
Rosewood						
Brazilian	*Dalbergia nigra*	P T C F	L	A	3	Dark-brown with black streaks
East Indian	*D. latifolia*	P F	L		3	Dark-purple to ebony
Sapele	*Entandrophragma cylindricum*	C F	A	A	2	Dark red-brown
Teak	*Tectona grandis*	P C F	A	L	3	Tawny-yellow to light-brown
Tupelo	*Nyssa aquatica*	P	A	A	1	Creamy to yellowish with brownish-streaked heartwood
Walnut, black	*Juglans nigra*	P T C F	A	A	3	Gray-brown to dark-brown
Wenge	*Milletia laurentii*	P	L	R	3	Dark-brown
Zebrawood	*Microberlinia brazzavillensis*	P	A		3	Straw and dark-brown

Common Uses
P = Paneling
T = Trim
C = Cabinetry
F = Furniture

Availability
R = Rare
L = Limited
A = Generally available

Cost Range
1 = Moderate
2 = High
3 = Very expensive

SEASONING OF WOOD AND DIMENSIONAL CHANGES

Wood shrinkage can cause problems in a completed structure, from unsightly cracking in finish woodwork to the cumulative settlement of several wood structural components bearing on one another. Table 4D–4 gives recommended moisture values of various wood items at time of installation for different parts of the United States, and Figure 4D–1 shows recommended moisture content values for interior wood use.

For more exacting situations, the dimensional change of wood components within the limits of 6% to 14% can be estimated using the following formula.

FORMULA: $\Delta D = D_i \times [C_t \times (M_f - M_i)]$

where:

ΔD = change in dimension
D_i = dimension in inches or other units at start of change
C_t = dimensional change coefficient (C_t for shrinkage in tangential direction, C_r for radial direction; radial shrinkage is shrinkage in the dimension perpendicular to the radial lines of tree growth)

Coefficients are given in Table 4D–5. For boards that are not truly flat or quarter-sawn, use the tangential coefficient.

M_f = moisture content in percent at end of change
M_i = moisture content in percent at start of change

Table 4D-4
RECOMMENDED MOISTURE CONTENT VALUES FOR VARIOUS WOOD ITEMS AT INSTALLATION TIME (in percent)

	Interior (woodwork, flooring, furniture, wood trim, laminated timbers, cold-press plywood)	**Exterior** (siding, wood trim, framing, sheathing, laminated timbers)
Most Areas of U.S.		
Average (2)	8	12
Individual pieces	6–10	9–14
Southwestern Area (1)		
Average (2)	6	9
Individual pieces	4–9	7–12
Damp Coastal Areas (1)		
Average (2)	11	12
Individual pieces	8–13	9–14

(1) See Figure 4D–1.
(2) To obtain a realistic average, test at least 10% of each item.

Source: Wood Handbook: Wood as an Engineering Material, *Forest Products Laboratory.*

Table 4D-5

COEFFICIENTS FOR DIMENSIONAL CHANGE DUE TO SHRINKAGE OR SWELLING WITHIN MOISTURE CONTENT LIMITS OF 6 TO 14 PERCENT

Species	Dimensional change coefficient [1]	
	Radial C_R	Tangential C_T
HARDWOODS		
Alder, red	0.00151	0.00256
Apple	.00205	.00376
Ash:		
Black	.00172	.00274
Oregon	.00141	.00285
Pumpkin	.00126	.00219
White, green	.00169	.00274
Aspen, quaking	.00119	.00234
Basswood, American	.00230	.00330
Beech, American	.00190	.00431
Birch:		
Paper	.00219	.00304
River	.00162	.00327
Yellow, sweet	.00256	.00338
Buckeye, yellow	.00123	.00285
Butternut	.00116	.00223
Catalpa, northern	.00085	.00169
Cherry, black	.00126	.00248
Chestnut, American	.00116	.00234
Cottonwood:		
Black	.00123	.00304
Eastern, southern	.00133	.00327
Elm:		
American	.00144	.00338
Rock	.00165	.00285
Slippery	.00169	.00315
Winged, cedar	.00183	.00419
Hackberry	.00165	.00315
Hickory:		
Pecan	.00169	.00315
True hickory	.00259	.00411
Holly, American	.00165	.00353
Honeylocust	.00144	.00230
Locust, black	.00158	.00252
Madrone, Pacific	.00194	.00451
Magnolia:		
Cucumbertree	.00180	.00312
Southern	.00187	.00230
Sweetbay	.00162	.00293
Maple:		
Bigleaf	.00126	.00248
Red	.00137	.00289
Silver	.00102	.00252
Sugar, black	.00165	.00353
Red oak:		
Commercial red	.00158	.00369
California black	.00123	.00230
Water, laurel, willow	.00151	.00350
White oak:		
Commercial white	.00180	.00365
Live	.00230	.00338
Oregon white	.00144	.00327
Overcup	.00183	.00462
Persimmon, common	.00278	.00403
Sassafras	.00137	.00216
Sweetgum	.00183	.00365
Sycamore, American	.00172	.00296
Tanoak	.00169	.00423
Tupelo:		
Black	.00176	.00308
Water	.00144	.00267
Walnut, black	.00190	.00274
Willow:		
Black	.00112	.00308
Pacific	.00099	.00319
Yellow-poplar	.00158	.00289

SOFTWOODS					
Baldcypress	.00130	.00216	Larch, western	.00155	.00323
Cedar:			Pine:		
Alaska-	.00095	.00208	Eastern white	.00071	.00212
Atlantic white-	.00099	.00187	Jack	.00126	.00230
Eastern redcedar	.00106	.00162	Loblolly, pond	.00165	.00259
Incense-	.00112	.00180	Lodgepole, Jeffrey	.00148	.00234
Northern white-[2]	.00101	.00229	Longleaf	.00176	.00263
Port-Orford-	.00158	.00241	Ponderosa, Coulter	.00133	.00216
Western redcedar[2]	.00111	.00234	Red	.00130	.00252
Douglas-fir:			Shortleaf	.00158	.00271
Coast-type	.00165	.00267	Slash	.00187	.00267
Interior north	.00130	.00241	Sugar	.00099	.00194
Interior west	.00165	.00263	Virginia, pitch	.00144	.00252
Fir:			Western white	.00141	.00259
Balsam	.00099	.00241	Redwood:		
California red	.00155	.00278	Old-growth[2]	.00120	.00205
Noble	.00148	.00293	Second-growth[2]	.00101	.00229
Pacific silver	.00151	.00327	Spruce:		
Subalpine, corkbark	.00088	.00259	Black	.00141	.00237
White, grand	.00112	.00245	Engelmann	.00130	.00248
Hemlock:			Red, white	.00130	.00274
Eastern	.00102	.00237	Sitka	.00148	.00263
Western	.00144	.00274	Tamarack	.00126	.00259
IMPORTED WOODS					
Andiroba, crabwood	.00137	.00274	Light red "Philippine mahogany"	.00126	.00241
Angelique	.00180	.00312	Limba	.00151	.00187
Apitong, keruing[2] (All *Dipterocarpus* spp.)	.00243	.00527	Lupuna	.00126	.00230
Avodire	.00126	.00226	Mahogany[2]	.00172	.00238
Balsa	.00102	.00267	Meranti	.00126	.00289
Banak	.00158	.00312	Nogal[2]	.00129	.00258
Cativo	.00078	.00183	Obeche	.00106	.00183
Emeri	.00106	.00169	Okoume	.00194	.00212
Greenheart[2]	.00390	.00430	Parana pine	.00137	.00278
Iroko[2]	.00153	.00205	Pau marfim	.00158	.00312
Ishpingo[2]	.00125	.00205	Primavera	.00106	.00180
Khaya	.00141	.00201	Ramin	.00133	.00308
Kokrodua[2]	.00148	.00297	Santa Maria	.00187	.00278
Lauans:			Spanish-cedar	.00141	.00219
Dark red "Philippine mahogany"	.00133	.00267	Teak[2]	.00101	.00186
			Virola	.00183	.00342
			Walnut, European	.00148	.00223

[1] Per 1 pct. change in moisture content, based on dimension at 10 pct. moisture content and a straightline relationship between the moisture content at which shrinkage starts and total shrinkage. (Shrinkage assumed to start at 30 pct. for all species except those indicated by footnote 2.)

[2] Shrinkage assumed to start at 22 pct. moisture content.

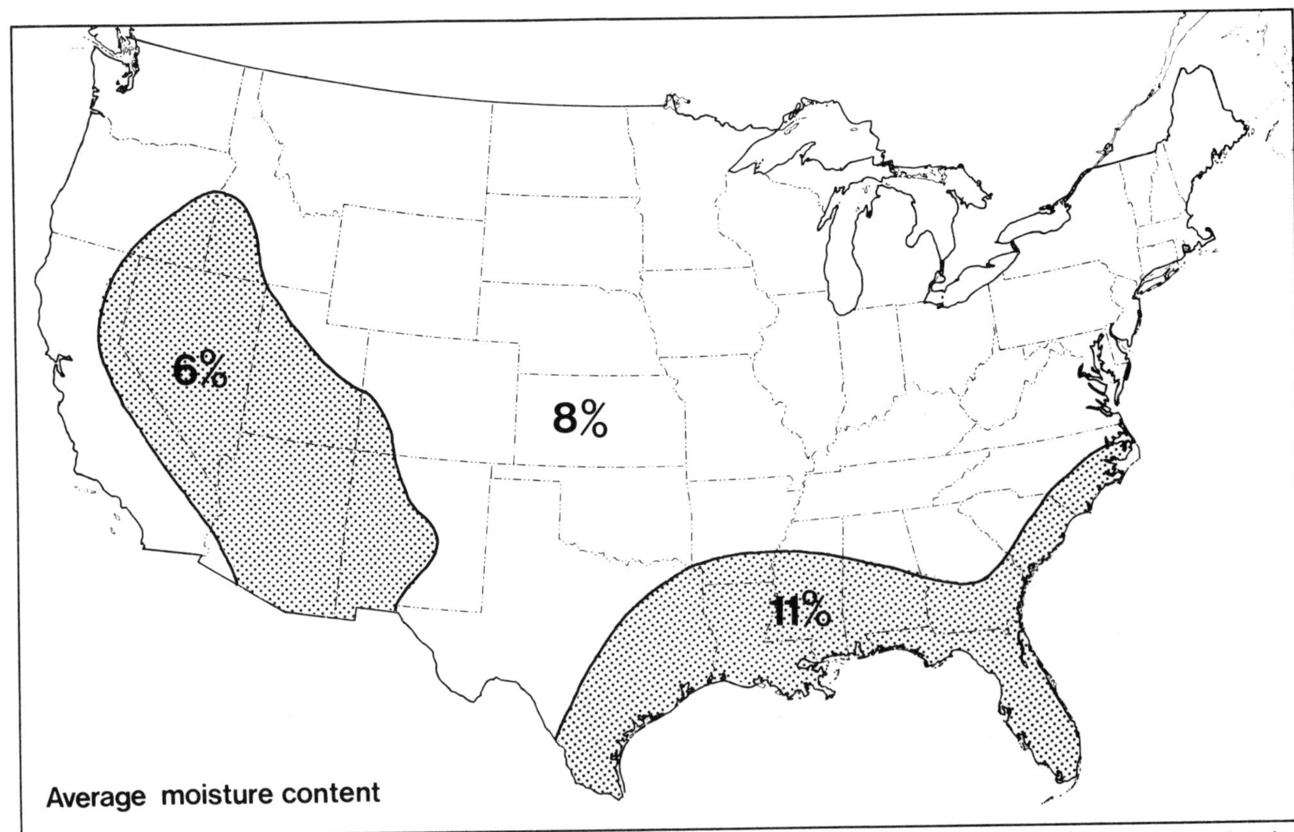

Source: Wood Handbook: Wood As an Engineering Material, *Forest Products Laboratory.*

Figure 4D-1: Recommended Average Moisture Content for Interior Use of Wood Products

PART 4E

Thermal and Moisture Protection

The following tables give some commonly needed reference information in tabular format for proper selection of building materials for thermal and moisture protection. In each case, knowing the circumstances of your building project, you can consult the appropriate table to assist you in making a preliminary decision.

For example, in selecting the proper sealant for a building condition, you will know the expected joint movement, the joint width, the materials to be sealed, and the environmental conditions the sealant must resist. By consulting Table 4E-3 you need only review the columns with the variables satisfying your criteria to find the recommended sealant types.

TABLE SHOWING SHINGLES

Table 4E-1
WOOD SHINGLES

Grade	Size	Weight (lbs./sq.)	Description
Red Cedar Shingles			
No. 1 Blue Label	24 (in.) (royals) 18 (in.) (perfections) 16 (in.) (XXXXX)	192 158 144	The premium grade of shingles for roof and sidewalls; 100% heartwood, 100% clear, and 100% edge-grain.
No. 2 Red Label	24 (in.) (royals) 18 (in.) (perfections) 16 (in.) (XXXXX)	192 158 144	A good grade for most applications; not less than 10 in. clear on 16 in. shingles; 11 in. clear on 18 in. shingles, and 16 in. clear on 24 in. shingles; flat grain and limited sapwood are permitted.
No. 3 Black Label	24 (in.) (royals) 18 (in.) (perfections) 16 (in.) (XXXXX)	192 158 144	A utility grade for economy applications and secondary buildings; guaranteed 6 in. clear on 16 in. and 18 in. shingles, 10 in. clear on 24 in. shingles.

No. 4 Under-coursing	18 (in.) (perfections) 16 (in.) (XXXXX)	60 60	A low grade for under-coursing on double-coursed sidewall application.
No. 1 or No. 2 rebutted-rejointed	18 (in.) (perfections) 16 (in.) (XXXXX)	60 60	Same specifications as No. 1 and No. 2 grades above but machine trimmed for exactly parallel edges with butts sawn at precise right angles; used for sidewall application where tightly fitting joints between shingles are desired; also available with smooth-sanded surface.
No. 1 Machine grooved	18 (in.) (perfections) 16 (in.) (XXXXX)	60 60	Same specifications as No. 1 and No. 2 grades above; used at maximum weather exposures and always applied at the outer course of double-coursed sidewalls.
No. 1 or No. 2 Dimension	23 (in.) (royals) 18 (in.) (perfections) 16 (in.) (XXXXX)	192 158 14	Same specifications as No. 1 and No. 2 grades except they are cut to specific uniform widths and may have butts trimmed to special shapes.
Red Cedar Shakes			
No. 1 Handsplit and resawn	18 (in.) × 1/2 to 3/4 18 (in.) × 3/4 to 1 1/4 24 (in.) × 1/2 to 3/4 24 (in.) × 3/4 to 1 1/4 32 (in.) × 3/4 to 1 1/4	220 250 280 350 450	These shakes have split faces and sawn backs; cedar blanks or boards are split from logs and then run diagonally through a bandsaw to produce two tapered shakes from each.
No. 1 Tapersplit	24 (in.) × 1/2 to 5/8	260	Produced largely by hand, using a sharp-bladed steel froe and a wooden mallet; the natural shinglelike taper is achieved by reversing the block, end-for-end, with each split.
No. 1 Straightsplit (barn)	18 (in.) × 3/8 24 (in.) × 3/8	200 260	Produced in the same manner as tapersplit shakes except that by splitting from the same end of the block, the shapes acquire the same thickness throughout.

Source: *Red Cedar Shingle & Handsplit Shake Bureau.*

TABLE SHOWING HOW TO SELECT THE CORRECT R VALUE OF BUILDING INSULATION

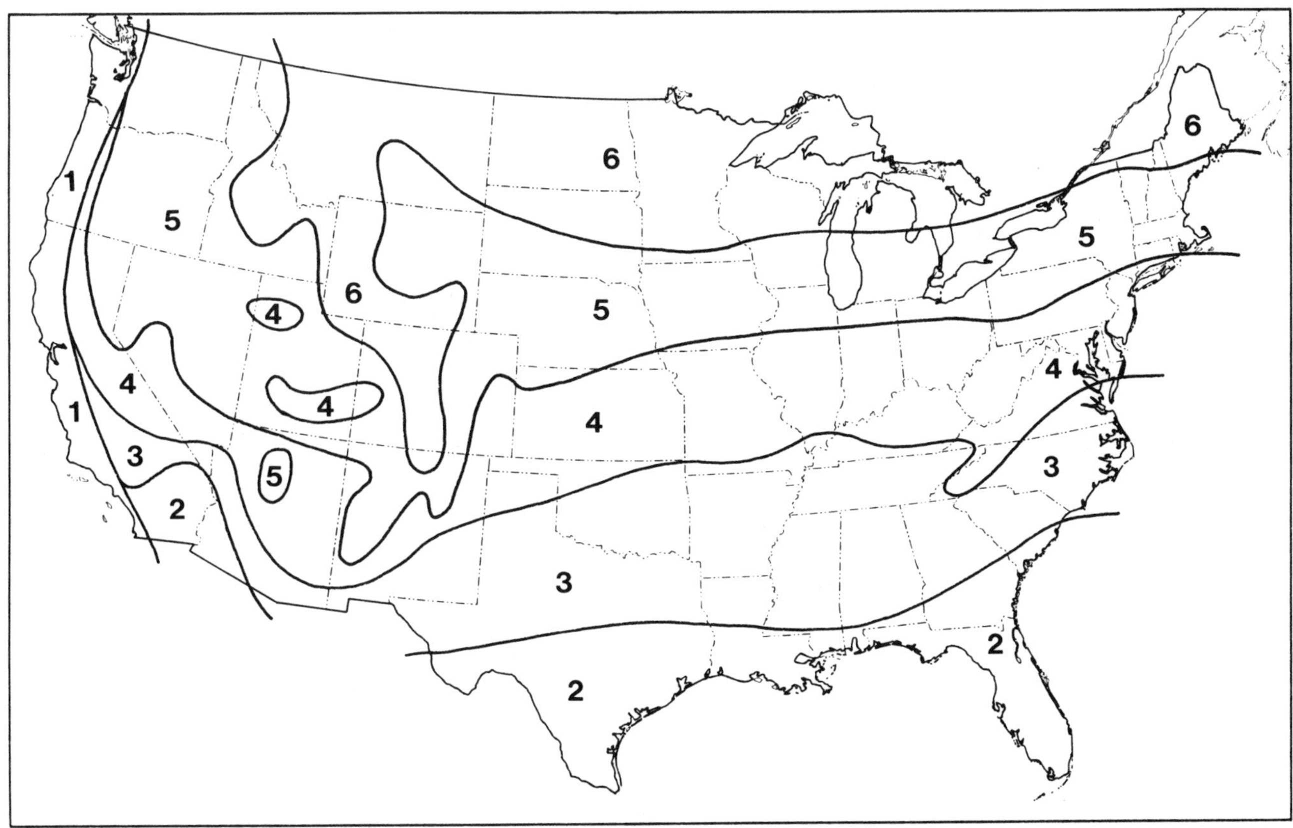

Figure 4E-1: Map of Recommended Insulation Zones in the U.S.

Table 4E-2
RECOMMENDED MINIMUM THERMAL RESISTANCES (R) OF INSULATION
(See Figure 4E-1 for Zones.)

Zone	Ceiling	Wall	Floor
1	19	11	11
2	26	13	11
3	26	19	13
4	30	19	19
5	33	19	22
6	38	19	22

TABLE SHOWING GUIDELINES FOR SELECTING SEALANTS

Table 4E-3
COMPARATIVE PROPERTIES OF SEALANTS

		Sealant Types									
		Oil Base	Butyl	Acrylic, Water Base	Acrylic, Solvent Base	Polysulfide, One Part	Polysulfide, Two Part	Polyurethane, One Part	Polyurethane, Two Part	Silicone	Notes
Recommended maximum joint movement, %		±5	±7.5	±7.5	±12.5	±12.5 to ±25	±25	±12.5 to ±15	±25	±25	(1)
Life expectancy (in years)		5–10	10+	10	15–20	20	20	20+	20+	20+	
Maximum joint width (in inches)		1/4	1/2	1/2	3/4	3/4	1	3/4	1–2	3/4	(2)
Weight shrinkage (in %)		10+	5–10	15	15	10	10	10	10	4	
Adhesion to:	Wood	●	●	●	●	●	●	●	●	●	(3)
	Metal	●	●	●	●	●	●	●	●	●	
	Masonry	●	●	●	●	●	●	●	●	●	(3)
	Glass	●	●	●	●	●	●	●	●	●	
	Plastic		●	●	●					●	

		Sealant Types									
		Oil Base	Butyl	Acrylic, Water Base	Acrylic, Solvent Base	Polysulfide, One Part	Polysulfide, Two Part	Polyurethane, One Part	Polyurethane, Two Part	Silicone	Notes
Curing time (in days)		120	120	5	14	14+	7	7+	3–5	5	
Maximum elongation (in %)		15	40	60	60+	300	600	300+	400+	250+	
Self-leveling available		n/a	n/a		●	●	●		●	●	
Non-sag available		n/a	n/a	●	●	●	●	●	●	●	
Resistance to: (see legend)	Ultraviolet	1–2	2–3	1–3	3–4	2	2–3	3	3	5	
	Cut/tear	1	2	1–2	1	3	3	4–5	4–5	1–2	
	Abrasion	1	2	1–2	1–2	1	1	3	3	1	
	Weathering	1–2	2	1–3	3–4	3	3	3–4	3–4	4–5	
	Oil/grease	2	1–2	2	3	3	3	3	3	2	
	Compression	1	2–3	1–2	1	3	3	4	4	4–5	
	Extension	1	1	1–2	1	2–3	2–3	4–5	4–5	4–5	
	Water immersion	2	2–3	1	1–2	3	3	1	1	3	

(1) Some high performance urethanes and silicones have movement capabilities as high as ±50%.
(2) Figures given are conservative. Verify manufacturers' literature for specific recommendations.
(3) Primer may be required.

Legend:
1 = Poor
2 = Fair
3 = Good
4 = Very good
5 = Excellent

Table 4E-4
STANDARD SEALANT SPECIFICATIONS*

	Type of Sealant	ASTM	Canadian Specification	Previous Federal Specifications
	Polysulfides			
TWO PART	1A-Self-Leveling	Type 1 C-920 Type M Grade P Class 25	CAN 2-19.24-M80, Type 1	TT-S-00227E, Type I Class A
TWO PART	1B-Non-Sag	Type II ASTM C-920 Type M Grade NS Type 12 1/2	CAN 2-19.24-M80, Type 2	TT-S-00227E, Type II Class A
ONE PART	1C-Self-Leveling	ASTM Type 5 Grade P, Class 25	CAN 2-19.13-M82 Type 1	TT-S-00230C, Type I Class A
ONE PART	1D-Non-Sag	ASTM Type 5 Grade NS Type 12 1/2	CAN 2-19.13-M82, Type 2	TT-S-00230C, Type II Class A
	Urethanes			
TWO PART	2A-Self-Leveling	ASTM C-920 Type M Grade P Class 25	CAN 2-19.24-M80, Type 1	TT-S-00227E, Type 1 Class A
TWO PART	2B-Non-Sag	ASTM C-920 Type M Grade NS Class 25	CAN 2-19.24-M80, Type 2	TT-S-00227E, Type II Class A
ONE PART	2C-Self-Leveling	ASTM C-920 Type S Grade P Class 25	CAN 2-19.13-M82, Type 1	TT-S-00230C, Type I Class A
ONE PART	2D-Non-Sag	ASTM C-920 Type S Grade NS Class 25	CAN 2-19.13-M82, Type 2	TT-S-00230C, Type II Class A

	3 Silicones	ASTM C-920 Type S Grade NS Class 25 New designation now in consideration by ASTM Committee C-24	CAN 2-19.13-M82, Class 25 CAN 2-19.13-M82, Class 40	TT-S-01543A Class A Vertical Surfaces Only
ONE PART	*4 Acrylics*		19-GP-5M	
ONE PART	*5 Acrylic Latex*	ASTM-C-834-76	19-GP-17M	ASTM-C-834-76
ONE PART	*6 Acoustical Sealant*		19-GP-21M	
ONE PART	*7 Butyl*	TT-S-001657	19-GP-14M	TT-001657
ONE PART	*8 Oil Based*	TT-C-598C	19-GP-6M	TT-C-598C
	9 Preformed Compressible and Non-Compressible Fillers Such as: a. Preformed compression seals (Neoprene) b. Preformed impregnated open cell foam sealant c. Preformed non-impregnated closed cell foamed sealant			

Note: These preformed products can be used in most joint situations. Please consult manufacturers' literature and specifications when their use is desired.

*For other specifications, consult the Sealant & Waterproofers Institute.

Source: *Sealant and Waterproofers Institute. Reproduced with permission.*

PART 4F

Doors and Windows

The selection and design of doors and glass building components is complicated by the many conditions under which they must perform. The tables in this part provide easy-to-use guidelines to assist you in making such selections. Tables 4F–1 through 4F–6 give concise data on doors, frames, and hardware selection. Tables 4F–7 through 4F–12 outline the various properties of glass and the selection and design of glazing materials.

TABLES SHOWING DOOR AND HARDWARE SELECTION

Table 4F–1
FIRE DOOR CLASSIFICATIONS

Fire Door Rating (in hours)	Opening Class	Use of Wall	Rating of Wall (in hours)
3	A	Fire walls Fire separations	3 or 4
1 1/2	B	Vertical shafts Exit stairs Fire separations	2
1	B	Vertical shafts Exit stairs Fire separations	1
3/4	C	Fire-resistive partitions Corridors Hazardous areas	1
1/2		Limited application	1 or less
1/3 (20 min.)		Corridors Smoke barriers	1 or less
1 1/2	D	Severe exterior exposure	2 or more
3/4	E	Exterior exposure	1 or less

Table 4F-2
HINGE WEIGHT SELECTION

Door Type	Estimated Frequency (daily)	Frequency Classification	Hinge Type
Large department store entrance	5000		
Large office building entrance	4000		
Theater entrance	1000		
School entrance	1250	High	Heavy weight, ball bearing
School toilet door	1250		
Store or bank entrance	500		
Office building door	400		
School corridor door	80		
Office building corridor	75	Medium	Standard weight, ball bearing
Store toilet door	60		
Residential entrance	40		
Residential door	25		
Residential corridor door	10	Low	Standard weight, plain bearing hinge
Residential closet door	6		

Table 4F-3
HINGE SIZING

Door Thickness (in inches)	Door Width (in inches)	Height of Hinge (in inches)
3/4 to 1 1/8	to 24	2 1/2
1 3/8	to 32	3 1/3
1 3/8	over 32 to 37	4
1 3/4	to 36	4 1/2
1 3/4	over 36 to 48	5
1 3/4	over 48	6
2, 2 1/4, 2 1/2	to 42	5 (heavy wt.)
2, 2 1/4, 2 1/2	over 42	6 (heavy wt.)

1. The width of the hinge is determined by the width of the door and the clearance required around jamb trim. One rule of thumb is the width of the hinge equals twice the door thickness, plus trim projection, minus 1/2 inch. If the fraction falls between standard sizes, use the next larger size. This is based on back set of 1/4 inch.
2. The height of the hinge is determined by the door thickness and the door width as indicated in Table 4F-3.
3. The number of hinges is determined by the height of the door:
   Doors up to 60 in. high, 2 hinges (1 pair)
   Doors 60 in. to 90 in., 3 hinges (1 1/2 pairs)
   Doors 90 in. to 120 in., 4 hinges (2 pairs)

Table 4F-4
WEIGHTS OF DOORS

Door Type	Thicknesses (in inches)				
	1 3/8	1 3/4	2	2 1/4	2 1/2
Ash	4.5	5.25	6	6.75	7.5
Birch	3.75	4.3	5	5.65	6.25
Fir	3	3.5	4	4.5	5
Mahogany	4.5	5.25	6	6.75	7.5
Oak	6	7	8	9	10
White pine	3	3.5	4	4.5	5
Hollow core	2	2.5			
Solid core	3.5	4.5	5	5.5	
Plastic laminate with particleboard core	4.5	5.5			
Hollow metal, 16 ga.	5.75	5.75	5.75	6	
Metal, 16 ga. with mineral core	6	6.25			

Note: Weights given in pounds per square foot.

Table 4F-5
RECOMMENDED METAL GAGES OF DOORS AND FRAMES

Building Type	Frame Gage	Door Face Gage
Apartments		
Main entrance	12	16
Apartment entrance	14 or 16	16
Bedroom	16	18
Bathroom	16	18
Stairwell	12 or 14	16
Schools		
Entrances	12	16
Classroom	14	16
Toilet	12 or 14	16
Gymnasium	12 or 14	16
Cafeteria	12 or 14	16
Stairwell	12 or 14	16
Hotels/motels		
Main entrances	12	16
Room entrance	14 or 16	16
Bathroom	16	18
Closet	16	18
Stairwell	12 or 14	16
Storage and utility	14 or 16	16

Table 4F-5 (Continued)

Building Type	Frame Gage	Door Face Gage
Hospitals		
Main entrances	12	16
Patient room	14	16 or 18
Stairwell	12 or 14	18
Operation and exam	12 or 14	16
Kitchen	12 or 14	16
Industrial		
Entrances	12	16
Offices	14 or 16	16 or 18
Production	12	16
Toilets	12 or 14	16
Tool and trucking	12	16
Offices		
Entrances	12	16
Individual offices	16	18
Closets	16	18
Toilets	12 or 14	16
Stairwell	12 or 14	16
Mechanical rooms	12 or 14	16

Table 4F-6
HARDWARE FINISHES

BHMA #	US #	BHMA Finish Description
605	US3	Bright brass, clear coated
606	US4	Satin brass, clear coated
609	US5	Satin brass, blackened, relieved, clear coated
611	US9	Bright bronze, clear coated
612	US10	Satin bronze, clear coated
613	US10B	Satin bronze, dark oxidized, oil rubbed
616	US11	Satin bronze, blackened, relieved, clear coated
617		Bright bronze, dark oxidized, relieved, clear coated
618	US14	Bright nickel, clear coated
619	US15	Satin nickel plated, clear coated
620		Satin nickel, blackened, relieved, clear coated
622	US19	Flat black
623	US20	Light oxidized, statuary bronze, clear coated
624	US20A	Dark statuary bronze, clear coated
625	US26	Bright chromium plate
626	US26D	Satin chromium plate
627	US27	Satin aluminum, clear coated
628	US28	Satin aluminum, clear anodized
629	US32	Bright stainless steel
630	US32D	Satin stainless steel

BHMA: Builders Hardware Manufacturer's Association.

TABLES SHOWING SELECTION AND DESIGN GUIDELINES FOR GLASS

Table 4F-7
STANDARD CLASSIFICATION OF FLAT GLASS

Type I—Transparent Glass, Flat

Class 1—Clear

q^1 Mirror select
q^2 Mirror
q^3 Glazing select
q^4 Glazing A
q^5 Glazing B
q^6 Greenhouse

Class 2—Tinted, Heat Absorbing, and Light Reducing

Quality q^3 Glazing select
Quality q^4 Glazing A
Quality q^5 Glazing B
Style A Higher light transmittance
Style B Lower light transmittance

Class 3—Tinted, Light Reducing

q^3 Glazing select
q^4 Glazing A
q^5 Glazing B

Type II—Patterned and Wired Glass, Flat

Class

1 Translucent
2 Tinted, heat absorbing, and light reducing
(A and B applies to Class 2 only)
Style A Higher light transmittance
Style B Lower light transmittance
3 Tinted, light reducing

Form (Classes 1, 2, and 3)

1 Wired, polished both sides
2 Patterned and wired
3 Patterned

Quality

q^7 Decorative
q^8 Glazing

Finish

f^1 Patterned one side
f^2 Patterned both sides

Mesh (Forms 1 and 2)

m^1 Diamond
m^2 Square
m^3 Parallel strand
m^4 Special

Pattern (Forms 2 and 3)

p^1 Linear
p^2 Geometric
p^3 Random
p^4 Special

Table 4F-8
TYPICAL GLAZING U VALUES

Glass Thickness	Typical Winter U Values (night)					
	Clear Single Glass	*Double Glazing, Air Space*		*Triple Glazing, 2 Air Spaces*		
		1/4 in.	1/2 in.	1/4 in.	3/8 in.	1/2 in.
1/8 in.	1.13	0.57	0.49	0.39	0.36	0.32
3/16 in.	1.12	0.56	0.49	0.38	0.35	0.31
1/4 in.	1.10	0.56	0.49	0.38	0.35	0.31
1/8 in. Low e	0.87	0.52	0.40	pyrolitic coated		
1/8 in. Low e	n/a	0.38	0.31	vacuum coated		

Table 4F-9
SOUND REDUCTION THROUGH VARIOUS GLASS CONSTRUCTIONS

Glass Thickness, Construction	Average Sound Transmission Loss (in 125-4000Hz dB)	Loudness Reduction Compared to 1/4 Inch Float Glass (in %)	STC Rating
Single-Layer Glazing			
SS float	23.5	—	26
DS float	24.1	—	29
1/4 in.	26.5	—	29
5/16 in.	28.8	15	29
3/8 in.	29.7	20	30
1/2 in.	31.5	29	33
5/8 in.	34.5	42	30
3/4 in.	34.6	43	33
7/8 in.	35.4	46	32
1 in. insulating	30.7	23	31
Laminated Glass			
1/4 in. 2 plies 1/8 in.	30.2	23	33
1/2 in. 2 plies 1/4 in.	33.6	39	36
1/2 in. 1 ply 3/8 in., 1 ply 1/8 in.	35.7	47	36
5/8 in. 4 plies 1/8 in.	36.3	49	38
3/4 in. 2 plies 3/8 in.	38.9	58	38
3/4 in. 3 plies 1/4 in.	38.7	57	39
1 in. 6 plies 1/8 in.	39.8	60	41

Table 4F-9 (Continued)

Glass Thickness, Construction	Average Sound Transmission Loss (in 125–4000Hz dB)	Loudness Reduction Compared to 1/4 Inch Float Glass (in %)	STC Rating
2 Lites of Glass Separated by Air Space			
1/2 in. and 1/4 in. with 2 in. air space	38.1	55	39
1/2 in. and 1/4 in. with 4 in. air space	39.3	59	40
1/2 in. and 1/4 in. with 6 in. air space	40.0	61	42
3/4 in. and 3/8 in. with 6 in. air space	40.6	62	40
1/2 in. and 1/4 in. laminated with 6 in. air space	42.6	67	44
1 in. insulating and 1/4 in. with 6 in. air space	40.4	62	40

Notes:

1. Laminated glass values based on 0.045 in. plastic interlayer.
2. Values for 2 lites of glass separated by air space are based on assembly without absorbent perimeter material. Addition of a good absorbent will increase average transmission loss by 3 to 5 dB.

Source: Flat Glass Marketing Association Glazing Manual *(1986 Edition).*

Table 4F-10
TYPICAL FACE AND EDGE CLEARANCE AND BITE FOR GLASS FRAMING

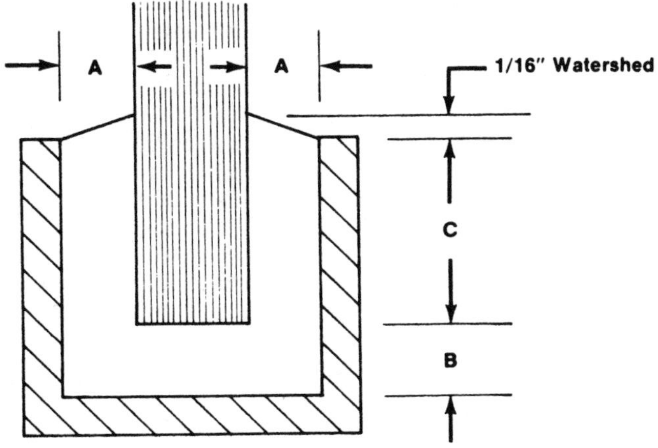

Thickness		Minimum Clearance		
inches	mm	A = Face	B = Edge	C = Bite
Monolithic Glass				
S.S.	2.5	1/16	1/8	1/4
1/8-D.S.[1]	3	1/8	1/8	1/4
1/8-D.S.[2]	3	1/8	1/4	3/8
3/16[1]	5	1/8	3/16	5/16
3/16[2]	5	1/8	1/4	3/8
1/4	6	1/8	1/4	3/8
5/16	8	3/16	5/16	7/16
3/8	10	3/16	5/16	7/16
1/2	12	1/4	3/8	7/16
5/8	15	1/4	3/8	1/2
3/4	19	1/4	1/2	5/8
7/8	22	1/4	1/2	3/4
Insulating Glass				
1/2	12	1/8	1/8	1/2
5/8	15	1/8	1/8	1/2
3/4	19	3/16	1/4	1/2
1	25	3/16	1/4	1/2
Ceramic-Coated Spandrel Glass				
1/4	6	3/16	1/4	1/2

1—Annealed Glass only.
2—Tempered Glass only.

Note: Typical clearances above may vary by manufacturer, particularly for some special products or applications. Follow the recommendations of the glass manufacturer, fabricator, or sealant supplier for individual instances.

Source: Flat Glass Marketing Association Glazing Manual *(1986 Edition).*

Table 4F-11
REFLECTIVE GLASS PERFORMANCE
Range of Shading Coefficients and U Values

Color	Light Trans.	1/4 in. Monolithic		1 in. Insulating	
		S.C.	U	S.C.	U
Wet Chemical or Vacuum Deposition					
Silver	8%	0.21–0.28	0.77–0.93	0.08–0.22	0.30–0.50
	14%	0.29–0.35	0.80–0.99	0.12–0.30	0.32–0.52
	20%	0.36–0.41	0.82–1.02	0.16–0.34	0.35–0.54
Golden	8%	0.17–0.27	0.66–0.90	0.08–0.18	0.27–0.48
	14%	0.20–0.34	0.69–0.97	0.12–0.24	0.28–0.52
	20%	0.24–0.40	0.96–1.06	0.14–0.28	0.29–0.54
Earthtone	8%	0.26–0.36	0.86–0.92	0.18–0.24	0.42–0.51
	14%	0.32–0.40	0.92–0.98	0.22–0.30	0.44–0.53
	20%	0.38–0.45	0.98–1.03	0.22–0.30	0.32–0.55
Low e: Clear	74%	n.a.	n.a.	0.64–0.74	0.31–0.35
Bronze	43%	n.a.	n.a.	0.44–.50	0.31–0.35
Gray	39%	n.a.	n.a.	0.42–0.48	0.31–0.35
Pyrolitic Deposition					
Bronze	21%	0.45	1.10–1.13	0.34	0.49–0.57
Gray	17%	0.44	1.10–1.13	0.33	0.49–0.57
Green	30%	0.40	1.10–1.13	0.30	0.49–0.57
Low e: Clear	72%	0.87	0.88–0.76	0.78–0.83	0.39–0.44
Bronze	47%	n.a.	n.a.	0.58	0.39–0.45
Gray	41%	n.a.	n.a.	0.55	0.39–0.45
Green	63%	n.a.	n.a.	0.57	0.39–0.45
Float Glass (uncoated)					
Clear	88%	0.93	1.10–1.13	0.80	0.49–0.56
Bronze	52%	0.71	1.10–1.13	0.55	0.49–0.57
Gray	43%	0.69	1.10–1.13	0.57	0.49–0.57
Green	75%	0.69	1.10–1.13	0.55	0.49–0.57

Note: Pyrolitic Low e data are for 3/16 in. glass and for 7/8 in. i.g. unit.

Source: Flat Glass Marketing Association Glazing Manual *(1986 Edition).*

Table 4F-12
OVERALL BOW ALLOWANCE FOR TEMPERED, HEAT-STRENGTHENED, AND SPANDREL GLASS

	Nominal Glass Thickness					
Length of Edge (in inches)	1/8 in.–5/32 in. 3/16 in.	7/32 in.	1/4 in.	5/16 in.	3/8 in.	1/2 in.– 7/8 in.
0–18 in.	1/8 in.	3/32 in.	1/16 in.	1/16 in.	1/16 in.	1/16 in.
18–36 in.	3/16 in.(a)	5/32 in.	1/8 in.	3/32 in.	3/32 in.	1/16 in.
36–48 in.	9/32 in.	7/32 in.	3/16 in.	5/32 in.	1/8 in.	3/32 in.
48–60 in.	3/8 in.	5/16 in.	9/32 in.(a)	7/32 in.	3/16 in.	1/8 in.
60–72 in.	1/2 in.	7/16 in.	3/8 in.	9/32 in.	1/4 in.	3/16 in.
72–84 in.	5/8 in.	9/16 in.	1/2 in.	11/32 in.(a)	5/16 in.(a)	1/4 in.
84–96 in.	3/4 in.	11/16 in.	5/8 in.	7/16 in.	3/8 in.	9/32 in.
96–108 in.	7/8 in.	13/16 in.	3/4 in.	9/16 in.	1/2 in.	3/8 in.
108–120 in.	1 in.	15/16 in.	7/8 in.	11/16 in.	5/8 in.	1/2 in.
120–132 in.		1 1/16 in.	1 in.	13/16 in.	3/4 in.	5/8 in.
132–144 in.		1 3/16 in.	1 1/8 in.	15/16 in.	7/8 in.	3/4 in.
144–156 in.		1 5/16 in.	1 1/4 in.	1 1/16 in.	1 in.	7/8 in.

From *GTA Engineering Standards Manual,* Section 8.1, page 7.
(a) Values are 1/32 in. less for Spandrel.
Note: The above GTA Standards are slightly less than in ASTM C1048–85 in a few instances.

Source: Flat Glass Marketing Association Glazing Manual *(1986 Edition).*

PART 4G

Finishes

The tables in this part provide methods for selecting some common finish materials. The information is presented in tabular format for easy use. Simply go to the table covering the material of interest and look in the row or column for the requirements of your project and other criteria. Then follow the corresponding column or row to the recommended selection of the particular finish material type.

Tables 4G–1 through 4G–3 will assist you with wood flooring, resilient flooring, and carpeting. Tables 4G–4 through 4G–6 provide information on ceramic tile.

TABLES SHOWING FLOORING

Table 4G-1
WOOD STRIP FLOORING GRADES

Oak, Unfinished		
Grade	*Bundles*	*Appearance Notes*
Clear	1 1/4 ft. and up Average length: 3 3/4 ft.	Best grade with the most uniform color. Plain sawn is standard with quarter sawn available on special order only.
Select	1 1/4 ft. and up Average length: 3 1/4 ft.	Limited character marks, unlimited sound sap; plain sawn is standard with quarter sawn on special order only.
No. 1 common	1 1/4 ft. and up Average length: 2 3/4 ft.	Variegated appearance, knots, worm holes, and other character marks; light and dark colors; imperfections filled and finished.
No. 2 common	1 1/4 ft. and up Average length: 2 1/4 ft.	Rustic appearance; has all characteristics of the species; red and white oak may be mixed; economical floor after knot holes, worm holes, checks, and other imperfections are filled and finished.
Some Combination Grades Select and better (special order only) 1 1/4 ft. shorts (lengths 9 in. to 18 in. red and white oak mixed) No. 1 common and better shorts		

Oak, Prefinished		
Grade	*Bundles*	*Appearance Notes*
Prime	1 1/4 ft. and up Average length: 3 1/2 ft.	Excellent appearance with natural color variations permitted. Limited character marks, unlimited sap. Special order.
Standard	1 1/4 ft. and up Average length: 2 3/4 ft.	Variegated appearance with varying sound wood characteristics of species.
Tavern	1 1/4 ft. and up Average length: 2 1/4 ft.	Rustic appearance with all wood characteristics of species. Economical floor.
Some Combination Grades Standard and better (average length 3 ft.) Tavern and better (average length 3 ft.)		
Beech, Birch, and Maple		
Grade	*Bundles*	*Appearance Notes*
First grade	2 ft. and up	Best appearance, practically clear; special order, check with local supplier for grades and species available.
Second grade	2 ft. and up	Variegated appearance; varying sound wood characteristics of species.
Third grade	1 1/4 ft. and up	Rustic appearance; serviceable, economical floor after filling.
Some Combination Grades Second and better Third and better		
Pecan:		
Grade	*Bundles*	*Appearance Notes*
First grade	2 ft. and up	Excellent appearance; natural color variation, limited character marks.
Second grade	1 1/4 ft. and up	Variegated appearance; varying sound wood characteristics of species.
Third grade	1 1/4 ft. and up	Rustic appearance; serviceable floor after filling.
Some Combination Grades First grade red (special order, face is all heartwood) First grade white (special order, face is all bright sapwood) Second grade red (special order, face is all heartwood)		

Table 4G-2
RESILIENT FLOORING PROPERTIES

		Types						
		Vinyl Tile	Sheet Vinyl	Rubber Tile	Cork	Vinyl-Faced Cork	Linoleum Sheet	Asphalt Tile
Common sizes		9 × 9 12 × 12	6 ft., 9 ft., 12 ft. wide	9 × 9 12 × 12	6 × 6 9 × 9	9 × 9 12 × 12	6 ft., 12 ft. wide	9 × 9 18 × 18
Thickness		1/16, 1/8	0.071–0.10	0.08–0.125	1/8–5/16	1/8	0.065–0.125	1/8
Use*		B, O, S	B, O, S	B, O, S	S	S	S	B, O, S
Load limit, psi		200	75–100	200	75	75–150	75	25
Flame spread		45–75	45–75	75	—	—	—	75
Smoke developed		425	425	100	—	450	—	—
Resistance to:	Alkalis	4–5	3–5	4	1	4	2	1
	Cigarette burns	1–4	1–3	4	2	2	1–2	1
	Grease/oil	5	5	3	2	5	5	1
	Indentation	2–5	2–5	2	2	3	2	2
	Stains	2–5	2–5	4–5	1–2	2–4	4	2
Properties:	Durability	4–5	3–4	4	1	2	3	2
	Ease of maintenance	3–4	4	2–3	1–2	3–4	2	2
	Resilience	1–4	2–4	4	5	3	2	1
	Quietness	1–4	2–4	4	5	3	2	1

*B = Below grade
O = On grade
S = Above grade

1 = Poor
2 = Fair
3 = Good
4 = Very good
5 = Excellent

Table 4G-3
CARPET PROPERTIES

			Fibers					
			Wool	*Nylon*	*Acrylic*	*Modacrylic*	*Polyester*	*Olefin (Polypropylene)*
Typical Construction	Process	Tufted	●	●	●		●	●
		Woven	●	●	●	●		
		Needle punched		●				
		Fusion bonded	●	●	●			
	Face weight (in oz./yd.)		30–55	20–40	25–42	40	32–55	26
	Total weight (in oz./yd.)		62–100	67–85	66–80		70–104	
	Pitch		189	270	216	216		216
	Stitches per inch		8-9	7.5–11.25	8.75–11	7–9	7–9	12
	Pile height (in inches)		5/16–9/16	1/8–5/8	7/32–7/16	3/16–15/64	9/16–13/16	5/16
	Surface	Level loop	●	●	●		●	
		Cut pile	●	●	●	●		●
		Cut/loop		●	●	●		
		Level loop/random shear		●	●			

Table 4G-3 (Continued)

		Fibers					
		Wool	*Nylon*	*Acrylic*	*Modacrylic*	*Polyester*	*Olefin (Polypropylene)*
	Flame spread Smoke developed, max.	55 160	35 190	25 160	20 60	20 410	80 —
Resistance to:	Abrasion	4–5	5	3	3	3–4	4
	Acids	2	4–5	3	3	4	4
	Alkalis	2	4–5	4	4	4	4
	Burns	3	2	2	2	3	2
	Crushing	4–5	3	3	3	2–3	1–2
	Insects and fungi	2–5*	4–5	4–5	4–5	4	4–5
	Moisture	2	2	3	3	3	5
	Soiling	3–4	3	3–4	3–4	4	4–5
	Staining	2–3	4	4	4	3	4–5
	Static buildup	2–4*	1–4*	3	3	3	4–5
	Sunlight	3–4	2	3	2–3	2–3	2–4
Properties	Durability	4–5	5	3–5	3–5	4	3
	Ease of maintenance	4–5	3	3–5	3–5	3–4	5
	Resilience	5	3	2	2	2	1
	Appearance retention	5	3–5	3–5	3–5	3–5	3

*Depends on treatment Legend: 1 = Poor 2 = Fair 3 = Good 4 = Very good 5 = Excellent

TABLES RELATING TO CERAMIC TILE

Use Table 4G–4 to find the Performance Level required. Then consult Table 4G–5 and choose the installation that meets or exceeds it. For example, Method F113, rated Heavy, can also be used in any area requiring lower Performance Level.

Table 4G-4
CERAMIC TILE FLOOR PERFORMANCE LEVEL REQUIREMENT GUIDE

General Area Descriptions		Recommended Performance-Level Rating
Office space, commercial, reception areas	General	Light
Public space in restaurants, stores, corridors, shopping malls	General	Moderate
Kitchens	Residential Commercial Institutional	Residential or Light Heavy Extra heavy
Toilets, bathrooms	Residential Commercial Institutional	Residential Light or Moderate Moderate or Heavy
Hospitals	General Kitchens Operating rooms	Moderate Extra heavy Heavy—use Method F122
Food plants, bottling plants, breweries, dairies	General	Extra heavy
Exterior decks	Roof decks Walkways and decks on grade	Extra heavy—use Method F103 Heavy, Extra heavy—use Method F101 or F102
Light work areas, Laboratories, Light receiving and shipping, etc.	General	Moderate or Heavy

Notes: Consideration must also be given to (1) wear properties of surface of tile selected, (2) fire-resistance properties of installation and backing, (3) slip resistance.

Tile used in installation tests listed in Selection Table were unglazed unless otherwise noted. Unglazed Standard Grade tile will give satisfactory wear, or abrasion resistance, in installations listed. Decorative glazed tile or soft body decorative unglazed tile should have the manufacturer's approval for intended use. Color, pattern, surface texture, and glaze hardness must be considered in determining tile acceptability on a particular floor.

For waterproof floors (to prevent seepage to substrate or story below), refer to Methods F121 and F122, and also specify setting method desired.

Table 4G-5
CERAMIC TILE FLOOR INSTALLATION PERFORMANCE GUIDE

Maximum Performance Level	Handbook Method Number	Page	Description	Grout	Comments On Use
RESIDENTIAL: Normal residential foot traffic and occasional 300 pound loads on soft (70 or less Shore A Durometer) rubber wheels. (Equivalent to passing test cycles 1 thru 3 of ASTM Test Method C 627.)	F116	14	Organic adhesive on concrete Ceramic mosaic or glazed floor tile	Wet cured[b] 1 pc: 1 sand	Dry-Set or Latex-portland cement mortar preferred
	F142	17	Organic adhesive on wood Ceramic mosaic or quarry tile	Latex-portland cement	Residential, low cost, bathroom, foyer
	F143	18	Epoxy mortar on wood Ceramic mosaic tile	Wet cured[b] 1 pc: 1 sand	High bond strength in residential use
	TR711	30	Epoxy adhesive over existing resilient tile Ceramic mosaic or quarry tile	Latex-portland cement	Residential renovation
LIGHT: Light commercial and better residential use, 200 pound loads on hard (100 or less Shore A Durometer) rubber wheels. (Equivalent to passing test cycles 1 thru 6 of ASTM Test Method C 627.)	F141	17	Portland cement mortar on wood Ceramic mosaic tile	1 pc: 1 sand	Depressed wood subfloor in residence
	F143	18	Epoxy mortar on wood Ceramic mosaic tile	ANSI A118.3 epoxy	Best for wood subfloors
	F144[a]	18	Latex-Portland cement mortar on glass mesh mortar unit. Ceramic mosaic or quarry tile	Latex-portland cement	Light weight installation over wood subfloor
	RF912[a] RF917	34	Glass mesh mortar unit / matting	Commercial portland cement	Concrete subfloor
MODERATE: Normal commercial and light institutional use, 300 pound loads on rubber wheels and occasional 100 pound loads on steel wheels. (Equivalent to passing test cycles 1 thru 10 of ASTM Test Method C 627.)	F112	13	Dry-Set mortar on cured mortar bed Ceramic mosaic tile	Wet cured[b] 1 pc: 1 sand	Economy for smooth surface
	F113	13	Dry-Set mortar on concrete[c] Ceramic mosaic tile	Latex-portland cement	Economy
	F113 F115	13 14	Dry-Set mortar on concrete[c] Ceramic mosaic tile	ANSI A118.3 epoxy	Mild chemical resistance
	F125	15	Conductive Dry-Set mortar Conductive tile	ANSI A118.3 epoxy	Hospital operating rooms, other special uses
	RF911[a] RF914, RF916	34 34	Glass mesh mortar unit / matting Portland cement mortar / matting	Commercial portland cement	Wood subfloor Concrete subfloor
HEAVY: Heavy commercial use, 200 pound loads on steel wheels, 300 pound loads on rubber wheels. (Equivalent to passing test cycles 1 thru 12 of ASTM Test Method C 627.)	F111 F112	13 13	Portland cement mortar Ceramic mosaic tile	1 pc: 1 sand	Smoothest floor surface
	F112	13	Dry-Set mortar on cured mortar bed Quarry Tile	Wet cured[b] 1 pc: 2 sand	Economy for smooth surface
	F113	13	Dry-Set mortar on concrete Ceramic mosaic tile	Wet cured[b] 1 pc: 1 sand	Best general thin-set method
	F125	15	Conductive Dry-Set mortar Conductive tile	Wet cured[b] 1 pc: 1 sand	Hospital operating rooms, other special uses
	RF913, RF915[a] RF918	34 34	Portland cement mortar / matting Portland cement mortar / matting	Commercial portland cement	Wood subfloor Concrete subfloor
EXTRA HEAVY: Extra heavy commercial use, high impact service; meat packing areas, institutional kitchen, industrial work areas, 300 pound loads on steel wheels. (Equivalent to passing test cycles 1 thru 14 of ASTM Test Method C 627.)	F111 F112 F101	13 13 12	Portland cement mortar Quarry tile or Packing house tile	1 pc: 2 sand	Smooth, hard service best ceramic tile floor
	F113 F102	13 12	Dry-Set mortar on concrete Quarry tile or packing house tile	Wet cured[b] 1 pc: 2 sand	Best general thin-set method
	F113 F114 F115	13 14 14	Dry-Set mortar on concrete Quarry tile or Packing house tile	ANSI A118.3 epoxy	General, on concrete, for mild chemical resistance
	F143	18	Epoxy mortar on wood Quarry tile or packing house tile	ANSI A118.3 epoxy	Hard service on wood subfloor, chemical resistance
	F131 F132	16 16	Epoxy mortar on concrete Quarry tile or packing house tile	ANSI A118.3 epoxy	Chemical resistance
	F134	17	Chemical resistant mortar on acid resistant membrane, packing house tile[d]	Furan or ANSI A118.3 epoxy	For continuous or severe chemical resistance

Selection Table Notes:

Tests to determine Performance Levels utilized representative products meeting recognized industry standards: Dry-Set mortar—TCA Formula 759; epoxy mortar and grout—TCA Formula AAR-II; and epoxy adhesive—TCA Formula C-150.

a. Data in Selection Table based on tests conducted by Tile Council of America, except data for F144 and RF900 Methods, which are based on test results from an independent laboratory through Ceramic Tile Institute.

b. Floor covered after grouting with polyethylene sheeting. Water added to entire surface on second day and sheeting replaced.

c. Rates "Heavy" if Dry-Set is wet cured for three days before grouting.

d. Floor may show surface wear under constant steel wheel traffic.

Table 4G-6
CERAMIC TILE GROUT GUIDE

	Printed through the courtesy of the Materials & Methods Standards Association. A rubber faced trowel should be used when grouting glazed tile with sanded grout.	GROUT TYPE: Commercial Portland Cement		Sand-Portland Cement	Dry-Set	Latex Portland Cement (3)	Epoxy (1) (6)	Furan (1) (6)	Silicone or Urethane (2)	Modified Epoxy Emulsion (3) (6)
		Wall Use	Floor Use	Wall-Floor Use	Wall-Floor Use					
TILE TYPE	GLAZED WALL TILE (More than 7% absorption)	•			•	•			•	
TILE TYPE	CERAMIC MOSAICS	•	•	•	•	•	•		•	•
TILE TYPE	QUARRY, PAVER & PACKING HOUSE TILE	•	•	•		•	•	•		•
AREAS OF USE	Dry and intermittently wet areas	•	•	•	•	•	•	•	•	•
AREAS OF USE	Areas subject to prolonged wetting	•	•	•	•	•	•	•	•	•
AREAS OF USE	Exteriors	•	•	•	•	•(4)	•(4)	•(4)		•(4)
PERFORMANCE	Stain Resistance (5)	D	C	E	D	B	A	A	A	B
PERFORMANCE	Crack Resistance (5)	D	D	E	D	C	B	C	A Flexible	C
PERFORMANCE	Colorability (5)	B	B	C	B	B	B	Black Only	Restricted	B

(1) Mainly used for chemical resistant properties.
(2) Special tools needed for proper application. Silicone, urethane and modified polyvinylchloride used in pregrouted ceramic tile sheets. Silicone grout should not be used on kitchen countertops or other food preparation surfaces unless it meets the requirements of FDA Regulation No. 21, CFE 177.2600.
(3) Special cleaning procedures and materials recommended.
(4) Follow manufacturer's directions.
(5) Five performance ratings—Best to Minimal (A B C D E).
(6) Epoxies are recommended for prolonged temperatures up to 140F, high temperature resistant epoxies and furans up to 350F.

SECTION 5

Reference Data

Table 5-1
WEIGHTS OF MATERIALS

Basic Materials		
Material	**Weight** (in lb. per cu. ft.)	**Weight** (in kg. per cu. m)
Liquids		
Water, 4° C, max. density	62.428	1000
Water, 100° C	59.830	958
Ice	57	913
Snow (fresh fallen)	8	128
Note: Use snow load as required by local building department.		
Sea water	64	1025
Gasoline	42	672
Refined petroleum	50	800
Soil, Sand, Gravel		
Earth, dry and loose	76	1217
Earth, dry and packed	95	1522
Earth, moist and loose	78	1249
Earth, moist and packed	96	1538
Earth, mud, packed	115	1842
Clay, dry	63	1009
Clay, damp and plastic	110	1762
Sand/gravel, dry and loose	90–105	1442–1682
Sand/gravel, dry and packed	100–120	1602–1922
Sand/gravel, wet	118–120	1890–1922
Wood (at 12% moisture content)		
Ash, white	41	657
Aspen	27	433
Birch, yellow	43	689
Cedar, northern white	22	352
Cedar, western red	23	368
Cherry, black	35	561
Cypress	32	513
Ebony	63	1009
Fir, Douglas (coast region)	34	545
Hemlock, western	30	481
Hickory	51	817
Mahogany, African	31	497
Mahogany, Honduras	32	513
Maple, hard	44	705
Maple, soft	33	529
Oak, red	44	705
Oak, white	47	753
Pine, northern white sugar	25	400
Pine, southern shortleaf	35	561
Pine, southern longleaf	41	657
Pine, ponderosa	28	449

Basic Materials		
Material	**Weight** (in lb. per cu. ft.)	**Weight** (in kg. per cu. m)
Poplar, yellow	28	449
Redwood	28	449
Rosewood	50	800
Spruce, sitka	27	433
Teak	43	689
Walnut, black	39	625
Metals		
Aluminum, cast	165	2643
Brass, cast, rolled	534	8554
Bronze, commercial	552	8842
Copper, cast, rolled	556	8906
Iron, wrought	480	7689
Lead	710	11,373
Lead sheet, 1/8 in.	6–8	96–128
Magnesium, alloys	112	1794
Monel metal	556	8906
Nickel	565	9050
Tin	459	7352
Stainless steel, rolled	492–510	7881–8169
Steel, rolled, cold-drawn	490	7849
Zinc, rolled, cast, sheet	449	7192
Stone		
Granite	157–187	2515–2995
Indiana limestone	144	2307
Limestone	117–175	1874–2803
Marble	163–172	2611–2755
Sandstone	119–168	1906–2691
Shale	172	2755
Slate	168–180	2691–2883
Miscellaneous Solids		
Asphalt	81	1297
Books	65	1041
Concrete, reinforced stone	150	2403
File cabinets, letter size, weight per 36 in. drawer	60–70/drawer	27–32 drawer
Glass, common	156	2499
Glass, plate	160	2563
Mortar, cement	130	2082
Paper	58	929
Particleboard	45	721
Terra cotta, voids filled	120	1922
Terra cotta, voids unfilled	72	1153

Table 5-1 (Continued)

Material	Weight (in lb. per sq. ft.)	Weight (in kg. per sq. m)
Construction Materials and Assemblies		
Exterior Walls		
Brick, 4 in.	40	195
Brick, 8 in.	80	391
Concrete block, lightweight		
4 in.	20	98
6 in.	28	137
8 in.	35	171
12 in.	55	269
Concrete block, heavy aggregate		
4 in.	30	146
6 in.	42	205
8 in.	55	269
12 in.	85	415
Frame walls		
2 × 4 studs @ 16 in. o.c., 5/8 in. gypsum board, insulated, 3/8 in. siding	11	54
2 × 6 studs with same construction as above	12	59
Stud walls with brick veneer	44	215
Windows, glass, frame, sash	8	39
Fiberboard, 1/2 in.	0.75	3.7
Glass curtain wall (approx.)	10–15	49–73
Gypsum sheathing, 1/2 in.	2	9.8
Insulation (per in. thickness)		
Fiberglas, rigid	0.71	3.5
Mineral fiber batt	0.21–0.33	1.03–1.61
Loose fill vermiculite	0.38–0.58	1.86–2.83
Polystyrene foam	0.15–0.2	0.73–0.98
Rigid expanded Perlite	0.9	4.39
Plywood, 1/2 in.	1.5	7.3
Plywood, 3/4 in.	2.2	10.7
Plywood, 1 1/8 in.	3.3	16.1
Floors and Floor Finishes		
Concrete, reinforced, 1 in.		
Stone	12.5	61
Lightweight	6–10	29.3–48.8
Slag	11.5	56.1
Concrete, plain, 1 in.		
Stone	12	58.6
Lightweight	3–9	14.6–43.9
Slag	11	53.7
Steel deck (normal span)		
0.0295 in.	2.0	9.8
0.0358 in.	2.5	12.2
0.0474 in.	3.0	14.6
Wood joists with double wood floor		
2 × 6 @ 12 in. o.c.	6	29.3
2 × 6 @ 16 in. o.c.	5	24.4
2 × 8 @ 12 in. o.c.	6	29.3
2 × 8 @ 16 in. o.c.	6	29.3
2 × 10 @ 12 in. o.c.	7	34.2

Construction Materials and Assemblies		
Material	**Weight** (in lb. per sq. ft.)	**Weight** (in kg. per sq. m)
2 × 10 @ 16 in. o.c.	6	29.3
2 × 12 @ 12 in. o.c.	8	39.1
2 × 12 @ 16 in. o.c.	7	34.2
Ceramic or quarry tile (3/4 in.) on 1/2 in. mortar bed	16	78
Ceramic or quarry tile (3/4 in.) on 1 in. mortar bed	23	112
Ceramic or quarry tile (1/2 in.), thinset	6	29.3
Ceramic tile (5/16 in.)	3.2	15.6
Granite tile		
3/8 in.	6	29.3
1/2 in.	9	43.9
Gypsum fill	6	29.3
Hardwood flooring (7/8 in.)	2.5	12.2
Hardwood flooring (5/16 in.)	1.25	6.1
Marble (3/4 in.) and setting bed	30	147
Marble tile (1/4 in.)	3.7	18.1
Slate (per in.)	15	9.4
Subflooring (3/4 in.)	3	14.6
Terrazzo		
Sand cushion (2 1/2 in. thick)	27	132
Bonded (1 3/4 in. thick)	18	88
Monolithic (1/2 in.)	7	34
Wood block (2 in. on mastic)	3	14.6
Roofs		
Asphalt shingles	2	9.8
Built-up roofing		
4 ply with gravel	5.5	26.9
5 ply with gravel	6	29.3
Cement tile	16	78
Clay tile, shingle type	8–16	39–78
Concrete roof tile	9.5	46
Copper or tin	1	4.9
Decking, 2 in. Douglas fir	5	24.4
Decking, 3 in. Douglas fir	8	39.1
Decking, steel	2.2–3.6	10.7–17.6
Fiberboard, 1/2 in.	0.75	3.7
Single ply roofing		
EPDM, 60 mil	0.38	1.86
PVC, 45 mil	0.30	1.46
Add for ballast	10–15	49–73
Modified bitumen	1.5	7.32
Add for ballast	4	20
Hypalon, 45–50 mil	0.30–0.34	1.46–1.66
Average single ply with insulation	1	4.88
Slate, 3/8 in.–1/2 in.	14–18	68–88
Waterproofing membranes		
Bituminous, gravel covered	5.5	27
Bituminous, smooth surface	1.5	7.3
Liquid applied	1	4.88
Wood sheathing (per in.)	3	14.7
Wood shingles	3	14.7

Table 5-1 (Continued)

Construction Materials and Assemblies		
Material	**Weight** (in lb. per sq. ft.)	**Weight** (in kg. per sq. m)
Partitions		
2 × 4 wood stud, 1/2 gypsum board each side	8	39
2 × 4 wood stud, plastered each side	20	98
4 in. lightweight concrete block	20	98
6 in. lightweight concrete block	28	137
Metal stud framing, 2 1/2 in., 3 5/8 in.		
1/2 gypsum board each side	5	24.4
5/8 gypsum board each side	6	29.3
Two layers 1/2 in. each side	9	43.9
Two layers 5/8 in. each side	10	48.9
Gypsum wallboard, 3/8 in.	1.4	6.8
Gypsum wallboard, 1/2 in.	1.8	8.8
Gypsum wallboard, 5/8 in.	2.3	11.2
Ceilings		
Suspended acoustical ceilings		
5/8 in. or 3/4 in. tile with grid	1	4.9
5/8 in. or 3/4 in. rated ceiling	1.3	6.4
Suspended gypsum board ceiling (5/8 in.)	3	14.7
Suspended metal lath and plaster		
Cement plaster	15	73
Gypsum plaster	10	48.8
Wood furring suspension system	2.5	12.2
Wall Finishes		
Ceramic mosaic tile (1/4 in.)	2.5	12.2
Ceramic tile (5/16 in.)	3.2	15.6
Marble tile (1/4 in.)	3.7	18.1
Marble (3/4 in. standard-set method)	11	54
Plaster (1/2 in.)	4.5	22
Quarry tile (1/2 in.)	5.8	28.3
Glazing		
1/8 in.	1.65	8.06
1/4 in.	3.29	16.06
3/8 in.	4.94	24.12
1/2 in.	6.58	32.13
3/4 in.	9.87	48.19
1/4 in. wire glass	3.5	17.1
1 in. insulating (1/4 in. lites)	7	34.2
Fire protection glass (Trade name: Contraflam®)		
30 minute (31mm)	10.2	50
60 minute (41mm)	13.3	65
90 minute (72mm)	20.5	100
Glass block, 3 7/8 in.	16	78
Glass block, 3 1/8 in.	12	59
Glass block, solid, 3 in.	34	166
Polycarbonate glazing, 1/4 in.	1.56	7.6

Note: Add 5 lbs. per sq. ft. (24.4 kg. per sq. m) for each face plastered.

Table 5-2
MINIMUM UNIFORMLY DISTRIBUTED LIVE LOADS

Occupancy or Use	Live Load (in lbs./sq. ft.) ANSI 58.1	UBC-1985
Access floor systems		
Office use		50 (1)
(plus 10 psf for partitions)		
Computer use		100 (1)
Air-conditioning (machine space)	200 (6)	
Amusement park structure	100 (6)	
Apartments (see residential)		
Armories and drill rooms	150	150
(UBC requirement for drill rooms: 100)		
Assembly areas and theaters		
Fixed seats	60	50
Lobbies	100	
Movable seats	100	100
Platforms (assembly)	100	125
Stage floors	150	125
Bakery	150	
Balconies		
Exterior	100	
Exterior, on one- and two-family residences only and not exceeding 100 sq. ft.	60	60
Interior (fixed seats)	60	
Interior (movable seats)	100	
Boathouse, floors	100 (7)	
Boiler room, framed	300 (6)	
Bowling alleys, poolrooms, and similar recreational areas	75	
Broadcasting studio	100	
Catwalks	25	
Ceiling, accessible furred	10	
Cold storage		
No overhead system	250 (8)	
Overhead system		
Floor	150	
Roof	250	
Computer equipment	150 (7)	
Corridors		
First floor	100	
(other floors, same as occupancy served except as indicated)		
Dance halls and ballrooms	100	100
Decks (patio and roof)		
Same as area served, or for the type of occupancy accommodated		
Dining rooms and restaurants	100	
Dormitories		
Non-partitioned	80	
Partitioned	40	
Elevator machine rooms	150 (6)	
Fan room	150 (6)	
File room		
Duplicating equipment	150 (7)	
Card	125 (7)	
Letter	80 (7)	

Table 5-2 (Continued)

Occupancy or Use	Live Load (in lbs./sq. ft.) ANSI 58.1	UBC-1985
Fire escapes	100	
On single family dwellings only		
Foundries	600 (6)	
Fuel rooms, framed	400	
Garages (passenger cars only)	50	50 (1)
Garages, general storage, and/or repair		100 (1)
For trucks and buses, use AASHTO lane loads. See local building code for concentrated load requirements.		
Garages, trucks	(3)	
Greenhouses	150	
Gymnasiums, main floors, and balconies	100	100
Hangars	150 (3)	
Hospitals		
Operating rooms, laboratories	60	
Private rooms	40	40 (1)
Wards	40	40 (1)
Corridors above first floor	80	
Hotels (see Residential)		
Kitchens, other than domestic	150 (6)	
Laboratories, scientific	100	
Laundries	150 (6)	
Libraries		
Reading rooms	60	60 (1)
Stack rooms, not less than[2]	150	125 (1)
Corridors above first floor	80 (7)	
Manufacturing		
Light	125	75 (1)
Heavy	250	125 (1)
Ice	300	
Marquees and canopies	75	60
Morgue	125	
Office buildings		
File and computer rooms shall be designed for heavier loads, based on anticipated occupancy		
Business machine equipment	100 (6)	
Files (see File room)		
Lobbies	100	
Offices	50	50 (1)
Partitions, movable		20
Penal institutions		
Cell blocks	40	
Corridors	100	
Printing plants		
Composing rooms	100	100 (1)
Linotype rooms	100	100 (1)
Paper storage	(9)	
Press rooms	150 (6)	150 (1)
Public rooms	100	
Residential		
Dwellings (one and two family)		
Uninhabitable attics without storage	10	
Uninhabitable attics with storage	20	

Occupancy or Use	Live Load (in lbs./sq. ft.) ANSI 58.1	UBC-1985
Habitable attics and sleeping areas	30	40
All other areas	40	40
Hotels and multifamily houses, private rooms, and corridors serving them	40	
Hotels and multifamily houses, public rooms, and corridors serving them	100	
Rest rooms	60	50 (10)
Rinks		
Ice skating	250	
Roller skating	100	
Schools		
Classrooms	40	40 (1)
Corridors above first floor	80	40 (1)
Sidewalks, vehicular driveways, and yards subject to trucking	250 (3)	250
Stadium and arena bleachers	100 (4)	100
Stairs and exitways	100	100 (5)
Storage warehouse		
Light	125	125
Heavy	250	250
Hay or grain	300 (7)	
Stores, retail		
First floor	100	75 (1)
Upper floors	75	75 (1)
Stores, wholesale, all floors	125	100 (1)
Telephone exchange	150 (6)	
Theaters		
Dressing rooms	40	
Grid-iron floor or fly gallery	60	
Well beams: 250 lb./ft./pair		
Header beams, 1000 lb./ft.		
Pin rail, 250 lb./ft.		
Projection room	100	
Transformer rooms	200 (6)	
Vaults, in offices	250 (7)	
Walkways and elevated platforms (other than exitways)	60	
Yards and terraces (pedestrian)	100	

Notes:

(1) Verify concentrated load requirements with local building code.

(2) The weight of books and shelving shall be computed using an assumed density of 65 lbs. per cu. ft. and converted to a uniformly distributed load; this load shall be used if it exceeds 150 psf.

(3) AASHTO lane loads should be considered.

(4) For detailed recommendations, see American National Standard for Assembly Seating, Tents, and Air-Supported Structures, ANSI/NFPA 102-1978.

(5) Stairs shall be designed to support a 300 lb. concentrated load placed in a position that would cause maximum stress.

(6) Use weight of actual equipment when greater.

(7) Increase when occupancy exceeds this amount.

(8) Plus 150 lbs. for trucks.

(9) Paper storage 50 lb./ft. of clear story height.

(10) Shall not be less than occupancy with which they are associated.

Table 5-3
DECIMALS OF A FOOT

Fraction	Decimal	Fraction	Decimal	Fraction	Decimal
		4	0.3333	8	0.6667
1/8	0.0104	4 1/8	0.3438	8 1/8	0.6771
1/4	0.0208	4 1/4	0.3542	8 1/4	0.6875
3/8	0.0313	4 3/8	0.3646	8 3/8	0.6979
1/2	0.0417	4 1/2	0.3750	8 1/2	0.7083
5/8	0.0521	4 5/8	0.3854	8 5/8	0.7188
3/4	0.0625	4 3/4	0.3958	8 3/4	0.7292
7/8	0.0729	4 7/8	0.4063	8 7/8	0.7396
1	0.0833	5	0.4167	9	0.7500
1 1/8	0.0938	5 1/8	0.4271	9 1/8	0.7604
1 1/4	0.1042	5 1/4	0.4375	9 1/4	0.7708
1 3/8	0.1146	5 3/8	0.4479	9 3/8	0.7813
1 1/2	0.1250	5 1/2	0.4583	9 1/2	0.7917
1 5/8	0.1354	5 5/8	0.4688	9 5/8	0.8021
1 3/4	0.1458	5 3/4	0.4792	9 3/4	0.8125
1 7/8	0.1563	5 7/8	0.4986	9 7/8	0.8229
2	0.1667	6	0.5000	10	0.8333
2 1/8	0.1771	6 1/8	0.5104	10 1/8	0.8438
2 1/4	0.1875	6 1/4	0.5208	10 1/4	0.8542
2 3/8	0.1979	6 3/8	0.5313	10 3/8	0.8646
2 1/2	0.2083	6 1/2	0.5417	10 1/2	0.8750
2 5/8	0.2188	6 5/8	0.5521	10 5/8	0.8854
2 3/4	0.2292	6 3/4	0.5625	10 3/4	0.8958
2 7/8	0.2396	6 7/8	0.5729	10 7/8	0.9063
3	0.2500	7	0.5833	11	0.9167
3 1/8	0.2604	7 1/8	0.5938	11 1/8	0.9271
3 1/4	0.2708	7 1/4	0.6042	11 1/4	0.9375
3 3/8	0.2813	7 3/8	0.6146	11 3/8	0.9479
3 1/2	0.2917	7 1/2	0.6250	11 1/2	0.9583
3 5/8	0.3021	7 5/8	0.6354	11 5/8	0.9688
3 3/4	0.3125	7 3/4	0.6458	11 3/4	0.9792
3 7/8	0.3229	7 7/8	0.6563	11 7/8	0.9896

Table 5-4
DECIMALS OF AN INCH

Fraction	Decimal	Fraction	Decimal
1/32	0.0313	17/32	0.5313
1/16	0.0625	9/16	0.5625
3/32	0.0938	19/32	0.5938
1/8	0.1250	5/8	0.6250
5/32	0.1563	21/32	0.6563
3/16	0.1875	11/16	0.6875
7/32	0.2188	23/32	0.7188
1/4	0.2500	3/4	0.7500
9/32	0.2813	25/32	0.7813
5/16	0.3125	13/16	0.8125
11/32	0.3438	27/32	0.8438
3/8	0.3750	7/8	0.8750
13/32	0.4063	29/32	0.9063
7/16	0.4375	15/16	0.9375
15/32	0.4688	31/32	0.9688
1/2	0.5000	1 in.	1.0000

CONVERSION FACTORS

The following conversion factors represent some of the more common units used by architects, engineers, and interior designers. They include both the English system of measurement and the International System (SI). The conversion factors are written without scientific notation except for very small or very large numbers, which are indicated by a number between one and ten followed by the letter *E* (exponent) and a plus or minus sign and another number. This indicates the power of 10 (positive or negative) by which the base number must be raised to obtain the correct value.

An asterisk (*) after the conversion number indicates that it is an exact value and that all subsequent digits are zero.

Conversion factors are based on *The International System of Units—Physical Constants and Conversion Factors,* Second Revised Edition, NASA Publication SP-7012 (1973); *Metric (SI) Units in Building Design and Construction,* ASTM E621, and derived calculations.

Table 5-5
CONVERSION FACTORS

Given	Multiply by	To Obtain
Length		
Centimeters	0.0328084	Feet
Centimeters	0.3937	Inches
Feet	0.3048	*Meters
Feet	1.89394 E-4	Miles, statute
Feet	1.64468 E-4	Miles, nautical
Feet	304.8	*Millimeters
Inches	2.54000	*Centimeters
Inches	.02540	*Meters
Kilometers	.62137	Miles, statute
Kilometers	.53959	Miles, nautical
Meters	3.28084	Feet
Meters	39.37	Inches
Meters	1.09361	Yards
Miles, statute	1.609344	*Kilometers
Miles, statute	.8684	Miles, nautical
Miles, nautical	6080.204	Feet
Miles, nautical	1.852	*Kilometers
Miles, nautical	1.1516	Miles, statute
Millimeters	3.28083 E-3	Feet
Millimeters	0.03937	Inches
Yards	.9144	*Meters
Area		
Acre	43,560	Square Feet
Acre	4840	Square Yards
Acre	4046.87	Square Meters
Acre	.004046857	Square Kilometers
Hectares	10,000	*Square Meters
Hectares	2.47104	Acres
Hectares	1.076387 E+5	Square Feet
Hectares	.00386101	Square Miles
Square Centimeters	.1550	Square Inches
Square Feet	.09290304	*Square Meters
Square Inches	6.4516	*Square Centimeters
Square Inches	645.16	*Square Millimeters
Square kilometers	247.104	Acres
Square kilometers	0.3861	Square miles
Square meters	10.7639	Square feet
Square meters	1.19599	Square yards
Square miles	2.58999	Square kilometers
Square millimeters	0.001550	Square inches
Square yards	0.83612736	*Square meters
Volume		
Acre-foot	1233.489	Cubic meters
Acre-foot	325,853	Gallons, U.S.
Board feet	144	Cubic inches
Board feet	0.0833	Cubic feet
Board feet	0.002359737	Cubic meters
Cubic centimeters	3.53145 E-5	Cubic feet

Given	Multiply by	To Obtain
Cubic centimeters	0.06102	Cubic inches
Cubic feet	0.028317	Cubic meters
Cubic feet	6.22905	Gallons, British Imperial
Cubic feet	7.48055	Gallons, U.S.
Cubic feet	28.3170	Liters
Cubic inches	16.38716	Cubic centimeters
Cubic meters	35.3147	Cubic feet
Cubic meters	423.776	Board feet
Cubic meters	1.30795	Cubic yards
Cubic yards	0.764555	Cubic meters
Fluid ounces	29.5735	Milliliters
Gallons, British Imperial	0.160538	Cubic feet
Gallons, British Imperial	1.20091	Gallons, U.S.
Gallons, British Imperial	4.54596	Liters
Gallons, U.S.	0.832702	Gallons, British Imperial
Gallons, U.S.	0.133680	Cubic feet
Gallons, U.S.	231	Cubic inches
Gallons, U.S.	3.7854	Liters
Liters	0.219975	Gallons, British Imperial
Liters	0.26417	Gallons, U.S.
Liters	0.353147	Cubic feet
Milliliters	0.033814	Fluid ounces (U.S.)
Mass and Weight		
Grams	0.001	*Kilograms
Grams (avoirdupois)	0.001771845	Kilograms
Grams (troy or apothecary)	0.0038879346	*Kilograms
Grams	0.035274	Ounces
Kilograms	2.204623	Pounds
Kilograms	0.000984207	Long tons
Kilograms	0.001102311	Short tons
Ounces (avoirdupois)	0.028349523	Kilograms
Ounces (avoirdupois)	28.34952	Grams
Pounds	0.45359237	*Kilograms
Pounds	0.0004464	Long tons
Pounds	0.000453592	Metric tons
Tons (long)	1016.0469	Kilograms
Tons (long)	2240	Pounds
Tons (long)	1.01605	Metric tons
Tons (long)	1.120	Short tons (2000 lbs.)
Tons (metric)	1000	*Kilograms
Tons (metric)	2204.62	Pounds
Tons (metric)	0.98421	Long tons
Tons (metric)	1.10231	Short tons
Tons (short, 2000 lbs.)	907.18474	*Kilograms
Mass per Unit Area		
Grams per square meter	0.029494	Ounces per square yard

Table 5-5 (Continued)

Given	Multiply by	To Obtain
Grams per square meter	3.27706 E-3	Ounces per square foot
Kilograms per square centimeter	14.2234	Pounds per square inch
Kilograms per square meter	0.204816	Pounds per square foot
Ounces per square yard	33.9057	Grams per square meter
Pounds per square foot	4.882428	Kilograms per square meter
Pounds per square inch	0.07031	Kilograms per square centimeter
Mass per Unit Length		
Kilograms per meter	0.671969	Pounds per foot
Pounds per foot	1.48816	Kilograms per meter
Mass per Unit Volume		
Kilograms per cubic meter	0.062428	Pounds per cubic foot
Kilograms per cubic meter	1.68556	Pounds per cubic yard
Pounds per cubic foot	16.018463	Kilograms per cubic meter
Pounds per cubic inch	27,679.9	Kilograms per cubic meter
Energy		
Btu (international)	1055.056	Joules
Btu per minute	17.572504	Watts
Btu per hour	0.293071	Watts
Btu per pound	2.326	Kilojoules/kilogram
Btu per square foot per hour	3.15459	Watts per square meter
Btu per pound-F°	4.1868	KJ(kg − K)
Btu per inch per hour per square foot per F° (thermal conductivity, k)	0.144228	Watts per meter Kelvin
Btu per hour per foot per F°	1.73073	Watts per meter Kelvin
Btu per hour per square foot per F° (thermal conductance, c, U)	5.67826	Watts per square meter Kelvin
Hour per square foot per F° per Btu (thermal resistance, R)	0.176110	Square meter Kelvin per watt
Horsepower (electric)	746	*Watts
Joule	1.0	*Newton-meter
Joule	1.0	*Watt-second
Kilojoule	0.947817	Btu
Kilowatt	1.34102	Horsepower
Kilowatt hour	3,600,000.0	*Joule
Therm	100,000	Btu
Therm	105.5056	Mega joules
Ton (refrigeration)	3.516800	Kilowatts

Given	Multiply by	To Obtain
Watt	3.41214	Btu per hour
Watts per square foot	10.76391	Watts per square meters
Watts per square meter	0.316998	Btu per square foot per hour
Watts per square meter Kelvin	0.176110	Btu per hour per square foot per F°
Watts per meter Kelvin	0.577789	Btu per hour per foot per F°
Volume per Unit Time		
Cubic feet per minute	0.0004719474	Cubic meters per second
Cubic feet per second	0.02831685	Cubic meters per second
Cubic meters per second	15,580.32	Gallons (U.S.) per minute
Cubic meters per second	35.3147	Cubic feet per second
Cubic meters per second	2118.882	Cubic feet per minute
Gallons (U.S.) per minute	0.0000630902	Cubic meters per second
Liters per second	2.11888	Cubic feet per second
Liters per second	15.8503	Gallons per minute
Light		
Candela per square inch	1550.003	Candela per square meter
Candela per square foot	10.66391	Candela per square meter
Candela per square meter	0.291864	Footlamberts
Footcandle (lumens per square foot^2)	10.76391	Lux
Footlambert	3.426259	Candela per square meters
Lambert	3183.009	Candela per square meter
Lumens per square foot	10.76391	Lumens per square meter
Lux	0.092903	Lumens per square foot (footcandle)
Second Moment of Area		
Millimeters^4	2.40251 E-6	Inches^4
Inches^4	416,231	Millimeters^4
Inches^4	0.416231 E-6	Meters^4
Moment of Inertia		
Kilogram-meters^2	23.7304	Pound-inches^2
Kilogram-meters^2	3417.17	Pound-inches^2
Pound-inches^2	292.640	Kilogram-millimeters^2

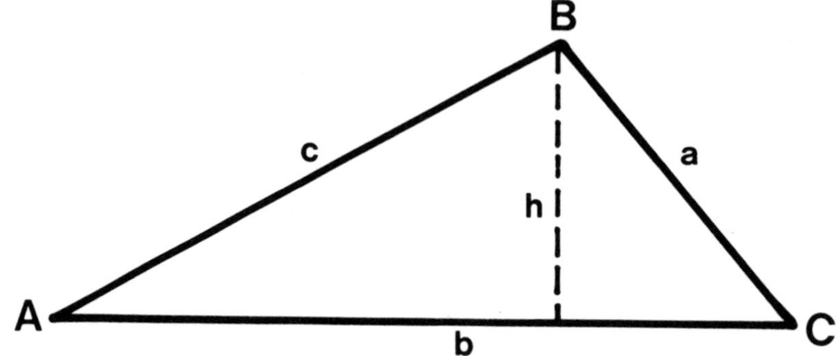

Figure 5-1: Properties of Obtuse Triangles

FORMULA:

$$a^2 = b^2 + c^2 - 2bc \cos A$$
$$b^2 = a^2 + c^2 - 2ac \cos B$$
$$c^2 = a^2 + b^2 - 2ab \cos C$$

$$s = \frac{a + b + c}{2} \qquad h = b\,\frac{\sin A \sin C}{\sin (A+C)}$$

$$\text{area} = \sqrt{s(s-a)(s-b)(s-c)} \qquad \text{area} = \frac{ab \sin C}{2}$$

$$\text{diameter of circumscribed circle} = \frac{a}{\sin A} = \frac{b}{\sin B} = \frac{c}{\sin C}$$

Known	To Find	Use
a b c s	A	$\tan 1/2\, A = \sqrt{\frac{(s-b)\,(s-c)}{s(s-a)}}$
a b c s	B	$\tan 1/2\, B = \sqrt{\frac{(s-a)(s-c)}{s(s-b)}}$
a b c s	C	$\tan 1/2\, C = \sqrt{\frac{(s-a)(s-b)}{s(s-c)}}$
a b C	c	$c = \sqrt{a^2 + b^2 - 2ab \cos C}$
a b C	A	$\tan A = \frac{a \sin C}{b - a \cos C}$
a A B	b	$b = \frac{a \sin B}{\sin A}$
a A B	c	$c = \frac{a \sin (A+B)}{\sin A}$
a b A	B	$\sin B = \frac{b \sin A}{a}$
a b A	c	$c = \frac{b \sin C}{\sin B}$
a c A	C	$\sin C = \frac{c \sin A}{a}$

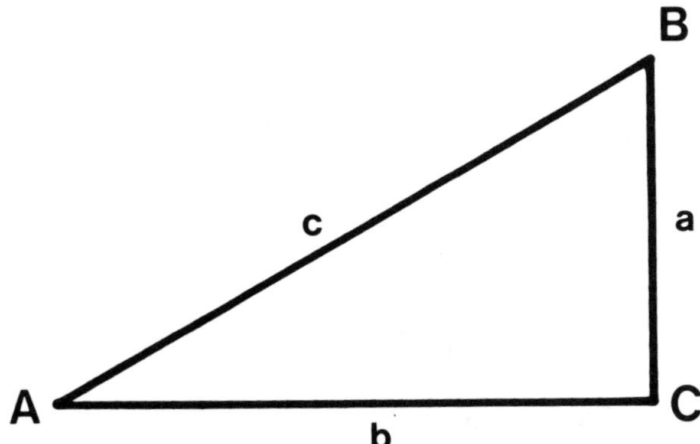

Figure 5-2: Properties of Right Angles

FORMULA: $a^2 + b^2 = c^2$

$\sin A = \frac{a}{c}$ $\qquad$ $\sin B = \frac{b}{c}$

$\cos A = \frac{b}{c}$ $\qquad$ $\cos B = \frac{a}{c}$

$\tan A = \frac{a}{b}$ $\qquad$ $\tan B = \frac{b}{a}$

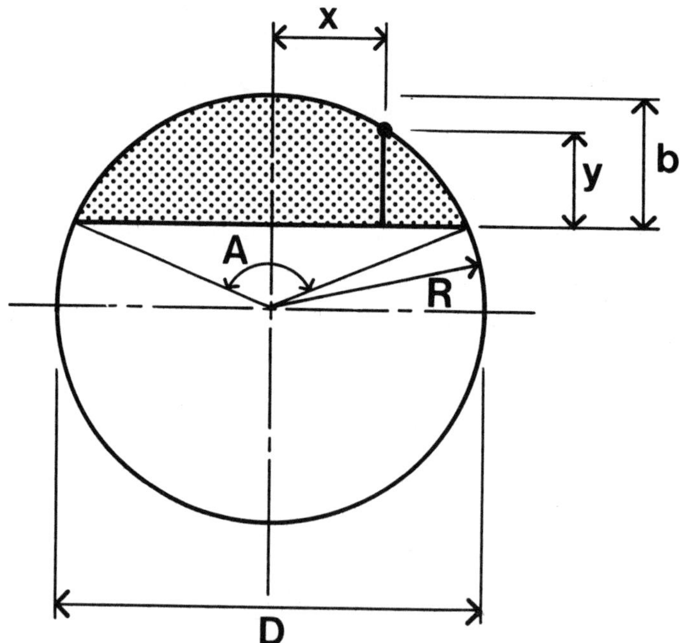

Figure 5-3: Properties of the Circle

FORMULA:

$\pi = 3.141592653$

Circumference $= \pi D$

Area $= \pi R^2$

rise $b = 2R \sin^2 \dfrac{A}{4} = R + y - \sqrt{R^2 - x^2}$

$y = b - R + \sqrt{R^2 - x^2}$

$x = \sqrt{R^2 - (R + y - b)^2}$

Diameter of a circle circumscribed about a square equals 1.414121 side of square.

Side of a square inscribed in a circle equals 0.70711 diameter of the circle.

Diameter of a circle of equal periphery as square equals 1.27324 side of square.

Side of a square of equal periphery as circle equals 0.78540 diameter of circle.

$360° = 2\ \pi$ radians = 6400 mils

1 radian = 57.2957795 degrees

1 radian = 57 degrees 17 feet 44.80625 inches

1 degree = 0.01745329252 radians

1 mil = 0.05625 degrees = 0.00098175 radians

1000 mils = 0.98175 radians = 56.25 degrees

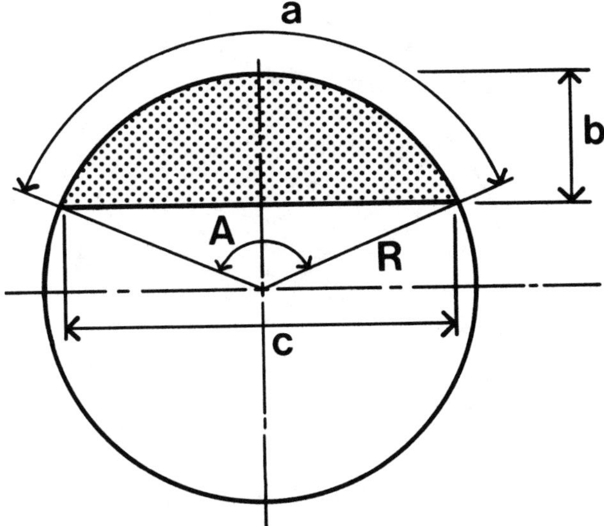

Figure 5-4: Properties of Circular Segments

$$\text{arc } a = \frac{\pi RA}{180} = 0.017453 \text{ RA}$$

$$\text{chord } c = 2\sqrt{2bR - b^2} = 2R \sin \frac{A}{2}$$

$$\text{area of segment} = \frac{(aR) - c(R - b)}{2}$$

$$\text{angle } A = \frac{180a}{\pi R} = 57.29578 \frac{a}{R}$$

$$\text{radius } R = \frac{4b^2 + c^2}{8b}$$

$$\text{rise } b = R - 1/2\sqrt{4R^2 - c^2} = \frac{c}{2} \tan \frac{A}{4}$$

where:

R = radius of circle
A = angle of the sector defining the segment in degrees
a = length of the arc of the segment
b = rise of the segment
c = length of the chord

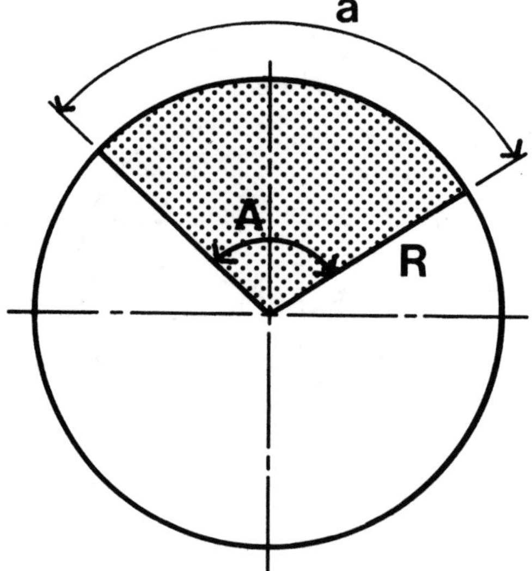

Figure 5-5: Properties of Circular Sectors

$$\text{arc a} = \frac{\pi RA}{180} = 0.017453\ RA$$

$$\text{area of sector} = \frac{aR}{2} = (\text{area of circle})\ \frac{A}{360}$$

$$\text{area of sector} = 0.0087266\ AR^2$$

$$\text{angle A} = \frac{180a}{\pi R} = 57.29578\ \frac{a}{R}$$

where:

R = radius of circle
A = angle of the sector
a = length of the arc of the sector

Equilateral Triangle

FORMULA:

$$\text{Area} = \frac{a^2}{4}\sqrt{3}$$

$$h = \frac{a}{2}\sqrt{3}$$

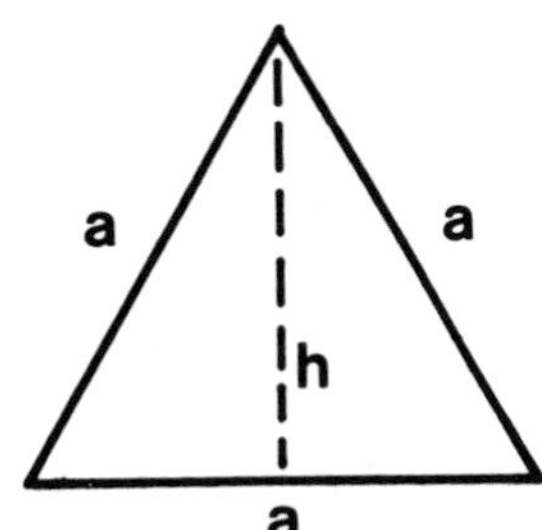

Parallelogram

FORMULA:

$$\text{Area} = bh$$
$$\text{Area} = ab \sin A$$
$$d(1) = \sqrt{(b + h \cot A)^2 + h^2}$$
$$d(2) = \sqrt{(b - h \cot A)^2 = h^2}$$

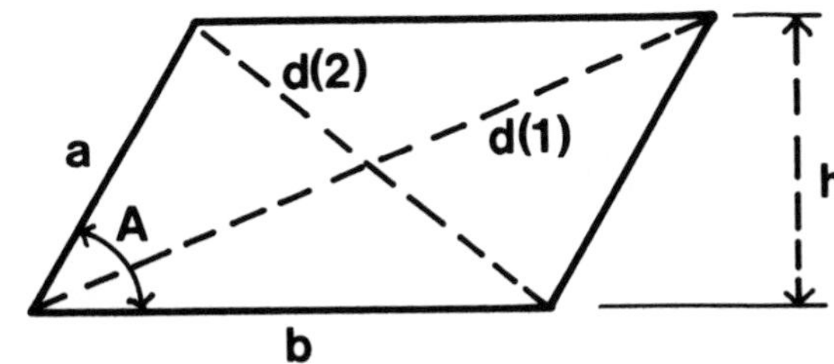

Trapezoid

FORMULA:

$$\text{Area} = 1/2\ (a + b)h$$

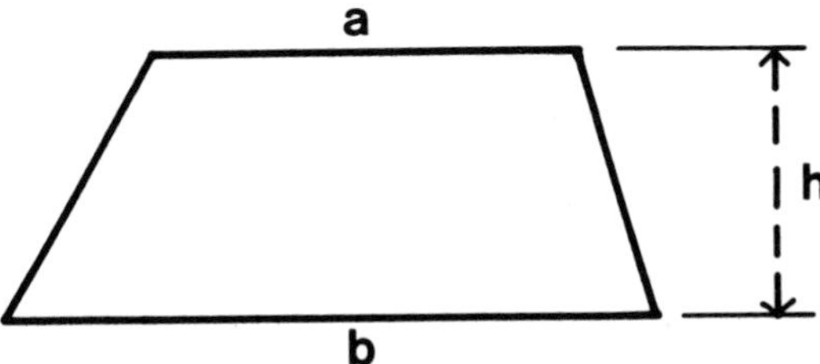

Ellipse

FORMULA:

$$\text{Area} = \pi ab$$

Approximate perimeter $= \pi \sqrt{2(a^2 + b^2)}$

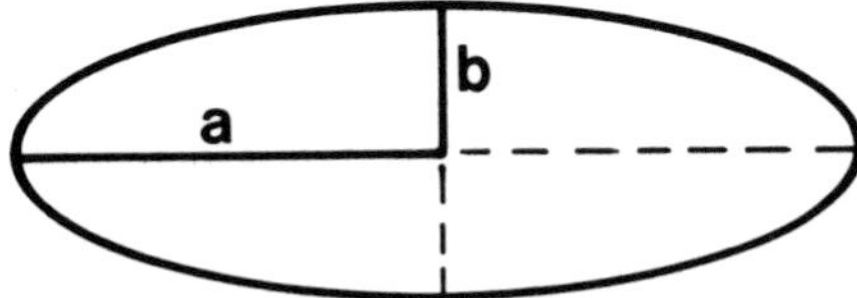

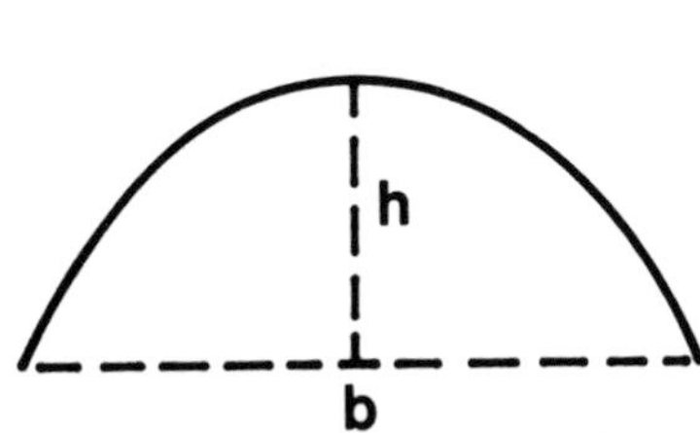

Parabola

FORMULA:

$$\text{Area} = 4/3\ bh$$

$$\text{Length of arc} = \sqrt{4h^2 + b^2} + \frac{b^2}{2h} \cdot \log_e \frac{2h + \sqrt{4h^2 + b^2}}{b}$$

Figure 5-6: Formulas of Plane Geometric Figures

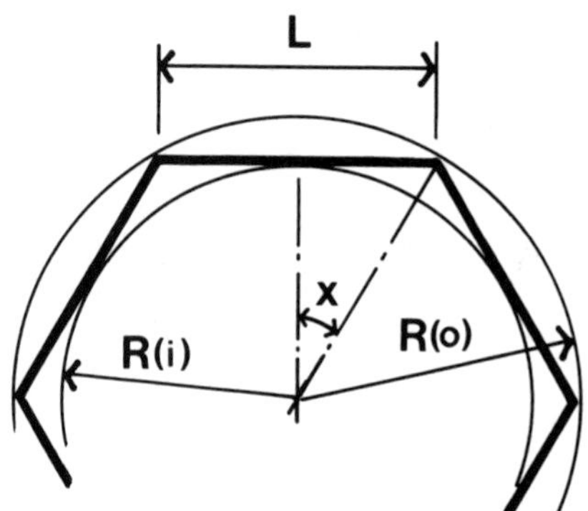

Regular Polygons

FORMULA:

$$\text{Area of regular polygon} = 1/4\ nL^2 \cot \frac{180}{n}$$

where:

n = number of sides
L = length of side

$$x = \frac{180}{n}$$

$$R(i) = \frac{L}{2 \tan x}$$

$$R(o) = \frac{L}{2 \sin x}$$

$$L = 2\sqrt{R(o)^2 - R(i)^2}$$

Polygon	Sides	Area	Radius of Inscribed Circle	Radius of Circumscribed Circle
Triangle, equilateral	3	$0.43301L^2$	0.28867L	0.57735L
Square	4	$1.00000L^2$	0.50000L	0.70710L
Pentagon	5	$1.72048L^2$	0.68819L	0.85065L
Hexagon	6	$2.59808L^2$	0.86602L	1.00000L
Heptagon	7	$3.63391L^2$	1.0383L	1.1523L
Octagon	8	$4.82843L^2$	1.2071L	1.3065L
Nonagon	9	$6.18182L^2$	1.3737L	1.4619L
Decagon	10	$7.69421L^2$	1.5388L	1.6180L

Figure 5-7: Formulas of Regular Polygons

Single Present Worth (SPW)

FORMULA:

$$P = F \left[\frac{1}{(1 + 1)^n} \right]$$

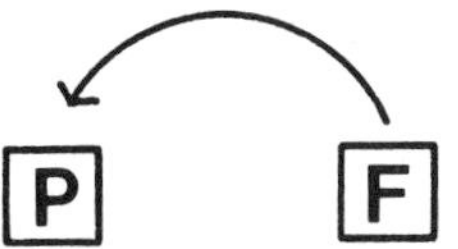

Uniform Present Worth (UPW)

FORMULA:

$$P = A \left[\frac{(1 + i)^n - 1}{i(1 + i)^n} \right]$$

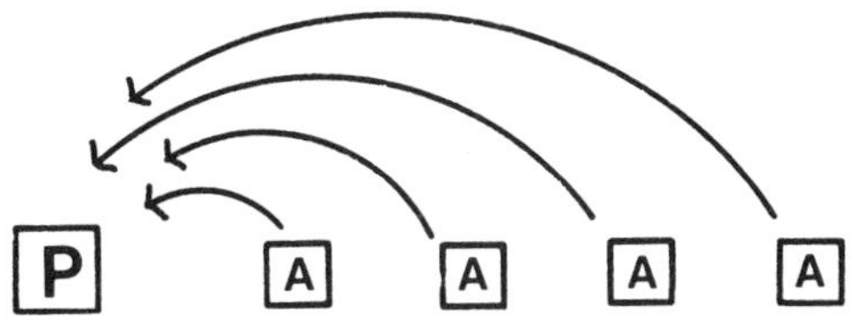

Uniform Present Worth Modified for Escalation (UPW*)

FORMULA:

$$P = A \left[\frac{1 + E}{i - E} \left[1 - \left(\frac{1 + E}{1 + i} \right)^n \right] \right]$$

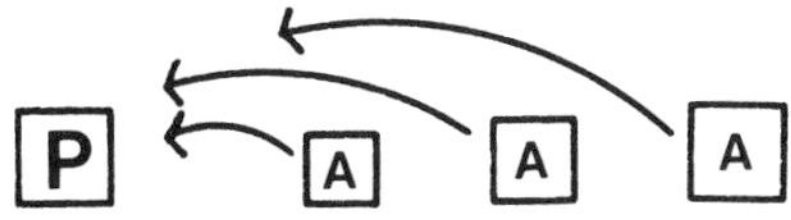

Uniform Capital Recovery (UCR)

FORMULA:

$$A = P \left[\frac{i(1 + i)^n}{(1 + i)^n - 1} \right]$$

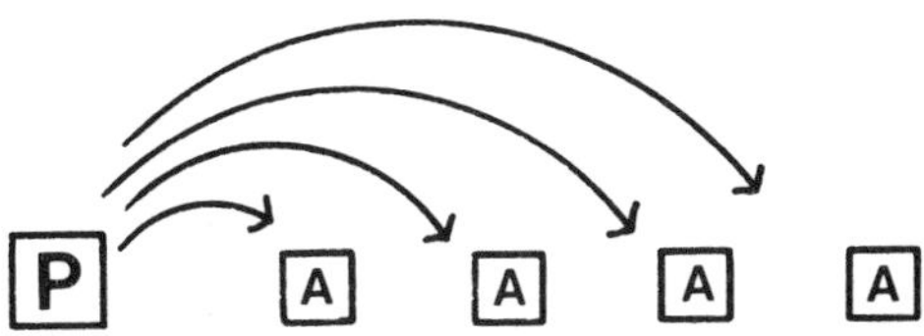

Uniform Sinking Fund (USF)

FORMULA:

$$A = F \left[\frac{i}{(1 + i)^n - 1} \right]$$

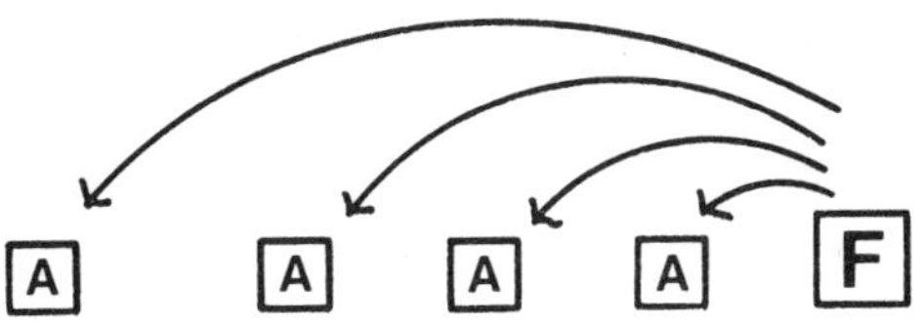

where:

P = present sum of money
F = future sum of money
A = end of period payment or receipt for n periods
i = discount rate (interest rate)
n = number of periods (years)
E = escalation rate

Figure 5-8: Life Cycle Cost Formulas

Index

N

O

P

R

S

T

V

W